# Northern Ireland Environmental Law

# NORTHERN IRELAND ENVIRONMENTAL LAW

Sharon Turner and Karen Morrow

*Consultant Editor*

Neil Faris

GILL & MACMILLAN

Gill & Macmillan Ltd
Goldenbridge
Dublin 8
with associated companies throughout the world

0 7171 22743

Index compiled by June Stein
Tables compiled by Neil Steen
Print origination by Typeform Repro Ltd
Printed in Great Britain at the University Press, Cambridge

This book is printed on acid-free paper

A catalogue record is available for this book from the British Library.

1 3 5 4 2

# Contents

## PART ONE

## PART TWO

## PART THREE

## Chapter Eleven   Environmental Impact Assessment     **495**

We dedicate this book firstly to all the trees that died in its making in the hope that it may save a few others by contributing towards the preservation and improvement of Northern Ireland's environment. Secondly, we want to express our appreciation to our families and long-suffering partners, Roddy Clarke and Michael Crilly, without whose patience and support this book would never have been completed.

# Foreword

The last twenty years have seen a vast increase in the attention paid to environmental matters, by scientists, politicians, lawyers and the public. This interest in the environment has generated a vast amount of legislation and a growing stream of litigation, which in turn have led to a rapidly increasing amount of writing about the law. The day is long gone when my book shelves, far less my bank balance, could cope with all of the books published on environmental law. This volume adds to the ever-lengthening list of books on this subject but has the rare virtue of offering something wholly new.

On too many occasions when new areas of the law develop, the needs of smaller jurisdictions are ignored. Those working in such jurisdictions have to make do with works written for elsewhere and constantly make their own conversions and adaptations to cope with the local legal and administrative position. Those wishing to observe from outside have no guide to the particularities of the law and will tend to abandon the attempt to understand or discuss what is happening, unsure of their grasp of the local variations from the position which they know. No longer is this the case for environmental law in Northern Ireland. Those working with the law there now have a comprehensive guide to the law which affects them, and those who purport to write about UK law have no excuse for not dealing with the law in all parts of the United Kingdom.

As an observer from outside (literally, as I regularly see the Ballylumford power station while on holiday in Kintyre), it is now a simple task to discover the state of the law across the North Channel. Two points stand out. The first is the extent to which the wholly unsatisfactory legislative arrangements for Northern Ireland have meant that the law there has lagged behind what are widely accepted to be beneficial developments in Great Britain. This is so even where there is a clear obligation to adjust the law to fit European Community requirements. Northern Ireland would provide plenty of business for the European Court of Justice if formal enforcement action were taken in relation to every failure to implement, timeously and completely, Community environmental legislation. The second, also in part related to the delay in translating government policy into action in Northern Ireland, is that the changes to the administrative structures in Great Britain which have separated regulators and regulated, 'gamekeepers and poachers', have not progressed as far in Northern Ireland. It by no means follows that what is appropriate for other parts of the UK is the best for Northern Ireland, but it will be much more satisfactory when one can be confident that the differences are the result of a proper consideration of the needs of each jurisdiction, not simply the product of inertia and delay.

There are indications that an effort is being made to catch up, as illustrated by some of the draft measures discussed in this book. Further changes will doubtless follow and new editions of this work will be required, and be as welcome as this first account of the law in Northern Ireland. There are no signs as yet that environmental legislation and litigation are finite resources, and it appears that for environmental lawyers, a sustainable future lies ahead.

*Colin T Reid*                                                                                    *September 1996*
*Professor of Environmental Law*
*University of Dundee*

# Preface

This has been the best and the worst of times to write a book on environmental law in Northern Ireland. During the past few years the substantive and structural elements of environmental regulation in the United Kingdom, and not least the Province, have changed fundamentally. As a result, this has been an exciting time for environmentalists and a challenging one for the law. A book which addresses the unique legal and environmental context which exists in Northern Ireland has, in our opinion, been long overdue; we hope that in writing this book we have made a positive contribution to the status and understanding of environmental law in this jurisdiction. It has been our intention to map out the current state of environmental institutions, policy and law for the practitioner and it our hope that while this book will prove useful to the legal profession it will also provide a valuable resource to other environmental professionals. There is perhaps no other area of the law which embraces such a wide range of disciplines and topics and, while we have only touched the 'tip of the iceberg', we feel that this book should provide a sound starting point for the development of a detailed knowledge of environmental law as it pertains to Northern Ireland.

This book reflects the law as it stood on 31 March 1996. With this in mind, we would like to draw the reader's attention to the fact that on 1 April 1996 the Environment Agency (for England and Wales) and the Scottish Environmental Protection Agency came into operation. Closer to home, the same date saw the DoE(NI) embracing the 'Next Steps' initiative and, as a result, the Department's Environment Service (with which this book is chiefly concerned) became the Environment and Heritage Service. The text highlights these changes and their implications. The powers of the new Agencies closely reflect their antecedents and the reader should therefore substitute the new titles as appropriate in his reading of the text. Substantive law is also in a state of fundamental transition in Northern Ireland. Throughout the text we have endeavoured to alert the reader to the main themes of imminent legislation; however, we must emphasise that the precise details of the current proposals for draft legislation may change before the legislation is finally made. The manifest influence of EC law in the formulation of environmental law and policy in the Province will become abundantly clear in the pages that follow. Given that European environmental legislation is adopted under the EC Treaty, we have for the sake of accuracy referred to EC (rather than EU) law throughout the text.

Finally, we would like to acknowledge the following: (i) we are indebted to Nigel High's excellent work on EC environmental law and to Simon Ball and Stuart Bell's book on environmental law in England and Wales; (ii) the book contains extracts from previous works published by the authors in the *Irish Journal of Taxation, Tolly's VAT Planning 1996–97* (Tolly's London), *Tolly's Environmental Handbook* (ed. by Freshfields Environmental Group, forthcoming), and *One Hundred and Fifty Years of Irish Law* (SLS Legal Publications and Roundhall, Sweet & Maxwell, 1996).

*Sharon Turner and Karen Morrow*                                        *16 October 1996*

# Preface

# A Practitioner's View

Turner and Morrow's *Northern Ireland Environmental Law* is a treasure-trove for the student of law and legal practitioner alike. But environmental law is not the exclusive domain of those 'learned in the law'; everyone in the business and commercial life of Northern Ireland has a vital interest in the proper management and regulation of the environment, and everyone as a citizen has a right to contribute to the decision making on the environment and to the enforcement of environmental law.

This book not only informs, but raises questions, sometimes troubling questions, about the quality of environmental management and the decision making process in Northern Ireland. Consider, for instance, that Northern Ireland still does not have an independent environmental protection agency to match those in our neighbouring jurisdictions. It may well be that there are benefits of the stewardship of the Department of the Environment for Northern Ireland over so many aspects of environmental management and regulation in Northern Ireland. Certainly, this book demonstrates the startlingly wide scope of the Department's powers and influence. The authors' comments at pages 27 and 31 will repay careful reading and are worthy of reflection.

For everyone has a part to play in what may be called the process of sustainable development; the World Commission on the Environment and Development in 1987 defined it as: 'development that meets the needs of the present without compromising the ability of future generations to meet their own needs'. The Government in London made an early commitment to the process in a series of White Papers and other reports including in particular *This Common Inheritance* in 1990. In 1993 the Department of the Environment for Northern Ireland did initiate the *Growing a Green Economy Initiative* for Northern Ireland. This was taken forward, at least to some extent, by a working group which published a report in December 1994. But it took the Department until March 1996 to publish its response, and most of the drive now seems to have gone out of the Initiative.

This book helps us all to realise that we should not leave these issues solely in the hands of Government. One of the key documents at the Rio Summit in 1992 was *Agenda 21*. This is an 'action plan' for the environment, which emphasises that the way towards sustainable development involves everyone.

Turner and Morrow's book should therefore be in the hands of everyone in Northern Ireland engaged in that task.

*Neil C Faris, Consultant Editor*                                          *September 1996*
*Partner and Head of Consultancy*
*Cleaver Fulton & Rankin*
*Solicitors*
*Belfast*

# Acknowledgments

We would like to take this opportunity to thank the many people who have helped to make this book what it is; however, the authors accept final responsibility for its contents. Although it is impossible to thank everyone by name, we are particularly indebted to the following people: Our publishers and particularly our editors, Finola O'Sullivan and Deirdre Greenan, for their considerable forbearance in the light of Northern Ireland's rapidly changing environmental law. The staff of the DoE(NI)'s Environment Service (as they then were), particularly David Bell, George Kearns, Norman Simmons, Sheila McConville, Rodney Thomas, Margaret Rainey, Wallace Lawson, Samuel J. Clark, James Wilkinson and all the staff of DoE(NI) libraries. We would also like to thank Nigel Carr of the IRTU (DED), Clive Mellon from the RSPB (NI Branch) and the staff of both the Belfast City Council Environmental Information Office and the Belfast City Council Environmental Health Unit, all of whom were extremely helpful. We are indebted to our colleagues at the Law Faculty at the Queen's University of Belfast for their practical and moral support throughout the preparation of the book; we would particularly like to acknowldege the following individuals: Grainne McKeever and Dorit Stuemper (our research assistants); Professor Brigid Hadfield (for her formidable proofing skills); Dr Joseph McMahon (Research Director) and Professor Norma Dawson (Dean and Director) for their help and encouragement.

# Table of Cases

## DOMESTIC

# EC

## TA

# Table of National Legislation

## ACTS

# ORDERS

# REGULATIONS

## ACTS OF THE OIREACHTAS

# Table of EC Legislation

## THE TREATY

## REGULATIONS

## DIRECTIVES

## DECISIONS

# Acronyms and Abbreviations

| | |
|---|---|
| ACO: | Access to the Countryside (NI) Order 1983 |
| AONB: | Area of Outstanding Natural Beauty |
| ARCI: | Alkali and Radiochemical Inspectorate |
| ASCOBANS: | The Agreement on the Conservation of Small Cetaceans in the Baltic and North Seas. |
| ASSI: | Area of Special Scientific Interest |
| BAT: | Best Available Techniques |
| BATNEEC: | Best Available Techniques Not Entailing Excessive Costs |
| BPEO: | Best Practicable Environmental Option |
| BPM: | Best Practicable Means |
| CAO: | Clean Air (NI) Order 1981 |
| CAP: | Common Agricultural Policy |
| CEQ: | Council on Environmental Quality (USA) |
| COPA: | Control of Pollution Act 1974 |
| CNCC: | Council for Nature Conservation and the Countryside |
| CZM: | Coastal Zone Management |
| DANI: | Department of Agriculture for Northern Ireland |
| DED: | Department of Economic Development |
| DoE: | Department of the Environment (Great Britain) |
| DoE(NI): | Department of the Environment for Northern Ireland |
| EA: | Environment Agency (England and Wales) |
| ECJ: | European Court of Justice |
| EHS: | Environment and Heritage Service |
| EIA: | Environmental Impact Assessment |
| EIONET: | European Environment Information and Observation Network |
| EIL: | Environmental Impairment Liability |
| EMAS: | Eco-Management and Audit Scheme (EC) |
| EMS: | Environmental Management System |
| ENFO: | Environmental Information Service (Ireland) |
| ES: | Environment Service |
| ESA: | Environmentally Sensitive Area |
| HMIP: | Her Majesty's Inspectorate of Pollution |
| IPC: | Integrated Pollution Control |
| ISO: | International Standards Organisation |
| IRTU: | Industrial Research and Technology Unit (DED) |
| LRTAP: | Long-Range Transboundary Atmospheric Pollution |
| MAFF: | Ministry of Agriculture, Fisheries and Food |
| MNR: | Marine Nature Reserve |
| MtC: | Million tonnes of Carbon |
| Mw: | Megawatts |
| MWIP: | Municipal Waste Incineration Plant |
| NCALO: | Nature Conservation and Amenity Lands (NI) Order 1985 |
| NEPA: | National Environmental Policy Act 1969 (USA) |
| NFFO: | Non-Fossil Fuels Order 1994 |

| | |
|---|---|
| NIE: | Northern Ireland Electricity |
| NIEL: | Northern Ireland Environment Link |
| NR: | Nature Reserve |
| NNR: | National Nature Reserve |
| NRA: | National Rivers Authority |
| NVQ: | National Vocational Qualification |
| OECD: | Organisation for Economic Co-operation and Development |
| OJ: | Official Journal of the EC |
| RCEP: | Royal Commission on Environmental Pollution |
| SAC: | Special Areas of Conservation |
| SEPA: | Scottish Environmental Protection Agency |
| SPA: | Special Protection Area |
| SSSI: | Site of Special Scientific Interest |
| RSPB: | Royal Society for the Protection of Birds |
| UKAS: | United Kingdom Accreditation Service |
| UNCED: | United Nations Conference on Environment and Development |
| UNEP: | United Nations Environment Programme |
| UWWT: | Urban Waste Water Treatment Regulations (NI) 1995 |
| WA: | Water Act (NI) 1972 |
| WO: | Wildlife (NI) Order 1985 |
| WSSO: | Water and Sewerage Services (NI) Order 1973 |

# PART ONE

# CHAPTER ONE

# Environmental Policy and Legislation in Great Britain

## Introduction

Environmental law is regarded by many as a 'new' subject, and indeed it is true to say that in its modern incarnation, as a discrete discipline within the law, this is so. It would, however, create a very misleading impression if the reader was left with the idea that this branch of law is entirely novel, since its antecedents—the topics now encapsulated under the umbrella term 'environmental law', in both statute and common law—reach far into our legal history.[1]

While it is imperative to resist the temptation to adopt a revisionist view of the law—ascribing to it motives and objectives that would be anachronistic if applied to the social and political context of the legal instrument or policy in question—it is still possible to identify within our legal tradition benefits and detriments, both direct and indirect, flowing to the environment from legal intervention. What follows is not an attempt to provide a comprehensive catalogue charting the development of environmental law from its earliest origins—such a task would be enormous and certainly beyond the scope of this text: instead this chapter aims to furnish the reader with a 'thumbnail sketch' giving a flavour of the changing shape of the law and illustrating its development.

## PART I THE ORIGIN OF MODERN ENVIRONMENTAL LAW: THE NINETEENTH CENTURY

Both common law and legislative provision, in the attempt to promote the interests of landowners and industry, respectively, provide examples of law having a significant environmental impact. Innovative legislation and the extension of existing common law rules to deal with novel problems came into their own in the wake of the industrial revolution and the urbanisation that was its inevitable result.

The industrial revolution generated the capacity for humankind to make an impact on the environment that was more widespread and at the same time more concentrated than at any previous stage of history. With the power to harness and exploit nature on a grand scale came the attendant problems of pollution and disputes between conflicting activities utilising the environment. As a relatively homogeneous agrarian life-style was superseded by the new shape of society, the social tensions generated by the impacts of industrialisation often resulted in the need for legal intervention.

---

1. Prof. Garner, 'Is environmental law a real subject?' NLJ, vol. 142, no. 580, 11 Dec. 1992.

It was through litigation based on disputes between individuals that the law was first called upon to deal with environmental difficulties. The fairly rudimentary legal control that resulted was very much a product of its time; any protection that was offered to the environment was purely incidental to the prime objective of the law in question.

## The common law and environmental protection

The following examples demonstrate this phenomenon. The common law, with its lengthy history and evolutionary character, was pressed into service to deal with what we would now term pollution problems under the well-established tort of nuisance (which by definition concerns itself with protecting the individual's interest in land). A famous example of this is found in *St Helen's Smelting Co. Ltd v. Tipping*.[2] The plaintiff purchased an estate in June 1860. This estate was situated within one-and-a-half miles of the defendant's copper smelting plant, which began particularly intense operations in September of that year. One result of the increase in production was that emissions from the plant caused damage to vegetation on the plaintiff's property (we would now term the mechanism by which this occurred 'acid deposition'). The court was placed in the difficult position of attempting to balance the well-established traditional right to the enjoyment of one's property with the emerging consequences of otherwise beneficial industrial activity.

The House of Lords found for the plaintiff, since tangible damage to his property was established on the facts as a result of the defendant's activities; in the circumstances the by-product of industrial activity—pollution—was held to amount to a nuisance. This appears to be a very promising outcome with regard to the common law acting as an agent of environmental control, but the significance of the decision was severely limited by several factors, some legal and some social.

In the *St Helen's* case the court was extremely careful to differentiate between an alleged nuisance that caused physical damage to a plaintiff's property (where it was quite prepared to intervene) and an alleged nuisance that interfered only with the plaintiff's 'use and enjoyment' of his property, i.e. with the peace required to comfortably enjoy the occupation of his land. In cases where the latter problem emerged, Lord Westbury LC made it clear, albeit *obiter*, that the availability of a remedy:

> must undoubtedly depend greatly on the circumstances of the place where the thing complained of actually occurs. If a man lives in a town, it is necessary that he should subject himself to the consequences of those operations of trade which may be carried on in his immediate locality, which are actually necessary for trade and commerce . . . and for the benefit of the town and of the public at large.

The *St Helen's* case clearly shows the limitations of common law control in this context; interference with traditional property rights left the judges on familiar ground while other, less tangible but no less real, consequences of industrial

---

2.  (1865) 11 HL Cas 642.

activity brought them into uncharted territory, where complex questions of cost-benefit analysis between individual rights and social utility were brought to the fore. Indeed in the case of nuisances that interfered with the use and enjoyment of land the *St Helen's* decision allowed scope for considerable regional variations in the standard of interference with another's property that would amount to actionable nuisance.

The utility of the nuisance action as a tool of environmental protection was further limited by the fact that the plaintiff is generally required to demonstrate that he has a legally recognised proprietary interest in the land affected by the alleged nuisance,[3] for example land ownership or tenancy. Many of those most closely affected by industrial pollution at this time were factory workers living in dwellings owned by their employers who could not establish the requisite legal interest on which to base an action. Indeed, even if an interest in land was established, obtaining relief remained a costly and cumbersome business; originally proceedings at both common law and equity were required in the first instance to obtain damages for injury caused (causation itself was problematic, as scientific understanding of pollution was, at that stage, rudimentary to say the least) and in the second instance to seek the equitable remedy of an injunction to prevent future damage. Recourse to the courts in cases of nuisance caused by polluting activities remained therefore the preserve of the privileged few.[4]

It became abundantly clear at a fairly early stage that the common law, with its evolutionary nature and case-by-case approach, could not hope to supply uniform standards for the use and enjoyment of land. It was also readily apparent that the courts felt profoundly uncomfortable in attempting to develop law that balanced the interests of landowners against industry. In addition, the peculiar characteristics of the common law and the adversarial nature of litigation did not allow other interests to be fully represented or weighed in the nuisance equation.

## Legislation and environmental protection

### *Public health and private Acts of Parliament*

The problem of industrial pollution and its impact on society, however, remained a very real and increasing source of social difficulties. The next attempt at intervention eschewed the common law and concentrated on legislative action. The approach taken in this first wave of 'environmental' legislation was shaped by perception of the problems caused by industrial pollution and urbanisation; these were primarily characterised by concern for human health.

It was clear from an early stage that urban living, with unprecedented population growth and concentration making traditional forms of sanitation hopelessly inadequate and epidemics killing tens of thousands commonplace,

3. *Malone v. Laskey* [1907] 2 KB 141 represents the traditional legal viewpoint on the plaintiff's status in relation to a nuisance action. The situation may perhaps have been altered in *Khorasandjian v. Bush* [1993] QB 727, in which a plaintiff who was resident in her parents' house (and thus lacking a proprietary interest in the property) made a successful nuisance claim in respect of malicious phone calls.
4. For detailed discussion of historical limitations on the utility and availability of nuisance actions see A. Ogus and G. Richardson, 'Economics & the Environment: A Study of Private Nuisance', 1977 CLJ, 284.

posed a huge threat to the health of the nation and in turn to its economic performance. Legislation emerged through an unlikely combination of philanthropy (which also greatly influenced working conditions through legislation such as the Factory Acts, the precursors of modern safety at work legislation) and the pressure generated by the 'enlightened self-interest' of industrialists seeking a healthy work force in order to make their businesses competitive.

The earliest legislation that emerged was in the form of private Acts of Parliament prompted by petitions from the local councils in whose areas industry was concentrated and where the problems of pollution and its consequent impact on health were at their clearest and most acute.

## Public health and public Acts of Parliament

The obvious utility of localised laws directed towards dealing with environmental problems was quickly realised, and this in turn precipitated the second wave of legislative action, this time on a national scale and promoted by the government, culminating in the mandatory provisions of the Public Health Act 1875. The 1875 Act was a landmark for environmental law, in that it represented an attempt to impose a uniform approach to controlling basic health hazards in the human environment, rather than allowing the traditional approach of voluntarism and consequent regional variations in standards to continue. The 1875 Act was merely the foundation for modern public health law; its provisions were much amended as knowledge of the environment and medicine improved. The standards required by statute followed suit, culminating in the Public Health Act 1936.

## Industrial pollution legislation

The same approach was also exhibited in dealing with industrial pollution, localised legislative initiatives like the Smoke Nuisance Abatement (Metropolis) Act 1853 providing the impetus for a new nationwide approach to pollution control in the provisions of the revolutionary Alkali Act 1863.

In addition to being the world's first national statutory pollution control regime, the 1863 Act created the world's first state environmental agency, the Alkali Inspectorate. This Inspectorate was charged with the responsibility of ensuring a professional and scientific approach to the setting of environmental standards and their enforcement. The 1863 Act was also much amended, culminating in consolidation in the Alkali &c. Works Regulation Act 1906.

The legislation adopted a command and control strategy for dealing with pollution.[5] Alkali works as defined in section 27 were required to be registered under section 9(1) and to operate within the terms of their registration (under section 9(2)), otherwise their owners would be guilty of an offence under section 9(8). Owners were required by section 2 to use the 'best practicable means'[6] to prevent the emission of noxious gases and to render harmless any gases that were

5. See chap. 13 for fuller discussion of this and other legal strategies for controlling activities that have an impact on the environment.
6. As defined by s. 27, 'best practicable means' not only referred to the provision and maintenance of appropriate equipment but also covered their manner of use and their effective supervision.

emitted. The best practicable means approach (which was added to the original legislative approach by the Alkali Act 1874) continued to represent the dominant legislative approach to environmental regulation in the UK until 1990.

## Emerging trends and patterns in British environmental law

The pattern established in the early development of laws affecting the environment in the nineteenth century displayed several characteristics which have continued to shape the legal approach to environmental problems into the last quarter of the twentieth century.

### A reactive approach

These characteristics include a reactive, crisis-led approach to environmental problems, usually with an anthropocentric dimension playing an important role. The Clean Air Act 1956 (which, among other things, introduced controls on smoke emissions) was passed as a result of public pressure generated by the deaths of almost four thousand people as a result of smog in London in 1952.[7] The 1956 Act provides a good example of disaster-driven legislation and exhibits the same attempt to respond to environmental factors affecting public health as the Public Health Act 1875, which introduced provisions for municipal sewerage systems in response to repeated cholera and typhoid epidemics.

### A fragmented approach

In addition to being crisis-driven and therefore based on pragmatism rather than a clearly thought-out strategic policy, legislation covering the environment was also geographically fragmented, with legislation affecting the constituent nations of the UK being introduced at sometimes widely differing times and in slightly different terms. For example, the Public Health Act 1875, dealing with England and Wales, was largely replicated in Ireland in the Public Health (Ireland) Act 1878, but similar provision was not made for Scotland until the passing of the Public Health (Scotland) Act 1897.

Almost from its inception, environmental legislation has distinguished those complex, scientific issues deemed to be the appropriate province of centralised, professional state agencies from simple, non-technical aspects of environmental regulation, which are allocated to local government. For example, the work of the Alkali Inspectorate fell into the former category, while the administration of clean air legislation was ascribed to the latter.

For these diverse reasons the UK in the late nineteenth century (and indeed for much of the twentieth) had no coherent approach to legislation affecting the environment for the state as a whole. Environmental policy in any discrete and ordered sense had yet to even begin to emerge. Legislation, even that which was directly concerned with pollution control, remained capable of providing only incidental protection for the environment, aiming not to protect the environment for its own sake but rather to render the environment safe and exploitable for human beings.

---

7. See D. Elsom, *Atmospheric Pollution: A Global Problem,* 2nd ed., Oxford: Blackwell, 1992.

## PART II THE LAW OF GREAT BRITAIN AND THE ENVIRONMENT: DEVELOPMENTS IN THE EARLY TWENTIETH CENTURY

The first foundations of environmental law had been laid by the end of the nineteenth century and were being constantly strengthened and updated. Pollution control, albeit in an extremely rudimentary form, was firmly established. Public health laws evolved into a fairly detailed and comprehensive code, and it was from this area that one of the principal building blocks of modern environmental law, the modern Town and Country Planning System, was to grow.

Early provisions concerned with controlling the built environment aimed to secure the public health goal of slum clearance, for example the Housing, Town Planning etc. Act 1909. Later, more sophisticated and more far-reaching provisions, such as the Housing, Town Planning etc. Act 1919, emerged as the benefits of more comprehensive and positive environmental control became apparent.

The benefits of pre-emptive control of the environment, including the tackling of problems at source and preventing them rather than simply responding to crises, having become established in theory, wider practical use of these strategies followed. The manifest need for environmental and economic reconstruction after the Second World War acted as both a catalyst and a justification for extending the scope of the planning regime.

The decisive factor in establishing a modern planning system is to be found in the landmark provision nationalising the right to develop land, placing it under public control, in the Town and Country Planning Act 1947. This paved the way for a comprehensive and controlled regime of development control, a major element required in a successful planning system.

Slower to mature but no less vital was the use of the development plan, emerging in its modern two-tier form in the Town and Country Planning Act 1968. Planning of course has a direct effect on the physical environment in the allocation of land for different and perhaps conflicting activities. The indirect effect of planning on the effectiveness of other environmental control regimes must not, however, be underestimated, a point stressed by the Royal Commission on Environmental Pollution in its Fifth Report.[8]

Thus, by the latter part of the twentieth century the United Kingdom at last had a core group of laws providing more or less direct control mechanisms over the environment, which would offer the building blocks of modern environmental law, statutory controls over industrial pollution, well-developed public health controls, and an established planning system. It is, however, of paramount importance to recognise that while each of these strands of legislative activity did represent progress in controlling human impact on the environment, the fragmentation of responsibility that characterised their operation (both within central government departments and between central and local government) continued to raise barriers to an integrated approach towards environmental regulation.

There was no real political will to adopt a more co-ordinated approach to environmental issues at this time, for several reasons, chief among these being the

---

8. *Air Pollution Control: An Integrated Approach* (Cmnd 6371), London: HMSO, 1976.

rather limited state of scientific knowledge about the importance and extent of humankind's impact on the environment. The environment remained low on the political agenda as a result. The problems of fragmentation, the weakness of environmental controls and the low priority accorded to the environment on the political and therefore the legislative agenda have continued to dog the development of the law in this area until recent years, and indeed these issues have not been fully addressed even now.

## PART III THE MODERNISING OF ENVIRONMENTAL LAW

### The environment on the international agenda: the 'first wave'

If one wishes to point to the milestone that establishes the beginning of modern environmental law and policy one need look no further than the UNCED Conference on the Human Environment in Stockholm in 1972 (the first 'Earth Summit'). This event, in addition to marking the genesis of modern international environmental law, also provided the catalyst for national and regional legal action in the sphere of the environment across the globe.

For the purposes of this text it is useful to note that the EC[9] quickly seized the initiative on environmental law, and, despite the understandable absence of the topic from the Treaty of Rome 1957, considerable and rapid progress was made, based on the consensus of the member states. EC policy on the environment was addressed in the first of five Environmental Action Programmes issued in 1973,[10] incidentally coinciding with the entry of the UK into the EC.

A series of Directives, dealing at first mainly with atmospheric and water pollution and later moving on to more complex issues such as waste, followed. The legal basis of EC environmental law was originally somewhat strained, Articles 100[11] and 235[12] initially supplying the required justification for EC action. The Single European Act 1987 finally introduced specific treaty provision for the environment in the form of Article 130. The Treaty on European Union 1992 further enhanced the status of environmental protection by incorporating it into the EC's objectives by amending Article 2 of the Treaty of Rome.

Legislation has been both abundant and innovative and has spurred the development of a more modern approach to environmental law in many of the EC's member states, not least in the UK.

### 'New' environmental law in Great Britain

In the UK, some interest in a modernised view of environmental problems had emerged in official circles in the period immediately before the Stockholm conference—as evidenced, for example, by the establishment of the Royal

---

9. For a detailed examination of EC environmental law see chap. 3 infra.
10. First Environmental Action Programme, OJ C112/1 20 Dec. 1973.
11. Art. 100 of the EEC Treaty was concerned with measures required to remove trade barriers between member states.
12. Art. 235 of the EEC Treaty provides a 'catch-all' clause allowing member states to grant additional powers to the EC to achieve its Treaty objectives.

Commission on Environmental Pollution[13] in 1970. In addition the Ministry of Housing and Local Government's report *Protection of the Environment: the Fight Against Pollution*[14] demonstrated a new commitment to action within the machinery of central government.

### Institutional change

The first practical manifestation of the Government's new attitude to the environment was the creation of a new central Department of the Environment in 1970.[15] The 'new' department was actually constituted by amalgamating the Ministries of Housing and Local Government, Public Building and Works, and (temporarily) Transport. This move did not in fact represent great progress in environmental policy on anything more than a symbolic level, since what was involved was arguably more a change of title for the Ministry of Housing and Local Government[16] than a change of governmental priorities.

In addition, the impact of the creation of the DoE must be seen in context. It was, and remains, by no means the only central government Department with a role and a responsibility in respect of the environment. Other ministries—notably MAFF and the Departments of Transport, Energy, and Trade and Employment—have long played and continue to play an important part in shaping the state's dealings with the environment. The DoE as a new department (and one with a split administrative personality and priorities) found itself in a weak position vis-à-vis the long-established 'big guns' of the central government machine. The establishment of the DoE was, however, a necessary precursor of more substantive governmental activity, and it did place planning and pollution control in the hands of a single department, providing the potential for a more integrated approach to governing the environment than had hitherto been the case.

### New legislative developments in Great Britain

The landmark legislation of this period in the UK was the Control of Pollution Act 1974 (COPA), which has proved instrumental in shaping current environmental law in the UK, not least by providing a baseline against which legal progress in dealing with environmental problems could be measured. The Act was ambitious for its time, representing as it did the first serious attempt to update the largely nineteenth-century law of pollution control that continued to hold sway throughout the UK.[17]

The 1974 Act dealt primarily with controlling water pollution and with

---

13. The RCEP (established in 1970) is one of a small number of permanent Royal Commissions providing a pool of experts from a range of disciplines, with a roving remit to advise Parliament on environmental issues.
14. Cmnd 4373, 1970.
15. See chap. 1 of J. McCormick, *British Politics and the Environment*, London: Earthscan, 1991 for a brief discussion of the origins of the DoE.
16. As late as 1989 those concerned specifically with environmental matters accounted for only 10 per cent of the total complement of DoE staff (McCormick, ibid.).
17. The COPA applied only to England and Wales. For an overview of the equivalent provisions applicable in Scotland and other Scottish environmental law see C. Reid, ed. *Green's Guide to Environmental Law in Scotland*, London: Sweet and Maxwell, 1992.

introducing a standardised approach to licensing the disposal of waste, applying command and control strategies to the latter class of pollution for the first time. While COPA was innovative in some respects, not least in the introduction of a comprehensive waste deposit licensing regime and registers of environmental information that were to be open to the public,[18] it was even at the outset outdated in others; for example, the definition of pollution used in section 7 of the Act remained determinedly old-fashioned and anthropocentric in its outlook.

The biggest failing of COPA, however, lay not in the Act itself but in the government's failure to bring many of its provisions into operation. For example, the most basic provisions concerning registers of environmental information in the water sector still remained unimplemented for a decade after the passing of the Act.[19] The government also failed to promote the full exploitation of the potential of COPA in other ways. For example, the DoE quickly fell hopelessly behind schedule in producing the guidance needed to flesh out the bones of Part I of the Act. This guidance was essential to enable local authorities to carry out their new responsibilities in respect of waste licensing and disposal, and without it the legislative regime was incomplete, lacking in detail, direction, and uniformity.

Many of the provisions of COPA were obsolete before they began to operate or before they reached maturity in practice. A new wave of environmental legislation and, for the first time, something approaching a rudimentary government environmental policy had, however, begun to emerge by the late nineteen-eighties, which will take British environmental law forward into the next century. The reasons for renewed governmental interest in the environment were complex, involving a combination of political and scientific factors; the surface of which we will merely skim here.

### The environment on the domestic political agenda

As will become readily apparent throughout this text, the swift and very public rise to prominence of the environment as a political issue, and its emergence as a central part of the legal agenda of the EC, has proved the motive force in the development of much of the substantive environmental law applicable in the United Kingdom. The legal impact of the EC's activities is clearly visible, but the impact of more nebulous political pressure generated by the airing of environmental issues should not be underestimated. One concrete example of political pressure leading to action in the UK centred on the Green Party's gaining an unprecedented 15 per cent of the vote in the elections to the European Parliament in 1989.[20] As a direct result, all the main political parties stressed environmental issues as part of their appeal to the electorate at the next general election.[21] In retrospect it seems strange that it took the shock of the 1989 election

---

18. Registers, though an innovative concept, proved less impressive in practice. Access to them was often problematic and the information they contained so arcane as to be virtually useless to those without special training. See T. Burton, 'Access to Environmental Information: The UK Experience of Water Registers', 1 JEL 1989, 192.
19. Burton, ibid., points out that the registers of information concerning water pollution promised by the COPA were only set up in 1984.
20. McCormick, supra.
21. Such was the perceived voter appeal of environmental issues that even fringe parties like Militant made environmental commitments in their manifestos.

to bring home to the main political parties the potential significance of environmentally sound policies as a vote winner, since the British environmental lobby is the oldest, best organised and most widely supported in the world. In 1990 membership of environmental non-governmental organisations in the UK was estimated at about 4.5 million, or 8 per cent of the population.[22] Government policy changed markedly on a domestic level; for example, Margaret Thatcher's attitude to the environment changed from describing it as a 'humdrum issue' during the Falklands crisis to 'one of the greatest challenges of the late twentieth century' in 1988.[23]

At the same time as the developments just alluded to, growing scientific concern over global warming and ozone depletion had placed environmental issues in a new position of prominence on the global political and legal agendas.

### The emergence of a domestic environmental policy

Concrete action soon followed political rhetoric, and Britain's first white paper on the environment—*This Common Inheritance: Britain's Environmental Strategy*[24] —was published in 1990. *This Common Inheritance* performed a dual role, representing both a baseline survey of action to date and a statement of intent for future action. The report gave wide coverage to environmental issues, dealing with global and national aspects, covering sectoral approaches to environmental regulation and dealing with environmental action in the constituent nations of the UK.

The Government expressed its commitment to developing environmental policies in paragraph 1.6 of the report, emphasising the need to:

> ensure that…policies fit together in every sector; that we are not undoing in one area what we are trying to do in another; and that policies are based on a harmonious set of principles rather than a clutter of expedients.

The Government sought to identify clear foundations for environmental action, underlining the 'ethical imperative of stewardship' as the basis of all environmental policies.[25] The 'stewardship commitment' as expressed in *This Common Inheritance* enshrines aspects of intergenerational justice and wider sustainable development and is to be achieved by acting on the best evidence and analysis,[26] adopting the precautionary principle,[27] opening up environmental decision-making and practices[28] and employing the best instruments (including market mechanisms[29]) for achieving environmental objectives.[30]

The Government went some way towards achieving integration of

---

22. See McCormick, supra, chap. 2, 'The Environmental Lobby', for a brief history of the rise of environmental pressure groups in Britain.
23. McCormick, ibid.
24. Cm 1200, 1990.
25. Para. 1.14.
26. Para. 1.16–1.17.
27. Para. 1.18–1.19.
28. Para. 1.20–1.21.
29. These will be discussed briefly in chap. 13 infra.
30. Para. 1.24–1.25.

environmental issues into other policy areas by requiring each government department to consider its own impact on the environment. Central government departments were also required to designate a minister to be responsible both for their own environmental policy[31] and to work on a ministerial committee charged with developing a co-ordinated approach to environmental issues.[32] In addition, a commitment was made to produce annual departmental reports charting progress on environmental initiatives.[33] Annual reports updating *This Common Inheritance* itself also provide a means both of charting general progress on the environment and allowing the progress of individual policies to be followed.

*This Common Inheritance* for practical purposes represents a new maturing in environmental policy in the UK and demonstrates a more structured and coherent approach to environmental issues than was previously possible.

## Institutional developments

While the development of environmental policy was crucial to the modernisation of environmental law in Britain, it did not represent the only means nor indeed the only motivation for the modification of environmental governance that has occurred in recent years. The maturing of environmental policy has had its parallel in the development of improved institutions in the environment sector.

### Her Majesty's Inspectorate of Pollution Control

HMIP was set up in 1987, not as the result of any drive to promote specific benefits to the environmental regulatory system but rather as part of a more general move to render central government institutions more efficient. It was not a new body but rather unified those elements of operational pollution control already located within the DoE;[34] the Air Pollution Inspectorate of the Health and Safety Executive[35] and the Radiochemical, Hazardous Waste and Water Inspectorates. HMIP constituted one of the four directorates in the Department's Environmental Protection Group, the others being the Directorate of Pollution Control, the Directorate of Air, Noise and Waste, and the Central Directorate of Environmental Protection.[36]

HMIP provided an opportunity for the industrial pollution control regime to attempt to escape from the tarnished image it had developed in its long and rather undistinguished history. It suffered, however, from many of the problems that had dogged its constituent parts; it continued to be chronically understaffed and underfunded and to have difficulty in establishing a distinct identity, subsumed as it was within the DoE.

*This Common Inheritance* introduced a solution to some of these problems by announcing that HMIP was to become a 'Next Steps' Agency, in the model

---

31. Para. 18.4.
32. Para. 18.3.
33. Para. 18.5.
34. The DoE's operational role was at that time very limited and has since decreased even further.
35. Previously known as the Alkali and Clean Air Inspectorate, the successor of the original Alkali Inspectorate.
36. See chap. 3 of Ball and Bell, *Environmental Law*, 3rd ed., London: Blackstone, 1995, for a brief history of the development of the DoE.

established by the popular National Rivers Authority (see below), though this move itself was not without drawbacks. The 'Next Steps' Initiative went much further than dealing with the environmental sector; it was essentially geared to allowing central government departments to divest themselves of operational functions[37] by creating largely autonomous agencies to deal with the day-to-day business of the state. Ministerial responsibility—the traditional means of ensuring the government's accountability for the activities of the wider executive—is less relevant to the new non-departmental public bodies created under the 'Next Steps' Initiative, since responsibility for operational decisions lies with the director of the agency in question and not with the minister in charge of the parent department. Traditional checks on the executive, such as parliamentary questions, have thus lost much of their potency; questions, instead of being dealt with by ministers in the House of Commons, are now forwarded to the director of the agency in question and will be answered in writing by the director. The only traditional form of accountability to Parliament which remains is rather less direct and certainly has a lower profile; the director of a 'Next Steps' Agency is responsible to Parliament, under the auspices of the Public Accounts Committee, for the way in which that agency uses public money.

HMIP's profile was further raised by its enhanced responsibilities in respect of industrial pollution control under Part I of the Environmental Protection Act 1990 (see below).

### *The National Rivers Authority*

The National Rivers Authority was set up in England and Wales[38] under the Water Act 1989.[39] This Act made long-overdue changes to the regulatory regime for water, but its prime aim was to carry through the Government's privatisation of the water industry. The Government had not initially intended to create a body like the NRA, having envisaged the privatised water companies being self-regulating. Such a situation would have broadly reflected the previous regulatory regime contained in the Water Act 1973, under which the ten Regional Water Authorities held both regulatory and operational powers, creating the much-criticised 'poacher-gamekeeper' combination. The Government was forced to delay its privatisation programme and to introduce a separate regulatory regime by a threat made by the Council for the Protection of Rural England to take the Government to the European Court of Justice, since the legislation as originally envisaged would have constituted a breach of EC law.

The NRA was charged with responsibility for regulating the majority of industrial discharges[40] to the aquatic environment (in consultation with HMIP)

---

37. The line between policy and operational issues is not always clear and has been the subject of public concern, for example in respect of the very public row on prison security between Michael Howard and the head of the prisons agency.
38. For details of the law in Scotland see *Green's Guide,* supra.
39. This gargantuan piece of legislation was split into five separate Acts in 1991; the NRA's powers are delineated by the Water Resources Act 1991.
40. The NRA was not given responsibility for the discharge of trade effluent to sewers, which is covered by the provisions of the Water Industry Act 1991 and falls under the ultimate control of the Director-General for Water Services.

and with some operational responsibilities, including regulating water flows and extractions, flood defence, navigation, and recreation. It operates on the basis of what has become known as 'integrated river basin management', taking an holistic approach to the whole water resource. In carrying out its specific duties the NRA is subject, under section 16 of the Water Resources Act 1991, to a general 'environmental' duty to:

> promote conservation and enhancement of natural beauty or amenity of inland or coastal waters and associated lands, flora and fauna and recreation.

The NRA swiftly gained the respect and support of many eminent environmental non-governmental organisations, not least the Council for the Protection of Rural England and the World Wide Fund for Nature, no doubt in part because of its aggressive prosecution strategy; it initiated no less than 3,997 successful prosecutions for offences concerning the water environment in its first year of operation.[41]

### The new Environment Agency

The Government, after several years of discussion, made provision in the Environment Act 1995[42] for two new agencies,[43] to be modelled on the successful format established by the NRA. The Environment Agency (EA)[44] in England and Wales and the Scottish Environmental Protection Agency (SEPA),[45] which are due to come into operation on 1 April 1996, represent a new departure for environmental governance in Great Britain. The agencies bring together for the first time most aspects of environmental regulation in a single unit, thus more accurately reflecting the integrated and holistic nature of the physical environment in the institutional arrangements designed to deal with its problems. The agencies will assume responsibility for the tasks formerly undertaken by HMIP and the NRA (and their Scottish equivalents) together with waste regulation and waste disposal regulatory responsibilities.[46]

We shall look briefly at the EA. The Act lays out (in section 4(1)) the Agency's principal aim:

> (subject to and in accordance with the provisions of this Act or any other enactment and taking into account any likely costs) in discharging its functions so to protect or enhance the environment, taken as a whole, as to make the contribution towards attaining the objective of sustainable development . . .[47]

---

41. See Ball and Bell, supra.
42. For a detailed commentary see Peter Lane and Monica Peto, *Blackstone's Guide to the Environment Act 1995,* London: Blackstone, 1995.
43. These agencies will cover England and Wales and Scotland, respectively; institutional arrangements in Northern Ireland are also set to change but in a rather different manner from their British counterparts; see chap. 2.
44. Covered by chap. 1, subss 1–19 of the Act.
45. Covered by chap. 2, subss 20–36 of the Act.
46. Some of the functions themselves are amended by the 1995 Act; see Lane and Peto, supra.
47. That is, a commitment to using ministerial guidance issued under s. 4(2) to promote the attainment of the objective of sustainable development by the agency in the discharge of its functions.

The EA's general functions with relation to pollution control are laid out in section 5, while section 6 makes like provision for water. These functions are subject to the Agency's general environmental and recreational duties contained in section 7; these duties involve general requirements placed on the Secretary of State for the Environment and the Agency (by section 7(1)(*a*)):

> so to exercise any power conferred on him or it . . . as to further the conservation and enhancement of natural beauty and the conservation of flora, fauna and geological or physiographical features of special interest.

Special coverage is given, among other things, to the protection and conservation of buildings, sites and objects of archaeological, architectural, engineering or historical interest (section 7(1)(*c*)(i)), along with more traditional environmental factors—flora and fauna (section 7(1)(*c*)(ii))—in proposals relating to the Agency's functions. The Agency is also called on to consider the economic and social well-being of rural communities in its proposals (section 7(1)(*c*)(iii)).

The new agencies seem to represent a good opportunity to allow the environmental regulatory regime in Great Britain to gain in strength and to reach maturity—though one note of caution should be sounded. In Britain the government has gained a reputation among environmentalists for showing a marked propensity to tinker with the institutions that deliver environmental regulation in preference to dealing with more substantive issues. The success of the new agencies will depend on many factors, not least the perennial problems of securing adequate funding and staff. If governmental support is not forthcoming then the agencies will not realise their full and considerable potential.

## Environmental legislation

### *The Environmental Protection Act 1990*

The Environmental Protection Act 1990[48] represented a major development in British environmental law and the foundation for future developments (including the Environment Act 1995). The 1990 Act overhauled and updated the regulatory regime for waste (Part II building on lessons learned from the shortcomings of the COPA regime in practice), the rather elderly statutory nuisance system (which was largely nineteenth-century in its content, substantially updated by Part III), litter (Part IV), and the new, previously uncharted area of genetically modified organisms (Part VI).

The most innovative aspect of the 1990 Act, however—the Government's 'big idea' in environmental law—was found in Part I of the Act, which introduced the system of integrated pollution control (IPC). This was first suggested as the way forward for modern environmental legislation by the Royal Commission on Environmental Pollution in its Fifth Report in 1976.[49] The idea was simple; a fragmented system of environmental laws and institutions was identified as leading to potential regulatory conflict and possibly even adverse consequences

---

48. Stephen Tromans has produced an invaluable commentary on the 1990 Act, *The Environmental Protection Act 1990*, 2nd ed., London: Sweet and Maxwell, 1993.
49. Op. cit.

for the environment. The RCEP suggested that a system of environmental governance be developed which, instead of taking a traditional sectoral approach to pollution control, looked at the environment as a whole, allowing the 'best practicable environmental option' (BPEO)[50] to be chosen for dealing with pollution. The means to be employed to achieve the BPEO were broader than the old 'best practicable means' requirement, the 1990 Act introducing instead the requirement of the 'best available techniques[51] not entailing excessive costs' (BATNEEC)[52] as a general condition to be complied with by every authorisation issued under the IPC regime.

While IPC applies only to the most polluting industrial processes, as laid down in the Environmental Protection (Prescribed Processes and Substances Regulations) 1991[53] (as amended), it represents a revolutionary concept in environmental regulation in that it allows for a single licensing system to be operated by a single agency (initially HMIP in consultation with the NRA where appropriate; the EA will take over this responsibility). IPC seems set to dominate the agenda for environmental regulation well into the next century, since it is to be the subject of EC legislation.[54]

Development in environmental institutions and in substantive environmental legislation in Britain has been particularly frenetic within the last decade—so much so that there has been little time to gauge the success or otherwise of the various initiatives outlined above. At the time of writing another stage of upheaval is about to begin with the establishment of the new environment agencies. There does seem to be some reason for optimism in looking to the future, however, since logic would appear to dictate that the environmental laws and institutions best fitted to deliver effective environmental regulation are those that replicate the holistic nature of the environment itself rather than being fragmented by historical accident or for administrative convenience.

---

50. The BPEO involves a co-ordinated approach to decision-making, identifying the alternatives available for dealing with the pollution generated by any particular industrial process and choosing the disposal option that is least harmful to the environment as a whole. For details see the RCEP Twelfth Report, *Best Practicable Environmental Option* (Cm 310), London: HMSO, 1988.
51. This includes not just plant and machinery but also training of the work force, building design, etc.
52. The BATNEEC requirement is found in s. 7(2)(*a*) of the 1990 Act.
53. SI 1991 No. 472.
54. Integrated pollution control is currently the subject of a draft Directive.

# CHAPTER TWO

# Environmental Law and Policy in Northern Ireland

## Introduction

For a variety of reasons, primarily historical, political, and geographical, Northern Ireland has a legal system which, while reflecting closely that of England and Wales, is at the same time both distinct and distinctive. The uniqueness of the Northern Ireland legal system is clearly demonstrated in the environmental laws that apply in this jurisdiction. It is, however, unfortunate that, as will be amply illustrated in the chapters which follow, the state of environmental law in Northern Ireland demonstrates some of the worst defects of the Northern Ireland legal system. This is particularly so with regard to the prevalence of antiquated legislation and in the frequent failure to secure the timely implementation of EC legislation. Questions of accountability and the ability of the administration to respond to local opinion are also thrown into sharp relief by environmental governance in Northern Ireland.

As well as featuring a distinctive corpus of environmental law, Northern Ireland also features unique arrangements both in the institutions with responsibility for the environment and in the evolution and development of environmental policy. These areas will form the basis for discussion in this chapter, with the substantive law forming the subject of the bulk of the text to follow.

It will already be apparent that the mechanisms adopted by the government to carry out environmental functions in Great Britain (and most particularly in England and Wales[1]) have been subject to frequent criticism and change, particularly since 1987. Northern Ireland's environmental institutions and laws have for many years been subject to similar pressures.

## PART I ENVIRONMENTAL POLICIES AND INSTITUTIONS UNDER THE NORTHERN IRELAND PARLIAMENT, 1922–72

### The Government of Ireland Act 1920

As one would expect in a statute from this era, the environment was not a policy priority area when it came to the division of responsibilities between the

---

1. Changes have also occurred in Scotland, although these have been for the most part less marked than south of the border (the focus of government activity having been, until the passage of the Environment Act 1995, on adapting the role of existing agencies rather than creating new ones); see C. Reid, ed. *Green's Guide to Environmental Law in Scotland* for a survey of the law; London: Sweet & Maxwell, 1992.

Westminster Parliament and the devolved legislatures[2] provided for in the Government of Ireland Act 1920. Laws affecting the environment fell under the general legislative competence of the Northern Ireland Parliament laid out in section 4 of the Act, namely:

> to make laws for the peace, order and good government of . . . Northern Ireland. . . .

This wide grant of power[3] was, however, hedged about by limitations in the form of 'excepted matters',[4] listed in section 4. Firstly there was a general territorial limitation placed on the legislative competence of the Northern Ireland parliament; it was only competent to legislate:

> in respect of matters exclusively relating to that portion of Ireland within [its] jurisdiction . . .

This general geographical limitation is of considerable practical significance, particularly in the environmental sector (though the issue is relevant to other policy areas), since the shape of the political institutions created by the 1920 Act was based on political compromise rather than an attempt to address issues at the optimum level on the ground; environmental problems (like many other subjects) are not neatly delineated by political borders.

Other subject-specific exceptions followed; these included, as one would expect, prohibitions on legislation concerning the Crown (section 4(1)(1)), foreign affairs, including war (section 4(1)(2)) and treaties (section 4(1)(4)), and the military (section 4(1)(3)).

Further limitations were imposed by the provisions of section 9 of the Act, delineating 'reserved matters'; these functions were, for the time being, to remain in the hands of the Westminster parliament but could in the future present opportunities for further devolution.

## Environmental matters within Northern Ireland

Internal arrangements in Northern Ireland were, like those in Great Britain at the time, vague on the question of environmental responsibility. Environmental issues were covered within the remit of traditional subject-specific departments—primarily the Ministry of Development, but other departments, notably Finance, and Health and Social Services, continued to play a highly influential role. It would be many years before the environment gained a sufficiently high political profile to emerge as the basis for a discrete department displaying even a nominal environmental ethos.

---

2. Of course the Government of Ireland Act 1920 never came into force in the southern part of the island. Its provisions, however, were not altered to fit the peculiarities of the Northern Ireland micro-state to which it eventually applied. For a wider discussion of the import of the 1920 Act see B. Hadfield, *The Constitution of Northern Ireland*, Belfast: SLS 1989.
3. Lord Thankerton in *Government of Ireland Act 1920 and Finance Act* (NI) *1934, s. 3, Re a Reference under* [1936] AC 352, stated: 'The Government of Northern Ireland has a sovereign Parliament, except in so far as certain powers are reserved.'
4. Excepted matters were those that it was considered necessary to retain at Westminster in order to retain the supremacy of the British parliament in respect of the external affairs of the United Kingdom and matters of national concern.

Some progress was made, however, in modernising domestic arrangements. The Town and Country Planning System began to emerge, based on a partial adaptation of the ground-breaking British system.[5] The utility of this process of adaptation was limited, however, by the fact that the British system, together with the network of ministerial guidance underpinning it, was tailored specifically to British needs and was not always fitted in scale, approach or content to the rather different Northern Ireland context. The Northern Ireland planning system quickly fell behind that in Great Britain, its initial momentum soon being lost, and the permissive and unsophisticated Planning and Housing (NI) Act 1931 dominated the law until the reintroduction of direct rule.

The way in which the planning system dealt with the environment under the Stormont government was determined by the government's policy priority of providing for the economic stability of the still young state. The exploitative provisions of the New Industries Development Acts (NI) 1932 and 1937 typified the government's approach, encouraging, indeed actively promoting, development as top priority.

If the Northern Ireland state's progress in making use of the potential of the planning system as an active tool for environmental control was less than edifying, its record in the development of other environmental control law and techniques was, if anything, even worse. The decidedly archaic provisions of the Public Health (Ireland) Act 1878 continued to dominate sanitary arrangements. The equally dated Alkali &c. Works Registration Act 1906 remained the focus for the regulation of industrial pollution. While the situation in Northern Ireland betrayed a marked degree of government indifference to the environment as an issue requiring state action, the lack of interest this evidenced could perhaps be described as different in degree rather than in kind from that displayed for much of the period in both Great Britain and Ireland.

When the environment finally rose to prominence on the international agenda in the late nineteen-sixties and early seventies and came to the fore on the domestic political agenda in Great Britain, its progress to prominence in Northern Ireland was retarded by the wider political crisis that had by this time engulfed the state.

## The political crisis and environmental issues in Northern Ireland

The next major change in environmental governance in Northern Ireland came about as the result of wider political pressure and compromise. Responsibility for the environment was taken out of the hands of local authorities, primarily because of its historical attachment to the politically contentious housing issue. The blueprint for wide institutional change within Northern Ireland, although reaching its ultimate execution under direct rule, was put in place (admittedly under severe domestic and external political pressure) by the Northern Ireland government.

The agenda for future change affecting the environment was part of a wider programme of institutional change initiated by the NI Prime Minister in a speech in the House of Commons on 17 December 1970. The main changes in respect of

---

5. See J. Hendry, 'The control of development and the origins of planning in Northern Ireland' in M. Bannon (ed.), *Planning: The Irish Experience, 1920–88,* Dublin: Wolfhound, 1989.

the environment were to be generated by proposed changes in the role of local government laid down by the Ministry of Development in its consultative document *Reorganising of Services.*[6] The strategy adopted involved marginalising the local political contribution in order to eliminate the endemic discrimination in the provision of local government services that had grown up since partition. The Ministry's scheme aimed to solve several problems at once; for our purposes the most important aims were to set up a new (less powerful but at the same time more representative) system of district councils and:

> to organise and to discharge in a planned and co-ordinated way, the regional functions under town and country planning (including urban renewal and town and village centre development), roads, traffic management, water supply and sewerage . . .

which were to be assigned to the Ministry of Development. Other priorities included liaison by the Ministry in its functions with the new district councils, the new Northern Ireland Housing Executive and the new education and library boards and health and social services boards.

The basic role and functions of the Ministry of Development became, by courtesy of a fashionable name change, the province of the Department of the Environment (DoE(NI)).

The relationship between central and local government in the provision of environmental services in Northern Ireland was shaped into its modern form at this time; the role given to local government was clearly established as subsidiary to that projected for the new central Department. The responsibilities to be designated for local government were clearly delineated to include:

- entertainment, culture and recreation[7]
- environmental health[8]
- cleansing and sanitation[9]
- protective services[10]
- regulatory services[11]
- cemeteries etc.
- gas undertakings
- markets and abattoirs.

While the functions given to district councils were all important in their own right, they were less than high-powered; they remained almost solely concerned with the operational aspects of a fairly mechanical range of functions.

Not only did the changes instituted in the early nineteen-seventies see the range and scope of local government contribution to the environmental governance of Northern Ireland curtailed but the role of central agencies—particularly of course the Department of the Environment but also the Department of Economic

---

6. Belfast: HMSO 1971.
7. This included responsibility for parks and urban landscaping.
8. This included responsibility for nuisances, clean air zoning and pest control.
9. This included responsibility for domestic and trade refuse collection and street cleansing.
10. For example water safety.
11. The environmental aspects of these powers demonstrate the rather prosaic nature of the whole class of powers they cover: the creation of building bylaws (subject to statutory direction), controlling dangerous buildings and places and dealing with petroleum storage.

Development (DED) and the Department of Agriculture for Northern Ireland (DANI)—was at the same time greatly expanded.

### Some problems resulting from Northern Ireland's unique system of environmental governance

The central government departments within Northern Ireland have, like their counterparts in Great Britain, an extensive role to play in the development of the strategic policy level of executive action with respect to the environment. However, in contrast to arrangements elsewhere, central departments in Northern Ireland have, since the early nineteen-seventies, had an enhanced role to play in the operational delivery of environmental governance and services that far outstrips that of the equivalent institutions in Great Britain.

One example of the dominance of central departments (and of the problems this can cause) is readily apparent in the context of town and country planning.[12] The DoE(NI) is the sole planning authority in Northern Ireland; its many responsibilities include:

- policy
- regional planning
- research
- urban renewal
- development control
- the preparation and review of area plans.

The DoE's planning service is therefore the holder of responsibilities in Northern Ireland that in effect amalgamate the roles played in Great Britain by the DoE and local government. On the mainland the DoE's role is primarily supervisory, whereas local government plays the primary role in carrying out development control and plan-making functions.[13] The result of this amalgamation is two-fold. The removal of the local political element from the planning system arguably decreases both the openness of the planning system and its incentive to respond to local people's needs and views; secondly, in addition to becoming less democratic, the system is also perceived as more 'professional' or technocratic, run by experts in planning issues and rather mystifying to the general public. The situation with regard to planning issues is replicated in the provision of other environmental services and regulation within Northern Ireland.

In addition to the problems inherent in the way planning functions have been allocated to the DoE(NI), further difficulties are also apparent in respect of its pollution control problems. For example, the DoE(NI) is charged with responsibility for regulating the aquatic environment in Northern Ireland.[14] Its responsibilities in this sector range from managing water resources (flow and abstraction etc.) to the control of pollution and the provision of water supply and sewerage services. The last function sits uneasily with the others, most particularly pollution control, since it places the Department (despite the different tasks in

---

12. For an examination of the operation of the planning system in Northern Ireland see A. Dowling, *Northern Ireland Planning Law,* Dublin: Gill & Macmillan, 1995.

13. In Northern Ireland, local authorities, far from initiating plans and running the development control system, find their role reduced to that of statutory consultees.

14. See chap. 4.

question being carried out by different branches of the organisation—the Water Executive and the Environment Service, respectively) in the unenviable position of being both poacher and gamekeeper. The current situation in which the DoE(NI) finds itself in regulating the water resource within Northern Ireland is rather like that of Regional Water Authorities in England and Wales before the privatisation of the water industry and the creation of the National Rivers Authority in 1989. The DoE(NI) is expected to regulate polluting discharges by industry while at the same time carrying operational responsibility for one of the most potentially environmentally damaging aspects of all human activity, and some conflict of interest would appear to be inevitable.

### Pressure for change: the impact of EC membership

While it is clear that domestic political pressure played the most significant part in reshaping the distribution of power between the central and local tiers of government in Northern Ireland, the same could not be said for the substantive law for which they are responsible. In Northern Ireland, as in the rest of the United Kingdom, the motive force for the modernisation of environmental laws has come from the pressure generated by the EC's gradual but pervasive extension of its competence into environmental issues. The nature and extent of the EC's influence is discussed in chapter 3.

## PART II THE CURRENT STRUCTURE AND RESPONSIBILITIES OF DoE(NI)

Pending imminent reorganisation of responsibility for many of the DoE(NI)'s operational functions—to transfer them into the hands of 'Next Steps' Agencies (which will be discussed below)—the organisation is currently tackling its diverse range of responsibilities in the following manner.[15]

### Water

The water environment in Northern Ireland continues to be organised on the same basis as that introduced in the early nineteen-seventies. The substantive legal provisions applicable are still centred on the Water Act (Northern Ireland) 1972 (as amended) and the Water and Sewerage Services (Northern Ireland) Order 1973[16] (as amended).[17]

The administrative structure of the Water Executive dealing with the operational aspects of the aquatic environment is divided between a head office with responsibility for policy issues and four divisional offices responsible for carrying out practical functions, located in Belfast, Ballymena, Craigavon and Derry. The geographical division of responsibility is based loosely on the catchment patterns of the main waterways in Northern Ireland. This factor, together with the fact that the wide range of the DoE(NI)'s responsibilities enable

---

15. For a brief overview of the DoE(NI)'s framework and its responsibilities see *Your Guide to DoE Services,* Belfast: DoE (NI) 1992 (part of the Citizen's Charter Initiative).
16. SI 1973 No. 70.
17. See chap. 5.

it to cover not just pollution control but also resource management issues, allows the regulatory regime the potential to offer an holistic approach to governing the water resource.

## Roads

The Roads Service within the DoE(NI) plans and builds new roads and also maintains the existing 15,000 miles of road and 4,300 miles of footpath in Northern Ireland. The service also deals with tackling traffic congestion.

## Works

The Department of Works is, as its name suggests, responsible for carrying out construction-based projects. This task is increasingly achieved by tendering works out to the private sector.

## Planning

The DoE(NI) Planning Service is divided into a central office and eight local planning offices, located in Ballymena, Belfast, Coleraine, Craigavon, Downpatrick, Enniskillen, Derry and Omagh. The Planning Service deals with approximately 18,000 planning applications annually, an average of 90 per cent of which are approved.[18] This statistic is rather worrying if one perceives the role of planning as being more than merely permissive.

The planning system in Northern Ireland has been subject to investigation and report on several occasions,[19] both in respect of specific planning issues (such as W. H. Cockcroft's *Review of Rural Planning Policy*[20]) and as part of the wider system of environmental control in Northern Ireland in the Rossi Report.[21] This report was particularly critical of the failure of the Northern Ireland planning system to adequately enforce countryside protection policies,[22] a phenomenon resulting in, among other things, the prevalence of 'bungalow blight'. As the CNCC (see below) stated in its evidence to the Rossi Committee, the policy of the DoE(NI) Planning Service on building houses in the countryside has led to an unenviable reputation for the planning system in Northern Ireland:

> Northern Ireland is cited by Planning Departments in Scotland and Wales as the worst case example, on no account to be followed.[23]

In the light of such criticism it is not surprising that the structure and operation of the Town and Country Planning System in Northern Ireland are once again the subject of scrutiny, this time by the House of Commons Select Committee on Northern Ireland.

---

18. See *Your Guide to DoE Services,* supra.
19. See Dowling, *Northern Ireland Planning Law,* supra.
20. London: HMSO, 1978.
21. House of Commons Environment Committee, *Environmental Issues in Northern Ireland,* HC 39(1990).
22. Para. 99.
23. Evidence, pp 15 and 16.

## The DoE(NI) Environment Service

While it is readily apparent that the aforementioned parts of the DoE(NI) play a very significant role in shaping Northern Ireland's environment, the specific focus for environmental regulation within the Department lies within the remit of the relatively new Environment Service (ES). The ES was set up in November 1990 as a key part of the Government's strategy designed to respond to the serious criticism of the structures for dealing with environmental protection in Northern Ireland expressed in the Rossi Report.

Another key part of the Government's response to the Rossi Report, and one of considerable importance for the ES in practice, was a commitment to deal with the chronic problem of the 'legislation lag' that had built up in Northern Ireland environmental law. This problem, which was particularly acute with regard to the provisions of EC law, required the devotion of considerable financial and legislative resources to updating existing legislative provision and to considering greater use of simultaneous legislation covering the whole UK in future. Progress has been slow but, at least as far as clearing the legislative backlog is concerned, the fruit of this policy commitment is finally beginning to be seen, as for example in the provisions of the Water and Sewerage Services (Amendment) (Northern Ireland) Order 1993[24] and the proposals for draft Orders on Waste and Contaminated Land and Industrial Pollution Control 1996 (see chapters 6 and 4, respectively).

The Environment Service emerged from an amalgamation of the existing Environmental Protection Division and the Conservation Service. The development of the ES was, however, of greater significance than a merely cosmetic rearranging of administrative structures. The profile of environmental regulation was considerably enhanced by the inclusion of the Service's Director on the DoE(NI)'s senior policy-making body, the Departmental Board.

## The remit of the Environment Service

The ES has a broad remit, its responsibilities straddling both operational and policy-based dimensions of the regulation of pollution in all environmental media, the conservation of the natural environment, and preservation of the built and historical environment. The ES also generates environmental information, particularly through the publication of its own biennial reports and through co-ordinating the Northern Ireland dimension in the UK-wide annual updates to *This Common Inheritance.*

The considerable breadth of the ES's role is most readily appreciated when it is recognised that the equivalent functions are carried out in England by a combination of the DoE, the Department of National Heritage, the Ministry of Agriculture, Fisheries and Food, the National Rivers Authority, Her Majesty's Inspectorate of Pollution, English Nature, English Heritage, the Royal Commission on Historic Monuments, and local authorities.

While such broad coverage of environmental governance functions allows in theory for an extremely co-ordinated and holistic approach to environmental control, the reality of the ES is that of a relatively small and underfunded agency

---

24. SI 1993 No. 3165.

struggling with a gargantuan regulatory role. The ES has been strengthened since its inception in the attempt to better equip it for its task. Staff numbers have been augmented, rising from 314 in 1990 to 408 in 1993[25] (though this had fallen to 370 by 1995[26]). Funding for environmental regulation in Northern Ireland has increased markedly, particularly in the early years of the service, from £6,456,000 (1989/90) to £17,800,000 (1992/93).[27]

### The structure of the Environment Service

The ES is organised in three directorates: Environmental Protection, Conservation (of both the natural and built environment) and Policy and Finance. The directors of each of these groupings, together with the ES's general director, head the service.

The responsibilities of each directorate are as follows:

*Environmental Protection*

- water quality functions (dealing with both pollution control and emergencies);
- the functions of the Alkali and Radiochemical Inspectorate (dealing with industrial air pollution and radioactivity);
- provision for environmental health (providing specialist technical advice to both central and local government).

(Waste management will be added to this directorate's responsibilities under the draft Waste and Contaminated Land Order 1996.)

*Conservation*

- the protection of habitats and species;
- the protection of the countryside and coast;
- the creation and operation of nature reserves and country parks;
- the protection of historic monuments;
- the protection of historic buildings.

*Policy and Finance*

- developing the ES's policy;
- setting out the ES's financial strategy;
- co-ordinating the ES's legislative programme;
- the provision of advice to ministers.

---

25. See Minutes of Evidence to House of Commons Environment Committee, session 1992–93, HC 861-1, part 1, annex A, para. 2.3. Some 60 per cent of the service's staff are non-industrial, being either professionals or administrators.
26. *Environment Service Report,* 1993–95, London: HMSO, 1993.
27. *Environment Service Report, 1991–93,* London: HMSO, 1993. The budget allocation above represented an increase of 23.5 per cent on that for the previous year.

The ES is supported in carrying out appropriate functions by specialist advice from the Council for Nature Conservation and the Countryside[28] (CNCC), the Historical Monuments Council, and the Historic Buildings Council.

The ES has, in order to better carry out its many tasks, developed working links with the other services located within the DoE(NI) and with other Northern Ireland Departments, particularly DANI, with a view to integrating environmental concerns with other aspects of government activity. The ES has also actively fostered ties with its counterparts in Great Britain and Ireland. The EC approved a joint initiative for the development of border areas between Northern Ireland and the Republic as part of the EC's INTERREG scheme in July 1991, which gives cross-border environmental co-operation a practical dimension.[29]

### The corporate aim of the Environment Service

The Service's aim in all its many tasks, as expressed in the first of its biennial reports in 1993,[30] is:

> to protect and conserve the natural and man-made environment and to promote its appreciation for the benefit of present and future generations.

To this end the ES has produced a corporate plan[31] setting out its plans and priorities for future action.

## Criticism of environmental governance in Northern Ireland: continued pressure for change

### The Rossi Report, November 1990 — signs of progress

The relatively poor record of the DoE(NI) in environmental protection in Northern Ireland, though long a source of disquiet within the Province, was not a priority for the UK government until the true extent of the inadequacies that existed was thrown into the political spotlight by a highly critical report issued by the House of Commons Select Committee on the Environment. The Rossi Report was extremely critical of many aspects of environmental governance in Northern Ireland. It made some twenty-nine recommendations for improvements in the substantive law, in policy and on an institutional level. The Rossi Report was instrumental in the foundation of the ES (as discussed above).

In the area of substantive law, emphasis was laid on updating compliance with EC Directives[32] and on minimising current and future disparities between the

---

28. The CNCC was set up in 1989 in response to the recommendations of J. P. Balfour's report *A New Look at the Northern Ireland Countryside,* London: HMSO, 1994. The CNCC is, however, not the high-profile independent equivalent of (what is now known as) English Nature, which was recommended in the Balfour Report; instead it is a body consisting of eighteen voluntary experts with a stipendiary chairman and deputy located within the DoE(NI), which 'supports' its work by providing it with two secretarial staff.
29. Minutes of Evidence to HC Environment Committee, part 1, annex A, para. 13.4.
30. *Environment Service Report, 1991–93,* London: HMSO, 1993.
31. *Environment Service Corporate Plan, 1994–97.*
32. Rec. 1, para. 32.

environmental law applicable in Northern Ireland and that in the rest of the UK.[33] In the policy arena, recommendations included increasing the resources applied to the designation of historic monuments and conservation areas[34] and the designation of areas of special scientific interest (ASSIs).[35]

Waste disposal issues, the need for coherent regional waste licensing within the province and contaminated land also received attention.[36] Improvements in water and air pollution controls were also suggested.[37]

The Committee's recommendations regarding institutional arrangements included emphasising the need for the DoE(NI) to develop a more positive approach to and a higher profile in conservation issues.[38] The Committee also recommended more sweeping change in the form of an environment agency for Northern Ireland,[39] for the following reasons:

> A Northern Ireland environmental agency could develop its own character, could be a focus for local pride in the environmental heritage and could play a full part in relationships with other national agencies and contribute to United Kingdom conservation.

The Committee suggested that such an agency should combine those functions exercised in England and Wales by English Heritage, the National Rivers Authority, Her Majesty's Inspectorate of Pollution, the Countryside Commission, and the Nature Conservancy Council.[40]

### The Government's response, March 1991

The Government's response to the Rossi Report is best described as mixed, ranging from positive action in setting up and supporting the ES to inertia on some of the Committee's more ambitious recommendations. For example, the Government was of the opinion that the small size of the Northern Ireland jurisdiction did not justify the creation of a separate environment agency. The Government did, however, promise action on other highlighted problem areas that appeared in the report, notably in respect of the legislative backlog.

### The DoE(NI) memorandum from Minutes of Evidence to the House of Commons Environment Committee (HC 861-1, session 1992/93)

Despite the recommendations of the Rossi Report and imminent change elsewhere in the UK, the Government expressed a wish to hold its fire on institutional changes within Northern Ireland until the proposed agencies for England and Wales and Scotland were operating.[41] Several reasons were given for this

---

33. Rec. 2, para 33.
34. Rec. 3, para. 40.
35. Rec. 4 and 5, para. 45 and 47.
36. Rec. 8, 9, 10, and 11, para. 61, 64, 68, and 71.
37. Rec. 12–17, para. 76, 77, 79, 80, 82, and 84; rec. 18 and 29, para. 88 and 96.
38. Rec. 25, para 124.
39. Rec. 26, para 129.
40. The latter functions have, since the Environmental Protection Act 1990 came into effect, been exercised by English Nature.
41. Minutes of Evidence to HC Environment Committee, part 2, annex A, para. 26.5.

reluctance to replicate British regulatory structures in Northern Ireland. These included the fact that the major functions suggested for the new agencies in Great Britain, with the exception of waste regulation, are already under the control of the Environment Service.[42] (Waste regulation too is to fall under the remit of the ES under the Draft Waste Order 1996.) As a result, it was claimed that many of the benefits of a unified agency are 'already being achieved' within the DoE(NI).

In addition it was pointed out that the Environment Service itself was relatively new and, given the augmentation of its resources, was just beginning to make a significant impact on the Northern Ireland environment,[43] and the Department wished to build on its success.

Finally, the DoE(NI) expressed the opinion that change in Northern Ireland's environmental governance should now be focused on:

> providing primary legislation, developing policies and securing professional expertise to address environmental issues to the point where arrangements in Northern Ireland have caught up with the rest of the United Kingdom . . .[44]

concentrating on substantive issues rather than tinkering with the institutions designed to deal with them.

### The shape of things to come

The DoE(NI) in its evidence to the House of Commons Environment Committee in 1993, while expressing a broadly negative view on the prospect of introducing a unified independent environment agency for Northern Ireland, was careful to mention that the Government was 'committed to keeping under review' Northern Ireland's environmental institutions. The result of this review has not, however, been a commitment to replicate the new environment agencies for England and Wales and Scotland in Northern Ireland but instead to extend the 'Next Steps' Initiative to environmental governance in the Province.

### The 'Next Steps' Initiative

Successive Conservative governments from 1979 onwards expressed a progressive concern with the cost of the civil service to the public purse and with pursuing efficiency in the delivery of public services. This concern eventually came to fruition in the policy arena with the Ibbs Report, *Improving Management in Government: The Next Steps,* delivered to the Prime Minister in 1988.[45] This report set out the thinking behind, and gave its name to, the 'Next Steps' Initiative. The report concluded that the civil service was too cumbersome[46] and too diverse to be viably and efficiently managed as a single body. The suggested remedy to the problem of managing the machinery of state was to separate those functions that were the essential province of central government[47] from the operational and

---

42. Ibid., para. 26.6.
43. Ibid., para. 26.8.
44. Ibid.
45. London: HMSO 1988.
46. With over 600,000 staff.
47. Servicing ministers and managing departments.

service delivery aspects of state activity, the latter to be carried out by the new 'Next Steps' bodies. The streamlined core departments would be responsible for sponsoring the activities of the 'Next Steps' agencies. These agencies, headed by their own directors, would manage their own budgets,[48] employ their own personnel, and have full responsibility for the day-to-day delivery of their services.

The 'Next Steps' proposals found favour with the Government and were implemented swiftly in Great Britain. By 1992 some seventy agencies had been set up, employing some 200,000 people.[49] By 1997 this number should have grown to 400,000 (three-quarters of the civil servants in the UK).[50]

The creation of 'Next Steps' agencies has already raised questions of accountability in Great Britain; the problems are likely to be even more acute in the context of the 'limited democracy' currently operating in Northern Ireland.[51]

### *'Next Steps' and the environment in Northern Ireland*

The 'Next Steps' Initiative began to make its effects felt in Northern Ireland with the creation of five agencies sponsored by the DoE(NI) in 1991; the Rate Collection Agency, the Public Records Office of Northern Ireland, the Driver and Vehicle (NI) Licensing and Testing Agencies, and the Ordnance Survey of Northern Ireland. The first wave of agencies created concerned themselves with fairly technical, non-controversial areas.

The next stage of the 'Next Steps' Initiative in Northern Ireland is likely to be more problematic. In April 1996 the Planning Service, the Construction Service, the Environment and Heritage Service, the Land Registers of Northern Ireland, the Roads Service and the Water Service come on stream as 'Next Steps' agencies. The new organisational structure of the DoE(NI) is laid out in the diagram below (the second tranche of 'Next Steps' agencies are in bold type).

### DoE Permanent Secretary

#### *Deputy Secretaries*

| Planning, environment and property services | Urban regeneration | Resources, housing and local government | Central Policy and Management Unit | Roads, transport, water and fire policy |
|---|---|---|---|---|

#### *Agencies*

| | | |
|---|---|---|
| **Planning Service** | Rate Collection Agency | **Water Service** |
| **Construction Service** | Ordnance Survey | **Roads Service** |
| **Environment and** | **Land Registers** | Driver and |
| **Heritage Service** | Public Records | Vehicle Licensing |
| | | Driver and |
| | | Vehicle Testing |

---

48. Subject to the supervision of the relevant streamlined central government department.
49. For a more detailed discussion of the 'Next Steps' Initiative see A. Bradley and K. Ewing, *E. C. S. Wade and A. W. Bradley: Constitutional and Administrative Law*, 11th ed., London: Longman, 1993.
50. Malcolm Moss (NI Environment Minister), reported by Gary Grattan in *Belfast Telegraph*, 27 Mar. 1996.
51. See, for example, G. Drewry's comments on the implications of the 'Next Steps' Initiative, PL (1988), 505 and PL (1990), 322.

Most of the second tranche of DoE(NI)-sponsored agencies are actually involved in the provision of environmental services, a function already rendered technocratic rather than democratic in many important respects because of the peculiarities of local government in Northern Ireland. Some commentators have expressed the fear that 'Next Steps' status will render the provision and regulation of services by the DoE(NI) even less accountable to Parliament and MPs than is now the case. This stated, while most environmental functions in the Province will remain, as they have been since the reintroduction of direct rule, under the control of the DoE(NI), the introduction of agencies could allow the various parts of the former 'superdepartment' to assert an independent identity. This could actually have benefits in encouraging a system of environmental governance that is more open and accountable to the public. The changes should certainly help to make the maze of DoE(NI) services accessible to the general public and environmental interest groups.

Despite the possible positive effects of the move to 'Next Steps' status, other more negative considerations also arise. First, it seems to be at variance with Government policy on environmental institutions in Great Britain, where the regulation of most significant environmental functions is to be combined within the remit of the new environment agencies for England and Wales and Scotland, to introduce fragmentation in the DoE(NI) through extending the 'Next Steps' initiative in the manner proposed. Northern Ireland's Environment Minister, Malcolm Moss, is keen, however, to stress that the need for co-operation between the new agencies has been recognised and:

> will be the subject of a 'common corporate framework'[52] which is to cover attaining policy targets and common objectives. The new agencies will be required in many areas of activity to 'combine their efforts to meet wider objectives.'[53]

It is to be hoped that the pattern of progress and modernisation in environmental regulation in Northern Ireland, notably exhibited by the Environment Service, will be encouraged rather than hindered by new institutional arrangements. Only time will tell.

### *Stop Press*

Appendix A contains more detailed information on the new Environment and Heritage Service (EHS).

---

52. Comments reported by Gary Grattan, *Belfast Telegraph*, 27 Mar. 1996.
53. Ibid.

# CHAPTER THREE

# European Environmental Law and Policy

## Introduction

As is the case throughout GB, EC environmental law and policy has exerted, and will continue to exert, an enormous influence on the nature and direction of environmental regulation in Northern Ireland. The purpose of this chapter is threefold. First, it is intended to provide a brief outline of the origins and direction of EC environmental law and policy in its own right. Second, it is intended to focus on the overall impact of EC environmental law and policy on environmental regulation in Northern Ireland and, in particular, on the extent to which it can be enforced by private parties in courts in Northern Ireland. Finally, it is intended to examine the role of the new EC Environment Agency and the European Environment Information and Observation Network (EIONET).

## PART I THE EMERGENCE OF EUROPEAN ENVIRONMENTAL LAW AND POLICY

When the EEC (as it was then known) was established in 1957, the Treaty of Rome contained no reference to the concept of environmental protection and did not confer any competence on the EEC to develop an environmental policy. The reasons for this are twofold. Firstly, the draftsmen of the original EEC Treaty perceived economic integration as the *raison d'être* of the EEC, and secondly, environmental protection had not yet emerged as a significant political issue in the nineteen-fifties. Although EC measures that had an environmental dimension were adopted during the late sixties and early seventies —for example, measures designed to control vehicle emissions, noise from vehicles, and the labelling of chemicals—they were adopted primarily for economic reasons. The emergence of EC environmental policy can be dated to the Paris Declaration, issued in 1972 by EC heads of state and government, which stated:

> Economic expansion is not an end in itself. Its first aim should be to enable disparities in living conditions to be reduced. It must take place with the participation of all the social partners. It should result in an improvement in the quality of life as well as in standards of living. As befits the genius of Europe, particular attention will be given to intangible values and to protecting the environment, so that progress may really be put at the service of mankind.[1]

---

1. Bull. EC-1972. See also the arguments posed by the Commission for an EC environmental policy, Commission, Sixth General Report (1972), 8.

The Declaration requested that a programme of action on the environment be drawn up by the Commission, and a year later the EC's First Environmental Action Programme (1973–76) was adopted.[2] The rapid development of EC environmental policy from the Paris Declaration to the present day, and the legal basis on which it is premised, are well documented in specialist texts, and therefore it is not intended to provide a detailed account of this process in the present book.[3] Suffice it to say, that environmental policy has become firmly established within the EC's sphere of competence, so much so that environmental standards adopted at European level now exert an enormous influence on almost every area of environmental regulation within the national legal systems of the member states.

In 1987 the Single European Act amended the Treaty of Rome to include a new Environmental Title (Articles 130r, s, and t), which gave, for the first time, an explicit legal basis for EC environmental legislation. This has since been amended and strengthened by the Treaty on European Union (Maastricht Treaty) in 1992. Article 130r(1), Title XVI (as amended by the Maastricht Treaty), states that:

> Community policy on the environment shall contribute to pursuit of the following objectives:
>
> — preserving, protecting and improving the quality of the environment;
>
> — protecting human health;
>
> — prudent and rational utilisation of natural resources;
>
> — promoting measures at international level to deal with regional or worldwide environmental problems.

The key principles underlying Community environmental policy are set out in Article 130r(2) of the EC Treaty, as amended by the Maastricht Treaty. Article 130r(2) states that:

> Community policy on the environment shall aim at a high level of protection taking into account the diversity of situations in the various regions of the Community. It shall be based on the precautionary principle and on the principles that preventative action should be taken, that environmental damage should as a priority be rectified at source and that the polluter should pay. Environmental protection requirements must be integrated into the definition and implementation of other Community policies . . .

It should be noted that in *R. v. Secretary of State for Trade and Industry, ex parte Duddridge*,[4] an application for judicial review was brought to challenge the decision of the Secretary of State not to issue regulations under the Electricity Act 1989 restricting electromagnetic fields from the electric cables being laid as part of the national grid. In effect, it was argued, that in failing to adopt the precautionary principle the Secretary of State was in breach of EC law. The Court of Appeal

---

2. OJ C112, 20 Dec. 1973.
3. See, for example, Nigel Haigh, *Manual of Environmental Policy: The EC and Britain,* London: Longman, 1992; Krämer, *EC Treaty and Environmental Law,* 2nd ed., London: Sweet and Maxwell, 1995; R. Malcolm, *A Guidebook to Environmental Law,* London: Sweet and Maxwell, 1994, pp 52–60; Ball and Bell, *Environmental Law* 3rd ed,. London: Blackstone Press, 1995, chap. 4.
4. Unreported, *Times,* 26 Oct. 1995.

ruled that because Article 130r was worded in the future tense it was clear that it did not create directly enforceable obligations to protect the environment. In the court's opinion the wording of Article 130r made it clear that it was intended that the Community would go on to enact legislation which implemented the objectives listed in Article 130r.

It should also be noted that the Maastricht Treaty has introduced a general principle of subsidiarity, which requires that action only be taken at Community level where this would be more effective than action by the member states. This concept is enshrined in Article 3b of the EC Treaty, which states:

> . . . the Community shall take action . . . only if and insofar as the objectives of the proposed action cannot be sufficiently achieved by the Member States and can therefore, by reason of the scale or effects of the proposed action, be better achieved by the Community.

Although much has been said and written about the implications of subsidiarity, the exact impact of this principle is not yet entirely clear. In relation to its impact in the context of environmental protection, Ball and Bell point out that the Community has resisted attempts by the UK to use the principle of subsidiarity to justify a request that certain environmental measures be amended (including Directives on air quality, bathing water, and drinking water) and that others be discontinued (including the proposed Directives on the ecological quality of water, landfill, and extensions of the Environmental Impact Assessment Directive).[5]

## European Environmental Action Programmes

Since the adoption of the First Environmental Action Programme, the EC has adopted four further Action Programmes on the environment, namely, 1977–81,[6] 1982–86,[7] 1987–92,[8] and 1993–2000.[9] These Action Programmes fulfil two essential purposes. First, the Programmes set out the Commission's proposals for the adoption of specific pieces of environmental legislation during the following years and, second, they set out the Commission's views on the future direction of EC environmental policy. It is important to note, however, that although the Action Programmes provide a framework for the development of environmental policy, they are not legally binding documents. The First Environmental Action Programme set out the EC's basic aims in the context of environmental protection and the key principles that would inform action in this regard. Overall, this programme was characterised by a reactive approach, in that it essentially focused on the control of pollution and on the adoption of remedial measures. The Second and Third Environmental Action Programmes adopted a more long-term view, in that they sought an overall improvement in environmental quality as well as a reduction in pollution. During the period of these two Action Programmes the EC adopted over a hundred environmental measures and signed twenty international environmental agreements. The Third Environmental Action Programme signalled

---

5. Ball and Bell, op. cit., 83–4.
6. OJ C139, 13 June 1977.
7. OJ C46, 17 Feb. 1983.
8. OJ C328, 7 Dec. 1987.
9. OJ C138, 17 May 1993.

a shift in Community environmental policy towards placing greater emphasis on preventive action. This change in emphasis was more fully developed in the Fourth Environmental Action Programme, which in effect raised environmental policy to a position of central importance in that it was perceived to be an essential component in the formulation of EC policy in economic, industrial and social contexts.

The Fifth Environmental Action Programme, *Towards Sustainability,* which will guide the development of EC environmental policy to the end of the century, departs from the traditional 'shopping list' of issues to be dealt with that characterised previous Action Programmes and instead attempts to set out a new approach to environmental protection which is designed to put the Community on the path towards sustainable development. The Fifth Environmental Action Programme identifies five principal 'target sectors' that have a particular impact on the environment and are central to achieving sustainable development, namely, industry, energy, agriculture, tourism, and transport. In effect these are the five sectors in which environmental issues are likely to be dealt with at EC level in the future. The Action Programme emphasises the need to integrate environmental protection into the formulation of Community policy in other sectors and also stresses the importance of using a wider variety of policy instruments, in particular, market and financial mechanisms, to supplement traditional legislation based on the 'command and control' approach to environmental protection. Finally, the Fifth Environmental Action Programme emphasises that the resolution of environmental problems is a responsibility which must be shared between a wide range of 'actors', in particular, governments, industry, and the general public.

## European approaches to Environmental Regulation

In giving expression to the fundamental principles and objectives underlying EC environmental policy as laid down in Article 130r(1) and (2) of the EC Treaty, Community environmental legislation has employed a wide variety of approaches to the problem of pollution control. Given the vast quantity of environmental legislation that has been adopted by the Community to date, it is difficult to provide a comprehensive list of these approaches. Nigel Haigh[10] has, however, identified the following as the eight principal approaches reflected in contemporary EC environmental law (some of which have been used in combination, while others are used to address specific situations):
(i) the imposition of emission standards for point discharges;
(ii) environmental quality standards, which address the use to be made of the environmental medium (i.e. drinking and bathing water) and address pollution from more diffuse sources;
(iii) product standards, which control the composition or construction of specific products;

---

10. Haigh, supra, chap. 3, pp 4–8. It should also be noted that the UK and EC have traditionally differed in the use of quality objectives and emission standards. The nature of this difference in approaches to pollution control is addressed in the context of water quality control in chap. 5 and is discussed in more detail by Haigh at pp 8–11.

(iv) process or operating standards, designed to regulate emissions from the process or to protect workers;

(v) exposure standards, which regulate the amount of pollutant to which targets may be exposed (e.g. regulating the amount of lead in drinking water);

(vi) total emission or 'bubble' standards, which impose an upper limit on all emissions of specific pollutants regardless of the source of the pollutant (e.g. the imposition of total emission standards for sulphur dioxide for large combustion plants in individual member states);

(vii) preventive controls; and

(viii) biological controls.

The Community is now beginning to embrace a 'cross-media' or 'integrated' approach to pollution control in order to tackle those pollutants which have the capacity to have an impact on all environmental media (e.g. the proposed Integrated Pollution Prevention and Control Directive). Integrated pollution control or IPC in effect requires consideration of the impact of pollutants on all environmental media (land, air, and water). The Community is also moving towards greater use of fiscal or market mechanisms to supplement the traditional 'command and control' approach to environmental regulation, particularly in the context of vehicle emissions.

Finally, it should also be noted that the EC often regulates by means of what is referred to as a 'Framework' Directive. Ball and Bell identify two separate types of Framework Directives.[11] On the one hand there is the Framework Directive which sets out a regime of controls and principles that will be applied in the future by reference to specific limit values laid down in further 'daughter' Directives on specific pollutants regulated within the general framework of control. An example of such a Directive is the Framework Directive on Dangerous Substances in Water. On the other hand the EC has also employed a more flexible form of Framework Directive which essentially sets out general procedures and requirements but leaves member states to adopt specific standards. The Framework Directive on Waste 75/442EEC, as amended, is an example of this type of Framework Directive.

## PART II THE IMPACT OF EUROPEAN ENVIRONMENTAL POLICY IN NORTHERN IRELAND

As is the case throughout the UK, EC environmental law and policy has exerted, and will continue to exert, an enormous influence on the nature and direction of environmental regulation in Northern Ireland. Over 200 pieces of environmental legislation have been adopted by the EC during the past two decades, the overall effect of which has been to considerably strengthen the protection afforded to Northern Ireland's environment as a whole. The precise nature and extent of the influence exerted by European environmental law in the Province is too great to detail in any meaningful way in the present context; however, it should be noted that the EC dimension to all areas of environmental law covered in this book is

---

11. *Environmental Law,* 3rd ed, London: Blackstone Press, 1995, pp 80–81.

addressed in detail in individual chapters. Existing and forthcoming Northern Ireland legislation on almost every aspect of the protection afforded to all environmental media (land, water and air) has been fundamentally influenced by standards set and approaches agreed at European level. Similarly, the Community has exerted a significant influence on the nature and level of protection afforded in Northern Ireland to individual species and their habitats. Community law has considerably strengthened the public's right of access to environmental information and the public's right to be consulted in decision-making concerning the application or operation of legislative controls in specific contexts. The implementation of European environmental standards has also ensured the gradual consolidation of the 'polluter pays' principle as a fundamental concept underlying environmental regulation in Northern Ireland. European environmental standards have also been responsible for the introduction of wider environmental controls such as environmental impact assessments, eco-labelling and eco-management and audit schemes. More recently Community environmental policy has started to influence areas such as countryside management and the provision of public access to the countryside, which have traditionally been determined entirely by national standards. Similarly, the direction of national energy policies, traditionally a preserve jealously guarded by national governments, is being shaped by policies adopted at European level.

## The implementation of EC environmental law in Northern Ireland

There are two basic sources of EC law, namely, Treaty law, which is referred to as the 'primary' law of the Community, and 'secondary legislation', namely, Regulations, Decisions and Directives adopted by Community institutions under Article 189 of the EC Treaty. The bulk of EC environmental law is contained in the form of Directives, which set out specific objectives to be achieved and which member states are then required to implement into national law by a specified date. The implementation periods vary according to the difficulties posed in achieving implementation. Although Directives are ideally suited to the process of harmonising national rules to a common European standard, in that they set out specific objectives to be achieved but leave member states with discretion as to the form and method of implementation and also afford member states a period of grace within which to complete implementation before the measure becomes legally effective, there are two important weaknesses in the effectiveness of this legislative form. The first concerns the problems of non-implementation or faulty implementation of EC environmental Directives, while the second concerns the imbalances in the enforcement of EC Directives in national courts.

One of the major problems facing the European legal system is the widespread failure among member states to implement Directives correctly and within the specified period. Although this problem pervades all areas of Community activity, it is particularly acute in the context of environmental Directives.[12] The European Court of Justice has repeatedly stated that member states are under an obligation to

---

12. Krämer, supra, chap. 5.

ensure complete and effective implementation of EC Directives by the implementation deadline specified in each Directive. However, the question as to what constitutes full and effective implementation often gives rise to considerable confusion. Although the European Court of Justice has addressed the nature of full and effective implementation on many occasions, the following extract from a ruling given in the context of an enforcement action taken against Germany for failing to implement the Groundwater Directive encapsulates the Court's position in this regard:

> . . . the transposition of a Directive into domestic law does not necessarily require that its provisions be incorporated formally and verbatim in express, specific legislation; a general legal context may, depending on the content of the Directive, be adequate for the purpose provided that it does indeed guarantee the full application of the Directive in a sufficiently clear and precise manner so that, where the Directive is intended to create rights for individuals, the persons concerned can ascertain the full extent of their rights and, where appropriate, rely on them before the national courts. . . . The fact that a practice is consistent with the protection afforded under a Directive does not justify failure to implement that Directive in the national legal order by means of provisions which are capable of creating a situation which is sufficiently precise, clear and open to permit individuals to be aware of and enforce their rights. As the Court held in its judgment in Case C-339/87 Commission v. Netherlands . . . in order to secure full implementation of Directives in law and not only in fact, member states must establish a specific legal framework in the area in question.[13]

In essence, the Court has made it clear that a Directive must be implemented by means of formal legislation which is consistent with the requirements of the Directive. Where the existing legal context does not ensure implementation of a Directive, new legislation will have to be introduced specifically for these purposes. Such legislation will have to be enacted before the expiry of the implementation deadline specified in the Directive. The Court has ruled that implementation by means of administrative practice (i.e. administrative circular), even one which is consistent with the requirements of the Directive, will not constitute correct implementation on the grounds that it is contrary to the demands of legal certainty. In Case C-337/89 *Commission v. UK*,[14] the European Court of Justice held that, even when a member state has achieved correct formal implementation of a Directive, a failure to implement the Directive in practice will be regarded as a failure to achieve full and effective implementation. Finally, it is worth noting the very interesting point, recently raised by Ball and Bell, that where a member state introduces legislation for the purposes of implementing a Directive which simply repeats the language of the Directive verbatim and makes

---

13. Case C-131/88 *Commission v. Federal Republic of Germany* [1991] 1 ECR 825 at para. 6. See also the rulings of the European Court in Case 363/85 *Commission v. Italy* [1987] ECR 1733 and Case C-339/87 *Commission v. Netherlands* [1990] ECR I-851.
14. [1992] I-ECR 6103. In this regard see: Krämer, *EC Treaty and Environmental Law*, London: Sweet & Maxwell, pp 140–41. Case C-337/89 is discussed further in chap. 5, Part V, section 2.

no attempt to explain the precise scope or meaning of the terms used, such legislation will arguably not constitute full and effective implementation.[15] In essence, the government's failure, as Ball and Bell put it, to 'translate' the language of the Directive (which is often unclear and difficult) so that the precise nature of the obligations imposed and rights conferred by the Directive are clear, the individual is unable to ascertain the full extent of the rights which they can enforce before their national court. Similarly, individuals may be unable to ascertain the extent of their obligations under the legislation in question. In effect, this implementation practice is contrary to the requirements of legal certainty. The Environmental Information Regulations (NI) 1993, the Conservation (Natural Habitats, etc.) Regulations (NI) 1995 and the Pollution of Groundwater by Dangerous Substances Regulations (NI) 1994, which implement Directive 90/313/EEC on freedom of access to environmental information, the Habitats Directive 92/43/EEC and the Groundwater Directive 80/68/EEC, are good examples of this practice in Northern Ireland.

The late implementation of environmental Directives is a major problem in Northern Ireland. Throughout this book it will be made clear that environmental Directives are normally implemented in Northern Ireland long after the deadline for implementation has expired—in many instances the delay spans several years—with the result that the Government is often in breach of its Community obligation to ensure implementation throughout the UK. The House of Commons Environment Committee report *Environmental Issues in Northern Ireland* noted information from European Commission officials to the effect that 'out of the total of just five referrals of the United Kingdom to the European Court of Justice relating to environmental legislation, no fewer than two related to delays in transposing EC law into the law of Northern Ireland.'[16] In *Commission v. UK,*[17] which concerned the UK's failure to implement the Drinking Water Directive, the UK argued that the delay in implementing the Directive in Northern Ireland was due to the complicated legislative procedure governing the enactment of legislation for Northern Ireland. The European Court of Justice rejected this as a legitimate excuse for failing to implement the provisions of the Directive in Northern Ireland by the implementation date. In effect, member states agree the implementation dates for individual Directives and therefore are required to ensure compliance. The Environment Committee Report pointed out that the procedure of implementing EC Directives in Northern Ireland usually begins only after the requirements laid down by the Directive have been implemented in Great Britain, and the procedure of adopting an Order in Council (which is the normal means of law-making for Northern Ireland) itself takes a minimum of sixty-four weeks. The DoE(NI), for its part, explained the reasons for the delay in the following terms:

---

15. Ball and Bell, *Environmental Law* 3rd ed., London: Blackstone Press, 1995, p. 86.
16. House of Commons Environment Committee, First Report: *Environmental Issues in Northern Ireland,* HC 39(1990), para, 26.
17. Case C-337/89 *Commission v. UK* [1992] I-ECR 6103. For further detail on the background to this case and the communications between the Commission and the UK, see Haigh, supra, chap. 4.4, pp 4–8.

> Some parts of it are delayed because draft Directives are changing. In other parts it is because either that it has been thought that other priorities in terms of work were more important, until we had extra staffing, or it was that we did not think it was directly relevant or the work was going on and one cannot always get things done immediately.[18]

The Environment Committee's report concluded that:

> as a matter of general principle we consider that the Government should ensure that environmental legislation is consistent throughout the United Kingdom—the environment itself makes no distinction between different legal jurisdictions. With respect to EC legislation, the United Kingdom is under a legal obligation to implement the requirements of Directives *throughout the country* within the specified time-limits. We find it unacceptable that the United Kingdom should be exposed to possible infringement proceedings before the European Court because of delays in Northern Ireland legislation . . . We welcome the Government's commitment to transpose the backlog of existing EC Directives as soon as possible and recommend that sufficient resources be allocated to meet the stated targets. For future legislation, we recommend that the Government review its practices to ensure that implementation in Northern Ireland is carried out simultaneously with the rest of the country.[19]

Although there does not appear to have been any concerted attempt to ensure simultaneous implementation of Environment Directives throughout the UK in the wake of these recommendations, it is important to note that a wide range of new environmental legislation has been enacted in Northern Ireland during the past three years, the great majority of which has been introduced for the purpose of implementing EC Directives. In addition, the DoE(NI) is in the process of introducing major new reforms in relation to industrial pollution control, waste control, and the regime of discharge consents which controls discharges of trade and sewage effluent and other polluting matter into Northern Ireland's inland, coastal and ground waters; these reforms, when enacted, will effectively ensure the implementation of several major EC environmental Directives in Northern Ireland.

### Remedies for non-compliance with European law

There are two principal means by which private parties can seek redress for the state's failure to implement European law. The first approach is laid down in Article 169 of the EC Treaty, which essentially empowers the European Commission to take enforcement proceedings against a defaulting member state for non-compliance with European law. The second, and more effective approach as far as private parties are concerned, has been developed in recent years by the European Court of Justice. In essence, the Court of Justice has ruled that the state may be liable in damages where an individual has sustained loss as a result of the

---

18. House of Commons Environment Committee, First Report: *Environmental Issues in Northern Ireland,* HC 39(1990), para. 30.
19. Ibid., para. 31–2.

state's failure to comply with European law. Before turning to address each of these remedies in more detail, it should be noted that where national law is inconsistent with EC law, it may often be possible to enforce the terms of European law either directly or indirectly in a national action and thereby circumvent domestic legislation which is incompatible with the Treaty or EC legislation. In effect, these principles afford a means by which rights and obligations contained in EC provisions can be relied on in national disputes, even where the state has failed to implement the requirements of EC law into national law, or, where the state has introduced national legislation which is inconsistent with EC law. The principles operating in this regard are outlined below (page 51).

### Enforcement actions under Article 169

Article 169 of the EC Treaty empowers the Commission to take enforcement proceedings before the European Court of Justice against a member state that has failed to comply with its EC law obligations. Although private parties may contact the Commission and alert it to possible state infringements of EC law, private parties do not have the power to compel the Commission to take enforcement proceedings; the Commission retains total discretion in this regard. If enforcement proceedings are taken by the Commission, the Commission will seek a declaration from the European Court confirming the infringement and requiring the state in question to take action to remedy the breach. Member states are obliged to comply with the terms of a Court declaration under Article 169 and may be prosecuted again under Article 169 for failing to do so. It should also be noted that the Treaty on European Union inserted a new power into the EC Treaty (Article 171) whereby the European Court of Justice may impose financial penalties on defaulting member states. Although it is unclear from the wording of Article 171 how these penalties will be calculated and who the recipient of the fine will be, penalties imposed under Article 171 have the potential to be very large. It should also be noted that the Commission has suggested that Community funds provided for environmental matters be withheld from member states which fail to comply with the obligation to implement EC environmental standards.[20]

In the specific context of environmental law, it is important to note that the Commission has embarked on a more rigorous policy of enforcement in relation to failures to implement EC environment Directives. In addition, the Commission has made it clear that the delays in implementing environmental Directives in Northern Ireland caused by the UK's system of making separate provision for the Province will not be regarded as a legitimate defence against proceedings under Article 169.[21] Although the individual does not have the power to force the Commission to act in any given situation, the Commission's decision to police the implementation of environmental Directives more closely and the European Court's new power to impose financial sanction under Article 171, will

---

20. Ball and Bell, supra, at p. 65.
21. HC 372 (1989-90) and HC 39 (1990-92). For a fuller explanation of the procedure under Article 169, see: Steiner, *Textbook on EC Law*, 4th ed., London: Blackstone Press, 1995 and Hartley, *The Foundations of European Community Law*, 2nd ed., London: Clarendon Press: 1995.

undoubtedly increase the pressure on member states to ensure full and effective implementation of environmental Directives.

### State liability in damages for failing to comply with European law

In the past six years the European Court of Justice has delivered a series of landmark decisions in which the Court has established and developed the principle of state liability in damages for failing to comply with EC law. Although this new principle of state liability is still developing, it is clear at this stage that member states are now under considerable pressure to ensure compliance with EC law obligations and, in particular, to ensure the timely and correct implementation of Directives.

The principle of state liability was first established in Case C-6/90 *Francovich v. Italy*[22] in which the European Court of Justice ruled that, in certain circumstances, an individual could take an action in damages against a member state to obtain compensation for loss sustained by him as a result of the state's failure to implement a Directive. In this instance enforcement proceedings had been brought some years earlier against the Italian Government concerning its failure to implement the Directive in question. However, despite a ruling from the European Court of Justice that Italy was in breach of its obligation to implement, the Italian Government continued in its failure to introduce the necessary implementing measures. Francovich (a private individual) brought an action against the Government in his national court in which he sought to enforce the terms of the Directive against the state or, alternatively, to be compensated for loss sustained as a result of the Government's failure to implement the rights contained therein (i.e. a loss of wages from his insolvent employer to which he was entitled under the Directive).

A reference was sent by the Italian court seeking guidance on the arguments posed by Francovich. The European Court of Justice ruled that the Directive in question could not be directly enforced against the state because it failed to comply with the conditions for direct effect (outlined below at page 51). However, the Court went on to rule that a failure to implement a Directive constituted a breach of a fundamental Community law obligation and that where an individual sustained loss as a result of that failure, a member state could be held liable in damages, provided the following three conditions were satisfied:

 (i) the Directive at issue must confer rights upon the individual;
(ii) the content of those rights must be capable of being identified on the basis of the Directive in question;
(iii) there must be a causal link between the state's failure and the damage suffered by the person affected.

Although the *Francovich* ruling considerably increases the pressure on member states to ensure the timely and correct implementation of Directives and considerably lessens any incentive not to implement them, the following points should be noted regarding its application in relation to environmental Directives. Although certain Directives, such as the Freedom of Access to Environmental Information Directive and the Drinking Water Directive, explicitly confer rights

---

22.  [1993] 2 CMLR 66.

on individuals, there are many Directives in this field which are designed principally to protect the environment. However, even where a Directive does not explicitly confer rights on individuals, Ball and Bell argue that 'most Directives laying down standards can be interpreted as conferring implied rights on individuals.'[23] The European Court of Justice has not yet ruled on whether the Directive must confer such rights explicitly or whether an implicit conferral of rights would suffice to invoke the state's liability in damages.

Compliance with the second condition will be determined on a case-by-case basis, and the European Court of Justice will be the final arbiter in this regard. Finally, Ball and Bell point out that the third condition may pose some difficulties in the environmental context, because 'in most situations the harm will be caused by an operational failure rather than by the Government's non-implementation.'[24] It should also be noted that the third condition in effect prevents the *Francovich* principle being used to obtain a ruling that a member state has failed to comply with its duty to implement; it is essential that some form of loss or harm be sustained by the plaintiff.

Although the ruling in *Francovich* made it clear that member states could be held liable in damages for a failure to implement a Directive on time, one of the questions left unanswered by *Francovich* was whether the principle would also apply beyond the particular situation raised in that case. In other words, would the *Francovich* principle apply to situations where a Directive was implemented incorrectly or where implementation was incomplete or was inadequate in practice? In addition, questions were raised as to whether it would also apply to other forms of failure to comply with Community law, for example, whether it would apply where a member state introduced legislation that was contrary to EC law.

On 5 March 1996 the European Court of Justice answered many of these questions in its rulings on Case C-46/93 *Brasserie du Pêcheur v. Germany* and Case C-48/93 *R. v. Secretary of State for Transport, ex parte Factortame (No. 3)*.[25] Each case concerned national laws which had been declared by the European Court of Justice (during the course of enforcement proceedings under Article 169) to be inconsistent with EC law. The former case concerned a German beer purity law which prohibited the import of beers containing additives and which was deemed to be incompatible with Article 30 of the Treaty; while the latter concerned certain provisions of the UK's Merchant Shipping Act 1988 which were deemed to be incompatible with Article 52 of the Treaty. In each case, the enforcement of the national laws in question resulted in financial loss for the plaintiff company; Brasserie du Pêcheur was forced to discontinue imports of beer into Germany, while Factortame, a Spanish fishing company, was forced to cease fishing in UK waters.

The essential question posed to the European Court in these two cases was whether the principle of state liability laid down in *Francovich* could be extended to cover the breaches of EC law in these situations. In other words, did the

---

23. Ball and Bell, *Environmental Law,* 3rd ed., London: Blackstone Press, 1995 at p. 66.
24. Ibid.
25. Unreported (Full Court) 5 March 1996 (*Financial Times,* 12 Mar. 1996). A single judgment was delivered in respect of both actions, as identical issues were raised.

principle of state liability cover only instances of non-implementation of Directives, or, could a member state be held liable in damages for loss sustained as a result of other forms of breaches of EC obligations? The Court ruled that member states could be held liable in damages for loss sustained by individuals for breaches of EC law for which the state could be held responsible, including the adoption of legislation which was incompatible with EC law. The German Government argued that member states should be held liable in damages only for loss sustained by individuals in situations where the measure of EC law in question was not capable of direct enforcement in the national court. The Court rejected this argument and stated that the right to reparation is the necessary corollary of the direct effect of the Community provision whose breach caused the damage in question. In other words, the Court took the view that the principle of direct effect (explained at page 51) and the right to reparation could not be regarded as mutually exclusive. Therefore, the fact that the provision of EC law in question is directly effective will not act as a barrier to an action in damages against the state for loss sustained as a result of the state's breach of the provision in question. The Court went on to rule that it did not matter which branch of the state was responsible for the breach. In effect, the state will be equally liable regardless of whether the breach was caused by the legislature, the executive or the judiciary.

Having made it clear that the principle of state liability for breaches of EC law extends beyond the non-implementation of Directives, the European Court then went on to address the conditions which would govern the state's liability in situations not involving the non-implementation of Directives. Before outlining the Court's ruling in this regard, it is important to make the following points. One of the most controversial questions raised in the wake of the *Francovich* ruling was whether the state could be held liable in damages for breaches of EC law where the state had misunderstood what was required of it under EC law. The obligation to implement Directives laid down in Article 189 of the Treaty is clear, and in *Francovich* the Italian Government had been left in no doubt as to its failure to comply with this obligation as a result of an enforcement action taken under Article 169 of the Treaty. However, there are many areas in which the requirements of EC law are more ambiguous, for example, where the member state is left with a wide degree of discretion in complying with EC law. Therefore, the question facing the European Court of Justice in *Brasserie du Pêcheur* and *Factortame (No. 3)* concerned the conditions under which a state should be held liable in damages for breach of EC law where its obligations under EC law are less clear. Should the conditions laid down in *Francovich* apply, or should more rigorous conditions be developed?

The European Court took the opportunity in *Brasserie du Pêcheur* and *Factortame (No. 3)* to address the extent of the member states' liability in this context. In addressing this issue the Court started by pointing out that:

> [a]lthough Community law imposes state liability, the conditions under which that liability gives rise to a right to reparation depend on the nature of the breach of Community law giving rise to the loss and damage . . .

In effect, the Court ruled that where the member state is acting in an area in which it has wide discretion under EC law, the conditions governing the state's liability in damages will differ from those governing liability where very little discretion is left to the state in complying with the requirements of EC law. Where the member state retains a wide discretion in complying with EC law the Court ruled that the conditions governing the state's liability '. . . cannot, in the absence of particular justification, differ from those governing the liability of the Community in like circumstances.' In other words, the Court acknowledged that the principles governing the Community's liability in damages under Article 215(2) of the Treaty are relevant to the conditions governing the member state's liability where the state was left with a degree of discretion in complying with the requirements of EC law which is comparable to that accorded to the Community institutions in implementing Community policy. In such circumstances the Court ruled that member states can be held liable in damages for loss sustained by the individual if the following conditions are satisfied:

(i) the rule of law infringed must be intended to confer rights on individuals;

(ii) the breach must be sufficiently serious; and

(iii) there must be a direct causal link between the breach of the obligation resting on the state and the damage sustained by the injured parties.

In the Court's opinion, these three conditions correspond in substance to the conditions governing the Community's liability in damages under Article 215 of the Treaty, and as is the case under *Francovich,* the national court has sole jurisdiction to determine whether these conditions have been satisfied in relation to a particular breach of EC law. The first and third of these conditions are clearly identical to those laid down in *Francovich* concerning the state's liability for non-implementation of a Directive. However, the requirement that the breach be 'sufficiently serious' is particular to the rulings in *Brasserie du Pêcheur* and *Factortame (No. 3).* Although the Court did not explain the relationship between the *Francovich* ruling on the one hand and *Brasserie du Pêcheur* and *Factortame (No. 3)* on the other, the Court suggested that the conditions laid down in *Brasserie du Pêcheur* and *Factortame (No. 3)* will govern liability only in situations where Community law has left the state with a wide discretion in deciding how to implement Community policy which is comparable to the discretion of the Community institutions in this regard. It would appear, therefore, that the conditions laid down in *Francovich* will apply where the member state has very little or no discretion in what steps must be taken to comply with EC law, as is the case in the context of the obligation to implement EC Directives into national law.

The main problem posed by the conditions laid down in *Brasserie du Pêcheur* and *Factortame (No. 3)* concerns the meaning of the concept of a 'sufficiently serious' breach. The European Court of Justice stated that the 'decisive test' for determining whether the breach of Community law is sufficiently serious to expose the state to liability in damages is whether the member state concerned 'manifestly and gravely disregarded the limits on its discretion'. Although the national court hearing the action has sole jurisdiction to make the final determination as to whether or not a particular breach of EC law is sufficiently serious, the European Court identified the following factors which the national court 'may' take into account in making this assessment:

> . . . the clarity and precision of the rule breached, the measure of discretion left by that rule to the national or Community authorities, whether the infringement and the damage caused was intentional or involuntary, whether any error of law was excusable or inexcusable, the fact that the position taken by a Community institution may have contributed towards the omission, and the adoption or retention of national measures or practices contrary to Community law.

A number of points must be noted concerning these factors. First, this list of factors is not exhaustive. In effect, further factors may be taken into consideration by the national judge, and indeed, further factors may be identified by the European Court itself in the future as being relevant to this assessment. Second, it is important to note that the national judge has a discretion in deciding whether to consider any or all of these factors. Third, the European Court made no attempt to attach particular importance to any individual factor. Fourth, the European Court specifically rejected the suggestion that the state's liability might be subject to proof that the state was at fault. The Court of Justice ruled that:

> . . . the obligation to make reparation for loss or damage caused to individuals cannot . . . depend upon a condition based on any concept of fault going beyond that of a sufficiently serious breach of Community law. Imposition of such a supplementary condition would be tantamount to calling into question the right of reparation founded on the Community legal order.

Although the national court is given considerable flexibility in applying the principle of state liability laid down in *Brasserie du Pêcheur* and *Factortame (No. 3)*, the Court of Justice went on to point out that:

> [o]n any view, a breach of Community law will clearly be sufficiently serious if it has persisted despite a judgment finding the infringement in question to be established, or a preliminary ruling or settled case-law of the Court on the matter from which it is clear that the conduct in question constituted an infringement.

In effect, where it is clear to the member state, either as a result of a successful enforcement action taken against the Government under Article 169 or from the case law of the European Court, that it is in breach of EC law, then such a breach must be characterised by the national judge as being 'sufficiently serious'. While the European Court stated that it could not substitute its assessment for that of the national court, it is clearly prepared to identify certain types of breaches which must be regarded as sufficiently serious for these purposes, thereby limiting the national judge's discretion to determine the state's liability. However, it should be stressed, that while the existence of a successful enforcement action against the member state would invoke the state's liability, a Commission action under Article 169 is not a pre-condition to liability under *Brasserie du Pêcheur* and *Factortame (No. 3)*.

Having set out the conditions governing liability where the member state has a wide discretion under EC law, the Court of Justice then went on to address the rules governing the actual mounting of such a claim before the national courts. In essence, the Court ruled that while Community law determines the conditions which must be satisfied to invoke the right to reparation laid down in *Brasserie du Pêcheur* and *Factortame (No. 3)*, this right must be exercised in accordance with domestic rules on liability. However, national provisions governing such actions must satisfy the requirements of equivalence and effectiveness, namely, they must not be less favourable than those relating to similar domestic claims and must not render it impossible or excessively difficult to obtain reparation in practice (the impact of European law on national procedural rules is addressed in more detail at page 54). In this regard it should be noted that the Court pointed out that the requirement under UK law that one must prove misfeasance in public office on the part of the executive in order to obtain reparation for a loss sustained as a result of the adoption of an illegal measure was incompatible with the principle established in *Brasserie du Pêcheur* and *Factortame (No. 3)*. It is extremely difficult to prove misfeasance in public office and, therefore, were it to be applied as a pre-condition to taking an action against the UK Government under *Brasserie du Pêcheur and Factortame (No. 3)*, it would virtually be impossible to mount an action against the executive and, therefore, to take a successful action under *Brasserie du Pêcheur* and *Factortame (No. 3)* within the UK. Finally, the Court stated that the reparation awarded must be 'commensurate with the loss or damage sustained' so as to ensure the effective protection of the individual's rights under EC law and, once again, national laws governing the extent of damages to be awarded must satisfy the principles of equivalence and effectiveness. However, the Court also pointed out that the national judge may inquire as to whether the injured person:

> . . . showed reasonable diligence in order to avoid the loss or damage or limit its extent and whether, in particular, he availed himself in time of all the legal remedies available to him.

The Court went on to say that the 'total exclusion of loss of profit as a head of damage' in this context would be incompatible with Community law and, similarly, that national rules could not prevent awards of exemplary damages if such an award could be awarded under a similar action based on national law.

Turning then to the facts of the *Brasserie du Pêcheur* and *Factortame (No. 3)* cases, the Court pointed out that the German and UK Governments were both acting in areas in which the state retained a wide discretion in complying with EC law. The Community had not yet introduced legislation harmonising the quality of beer, whereas the implementation of the common fisheries policy left a margin of discretion to the member states and the registration of vessels fell within the jurisdiction of national governments. In effect, the Court concluded that the UK and German Governments 'were faced with situations which involved choices comparable to those made by the Community institutions when they adopt legislative measures pursuant to a Community policy' and therefore that their liability must be assessed in light of the conditions laid down in *Brasserie du Pêcheur* and *Factortame (No. 3)* rather than those laid down in *Francovich*. The Court ruled that both the UK and Germany were guilty of a 'sufficiently serious' breach of EC law given that both Governments had persisted in enforcing the national laws in question despite the fact that the Commission had taken successful enforcement actions against both Governments concerning the national provisions in question. In addition, the Court ruled that the two other conditions governing liability were satisfied and that both Governments were therefore liable in damages.

The ruling in *Brasserie du Pêcheur* and *Factortame (No. 3)* is clearly of enormous significance to anyone dealing with any aspect of EC law. However, the full meaning and extent of the Court's very complex ruling will become clear in the coming years. Some further guidance as to the application of the *Brasserie du Pêcheur* and *Factortame (No. 3)* ruling has been provided by the Court's recent decision in Case C-392/93, *R. v H.M. Treasury, ex parte British Telecommunications plc*.[26] In the *BT* case the Court applied the principles laid down in *Brasserie du Pêcheur* and *Factortame (No. 3)* to a situation where the state had *incorrectly* implemented the provisions of a Directive into national law. The Court ruled that the principles laid down in *Brasserie du Pêcheur* and *Factortame (No. 3)* governing state liability would apply in these circumstances because the state had a wide discretion and was acting in a legislative capacity. The Court ruled that this restrictive approach was justified, in particular, by the:

> . . . concern to ensure that the exercise of legislative functions is not hindered by the prospect of actions for damages whenever the general interest requires the institutions or member states to adopt measures which may adversely affect individual interests.

In the specific context of the *BT* case, the Court ruled that it had sufficient information as to the facts of the national action to rule that the breach of EC law in question was not 'sufficiently serious' because the Government had not manifestly and gravely disregarded the limits imposed on the exercise of its discretion. In the Court's opinion the provision of the Directive which had been incorrectly implemented was sufficiently broad to reasonably bear the interpretation given to it by the Government. The Court pointed out that other member states had also given the same interpretation to this provision and, in addition, that the Court's case-law provided no guidance as to the correct meaning of the provision in question and, finally, that the Commission had not raised any objections when the national implementing measure was adopted in 1992.

From the case law that has been delivered thus far the position on state liability can be broadly summarised as follows:

(*a*) If a member state breaches its obligations under EC law in an area in which it has little or no discretion under EC law, the state will be liable under the principles laid down in *Francovich* in damages for loss sustained by the individual as a result of the breach. It is clear from the *Francovich* ruling that a failure to introduce national legislation for the purposes of discharging the obligation under Article 189 of the Treaty to implement a Directive will invoke liability under the *Francovich* conditions. In this regard the *Francovich* ruling will provide a potent remedy for the private party who is unable to directly enforce the provisions of a Directive because they either: (i) fail the test for direct effects (outlined at page 51) or, (ii) because the defendant in the case is also a private entity (a Directive cannot be directly enforced between private parties (see page 52)) and the national judge deems it impossible to give indirect effect (see page 53) to the terms of the Directive in question. The

---

26.  [1996] 3 WLR 203.

implications of the *Francovich* ruling in the context of non-implementation of EC environment Directives are considered at pages 42–3.

However, it is as yet unclear whether the *Francovich* conditions will apply only to non-implementation or whether the Court will go on in later cases to identify other forms of breaches which fall within the *Francovich* ruling, i.e. breaches of EC law in contexts in which the state has little or no discretion under EC law. It should be noted that a failure to implement a Directive correctly would appear to fall within the more stringent conditions laid down in *Brasserie du Pêcheur* and *Factortame (No. 3)*. However, it is not entirely clear whether this will automatically be the case simply because the state is acting in a legislative capacity or whether the terms of the particular Directive in question must also confer wide discretion on the state.

(*b*) The ruling in *Brasserie du Pêcheur* and *Factortame (No. 3)* will apply to loss caused as a result of a member state's breach of EC law provided the state is acting in a context in which it has a wide discretion under EC law in terms of what action is necessary to implement or comply with EC policy. Clearly this will encompass a much wider range of possible situations. However, the conditions governing liability are also more difficult to establish because one must establish that the breach is sufficiently serious. It should be noted, however, that the European Court clearly intends to hold those states who realised that they were in breach of EC law, but persisted, liable in damages for loss caused by their breach. It should also be emphasised that the state's liability under *Brasserie du Pêcheur* and *Factortame (No. 3)* will extend to all organs of state, i.e. to judicial, executive and legislative action. In this regard it should be emphasised that the European Court's case law makes it clear that the concepts of the judical and executive branches of state will be interpreted broadly.

The Court's case law concerning the notion of a national court or tribunal for the purposes of the Preliminary Ruling Procedure under Article 177 of the EC Treaty gives a clear indication of the approach which the European Court is likely to take to the interpretation of the judicial branch of state for the purposes of state liability. In essence, the Court of Justice has consistently emphasised that the question as to what constitutes a national court or tribunal for the purpose of Article 177 is a question of Community law to be determined by the European Court itself. In this regard the Court has ruled that the notion of a court or tribunal will cover those bodies which are ordinarily regarded as belonging to the judiciary under national law. However, the Court has also made it clear that bodies which perform a 'judicial function' will also be included regardless of the fact that the body is not regarded as a court or tribunal under national law. While the concept of a 'judicial function' is, as Hartley points out, 'notoriously difficult to pin down',[27] the central thrust of the European Court's case-law in this regard is that the body in question must have the power to give binding decisions as to the legal rights and obligations of private parties and, in addition, the body must be performing its judicial function subject to the approval and with the assistance of the public authorities.[28]

---

27. T.C. Hartley, *The Foundations of European Community Law*, 2nd ed., Clarendon Press 1994, p. 276.
28. The European Court's case-law on the concept of a court or tribunal is extensive. However, Hartley, ibid., and Steiner, *Textbook on EC Law*, 4th ed., London: Blackstone Press, 1995, p. 325, provide excellent commentaries on the Court's work in this context.

Turning then to the context of environmental regulation in Northern Ireland, it would appear that bodies such as the Water Appeals Commission, Planning Appeals Commission, DoE(NI) (particularly its Environment Service), the DED, and DANI all perform judicial functions subject to public control. Therefore, if the European Court translates its approach to the concept of a court or tribunal under Article 177 to the context of state liability under *Brasserie du Pêcheur* and *Factortame (No. 3)*, these bodies would be capable of invoking the state's liability in damages for loss sustained as a result of an incorrect application of EC environmental law.

In Case C-188/89 *Foster v. British Gas plc*[29] the European Court of Justice made it clear that the concept of the state should be interpreted broadly for the purposes of the direct enforcement of Community law. In effect, the Court ruled that the state would include public bodies or 'an emanation of the state' which the Court defined as:

> . . . a body, whatever its legal form, which has been made responsible, pursuant to a measure adopted by the state, for providing a public service under the control of the state and has for that purpose special powers beyond those which result from the normal rules applicable in relations between individuals.[30]

Given that state departments within Northern Ireland play such a central role in the operation of the system of environmental governance, both in their own right and through the sponsorship of 'Next Steps' Agencies, their activities would undoubtedly be covered by the ruling in *Brasserie du Pêcheur* and *Factortame (No. 3)* for the purposes of state liability.

At the time of writing, the European Court has yet to deliver its rulings in Case C-5/94 *Hedley Lomas* and Case C-178/94 *Dillenkofer* in which the scope of the principles laid down in *Brasserie du Pêcheur* and *Factortame (No. 3)* will be addressed further. In terms of identifying a specific NI example of potential state liability under the *Brasserie du Pêcheur* and *Factortame (No. 3)* principles, one could point to the implementation of the Groundwater Directive in NI. Although the terms of the Groundwater Directive, taken in isolation, are somewhat ambiguous as to the nature of the obligations imposed on member states to prevent water pollution due to discharges of dangerous substances to groundwater, the European Court of Justice gave a series of unequivocal rulings in the late nineteen-eighties in which the requirements of the Groundwater Directive were interpreted in some detail (see chapter 5, Part VII, section 2). Despite the fact that the terms of the Directive and the precise extent of the member states' obligations in terms of implementing the Directive were made clear by the European Court of Justice, the DoE(NI) introduced legislation for the purposes of implementing the requirements of the Directive in Northern Ireland in 1994 which arguably fail to comply with the UK's clear Community obligations in this context. It is submitted that, based on the Court's decision in the *BT Case,* the DoE(NI) has committed a 'sufficiently serious' breach of Community law. The European Court of Justice made it clear in Case C-131/88

---

29. [1990] ECR I-3313
30. para. 20.

*Commission v. Federal Republic of Germany.*[31] The Court's ruling in this case and the Northern Ireland legislation introduced to implement the Groundwater Directive are addressed in detail in Chapter 5, Part VII, section 2. The Groundwater Directive is intended to confer rights on the individual, and so it would appear that if a private party sustains damage as a result of the DoE(NI)'s failure to comply with its EC obligations in this context, the UK will be held liable in damages under the principles laid down in *Brasserie du Pêcheur* and *Factortame (No. 3)*. In this regard, it is worth noting that if permission is given to allow the establishment of a landfill at Magheramorne, consequent upon the public inquiry (1996) into the suitability of the site, it is arguable that should a private party sustain damage as a consequence of detriment to groundwater, that the DoE(NI) would, in the final analysis, be susceptible to an action in damages.

## The enforcement of European law in national courts

The dual doctrines of supremacy and direct effect explain the basis on which and the extent to which Community law can be enforced by private entities in national courts. In brief, the doctrine of supremacy states that EC law will prevail over all forms of conflicting national law. National courts are in effect prevented from applying conflicting national provisions and national parliaments are obliged to repeal all existing national measures that conflict with EC provisions and must refrain from enacting any new conflicting measures. The doctrine of direct effect states that Community measures that are clear and precise, unconditional and require no further legislation to render them legally effective can be directly enforced by private entities in national courts. The principle of direct effect extends to all forms of EC law, i.e. Treaty Articles, Regulations, Decisions, and Directives. Since the European Court of Justice established these two fundamental principles in the nineteen-sixties,[32] it has gone on to declare numerous Articles of the EC Treaty and provisions of secondary legislation to be directly effective. Direct effect in fact is now the norm, not the exception. The dual doctrines of supremacy and direct effect thus enable private parties to override conflicting national provisions and to directly enforce rights and obligations contained in EC provisions in their national courts. While these principles provide private parties with powerful tools, the following points should be noted concerning the direct effectiveness of EC Directives:

1. A Directive is not capable of being directly enforced in national courts until the time limit for implementation has expired. Although the obligation imposed on member states to implement a Directive is binding from the moment a Directive is enacted by the EC, member states are given a period of grace in which to complete the implementation process, during which the rights and obligations contained in the Directive cannot be directly enforced in national actions. However, once this deadline has expired, and provided the provisions of the Directive are clear and unconditional, the requirements laid down in a Directive can be directly enforced. The Directive will be enforced regardless of

---

31. [1991] 1 ECR 825.
32. It is impossible within the scope of the present chapter to explain the development of these principles in any detail. For further reading on the case law surrounding supremacy and direct effect see J. Steiner, *Textbook on EC Law* 4th ed., London: Blackstone, 1995, chap. 2 and 3.

any conflicting national law. In the event that there is some uncertainty as to whether the provisions of a particular Directive satisfy the conditions for direct effect, the European Court of Justice can be called on to deliver an authoritative ruling on this question under the Preliminary Reference Procedure contained in Article 177 of the EC Treaty.[33] It should be noted that in some instances EC environment Directives do not lay down precise standards; this lack of precision will be a barrier to direct enforcement. It should also be noted that Directives are the only form of Community law that require formal implementation, and therefore Articles of the Treaty, Regulations and Decisions are, in principle, capable of direct enforcement from the moment of enactment.

2. In the event that the Government introduces measures which implement a Directive incorrectly or which do not completely implement the Directive, or where there is inadequate implementation in practice, the original Directive can be enforced directly, provided it satisfies the conditions for direct effect and the time limit for implementation has expired.

3. In *Marshall v. Southampton and South-West Hampshire Area Health Authority*[34] the European Court of Justice ruled that EC Directives are only capable of being enforced 'vertically' against the state or an emanation thereof; they cannot be directly enforced 'horizontally' by one private party against another. Although the European Court of Justice has ruled that Articles of the Treaty, Regulations and Decisions are all capable of full direct effects (i.e. against the state and against other private parties), it has consistently refused to allow the direct enforcement of Directives between private parties. Despite compelling arguments raised by three Advocates-General to extend full direct effectiveness to Directives, the European Court has recently confirmed its stance in this regard in *Faccini Dori v. Recreb SRL*.[35] The essential rationale underlying the extension of direct effect to Directives is the need to prevent member states from relying on their own failure to implement a Directive as a means of preventing private parties from enforcing the rights and obligations contained therein. However, one of the principal reasons justifying the limitation imposed on the direct effect of Directives is that private parties do not have the power to implement Directives and, therefore, should not have unimplemented Directives enforced against them. This split in the direct effect of Directives has generated considerable criticism, not least because of the imbalance in the effectiveness of this most important form of EC law and the arbitrary injustice suffered by private parties whose capacity to enforce EC law rights and obligations is limited simply by the nature of the

---

33. In this regard it is important to note the apparent reluctance on the part of judges in the UK to make references in recent environmental law cases in which the correct interpretation of the EC Directives in question was unclear. See *Twyford Parish Council v. Secretary of State for Transport* [1992] JEL 273; *Wychavon DC v. Secretary of State for the Environment and Velcourt Ltd* [1994] JEL 351; *Petition of the Kincardine and Deeside DC* [1991] SCLR 729; and the Court of Appeal decision in *R. v. Secretary of State for the Environment, ex parte RSPB*, in which the Government's failure to designate an area known as Lappel Bank as an SPA under the Wild Birds Directive was being challenged (unreported, 18 Aug. 1994). It should be noted, however, that the House of Lords has since made a reference to the European Court of Justice in this case, and the ruling is awaited.

34. [1986] ECR 723.

35. [1994] ECR I-3325.

defendant.[36] The split in the direct effect of Directives has important implications in the field of environmental protection. In essence, although a private party may rely on the doctrine of direct effects to enforce the terms of a Directive against the state, the standards laid down in an environmental Directive will not be directly enforceable against private companies which fail to comply with those standards; this constitutes a significant limitation in the effectiveness of EC Directives given the polluting effect of many activities carried out by private companies. The split in the direct effect of Directives also has the result of affording greater protection to private bodies, whose potential to generate pollution is as great as many public bodies.

4. Although the imbalance in the direct effect of Directives significantly limits the effectiveness of EC environmental Directives, it is important to note that the European Court of Justice has provided a number of means by which this split can be circumvented. In *Foster v. British Gas plc*[37] the European Court made it clear that the concept of the state must be interpreted broadly to include bodies under state control. The Court stated that:

> a body, whatever its legal form, which has been made responsible pursuant to a measure adopted by the state, for providing a public service under the control of the state, and has for that purpose special powers beyond those which resulted from the normal rules applicable in relations between individuals, is included among the bodies against which the provisions of a Directive capable of having direct effect might be relied upon.

In essence, the Court has sought to render as wide a range of bodies as possible susceptible to the direct enforcement of Directives. It must be noted, however, that although the European Court of Justice defines the concept of the state broadly, it falls to the national court to decide whether the particular body involved in a specific case actually falls within this definition.[38]

In Case 14/83 *Von Colson v. Land Nordrhein-Westfalen*[39] and Case C-106/89 *Marleasing v. Comercial Internacional de Alimentación*[40] the Court introduced and developed the concept of 'indirect effect', which states that national courts are under an obligation to interpret national law so as to give effect to the spirit and purpose of relevant EC provisions. In essence, the concept of indirect effect operates to enable EC provisions to be indirectly enforced in national courts by means of the judicial interpretation of national law. Although some uncertainty surrounds the extent of the interpretative obligation imposed on national

---

36. For discussion of the Advocate-Generals' arguments in favour of full horizontal direct effect for Directives see S. Turner, 'Horizontal direct enforcement of Directives rejected' (1995) vol. 46 NILQ 244. For a more detailed discussion of the enforcement of Directives in national courts see S. Prechal, *Directives in European Community Law: A Study of Directives and their Enforcement in National Courts* Oxford: Clarendon Press 1995.
37. [1990] 3 All ER 897. For further discussion of the application of this test by the European Court of Justice and national courts see Prechal, ibid., pp 77–85.
38. See, for example, the recent decision in *Griffen v. South-West Water Services Ltd* [1995] Water Law 5, where it was decided that a privatised water company fell within the definition of an emanation of the state.
39. [1986] 2 CMLR 430.
40. [1992] 1 CMLR 305.

judges, the European Court of Justice has made it clear that national judges must interpret all relevant national law so as to give effect to European provisions in that field. The House of Lords in *Webb v. EMO Air Cargo*[41] accepted that all relevant national law would be susceptible to the principle of indirect effect, regardless of when or why the national legislation was enacted. However, the House of Lords went on to state that judges in the UK would only be obliged to give indirect effect to EC law in so far as it is possible to do so within the limitations of national rules of statutory interpretation. In effect, the House of Lords has made it clear that the principle of indirect effect will not operate to introduce direct effect 'by the back door' in the UK. Although the principle of indirect effect offers private parties a possible means of enforcing the provisions of EC environmental Directives against another private entity, it is not as reliable a tool of enforcement as the principle of direct effect, because it is dependent on the process of judicial interpretation, which itself is a subjective process.

Finally, it should be noted that the European Court's recent decision in Case C-6/90 *Francovich v. Italy*[42] (discussed at page 42) affords private parties a right to damages for any loss sustained by the Government's failure to implement a Directive in certain situations. This decision is widely regarded as removing the distinction between the vertical and horizontal direct effectiveness of Directives. It is important to note that while this ruling may enable a private party to obtain compensation for loss sustained as a result of non-implementation, it does not enable the private party to enforce the actual requirements of the Directive. So in terms of environmental protection, there may be compensation for loss sustained, but the environmental protection element of the Directive will not be enforced directly. In addition, as already explained above, the nature of EC environmental Directives may limit the application of the ruling in *Francovich* in the field of environmental law.

## The impact of European law on national procedural rules

The European Court of Justice has developed a considerable body of case law concerning the operation of national procedural rules which govern actions taken in national courts that are based on EC rights and obligations. It is impossible within the present confines to elaborate on the Court's rulings in this regard in much detail. However, the following general points should be noted:[43]
1. National procedural rules governing actions taken before national courts which are based on EC law rights and obligations must comply with the principles of 'effectiveness' and 'non-discrimination' or 'equivalence'. In essence, this means that national procedural rules must not be framed in such a way as to render it virtually impossible to exercise the EC law rights in practice. In addition, the procedural conditions governing the enforcement of EC law rights must not be less favourable than those which apply to comparable actions based on national law.

---

41. [1992] 4 All ER 929.
42. [1993] 2 CMLR 66.
43. For further discussion of the case law in this area see Prechal, supra, pp, 145–87.

2. Any national procedural rules that pose an obstacle to the effective enforcement of EC law in national courts must be removed and, if necessary, a new remedy must be created to ensure the effective enforcement of EC law. For example, in the seminal case of *R. v. Secretary of State for Transport, ex parte Factortame (No. 1)*[44] the European Court of Justice ruled that the House of Lords was obliged to grant interim relief against the Crown in order to ensure that the Community law in question could be enforced effectively, even though such relief was regarded as unconstitutional under national law. In effect, the House of Lords was obliged to grant an injunction to suspend the operation of a national statute pending a final ruling from the European Court of Justice as to whether the statute was contrary to EC law. Ball and Bell point out that the ruling in *Factortame (No. 1)* has important implications in the field of environmental law; in particular they point out that:

> in many typical environmental cases the applicant will either fail to establish locus standi for a judicial review action, or will be unable to bring an action in tort because it has no interest that the law recognises (for example, the plaintiff may be an amenity group, or may have suffered only economic loss). The judgment in *Factortame*, relying on Article 5 of the Treaty,[45] suggests it is strongly arguable that such restrictive national laws should be dispensed with where a matter of EC law is concerned.[46]

## Challenging the validity of EC legislation

Only the European Court of Justice has the jurisdiction to rule on the validity of EC provisions, and Articles of the Treaty are immune from such challenge. Private parties may gain access to the European Court of Justice for the purpose of challenging the validity of EC secondary legislation (Regulations, Decisions, and Directives) either indirectly by means of a preliminary reference (under Article 177) from a national court to the European Court seeking a ruling on a question of validity or directly under Article 173 of the EC Treaty. It is important to note that although Article 173 provides private parties with a means of mounting a direct action for judicial review before the European Court of Justice, in practice, the Court has interpreted the requirements governing *locus standi* for private parties so restrictively that it is almost impossible to establish admissibility under Article 173. As a result, while the preliminary reference procedure provides only indirect access, it has emerged in practice as the most accessible avenue to the European Court of Justice for the purpose of obtaining rulings on the validity of EC law.[47] The principal weakness posed by the reference procedure for private parties is

---

44. [1990] 3 CMLR 1.
45. Art. 5 states that member states are required to 'take all appropriate measures, whether general or particular, to ensure fulfilment of the obligations arising out of [the Treaty] or... resulting from action taken by institutions of the Community.'
46. Ball and Bell, supra, p. 67. It should be noted that Ball and Bell go on to discuss other possible applications of the *Factortame* principle in the context of environmental protection.
47. For further discussion of the relationship between Arts. 177 and 173 in terms of the extent to which the validity of EC measures can be challenged using both remedies simultaneously see S. Turner, 'Challenging EC law before a national court: a further restriction of the rights of natural and legal persons?' (1995) Irish Journal of European Law, pp 68–87.

that, with few exceptions, the national judge retains complete discretion to decide whether to make a reference in a particular case.[48]

## Obligations to report on progress in implementing European environmental Directives into national law

Many of the early EC environment Directives required member states to submit periodic reports to the Commission so that the Commission could assess whether European environment standards were being fully and correctly implemented into national law. In 1991 the Commission reported that member states were failing to adequately comply with their reporting obligations.[49] In essence, the Commission stated that not all member states systematically submitted implementation reports, and also that national reports did not provide sufficiently detailed evidence as to whether national measures adopted for the purposes of implementing EC standards actually achieved their objective. Instead they tended to provide a brief report of the technical and administrative measures that were already in force or were specially enacted in order to implement the EC measure in question.

In an effort to harmonise and improve the reporting requirements included in certain existing environment Directives, the Community adopted Directive 91/692/EEC,[50] which in effect amended various major environment Directives so that member states are now required to report to the Commission on the implementation of these Directives every three years. The national submission must take the form of a sectoral report in which the implementation of several relevant Directives is reviewed. For example, the first national report on water must cover the period 1993–95 and must address the implementation of several EC Directives concerning water pollution (see below).

Under the amended system of reporting, the Commission is required to send each member state a questionnaire or outline six months before the beginning of the period which the report must cover; the questionnaire or outline is intended to provide the basis of the national implementation report. The national reports must then be sent to the Commission within nine months of the end of the period of the report; the Commission is then obliged to publish a report on implementation for that three-year period. The report must be published within nine months of receipt of the national reports.

The following is a list of the sectoral implementation reports required by Directive 91/692/EEC, the periods they must cover, and the Directives which must be addressed in each sectoral report:

### Water

The first national report must cover the period 1993–95 and must report on the implementation of the following Directives:

- 76/464/EEC— Emissions of dangerous substances into water

---

48. For further reading on the operation and scope of Arts. 177 and 173 see Steiner, supra, chap. 24 and 26.
49. Commission, *Monitoring Application of Community Legislation*, 8th Report (OJ C338/1, p. 204 et seq.). See also Krämer, supra, pp 140–42.
50. OJ L377, 31 Dec. 1992.

- 82/176/EEC— Daughter Directive
- 84/156/EEC— Daughter Directive
- 84/491/EEC— Daughter Directive
- 86/280/EEC— Daughter Directive
- 75/440/EEC— Quality of surface water intended for the abstraction of drinking water (*annual* report required from 31 December 1993)
- 78/176/EEC— Waste from the titanium dioxide industry
- 78/659/EEC— Quality of water for freshwater fish
- 79/869/EEC— Sampling and analysis of surface water intended for the abstraction of drinking water
- 79/923/EEC— Quality of water required for shellfish
- 80/68/EEC — Groundwater
- 80/778/EEC— Drinking water (*annual* report required from 31 December 1993)

*Air*

The first national report must be sent to the Commission for the period 1994–96 and must address the following Directives:

- 75/716/EEC— Sulphur content of gas oil
- 80/779/EEC— Air quality (smoke and sulphur dioxide) (*annual* reports must be submitted)
- 82/501/EEC— Major accident hazards ('Seveso' Directive)
- 82/884/EEC— Air quality (lead) (*annual* report must be submitted)
- 84/360/EEC— Air Framework Directive on industrial emissions
- 85/203/EEC— Air quality (nitrogen dioxide)
- 87/217/EEC— Emissions of asbestos to the environment

*Waste*

The first national report must be submitted for the period 1995–97 and must address the implementation of the following Directives:

- 75/439/EEC— Disposal of waste oils
- 75/442/EEC— Imports and exports of waste
- 76/403/EEC— Disposal of PCBs
- 78/319/EEC— Toxic and dangerous waste
- 84/631/EEC— Transfrontier shipments of toxic waste
- 85/339/EEC— Containers for liquids
- 86/278/EEC— Use of sewage sludge on agricultural land

With the exception of the Seveso Directive, all the above Directives are addressed throughout this book. In addition, it should be noted that Directive 91/271/EEC on Urban Waste Water Treatment imposes a reporting obligation, as does the Wild Birds Directive 79/409/EEC and the Habitats Directive 92/43/EEC. It should also be noted that these national implementation reports are likely to come within the categories of environmental information to which the public have a right of access under the Environmental Information Directive, discussed in chapter 12.

## PART III  THE EUROPEAN ENVIRONMENT AGENCY AND EIONET

In 1990 the EC adopted Regulation EEC/1210/90,[51] which established the European Environment Agency and the European Environment Information and Observation Network (EIONET). The purposes of the Agency and Network are twofold. First, they are intended to provide both the Community and the member states with 'objective, reliable and comparable information at European level' that will enable them to develop the requisite environmental protection measures and also to assess the results of such measures. Second, it is intended that such information will ensure that the public 'is properly informed about the state of the environment,' and to this end the Regulation requires that the information provided must be 'accessible' (Article 1.2). Article 6 of the Regulation provides that all environmental data supplied to the European Environment Agency or emanating from the Agency may be published but must be made accessible to the public, subject to Commission and member states' rules on the dissemination of information, in particular rules on confidentiality. The more detailed outline of the Agency's areas of activity provided below will identify the nature of the environmental information that should be available to the public. Although Regulation EEC/1210/90 was adopted in 1990, the Agency could not begin to operate until its location was agreed between the member states. Three years later it was agreed that the Agency would be located in Copenhagen, and at the end of 1994 the Agency was opened to the public. The Commission is required to submit a report reviewing the Agency's work two years after the Agency becomes operational (i.e. by October 1996); the Council of Ministers will then decide whether the Agency should be assigned further tasks.

Before embarking on a more detailed consideration of the Agency's mandate and the operation of EIONET, it is important to note that although neither the Agency nor the EIONET has an inspectorate capacity, both will play a significant role in reinforcing existing EC powers to monitor the implementation of EC environment standards within the legal systems of each member state and, in particular, will considerably support the reporting obligations imposed on member states under many EC environmental Directives (outlined above). In addition, the executive director of the Agency has argued that the information collected and generated by the Agency and information network should contribute to environmental protection throughout Europe by:

> . . . providing early warning of impending environmental problems; ensuring that [approaches to environmental regulation are based on] *informed* choice; helping to improve the design of policy instruments; monitoring and evaluating the effectiveness of regulations and other actions; empowering the public, NGOs and business to take action; spotlighting deficiencies in the data, so that the scientific community can start filling the gaps; highlighting the inadequacies at member state level, so that improvements in both data gathering and enforcement capacities

---

51.  OJ L120, 11 May 1990.

are encouraged; disseminating details of good practice, both in data collection and in environmental technology.[52]

To meet the objectives set out by Regulation EEC/1210/90, Article 2 of the Regulation gives the Environment Agency ten specific tasks:

1. to establish and co-ordinate the European Environment Information and Observation Network (explained below). In this regard the Agency is responsible for the collection, processing and analysis of data. It is also required to continue the work started under CORINE;[53]
2. to provide the EC and the member states with the objective information necessary for formulating and implementing effective environmental policies;
3. to record, collate and assess data on the state of the environment, to draw up expert reports on the quality, sensitivity and pressures on the environment within the territories of the member states and to provide uniform assessment criteria for environmental data to be applied in all member states; this data will assist the Commission in its task of ensuring that EC environmental legislation is implemented correctly;
4. to help ensure that environmental data at European level is comparable and, where necessary, to encourage the harmonisation of measurement methods throughout the Community;
5. to promote the incorporation of European environmental information into international environment monitoring programmes;
6. to ensure the broad dissemination of reliable environmental information and to publish a report on the state of the environment every three years;
7. to stimulate the development and application of environmental forecasting techniques;
8. to stimulate the development of methods of assessing the cost of damage to the environment and environmental preventive protection and restoration policies;
9. to stimulate the exchange of information on the best available technologies for preventing or reducing damage to the environment;
10. to co-operate with other EC and international bodies and programmes.

---

52. The executive director of the European Environment Agency, Domingo Jimenez-Beltran, delivered the first annual Cambridge Environmental Lecture in May 1995. The lecture dealt with the mandate of the agency and the EIONET and was published as 'The process of sustainable development and the role of the European Environment Agency' (1995) European Environmental Law Review 265.
53. In 1985 the EC adopted Decision 85/338/EEC (OJ L176, 6 July 1985), which established an experimental project known as CORINE authorising the Commission to gather, co-ordinate and ensure the consistency of information on the state of the environment and natural resources within the EC. In particular the CORINE programme focused on the collating of information in relation to four areas of priority concern, namely, acid deposition, protection of the Mediterranean environment, biotopes for conservation and improvement in the comparability and availability of environmental data and methods of analysing that data. Decision 85/338/EEC set up a four-year programme of work that started on 1 Jan. 1985; this was later extended for a further two years by Decision 90/150/EEC (OJ L81, 28 Mar. 1990). Regulation EEC/1210/90, which establishes the European Environment Agency and the EIONET, now makes provision for a permanent environmental information system which supersedes and develops the CORINE programme. For further information concerning the development of the CORINE programme see Haigh, supra, chap. 11.3, p. 1.

Article 3 requires the Agency to focus its work into two principal areas of activity:
 (i) gathering the information necessary to describe the present and foreseeable state of the environment in terms of its quality, the pressures being exerted on the environment, and the sensitivity of the environment and
(ii) furnishing information which can be used directly in the implementation of Community environmental policy; in this regard, priority is to be given to air quality and atmospheric emissions; water quality, pollutants and water resources; the state of the soil, of the fauna and flora and of biotopes; land use and natural resources; waste management; noise emissions; chemical substances that are hazardous for the environment; and coastal protection.

Article 3 goes on to specify that the Agency's work should cover, in particular, transfrontier, plurinational and global phenomena. It must also take the socio-economic dimension into account and must avoid duplicating the activities of other institutions and bodies. Finally, it should be noted that the Agency is required to seek co-operation with other EC and international bodies and in particular with the Joint Research Centre (measurement methods) and Statistical Office (statistics information). In August 1995 the Agency published *Europe's Environment: The Dobřiš Assessment* which is the first pan-European analysis of the state of the environment.[54]

As already stated, the European Environment Agency is required to establish and co-ordinate the European Environment Information and Observation Network (EIONET). The structure of the EIONET is made up of three parts, namely:
  (i) the 'Main Component Elements' (member states must designate the main component elements of national environment information networks; thus far, 450 MCEs have been designated throughout the EC);
 (ii) the 'National Focal Points' (each member state must designate a principal contact point with the Agency to co-ordinate and/or transmit national information to the Agency and other national elements of the network); and
(iii) the 'Topic Centres' (member states may suggest institutions and organisations within their territories that could co-operate with the Agency on specific topics). The structure of the EIONET was confirmed by the Agency's management board in October 1994, and detailed procedures for the exchange of information within the EIONET and with the Environment Agency are at present being established.

---

54. The Agency will also publish a summary of the *The Dobřiš Assessment.* A statistical compendium to the full report, produced by Eurostat, is also available under Catalogue No. CA-82-94-488-EN-C (+Dr, Fr). The Agency can be contacted at: Kongens Nytorv 6, DK-1050, Copenhagen K, Denmark. Tel: + 4533 36 7100;  Fax: + 45 33 36 7199.

# PART TWO

PART TWO

# CHAPTER FOUR

# Air Pollution

## Introduction

The prevention and control of air pollution is without doubt one of the most difficult environmental problems facing both individual governments and the international community as a whole. The sources of air pollution are varied, ranging from toxic emissions from industrial processes to domestic activities such as lighting fires not to mention exhaust emissions from the ubiquitous motor car. To compound the problem, air is a highly mobile environmental medium, with the result that emissions have the capacity not only to pollute local air but also to cause international or indeed global atmospheric pollution.

The discovery of phenomena such as acid rain, the ozone hole and global warming, all global processes resulting from atmospheric pollution, have made it clear that effective air pollution control is no longer an issue for individual governments, no matter how environmentally conscious, but instead requires concerted international co-operation across a wide spectrum of human activities. As is the case in Great Britain and in countries throughout the European Community, the legislative framework which has evolved to control air pollution in Northern Ireland reflects the growing international dimension of regulation in this context.[1] With the exception of controls exerted on domestic and some industrial emissions of smoke, grit, and dust, contemporary legislation in Northern Ireland governing all aspects of air pollution has either been shaped by, or developed in, response to initiatives developed at either EC or international level. The EC, as the principal influence in this context, has tackled the problem of air pollution from a number of angles and has developed a wide variety of regulatory mechanisms to give effect to its policies. These include product standards, environmental quality standards, emission limit values, 'bubble' emission limits, production limits, substance-oriented standards, and, more recently, financial or market-based instruments of control; their specific application in particular contexts will be highlighted and explained in each section of this chapter.[2] It should be noted, however, that as is the case in the context of many other spheres of environmental regulation, the process of implementing EC Directives concerning air pollution has been much slower for Northern Ireland than for the rest of the UK.

The Clean Air (NI) Order 1981 is the principal legislative mechanism for controlling emissions of smoke, grit, dust and fumes from both industrial and domestic sources in Northern Ireland (excluding emissions from the most

---

1. For a historical overview of the emergence of legal controls on air pollution, see Ball and Bell, *Environmental Law,* 3rd ed., London: Blackstone Press, 1995, pp 321–7.
2. Nigel Haigh identifies these mechanisms as the principal approaches adopted by the EC to air pollution and provides a detailed explanation of each in his *Manual of Environmental Policy: the EC & Britain*, London: Longman, 1992, chap. 6.

polluting industrial and commercial activities, which are regulated under the Alkali &c. Works Regulation Act 1906). The Clean Air (NI) Order 1981 (hereafter referred to as the CAO) is enforced by Northern Ireland's twenty-six district councils and is based on the system of control first introduced in Great Britain in the nineteen-fifties for the purposes of combating smog in urban environments. Its provisions are essentially identical to those applying in Great Britain under the Clean Air Act 1956, as amended by the Clean Air Act 1968. These provisions have since been consolidated with minor amendments in the Clean Air Act 1993. The CAO establishes an area of control which is entirely separate from all other sections of air pollution legislation. However, the creation of smoke control areas under the CAO has been vital to the process of implementing EC Directives concerning ambient air quality in Northern Ireland.

At the time of writing, emissions into the air from Northern Ireland's most polluting industrial processes are regulated under the system of control laid down in the Alkali &c. Works Regulation Act 1906, as amended, which is based on use of the 'best practicable means' (BPM). It is important to note, however, that Northern Ireland's approach to industrial pollution control is currently in a state of transition. In March 1996 the DoE(NI) published the proposal for a draft Industrial Pollution Control (NI) Order 1996, which, when enacted, will introduce a considerably strengthened three-tier regime of industrial pollution control that incorporates a system of integrated pollution control (IPC) for those processes with the greatest capacity for generating pollution and which requires compliance in terms of the 'best available techniques not entailing excessive cost' (BATNEEC) and, in certain instances, consideration of the 'best practicable environmental option' (BPEO). In effect, the proposed Industrial Pollution Control (NI) Order 1996 will ensure full implementation of the Air Framework Directive 84/360/EEC in Northern Ireland, it will provide the legislative basis for the implementation of the proposed Integrated Pollution Prevention and Control Directive,[3] soon to be adopted by the EC, and it will bring Northern Ireland standards on industrial pollution control into line with those now governing industrial processes in Great Britain while tailoring those standards specifically to suit the circumstances of the industrial base operating within the Province.

Other EC Directives concerning industrial processes are at various stages of implementation in Northern Ireland. The Asbestos Directive has been fully implemented in Northern Ireland as far as emissions into the air and water are concerned, the Large Combustion Plants Directive has been partially implemented, while the Municipal Waste Incinerator Directives have yet to be formally implemented. EC Air Quality Directives have been fully implemented in Northern Ireland however, both the EC and the UK are in the process of introducing significant changes to their systems of air quality control. There has been full implementation in Northern Ireland of the numerous Directives concerning the prevention and control of motor vehicle air pollution. However, vehicle emission standards in particular, and transport policy in general, are under close scrutiny because of mounting concern throughout the EC about the detrimental impact of vehicle emissions on air quality.

---

3. COM (93) 423 final.

A number of measures have been introduced by the EC to combat the problem of acid rain, and these are partially implemented in Northern Ireland. Measures adopted by the EC to combat ozone depletion have been introduced in the form of Regulations, obviating the need for specific implementation in Northern Ireland; EC Regulations simply take effect for the UK as a whole from the moment of enactment. The European Commission has also been actively encouraging member states to address the extremely complex problem of global warming. However, because action in relation to this issue would require, in particular, a reduction in emissions of carbon dioxide as the principal greenhouse gas, thereby necessitating fundamental changes in our consumption of energy, member states have thus far resisted significant action in this regard; any action which has been taken is addressed in chapter 10.

Finally, it is important to note the active role played by the EC in the development of standards concerning the public availability of information concerning air pollution. In addition to the adoption of the Environmental Information Directive (discussed in chapter 12), several other Directives, such as the Air Framework Directive 84/360/EEC on industrial air pollution, the forthcoming Integrated Pollution Prevention and Control Directive, and the Air Quality Directives, all require greater public consultation in the decision-making process involved in the control of industrial pollution and greater public access to information concerning the application of such controls to specific industrial processes. Similarly, several Directives require member states to monitor the presence of specific pollutants and their effects on the environment and to share information gathered with the Commission and with other member states.

This chapter will address all areas of air pollution control which currently affect Northern Ireland. These sections are as follows:

- Part I        Emissions of smoke, dust, grit and fumes from both domestic and industrial sources
- Part II       Emissions from industrial plants other than smoke, dust, grit and fumes
- Part III      Emissions from large combustion plants
- Part IV       Emissions of asbestos into the air
- Part V        Emissions from municipal waste incinerators
- Part VI       Cable burning
- Part VII      Air quality standards
- Part VIII     Motor vehicle pollution
- Part IX       The international dimension
- Part X        Forest damage caused by air pollution
- Part XI       Information concerning air pollution

## PART I EMISSIONS OF SMOKE, DUST, GRIT AND FUMES

Emissions of smoke, dust, grit and fumes from all fires and furnaces, whether domestic or industrial (except for works regulated under the system of industrial pollution control outlined in Part II of this chapter) are regulated by the Clean Air (Northern Ireland) Order 1981,[4] which repeals the Clean Air Act

---

4. SI 1981/158.

(NI) 1964.[5] In effect, the Clean Air (NI) Order 1981 (referred to as the CAO) provides a comprehensive control mechanism for emissions of smoke, dust, grit and fumes. It establishes an entirely separate system of control from that regulating emissions of noxious and offensive gases and emissions of smoke, grit and dust from those industrial and commercial activities which are regulated under the system of industrial air pollution control laid down under the Alkali &c. Works Regulation Act 1906, outlined in Part II of this chapter. The provisions of the CAO are essentially identical to those applying in Great Britain under the Clean Air Act 1956, as amended by the Clean Air Act 1968. However, these provisions have since been consolidated with minor amendments in the Clean Air Act 1993.

Over the years various pieces of subordinate legislation have been made by the DoE(NI) which supplement the terms of the CAO. In addition, the CAO has been amended by the Local Government (Miscellaneous Provisions) (Northern Ireland) Order 1985.[6] Article 39 of the CAO provides that the Order itself will be enforced by the district councils, and nothing in article 39 may be construed as extending to the enforcement of the Alkali &c. Works Regulation Act 1906 or to the enforcement of any building bylaws. Article 40 sets out the application of the Public Health Acts (NI) 1878–1962 to the functions of the district councils under the CAO. Article 42 states that any premises which extend into the districts of two or more district councils will be treated for the purposes of the CAO as being wholly within such one of those districts as may be agreed upon by those councils. The terms of article 42 have been amended by the Local Government (Miscellaneous Provisions) (NI) Order 1985, which provides that the phrase 'or, in default of agreement, as may be determined by the DoE(NI)' be omitted from article 42. Finally, before embarking on a more detailed examination of the CAO, it should be noted that the proposal for the draft Industrial Pollution Control (NI) Order 1996, when enacted, will make various further amendments to the provisions of the CAO.

## SECTION 1. DARK SMOKE

### Article 3

#### *Prohibition on emissions of 'dark smoke' from chimneys under article 3*

Article 3(1) of the Clean Air (NI) Order 1981 provides that it is an offence to emit 'dark smoke' from 'a chimney of any building'. Article 3 does not, therefore, cover smoke from outdoor fires, and in *Clifford v. Holt*[7] it was decided that the term 'building' would include parts of a recognised structure. In the event that this provision is contravened, the 'occupier of the building' is guilty of an offence. Where different parts of a building are occupied by different people, article 2(4) of the CAO provides that the term 'occupier of a building' will be construed as a reference 'to the occupier or other person in control of the part of the building in which the relevant fireplace is situated.' Article 3(4) extends the prohibition to 'chimneys serving the furnace of any boiler or industrial plant (being a boiler or

---

5.  c. 16.
6.  SI 1985/1208.
7.  [1899] 1 Ch 698.

plant attached to a building or for the time being fixed to or installed on any land).'
In this context 'the person having possession of the boiler or plant' will be the person deemed guilty of an offence in the event that article 3 is violated.

The term 'smoke' is defined by article 2(2) as including 'soot, ash, grit and gritty particles emitted in smoke,' while 'dark smoke' is defined by article 2(3) as:

> smoke which, if compared in the appropriate manner with a chart of the type known on the 9th June 1964 as the Ringelmann Chart, would appear to be as dark as or darker than shade 2 on that chart; but—
>
> (a) in proceedings brought under article 3, 4 or 23, the court may be satisfied that smoke is or is not dark smoke as so defined notwithstanding that there has been no actual comparison of the smoke with a chart of that type; and
>
> (b) in particular, and without prejudice to the generality of the preceding provisions of this paragraph, if any method is prescribed for ascertaining whether smoke is dark smoke as so defined, proof in any such proceedings that that method was properly applied, and that the smoke was ascertained by that method to be or not to be dark smoke as so defined, shall be accepted as sufficient.

Article 2(2) of the CAO defines the term 'chimney' as including:

> structures and openings of any kind from or through which smoke, grit, dust or fumes may be emitted, and in particular, includes flues, and references to a chimney of a building include references to a chimney which serves the whole or part of a building but is structurally separate from it.

### *Defences to proceedings for an offence under article 3*

Article 3(3) affords the defendant a number of statutory defences to proceedings brought under article 3. It is a defence to prove:

> (a) that the contravention complained of was solely due to the lighting up of a furnace which was cold and that all practicable steps had been taken to prevent or minimise the emission of dark smoke [the term 'practicable' being defined in article 2(2) as meaning reasonably practicable having regard, amongst other things, to local conditions and circumstances, to the financial implications and to the current state of technical knowledge]; or
>
> (b) that the contravention complained of was solely due to some failure of a furnace or of apparatus used in connection with a furnace and that—
>
>> (i) that failure could not reasonably have been foreseen, or, if foreseen, could not reasonably have been provided against; and
>>
>> (ii) the contravention could not reasonably have been prevented by action taken after the failure occurred; or
>
> (c) that the contravention complained of was solely due to the use of unsuitable fuel and that—
>
>> (i) suitable fuel was unobtainable; and
>>
>> (ii) the least unsuitable fuel which was available was used; and

(iii) all practicable steps [defined as above] had been taken to prevent or minimise the emission of dark smoke as a result of the use of that fuel; or

(*d*) that the contravention complained of was due to a combination of two or more of the causes specified in sub-paragraphs (a) to (c) and that the other conditions specified in those sub-paragraphs are satisfied in relation to those causes respectively.

A failure by the district council to satisfy the notification procedure set out below (enforcement obligations) will also provide the defendant with a defence to proceedings in this context.

### Penalties incurred for breach of article 3

The penalties incurred for violation of the prohibition contained in article 3 are laid out in article 38(1) of the CAO. In effect, a person found guilty of an offence under article 3 will be liable on summary conviction to a maximum fine of £1,000 where dark smoke is emitted from the chimney of a private dwelling and to a maximum fine of £2,500 where dark smoke is emitted from any other chimney.

### District councils' enforcement powers and obligations

Articles 37 and 39 of the CAO set out district councils' powers in relation to the enforcement of article 3. Article 39(2) states that a district council 'may institute proceedings for an offence under Article 3 where any smoke affects any part of its district notwithstanding that the smoke is emitted from a chimney outside its district.' Article 37(1) imposes an obligation on district councils to notify 'as soon as may be' the person deemed liable under the CAO of the council's belief that an offence has been committed under article 3. If the notice is not given in writing then article 37(1) states that the district council must confirm the notification in writing before the end of 'the four days next following the day on which the council became aware of the offence.'

Article 37(2) provides that a failure to comply with the terms of article 37(1) will provide a defence to the defendant in proceedings brought in relation to an offence under article 3. In addition, article 37(2) provides that the notification requirements laid down in article 37(1) will be 'deemed not to have been complied with' if the district council fails to give the required notification 'before the end of the two days' next following the day of the offence, or, where the offence was committed after 13 March 1980, before the end of the four days next following the day of the offence. Article 62 of the Pollution Control and Local Government (NI) Order 1978[8] came into operation on 13 March 1980, which is the deadline specified in article 37(2) of the CAO. The presumption that article 37(1) has not been complied with will operate unless the contrary is proved. Article 37(3) empowers the district council to arrange for any of its officers to discharge its functions under article 37.

---

8. SR 1980 No. 97. Art. 62 was repealed by Sch. 5 to the CAO.

### Emissions from vessels

Article 27 of the CAO provides that article 3 also applies to emissions from 'vessels in waters' in the same way that it applies to buildings. References to the owner[9] of and to the master or other officer or person in charge of the vessel must be substituted for references to the 'occupier of the building' as used in article 3. References to a furnace include references to the vessel's engine. Article 27(2) and (3) detail the waters to which the article applies. With the exception of article 27, no other provision of the CAO applies to smoke, dust or grit emitted from a vessel. Article 29(4) provides that article 27 shall, with the omission of the reference in article 27(1) to the owner, apply to vessels owned by the Crown *other* than (i) vessels of Her Majesty's navy and (ii) Government ships[10] in the service of the Admiralty while employed for the purposes of Her Majesty's navy. Article 38(1)(*b*) provides that contravention of article 3 as applied under article 27 to vessels is punishable on summary conviction by a maximum fine of £5,000.

### Emissions from railway engines

The prohibition contained in article 3 also applies to emissions from railway locomotive engines in the same way as it applies to emissions from buildings (article 26). References to the owner (defined as above) of the engine must be substituted for references to the occupier of the building as used in article 3. The owner of a railway engine must 'use any practicable means[11] there may be' to minimise the emission of smoke from the engine's chimney. Failure to do so is an offence. With the exception of article 26, the provisions of the CAO do not apply to emissions of smoke, grit or dust from railway locomotive engines.

Article 28 empowers the district council to exempt any chimney from the operation of article 26 where, on an application to the council, the council considers that it is expedient to do so in order to enable investigation and research to be carried out into air pollution. Schedule 1 to the CAO will apply to an application under article 28.

### Exemptions from article 3

Article 3(2) states that the DoE(NI) may exempt certain emissions of smoke from the operation of article 3(1). The Dark Smoke (Permitted Periods) Regulations (NI) 1965,[12] Dark Smoke (Permitted Periods) (Vessels) Regulations (NI) 1965,[13] and the Clean Air (Emissions of Dark Smoke) (Exemption) Regulations (NI)

---

9. Art. 2(2) of the CAO provides that the term 'owner' has the same meaning as in the Public Health (Ireland) Act 1878 c. 52.
10. 'Government ship' is defined in art. 29(6) as having the same meaning as in s. 80 of the Merchant Shipping Act 1906 (c. 48).
11. Art. 2(2) defines 'practicable' as meaning reasonably practicable having regard, among other things, to local conditions and circumstances, to the financial implications, and to the current state of technical knowledge, and 'practicable means' includes the provision and maintenance of plant and the proper use of it.
12. SR No. 73.
13. SR No. 74.

1981[14] have all been adopted under this provision. In addition, article 28 of the CAO empowers the district council to exempt any chimney from the operation of article 3 where, on an application made to the council, it considers that it is expedient to do so in the interest of investigation and research into air pollution. Schedule 1 to the CAO governs the making of such an application.

## Article 4

### Prohibition of emissions of 'dark smoke' from industrial or trade premises under article 4

It is an offence under article 4(1) of the CAO to emit dark smoke from 'any industrial or trade premises'. Where article 4 is contravened, the 'occupier of the premises' is guilty of an offence. Article 4(1) does not apply to emissions of dark smoke from chimneys governed by article 3 (see above). 'Industrial or trade premises' are defined by article 4(5) as 'premises used for any industrial or trade purposes or premises not so used on which matter is burnt in connection with any industrial or trade process.' In *Sheffield CC v. ADH Demolition*[15] the court ruled that the term 'premises' as used in section 2 of the Clean Air Act 1993 (which is the equivalent, but not identical, provision applying in Great Britain) applied to the grounds of factories and to open areas such as demolition sites. Ball and Bell also suggest that section 2 of the 1993 Act also applies to 'open areas without any connection to industrial activities.'[16]

The meaning of the term 'emission of dark smoke' within the meaning of section 2 of the Clean Air Act 1993 was addressed by the High Court in *O'Fee v. Copeland Borough Council*.[17] In effect, the court was asked to consider the meaning of the term 'emission'. The question at issue was whether dark smoke which was witnessed rising from a fire burning on the appellant's farm could be regarded as an 'emission' for the purposes of the Act, even if the dark smoke remained within the boundaries of the land. In this case the Environmental Health Officer who witnessed the fire could give evidence that the smoke rising from the fire was 'dark smoke' but could not give evidence of the shade of the smoke at the point at which it crossed the boundaries of the land. The High Court ruled that the prohibition on emissions of dark smoke from land included movement above the surface of the ground, even though the 'dark smoke' remained within the boundaries of the land occupied. The court concluded that the purpose of the Clean Air Act 1993 was to prevent and control pollution of the air and, therefore, to exclude the air space immediately above the parcel of land on which the fire was burning would defeat the purposes of the Act.

---

14. SR No. 86.
15. (1984) 82 LGR 177.
16. Ball and Bell, *Environmental Law*, 3rd ed., London: Blackstone Press, 1995, p. 335.
17. Unreported, Queens Bench Division, 9 March 1995. For further commentary on this see *Environmental Law Monthly*, Monitor Press, January 1996, 2–4.

## Defences to proceedings for an offence under article 4(1)

Article 4(4) provides that it is a defence to proceedings under article 4(1) to prove that the contravention complained of was 'inadvertent and that all practicable[18] steps had been taken to prevent or minimise the emission of dark smoke'. As is the case under article 3, a failure on the part of a district council to satisfy the procedural requirements governing the enforcement of article 4 (as set out in article 37(1) and (2), outlined in the context of article 3) will constitute a defence to proceedings under article 4.

## Penalties incurred for breaches of article 4

Article 38(5), (6) and (7) sets out the penalties incurred for an offence under article 4(1). In effect, article 38(5) provides that a person found guilty of an offence under article 4 will be liable on summary conviction to a maximum fine of £2,500. Article 38(6) then makes general provision for repeated and continued offences under the CAO. It provides that where a person is convicted of an offence under the CAO and it is established that the offence was 'substantially a repetition or continuation of an earlier offence by him after he had been convicted of the earlier offence', that person will be liable on summary conviction to the greater of: (i) a maximum fine of £2,500 or (ii) a fine of £500 for every day on which the earlier offence was repeated or continued by that person within the three months following conviction. Article 38(7) provides that where a person would be liable under article 38(6) for a daily penalty, the court which convicts him of the earlier offence may fix a reasonable period from the date of conviction within which the defendant must comply with the CAO and any directions given by the court; where such a period is fixed, the daily penalty for repeated or continuing violation cannot be imposed in relation to any breach committed before the expiry of that period.

## District councils' enforcement powers and obligations

As with article 3, article 37 of the CAO sets out the district council's obligations to notify occupiers of offences under the terms of article 4. The details of these obligations are set out above in relation to article 3.

## Exemptions from article 4

Article 4(3) empowers the DoE(NI) to adopt regulations exempting emissions of dark smoke from industrial and trade premises caused by the burning of prescribed matter. The Clean Air (Emission of Dark Smoke) Regulations (NI) 1981[19] have been adopted pursuant to this power. In addition, article 28 empowers the district council to exempt any premises from the operation of article 4 where, on an application to the council, the council considers that it would be expedient to do so

---

18. Art. 2(2) defines 'practicable' as meaning 'reasonably practicable having regard, amongst other things, to local conditions and circumstances, to the financial implications and to the current state of technical knowledge.'
19. SR No. 340.

for the purposes of carrying out investigation and research into air pollution. The provisions of Schedule 1 to the CAO govern the making of an application under article 28.

## SECTION 2. SMOKE FROM FURNACES

## Article 5

### Certain furnaces to be so far as practicable smokeless

Article 5(1) provides that unless a furnace is, so far as practicable,[20] capable of being operated continuously without emitting smoke[21] when burning fuel of a type for which the furnace was designed, that furnace must not be *installed* either:

(a) in a building; or

(b) in any boiler or industrial plant[22] attached to a building or [which is] for the time being fixed to or installed on any land.

Article 5(12) provides that the prohibition contained in article 5(1)(b) also applies to:

(a) the attachment to a building of a boiler or industrial plant which already contains a furnace; [and]

(b) to the fixing to or installation on any land of any boiler or industrial plant which already contains a furnace.

Article 5(13) states that article 5 will also, apply to such furnace *reconstruction* works as may be prescribed by regulations in the same way as it applies to the installation of any furnace under article 5(1). This power has not been exercised.

Article 5 does not apply to the following types of furnaces:

1. where the installation of a furnace has begun, or an agreement for the purchase or installation of a furnace has been entered into, before 1 July 1965 (article 5(2));

2. furnaces designed solely or mainly for use for domestic purposes, not being furnaces of boilers with a maximum heating capacity of 16.12 kilowatts[23] or more per hour (article 5(11)).

### *Notice to, and approvals by, the district council*

Article 5(3)–(8) imposes an obligation to notify the district council of a proposal to install a furnace in a building, boiler or plant within the meaning of article 5(1),

---

20. 'Practicable' is defined in art. 2(2) as being reasonably practicable having regard, among other things, to local conditions and circumstances, to the financial implications, and to the current state of technical knowledge.

21. 'Smoke' is defined in art. 2(2) as including soot, ash, grit and gritty particles emitted in smoke.

22. 'Industrial plant' is defined in art. 2(2) as including any still, melting pot or other plant used for any industrial or trade purposes and also any incinerator used for or in connection with any such purposes.

23. The unit of measurement expressed in article 5(11) of the CAO has been amended by Sch. 2 to the Alkali &c. Works and Clean Air (Metrication) Regulations (NI) 1994 (SR No. 192), which implements, in part, Directive 80/181/EEC (OJ L39/40), as modified by Directive 89/617/EEC (OJ L357/28), concerning the harmonisation of national laws relating to units of measurement.

unless the furnace is being installed in accordance with plans and specifications which have been submitted to, and approved by, the district council for the purposes of article 5. A failure to either (i) notify the district council of the proposed installation or (ii) to install in accordance with plans and specifications approved by the district council for the purposes of article 5, is an offence under article 5(9) or (10). Article 5 does not impose an obligation to submit plans and specifications for approval, but it states that a date may be prescribed by regulations after which it will be impossible to install such furnaces as may be prescribed by regulations without first submitting plans and specifications of the furnace to the district council for approval. At the time of writing no such date has been laid down.

The terms of article 5(3)–(8) will now be outlined in more detail:

1. Article 5(4) provides that a furnace must not be installed in a building, boiler or plant (within the meaning of article 5(1)) unless notice of the proposal to install the furnace has been given to the district council. This provision does not apply to furnaces to which article 5(6) applies; the terms of article 5(6) are set out below.

2. Article 5(6) states that where plans and specifications for the installation of a furnace are submitted to the district council for approval for the purposes of article 5, the furnace to which the plans and specifications relate must not be installed in a building, or in any boiler or industrial plant attached to a building or for the time being fixed to or installed on any land, except in accordance with the approved plans and specifications. This provision applies whether or not plans and specifications are required to be submitted under article 5(5), outlined below.

3. If, for the purposes of article 5, a district council approves plans and specifications for the installation of a furnace, the installation of that furnace will be deemed to comply with the provisions of article 5(1) (article 5(3)).

4. The provisions of Schedule 1 to the CAO apply in relation to an application for approval by the district council of any plans and specifications submitted to the council for the purposes of article 5. However, the district council must not grant any application for approval under article 5 if the furnace in question is not, so far as is practicable, capable of being operated continuously without emitting smoke when burning fuel of a type for which the furnace was designed (article 5(8)).

5. Article 5(5) states that a date may be prescribed after which such furnaces as may be prescribed must not be installed in a building, boiler or plant (within the meaning of article 5(1)) unless plans and specifications of the furnace have been submitted to the district council for approval for the purposes of article 5. No such date has yet been prescribed.

6. Article 5(9) states that a person who either: '(*a*) installs a furnace in contravention of [article 5] (4), (5) or (6); or (*b*) on whose instructions a furnace is installed in contravention of any those paragraphs' will be guilty of an offence.

7. Article 5(10) provides that a person who either: '(*a*) installs a furnace in contravention of [article 5](1); or (*b*) on whose instruction a furnace is so installed' will be guilty of an offence *unless* it is a furnace to which article 5(6) applies.

### *Penalty incurred for breaches of article 5*

Article 38(2) sets out the penalty incurred for violation of article 5(9) where the breach is in respect of article 5(4). A person found guilty on summary conviction of such an offence will be liable to a maximum fine of £1,000.

Article 38(5), (6) and (7) sets out the penalties incurred for offences under article 5(10). The penalties imposed are identical to those outlined in relation to penalties for offences under article 4 of the CAO in section 1 above.

### *Exemptions from article 5(1)*

Article 28 empowers the district council to exempt any furnace, boiler or industrial plant from the operation of article 5(1) where, on an application to the council, it considers it expedient to do so in order to enable investigation and research to be carried out on air pollution. Schedule 1 to the CAO governs the making of an application under article 28.

### *Density meters under article 6*

Schedule 3 to the Local Government (Miscellaneous Provisions) (NI) Order 1985[24] repeals article 6 of the CAO concerning density meters.

## SECTION 3.  GRIT AND DUST FROM FURNACES

### Grit and dust from furnaces under article 7

In addition to controlling emissions of smoke, the CAO also regulates emissions of 'grit and dust'[25] from any furnace in which 'solid, liquid or gaseous matter is burnt' (article 7(5)). It does not apply to furnaces 'designed solely or mainly for domestic purposes and used for heating a boiler with maximum heating capacity of less than 16.12 kilowatts per hour'.[26]

Article 7(1) empowers the DoE(NI) to prescribe limits by means of regulations on the rates of emission of 'grit and dust' from the chimneys of furnaces to which article 7 applies. At the time of writing this power has not been exercised. Article 7(2) provides that it is an offence to emit grit or dust from a chimney serving a furnace to which article 7 applies on any day[27] at a rate which exceeds the limits that might be prescribed in regulations adopted by the Department under article 7(1). Where the prescribed limits are exceeded, the occupier of any building in which the furnace is situated will be deemed liable.

### *Defence to proceedings under article 7(2)*

It is a defence to prove that 'the best practicable means were used to minimise the alleged emission.' The term 'practicable' is defined in article 2(2) of the CAO as

---

24. SI 1985/1208.
25. Art. 2(2) defines 'grit and dust' as including solid particles of any kind.
26. The unit of measurement expressed in article 7 of the CAO has been amended by Sch. 2 to the Alkali &c. Works and Clean Air (Metrication) Regulations (NI) 1994 (SR 1994 No. 192), which implements, in part, Directive 80/181/EEC (OJ L39/40), as modified by Directive 89/617/EEC (OJ L357/28), concerning the harmonisation of national laws relating to units of measurement.
27. 'Day' is defined in art. 2(2) as a period of twenty-four hours beginning at midnight.

meaning 'reasonably practicable having regard, among other things, to local conditions and circumstances, to the financial implications, and to the current state of technical knowledge'; the phrase 'practicable means' is defined as including 'the provision and maintenance of plant and the proper use of it'.

## *Emissions of grit and dust where no limits have been prescribed under article 7(1)*

Article 7(4) provides that the occupier of a building containing a furnace governed by article 7, which is served by a chimney for which no emission limit has been prescribed under article 7(1), will be guilty of an offence 'if all practicable means there may be' are not employed to minimise the emission of grit or dust from that chimney.

## *Penalties incurred for breaches of article 7*

Article 38(5), (6) and (7) sets out the penalties incurred for any offence under article 7; the exact penalties imposed are outlined in the context of penalties imposed for breaches of article 4 of the CAO explained in section 1 above.

## *Exemptions from article 7*

Article 28 empowers the district council to exempt any chimney from the operation of article 7 where, on an application to the council, the council considers it expedient to do so in order to enable investigation and research to be carried out into air pollution. Schedule 1 to the CAO governs the making of an application under article 28.

## Fumes

Article 16 empowers the DoE(NI) to adopt regulations which apply all or some of the provisions of articles 7, 9, 10, 26(3), 27(4) and 29(1) to fumes in the same way as they apply to emissions of grit and dust. At the time of writing this power has not been used. Similarly the DoE(NI) is empowered to adopt regulations which apply the terms of article 5 to fumes in the same way as they apply to smoke. At the time of writing no such regulations have been adopted. The DoE(NI) may also make whatever modifications are necessary when these provisions are being applied to fumes.

## New furnaces to be fitted with plant to arrest grit and dust under articles 8 and 9

Articles 8(2) and 9(1) provide that a furnace of such a kind as may be prescribed by regulations in any building which is used in any building, 'to burn fuel or solid waste', must not be used to burn fuel or solid waste unless the furnace is provided with plant for arresting grit and dust (including solid particles of any kind (article 2(2)). Plans and specifications for such plant must have been submitted to and approved by the distict council for the purposes of articles 8 and 9, respectively. Such plant must also be properly installed, maintained, and used. The Department's power to prescribe the types of furnaces to be fitted with plant to arrest grit and dust has not been exercised to date.

### District council powers in relation to applications for approval

Article 8(5) and (6) governs the powers of the district council in relation to applications for approval for furnaces to which articles 8 and 9 apply. Paragraph (5) provides that Schedule 1 to the CAO will apply in relation to an application for approval by the district council of any plans and specifications submitted to that council for the purposes of articles 8 and 9. The district council cannot grant any application for approval under article 8 or 9 if the furnace in question does not comply with such minimum standards as may be prescribed by regulations for the concentration or the rate (or both) of emissions of grit and dust from furnaces to which articles 8 and 9 apply. No such regulations have been adopted. Schedule 3 to the Local Government (Miscellaneous Provisions) (NI) Order 1985[28] requires that article 8(7) and (8) concerning the referral to the DoE(NI) be repealed.

### Furnaces excluded from articles 8 and 9

Article 8 excludes furnaces:
  (i)   that were installed before 1 July 1965, or
  (ii)  whose installation began before 1 July 1965, or
  (iii) where an agreement for the purchase or installation of the furnace was entered into before 1 July 1965.
Article 9 excludes furnaces under identical conditions as those excluded under article 8 but uses the date of the coming into operation of article 62 of the Pollution Control and Local Government (NI) Order 1978[29] (i.e. 13 March 1980[30]) as the cut-off date.

### Offences under articles 8 and 9

Article 8(3) provides that the occupier of the building is guilty of an offence if a furnace used to burn fuel or solid waste is used in contravention of article 8(2). Article 9(1) provides that the occupier of the building is guilty of an offence if a furnace used to burn fuel or solid waste is, 'on any day', used in contravention of article 9(1).

### Penalties for offences under articles 8 and 9

Article 38(5), (6) and (7) sets out the penalties incurred for offences in this context; the exact penalties imposed are outlined in the context of penalties imposed for violation of article 4 of the CAO in section 1 above.

### Exemptions from articles 8 and 9

Article 28 empowers the district council to exempt any furnace from the operation of articles 8 and 9 where, on an application to the council, the council considers it expedient to do so in order to enable investigation and research to be carried out on air pollution. Schedule 1 to the CAO will apply to the making of an application under article 28.

---

28.  SI 1985/1208.
29.  SI 1978/1049.
30.  SR 1980 No. 97. Art. 62 itself was repealed by Sch. 5 to the CAO.

Article 10 of the CAO provides that furnaces within the meaning of article 9 can be exempted from the operation of article 9(1) either: (i) under regulations adopted by the DoE(NI) under article 10(1) (no such regulations have yet been adopted) or (ii) as a result of an application made by the occupier of a building to the district council under article 10(2). Article 10(2) provides that where a district council is satisfied that the emission of grit or dust from any chimney serving a furnace in the building will not be prejudicial to health[31] or a nuisance, if the furnace is used for a particular purpose without complying with article 9(1), the district council may exempt the furnace from the operation of article 9(1) for those purposes. It should be noted that Schedule 3 to the Local Government (Miscellaneous Provisions) (NI) Order 1985 requires that article 10(3), which laid down certain requirements concerning the format in which the application should be made, be repealed. As a result, the occupier of the building is not required to follow any particular format when submitting an application for exemption under article 10(2). Where the district council fails to determine the application and to give a written notice of its decision to the applicant within eight weeks of receiving the application, or such longer period as may be agreed in writing between the applicant and the council, the exemption will be regarded as having been granted to the furnace for the purposes specified in the application.

If a district council decides not to grant an exemption under article 10(2) it is obliged to give the applicant a written notification of its decision, stating its reasons. The applicant may bring an appeal against a decision to refuse an exemption. Article 10(5) requires that the appeal be brought to the DoE(NI) by the applicant within twenty-eight days of receiving notification of the district council's refusal. Article 10(6) empowers the DoE(NI) to either:

(i) confirm the decision to refuse the application;
(ii) grant the exemption for the purposes specified in the application; or
(iii) grant the exemption but vary the purposes for which the furnace may be used under the exemption.

The DoE(NI) is required to give the appellant written notice of its decision concerning the appeal and must also state the reasons for its decision.

Where an exemption is created either by regulation under article 10(1) or as a result of an application under article 10(2), the occupier of the building will be guilty of an offence if the furnace is used on any day for a purpose other than that for which it was exempted. Article 38(5), (6) and (7) sets out the penalties incurred for an offence under article 10. The exact penalties imposed in this regard are outlined above in section 1 in the context of penalties imposed for breaches of article 4 of the CAO.

## Measurement of grit, dust and fumes from furnaces under article 8

Article 11 makes provision for ensuring that emissions of grit, dust and fumes from furnaces within the meaning of article 8 can be made and recorded either by or in the presence of the district council. As stated above, article 8 applies to furnaces (of such a kind as may be prescribed) which are used to burn fuel or solid

---

31. The term 'prejudicial to health' is defined in art. 2(2) as being 'injurious, or likely to cause injury, to health'.

waste, excluding furnaces whose installation began before 1 July 1965, or which were installed, agreed to be installed or purchased before 1 July 1965. Article 11(1)–(4) empowers the district council to serve a notice on the occupier of a building in which such a furnace is situated, requiring that emissions of dust, grit or fumes from the furnace be measured and recorded. However, article 11(5)–(7) also empowers the occupier of such a building to request that the district council measure and record such emissions.

### District council powers to require that emissions be measured

Article 11(1) provides that the district council may, by notice in writing served on the occupier of the building, direct that the provisions of article 11(2) apply to a furnace within the meaning of article 8 used in the building. Article 11(2) sets out a variety of emission measurement requirements which the district council may apply to such a furnace. Where article 11(2) is applied to a furnace, the occupier of the building is obliged to comply with such measurement requirements as may be prescribed (this power has not been exercised). These requirements may relate to:

(a)  making and recording measurements from time to time of the grit, dust and fumes[32] emitted from the furnace;

(b)  making adaptations for that purpose to the chimney serving the furnace;

(c)  providing and maintaining apparatus for making and recording the measurements; and

(d)  informing the district council of the results obtained from the measurements or otherwise making those results available to it.

Article 11(4) states that it is an offence to fail to comply with any requirement under article 11(2). The occupier of a building will be held liable. In addition, where an occupier of a building has been required under article 11(2) to make and record measurements of grit, dust and fumes, the occupier is obliged by article 11(9) to permit the district council to be present during the making and recording of those measurements. Article 38(5), (6) and (7) sets out the penalties incurred for an offence under article 11. The exact penalties imposed in this regard are outlined above in section 1 in the context of penalties imposed for breaches of article 4 of the CAO.

Article 11(8) imposes an obligation on the district council to include a statement of the terms of article 11(5)–(7) in a direction issued under article 11(1). In effect, the district council is obliged to inform the occupier of a building that it is possible for the occupier to request that the district council measure and record emissions of dust, grit and fumes from a furnace within the meaning of article 8. The details of article 11(5)–(7) are outlined below. Article 11(3) empowers the district council to serve a subsequent written notice on the occupier of the building revoking any direction given under article 11(1). Such a revocation will not prejudice the power of the district council to issue another direction under article 11(3).

Article 11(5)–(7) empowers the occupier of a building in which a furnace

---

32.  The term 'fume' is defined in art. 2(2) as any airborne solid matter smaller than dust.

(within the meaning of article 8) is situated to request, by notice in writing, that the district council make and record measurements of grit, dust and fumes emitted from the furnace. The occupier of the building, or any subsequent occupier of the building, is entitled to withdraw such a notice by means of a subsequent notice in writing. Article 11(7) provides that where a notice to measure issued by the occupier of a building under article 11(5) is in force the district council is obliged, from time to time, to make and record measurements of the grit, dust and fumes emitted from the furnace to which the notice relates. Where such a notice is in force, the occupier of the building cannot be required to comply with any of the measurement requirements listed in article 11(2), with the exception of the requirement to make adaptations to the chimney serving the furnace for the purpose of carrying out the measurement referred to in article 11(2)(*b*).

### *Exemption from article 11*

Article 28 empowers the district council to exempt any furnace from the operation of article 11 where, on an application, the council considers that it is expedient to do so in order to allow research and investigation to be carried out into air pollution. Schedule 1 to the CAO applies to the making of an application under article 28.

### District council powers to gather information about furnaces and fuel consumed

To enable it to carry out its functions under articles 8–11, the district council has the power under article 12 of the CAO to require the occupier of any building to furnish such information about the furnaces in the building and the fuel or waste burned in those furnaces as the council in question may reasonably require for that purpose. Article 12(1) requires the district council to serve a written notice of the request on the occupier of the building. The occupier of the building is required to furnish the information requested within fourteen days or within such longer time as may be specified in the notice.

### *Offences under article 12*

Where a person has been duly served with a notice requesting such information, it is an offence under article 12(2) to fail to comply with the requirements of the notice within the time specified, or to furnish any information which the person in question knows to be false in any material particular. The person served with the notice will be deemed guilty of an offence in these circumstances.

### *Penalty incurred for breaches of article 12*

Article 38(5) sets out the penalty incurred for an offence under article 12. A person found guilty on summary conviction for an offence under article 12 will be liable to a maximum fine of £2,500.

### Grit and dust emissions from outdoor furnaces

Article 13(1) provides that articles 7–12 of the CAO will apply to the furnace 'of any boiler or industrial plant (being a boiler or plant attached to a building or for the time being fixed to or installed on any land)' in the same way as they apply to a furnace in a building. The remainder of article 13 makes various adjustments to the application of articles 7–12 to furnaces that are not in a building:

1. Article 13(2) provides that when articles 7–12 are applied to a furnace that is not in a building, the references in articles 7–12 to the 'occupier of the building' must be interpreted as being references to 'the person having possession of the boiler or plant.'

2. Article 13(3) provides that when the furnace in question is one which is 'already contained in any boiler or industrial plant,' being a boiler or plant attached to a building or for the time being fixed to or installed on any lands, the following adjustments must be made:

   (a) the references in article 8 and 9(3) to the installation of a furnace shall be interpreted as references to attaching the boiler or plant to the building or fixing it to or installing it on any land; and

   (b) the reference to the purchase of a furnace shall be construed as a reference to purchasing the boiler or plant.

## Section 4. Height of Chimneys

Article 14 sets out the position concerning the height of certain chimneys.[33] Article 14(1) provides that where it is proposed to erect a chimney, plans for that chimney, showing also where it is to be erected, must be submitted to the district council for its approval for the purposes of this article. Article 14(1) does not apply to chimneys governed by article 15, i.e. chimneys which serve a furnace (discussed below). In addition, article 14(1) does not apply to chimneys of buildings which are used, or are to be used, wholly for one or more of the following purposes:

   (i)   as a residence or residences;
   (ii)  as a shop or shops;
   (iii) as an office or offices.

### District council powers to approve a proposal to erect a chimney

Subject to the provisions of article 14(3), Schedule 1 to the CAO governs the making of an application to the district council for approval to erect a chimney within the meaning of article 14. Article 14(3) states that the district council shall not approve plans for the erection of a chimney under article 14 unless it is satisfied that the height of the chimney as shown in the plans will be sufficient to prevent, so far as is practicable, the smoke, grit or gases from becoming a nuisance or prejudicial to health, having regard to:

   (a) the purpose of the chimney;

   (b) the position and description of buildings near to it;

   (c) the levels of the neighbouring ground; and

   (d) any other matters requiring consideration in the circumstances.

---

33. See also the *Third Memorandum on Chimney Heights,* London: HMSO, which sets out guidelines on assessing chimney heights.

## District council powers where a chimney is erected in contravention of plans approved by the council for the purposes of article 14

Article 14(4) empowers the district council: (i) to pull down, alter or remove so much of the chimney as has been erected and (ii) to recover summarily any expenses incurred by the council in carrying out of the work described in (i) from the person who caused the erection in question to be carried out. Article 33 governs the district council's power to recover expenses together with interest under article 14.

## Height of chimneys serving a furnace

Article 15 controls the height of chimneys serving certain types of furnaces (furnaces covered by article 15 are discussed below). Article 15(1) provides that the occupier of a building must not 'knowingly cause or permit' a furnace to which article 15 applies to be used in the building to burn fuel or solid waste, unless:

(i) the height of the chimney serving the furnace has been approved under article 15 and

(ii) any conditions which were attached to the approval have been complied with.

Article 15(2) imposes an identical obligation on a person who has possession of a boiler or industrial plant (except 'an exempted boiler or plant'[34]) that is attached to a building or which is for the time being fixed to or installed on any land. Such a person must not knowingly cause or permit a furnace of the boiler or plant to be used to burn fuel or solid waste (as described in article 9(1)) unless the two conditions outlined above are complied with.

### *The furnaces to which article 15 applies*

Article 15(10) states that the provisions of article 15 will apply to the following types of furnaces:

(i) any furnace served by a chimney other than a chimney the construction of which was begun or the plans for which were passed before the date on which article 62 of the Pollution Control and Local Government (NI) Order 1978 came into operation (i.e. 13 March 1980);[35]

(ii) any furnace the combustion space of which has been increased since the date on which article 62 of the 1978 Order came into operation; and

(iii) any furnace the installation of which was begun after the date on which article 62 came into operation and which replaces a furnace which had a smaller combustion space;

not being a furnace forming part of a generating station as defined in the Electricity Supply (NI) Order 1972[36] other than a private generating station as so defined.

---

34. 'Exempted boiler or plant' is defined in art. 15(11) as meaning a boiler or plant which is used or is to be used wholly for any prescribed purpose. Thus far the Department has not exercised its power to exempt boilers or plants from the operation of article 15.
35. SR 1980 No. 97. Art. 62 itself was repealed by Sch. 5 to the CAO.
36. SI 1972/1072.

### Offences for breach of article 15(1) and (2)

The occupier of the building will be deemed guilty of an offence under article 15(1) if the requirements laid down in article 15(1) are violated on any day. Similarly, the person having possession of a boiler or plant as described in article 15(2) will be guilty of an offence for contravention of article 15(2) on any day. Article 38(5), (6) and (7) sets out the penalties for an offence under article 15; the exact penalties imposed in this regard are outlined in section 1 above in the context of penalties incurred for breaches of article 4 of the CAO.

### District council powers to approve the height of a chimney serving a furnace

Article 15(4) states that a district council cannot approve the height of a chimney for the purposes of article 15 unless it is satisfied that the height of the chimney will be sufficient to prevent, so far as practicable, the smoke, grit, dust, gases or fumes emitted from the chimney from becoming prejudicial to health or a nuisance. The term 'prejudicial to health' is defined in article 2(2) of the CAO as meaning 'injurious, or likely to cause injury, to health'. In making its decision in this regard the district council must have regard to the following factors:

(*a*) the purpose of the chimney;

(*b*) the position and descriptions of buildings near it;

(*c*) the levels of the neighbouring ground;

(*d*) any other matters requiring consideration in the circumstances.

Schedule 3 to the Local Government (Miscellaneous Provisions) (NI) Order 1985[37] requires that article 15(3), which sets out the format in which an application for approval should be submitted, be repealed. Article 15(5) empowers the district council to approve the height of a chimney for the purposes of this article without qualification. Similarly, the council is empowered to approve the height of such a chimney without subjecting the approval to conditions concerning the rate or quality of the emissions from the chimney. If the district council fails to determine an application for approval submitted under article 15 and fails to give the applicant written notification of its decision within two months of receiving the application (or within such longer period as may be agreed in writing between the applicant and the district council), article 15(6) provides that the approval sought will be regarded as having been refused.

If the district council decides not to approve the height of a chimney for the purposes of article 15, or decides to grant its approval subject to certain conditions, the district council is obliged to give the applicant[38] written notification of its decision, stating its reasons. Where the district council decides not to approve the height of the chimney, the council is obliged to specify the lowest height (if any) which it is prepared to approve unconditionally, or, the lowest height it is prepared to approve subject to specified conditions. If the council thinks fit, both pieces of information can be communicated to the

---

37. SI 1985/1208.
38. Art. 15(11) provides that where the original applicant notifies the district council that his interest in the application has been transferred to another person, references to the applicant under art. 15 will be construed as references to that other person.

applicant. Such information should be communicated to the applicant with the written notification of its decision to refuse the application as submitted.

### *The applicant's right to appeal under article 15*

The applicant may appeal a refusal by the district council within twenty-eight days of receiving written notification of the refusal. The appeal is brought to the DoE(NI). Article 15(8) empowers the DoE(NI) to:

(i) confirm the district council's decision;
(ii) approve the height of the chimney without qualification;
(iii) approve the height of the chimney subject to conditions concerning the rate and/or quality of emissions from the chimney;
(iv) cancel any conditions imposed by the district council; or
(v) substitute, for any conditions imposed by the council, other conditions which the district council had power to impose.

The DoE(NI) is obliged to give the appellant written notification of any decision on an appeal under article 15, stating the reasons for its decision. Where the DoE(NI) decides not to approve the height of the chimney, it is obliged, like the district council, to specify in the written notification the lowest height (if any) it is prepared to approve unconditionally or the lowest height it is prepared to approve subject to conditions or, if it thinks fit, to specify both.

### The application of articles 5, 7, 9, 10, 26(3), 27(4) and 29(1) to fumes

Article 16 empowers the DoE(NI) to adopt regulations which apply any or all of the provisions contained in articles 7, 9, 10, 26(3), 27(4) and 29(1) to fumes[39] in the same way as they apply to grit and dust. Similarly, the DoE(NI) is empowered to adopt regulations that apply the provisions of article 5 to fumes—in other words, to require that furnaces do not emit fumes so far as is practicable. No such regulations have been adopted to date.

## SECTION 5. SMOKE CONTROL AREAS

### The creation of smoke control areas

District councils are empowered under article 17(1) to declare, by means of an order confirmed by the DoE(NI), the whole or any part of the district of the council to be a smoke control area. At the time of writing a total of 103 smoke control areas have been declared in Northern Ireland, covering more than 130,000 dwellings, requiring as a minimum, the use of smokeless fuels and the installation of smokeless fires.[40] Schedule 2 to the CAO sets out the process that must be followed by the district council when making a smoke control order. Article 17(6) provides that any order made by a district council under article 17 may be varied or revoked by a subsequent order so made and confirmed.

A district council cannot exercise its power under paragraph 8 of Schedule 2 to

---

39. 'Fumes' are defined in art. 2(2) as any airborne solid matter smaller than dust.
40. *Environment Service Corporate Plan*, 1994–97, p. 25

postpone the coming into operation of an order under article 17 for a period of more than twelve months, or, for periods that amount in all to more than twelve months, without the consent of the DoE(NI).[41]

Article 41 sets out the powers of district councils to act jointly for the purposes of declaring an area to be a smoke control area. The consequences of such joint action are also addressed.

### The effect of being declared within a smoke control area

Once an area has been declared to be a smoke control area, article 17(2) provides that it is an offence to emit smoke on any day from a chimney of any building within the area. The occupier of that building will be deemed guilty of an offence. This provision is subject to the various exemptions and limitations that are in force under article 17 (below).

### District councils obligations to notify occupiers of offences under article 17

Article 37 imposes an obligation on district councils to notify, as soon as may be, the occupiers of an offence committed under article 17. If the notice is not in writing, article 37(1) provides that the district council is obliged to confirm the notice in writing 'before the end of the four days next following the day on which the council became aware of the offence'.

### Penalties incurred

Article 38(2) governs the penalty imposed for an offence under article 17(2). A person found guilty of an offence under article 17 will be liable on summary conviction to a maximum fine of £1,000.

### Defence to proceedings under article 17(2)

First, it is a defence to prove that 'the emission of smoke was not caused by the use of any fuel other than an 'authorised fuel''. Second, article 37(2) also provides that a failure on the part of the district council to comply with the notification obligations under article 37(1) (outlined above) will constitute a defence to proceedings under article 17. In this regard, article 37(2) goes on to provide that the notification requirements laid down in article 37(2) will be 'deemed not to have been complied with' if the district council has failed to give the required notification 'before the end of the two days' next following the day of the offence. Where the offence was committed after 13 March 1980, the relevant time sale is before the end of the four days next following the day of the offence (article 62 of the Pollution Control and Local Government (NI) Order 1978 came into operation on 13 March 1980, which is the deadline specified in article 37(2) of the CAO). The presumption that article 37(1) has not been complied with will operate unless

---

41. Art. 17(14) governs the coming into operation of a smoke control order made before art. 62 of the Pollution Control and Local Government (NI) Order 1978 came into effect, i.e. 13 Mar. 1980 (SR 1980 No. 97). Sch. 5 to the CAO has repealed art. 62 itself.

the contrary is proved. Third, it may also be a defence to prove that the emissions were made from an exempted building, fireplace, or chimney (see below).

The term 'authorised fuel' is defined in article 2(2) of the CAO as a fuel which the DoE(NI), having regard among other things to the sulphur content of the fuel, has prescribed as an authorised fuel for the purposes of the CAO. The following 'authorised fuel' regulations are at present in force in Northern Ireland: the Smoke Control Areas (Authorised Fuels) Regulations (NI) 1992[42] and the Smoke Control Areas (Authorised Fuels) (Amendment) Regulations (NI) 1993.[43] The 1992 Regulations revoke the Smoke Control Areas (Authorised Fuels) Regulations (NI) 1982[44] and the Smoke Control Areas (Authorised Fuels) Regulations (NI) 1986.[45]

## Proposed Regulations concerning authorised fuels

At the time of writing, the DoE(NI) has prepared two sets of draft Regulations, namely the Smoke Control Areas (Supply and Sale of Unauthorised Fuels) Regulations (NI) and the Sulphur Content of Solid Fuel Regulations (NI). These draft Regulations concern the sale and content of fuels in smoke control areas and are designed to strengthen the implementation of smoke control areas in Northern Ireland.

The first Regulations will introduce a ban on the sale of unauthorised fuels in smoke control areas, while the second set will limit the sulphur content of solid domestic fuel to 2 per cent. In an effort to ensure that the Regulations will be implemented effectively, the DoE(NI) proposes to include enforcement procedures, including a power of entry, which would enable authorised officers from district councils to enter trade premises, check solid fuel stocks and take random samples of those stocks for independent testing. It is intended that these Regulations will come into force in the near future.

## Variations, limitations and exemptions from the operation of article 17 in a smoke control area

Article 17(4) empowers a district council to introduce orders which:
- (i) make different provision for different parts of the smoke control area;
- (ii) limit the operation of article 17 to specified classes of building in the area; and
- (iii) exempt specified buildings or classes of buildings or specified fireplaces or

---

42. SR No. 70. Reg. 2 of the 1992 Regulations defines 'authorised fuels' as 'anthracite, briquetted fuels carbonised in the process of manufacture, coke, electricity, fluidised char binderless briquettes manufactured by the Coal Products Limited (as per 1993 Amendment Regulations), gas, low temperature carbonisation fuels, low volatile steam coals and the additional fuels described in Schedule 1.' Although most of the fuels prescribed as authorised fuels in Reg. 2 and Sch. 1 have previously been authorised fuels, there have been changes in the way in which the fuels are described in many cases. The descriptions reflect current manufacturing methods.
43. SR No. 7. The 1993 Regulations amend the 1992 Regulations by substituting 'Coal Products Limited' for 'National Coal Board' in the definition of authorised fuels. Reg. 3 of the 1993 Regulations amends Sch. 1 to the 1992 Regulations by prescribing three additional authorised fuels.
44. SR No. 216.
45. SR No. 313.

classes of fireplaces in the area from the operation of article 17, subject to such conditions and for such periods as may be specified in the order.

Article 17(12) provides that, notwithstanding paragraph 7 of Schedule 2 to the CAO, an order made by a district council under article 17 which varies a previous order so as to exempt specified buildings or classes of building or specified fireplaces or classes of fireplace from the operation of article 17, may come into operation on, or at any time after, the date of its confirmation. (Schedule 2 governs the making of smoke control orders in Northern Ireland.)

Article 17(7) empowers the DoE(NI) to prescribe, subject to conditions, classes of fireplace which may be used in a smoke control area for burning fuel other than an authorised fuel. In making such an exemption, the DoE(NI) must be satisfied that the class of fireplace can be used to burn unauthorised fuel without producing any smoke or a substantial quantity of smoke. Several exempted fireplace Regulations have been introduced by the DoE(NI) over the years. However, in 1992 the DoE(NI) introduced the Smoke Control Areas (Exempted Fireplaces) Regulations (NI) 1992,[46] which revoked and replaced, with amendments, these earlier measures.[47] Regulation 2 provides that the classes of fireplace prescribed in column (1) of Schedule 1 to the 1992 Regulations will, subject to the conditions prescribed in column (2), be exempted from the provisions of article 17. Regulation 3(1) and (2) provides that fireplaces which were manufactured before 1 February 1993 and which were authorised by Regulations revoked by the 1992 Regulations may be used, notwithstanding the revocation of earlier Regulations. Article 17(8) empowers the DoE(NI) to suspend or relax, by order, the operation of article 17 in relation to the whole or part of a smoke control area if at any time it appears necessary or expedient to do so. In this regard, the Department is required first to consult the district council, unless consultation is impracticable because of the urgency of the situation. Where such an order is made, or an order varying or revoking such an order, the district council is obliged, as soon as practicable, to take such steps as appear to the council to be suitable to bring the effect of the order to the attention of those affected by it (article 17(9)).

### The application of article 17 to chimneys serving the furnace of boilers or industrial plant

Article 17(10) provides that article 17 will apply to chimneys serving furnaces of any boiler or industrial plant (being a boiler or plant attached to a building or for the time being fixed to or installed on any land) in the same way as it applies to the chimney of a building as explained above. Where article 17 is applied to a chimney which serves the furnace of a boiler or industrial plant, article 17(11) requires:

(i)   that references to boilers or plant be substituted for references to 'building' in article 17 and

---

46.  SR No. 538.
47.  The following is a list of the Regulations revoked by the 1992 Regulations: SR&O (NI) 1970 No. 222; SR&O (NI) 1971 No. 74; SR&O (NI) 1971 No. 330; SR&O (NI) 1972 No. 180; SR 1974 No. 40; SR 1974 No. 275; SR 1977 No. 347; SR 1983 No. 405; SR 1985 No. 53.

(ii) that references to the person having possession of the boiler or plant be substituted for references to the occupier of a building.

### *Exemptions to article 17 for the purposes of research into air pollution*

Article 28 empowers the district council to exempt any chimney from the operation of article 17 where, on an application to the council, the council considers that it is expedient to do so in order to enable research and investigation to be carried out into air pollution. Schedule 1 to the CAO will apply to an application made under article 28.

### The application of the Air Quality Standards Regulations (NI) 1990, as amended, to smoke control areas

Regulation 9(1)–(8) of the Air Quality Standards Regulations (NI) 1990[48] empowers the DoE(NI) to direct district councils to create smoke control areas under article 17 of the CAO in order to comply with the requirements of Directive 80/779/EEC on air quality limit values and guide values for sulphur dioxide and suspended particulate set out in regulations 3 and 4 of the Air Quality Standards Regulations (NI) 1990, as amended. The requirements of the 1990 Regulations are discussed in Part VII of this chapter.

### Adaptations of fireplaces in private dwellings which are or will be within a smoke control area

Article 18(1) provides that if, after the confirmation of an order made by a district council under article 17, the owner or occupier of, or any person having an estate or interest in any private dwelling[49] which is or will be within a smoke control area as a result of the order, incurs expenditure on adaptations in or in connection with the dwelling to avoid contravening article 17, the district council:

(*a*) shall repay to the owner, occupier or other person seven-tenths of the expenditure so incurred; and

(*b*) may if it thinks fit also repay to the owner, occupier or other person the whole or any part of the remainder of that expenditure.

Article 18(1) does not apply to new dwellings.[50] Article 20 provides that where the person who would be entitled to payment by the district council under article 18(1) assigns his right to that payment to another person before the payment becomes payable and gives notice of the assignment to the council, the council

---

48. SR No. 145.
49. 'Private dwelling' is defined by art. 2(5) of the CAO as any building or part of a building used or intended to be used as such. A building or part of a building will not be excluded from the definition of a private dwelling because of the fact that the person who resides or is about to reside in it, or is required or permitted to reside in it, does so as a result of his employment or of holding an office.
50. 'New dwelling' is defined in art. 2(6) of the CAO as a dwelling which was either: (i) erected after 9 June 1964 or (ii) produced by conversion, after 9 June 1964, of other premises with or without the addition of premises erected after that date; a dwelling or premises will not be treated as erected or converted after 9 June 1964 for the purpose of this definition unless the erection or conversion was begun after that date.

will make the payment to that other person when it becomes payable. Article 18(2) provides that article 18(1) will not apply to any expenditure unless:

(i)   it is incurred before the coming into operation of the order declaring the area to be in a smoke control area *and* is incurred with the approval of the district council given for the purposes of article 18(1) and (2) (whether given before or after the expenditure is incurred), or

(ii)  the expenditure is reasonably incurred in carrying out adaptations required by a notice given under article 18(3).

Article 18(2) also provides that in both cases the adaptations must be carried out to the satisfaction of the district council.

### Power of the district council to require that adaptations be carried out

Article 18(3) provides that a district council may require that adaptations be carried out in or in connection with a dwelling which is or will be within a smoke control area in order to avoid contravention of article 17.[51] In this regard the council must serve a written notice on the person 'appearing to them to be the owner or occupier of a private dwelling'. Such a notice will require the adaptations to be carried out within such period as may be specified in the notice. The period must not be less than twenty-one days from the service of the notice; the period may also be extended by written permission of the council (article 18(4)). Where the district council does serve a notice under article 18(3), the council is obliged to inform 'each other person' on whom a notice may be served of the fact that such a notice has been served (article 18(5)).

### Appealing a notice to carry out adaptations

Article 18(6) entitles a person on whom a notice under article 18(3) is served to appeal the notice to a court of summary jurisdiction. The appeal must be brought within twenty-one days of the service of the notice or within such longer period as the district council may in writing allow. Article 18(6) sets out the following grounds of appeal:

(a)  that the notice is not justified by the terms of [article 18](3);

(b)  that there has been some informality, defect or error in, or in connection with, the notice;

(c)  that the district council has refused unreasonably to approve the execution of alternative adaptations, or that the adaptations required by the notice to be carried out are otherwise unreasonable in character or extent, or are unnecessary;

---

51.  As a general matter it should be noted that art. 20 contains a number of technical provisions concerning: (i) the meaning of the phrase 'adaptations in or in connection with a dwelling to avoid contravention of Article 17,' as used in art. 18 and 19, (ii) the meaning of references to expenditure or expenses incurred in the execution of works as used in art. 18 and 19, and (iii) the district council's power to control the types of appliances being installed during the adaptation of a dwelling in order to avoid contravention of art. 17. Art. 21 confers power on the head of the DoE(NI) to vary or add to the list of works and appliances referred to in art. 20(1). Art. 20(1) lists the specific works which come within the phrase 'adaptations in or in connection with a dwelling' used in articles 18 and 19. The Clear Air Act (Grant Extension) Order (NI) 1969 (SR&O No. 57) has been adopted under art. 21.

(*d*) that the time within which the adaptations are to be carried out is not reasonably sufficient for the purpose;

(*e*) that the notice might lawfully have been served on the occupier of the dwelling in question instead of on the owner, or on the owner instead of the occupier, and that it would have been equitable for it to have been so served.

Article 18(7) empowers the court to which the appeal is brought to confirm, revoke or vary the order, as it thinks fit. Article 18(7) also provides that where the appeal is based on the grounds in paragraph (*b*) above, the court must dismiss the appeal if it is satisfied that the informality, defect or error was not a material one. Where the appeal is based on the grounds outlined in paragraph (*e*), article 18(8) provides that the appellant is required to serve a copy of his notice of appeal on each person referred to in the notice and in addition, that the court, on hearing the appeal, may make such order as it thinks fit with respect to:

(*a*) the person by whom the adaptations are to be carried out;

(*b*) whether that person is to bear the whole or part of the cost of carrying out the adaptations, and the proportion which any such part is to bear to that cost; and

(*c*) whether any other person is to make to that person a contribution towards that cost, and the proportion which such contribution is to bear to that cost.

Article 18(9) provides that the court, in exercising its powers under article 18(8), should have regard, as between an owner and an occupier, to the terms and conditions (whether contractual or statutory) of the tenancy and to the nature of the adaptations to be carried out.

## Consequences of failing to comply with a notice served under article 18(3)

If a notice served under article 18(3) is not complied with, article 18(10) empowers the district council to carry out the adaptations which were required to be carried out by the notice. Such work can be carried out either:

(*a*) after the expiration of the time within which the adaptations were required by the notice to be carried out; or

(*b*) if on an appeal brought against the notice, the notice has been confirmed with or without variation, after the expiration of twenty-one days from the final determination of the appeal or such longer period as the court in determining the appeal may fix . . .

The district council may carry out the adaptations with any variation made by the court. Where the council carries out adaptations under its powers in article 18(10), it is entitled to recover the 'appropriate fraction' of the 'relevant expenses' from the person on whom the notice was served under article 18(3) where an order is not made by a court under article 18(8).[52] Where an order is made by a court pursuant to article 18(8), the council is entitled to recover:

(i) the 'appropriate fraction'[53] of the 'relevant expenses'[54] from the person who, under the order, is to bear the whole of the cost of carrying out the adaptation or

(ii) the 'appropriate fraction' of so much of the 'relevant expenses' as bears to the 'relevant expenses' the same proportion as that fixed under article 18(8)(*b*) or (*c*) from any person who is required by an order to bear part of, or make a contribution towards, the cost of carrying out the adaptations.

## Power of district councils to make grants towards adaptations carried out in certain premises to avoid contravention of article 17

Article 22(2) provides that if, after the confirmation of an order adopted by a district council under article 17, the owner or occupier of any premises or part of any premises to which article 22 applies incurs expenditure on adaptations in or in connection with the premises or part of the premises, to avoid contravening article 17, the district council may repay to him the whole or any part of that expenditure.[55] Article 22 applies to 'any premises or part of any premises being or being part of a hereditament which in any valuation list prepared by the Commissioner of Valuation is distinguished as exempt under article 41 of the Rates (NI) Order 1977[56] and that the Commissioner certifies is so distinguished as being a hereditament of a description mentioned in article 41(2)(*b*) or (*c*)'. Article 22(2) requires that the premises in question 'will be within' a smoke control area as a result of the district council's order under article 17.

---

52. Art. 33 sets down detailed provisions governing the district council's power to recover expenses, together with interest recoverable under art. 18. It should also be noted that art. 19 makes provision for the DoE(NI) to contribute towards certain expenses incurred by district councils in carrying out adaptations under art. 17 and 18. Art. 21 confers power on the head of the DoE(NI) to vary the amounts of the contributions referred to in art. 19(3) and to extend the provisions of art. 19 to any class of new dwelling. Such variations must be made with the approval of the head of the Department of Finance and subject to affirmative resolution. The Clean Air Act (Grant Extension) Order (NI) 1969 (SR&O No. 57) has been adopted in this regard.

53. 'Appropriate fraction' is defined in art. 18(12) as meaning three-tenths or such smaller fraction as the district council may in any particular circumstances determine. It should be noted that art. 21 empowers the head of the DoE(NI) to vary the amounts of repayments referred to in art. 18(1)(*a*) and to make corresponding variations of the fraction to be used in relation to the amounts recoverable under art. 18(11) and to extend the provisions of art. 18 to any class of new dwelling. Such variations must be made with the approval of the head of the Department of Finance, subject to affirmative resolution. The Clean Air Act (Grant Extension) Order (NI) 1969 (SR&O No. 57) has been adopted by the DoE(NI) in this regard.

54. 'Relevant expenses' is defined in art. 18 (12) as the expenses reasonably incurred by the district council in carrying out the adaptations.

55. Art. 22(3) states that art. 20 will apply for the interpretation of art. 22 in the same way as it applies to the interpretation of art. 18 and 19; see notes 51–3, supra. However, references in art. 20 to 'a dwelling' should be regarded as references to 'any premises or part of any premises' to which art. 22 applies.

## Section 6. Smoke nuisances

### Abatement of smoke nuisances

Article 23(1) provides that where smoke is a nuisance to any of the inhabitants of a neighbourhood it will be regarded as a nuisance within the meaning of section 107 of the Public Health (Ireland) Act 1878.[57] The provisions of the 1878 Act (except section 288, saving for mines etc.) will apply to such nuisances, subject to the provisions of article 23 of the CAO. Article 23(1) does not apply to:

(a) smoke emitted from a chimney of a private dwelling; or

(b) dark smoke emitted from a chimney—

   (i) of a building; or

   (ii) serving the furnace of a boiler or industrial plant attached to a building or for the time being fixed to or installed on any land; or

(c) dark smoke emitted otherwise than as mentioned in sub-paragraph (b) from industrial or trade premises within the meaning of Article 4 [meaning premises used for any industrial or trade purposes, or premises not so used on which matter is burnt in connection with any industrial or trade process] (see page 70).

Article 37(1) and (2) obliges the district council to notify 'as soon as may be' the person deemed liable under article 23 of their belief that a violation of article 23 has occurred. If notification has not been given in writing, the district council is obliged to confirm the notification in writing 'before the end of the four days next following the day' on which the council became aware of the offence. In any proceedings brought under article 23 where smoke is emitted from a chimney, it is a defence to prove that 'the best practicable means had been employed to prevent the nuisance.' A failure on the part of the district council to comply with the notification requirements under article 37 will also provide the defendant with a defence.

Article 38(7) of the CAO gives the court hearing the action power to make provision for the imposition of a deadline by which a smoke nuisance must be stopped and, also, for the imposition of daily penalties where the nuisance is continued or repeated after that deadline has expired. Article 28 empowers the district council to exempt any chimney from the operation of article 23 where, on an application to the district council, the council considers that it is expedient to do so in order to enable research and investigation to be carried out into air pollution. Schedule 1 to the CAO will apply to an application under article 28.

### New building over-reaching adjacent chimneys

Article 24 provides that where any person erects or raises a building to a height greater than an adjoining building, and any chimneys or flues of an adjoining

---

56. SI 1977/2157.
57. 1878 c. 52.

building are in a party wall between the two buildings or are 1.83 metres[58] or less from the nearest part of the taller building, the district council may by notice in writing require the person erecting the taller building to build up the chimneys or flues of the adjoining buildings, if it is reasonably practicable to do so, so that the top of the chimneys or flues will be of the same height as the top of the chimneys of the taller building or the top of the taller building, whichever is the higher. The council's notice may specify the time within which such work is to be carried out.

In addition, the council's notice may require the owner or occupier of the adjoining (lower) building to allow the person erecting the taller building to enter the lower building and carry out such work as may be necessary to comply with the notice served on him.

Article 24 also provides that if the owner or occupier of the lower building serves a counter-notice on the person erecting the taller building and the district council to the effect that they wish to carry out the work themselves, then the owner or occupier of the lower building must comply with the council's notice to build up the chimneys or flues, and may recover expenses reasonably incurred from the person erecting the taller building. A counter-notice must be served within fourteen days of the date on which the council's notice was served on the owner or occupier of the lower building. The terms of article 24 only apply to the erection or raising of a building occurring after 13 March 1980 (i.e. the date on which article 62 of the Pollution Control and Local Government (NI) Order 1978 came into effect).[59]

### Appealing a notice served by the district council under article 24

Article 24(2) entitles both the person erecting the taller building and the owner or occupier of the lower building to appeal a notice served on them by the district council. The appeal will be taken to a court of summary jurisdiction.

### Offences under article 24

Article 24(3) provides that if the person erecting the taller building fails to comply with the terms of the district council's notice, he will be guilty of an offence. However, an offence will not have been committed if the owner or occupier of the lower building has:

(i)   refused to allow entry to that building or has refused to allow the carrying out of any work which was necessary to comply with the notice, or

(ii)  has served a counter-notice.

Article 24(3) also provides that if the owner or occupier of the lower building fails to comply with a notice served under article 24(1) or, having served a counter-notice, fails to comply with the terms of the district council's notice, he will be guilty of an offence. Article 24(3) entitles the district council to carry out

---

58.  The unit of measurement expressed in art. 24(1) has been amended by Sch. 2 to the Alkali &c. Works and Clean Air (Metrication) Regulations (NI) 1994 (SR 1994 No. 192), which implements in part Directive 80/181/EEC (OJ L39/40, 20 Dec. 1980), as modified by Directive 89/617/EEC (OJ L357/28, 7 Dec. 1989), concerning the harmonisation of national laws relating to units of measurement.

59.  SR 1980 No. 97. Art. 62 itself was repealed by Sch. 5 to the CAO.

such work as may be necessary to comply with the notice served under article 24(1) and to recover the expenses reasonably incurred in so doing from the person on whom the notice was served.

### *Penalty incurred*

Article 38(3) sets out the penalty incurred for an offence under article 24(3). In effect, a person guilty on summary conviction of an offence under article 24(3) will be liable to a maximum fine of £200.

## SECTION 7. SPECIAL CASES

### The relationship between the Clean Air (NI) Order 1981 and the Alkali &c. Works Regulation Act 1906

Article 25 of the CAO governs the relationship between these two provisions. Subject to the provisions of article 25, articles 3–24 of the CAO do not apply to works registered under the Alkali &c. Works Regulation Act 1906 (considered in Part II of this chapter), which currently governs industrial air pollution in Northern Ireland. The terms of article 25 are quite complex and are outlined at the relevant junctures in Part II of this chapter. However, the principal provision laid down in article 25 for present purposes is that the controls imposed by the Alkali Act will apply to smoke, grit and dust emitted from registered works in the same way as they apply to emissions of noxious and offensive gases from such works.

### Railway engines and vessels

The terms of articles 26 and 27 which appy to emissions from railway engines and vessels (and exemptions from article 26) have been discussed above in section 1 in the context of emissions of dark smoke under article 3.

### Exemptions for purposes of investigations and research

Article 28 empowers district councils to exempt chimneys, furnaces, boilers and plants from the operation of certain articles of the CAO where the council considers, on an application for exemption, that it would be expedient to do so for the purposes of investigation and research into air pollution. The provisions of Schedule 1 to the CAO will govern the making of an application for exemption under article 28.

The following articles are eligible for exemption under the CAO:

- (*a*) any chimney from the operation of Articles 3, 7, 17, 23 and 26;
- (*b*) any furnace, boiler or industrial plant from the operation of Article 5(1);
- (*c*) any premises from the operation of Article 4;
- (*d*) any furnace from the operation of Articles 8, 9, and 11.

**Crown premises**

Article 29(1) imposes an obligation on district councils to report any of the following to the Government department responsible:

> (a)   emissions of dark smoke,[60] or of grit and dust[61] from any premises[62] which are under the control of any Government department[63] and are occupied for the public service of the Crown[64] or for any of the purposes of any Government department; or
>
> (b)   emissions of smoke, whether dark smoke or not, from any such premises which are within a smoke control area; or
>
> (c)   emissions of smoke, whether dark smoke or not, from any such premises which appear to the council to constitute a nuisance to any of the inhabitants of the neighbourhood; or
>
> (d)   emissions of dark smoke from—
>
>> (i)   any vessel of Her Majesty's navy; or
>>
>> (ii)  any Government ship in the service of the Admiralty while employed for the purposes of Her Majesty's navy
>
> which appear to the council to constitute a nuisance to any of the inhabitants of the neighbourhood.

The district council's obligation under article 29(1) will not be invoked unless the council considers it appropriate to inform the government department responsible for any of the above emissions. Article 29(2) imposes an obligation on a government department which receives a report under article 29(1) to enquire into the circumstances. If the inquiry reveals that there is a cause for complaint, the department in question is obliged to employ all practicable means for preventing or minimising the emission of the smoke, grit or dust or, as the case may be, abating the nuisance and preventing a recurrence of it.

**Application of article 29 to premises occupied for the service of a visiting force**

Article 29(5) governs the application of article 29 to emissions from premises which are occupied for the service of a 'visiting force', meaning any such body, contingent or detachment of the forces of any country which constitute a visiting force for the purposes of any of the provisions of the Visiting Forces Act 1952.[65]

---

60.  The term 'dark smoke' is defined in s. 1 of the CAO in the context of art. 3 of the CAO.
61.  The term 'grit and dust' is defined by art. 2(2) of the CAO as including 'solid particles of any kind'.
62.  Art. 29(3) identifies the types of interests which may subsist in the premises in question which will or, as the case may be, will not affect the application of art. 29.
63.  'Government department' is defined as including a department of the government of the United Kingdom.
64.  'Crown' is defined in art. 29(6) as including the Crown in right of Her Majesty's Government in the United Kingdom.
65.  c. 67.

## Section 8. Miscellaneous

### Heating and cooking arrangements in buildings

Article 30 of the CAO states that requirements may be prescribed as to the provision of heating and cooking arrangements in buildings which are designed to prevent, so far as is practicable, the emission of smoke. Regulations introduced under article 30 will be deemed to be made in accordance with the provisions of the Building Regulations (NI) Order 1979.[66] Schedule 4, Part II, to the CAO amends Schedule 2 to the Building Regulations (NI) Order 1979.

The New Buildings (Prevention of Emissions of Smoke) Regulations (NI) 1969[67] were introduced pursuant to article 30. (These measures were originally adopted under the Clean Air Act (NI) 1964, which was consolidated by the CAO. However, they are now deemed to be adopted pursuant to article 30 of the CAO.) The 1969 Regulations prescribe the types of appliance which may be installed in the areas specified in the Schedule, and set out the conditions under which compliance with the Regulations may be dispensed with.

### Powers of district councils as to research and publicity

Article 31 lists the types of activities that district councils are empowered to arrange or contribute to in the context of research into and publicity concerning air pollution. They include (a) delivery of lectures and holding of discussions concerning air pollution, (b) arranging displays of pictures, films, exhibitions or models concerning air pollution, and (c) making a financial contribution towards the costs of any of the activities mentioned in (b).

### Powers of the county court to authorise work and order payments

Article 32 provides that 'if works are reasonably necessary in or in connection with a building in order to enable the building to be used without contravention of any of the provisions of [the CAO],' the occupier of the building may:

1. apply to the county court for an order enabling him to carry out the works described above if he has been prevented from doing so, by reason of the nature of his interest in the building, without the owner's consent (or some other person having an estate or interest in the building), but he is unable to obtain consent; and

2. apply to the country court for an order directing the owner or some other person having an estate or interest in the building to indemnify him (fully or in part) for the cost of carrying out such work if the occupier considers that the whole or part of that cost should be borne by such persons.

Article 32(1) empowers the county court to make such an order as appears to the court to be just where an application under article 32(1) is made.

Where the court is considering whether and, if so, what type of works are necessary, article 32(2) requires it to have regard to any difficulty there may be in obtaining, or in obtaining otherwise than at a high price, any fuels which would have to be used but for the execution of the works.

---

66. SI 1979/1709.
67. SR No. 6.

## Suspected offences in relation to motor vehicles

Article 34 provides that where a district council reasonably suspects that a motor vehicle is used so as not to comply with any regulations made under article 28(1)(*d*) of the Road Traffic (NI) Order 1981[68] (smoke, fumes, vapour, sparks, ashes or grit from motor vehicles), the council must, in cases where it seems proper to do so, report the description of the vehicle, and any other circumstances that appear to the council to be relevant, to the DoE(NI). The DoE(NI) must cause the matter to be investigated.

## Extension of the CAO to certain gaseous emissions

Article 35(1) empowers the DoE(NI) to adopt regulations that make provision for the reduction or control of gaseous emissions from a chimney where the Department is satisfied that practicable means exist for doing so. The Department must consult such organisations as appear to it to be representative of interests substantially affected before adopting such regulations. Regulations adopted under article 35(1) may contain such consequential and incidental provisions and may make such adaptations of the CAO as appear to the Department to be necessary or expedient for the purposes of giving effect to article 35. These powers have not been used to date.

### SECTION 9. ADMINISTRATION AND ENFORCEMENT OF THE CAO

## Unjustified disclosures of information

Article 36 provides that a person who discloses any information relating to any trade secret which has been furnished to, or obtained by, them under the CAO or in connection with the execution of the CAO is guilty of an offence. Such a disclosure will not constitute an offence if it is made in any of the following circumstances:

(*a*) with the consent of the person carrying on that undertaking; or

(*b*) in connection with the execution of this Order; or

(*c*) for the purposes of any legal proceedings arising out of this Order or of any report of such proceedings.

Article 38(4) sets out the penalty for an offence under article 36. In effect, a person found liable for an offence under article 36 will be liable on summary conviction to a maximum fine of £2,500 or to a maximum period of three months' imprisonment, or to both.

## PART II EMISSIONS FROM INDUSTRIAL PLANTS

As is the case throughout the EC, industrial processes in Northern Ireland are a potent source of pollution. The existing approach to the regulation of industrial pollution in Northern Ireland is essentially to control industrial emissions to air, discharges to water and deposits to land under separate legislation. Industrial emissions to air are regulated by two pieces of legislation. The Alkali &c. Works

---

68. SI 1981/154.

Regulation Act 1906, as amended, imposes a system of industrial air pollution control based on use of the 'best practicable means' for preventing or minimising emissions of noxious and offensive gases and smoke, grit and dust from the most polluting industrial processes (i.e. 'alkali works' and 'scheduled works'). The Clean Air (NI) Order 1981 regulates all other industrial emissions of smoke, dust, grit and fumes. Industrial emissions into water are currently governed by the Water Act (NI) 1972, as amended, which imposes a system of discharge consents for discharges of trade effluent and other polluting matter into inland, coastal and ground waters. The disposal of controlled waste on land is governed by the licensing system established under the Pollution Control and Local Government (NI) Order 1978 and under measures adopted pursuant to the 1978 Order.

Since the early nineteen-eighties, fundamental changes have been introduced, on both an EC and a national level, in the regulation of industrial pollution which essentially require the introduction of more stringent and coherent controls on industrial processes, the implementation of the 'polluter pays' principle, greater public consultation in the operation of the system of control, and the provision of greater public access to information concerning the application of the control regime to specific industries. The Environmental Protection Act 1990, as amended by the Environment Act 1995, which now governs industrial pollution control in Great Britain, requires that a system of integrated pollution control (IPC) be used when determining whether to authorise the carrying on of those industrial processes with the greatest capacity to generate pollution. In effect, IPC requires enforcing authorities to consider the total environmental effect of such processes (i.e. on land, water, and air) rather than simply their impact on one environmental medium, as is the case under traditional approaches to industrial pollution control. In addition, contemporary environmental law standards require that industrial pollution control regimes ensure that the 'best available techniques not entailing excessive cost' (BATNEEC) are used to prevent and minimise industrial pollution and, in the case of highly polluting processes, that the 'best practicable environmental option' (BPEO) is used to identify the most appropriate receiving environmental medium.

In March 1996 the DoE(NI) published the proposal for a draft Industrial Pollution Control (NI) Order 1996, which will, when enacted, implement contemporary EC and national approaches to industrial pollution control in Northern Ireland. In effect, the draft Order will introduce a three-tier system of industrial pollution control, which requires compliance in terms of the BATNEEC; and, in the case of the most polluting processes, regard will have to be had to the BPEO. In addition, the new control regime will introduce a system of integrated pollution control for Northern Ireland's most polluting industrial processes. The draft Order will also introduce more extensive enforcement powers and more stringent penalties for industrial pollution, it will implement the 'polluter pays' principle in this context through the introduction of a charging system for the administration and enforcement of the control regime, and it will create new public rights to information concerning the operation of the control regime as a whole. In essence, Northern Ireland is preparing to introduce standards which will not only implement the EC Air Framework Directive 84/360/EEC on industrial air pollution and provide the legislative basis on which to implement the Integrated Pollution Prevention and Control Directive soon to be adopted by the EC, but will also bring Northern Ireland standards on industrial pollution control into line with those currently operating in Great Britain under the Environmental Protection Act 1990, as amended by the Environment Act 1995.

Part II of this chapter is divided into three sections. Section 1 addresses the system of air pollution control laid down in the Alkali &c. Works Regulations Act 1906 which currently governs emissions from Northern Ireland's most polluting industrial processes (the terms of the Clean Air (NI) Order 1981, which currently govern all other industrial emissions to the air, are addressed in detail in Part I of this chapter). Section 2 addresses the requirements laid down under the Air Framework Directive 84/360/EEC on industrial air pollution, the move to integrated pollution control introduced in Great Britain for prescribed industrial processes, and the requirements to be introduced under the proposed Integrated Pollution Prevention and Control Directive. Section 3 then outlines the nature of the control regime proposed in the draft Industrial Pollution Control (NI) Order 1996.

### SECTION 1. EXISTING CONTROLS ON INDUSTRIAL POLLUTION IN NORTHERN IRELAND

At the time of writing, emissions from those industries with the greatest capacity for generating air pollution in Northern Ireland (i.e. chemical works, power stations, minerals works and lead works) are regulated under the Alkali &c. Works Regulation Act 1906, as amended.[69] In effect, the Alkali Act requires such industries (or 'works' as they are referred to in the Act) to register annually with the Alkali and Radiochemical Inspectorate (ARCI)—which is located within the DoE(NI)'s Environment Service and which administers and enforces the terms of the Alkali Act in Northern Ireland. In addition, such industries are required to employ the 'best practicable means' (BPM) for preventing emissions of pollutants to the atmosphere and for rendering any emissions harmless and inoffensive. Section 27 of the Alkali Act provides that the expression 'best practicable means' refers to all aspects of the process in question, i.e. the provision and efficient maintenance of appliances which are adequate for pollution control, the manner in which such appliances are used, and the 'proper supervision' by the owner of any operation from which such gases derive. It is important to note, however, that the Alkali Act does not define the specific requirements imposed on individual works by the BPM concept. The concept of BPM is a flexible one which is defined in relation to specific industrial processes and caters for local and individual circumstances. BPM Notes are normally drawn up by the Alkali and Radiochemical Inspectorate (ARCI) in consultation with interested parties. Such notes do not have statutory force and leave discretion with local inspectors to modify their application according to local conditions and the circumstances in individual plants.

---

69. c. 14. The Alkali Act has been extensively amended by a number of provisions, namely Sch. 7 to the Pollution Control and Local Government (NI) Order 1978 (SI 1978/1049), Sch. 4 to the Clean Air (NI) Order 1981 (SI 1981/158), the Alkali &c. Works Order (NI) 1991 (SR No. 49), the Alkali &c. Works (Amendment) Order (NI) 1994 (SR No. 104), and the Alkali &c. Works (Amendment No. 2) Order (NI) 1994 (SR No. 444). Other provisions have also amended parts of the Alkali Act; however, these amendments have since been replaced by amendments introduced by the above measures.

Ball and Bell summarise the objectives of the 'best practicable means' concept as follows:

> The phrase . . . incorporates both a scientific approach ('means') and a discretionary approach ('best' and 'practicable'). There [are] three main aims of the BPM legislation. First, there [is] a prohibition on any emission which could constitute a recognised health hazard. Secondly, emissions [have] to be reduced to the lowest level, always balancing that requirement with local conditions and circumstances, the current state of pollution control technology, the effects of the substances emitted, the financial effect upon a company using such equipment and the means that [are] to be used to control the emissions. Thirdly, where there [are] harmful emissions, the aim [is] that such emissions should be, so far as possible, diluted and dispersed.[70]

In effect, the BPM concept is operated by means of conciliation between the ARCI and industry, rather than by confrontation. Although the 'owner' of works governed by the Alkali Act is the principal person held liable for breaches of the Alkali Act, it is important to note that section 27 defines the term 'owner' widely to include 'any lessee, occupier or any other person carrying on any work to which this Act applies.' It should also be noted that the Alkali &c. Works and Clean Air (Metrication) Regulations (NI) 1994[71] substitute metric units for all imperial measurements in the Act, thereby implementing Directive 80/181/EEC,[72] as amended by Directive 89/617/EEC,[73] on the approximation of national laws relating to units of measurement.

## Control of emissions and BPM for 'alkali works'

Part I of the Alkali Act, as amended (sections 1 and 2), governs the condensation and emission of hydrochloric acid and the discharge of noxious or offensive gases from 'alkali works'. The term 'alkali works', for these purposes, was defined by section 27(1) as meaning every plant for: (i) 'the manufacture of sulphate of soda or sulphate of potash' in which hydrochloric gas is produced or (ii) 'the treatment of copper ores by common salt or other chlorides whereby any sulphate is formed' in which hydrochloric gas is produced. Section 27 of the Alkali Act defines the term 'noxious or offensive gas' as including specified gases and fumes.[74]

---

70. Ball and Bell, *Environmental Law,* 3rd ed., London: Blackstone Press, 1995, p. 285.
71. SR No. 192.
72. OJ L39/40, 20 Dec. 1980.
73. OJ L357/28, 7 Dec. 1989.
74. It should be noted that art. 25(4) of the Clean Air (NI) Order 1981 provides that the Alkali Act will have effect in relation to emissions of 'smoke, grit and dust' (see Part I, sections 1–3 of this chapter for the definition of these terms) from any work regulated by the Act in the same way as it applies to noxious or offensive gases. In effect, references to noxious or offensive gases in the Act should be interpreted as including those gases listed in s. 27 of the Alkali Act, as amended, *and* emissions of smoke, grit and dust. Art. 25(8) confers power on the DoE(NI), on the application of a district council, to exempt any work from the requirements of art. 25 or to make provision for defences to proceedings brought under art. 3 of the Clean Air (NI) Order 1981 in respect of emissions of dark smoke from the work or to proceedings brought under art. 23 of the Order in relation to a smoke nuisance caused by emissions of smoke from the work. The terms of art. 3 and 23 of the Clean Air (NI) Order 1981 are detailed in Part I of this chapter (sections 1 and 6 respectively).

However, this list has since been amended and considerably extended by article 3 of the Alkali &c. Works Order (NI) 1991, which now contains the current list of those gases regulated by the Alkali Act.[75] The 1991 Order, in effect, amends the Alkali Act so as to take account of the requirements of the Air Framework Directive 84/360/EEC (discussed below) and Directive 87/217/EEC[76] on the prevention and reduction of environmental pollution by asbestos.[77] Section 1(1) of the Alkali Act provides that every 'alkali work' must be carried on in such a way as to ensure (to the satisfaction of the ARCI) a 95 per cent condensation of the 'muriatic acid gas' (hydrochloric acid) emitted from the work and, in addition, that each cubic metre of air, smoke or chimney gases escaping from the work into the atmosphere contains not more than 0.46 gram of muriatic acid.[78] Section 1(2), as amended, provides that the owner of any alkali work, where work is carried on in violation of section 1(1), will be guilty of an offence and will be liable to the penalties set out in section 16A of the Act (discussed below).

Section 2, as amended, provides that the owner of every alkali work is obliged to use the best practicable means for: (i) preventing the escape of 'noxious or offensive gases'[79] through the exit flue of any apparatus used in any process carried on in the work, (ii) preventing the direct or indirect discharge of such noxious or offensive gases into the atmosphere, and (iii) rendering any noxious or offensive gases that are discharged 'harmless and inoffensive'. The requirements laid down in section 2 are subject to the qualification that the ARCI may not object to the discharge of any hydrochloric acid gas, smoke or gas into the atmosphere through a chimney or other final outlet if the amount of acid gas in each cubic metre of discharged air, smoke or gases does not exceed 0.46 gram.[80] If the owner of any alkali work fails, in the opinion of the court hearing the case, to use the best practicable means, he will be guilty of an offence and will be liable to the penalties laid down in section 16A, discussed below.

### Control of emissions and BPM for scheduled works

Part II (sections 6 and 7) of the Alkali Act regulates the most polluting industrial works, namely, the 'scheduled works' listed in the first Schedule to the Act. It is important to note that this list has since been amended and considerably extended[81] by article 4 of the Alkali &c. Works Order (NI) 1991 and, more recently, by article 3 of the Alkali &c. Works (Amendment) Order (NI) 1994 and article 3 of the Alkali &c. Works (Amendment No. 2) Order (NI) 1994. The works

---

75. Art. 25 of the Clean Air (NI) Order 1981 confers power on the DoE(NI) to vary or extend the list of works and the list of noxious and offensive gases that are regulated by the Alkali Act, and in doing so the Department may hold local or other inquiries on this subject.
76. OJ L85, 28 Mar. 1987.
77. The requirements of this Directive in relation to discharges of asbestos to water and emissions to air are also discussed in chap. 5 and Part IV of this chapter, respectively.
78. S. 16 of the Alkali Act, as amended by the Alkali &c. Works and Clean Air (Metrication) Regulations (NI) 1994 (SR No. 192), governs the calculation of the proportion of acid to a cubic metre of air, smoke or gases for the purposes of the Act. In effect, that proportion must be calculated at the temperature of 15°C and at a barometric pressure of 1 bar.
79. Note 74, supra.
80. Note 78, supra.
81. Note 75, supra.

listed in the 1991 Order in effect take account of the requirements laid down in the Air Framework Directive 84/360/EEC on industrial air pollution and Directive 87/217/EEC on the prevention and reduction of environmental pollution from asbestos. In effect, section 6 of the Alkali Act now provides that every 'sulphuric acid work' as defined in paragraph 1 of Schedule 2 to the Alkali &c. Works Order (NI) 1991 (as amended) must be carried on so as to secure (to the satisfaction of the ARCI) the condensation of the acid gases of sulphur or of sulphur and nitrogen which are produced in the process of manufacturing sulphuric acid in that work 'to such an extent that the total acidity of those gases in each [cubic metre] of residual gases after completion and process, and before admixture with air, smoke or other gases, does not exceed what is equivalent to [9.15 grams] of sulphuric anhydride.'[82]

In addition, section 6 provides that every hydrochloric (muriatic) acid work as defined in paragraph 8 of Schedule 2 to the Alkali &c. Works Order (NI) 1991, as amended, is carried on in such as way as to secure (to the satisfaction of the ARCI) the condensation of the hydrochloric acid produced in such work 'to such an extent that in each [cubic metre] of air, smoke or chimney gases escaping from the work into the atmosphere there is [no more than 0.46 gram of hydrochloric acid].'[83] Section 6(3), as amended, provides that the owner of any sulphuric acid work or of any hydrochloric acid work where work is carried on in violation of the requirements laid down in section 6 will be guilty of an offence and liable to the penalty laid down in section 16A of the Alkali Act. Section 7 then imposes an obligation on the owner of any scheduled work to use the best practicable means for: (i) preventing the escape of noxious or offensive gases[84] through the exit flue of any apparatus used in any process carried on in the work, (ii) preventing the direct or indirect discharge of such gases into the atmosphere, and (iii) rendering such gases, where discharged, 'harmless and inoffensive'. It should be noted, however, that the terms of section 7 are subject to the proviso that the ARCI cannot object:

(i)  to any hydrochloric (muriatic) acid gas in the air, in smoke or in gases discharged into the atmosphere through a chimney or other final outlet where the amount of such acid gas in each cubic metre of air, smoke or gases so discharged does not exceed 0.46 gram; or

(ii)  to any acid gases in the air, in smoke or in gases discharged into the atmosphere by a chimney or other final outlet receiving the residual gases from any processes for the concentration or distillation of sulphuric acid where the total acidity of such acid gases (including those from the

---

82. S. 16 of the Alkali Act, as amended by the Alkali &c. Works and Clean Air (Metrication) Regulations (NI) 1994 (SR No. 192), governs the calculation of the proportion of acid to a cubic metre of air, smoke or gases for the purposes of the Act. In effect, that proportion must be calculated at the temperature of 15°C and at a barometric pressure of 1 bar.

83. Ibid.

84. S. 27 of the Alkali Act contained the original list of those gases and fumes within the definition of the term 'noxious or offensive gas'; this list has since been amended and considerably extended by art. 3 of the Alkali &c. Works Order (NI) 1991, which contains the list of those gases now regulated by the Alkali Act. These amendments were introduced by the DoE(NI) under powers contained in art. 25 of the Clean Air (NI) Order 1981; see note 75, supra. See also note 74, supra, concerning emissions of smoke, grit and dust from works regulated by the Alkali Act.

combustion of coal) in each cubic metre of air, smoke or gases so discharged does not exceed what is equivalent to 3.43 grams of sulphuric anhydride.

Section 7(3), as amended, provides that if the owner of a scheduled works fails, in the opinion of the court hearing the case, to use the BPM he will be guilty of an offence and liable to those penalties laid down in section 16A below.

## Registration of works

Section 9(1) of the Alkali Act prohibits the carrying on of an 'alkali work' or a 'scheduled work' unless the work has a certificate of registration issued by the ARCI under the Act. The owner of an alkali work or a scheduled work who violates this provision will be guilty of an offence under section 9(8), as amended, and will be liable to the penalties laid down in section 16A of the Act, discussed below. To be eligible for a certificate of registration under the Act, the owner of the alkali work or scheduled work must apply for the certificate, and must do so in the manner prescribed by the Alkali &c. Works (Registration) Order (NI) 1981.[85] The 1981 Regulations govern the contents of the register of works and the information which must be detailed when making an application for a certificate of registration. In addition, a certificate of registration cannot be issued unless the application is made in the prescribed manner and the ARCI is satisfied that the work in question is furnished with such appliances as appear to it to be necessary to enable the work to be carried on in accordance with the terms of the Alkali Act which apply to that work. All works governed by the Alkali Act must be registered annually.

Section 9(7) provides that the owner of a registered work must send written notice of any change in the ownership of the work or in any of the particulars stated in the register concerning that work. Such notice must be sent to the ARCI within one month of such change; the register and certificate will be altered to take account of the change and no charge may be levied. However, where the owner fails to provide notice as required, the work will be regarded as not having a certificate of registration under the Alkali Act.

## Monitoring compliance

Section 12(1) of the Alkali Act confers various powers on the ARCI to monitor compliance with the requirements of the Act. In particular, an inspector may, 'at all reasonable times by day and night, without giving previous notice,' enter and inspect any work which is governed by the terms of the Alkali Act. In addition, an inspector may examine: (i) any process which causes the production of any noxious or offensive gas[86] and (ii) any apparatus which is used to condense such gas or which otherwise operates to prevent the discharge of such gas into the atmosphere or which renders such gas harmless and inoffensive when discharged. Similarly, an inspector may ascertain the quantity of gas discharged into the atmosphere and the quantity of gas condensed or otherwise dealt with, and may

---

85. SR No. 383. The 1981 Regulations repeal and replace the Order of the Local Government Board (27 Nov. 1906) which previously prescribed these conditions.
86. See note 74, supra, concerning the application of the Alkali Act to emissions of smoke, grit and dust from works regulated by the Act.

apply such tests and carry out such experiments and 'generally make all such inquiries as seems to him to be necessary or proper for the execution of his duties under [the Alkali Act].' It is important to note, however, that the inspector's powers under section 12(1) may not be exercised in such as way as to 'interrupt' the manufacturing process.

Section 12(2)–(4) then imposes a number of obligations on the owners of works governed by the Act which are designed to facilitate the ARCI in monitoring compliance with the requirements laid down in the Act. In effect, section 12(2) provides that the owner of a work which is governed by the Alkali Act must furnish the Chief Inspector of the ARCI with a sketch plan of those parts of the work in which any of the following are carried on: (i) processes causing the production of any noxious or offensive gas,[87] (ii) any process for the condensation of such gas, and (iii) any process for preventing their discharge into the atmosphere or for rendering discharged gases harmless and inoffensive. The plan must be kept secret, and the obligation to provide the plan is only invoked if one is requested.

Section 12(3) requires the owner of every work which is governed by the Alkali Act and his agents to provide every inspector with all the facilities necessary for entry, inspection, examination and testing under the Act. Where such facilities are not provided, or where the inspector is obstructed in the execution of his duty under the Act, the owner of the work in question will be guilty of an offence, as will every person who wilfully obstructs an inspector in the execution of his duty; a person found guilty on summary conviction for either of these offences will be liable to a maximum penalty of £500.

Finally, it should be noted that where the DoE(NI) is of the opinion that any work is likely to cause the production of any noxious or offensive gas,[88] the Department has the power under article 25 of the Clean Air (NI) Order 1981 to authorise an ARCI inspector to enter and inspect the work in question, even if the work is not regulated by the Alkali Act. The provisions of the Alkali Act will govern the inspector's power of entry and inspection (outlined above). It should be noted, however, that the Department's power in this respect does not extend to authorising the entry into or inspection of a work in connection with the emission of smoke, grit or dust.

## Penalties under section 16A

Schedule 4 to the Clean Air (NI) Order 1981[89] inserts section 16A into the Alkali &c. Works Regulation Act 1906, which sets out the penalties imposed for offences under the Alkali Act for which no express penalty is provided (i.e. an offence under sections 1, 2, 6, 7 or 9 of the Act). The fines laid down in section 16A have been raised by Schedule 3 to the Fines and Penalties (NI) Order 1984,[90] as amended by article 3(2) of the Criminal Justice (NI) Order 1994.[91] In effect, a person found guilty of an offence under sections 1, 2, 6, 7 or 9 will be liable on

---

87. Ibid.
88. Ibid.
89. SI 1981/158.
90. SI 1984/703.
91. SI 1994/2795.

summary conviction to a maximum fine of £5,000. However, where a person is convicted of an offence under any of these sections, and it is established to the satisfaction of the court hearing the action that the offence was 'substantially a repetition or continuation of an earlier offence by him after he had been convicted of the earlier offence,' that person will be liable on summary conviction to whichever is the greater of a maximum fine of £5,000, or, a fine of £500 for every day on which the earlier offence has been continued or repeated by that person within three months following conviction for the earlier offence.

## Enforcement powers and practice

Various sections of the Alkali Act, as amended, govern the taking of legal proceedings for contraventions of the Act. However, before outlining the details of those powers it should be noted that, thus far, the ARCI has not considered court action to be necessary to enforce the requirements laid down in the Act. Where a registered work fails to comply with the necessary emission standards, it would initially receive a warning letter after discussion between the owner of the work and the ARCI. If this approach does not ensure compliance, the ARCI issues an 'infraction letter', which details the violations at issue and specifies a time limit within which remedial action will have to be taken. In addition, the infraction letter will give the owner of the work notice that failure to comply with the terms of the Act may lead to legal action.

The *Environment Service Report* 1993–95 points out that responding to complaints about air pollution from registered works comprises an important dimension of the DoE(NI)'s work in relation to air pollution generally. The report notes that historically the majority of complaints concern dust emissions from quarry operations. New BPM standards were phased in recently for mineral works in Northern Ireland, which are designed to impose more stringent emission standards on such works. In addition, significant effort has been devoted to aluminium works, cement works, and power generation (emissions from power generation represent a substantial source of atmospheric pollution in Northern Ireland; these emissions are also regulated under the EC Large Combustion Plant Directive, which is discussed separately in Part III of this chapter). It should also be noted that the DoE(NI)'s Environment Service has conducted local surveys in recent years to assess the environmental impact of industrial installations. In this regard, surveys have been carried out on the concentration of nitrogen dioxide around Northern Ireland's four power stations, on soil levels around lead works, and on dioxin levels in undisturbed soils.[92] The DoE(NI)'s submission to the House of Commons Environment Committee in 1990, *Environmental Issues in Northern Ireland,* noted that 'virtually all registered works comply with the required emission standards. There are, however, a small number of sites where even with implementation of BPM complaints do arise mainly due to the proximity of dwellings and prevailing adverse climatic conditions.'[93] The Chief

---

92. For further details of the results of these surveys see *Environment Service Report,* 1991–93, pp 36–7, and the DoE(NI)'s submission to the House of Commons Environment Committee in 1990, contained in *House of Commons Environment Committee First Report: Environmental Issues in Northern Ireland,* HC 30-39 (1990), pp 54–5.
93. Ibid., p. 53.

Alkali Inspector has published a series of reports since 1982, under section 13 of the Alkali Act, detailing the work carried out by the ARCI in enforcing the provisions of the Act as they apply to Northern Ireland. The most recent of these reports, entitled the *Report of the Chief Alkali Inspector*, was published in 1995 by HMSO and covers the work of the Inspectorate in the years 1992–1993. The report notes that, by the end of 1993, 118 premises were registered under the Alkali Act. These accounted for a total of 206 registerable processes as compared to 188 in 1991. In the period of the report, a total of 110 complaints were investigated by the ARCI, 58 of which concerned mineral works. It was also noted that 97 of these complaints were dealt with within 24 hours of receipt. In addition, 730 visits were made by the ARCI to registered works during the calendar years 1992 and 1993 and a further 1,362 visits concerning radioactive and general air pollution matters were made in the same period. It should be noted that these reports also contain useful statistical information on the enforcement of the Alkali Act in Northern Ireland, and also new BPM notes; the next report from the Chief Alkali Inspector will be published in October 1996 and will cover the years 1994–95.

Legal proceedings for an offence under sections 1, 2, 6, 7 or 9 of the Alkali Act can only be brought by an inspector and with the sanction of the central authority (ARCI) (section 16A(3)). Where proceedings are brought in relation to an offence under this Act, it will be sufficient to allege that the work in question is a work governed by the Alkali Act and to state the name of the registered or ostensible owner of the work, or the title of the firm by which the employer of persons in such work is usually known (section 18, as amended). In addition, where legal proceedings are being brought against an owner for violation of sections 1, 2, 6 or 7, an inspector must serve the owner in question with written notice of the facts on which the Chief Inspector has based his conclusion that the requirements laid down in any of these sections have been violated and/or, as the case may be, the 'means' (BPM) which the owner has failed to use and the means which, in the Chief Inspector's opinion, would suffice to avoid contravention of the Alkali Act. This notice must be served at least twenty-one days before the hearing, and a copy of the notice must be produced before the court hearing the action. It should be noted that the Chief Inspector may base his opinion on facts which have been disclosed by his own examination or by an examination conducted by any other ARCI inspector (section 25).

Section 20 provides that where it is established that an offence has been committed in a work governed by the Alkali Act, the owner of the work will be deemed to have committed the offence and will be liable to pay the fine unless he can prove to the court's satisfaction that he has used: 'due diligence to comply with and to enforce the execution of [the Alkali Act], and that the offence in question was committed without his knowledge, consent, or connivance, by some agent servant or workman, whom he shall charge by name as the actual offender...' Where this is established to the court's satisfaction, the agent, servant or workman named will be liable to pay the fine and the costs of all the legal proceedings which may be taken either against himself or against the owner of the work in question. Section 20, as amended, also provides that an ARCI inspector may take legal proceedings against the person whom he believes to be the actual offender without first proceeding against the owner in any situation where he is satisfied that the owner of the works has used all due diligence to comply with and to enforce the terms of the Alkali Act and that the offence in question has been committed by that other without the knowledge, consent or connivance of the owner.

Section 18 provides that a person cannot be subject to a fine under the Act for more than one offence in respect of the same work in respect of any one day. Section 21 governs the delivery, sending and service of notices, summonses or other documents which must be or are authorised to be served on the owner of a works under the Act.

### Nuisance caused by works regulated by the Alkali Act

Where a complaint is made to a central authority by any sanitary authority on the basis of information provided by any of its officers, or by any ten inhabitants of their district, that any work regulated by the Alkali Act is being carried on (either within or outside the district) in contravention of the Act and that a nuisance[94] is thereby being caused to any of the inhabitants of the district, the central authority is obliged to make such inquiry into the matter as it thinks fit and just and, after the inquiry, may direct an ARCI inspector to take such proceedings as it thinks fit and just (section 22). The sanitary authority making the complaint may be required by the central authority to pay the expense of any such inquiry.

Finally, section 24 provides that where a nuisance arising from the discharge of any noxious or offensive gas or gases[95] is wholly or partially caused by the acts or defaults of the owners of several works regulated by the Alkali Act, any person who is injured by this nuisance may take legal proceedings against any one or more of the owners of the works in question and may recover damages from each defendant owner in proportion to their contribution to the nuisance; this is the position regardless of the fact that the act or default of any individual defendant would not separately have caused a nuisance. It is important to note, however, that section 24 does not authorise the recovery of damages from any defendant owner who can produce a certificate issued by the DoE(NI) to the effect that the defendant's works have been carried on in compliance with the requirements of the Alkali Act and were in compliance at the time when the nuisance arose.

## SECTION 2. EC AND BRITISH STANDARDS ON INDUSTRIAL POLLUTION CONTROL

In 1984 the EC took its first step towards the regulation of industrial air pollution with the adoption of Air Framework Directive 84/360/EEC.[96] This Directive was essentially adopted in response to mounting concern, in particular that of the

---

94. It should be noted that s. 29 of the Alkali Act provides that nothing in the Act will legalise any act or default which would, but for the operation of the Alkali Act, be deemed a nuisance or otherwise contrary to the law; nor will the operation of the Act deprive any person of any remedy by action, indictment or otherwise to which he would otherwise be entitled if the Alkali Act had not been enacted.

95. See note 74, supra, concerning the application of the Alkali Act to emissions of smoke, grit and dust from works regulated by the Act.

96. OJ L188, 16 July 1984. See: Haigh, supra, chap. 6, for a detailed discussion of the development of Directive 84/360/EEC and the requirements contained in the Directive.

Federal Republic of Germany, about the effects of acid deposition or 'acid rain' caused by industrial emissions throughout the EC. Although it has long been known that emissions from industrial plants posed a serious threat to the local environments in which they were based, it has only recently been accepted that such emissions also have the capacity to travel considerable distances, often crossing national frontiers, and to be deposited as 'acid rain', resulting in serious damage to vegetation and aquatic environments.

In the light of the international character of acid rain, the EC decided that emissions from industrial plants would be more effectively regulated at European than at national level.[97] Directive 84/360/EEC essentially requires member states to ensure that certain types of industrial plants (listed in Annex I to the Directive) have obtained prior authorisation from a competent authority. The Directive requires that authorisation be obtained when a new plant is being designed and in the event of a major alteration to an existing plant. In addition, the Directive requires that the authority responsible for issuing the authorisation be satisfied that all appropriate measures to ensure the prevention of air pollution have been taken (including the 'best available technology not entailing excessive cost'), that emissions from the plant will not cause significant air pollution (in particular those emissions listed in Annex II), that emission limit values will not be exceeded, and that account has been taken of air quality limit values (EC air quality standards are outlined in Part VII of this chapter). Furthermore, the Directive requires that applications for such authorisations and the ultimate decisions regarding those applications be made available to the public.

Directive 84/360/EEC is characterised as a 'Framework Directive', because it anticipates the adoption of further Directives which will lay down emission limit values based on BATNEEC for specific industries or processes. Thus far the EC has adopted 'daughter' Directives which set out emission limit values for large combustion plants, asbestos and municipal waste incinerators, each of which is discussed in more detail in Parts III–V respectively of this chapter.

Although Directive 84/360/EEC lays down an implementation date of 30 June 1987, the process of implementing the Directive in Northern Ireland law did not begin until 1987 and at the time of writing is still not complete. It should be said, however, that this delay is due not only to the normal legislative delays in implementing Directives in Northern Ireland but, also, to the fact that the DoE(NI)'s proposals for implementation have been overtaken by fundamental changes in both national and EC approaches to industrial air pollution control which have required the Department to revise its initial proposals for implementation.

The process of implementing Directive 84/360/EEC in Northern Ireland has spanned a number of stages to date. The first phase began in 1987 with the publication of the *Review of Public Health and Air Pollution Controls in Northern*

---

97. In this regard it should also be noted that the UK and EC are parties to the Geneva Convention on long-range transboundary air pollution, which, together with its attendant protocols regulating emissions of specific substances, is the principal international convention on acid rain. The UK is a major contributor to acid rain in Europe. For further details on acid rain see Part IX of this chapter and *Sustainable Development: the UK Strategy* (Cm 2426), London: HMSO, 1994, pp 49–55.

*Ireland: A Consultation Paper* which sets out, among other things, the DoE(NI)'s proposals for the implementation in Northern Ireland of Directive 84/360/EEC. However, in 1990 the Government enacted the Environmental Protection Act 1990, which introduced fundamental changes in the regulation of industrial pollution control in Great Britain. Part I of the 1990 Act introduced a two-tier system of control for industrial processes for Great Britain, which in effect went a step further than that contained in Directive 84/360/EEC. The first tier established an integrated pollution control (IPC) system for the most polluting industrial processes, which requires Her Majesty's Inspectorate of Pollution (HMIP) in England and Wales and Her Majesty's Industrial Pollution Inspectorate (HMIPI) in Scotland to issue a single authorisation which takes account of the total environmental effects of the polluting capacity of prescribed industrial processes and which controls emissions to all three environmental media—air, water, and land. In effect, IPC moves away from the sectoral approach to industrial pollution control reflected in Directive 84/360/EEC, whereby only the BATNEEC for preventing or minimising air pollution is required. The second tier introduced a local authority air pollution control (LAAPC) system for less polluting industrial process in Great Britain, which is enforced by local authorities but only controls emissions to air. By 1993, Directive 84/360/EEC was implemented in Northern Ireland in practice—but not to the exact requirements of the Directive—with the adoption of the Alkali &c. Works Order (NI) 1991[98] and the Environmental Information Regulations (NI) 1993.[99] In effect, the 1991 Order brought those plants which were not previously subject to air pollution control but which are listed in Annex I of Directive 84/360/EEC within the list of scheduled processes governed by the Alkali &c. Works Regulation Act 1906, as amended, while the 1993 Information Regulations made provision for public access to information concerning such processes.

The second phase in the implementation of Directive 84/360/EEC in Northern Ireland began in February 1993 with the publication of *Proposals for a New System of Air Pollution Control in Northern Ireland: A Consultation Paper.* The Consultation Paper proposed the enactment of a new Order in Council which would repeal the Alkali &c. Works Regulation Act 1906 in its application to Northern Ireland and introduce a new system of air pollution control referred to as APC. In light of the fact that Northern Ireland's industrial base only contains a small number of processes that emit any of the substances regulated by IPC to an environmental medium other than air, the DoE(NI) initially decided that it was unnecessary to introduce a specific system of IPC for industrial pollution in Northern Ireland and instead opted for a system of control which was tailored to Northern Ireland's particular needs. The 1993 Consultation Paper proposed a two-tier system of air pollution control (referred to as APC) based on BATNEEC, to be exercised by a Chief Inspector appointed by the DoE(NI) and district councils, respectively. The APC system was intended to ensure full implementation of Directive 84/360/EEC in Northern Ireland, and while it was not a formally

---

98. SR No. 49. The operation of the 1991 Order in relation to the Alkali &c. Works Regulation Act 1906 is explained in detail in Part II, section 1 of this chapter.

99. SR No. 45. The requirements laid down by the Environmental Information Regulations (NI) 1993 are addressed in detail in chap. 12.

integrated system of industrial pollution control, the DoE(NI) took the view that the existing involvement of the Department's Environment Service in the administration and enforcement of legislation governing industrial discharges to water, emissions to air and deposits to land would effectively ensure that the holistic approach required by IPC would be achieved, thus bringing Northern Ireland industrial pollution control into line with British standards.

However, since the beginning of the preparation of the Draft Order in Council, the European Commission submitted its proposal for a new Directive on Integrated Pollution Prevention and Control (IPPC).[100] The text of the Directive was agreed by the Council of Ministers on 23 June 1995. It was expected that the Directive would be formally adopted by the end of 1995; however, at the time of writing, the draft Directive has not yet been adopted. The IPPC Directive will enter into force three years after its adoption or enactment but will give member states a further eight years within which to implement its requirements. Although the eight-year implementation period appears lengthy on one level, in reality it represents a considerable achievement. Because of the substantial changes required to upgrade existing processes to the requisite standard, possible phasing-in periods of fourteen to twenty years were discussed.

The IPPC Directive will replace and repeal Directive 84/360/EEC and will require the implementation of a single integrated system of pollution control throughout the EC for discharges to all environmental media from certain categories of industrial plants, thereby bringing EC controls over the most polluting industrial processes into line with the more effective system of IPC already employed in Great Britain under the Environmental Protection Act 1990 and in several other member states. Given that the DoE(NI)'s proposed system of APC would not provide the necessary statutory basis for the implementation of the IPPC Directive, the Department was forced to return to the proverbial 'drawing-board' to extend the scope of the proposed Order in Council so as to provide for a system of IPC in Northern Ireland for those industrial processes with the greatest capacity for generating pollution. In March 1996, the DoE(NI) published the Proposal for a Draft Industrial Pollution Control (NI) Order 1996, an *Explanatory Document,* and a *Compliance Cost Assessment.* The system of industrial pollution control proposed in the Draft Order in Council will be discussed in section 3 below.

SECTION 3. REFORM OF INDUSTRIAL POLLUTION CONTROL IN
NORTHERN IRELAND

The proposal for a Draft Industrial Pollution Control (NI) Order 1996 in effect sets out the proposed control regime for industrial pollution in Northern Ireland. However, it is important to note that many of the details of the system are to be prescribed by regulation after the proposed Order has been enacted. The explanatory notes published by the DoE(NI) state that the proposed control regime will provide full implementation of the Air Framework Directive 84/360/EEC, the statutory basis for compliance with the proposed IPPC Directive, and will bring industrial pollution control in Northern Ireland into line with controls operating in

---

100. COM (93) 423 final.

Great Britain. In addition, the proposed Order: (i) introduces considerably increased penalties for pollution offences, (ii) provides greater enforcement powers for the enforcing authorities, (iii) ensures greater public consultation in the decision whether to grant authorisations, (iv) provides public access to information concerning the specific application of the control regime to industrial plants in Northern Ireland, and, finally, (v) ensures implementation of the 'polluter pays' principle in this context.

Rather than introducing the two-tier system of control operating in Great Britain, the proposed Order proposes the introduction of a three-tier system of control based on the use of the 'best available techniques not entailing excessive cost' (BATNEEC). Clauses 3–5 set out the following functional split:

(i) The first tier of control will regulate industrial processes in Northern Ireland with a 'high pollution potential'. In effect, the Chief Inspector will administer a system of 'integrated central control' or IPC for those processes falling within the first tier, which is designed to prevent or minimise pollution of the environment caused by the release of substances (to be prescribed) into any environmental medium.

(ii) The second tier will regulate industrial processes with the 'potential to cause serious pollution'. The Chief Inspector will administer a system of 'restricted central control' (i.e. not integrated control) for processes within the second tier, which is designed to prevent or minimise pollution of the environment caused by the release of substances (to be prescribed) into the air (but not any other environmental medium).

(iii) The third tier will concern industrial processes with 'significant but less potential for air pollution'. District councils will be given new powers to enforce and administer a system of 'local control' for processes falling within the third tier, which is designed to prevent or minimise pollution of the environment caused by the release of substances (also to be prescribed) into the air (but not any other environmental medium).

The Chief Inspector will be appointed by the DoE(NI) and will be based within the new 'Next Steps' agency which replaces the existing Environment Service, thereby maintaining central control within the DoE(NI) of the most polluting industrial processes. District councils will be conferred with new powers to regulate air pollution control in relation to the least polluting industrial processes. In addition, inspectors will be appointed by district councils and by the DoE(NI) to administer and enforce the proposed control regime. Provision is also made for the transfer of responsibility for certain processes from district council or local control to central control by the Chief Inspector. However, where such a transfer does occur, the Chief Inspector's powers will only extend to the release of polluting discharges to the air.

The system of control introduced under the proposed Order will be automatically applicable to all new processes established after the enactment of the Order. However, the proposed system of control will be phased in gradually for all existing industries. Subject to the phasing in of the new controls, the Alkali &c. Works Regulation Act 1906 will be repealed in its application to Northern Ireland. In addition, those provisions of the Clean Air (NI) Order 1981 and the Pollution Control and Local Government (NI) Order 1978 which relate to industrial pollution will also be repealed.

Although the proposed Order provides the operational framework for the proposed system of control, many of the details within this system will be prescribed by means of regulations adopted by the DoE(NI). In particular, the DoE(NI) will be empowered to adopt regulations which would:

(i) prescribe the industrial processes that will come within the three-tier system of control and designate those processes as falling within one or other of the tiers of control set out above;

(ii) specify the particular substances that may be released into the environment subject to the system of control laid down in the proposed Order; and

(iii) set quality objectives, specify standards and set limits for the concentrations or amounts of those substances that may be released by prescribed processes.

It is expected that those processes falling within the existing system of control under the Alkali &c. Works Regulation Act 1906, as amended, will come within the Chief Inspector's remit (i.e. the first or second tier of control). Once a process is prescribed by regulation as coming within the system of control contained in the proposed Order, then after a date to be prescribed, an authorisation from the relevant enforcement authority for that process will be required in order to carry on that process within Northern Ireland.

## Applications for and conditions of authorisation

Part I of Schedule 1 to the proposed Order governs the making of an application for authorisation. In effect, the Schedule empowers the DoE(NI) to prescribe the procedure for application. However, it is important to note that all applications for authorisation will have to be advertised to the public, unless the application is specifically exempted by regulations adopted by the DoE(NI). In addition, prescribed processes must be carried on in accordance with the terms of their authorisation.

Clause 7 governs the conditions of authorisation for all tiers of control. In effect, the Chief Inspector and district authorities must include such conditions in an authorisation as are appropriate for ensuring that in carrying on a prescribed process the best available techniques not entailing excessive cost (BATNEEC) will be used to prevent or minimise pollution. Where the application concerns a process designated for integrated central control which involves the release of prescribed substances to one or more environmental media, the authorisation must ensure that the BATNEEC will be used to minimise pollution to the environment as a whole, *having regard* to the 'best practicable environmental option' (BPEO) in relation to the substances which may be released. In addition, there will be an implied condition in every authorisation that the person carrying on the process to which the authorisation relates will use the BATNEEC to prevent or minimise pollution. The concepts of BATNEEC and BPEO will be discussed in greater detail below.

## Enforcement of the control regime

In line with the Government's commitment to implement the 'polluter pays' principle, clause 8 confers power on the DoE(NI) to impose fees and charges: (i) for the recovery of expenditure incurred by the enforcement authorities (Chief Inspector and district councils) in processing applications for authorisations and in making variations to authorisations, and (ii) in consideration for the subsistence of authorisations. Clause 8 would also enable enforcing authorities to revoke an authorisation where the holder of the authorisation fails to pay the charge due for the subsistence of the authorisation. The compliance cost assessment published by the DoE(NI) for the proposed Order states that the Order is not expected to lead to any significant increase in public expenditure; instead, additional costs incurred by the new regime will be recovered through the charging scheme provided for in the proposed Order.

Clause 9 provides that, once granted, an authorisation will be capable of being transferred from one person to another, but that the person assuming responsibility for the operation of the prescribed process will be bound by any conditions attached to the original authorisation. Clauses 10 and 11 will confer power on the enforcing authorities to vary the conditions attached to an authorisation (by means of a variation notice) and will also regulate the power of the operator to respond to such variations by means of introducing 'substantial changes' in the manner in which the prescribed process is operated. In addition, clauses 10 and 11 regulate the power of the holder of an authorisation to introduce a 'relevant change' (i.e. a change in the manner in which the process in question is operated which would alter the substances that would be released) and will enable the holder seeking to introduce such a change to request that the authorisation be varied to take account of the proposed change.

Clause 12 confers a general discretionary power on enforcing authorities to revoke an authorisation at any time by means of notice in writing. Without prejudice to the general nature of that power, the enforcing authority may also revoke the authorisation where it has reason to believe that the process to which the authorisation relates has never been carried on at all or has not been carried on for a year. In addition, the DoE(NI) is empowered to give directions to enforcing authorities as to whether the authorisation should be revoked under clause 12.

Clauses 13 and 14 will empower the enforcing authorities to issue enforcement and prohibition notices. In essence, where the enforcing authority is of the opinion that the holder of an authorisation is carrying on the process to which the authorisation relates in breach of any of the conditions of the authorisation, or is likely to breach any such condition, the enforcing authority will have the power to issue an enforcement notice detailing the nature of the contravention and also the steps which must be taken to remedy the situation. The DoE(NI) will also be empowered to give directions to the enforcing authority as to whether such a notice should be issued. A prohibition notice must be issued where the continued operation of the authorised process would involve an imminent risk of serious pollution of the environment. Once served, a prohibition notice has the effect of rendering the authorisation for the process in question ineffective. The DoE(NI) will also be empowered to give directions as to whether such a notice should be issued. Clause 15 provides for appeals to be brought against: (i) a refusal to grant an authorisation, (ii) the conditions attached to an authorisation, (iii) the various forms of notice which may be served (i.e. enforcement, prohibition, variation notices, etc.), (iv) a refusal to vary an authorisation, and (v) a decision by the enforcing authority that information relating to the individual or business is not commercially confidential and therefore should be made available for public inspection. Clause 15 and Schedule 2 to the proposed Order set out the procedures for the appeal; appeals will be lodged with the DoE(NI), which may delegate its powers in this matter.

Clause 17 confers extensive powers of entry and other related inspection powers on enforcing authorities to facilitate the execution of their functions under the proposed Order. In particular, the enforcing authorities will be empowered to carry out necessary examinations and investigations, sampling, testing, photographing, detention of substances and articles, and to requisition information. Schedule 3 to the proposed Order contains supplemental provisions concerning powers of entry. In addition, an inspector appointed by either the DoE(NI) or a district council under clause 16 will be empowered under clause 18 to take immediate action to seize and render harmless any article or substance found (on premises which he has power to enter) which he reasonably believes, in the circumstances in which he finds it, is a cause of imminent danger of serious pollution to the environment or serious harm to human health.

Clauses 19–22 and 29 govern the control of information under the proposed system of industrial pollution control. Clause 19 will enable the DoE(NI) to require enforcing authorities to provide such information concerning the discharge of their functions as the Department may require; the DoE(NI) and enforcing authorities may in turn serve a notice in writing on any person requiring them to provide such specified information as the authorities consider necessary to discharge their functions under the proposed Order.

Clause 20 requires enforcing authorities to maintain registers which would contain specified information concerning authorisations for the prescribed processes for which they are responsible under the proposed Order; these registers will be available for public inspection. In particular, the register will list: (i) applications made to that enforcing authority for authorisation under the proposed Order; (ii) authorisations which have been granted by that authority; (iii) variation notices, enforcement notices and prohibition notices issued by that authority; (iv) authorisations which have been revoked by that authority; (v) appeals brought under clause 15; (vi) convictions for offences under the proposed Order; and (vii) information obtained or furnished in pursuance of the conditions of authorisations or under any provision of the proposed Order. Clauses 21 and 22 provide that any of the above information can be excluded from public registers if either the Secretary of State concludes that it would be contrary to the interests of national security or the enforcing authorities (or DoE(NI) on appeal) decide that the information in question is commercially confidential.

Finally, clause 29 provides for the free exchange of information between the DoE(NI) and district councils on the one hand and the free exchange of information between district councils on the other, so as to facilitate the discharge of their respective duties under the proposed Order.

### Offences, penalties and legal proceedings under the proposed Order

Clause 23(1) and (2) lists the offences which will be created under the proposed Order and the penalties which will be imposed in the event of conviction. It should be noted as a general matter that under clause 23(6) an inspector (who is authorised by the DoE(NI) to do so) will be able to take proceedings before a magistrates' court in relation to any of the offences listed in clause 23(1), even if the inspector is not a barrister or solicitor. The offences listed in clause 23(1) are as follows:

1.  It will be an offence to carry on a prescribed process without authorisation from the relevant enforcing authority or to carry on a prescribed process in a manner which violates the conditions of the authorisation. A person convicted of such an offence will be liable on summary conviction to a maximum fine of £20,000 or to maximum term of imprisonment of three months, or to both; a person convicted on indictment will be liable to an unlimited fine or to a maximum term of imprisonment of two years, or to both.

2.  It will be an offence to fail to give notice (in the prescribed form and within the prescribed time) to the relevant enforcing authorities that an authorisation is being transferred to another person who will assume responsibility for carrying on the industrial process to which the authorisation relates. A person convicted of such an offence will be liable on summary conviction to a fine which does not exceed the statutory maximum, or, on conviction on indictment to an unlimited fine or to a maximum period of imprisonment of two years, or to both.

3.  It will be an offence to contravene any requirement or prohibition imposed by an enforcement notice or a prohibition notice. The penalties imposed in this regard will be identical to those outlined at number 1 above. In this regard it should also be noted that clause 24 will confer power on the enforcing authority to bring legal proceedings in the High Court where it is of the opinion that normal enforcement mechanisms for such an offence would be an ineffectual remedy against a person who has failed to comply with an enforcement or prohibition notice.

4.  It will be an offence to fail, without reasonable excuse, to comply with any requirement imposed under clause 17 by an inspector exercising his powers of entry and inspection etc. or to fail or refuse to provide facilities necessary for the discharge of his powers or to prevent any person from providing information requested by an inspector. A person found guilty of such an offence will be liable on summary conviction to a maximum fine of £5,000 (level 5 on the standard scale).

5.  It will be an offence to intentionally obstruct an inspector in the performance of his duties or powers. The penalty imposed for conviction will be identical to that outlined at number 2 above where the offence concerns the violation of clause 18. In all other cases a penalty of £5,000 will be imposed on summary conviction.

6.  It will be an offence to fail, without reasonable excuse, to comply with any requirement imposed by a notice issued by the DoE(NI) or the enforcing authorities under clause 19(2) requesting any person to provide information that the authorities consider necessary in order to exercise their powers or to discharge their duties under the proposed Order. The penalty for conviction will be identical to that outlined at number 2 above.

7.  It will be an offence to knowingly or recklessly make a false or misleading statement or to provide false or misleading information when making an application for an authorisation or for a variation thereof, to carry on a prescribed process or in response to a request for information by the DoE(NI) or the enforcing authority. The penalty imposed for conviction will be identical to that imposed at number 2 above.

8. It will be an offence to intentionally make a false entry in any record which was required to be kept under clause 7 concerning the authorisation. The penalty for conviction will be identical to that imposed at number 2 above.
9. It will be an offence to forge any document used in the control regime or to use such a document in such a way that it would be likely to deceive. The penalty for conviction will be identical to that imposed at number 2 above.
10. It will be an offence to falsely pretend to be an inspector. A maximum fine of £5,000 (level 5 on the standard scale) will be imposed on summary conviction.
11. It will be an offence to fail to comply with an order made by a court under clause 26 (which will empower the court to order remedial action where a person is convicted of any of the offences listed at numbers 1 and 3 above). The penalty imposed for conviction of such an offence will be identical to that outlined at number 1 above.

Clause 25 will govern the admissibility of evidence and burdens of proof in relation to legal proceedings for pollution offences under the proposed Order which concern prescribed processes designated for either integrated central control or restricted central control by the Chief Inspector, (i.e. the first and second tiers of control which regulate the most polluting processes). In effect, any information provided or obtained pursuant to or under a condition of an authorisation granted by the Chief Inspector (including any information provided or obtained or recorded by means of any apparatus) will be admissible in evidence in any proceedings, regardless of whether the proceedings are being taken against the person holding the authorisation or against some other person. Draft clauses 26 and 27 then confer powers on the court and on the Chief Inspector to order or arrange for remedial action to be taken where certain breaches of the proposed Order have occurred. If a person is convicted of an offence outlined at numbers 1 or 3 above, the court hearing the action will be empowered to order that person to take such action, within such time as may be specified, to remedy any matters that the convicted person has the power to remedy. An order to take remedial action may be made as an alternative to the penalties set out in clause 23 for such offences or may be in addition to such penalties. Where it is possible to remedy harm caused by breaches of the proposed Order outlined at numbers 1 or 3 above, the Chief Inspector will have the power to arrange for any reasonable steps to be taken towards remedying that harm and will also have the power to recover the costs of taking such steps from the convicted person.

Clause 32 will regulate offences committed by companies (bodies corporate). In effect, any person who was the director, general manager or company secretary or a member who managed the affairs of a body corporate at the time when the offence was committed, may be prosecuted and convicted of that offence if it is proved that the offence in question was committed with his consent or connivance, or, that he failed to exercise reasonable diligence, which would have prevented the commission of the offence. Such person's liability to legal prosecution will be in addition to any proceedings which may be brought against the company itself.

Clause 33 addresses the position where the offence is due to the act or default of someone other than the holder of the authorisation. In effect, such a person may be charged with and convicted of the offence regardless of whether or not legal proceedings for that offence are also taken against the person holding the authorisation for the prescribed process in question.

Clause 28 will regulate the relationship between authorisations issued under the proposed Order and other statutory controls governing the disposal of waste on land, the control of radioactive substances, and discharges to water. All the provisions of the proposed Order will also apply with certain modifications to the Crown and to Government departments.

## Definition of BATNEEC

Clause 7(10) states that references to BATNEEC 'include (in addition to references to any technical means and technology) references to the number, qualifications, training and supervision of persons employed in the process, and the design, construction, lay-out and maintenance of the buildings in which it is carried on.' Although it is clear from this definition that BATNEEC is a much wider concept than the BPM concept which underpins the system of industrial air pollution control laid down in the Alkali &c. Works Regulation Act 1906, the DoE(NI) has not provided any further guidance about the potential operation of this concept in Northern Ireland under the proposal for the Draft Order. Assistance in this regard can, however, be obtained from the DoE's guide to IPC[101] under the Environmental Protection Act 1990 and from the HMIP Manual on IPC, which includes internal guidance notes on IPC, and from academic discussion of these guidance notes. Although the IPC system established under the EPA 1990, as amended, creates only two tiers of control, the same concepts underlie both the British and the proposed Northern Ireland systems for industrial pollution control. It should also be noted at this juncture that very few applications for authorisations have thus far been refused under the EPA 1990 and, therefore, there are very few appeal decisions to call on for further guidance in this regard. Guidance can be gleaned from the terms of the Air Framework Directive 84/360/EEC and from Article 2.10 of the proposed IPPC Directive (which provides definitions of 'best available techniques') and from the Commission's discussion of the proposed IPPC Directive.

Before considering the meaning of the individual elements of BATNEEC, a number of general points should be noted about its application. The DoE Guidance Note points out that BATNEEC will be one of a number of factors taken into consideration in deciding whether to grant an authorisation in any given situation. In this regard, the Guidance Note emphasises that regardless of the dictates of BATNEEC, a release will not be tolerated which constitutes a health hazard either in the long or short term. During the course of a discussion of the BATNEEC concept as explained in the DoE Guidance Note, Leeson points out that:

> . . . in reducing emissions to the lowest practicable level, account will need to be taken of local conditions and circumstances, both of the process and the environment, the current state of knowledge, and the financial implications in relation to capital expenditure and revenue cost. Local conditions will of course include variable factors such as the configuration, size and so on of the individual plant. While much is therefore left to the

---

101. Draft guidance note (DoE news release no. 271), *The Meaning of BATNEEC.*

discretion of the enforcing authority, what is BATNEEC for one process is
likely to be so for other comparable processes.[102]

Turning then to available definitions of the individual elements of BATNEEC,
it should be noted that the interpretation provided in the DoE Guidance Note and
the definitions of BAT (EC formulation of BATNEEC) provided in the proposed
IPPC Directive are very similar. The term 'best' is defined in Article 2.10 of the
proposed IPPC Directive as meaning the 'most effective in achieving a high level
of protection for the environment as a whole, taking into account the potential
benefits and costs which may result from action or lack of action.' This term is
defined by the DoE Guidance Note as meaning the techniques which are the most
effective 'in preventing, minimising or rendering harmless polluting emissions.' In
this regard, Ball and Bell point out that the term 'best' is 'not an absolute term';[103]
the Guidance Note emphasises that a number of techniques may be equally
effective, and therefore all qualify under this term.

'Available' is defined by Article 2.10 of the proposed IPPC Directive as
meaning those techniques which have been 'developed on a scale which allows
implementation in the relevant industrial context, under economically viable
conditions, whether or not the techniques are used or produced inside the member
state in question, as long as they are reasonably accessible to the operator.' The
DoE Guidance Note provides a similar interpretation of 'available', in that it
stresses that availability does not necessarily imply that the technique is in
'general use' but does require that the technique be 'generally accessible'; this
does not imply that sources outside the UK are 'unavailable' for these purposes.
The fact that there is only a monopoly supplier of the equipment will not affect
availability for these purposes, provided it is sufficiently accessible.

The term 'techniques' is defined by Article 2.10 of the proposed IPPC Directive
as including 'both the technology used and the way in which the installation is
designed, built, maintained, operated and decommissioned. The techniques must
be industrially feasible, in the relevant sector, from a technical and economic point
of view.' The DoE Guidance Note provides a similar interpretation. It states that
'techniques' should be taken to mean 'the concept and design of the process, the
components of which it is made up and the manner in which they are connected
together to make the whole. It should also be taken to include matters such as staff
numbers, working methods, training, supervision and manner of operating the
process.'

The Commission also provided an explanation of the meaning and operation of
BAT in its proposal document for the IPPC Directive. The Commission stated that:

the definition of 'best' reinforces the need to take potential benefits and
costs into account in selecting BAT. The requirement of being the most
effective for achieving a high level of protection for the environment as a
whole can only be fulfilled by giving special consideration to all the items
listed in annex IV; it will not necessarily result in the most expensive
solution. The definition of 'available' makes it clear that techniques which
are available anywhere in the world are available for the purposes of this
Directive. Nor does it imply a multiplicity of sources. If there is a monopoly

---

102. J. D. Leeson, *Environmental Law,* London: Pitman, 1995, p. 46.
103. Ball and Bell, *Environmental Law,* 3rd ed., London: Blackstone Press, 1995, p. 309.

supplier, the technique counts as being available provided that it is accessible (within reason) to the operator. Finally, the definition of 'techniques' is intended to ensure that not only the technology itself is important, but so too is the way in which it is operated. Significant environmental gains can be made by improving the methods of operation of installations. It follows from this definition, and is made explicit in later Articles [of the IPPC Directive] that BAT will evolve, so providing a dynamic towards improved standards over time (and so the Directive should provide a continuing framework for industrial pollution control).[104]

The two dimensions to BATNEEC, namely 'best available techniques' and 'not entailing excessive cost', must be balanced against one another. However, it is unclear whether costs will exert the greater influence. In relation to this uncertainty, Ball and Bell point out that 'it is this unknown factor which could mean that the concept of BATNEEC will be much harsher than that of the traditional best practicable means.'[105] Ball and Bell cite HMIP's internal guidance notes on IPC, which form part of the HMIP Manual on IPC, as having made it clear that:

...when issuing authorisations [HMIP] will be viewing an application in terms of a process standard rather than purely looking at the emission levels. Operators will have to demonstrate the options that they have considered when selecting the best available techniques. However, [HMIP] have pointed out that in a situation where the best available technique is not put forward, the applicant must be able to justify the technique on the grounds that the selection of another option would involve entailing excessive cost.[106]

HMIP's internal guidance note stresses in this regard that the onus is on the operator of the process in question to 'describe excessive cost in absolute terms without reference to the cost of the product. The applicant must be able to demonstrate that the increased cost of the product produced by the best available technique is grossly disproportionate to any environmental benefit likely to accrue from that method of production. The extra cost must represent a significant fraction of the cost of the finished product.' Ball and Bell also note that 'the tone of the new guidance is that HMIP will certainly be looking towards the upgrading of existing plant with as much severity as the implementation of new plant.'[107]

Finally, Leeson's commentary on the application of 'not entailing excessive cost' to new and existing processes should be noted. In effect, he points out that the NEEC element to BATNEEC:

. . . is to be considered independently in its application to new and existing processes. In relation to new processes the presumption is that the best available techniques will be used. However, where in a particular case the best process offers a relatively modest gain in efficiency over the alternative at a disproportionate cost, it may be that that additional cost

---

104. COM (93) 423 Final, p. 14.
105. Note 103, supra, p. 310.
106. Ibid.
107. Ibid., p. 311. It should also be noted that HMIP's guidance note also addresses the possibility of relaxing BATNEEC requirements where substances are released but rendered harmless and also addresses the implications of geographical location or effects in terms of the dilution or dispersal of the pollutants.

should be considered excessive in this context and the alternative adopted. Judgment based on the individual circumstances will still govern the decision, though, so that if, for example, the emissions here were particularly dangerous, even the disproportionate cost would not be excessive.[108]

Leeson also points to the guidance offered in Articles 12 and 13 of the Air Framework Directive 84/360/EEC concerning the application of NEEC to existing processes. Article 13 applies to processes which were in existence before 1987 and provides that in applying measures for the gradual upgrading of existing plant in the categories listed in Annex I to the Directive, member states must take the following into account:

— the plant's technical characteristics;
— its rate of utilisation and length of its remaining life;
— the nature and volume of polluting emissions from it; and
— the desirability of not entailing excessive costs for the plant concerned, having regard in particular to the economic situation of undertakings belonging to the category in question.

**Definition of BPEO**

As is the case under Part I of the Environmental Protection Act 1990, the draft Northern Ireland Order makes no attempt to define the concept of BPEO. The concept was introduced by the Fifth Report of the Royal Commission on Environmental Pollution in 1976; and despite three further Royal Commission reports in which the nature and scope of BPEO have been addressed in some detail, in practice, BPEO has proved very difficult to 'pin down'.[109] In effect, while BATNEEC requires the application of the best available techniques to prevent and minimise discharges of pollutants, BPEO requires consideration of 'the most appropriate receiving environmental medium'.[110] The Royal Commission's Tenth Report, published in 1984, stated that the term BPEO meant 'the optimal allocation of the waste spatially; the use of different sectors of the environment to minimise damage overall'.[111] A year later the Eleventh Report developed this definition by stating that the objective of BPEO:

...is to find the optimum combination of available methods of disposal so as to limit damage to the environment to the greatest extent achievable for a reasonable and acceptable total combined cost to industry and the public purse.[112]

The Royal Commission's Twelfth Report on Environmental Pollution, published in 1988, was devoted entirely to a discussion of the concept of BPEO. In this report the Royal Commission stated that:

---

108. Note 102, supra, p. 46.
109. Ball and Bell, supra, p. 311.
110. Leeson, *Environmental Law,* London: Pitman 1995, p. 48.
111. Tenth Report of the Royal Commission on Environmental Pollution: *Tackling Pollution: Experience and Prospects* (Cmnd 9149), London: HMSO, 1984.
112. Eleventh Report of the Royal Commission on Environmental Pollution: *Managing Waste: The Duty of Care* (Cmnd 9675), London: HMSO, 1985.

a BPEO is the outcome of a systematic consultative and decision-making procedure which emphasises the protection and conservation of the environment across land, air and water. The BPEO procedure establishes, for a given set of objectives, the option that provides the most benefit or least damage to the environment as a whole, at acceptable cost, in the long term as well as in the short term.[113]

It should also be noted that the Twelfth Report of the Royal Commission provides a very detailed explanation of the steps which should be taken to arrive at a BPEO and the characteristics of a BPEO when identified. Leeson, who also refers to the above extracts from the Royal Commission reports as explaining the meaning and nature of BPEO, states that:

...instead of concentration on cost-effective techniques for reducing emissions [BPEO] . . . is primarily concerned to select the most appropriate or least damaging environmental alternative for the reception of the waste or polluting material. The term is wide enough, though, to include the reduction of such emissions by modification of processes and plant.[114]

Leeson goes on to state that:

...BPEO may be regarded as a more developed treatment of the factors potentially subject to review in considering the application of the 'best practicable means' test.[115]

During their discussion of the system of integrated pollution control operating in Great Britain, Ball and Bell point out that while:

...a BPEO assessment has a number of similarities with a formal environmental assessment, it is the distinguishing features which make the concept of BPEO both wider and narrower than the assessment of a construction project. It is narrower in the sense that with a BPEO assessment there is only a requirement to assess the effects of releases of substances upon air, water and land. It is, however, wider in that there is a requirement to assess the availability and relative cost-benefit ratios of other process options which could be used to deal with the releases.[116]

Finally, it should be noted that HMIP has published draft guidance on the steps to be taken when carrying out a BPEO assessment; and while the approach used has been criticised, Ball and Bell point out that 'the introduction of some formal guidance on the issue of carrying out a BPEO assessment is necessary in order for the concept to have any meaning'.[117]

---

113. Twelfth Report of the Royal Commission on Environmental Pollution: *Best Practicable Environmental Option* (Cm 310), London: HMSO, 1988.
114. Leeson, supra, p. 42.
115. Ibid., p. 43. Leeson also points out that the BPEO will be an important factor in planning applications for 'the location and operation of new and extended activities and processes, and in this context is one of the objectives of Environmental Impact Assessment,' which is addressed in chap. 11. For further discussion of BPEO see S. Tromans (ed.), *Best Practicable Environmental Option: A New Jerusalem,* London: UK Environmental Law Association 1987.
116. Ball and Bell, supra, p. 311. The concept of environmental impact assessment is addressed in chap. 11.
117. Ibid., p. 312.

## PART III EMISSIONS FROM LARGE COMBUSTION PLANTS

Directive 88/609/EEC[118] has been adopted for the purposes of regulating emissions of dust, sulphur dioxide ($SO_2$) and nitrogen oxides (NOx) from fossil-fuelled power stations and other large combustion plants such as oil refineries.

As a 'daughter' Directive to Air Framework Directive 84/360/EEC (discussed in Part II of this chapter), Directive 88/609/EEC also employs emission limits as the primary mechanism of control. However, it is important to note that Directive 88/609/EEC employs a variation on this mechanism, in that it imposes what is known as a 'bubble' limit. In essence the Directive allocates a total national emission limit for large combustion plants to each member state, which is then progressively reduced over time. The advantage of the 'bubble' or national limit is that it affords member states a degree of flexibility in relation to emission limits for individual plants but is subject to an overall national ceiling.

Although emissions of sulphur dioxide and nitrogen oxides are among the primary causes of acid rain (discussed at pages 107 and 150), it took five years of controversial negotiations before member states would agree to the adoption of legislation that would require the progressive reduction of such emissions. The UK, as the principal emitter of sulphur dioxide within the EC—because of the use of high-sulphur indigenous coal—was the most consistent objector to the adoption of the Directive. It ultimately changed its position on this issue in 1986 but managed to negotiate a derogation for new plants burning indigenous high-sulphur coal. The Directive only applies to plants which have a 'rated thermal input of 50 megawatts or more,' and certain types of combustion plants are excluded from the operation of the Directive. Different requirements are set out for 'new' and 'existing' plants. 'Existing plants' are defined as plants whose original construction licence or whose operating licence was granted before 1 July 1987. 'New plants' are defined as those licensed on or after 1 July 1987. Only those provisions of the Directive which cover 'existing plants' have been implemented in Northern Ireland; however, legislation implementing provisions relating to 'new plants' is expected during 1996. Minor amendments were made to Directive 88/609/EEC by Directive 94/66/EC, which in essence extended its scope to cover new coal-fired plants in the range of 50–100 MW thermal.

### Implementation in Northern Ireland

Directive 88/609/EEC has been implemented in Northern Ireland by the Large Combustion Plants (Control of Emissions) Regulations (NI) 1991[119] as far as existing plants are concerned; legislation implementing the Directive as far as new plants are concerned has yet to be introduced, although any new plant will, in practice, be required to comply with the permitted emission levels specified for sulphur dioxide and nitrogen oxides in the Directive. It should be noted that the Alkali and Radiochemical Inspectorate for Northern Ireland published a new 'best practicable means' (BPM) note in March 1993 for large combustion works with a

---

118. OJ L336, 7 Dec. 1988. Compliance date: 30 June 1990. See N. Haigh, supra, chap. 6.10 and N. Haigh, 'New Tools for European Air Pollution Control' (1989) International Environmental Affairs, Vol. 1., No. 1.
119. SR No. 449.

thermal capacity of between 50–500 MW.[120] The following is an outline of the requirements laid down by the 1991 Regulations.

### Maximum emission levels for existing plants

Directive 88/609/EEC imposes total national emission limits with phased reductions on each member state for sulphur dioxide and nitrogen oxides. The limits vary between member states. Annex I requires the UK to reduce sulphur dioxide emissions by 20 per cent in 1993, 40 per cent in 1998, and 60 per cent in 2003, using emission levels in 1980 as the base year. Annex II requires the UK to reduce emissions of nitrogen oxides by 15 per cent in 1993 and 30 per cent in 1998, using 1980 as the base year.

Member states are obliged to produce national programmes for the progressive reduction of total national emission of both sulphur dioxide and nitrogen oxides that comply with the limits imposed in Annex I and II, and these must be communicated to the European Commission by 31 December 1990. A programme that applies to Great Britain and Northern Ireland was submitted to the Commission in 1990. There are five combustion plants in Northern Ireland which come within the controls laid down in this Directive, namely the four large power stations at Kilroot, Ballylumford (Premier Power Station), Belfast West, and Coolkeeragh, and a smaller private station owned by Du Pont in Derry. Their emissions of sulphur dioxide will be reduced to 40 per cent of 1992 levels by the year 2003 as part of the national plan to reduce emissions from large combustion plants. The *Environment Service Report* 1993–95 states that Northern Ireland's sulphur dioxide emissions have falllen by 7.9 per cent over the period of the report, thereby keeping Northern Ireland's contribution to the national reduction programme on target.

The first steps have been taken to reduce emissions of nitrogen oxides from Northern Ireland power stations, namely, the fitting of low-NOx burners in two boilers at the Ballylumford plant. A register of permitted emission levels of sulphur dioxide and nitrogen oxides for existing plants in Northern Ireland, which complies with the UK plan, has been issued by the DoE(NI).[121] Regulation 3 of the Large Combustion Plants (Control of Emissions) Regulations (NI) 1991 imposes an obligation on the operator of existing plants in Northern Ireland to ensure that emissions of sulphur dioxide and nitrogen oxides from the plant do not exceed the permitted levels specified for that plant in the register in relation to the years specified in the register.

### Duty of the plant operator to monitor and provide information to the Chief Inspector

Regulation 4 imposes an obligation on the operator of the plant to monitor

120. A copy of the BPM note is contained in Appendix V of the *Report of the Chief Alkali Inspector: for the years 1992–1993*, London: HMSO, 1995.

121. Copies of this register are available from the DoE(NI)'s Environment Service, Air Legislation Section, Calvert House, 23 Castle Place, Belfast BT1 1FY. A copy of the UK National Plan is contained in Appendix IV of the *Report of the Chief Alkali Inspector: for the years 1992–1993*, London: HMSO, 1995.

emissions of sulphur dioxide and nitrogen oxides from the plant, using methods which have been approved by the Chief Inspector (DoE(NI) Environment Service). In addition, regulation 4 requires the operator of the plant to inform the Chief Inspector in writing:

(i) of the quantity of sulphur dioxide and nitrogen oxides emitted from the plant each month (such information must be conveyed to the Chief Inspector within fourteen days of the end of each month);

(ii) when emission levels of either sulphur dioxide or nitrogen oxides amount to 85 per cent of the permitted level (as described above) (such information must be conveyed 'forthwith');

(iii) of any change in circumstances relating to energy demand, the availability of fuel, or any other difficulty likely to affect the operation of that plant which is liable to cause a permitted level to be exceeded (such information must be conveyed to the Chief Inspector 'as soon as practicable').

### Variation of plant emission levels

Directive 88/609/EEC provides that targets can be modified in exceptional circumstances, for example where the demand for energy or the availability of fuels undergoes a substantial unexpected change. Regulation 5(1)(*a*) and (*b*) empowers the operator of a plant to request that the Chief Inspector vary the permitted levels for the plant. However, regulation 5(2) states that the Chief Inspector must not agree to such a request unless he is satisfied that the total emission levels permitted for that substance for Northern Ireland for the years concerned (as set out in the register) are unlikely to be exceeded.

### Directions by the Chief Inspector

Where the Chief Inspector considers that a permitted level is likely to be exceeded, regulation 6 empowers him to direct the operator of a plant, by notice in writing, to submit, within such reasonable period as may be specified, written particulars of the measures the operator proposes to take to achieve compliance with that level.

### Offences

Regulation 7 provides that an operator of a plant who fails to ensure that emissions of sulphur dioxide or nitrogen oxides do not exceed permitted levels as required under regulation 3 is guilty of an offence. Similarly, a failure on the part of an operator to discharge obligations imposed by regulations 4 and 6 would constitute an offence under regulation 7. Regulation 7(3) provides that where the commission of an offence by any person under these Regulations is due to the act or default of some other person, that other person will be guilty of the offence and may be charged with and convicted of the offence, whether or not proceedings are brought against the first-named person. In proceedings for an offence under the 1991 Regulations it is a defence to prove that the person charged took all reasonable precautions and exercised all due diligence to avoid the commission of such an offence by himself or any person under his control (regulation 7(2)). Regulation 7(4) provides that where the defence provided for in regulation 7(2) involves the allegation that the commission of the offence was due to the act or default of another person, the person charged cannot rely on such a defence, unless he has served a notice in writing on the prosecutor not less than seven clear days before the hearing, giving such information as was then in his possession to identify or assist in identifying that person. This rule can only be avoided where leave is given by the court.

### *Penalties*

Regulation 7(1) sets out the penalties for offences committed under these Regulations. In effect, an operator who either fails to discharge a duty to which he is subject under regulation 3 or who fails to comply with regulation 4 or a direction under regulation 6, will be liable on summary conviction to a maximum fine of £5,000 (level 5 on the standard scale) or, on conviction on indictment, to a maximum term of imprisonment of two years or a maximum fine of £5,000, or to both.

## *PART IV* EMISSIONS OF ASBESTOS INTO THE AIR

Directive 87/217/EEC[122] controls the emission of asbestos into air, water and onto land and is therefore an example of a 'substance-oriented' Directive, in that emissions of an individual substance into all environmental media are regulated by a single Directive.

Directive 87/217/EEC imposes a general duty on member states to ensure, as far as is reasonably practicable, that emissions of asbestos are reduced at source and prevented. The Directive controls the use and manufacture of asbestos, working with asbestos products and the demolition of buildings which contain asbestos and applies to blue asbestos (crocidolite), brown asbestos (amosite), white asbestos (anthophyllite, chrysotile, and actinolite), and tremolite. Like the Large Combustion Plant Directive, considered in Part III of this chapter, Directive 87/217/EEC is another daughter Directive adopted under Air Framework Directive 84/360/EEC (addressed in Part II, section 2) and as such lays down limit values for emissions of asbestos into the air. In addition, Directive 87/217/EEC requires that discharges of asbestos into the air be monitored regularly, using methods specified in an Annex to the Directive or equivalent methods. Compliance with BATNEEC is required where asbestos is used. However, this is subject to certain qualifications for emissions into air by existing plant set out in Directive 84/360/EEC.

Directive 87/217/EEC also supplements other EC Directives which control asbestos in relation to the protection of workers, waste, and the marketing and use of asbestos. It is important to note that while emissions of asbestos into all environmental media are regulated by Directive 87/217/EEC, its provisions have

---

122. OJ L85, 28 Mar. 1987. Compliance date: 31 Dec. 1988. See: N. Haigh, supra, chap 7.11 for a detailed explanation of the development of Directive 87/217/EEC and its requirements.

been implemented in Northern Ireland for each medium individually; only those provisions concerning emissions into the air are discussed in this chapter.

## Implementation in Northern Ireland

Directive 87/217/EEC is implemented in Northern Ireland (so far as emissions into the air are concerned) by the Control of Asbestos in the Air Regulations (NI) 1993,[123] the Alkali &c. Works Regulation Act 1906,[124] as amended, and the Control of Asbestos at Work Regulations (NI) 1988,[125] as amended. The relevant provisions of each implementing measure will be considered in turn.

### *The Control of Asbestos in the Air Regulations (NI) 1993*

*Limit value for the discharge of asbestos into the air during the use of asbestos*

Regulation 3(1) requires any person who has control of an asbestos work[126] to ensure that the concentration of asbestos[127] that is emitted through discharge ducts into the air during the 'use' of asbestos does not exceed 0.1 milligrammes of asbestos per cubic metre of air discharged. Directive 87/217/EEC requires that BATNEEC be employed where asbestos is used. The Chief Inspector[128] is empowered by regulation 3(2) to ensure that measurements of the concentration of asbestos so emitted are taken at regular intervals and that the sampling and analysis procedures and methods used to comply with regulation 3(1) are in accordance with those set out in the Annex to Directive 87/217/EEC or with any other procedure or method which gives equivalent results.

The 'use' of asbestos is defined in regulation 3(3) as activities which involve the handling of a quantity of more than 100 kilogrammes of raw asbestos per year and which concern:

(a) the production of raw asbestos[129] ore, excluding any process directly associated with the mining of the ore; or

(b) the manufacturing or industrial finishing or any of the following products using raw asbestos—

asbestos cement, asbestos cement products, asbestos fillers, asbestos filters, asbestos floor covering, asbestos friction products, asbestos

---

123. SR No. 170.
124. c. 14.
125. SR No. 74.
126. 'Asbestos work' is defined in reg. 3(3) as any work described in para. 54 of the first Schedule to the Alkali &c. Works Regulation Act 1906 (c. 14), as amended by the Alkali &c. Works Order (NI) 1991 (SR No. 49).
127. 'Asbestos' is defined in reg. 2(1) as meaning the following fibrous silicates: amosite (brown asbestos), actinolite, anthophyllite, chrysotile (white asbestos), crocidolite (blue asbestos), and tremolite.
128. 'Chief inspector' is defined in reg. 3(3) as meaning the person constituted as such pursuant to s. 10(1) of the Alkali &c. Works Regulation Act 1906 (c. 14), as amended by the Alkali &c. Works Order (NI) 1991 (SR No. 49). It also includes a deputy appointed under s. 10(5) of the 1906 Act, as amended.
129. 'Raw asbestos' is defined in reg. 3(3) as the product resulting from the primary crushing of asbestos ore.

jointing, packaging, and reinforcement materials, asbestos paper and card, or asbestos textiles.

*Control of environmental pollution by asbestos resulting from the working of products containing asbestos*

Regulation 4(1) provides that a person who undertakes activities involving the working[130] of products containing asbestos must ensure that those activities do not cause significant environmental pollution by asbestos fibres[131] or dust emitted into the air. Similarly, regulation 4(2) provides that any person undertaking the demolition of buildings, structures or installations containing asbestos and the removal from them of asbestos, involving the release of asbestos fibres or dust into the air, must ensure that 'significant environmental pollution'[132] is not caused as a result.

*Offences*

Regulation 5(1) provides that failure to comply with regulation 3(1) or 4 is an offence. Regulation 5(3) provides that where the commission of an offence under regulation 5(1) is due to the act or default of another person, that other person will be guilty of an offence and may be charged with and convicted of the offence, whether or not proceedings are brought against the first-mentioned person under regulation 5(1). Regulation 5(2) provides that in proceedings for an offence under the 1993 Regulations it is a defence to prove that the person charged took all reasonable precautions and exercised all due diligence to avoid the commission of such an offence by himself or by any person under his control.

*Penalties*

Regulation 5(1) sets out the penalties for offences under these Regulations. In effect, a person who fails to comply with requirements laid down in regulations 3(1) or 4 will be liable on summary conviction to a maximum fine of £5,000 (level 5 on the standard scale) or, on conviction on indictment, to a maximum fine of £5,000 or to a maximum term of imprisonment of two years, or to both.

### The Alkali &c. Works Regulation Act 1906, as amended

The discharge of certain noxious or offensive gases from certain types of works is subject to control under the Alkali &c. Works Regulation Act 1906. Article 25(9) of the Clean Air (NI) Order 1981[133] empowers the DoE(NI) to make orders amending or extending the lists of gases and of works scheduled in the 1906 Act.

---

130. The 'working of products containing asbestos' is defined in reg. 4(3) as activities other than the use of asbestos as defined at p. 125 which are liable to release asbestos into the environment.
131. 'Fibres' is defined in reg. 4(3) as having the same meaning as in Part BII of the Annex to Directive 87/217/EEC.
132. 'Significant environmental pollution' is defined in reg. 4(3) as having the same meaning as in Art. 7 of Directive 87/217/EEC.
133. SI 1981/158. The relevant terms of the Clean Air (NI) Order 1981 are outlined in detail in Part I, section 7 of this chapter.

The Alkali &c. Works Order (NI) 1991[134] extends and revokes all previous orders adopted under article 25(9). Schedule 2 to the 1991 Order extends the classes of premises from which emissions into the air must be controlled under the 1906 Act to premises on which certain asbestos works are carried out. The system of control laid down by the Alkali &c. Works Regulation Act 1906 is outlined in Part II, section 2 of this chapter.

## The Control of Asbestos at Work Regulations (NI) 1988, as amended by the Control of Asbestos at Work (Amendment) Regulations (NI) 1993

*Duties of the employer to protect employees and others from exposure to asbestos at work*

The Control of Asbestos at Work Regulations (NI) 1988 impose duties on employers for the protection of employees who may be exposed[135] to asbestos[136] at work and also for the protection of other persons who are or are liable to be affected by such work (regulation 3). Regulation 4 of the 1988 Regulations, as amended by the Schedule to the 1993 Regulations, provides that an employer must not carry out any work 'which exposes or is likely to expose any of his employees to asbestos,' unless (i) he has identified 'by analysis or otherwise' the type of asbestos involved before beginning the work in question or (ii) he assumes that the asbestos is not chrysotile alone for the purposes of these Regulations and has treated it accordingly.

In addition, regulation 5 obliges an employer in this situation to carry out an adequate assessment of the exposure involved. In particular, that assessment must identify the nature of the asbestos involved and the nature and degree of the exposure to asbestos and must determine the steps which are to be taken to prevent or reduce that exposure to the lowest level reasonably practicable.[137] Regulation 5, as amended, also states that this assessment must be reviewed regularly and a new assessment carried out when there is 'reason to suspect' that the existing assessment is no longer valid or when there is 'a significant change in the work to which the assessment relates.'

---

134. SR No. 49.
135. Reg. 2(2) of the 1988 Regulations states that for the purposes of these Regulations: '(*a*) any reference to an employee being exposed to asbestos shall be treated as a reference to the exposure of that employee to asbestos dust arising out of or in connection with any work with asbestos or with any product containing asbestos which is carried out by the employer; and (*b*) in determining whether an employee is exposed to asbestos or whether the extent of such exposure exceeds the action level or any control limit, no account shall be taken of any respiratory protective equipment which, for the time being, is being worn by that employee.'
136. 'Asbestos' is defined in reg. 2(1) of the 1988 Regulations as meaning any of the following minerals: crocidolite, amosite, chrysotile, fibrous actinolite, fibrous anthophyllite, fibrous tremolite, and any mixture containing any of these minerals.
137. Where work that exposed or was likely to expose employees to asbestos has been started before the coming into operation of the 1988 Regulations (i.e. before 25 Apr. 1988) or within twenty-eight days of that date, an employer will be deemed to be in compliance with the 1988 Regulations if he makes the assessment required by reg. 5 within twenty-eight days of the coming into force of these Regulations (reg. 5(3)).

*Plans of work*

Paragraph 4 of the Schedule to the 1993 Regulations inserts a new regulation 5A after Regulation 5 of the 1988 Regulations. Regulation 5A provides that an employer cannot undertake any work that involves the removal of asbestos from any building, structure, plant or installation or from a ship (including its demolition) unless the employer has prepared a suitable written plan of work which details how the work is to be carried out. The plan of work must be kept by the employer at least until the work in question has been completed. Regulation 5A also requires that the plan of work contain details of:

(a) the nature and probable duration of the work;

(b) the location of the place where the work is to be carried out;

(c) the methods to be applied where the work involves the handling of asbestos or materials containing asbestos; and

(d) the characteristics of the equipment to be used for—

(i) the protection and decontamination of those carrying out the work; and

(ii) the protection of others on or near the worksite.

*Notification of work with asbestos*

Regulation 6 requires the notification of work with asbestos in which an employee is or is liable to be exposed to a level of asbestos that exceeds or is liable to exceed the 'action level'.[138] Notification must be sent to the enforcing authority, unless this work has already been notified under other Regulations outlined in regulation 6.

*Information and training*

Regulation 7 obliges an employer to ensure that employees and other persons on premises where the work is conducted are provided with adequate information, instruction, and training.

*Prevention or reduction of exposure to asbestos*

Regulation 8(1) imposes an obligation on employers to prevent the exposure of employees to asbestos at work, or, where prevention is not reasonably practicable, the employer must reduce the exposure to the lowest reasonably practicable level by measures other than the use of respiratory protective equipment. If it is not reasonably practicable under regulation 8(1) to reduce the exposure to a level

---

138. Para. 1 of the Schedule to the 1993 Regulations amends the definition of the term 'action level' contained in reg. 2(1) of the 1988 Regulations so as to reduce the level in relation to exposure to chrysotile from 120 to 96 fibre-hours per millilitre of air. The definition now reads: 'Action level means one of the following cumulative exposures to asbestos over a continuous 12-week period when measured or calculated by an approved method namely: (a) where the exposure is solely to chrysotile, 96 fibre-hours per millilitre of air; or (b) where exposure is to any other form of asbestos either alone or in mixtures including mixtures of chrysotile with any other form of asbestos, 48 fibre-hours per millilitre of air; or (c) where both types of exposure occur separately during the 12-week period concerned, a proportionate number of fibre-hours per millilitre of air.'

which is below the specified 'control limits',[139] then employers must, in addition to taking the measures specified in regulation 8(1), provide employees with suitable respiratory protective equipment which will reduce the concentration of asbestos in the air inhaled by the employee to a concentration below those limits. Such equipment must be of an approved type or must conform to an approved standard for the purposes of the 1988 Regulations, as amended.

Paragraph 5 of the Schedule to the 1993 Regulations requires the insertion of subparagraph (1A) into regulation 8 after paragraph (1). Regulation 8(1A) provides that where employees may be exposed to asbestos in any manufacturing process or in the installation of any product, the prevention of such exposure must be achieved, where it is practicable, by substituting for asbestos a substance that, under the conditions of its use, does not create a risk to the health of the employees or creates a lesser risk than that created by asbestos. Regulation 8(1A) is stated to be 'without prejudice to the generality of regulation 8(1).' The obligation imposed by regulation 8(1A) is imposed on all employers.

Paragraph 5(2) of the Schedule to the 1993 Regulations requires that a new paragraph (4) be added to regulation 8 of the 1988 Regulations. Regulation 8(4) states that if an unforeseen event occurs that results in the escape of asbestos into the work-place at a concentration which is liable to exceed any applicable control limit, the employer is obliged to ensure that:

(a) only those persons who are responsible for the carrying out of repairs and other necessary work are permitted in the affected area and that those persons are provided with appropriate respiratory protective equipment and protective clothing; and

(b) employees and other persons who may have been affected by the event are informed of it forthwith.

Both employers and employees are obliged to make proper use of the protective respiratory equipment (regulation 9), while requirements are imposed on employers for the proper maintenance of such equipment (regulation 10). In addition, employers are obliged to provide and maintain clean protective clothing (regulation 11).

*Spread of asbestos*

Employers are also obliged to prevent the spread of asbestos from the work-place (regulation 12).

---

139. Para. 1 of the Schedule to the 1993 Regulations also amends the definition of the term 'control limit' contained in reg. 2 (1) of the 1988 Regulations so that certain concentrations of asbestos in the atmosphere are applicable only to chrysotile, and lower concentrations are applicable to all other forms of asbestos. Formerly the lower concentrations applied only to asbestos which consisted of, or contained, any crocidolite or amosite. The definition now reads: ' "Control limit" means one of the following concentrations of asbestos in the atmosphere when measured or calculated by an approved method, namely: (a) for chrysotile: (i) 0.5 fibres per millilitre of air averaged over any continuous period of 4 hours, or (ii) 1.5 fibres per millilitre of air averaged over any continuous period of 10 minutes; (b) for any other form of asbestos either alone or in mixtures including mixtures of chrysotile with any other form of asbestos: (i) 0.2 fibres per millilitre of air averaged over any continuous period of 4 hours, or, (ii) 0.6 fibres per millilitre of air averaged over any continuous period of 10 minutes.'

*Cleanliness of premises and plant*

Employers are required to ensure that the premises and plant involved in the work with asbestos are kept clean (regulation 13).

*Designated areas*

Regulation 14 requires that an area in which exposure to asbestos is or is liable to exceed the 'action level' or 'control limit' must be designated as an 'asbestos area'[140] (where an action level is concerned) or a 'respirator zone'[141] (where a control limit is concerned). Designated areas must be clearly and separately demarcated. Regulation 14 also provides that only limited entry can be allowed into those areas, that the employer must take suitable steps to prevent employees from smoking, eating or drinking in such areas, and that suitable alternative eating arrangements be provided. In addition, requirements are laid down for the wearing of protective respiratory equipment in respirator zones where the exposure to asbestos is likely to exceed a control limit.

*Air monitoring*

Regulation 15 obliges employers to take 'adequate steps' to monitor the exposure of employees at work to asbestos 'where such monitoring is appropriate for the protection of the health of those employees.' To this end an employer is obliged to keep 'a suitable record' of any monitoring which has been carried out; under the 1993 Regulations, as amended, that record must be kept for at least forty years where the exposure is such that a health record is required to be kept under regulation 16 (addressed below), and in any other case must be kept for at least five years.

*Medical surveillance of employees*

Employers are obliged by regulation 16 to maintain health records and regular medical surveillance of those employees who are liable to be significantly exposed to asbestos—i.e. whose exposure exceeds the action level defined in regulation 2(1), as amended by the Schedule to the 1993 Regulations. Such medical surveillance must be carried out either by 'an employment medical adviser' or by 'an appointed doctor' (both terms are defined in regulation 2(1) of the 1988 Regulations). A copy of these medical records must (under the 1993 Regulations, as amended) be kept for at least forty years from the date of the last entry made.

Regulation 16 lays down specific requirements concerning the nature of the medical surveillance which must be carried out, the provision of facilities for such examinations, and the issuing of certificates that such surveillance has been conducted. An employer is obliged to give employees access to their health records; the employer must be given 'reasonable notice' of such a request.

---

140. Reg. 2(1) of the 1988 Regulations provides that the terms 'asbestos area' and 'respirator zone' will be construed in accordance with reg. 14 of the 1988 Regulations.
141. Ibid.

### Washing and changing facilities

Regulation 17 requires that employers provide employees who are exposed to asbestos with 'adequate and suitable' washing and changing facilities and facilities for storing protective equipment.

### Storage, distribution and labelling of raw asbestos and asbestos waste

Regulation 18 and Schedule 2 to the 1988 Regulations regulate the storage, distribution and labelling of raw asbestos and asbestos waste.

### Supply of products containing asbestos

Regulation 19 provides that a person must not supply any product which contains asbestos for use at work unless the product is labelled in accordance with Schedule 2 to the 1988 Regulations.

### Exemption

Regulation 20 empowers the DoE(NI) to issue certificates which exempt any person or class of persons from the operation of the 1988 Regulations. However, the DoE(NI) may not grant such a certificate unless it is satisfied in the circumstances of the case, and having regard to any conditions attached to the exemption, that such an exemption would not prejudice the health or safety of any persons who are likely to be affected by the exemption.

### Codes of practice

Codes of practice, approved by the Health and Safety Agency for Northern Ireland under article 18(1) of the Health and Safety at Work (NI) Order 1978, will be published, as will guidance on the operation of these Regulations.[142]

### Offences and penalties

A person who violates the provisions of the 1988 Regulations, as amended, is guilty of an offence under article 31 of the Health and Safety at Work (NI) Order 1978 and will be liable, on summary conviction, to a fine not exceeding £5,000 (level 5 on the standard scale) or, on conviction on indictment, to an unlimited fine.

## PART V MUNICIPAL WASTE INCINERATORS

Directives 89/369/EEC[143] and 89/429/EEC[144] set down emission limit values for new and existing municipal waste incineration plants (MWIP), which are defined as plants that deal only with domestic, commercial and trade waste. These

---

142. These codes of practice may (when issued) be obtained from HMSO, 80 Chichester Street, Belfast BT1 4JY.
143. OJ L163, 14 June 1989. Compliance date: 1 Dec. 1990. See: N. Haigh, supra, chap. 6. 11 for a more detailed discussion of Directives 89/369/EEC and 89/429/EEC.
144. OJ L203, 15 July 1989. Compliance date: 1 Dec. 1990.

Directives do not cover incinerators which handle sewage sludge, chemical waste, toxic waste, or hospital waste. Dust, heavy metals, traces of dioxins and acidic gases are among the emissions primarily associated with municipal waste incinerators.

Directive 89/429/EEC on existing MWIP defines 'existing plants' as plants which were granted their first authorisation before the Directive's implementation deadline—1 December 1990. A timetable is set out in the Directive which stipulates the time limits within which existing plants must attain the standards specified for new plants in Directive 89/369/EEC. Directive 89/369/EEC sets down emission limit values for new MWIPs and also standards for the operation and monitoring of such plants. In addition, Directive 89/369/EEC provides that, as from 1 December 1990, these requirements must be attached to the prior authorisations which must be issued under the Air Framework Directive 84/360/EEC and Directive 75/442/EEC on waste. These Directives are addressed in Part II of the present chapter and chapter 6 respectively.

**Implementation in Northern Ireland**

Thus far, the MWIP Directives have not been formally implemented in Northern Ireland. However, it should be noted that 'existing' MWIPs in Northern Ireland with a capacity of 1 tonne per hour or greater are controlled under the Alkali &c. Works Regulation Act 1906.[145] At the time of writing there is only one such plant in Northern Ireland. In 1994 the Alkali &c. Works (Amendment) Order (NI) 1994[146] was enacted to bring all such MWIPs under the system of industrial air pollution control imposed by the Alkali Act, which, in practice, implements the emission standards laid down by both Directives. The enactment of the proposed Industrial Pollution Control (NI) Order 1996, scheduled for mid-1996, will ensure full implementation of the MWIP Directives in Northern Ireland. The provisions of the proposal for the draft Order are discussed in more detail in Part II, sections 2 and 3 of this chapter.

## *PART VI* CABLE BURNING

Article 56(1) of the Pollution Control and Local Government (NI) Order 1978[147] provides that a person who burns insulation from a cable with a view to recovering metal from the cable will be guilty of an offence unless the place at which the burning is carried out is a registered work pursuant to section 9 of the Alkali &c. Works Regulation Act 1906, as amended.[148] Article 56(2) provides that section 16A of the Alkali Act (as amended) will govern liability for an offence under article 56(1). The terms of the Alkali Act are addressed in detail in Part II, section 1 of this chapter.

---

145. c. 14. The Alkali Act is addressed in detail in Part II, section 1 of this chapter.
146. SR No. 104.
147. SI 1978/1049.
148. c. 14.

## PART *VII* AIR QUALITY STANDARDS

One of the most important initiatives undertaken by the EC in the context of air pollution control has been the introduction of a series of air quality Directives designed to improve ambient or ground-level air quality for the purposes of protecting human health and the environment. Directives 80/779/EEC,[149] 82/884/EEC[150] and 85/203/EEC[151] were introduced during the early nineteen-eighties to control concentrations of smoke and sulphur dioxide, lead and nitrogen dioxide, respectively.

Each of these Directives sets down air quality limit values for the pollutant in question and require member states to ensure that atmospheric concentrations of these pollutants do not exceed the limit values specified. In addition, these Directives require that specified sampling and measuring procedures be used and that monitoring stations be established.

The most recent air quality Directive, Directive 92/72/EEC[152] concerning ground-level ozone, was introduced in 1992. (It should be noted that the regulation of ground-level ozone is distinct from that of the upper atmosphere, discussed in Part IX of this chapter) Ground-level ozone is not emitted directly in any significant quantity but is formed by the action of sunlight on nitrogen oxides and volatile organic compounds (VOCs). VOCs are a major contributor to the formation of ground-level ozone and are emitted from a wide variety of sources. Road traffic is thought to be the largest source. However, other identified sources include the storage of petrol and its distribution from terminals to service stations, the use of solvents, oil refining, and a number of industrial processes. Unlike the other air quality Directives, Directive 92/72/EEC does not set down specific limit values. Nigel Haigh points to two principal reasons for this, namely: (i) scientists do not yet fully understand the process by which ozone is formed or the most effective means of preventing its formation, and (ii) the Commission realised when submitting its proposal for this Directive that limit values for ozone would be exceeded regularly by several member states. Indeed, member states even rejected the Commission's suggestion that such limits be adopted within five years of the adoption of the Directive.[153] Directive 92/72/EEC simply requires member states to establish ozone monitoring stations and to share information concerning ozone with the Commission and with other member states. By this means it is intended that a greater understanding will be developed of the process by which

---

149. Directive 80/779/EEC Sulphur Dioxide and Suspended Particulates (Smoke) OJ L229, 30 Aug. 1980; formal implementation date: 17 July 1982; mandatory compliance date: 1 Apr. 1993. Directive 80/779/EEC has been amended by Directives 81/857/EEC (OJ L39/1, 20 Jan. 1981) and 89/427/EEC (OJ L201/53, 14 July 1989). See: Haigh, supra, chap. 6.4 for a more detailed discussion of Directive 80/779/EEC.

150. Directive 82/884/EEC Lead OJ L378, 31 Dec. 1982; formal implementation date: 9 Dec. 1984; mandatory compliance date: 9 Dec. 1987. Directive 82/884/EEC has been amended by Directive 91/692/EEC. See: Haigh, ibid. chap. 6. 6 for a more detailed discussion of Directive 82/884/EEC.

151. Directive 85/203/EEC Nitrogen Dioxide OJ L87, 27 Mar. 1985; formal implementation date: 1 Jan. 1987; mandatory compliance date: 1 July 1987. See: Haigh, ibid. chap. 6. 5 for a more detailed discussion of Directive 85/203/EEC.

152. Directive 92/72/EEC Ozone OJ L297, 13 Oct. 1992; formal implementation date: 21 Mar. 1994. See: Haigh, ibid. chap. 6. 15 for a more detailed discussion of Directive 92/72/EEC.

153. Haigh, ibid., chap. 6. 15, p. 2.

ozone is formed, thus making it possible for legislation for the control of this form of air pollution to be introduced in the future.

Ambient air quality in the UK is monitored under the National Air Quality Survey and also under the recently established Enhanced Urban Network. There are at present nine sites throughout the UK in the national urban air quality monitoring network, including Belfast as the only site in Northern Ireland. Sulphur dioxide has been monitored in Templemore Avenue, Belfast, for some years under the national network. However, a further two sites in Belfast have been established, at Lombard Street and at Queen's University, as part of the first phase of the Enhanced Urban Network. The Lombard Street site monitors a range of pollutants, including sulphur dioxide, ozone, nitrogen dioxide, particulate matter (PM10—an exhaust pollutant mainly caused by diesel oil), and carbon monoxide. Black smoke is about to be included in this range for the first time. The site at Queen's University measures a range of hydrocarbons, including benzene and 1,3-butadiene, which is primarily associated with air pollution generated by traffic (legislative control of air pollution from motor vehicle emissions is outlined in Part VIII of this chapter).[154]

Thus far, two studies have been conducted on atmospheric concentrations of nitrogen dioxide in the UK, one in 1986 and another more recently in 1991. The *Environment Service Report* 1991–1993 stated that the results from the fifteen sites tested in Northern Ireland showed an increase in the levels of nitrogen dioxide over those measured in 1986. However, levels of nitrogen dioxide in Northern Ireland did not exceed EC limit values on either occasion. A more general increase of 35 per cent in atmospheric concentrations of nitrogen dioxide throughout the UK was recorded, which reflects a 38 per cent increase in emissions from motor vehicles over the period between the two tests. A long-term study of atmospheric concentrations of nitrogen dioxide has recently been begun with the participation of ten Northern Ireland district councils. The essential purpose of the study is to determine long-term trends and the relative effectiveness of various control mechanisms that have been introduced to curtail motor vehicle emissions in particular.

Atmospheric concentrations of smoke and sulphur dioxide in urban air have been monitored in Northern Ireland since the nineteen-fifties under the aegis of the UK National Survey of Air Pollution. During the early years of this survey Northern Ireland was shown to have cleaner air than much of the rest of the UK. More recently, however, Northern Ireland has emerged as a problem region as far as pollution from smoke and sulphur dioxide is concerned, because of continued widespread reliance on the burning of coal for domestic heating. The *Environment Service Report* 1993–1995 estimated that some 70 per cent of homes in Northern Ireland are heated by solid fuel, compared with just 12 per cent in Great Britain.

Although smoke and sulphur dioxide are emitted into the air from both industrial and domestic sources, the *Environment Service Report* 1991–1993 points out that it is now clear that the greatest problem is presented by the cumulative effect of all low-level emissions from domestic coal fires. Industrial

---

154. Air quality bands have been drawn up by the DoE(NI) to ensure compliance with EC and international requirements; copies are available from the Environment Service, Air Legislation Section, note 121, supra.

emissions are regulated under the Alkali &c. Works Regulation Act 1906 (most polluting industrial processes) and the Clean Air (NI) Order 1981 (less polluting processes). However, the imposition of Smoke Control Orders under article 17 of the Clean Air (NI) Order 1981 (discussed in detail in Part I, section 5) is identified by the Environment Service as playing a central role in implementing the limit values imposed by Directive 80/779/EEC for smoke and sulphur dioxide in Northern Ireland. Air quality in Northern Ireland has improved, although not as quickly as in Great Britain, where the widespread use of natural gas has helped significantly. Current concentrations of smoke and sulphur dioxide in Belfast, Derry and Newry still approach and sometimes exceed the limit values laid down in Directive 80/779/EEC, particularly during winter, when the air is static. In this regard the Environment Service has commented that 'averaged over the year, or even the winter months, the situation is fair, but the short term peaks do give rise to concern.'[155]

The Government has provided financial support for the creation of smoke control areas in Northern Ireland and during 1993/94 provided £1 million in funding to district councils to aid their creation. In addition, new Regulations are about to be introduced which limit the sulphur content of domestic solid fuel to 2 per cent and strengthen controls on sales of fuels in smoke control areas.[156] The Warren Spring Laboratory has also been commissioned to investigate and propose a strategy for reducing smoke and sulphur dioxide levels in areas which have exceeded or are at risk of exceeding the limits laid down in Directive 80/779/EEC.

## Future developments in air quality control

On a national level, the UK's Sustainable Development Strategy[157] has identified the progressive improvement of urban air quality as one of the key challenges facing national environmental policy. Shortly after the publication of this strategy document the Government published a Consultation Paper, *Improving Air Quality*,[158] outlining the Government's views on how this challenge might be tackled. In January 1995 a second Consultation Paper, *Air Quality: Meeting the Challenge*,[159] was published, which took account of responses to *Improving Air Quality* and the recommendations concerning air quality set out in the Eighteenth Report of the Royal Commission on Environmental Pollution on Transport and the Environment and sets out the cornerstone of Government policy on air pollution control.

155. *Environment Service Report,* 1991–93, 34; *Environment Service Report,* 1993–95, pp 26–8.
156. See Part II, Section 5 (p. 85) of this chapter for further details of these proposed regulations.
157. *Sustainable Development: The UK Strategy* HMSO: London (Cm 2426 1994), chap.7.
158. DoE 1994. The paper was issued on behalf of the DoE, DoE(NI), and Scottish Office Environment Department.
159. DoE 1995. The paper was issued on behalf of the DoE, DoE(NI), and Scottish Office Environment Department. See also the report of the Select Committee on the Environment on Volatile Organic Compounds (vol. 1), London: HMSO 1994. The Government's response to the Select Committee report was published on 27 June 1995 and is available from the Public Enquiries Unit of the DoE, tel. (0171) 2760900. See also *The Future of Air Quality Monitoring Networks in the UK: A Consultation Paper,* London: DoE 1994, which is available from the Air Quality Division of the DoE, Romney House, 43 Marsham Street, London SW1P 3PY.

In effect, the Government proposes the development of an integrated strategy for the management and improvement of air quality designed to achieve sustainable improvements both in the short term and long term and within this to establish clear, identifiable goals. The details of this strategy will be published in the near future. However, *Air Quality: Meeting the Challenge* sets out the policies which will inform that strategy and the means by which it will be given effect. These policies deal with the following three areas:

(i) The introduction of a new framework of national air quality standards and targets, focused on the nine most significant pollutants, namely ozone, benzene, 1,3-butadiene, sulphur dioxide, carbon monoxide, nitrogen dioxide, particles, polycyclic aromatic hydrocarbons (PAHs), and lead.

(ii) The introduction of new systems of local air quality management based on 'air quality management areas' established in those areas where air quality targets are unlikely to be met.

(iii) The effective control of emissions, particularly from vehicles.

At EC level the Council is currently considering a Commission proposal[160] for a new framework Directive on ambient air quality assessment and management, which would replace and harmonise the existing air quality Directives. The draft Directive contains broadly similar proposals to those put forward by the Government Consultation Paper *Improving Air Quality* and essentially proposes the introduction of three types of air quality objectives, namely, a limit value, a guide value, and an alert threshold. The proposed Directive would regulate atmospheric concentrations of over twenty substances. However, not all substances would be subject to all three types of control from the outset. It is intended that further 'daughter Directives' would be introduced at a later stage to gradually include those substances not originally subject to all three types of control and the Internet.

### Public information on air quality

In October 1990 public information became available on ambient air quality for the UK as a whole. Information on levels of air pollution are provided twice daily through Ceefax (teletext) and a free telephone number—0800 556677. In addition, bulletins are provided to the press, radio and television forecasting centres and the Internet.

### Implementation in Northern Ireland

Directives 80/779/EEC, 82/884/EEC and 85/203/EEC have all been implemented in Northern Ireland[161] by the Air Quality Standards Regulations (NI) 1990,[162] as amended by the Air Quality Standards (Amendment) Regulations (NI) 1994[163] and the Air Quality Standards (Amendment) Regulations (NI) 1996.[164] Directive

---

160. COM (94) 109 final.
161. See Haigh, supra, chap. 6 for a detailed discussion of the implementation of the Air Quality Directives in Great Britain.
162. SR No. 145.
163. SR No. 339.
164. SR No. 23.

92/72/EEC has been implemented in Northern Ireland by the Ozone Monitoring and Information Regulations 1994.[165] Each of these implementing provisions will be discussed in turn.

## The Air Quality Standards Regulations (NI) 1990 (as amended)

### Limit values for sulphur dioxide and suspended particulates in the atmosphere

Regulation 3(1) provides that the DoE(NI) must take appropriate measures to ensure that the concentrations of sulphur dioxide and suspended particulates (smoke) in the atmosphere, measured in accordance with regulation 4 (below), do not exceed the limit values given in Annex I to Directive 80/779/EEC. Regulation 3(2), which temporarily exempted Belfast, Derry and Newry and Mourne from the application of the limit values imposed by regulation 3(1), is revoked by the Air Quality Standards (Amendment) Regulations (NI) 1994. Regulation 4(1) requires that the DoE(NI) must ensure that stations for measuring the concentrations of sulphur dioxide and suspended particulates in the atmosphere are established and that these concentrations are measured in accordance with Annexes III and V to Directive 80/779/EEC. Regulation 4(2) requires that the measuring stations must be established at sites where pollution is thought to be greatest and where the measured concentrations are representative of local conditions, in particular in Belfast, Derry, Newry and Mourne, and in zones where the limit values referred to in regulation 3(1) are likely to be approached or exceeded.

### Limit value for lead in the air

Regulation 5 requires the DoE(NI) to take the necessary measures to ensure that the mean annual value for the concentration of lead in the air, measured in accordance with Regulation 6 (below), does not exceed the limit value of 2 micrograms of lead per cubic metre, expressed as an annual mean concentration. Regulation 6(1) requires that the DoE(NI) ensure that any sampling stations for measuring the concentrations of lead in the air which may be necessary to comply with Directive 82/884/EEC are installed and operated and that those stations calculate the mean value in accordance with the Annex to that Directive. Regulation 6(2) provides that such sampling stations must be installed at sites where individuals may be exposed to lead in the air continually for a long period and where, in the opinion of the DoE(NI), the limit value specified in regulation 5 is likely to be exceeded.

### Limit value for nitrogen dioxide in the atmosphere

Regulation 7, as amended by the Air Quality Standards (Amendment) Regulations (NI) 1994 and 1996, requires the DoE(NI) to take the necessary measures to ensure throughout Northern Ireland that the concentration of nitrogen dioxide in the atmosphere, measured in accordance with regulation 8 (below), does not exceed the limit value as defined in the first indent of Article 2 of Directive 85/203/EEC. Regulation 8(1) requires the DoE(NI) to ensure that any measuring

---

165. SR No. 440.

stations for measuring the concentration of nitrogen dioxide in the atmosphere which may be necessary to comply with the terms of Directive 85/203/EEC are established and that those stations measure the concentrations of nitrogen dioxide in the atmosphere in accordance with paragraph 4 of Annex III and IV to that Directive. Regulation 8(2) requires that those measuring stations must be established at sites selected in accordance with paragraphs 1–3 of Annex III to Directive 85/203/EEC and in particular in zones where the limit value referred to in regulation 7 is or is likely to be exceeded.

*Smoke control areas*

Regulation 9(1)–(8) empowers the DoE(NI) to direct district councils to prepare proposals for orders under article 17 of the Clean Air (NI) Order 1981[166] in order to comply with the requirements of Directive 80/779/EEC on air quality limit values and guide values for sulphur dioxide and suspended particulates. The terms of article 17 are outlined in Part I, section 5 of this chapter. The DoE(NI) itself has produced proposals for two sets of Regulations designed to contribute to the implementation of Directive 80/779/EEC concerning sulphur dioxide and suspended particulates (smoke).[167] The first introduces a ban on the sale of unauthorised fuels in smoke control areas, while the second imposes limits on the sulphur content of solid domestic fuel. Both sets of draft Regulations are scheduled to come into force in the near future.

**The Ozone Monitoring and Information Regulations 1994**

These Regulations require the Secretary of State to designate or establish measuring stations for the purpose of monitoring concentrations of ozone and also to set out the method to be used for measuring those concentrations. The Secretary of State is also required to take the necessary steps to inform the public where certain ozone concentration thresholds are exceeded. Ozone monitoring is carried out on a UK-wide basis by the DoE. Ozone is currently monitored in Northern Ireland at two locations, Lough Navar since 1987 and Belfast since 1992. Measurement is made using an ultraviolet absorption analyser, which calculates the absorption of UV light at a wavelength of 254 nanometres by ozone.[168] Bulletins to the press, radio and television forecasting centres, including health advice, are also arranged by the DoE.[169]

---

166. SI 1981/158. The terms of the Clean Air (NI) Order 1981 are discussed in detail in Part I of this chapter; the terms of art. 17 concerning smoke control areas are outlined in Part I, Section 5.
167. Both sets of draft Regulations are addressed in Part I, section 5, p. 85 of this chapter.
168. Standards and guidelines on ozone have been issued by the World Health Organisation, the EC, and the DoE. Copies of these standards are available from the DoE(NI), Environment Service, Air Legislation Section. A new air quality standard for ozone in the UK has been recommended by the Expert Panel on Air Quality Standards. This is based on the exposures likely to be harmful to human health and the potential for short-term respiratory symptoms. The standard is 50 ppb as a running eight-hour average. It is intended that monitoring data will be reported in terms of the number of days in which the standard is exceeded at any one site.
169. For further information in this regard contact the Public Enquiries Unit of the DoE, tel. (0171) 2760900.

# PART *VIII* MOTOR VEHICLE POLLUTION

In recent years it has been accepted that motor vehicle emissions are major contributors to air pollution and also that the effective control of such emissions is crucial to the attainment and maintenance of clean air. As with many areas of air pollution control, the regulatory framework which has evolved for the purposes of combating air pollution from motor vehicle emissions has been developed at EC rather than at national level.

In tackling this form of air pollution the Community has employed 'product standards' as the principal mechanism of control—in other words, requiring products to be constructed or constituted so as to comply with specified technical standards. Product standards have been used to prevent and control motor vehicle air pollution in two ways. On the one hand the EC has required that new and existing vehicles (and their components) be constructed and used so as to comply with technical standards for vehicle emissions, while on the other hand it has regulated the content and composition of the fuel used in vehicles. Although product standards have been used as the primary regulatory mechanism, it should be noted that financial or market-based instruments have also been introduced more recently as an additional means of combating motor vehicle air pollution. For example, member states have been allowed to introduce differences in the price of leaded and unleaded petrol as a means of encouraging the use of less-polluting unleaded petrol and, also, to introduce tax incentives to encourage motorists to install emission-reducing equipment in their vehicles, such as catalytic converters. It should be said, however, that while market-based instruments are likely to become a more central element in the EC's approach to the control of vehicle pollution in the future, for the present they remain a relatively minor part of its strategy in this context.

The remainder of this Part is divided into two sections. Section 1 deals with product standards concerning vehicle construction and use, while section 2 addresses product standards concerning fuel composition.

## SECTION 1. MOTOR VEHICLE CONSTRUCTION AND USE

Over the years the EC has adopted numerous Directives setting out technical standards for the construction and use of motor vehicles. However, only those Directives which introduce technical standards for vehicle emissions are relevant in the context of air pollution.

The first vehicle emission standards were laid down in 1970 by Directive 70/220/EEC,[170] which imposed limits on specified emissions from passenger cars. Over the years Directive 70/220/EEC has been amended on a number of occasions, with each amending Directive imposing more stringent controls on emissions from passenger cars while also expanding the range of emissions subject to regulation. In addition the EC has adopted a number of Directives which impose limit values on emissions from commercial and agricultural vehicles. The early emission standards were introduced primarily to prevent the creation of

---

170. OJ L76, 6 Apr. 1970.

barriers to the free movement of goods (and thereby distortions in competition) caused by the imposition of more stringent emission standards by individual member states. However, as the Community's environmental policy developed and concern as to the effects of motor vehicle pollution increased during the nineteen-eighties, Directives concerning vehicle emission standards became an important instrument of environmental protection. By the late nineteen-eighties Community policy concerning vehicle emissions had shifted from the imposition of optional emission standards to the imposition of mandatory standards, intended to be at least as severe as those now in force in the United States and designed to achieve total harmonisation of standards throughout the Community.

The first stage in the strategy to combat air pollution from motor vehicles is now in operation. Mandatory limit values, applying uniformly throughout the EC, have applied to all new vehicle types since 1 July 1992; such emission standards have also applied to all new registrations since 1 January 1993. As a result, EC environmental standards are now on a par with those applying in the United States, Sweden, and Switzerland. The imposition of emission standards has thus far proved successful. Emissions of pollutants have fallen continuously since 1970—by 85 per cent in the case of emissions from small vehicles and by 90 per cent for heavy vehicles.[171] The second stage of EC controls over vehicle emissions came into effect on 1 January 1996, bringing EC emission standards below American targets for 1994.[172]

In essence, the emission standards Directives provide that new models must be constructed so as to comply with technical standards concerning emissions before they can be granted 'type approval'. The term 'type approval' is used to describe the approval which a vehicle manufacturer must obtain for a new model before introducing it to the market, 'type approval' essentially meaning that the prototype of the new model conforms to specified design and construction standards. In addition, these Directives require existing vehicles to be maintained and used so as to comply with specified emission standards. A series of Type Approval Regulations and Construction and Use Regulations have been enacted over the years to implement the emission standards laid down in these Directives. The remainder of this section will briefly outline the standards which have been laid down in the vehicle emission Directives and the Regulations that have been introduced to implement their provisions in Northern Ireland.

### EC Directives concerning vehicle emission standards

#### *Passenger vehicle emission standards*

- Directive 70/220/EEC[173] introduced emission limit values for carbon monoxide and unburnt hydrocarbons from vehicles with petrol engines (excluding tractors and public works vehicles). It has been amended by the following Directives:

---

171. Dr Martin Bangemann, Vice-President of the European Commission, opening speech at a European symposium on 'Auto Emissions 2000', 'Stage 2000' of the European Regulations on Air Polluting Emissions of Motor Vehicles. Office for Official Publications of EC: Luxembourg (21 Sept. 1992).

172. Ibid.

173. OJ L76, 6 Apr. 1970. See: Haigh, supra, chap. 6. 8 for a more detailed discussion of Directive 70/220/EEC and its amending Directives.

- Directive 72/306/EEC[174] set limits on emissions of soot from diesel-engined vehicles other than tractors and public works vehicles.
- Directive 74/290/EEC[175] reduced further levels of carbon monoxide and hydrocarbon.
- Directive 77/102/EEC[176] introduced limits for nitrogen oxides.
- Directive 78/665/EEC[177] reduced emission limit values for CO, HC and NOx.
- Directive 83/351/EEC[178] further reduced limit values for CO, HC and NOx by 20–30 per cent and enlarged the scope of the Directive to cover diesel-engined vehicles, but did not set any emission limits for such vehicles.
- Directive 88/76/EEC[179] introduced emission limits based on engine size rather than vehicle weight, as was done in Directive 72/220. Different implementation dates for new registrations and new models are set out. It was a first step towards parity with American vehicle emission standards.
- Directive 88/436/EEC[180] introduced limit values for overall particulate (smoke) emissions from diesel-engined cars. Limits are based on mass rather than opacity of smoke.
- Directive 89/491/EEC[181] introduced various minor amendments some of which concern the use of unleaded petrol.
- Directive 89/458/EEC[182] introduced more stringent 'second-stage' limit values for emissions from smaller petrol and diesel-engined cars, requiring use of regulated three-way catalytic converters. It brought the EC into line with American and Japanese emission standards.
- Directive 91/441/EEC[183] extended emission limit values, which were introduced for small cars by Directive 89/458, to all new models and all new registrations. New-model cars were to be fitted with a three-way catalytic converter by 1 July 1992, and new registrations by 1 January 1993. The Directive also introduced a range of new requirements concerning emissions of carbon monoxide, VOCs, the durability of anti-pollution devices, improvements in test procedures, the introduction of more stringent 'second-stage' smoke emission limits for diesel-engined cars. The Council was committed to imposing even stricter emission limits on carbon monoxide, hydrocarbons, nitrogen oxides, VOCs and smoke by the end of 1993, to come into effect by the beginning of 1996. There was also a commitment to introduce new limits on carbon dioxide emissions from vehicles by the end of 1992, to come into effect by the beginning of 1993.

---

174. OJ L190, 20 Aug. 1972.
175. OJ L159, 15 June 1974.
176. OJ L32, 3 Feb. 1977.
177. OJ L223, 14 Aug. 1978.
178. OJ L197, 20 July 1983.
179. OJ L36, 9 Feb. 1988.
180. OJ L214, 6 Aug. 1988.
181. OJ L238, 15 Aug. 1989.
182. OJ L226 3 Aug. 1989.
183. OJ L242, 30 Aug. 1991.

*Commercial vehicles*

- Directive 88/77/EEC[184] introduced emission limit values for carbon monoxide, hydrocarbons and nitrogen oxides for diesel-engined commercial vehicles over 3.5 tonnes. This Directive is amended by the following two Directives:
  - Directive 91/542/EEC[185] which phased in over two stages more strict standards for emissions of carbon monoxide, hydrocarbons and nitrogen oxides from commercial vehicles (new models and new registrations). It also introduced smoke emission limits for commercial vehicles.
  - Directive 93/59/EEC[186] extended to light commercial vehicles (under 3.5 tonnes), emission limits equivalent to those applying to passenger cars under Directive 91/441. New models must comply by 1 October 1993, all new vehicles by 1 October 1994.

*Diesel engines for tractors*

- Directive 77/537/EEC[187] established limits on the opacity of diesel emissions from the engines of wheeled agricultural and forestry tractors.

*Testing vehicle emissions*

- Directive 92/55/EEC[188] laid down requirements for vehicle emission tests in roadworthiness tests.

*Type Approval Regulations in Northern Ireland*

The whole area of type approval is very technical and is governed by a vast network of Regulations. Given the technical nature of this area, it is intended only to explain the basic idea behind type approval and the essential framework of legislation operating in the area.

Put simply, there are two tiers of type approval operating in Northern Ireland. On the one hand there is the EC type approval system, and on the other hand there is the Northern Ireland type approval system. In effect, the Northern Ireland system covers those vehicles which fall outside the EC type approval system, namely, single vehicle, low volume, etc. In addition it should be noted that there is no type approval system in operation in Northern Ireland for heavier vehicles. It should also be noted that although there is provision in Northern Ireland law for type approval, the absence of motor manufacturing industries in Northern Ireland means that type approval has no practical effect.

The basic principle of EC type approval was laid down in Directive 70/156/EEC.[189] This was further amended by Directive 87/403/EEC[190] and more recently by Directive 92/53/EEC.[191] Essentially these Directives require member

---

184. OJ L36, 9 Feb. 1988.
185. OJ L295, 25 Oct. 1991.
186. OJ L186, 28 July 1993.
187. OJ L220, 29 Aug. 1977.
188. OJ L225, 10 Aug. 1992.
189. OJ L42, 23 Feb. 1970.
190. OJ L220, 8 Aug. 1987.
191. OJ L225, 10 Aug. 1992.

states to establish a system for granting EC type approval for light passenger vehicles. The Directives prohibit member states from registering or permitting the sale or entry into service of such vehicles unless they are accompanied by a valid EC certificate of conformity; they also prevent member states refusing the sale or entry into service of vehicles with a valid EC certificate of conformity. Similar provisions are made for motor vehicle parts. In order to receive EC type approval such models must comply with various EC standards, including EC vehicle emission standards.

These Directives are implemented for the UK as a whole by the Motor Vehicles (EC Type Approval) Regulations 1992;[192] the requirements laid down by the type approval Directives take effect under these Regulations from 1 January 1996. Before the introduction of the Motor Vehicles (EC Type Approval) Regulations 1992, the Motor Vehicles (Type Approval) (EEC) Regulations (NI) 1987,[193] as amended, governed the system of type approval for light passenger vehicles in Northern Ireland. The 1987 Regulations and their amending Regulations have been revoked in two stages by the Motor Vehicles (Type Approval) (EEC) (Revocation) Regulations (NI) 1994[194] and the Motor Vehicles (EC Type Approval) Regulations 1992.[195] As a result of these revocations a Northern Ireland manufacturer applying for the type approval of a light passenger vehicle must now apply to the Secretary of State under the 1992 Regulations, which apply to the whole of the UK.

Any passenger vehicles which fall outside the scope of Directive 92/53/EEC (i.e. single vehicle, low volume, etc.) are still required to obtain type approval under the Northern Ireland type approval system; the specific standards are set out in the Motor Vehicles (Type Approval) Regulations (NI) 1985.[196] The Road Traffic (Type Approval) (NI) Order 1985[197] introduces a specific system of type approval for motor vehicles for Northern Ireland.[198] The 1985 Order empowers the DoE(NI) to make type approval regulations prescribing requirements concerning the design, construction, equipment and marking of motor vehicles (Regulations adopted pursuant to these powers are outlined below). Article 31A(1) provides that where the DoE(NI) is satisfied, on an application made to it by the manufacturer of a motor vehicle to which type approval Regulations made by the DoE(NI) apply, and after examination of the motor vehicle:

(a) that the motor vehicle complies with the relevant type approval requirements; and

(b) that adequate arrangements have been made to secure that other motor vehicles purporting to conform with that motor vehicle in the

---

192. SI 1992/3107.
193. SR No. 306.
194. SR No. 240.
195. SI 1992/3107.
196. SR No. 294.
197. SI 1985/755.
198. The amendments to the 1981 Order are made without prejudice to existing powers contained in art. 28, Part IV of that Order. The terms of the type approval system are set out in art. 3 of the 1985 Order. The 1985 Order requires that the terms of reg. 3 be inserted into the 1981 Order; this results in the insertion of new art. 31A, 31B, 31C, 31D and 31E after art. 31 of the 1981 Order.

relevant aspects of design, construction, equipment and marking will
so conform in all respects or with such variations as may be
permitted,

the DoE(NI) may approve that motor vehicle as a type vehicle and, if so, will issue
a 'Type Approval Certificate' stating that the motor vehicle complies with the
relevant Type Approval Requirements and specifying the permitted variations
from the type motor vehicle for motor vehicles so conforming in all respects and
for vehicles so conforming with any such variations. Once a type approval
certificate has been issued to a manufacturer, the manufacturer may issue a
'certificate of conformity' in respect of each motor vehicle manufactured by him
which conforms with the type motor vehicle, stating that it conforms with the type
motor vehicle in relevant matters of design, construction, etc. For the purposes of
type approval, the term 'motor vehicle' also includes vehicle parts. The
requirements of the type approval system are applicable before, whether or not
they are applicable after, the motor vehicles are used on the road. Offences created
by the 1985 Order include the use on the road and the sale or supply of motor
vehicles which do not have an appropriate certificate in compliance with the
requirements laid down. Levels of fines incurred for such offences are listed in
regulation 5 of the 1985 Order; these provisions are inserted into Schedule 4 to the
1981 Order.

The 1985 Order also makes provision for appealing determinations of the
DoE(NI) in relation to applications for type approval and lays down powers of
entry and inspection for authorised officers to test conformity with type approval
requirements.[199] The Motor Vehicles (Type Approval) Regulations (NI) 1985,[200]
as amended, govern type approval for passenger and dual-purpose vehicles in
Northern Ireland. They have been adopted by the DoE(NI) pursuant to its powers
under regulation 3 of the Road Traffic (Type Approval) (NI) Order 1985.
Regulation 4 of the 1985 Regulations sets out the application procedure for type
approval for such vehicles. The 1985 Regulations require that type approval only
be given to new models which are designed in compliance with specified
standards, including the EC vehicle emission standards laid down in the Directives
listed above. Schedule 1 to the Motor Vehicle (Type Approval) Regulations (NI)
1985 contains a detailed table of type approval standards for numerous aspects of
motor vehicle construction.[201]

---

199. The Motor Vehicles (Type Approval and Approval Marks) (Fees) Regulations (NI) 1992 (SR No.
      227) prescribe the fees payable for the partial, consecutive and complete examination of vehicles
      or parts of vehicles and for the issue of documents in respect of vehicles to which the Northern
      Ireland Regulations apply. The 1992 Regulations revoke and replace the Motor Vehicles (Type
      Approval and Approval Marks) (Fees) Regulations (NI) 1990 (SR No. 220).
200. SR No. 294.
201. The following is a list the Regulations which have amended the provisions of Sch. 1 concerning
      vehicle emission standards: the Motor Vehicle (Type Approval) (Amendment) Regulations (NI)
      1987 (SR No. 389); the Motor Vehicle (Type Approval) (Amendment) Regulations (NI) 1988 (SR
      No. 405); the Motor Vehicle (Type Approval) (Amendment) Regulations (NI) 1990 (SR No. 84);
      the Motor Vehicle (Type Approval) (Amendment) Regulations (NI) 1992 (SR No. 508); the
      Motor Vehicle (Type Approval) (Amendment) Regulations (NI) 1995 (SR No. 38). The Motor
      Vehicle (Type Approval) (Amendment) Regulations (NI) 1995 revoke the Motor Vehicle (Type
      Approval) (Amendment No. 2) Regulations (NI) 1990 (SR No. 312).

## Construction and Use Regulations

The Motor Vehicles (Construction and Use) Regulations (NI) 1989,[202] as amended, govern the construction and maintenance of both passenger and goods vehicles in Northern Ireland. These Regulations have been adopted by the DoE(NI) pursuant to articles 28(1), 29(2), 214(1) and 218(1) of the Road Traffic (NI) Order 1981[203] and are enforced through the Motor Vehicle Testing Regulations (NI) 1989,[204] which consolidate, with amendments, the Motor Vehicle Testing Regulations (NI) 1975. The Motor Vehicle Testing (Fees) (Amendment) Regulations (NI) 1991[205] regulate fees payable for such tests and revoke the Motor Vehicle Testing (Fees) (Amendment) Regulations (NI) 1990.[206]

As with the type approval Regulations, these Regulations set out standards for the construction and use of numerous aspects of motor vehicles. Only Regulation 63 is of relevance to the issue of air pollution. Regulation 63(1)–(12) sets out a series of rules governing the construction, maintenance and use of vehicles on roads as far as emissions of smoke, visible vapour, grit, sparks, ashes, cinders or oily substances are concerned. These rules are expressed in relation to the provisions of Tables I and II of regulation 63, which require compliance with the EC vehicle emission standards listed above. In addition, Regulation 63 creates various exemptions for vehicles in particular circumstances. The 1989 Regulations have been amended on several occasions. However, Regulation 63 of the 1989 Regulations has only been amended by the following measures:[207]

- the Motor Vehicles (Construction and Use) (Amendment No. 2) Regulations (NI) 1991[208]
- the Motor Vehicles (Construction and Use) (Amendment No. 4) Regulations (NI) 1992[209]
- the Motor Vehicles (Construction and Use) (Amendment) Regulations (NI) 1993[210]
- the Motor Vehicles (Construction and Use) (Amendment) Regulations (NI) 1994.[211]

## SECTION 2. CONTROLS ON THE CONTENT AND COMPOSITION OF FUEL

As already stated, the EC has imposed controls on the content and composition of fuel as a means of reducing and preventing air pollution. In this regard the

---

202. SR No. 299.
203. SI 1981/154.
204. SR No. 234.
205. SR No. 357.
206. SR No. 223.
207. The DoE(NI) Transport Division has collated the amendments to reg. 63. However, because the DoE(NI) does not publish consolidations of single regulations, this has not been published. Copies of the consolidation are, however, available from the DoE(NI) Transport Division, Transport Legislation, Room G-31, Clarence Court, 10–18 Adelaide Street, Belfast BT2 8GB; tel. (01232) 540059; fax (01232) 540020.
208. SR No. 420.
209. SR No. 509.
210. SR No. 39.
211. SR No. 231.

Community has introduced Directives which lay down maximum content limits for lead and benzene in petrol and for sulphur in gas oils. The term 'gas oil' includes diesel oil which is used for motor vehicles but also light fuel oils used for household heating and cooking purposes. The term 'gas oil' does not include the heavier 'fuel oil' used in power stations and for industrial heating; as yet the member states have been unable to reach agreement on a draft Directive for fuel oil.

### Controls on lead and benzene in petrol

Directive 85/210/EEC[212] lays down a maximum lead and benzene content for petrol. Essentially the Directive requires member states to ensure the availability and balanced distribution of leaded petrol, defined by the Directive as containing between 0.4 and 0.15 grams of lead per litre. Member states are also required to reduce the maximum lead content of leaded petrol to 0.15 grams per litre once they consider it appropriate to do so. In addition, they are required to ensure that premium-grade unleaded petrol is available and also distributed in a balanced manner throughout their territories from 1 October 1989 (or before that date if they choose to). Unleaded petrol is required to be clearly labelled at the pump and must have a minimum octane number of 85.0 and a minimum research octane number of 95.0. Member states are also required to encourage the use of unleaded petrol in vehicles. Finally, the Directive requires that as of 1 October 1989 the benzene content of both leaded and unleaded petrol should not be in excess of 5.0 per cent by volume. Provision is also made for exemptions from these limits where a sudden change in the supply of oil or petroleum products occurs. The Commission must be informed of the use of a higher limit, and the exemption may only be used for a maximum of four months. Directive 87/416/EEC allows member states to actually ban the marketing of 'regular' leaded petrol; this Directive has not been implemented in the UK, because such petrol is not widely used in the UK.

### *Implementation in Northern Ireland*

Directive 85/210/EEC is implemented by the Motor Fuel (Composition and Content) Regulations 1994[213] for the UK as a whole, adopted by the Secretary of State for Transport under sections 30(1) and (3) and 63(1) of the Clean Air Act 1993 (c. 11). Directive 87/416/EEC is not implemented in the UK. The 1994 Regulations revoke and replace the Motor Fuel (Lead Content of Petrol) Regulations 1981,[214] as amended (which applied throughout the UK).

---

212. OJ L96, 3 Jan. 1985. This Directive replaces Directive 78/611/EEC (OJ L197, 22 July 1978) and is amended by Directive 87/416/EEC (OJ L225, 13 Aug. 1987). Member states are required to complete formal implementation of Directive 85/210/EEC by 1 Jan. 1986. See Haigh, supra, chap. 6. 7 for a more detailed discussion of the requirements and development of this Directive.
213. SI 1994/2295.
214. SI 1981/1523.

## Sulphur content of gas oil

Directive 87/219/EEC[215] requires that the sulphur content of gas oil must not exceed 0.3 per cent. However, a lower sulphur content of 0.2 per cent may be required by member states, firstly, where it is necessary to meet air quality standards laid down in Directive 80/779/EEC, or secondly, where it is necessary because of the damage caused to the environment or to the national heritage by total sulphur dioxide emissions. Directive 93/12/EEC[216] amends Directive 87/219/EEC in that it introduces a limit of 0.2 per cent sulphur by weight for all diesel fuels from 1 October 1994.

### Implementation in Northern Ireland

Directive 87/219/EEC is implemented by the Motor Fuel (Composition and Content) Regulations 1994[217] for the UK as a whole and the Oil Fuel (Sulphur Content of Gas Oil) Regulations (NI) 1991.[218] Each of these provisions will be outlined in turn.

### The Motor Fuel (Composition and Content) Regulations 1994[219]

Before the introduction of the 1994 Regulations, EC Directives concerning the lead content of petrol and the sulphur content of diesel fuel were implemented by separate Regulations, which applied throughout the UK, namely, the Motor Fuel (Sulphur Content of Gas Oil) Regulations 1976,[220] the Motor Fuel (Sulphur Content of Gas Oil) (Amendment) Regulations 1990,[221] the Motor Fuel (Lead Content of Petrol) Regulations 1981,[222] the Motor Fuel (Lead Content of Petrol) (Amendment) Regulations 1985,[223] and the Motor Fuel (Lead Content of Petrol) (Amendment) Regulations 1989.[224] All of these have been revoked and replaced by the Motor Fuel (Composition and Content) Regulations 1994, which now control the lead, benzene and sulphur content of motor fuels (defined as including petrol and diesel fuels) for the UK as a whole. Subject to the provisions of

---

215. OJ L91, 3 Apr. 1987; formal compliance: 1 Oct. 1994. See: Haigh, supra, chap. 6. 3, for a more detailed discussion of the development and requirements of this Directive. It should also be noted that Directive 87/219/EEC entirely replaces Directive 75/716/EEC (OJ L 307 27 Nov. 1975) which was the first EC Directive adopted in this regard.
216. OJ L74, 27 Mar. 1993.
217. SI 1994/2295. The 1994 Regulations revoke and replace the Motor Fuel (Sulphur Content of Gas Oil) Regulations 1976 (SI 1976/1989), as amended, which applied throughout the UK.
218. SR No. 235. The 1991 Northern Ireland Regulations revoke and replace the Oil Fuel (Sulphur Content of Gas Oil) Regulations (NI) 1979 (SR No. 21).
219. An assessment of the cost of compliance with the 1994 Regulations has been prepared, and copies can be obtained from the Department of Transport, Room C19/07, 2 Marsham Street, London SW1 3EB. Copies of the Institute of Petroleum publications referred to in Sch. 1 to these Regulations may be obtained from the Institute of Petroleum, 61 Cavendish Street, London W1M 8AR. Copies of the ASTM publications also referred to in Sch. 1 to these Regulations may be obtained from ASTM European Office, 27–29 Knowl Piece, Wilbury Way, Hitchin, Hertfordshire SG4 0SX.
220. SI 1976/1989.
221. SI 1990/1097.
222. SI 1981/1523.
223. SI 1985/1728.
224. SI 1989/547.

Regulation 4 (and Schedule 1), regulation 5 lays down requirements for the composition and content of leaded, unleaded and high-octane (super) unleaded petrols and for diesel fuel which are based on specified paragraphs contained in the following British Standard Specifications (or their equivalent in accordance with regulation 11):

- BS 4040: 1988 —    BS for leaded petrol, as amended on 29 June 1990 by Amendment no. 1
- BS EN 228: 1993 — BS for unleaded petrol (gasoline)
- BS 7800: 1992 —    BS for high-octane (super) unleaded petrol
- BS EN 590: 1993 — BS for automotive diesel fuel.

Some of the requirements set out in regulation 5 vary according to the time of year when the fuel is distributed or sold; and all these requirements must be read in the light of the rules set out in regulation 4 concerning the effect of these standards. Regulations 6 and 7 prohibit the distribution of non-complying fuel from a refinery or from an import terminal. Similarly, the sale of such fuel by retail at a filling station is prohibited. Regulation 8 sets out a number of exemptions from these prohibitions, including the distribution or sale of motor fuel for the purposes of certain tests or experiments concerning motor fuel, for use in an aircraft (other than a hovercraft), for use in vehicles constructed or adapted for use solely in competition or trials, or motor fuel which is in the process of being manufactured or blended. In addition, regulation 8(3) provides that it is not unlawful for a person to distribute or sell non-complying motor fuel if the failure to comply with the motor fuel composition and content requirements set out in these regulations is due to a mistake, to reliance on information supplied to that person, to the act or default of another person, or to an accident or some other cause beyond that person's control. However, regulation 8(3) also requires that the person in question must have taken all reasonable precautions and exercised all due diligence to avoid such failure by himself or any person under his control. Finally, regulation 9 empowers the Secretary of State to grant exemptions to specified persons or classes of person.

Regulation 12(1)–(4) sets out the position concerning motor fuel which was obtained before 1 October 1994, when the 1994 Regulations came into force. Regulation 12(3) provides that the Regulations revoked by the 1994 Regulations (listed above) will continue to have effect in relation to a person as regards motor fuel which came into his possession before 1 October 1994. Regulations 6 and 7 of the 1994 Regulations will not apply to such fuel. Regulation 12(4) sets out the position for a person who sells motor fuel by retail at a filling station. It provides that motor fuel which came into the possession of such a person before 1 October 1994 will continue to be regarded as having come into his possession before that date, despite the fact that it has been mixed with one or two deliveries of motor fuel which were made to him on or after that date. However, motor fuel will be regarded as having come into his possession after 1 October 1994 if it has been mixed with three or more deliveries of motor fuel which were made to him on or after that date.

*Oil Fuel (Sulphur Content of Gas Oil) Regulations (NI) 1991*

These Regulations were adopted by the DoE(NI) under articles 2(2) and 55(1), (3), (5) and (6) of the Pollution Control and Local Government (NI) Order 1978,[225] which require the DoE(NI) to consult representatives of oil producers and users of oil, representatives of manufacturers and users of plant and equipment for which oil fuel is used and also persons considered by the DoE(NI) to be conversant with the problems of air pollution. Regulation 3(2) prohibits the use, or causing or permitting to be used, in a furnace or engine to which these Regulations apply, gas oil[226] having a sulphur content which exceeds 0.3 per cent by weight when tested by the appropriate method,[227] as described in Regulation 4. The principal change introduced by these Regulations is the reduction of the maximum permitted amount of sulphur from 0.5 per cent by weight to 0.3 per cent by weight, as required by Directive 87/219/EEC.[228]

The prohibition in the 1991 Regulations applies to any furnace or engine *except:* (i) a furnace or engine used in a ship or (ii) a diesel engine used to propel a motor vehicle as defined in article 2(2) of the Road Traffic (NI) Order 1981.[229] Regulation 5 sets out a number of exemptions to the prohibition contained in Regulation 3. They include the use of gas oil already in the user's possession on 31 December 1988 which has a sulphur content of less than 0.5 per cent by weight when tested by the appropriate method; the production, treatment or use of gas oil which is in the course of being manufactured, processed or blended in the refining industry; in certain circumstances the use of gas oil in the fuel tank of a motor vehicle entering Northern Ireland from a state which is not a member of the EC; and the use of gas oil for the purpose of various types of tests or experiments in connection with the composition of oil fuel or the design or performance of any article which uses or is intended to use oil fuel or components or lubricants thereof. Regulation 6 also empowers the DoE(NI) to grant exemptions pursuant to Article 2.3 of Directive 87/219/EEC[230] on the approximation of national laws concerning the sulphur content of certain liquid fuels.

Regulation 7 of the 1991 Regulations reduces penalties incurred for violation of the prohibition in regulation 3. Where regulation 3 is violated, liability to

---

225. SI 1978/1049.
226. Reg. 2 defines gas oil as any oil fuel of which at least 85 per cent by volume, including distillation losses, distils at a temperature of 350°C when tested by the methods described in the first revision (Feb. 1985) of British Standard BS 2000, part 123: 1985, entitled 'British Standard Methods of Test for Petroleum and its Products, part 123, Distillation of Petroleum Products', which came into effect on 28 Feb. 1985.
227. Reg. 4(*a*) and (*b*) laid down the appropriate method of testing required by the Regulations. For the purposes of reg. 3(2) and reg. 5(*a*)(i), gas oil is tested by the appropriate method when: (i) it is tested by the method described in the Institute of Petroleum document *Sulphur Petroleum Products by Energy-Dispersive X-Ray Fluorescence (Non-Dispersive X-Ray Fluorescence)* published by the Institute of Petroleum as designation IP 336/81 (reapproved 1986) and (ii) the results of any such test are interpreted in accordance with the rules given in the first revision (Feb. 1981) of the British Standard entitled *Method for Determination and Application of Precision Data in Relation to Methods of Test for Petroleum Products,* published under the numbers BS 4306: 1981 and ISO 4259-1979, which came into effect on 27 Feb. 1981.
228. OJ L91, 30 Mar. 1987.
229. SI 1981/154.
230. OJ L91, 30 Mar. 1987.

conviction on indictment is excluded, and the maximum fine on summary conviction is reduced to £100.

## PART IX THE INTERNATIONAL DIMENSION

Although this chapter has focused primarily on the domestic legal controls imposed on atmospheric pollution, the most difficult problems arising in this context concern problems of global atmospheric pollution. In this regard, three principal phenomena can be identified, namely, acid rain, global warming or climate change, and the depletion of the ozone layer. It is impossible within the confines of this chapter to examine all three in detail; however, it must be emphasised that global atmospheric pollution poses some of the most intractable legal, political and economic problems currently facing the international community.

Put simply, acid rain is acid deposition caused by emissions of sulphur dioxide and nitrogen oxides into the atmosphere, primarily from electricity generation stations and road transport. Although it has long been known that emissions of sulphur dioxide have the capacity to harm local environments, the decision to remedy local pollution by means of building taller chimneys, which would disperse such emissions into the upper atmosphere, resulted in the 'export' of pollution. In effect, while the areas immediately surrounding the plants were protected, these emissions had the capacity to travel considerable distances, often across national boundaries, and to be deposited as acid rain, resulting in serious damage to vegetation and aquatic environments.

The UK is a major exporter of sulphur dioxide. Given the international nature of pollution from acid rain, this problem has had to be tackled on an international and regional level. Although the UK and EC have both signed the Geneva Convention on Long-Range Transboundary Air Pollution and its attendant protocols, more stringent and effective controls in this regard have been adopted by the EC itself. Emissions from power plants have been controlled under the Framework Directive 84/360/EEC on industrial air pollution and the Large Combustion Plant Directive 88/609/EEC. More stringent controls will be introduced under the forthcoming Integrated Pollution Prevention and Control Directive. The controls imposed under these provisions and their implementation in Northern Ireland are discussed in detail in Parts II and III of this chapter. In addition, the EC has been the prime mover in introducing more stringent controls on emissions from motor vehicles; such controls and their implementation in Northern Ireland are discussed in Part VIII of this chapter.[231]

The problem of global warming or climate change poses infinitely more difficult challenges to the international community. Briefly, the earth's surface is made habitable because 'greenhouse gases' in the atmosphere trap heat from the sun, thereby keeping the surface temperature constant. Carbon dioxide is the most important of these greenhouse gases. However, its presence in the atmosphere has

---

231. For further information on the nature and effect of acid rain and the action which has been taken in the UK to control such pollution see *Sustainable Development: The UK Strategy,* HMSO, chap. 7, and D. Rose, *The Dirty Man of Europe,* London: Simon and Schuster, 1990.

dramatically increased over the past century, primarily because of the burning of fossil fuels, namely coal and oil, which are the principal means of generating energy in industrialised countries throughout the world. The scientific community argues that increased levels of carbon dioxide in the atmosphere may lead to a rise in the earth's surface temperature, a change which might have the capacity to profoundly affect global climate patterns, resulting in massive disruptions to economic and social activity. Growing scientific certainty of the dangers of global warming has forced the international community to address the question of how best to meet the challenge posed by this most complex problem. Although the international community is deeply divided on the most appropriate substantive steps to be taken to tackle global warming, a broad international consensus has emerged to the effect that fundamental changes are necessary in individual and industrial attitudes towards energy consumption. The United Nations Framework Convention on Climate Change signed in 1992 in Rio de Janeiro at the UN Conference on Environment and Development ('Earth Summit') marked the first international attempt to introduce legal regulation in this context. However, as is explained in chapter 10, the law established in the Climate Change Convention is largely aspirational.[232] During the nineteen-nineties the EC Commission has submitted more specific proposals for substantive action in relation to carbon dioxide emissions, namely, the proposal to introduce taxes on carbon emissions and energy consumption policies designed to reduce emissions of carbon dioxide, promote the substitution of fossil fuels for less polluting fuels, and encourage energy-efficiency.[233] In effect, the primary function of the proposed tax is to bring about changes in individual and industrial attitudes to energy consumption, with revenue accumulation as a secondary goal. Thus far the European Council of Ministers has been unable to agree on the introduction of such a tax, and at the time of writing, the debate on this issue remains in a stalemate.[234]

In recent years the international community has devoted considerable attention to the depletion of ozone concentrations in the upper atmosphere caused by the discharge of ozone-depleting substances into the atmosphere. The stratospheric ozone layer acts as a protective shield against harmful ultraviolet radiation from the sun; depletion would undoubtedly have serious consequences for life as it has evolved on earth. The signing of the Vienna Convention for the Protection of the Ozone Layer in 1985 represented the international community's first attempt to address the problem of the 'ozone hole', in essence establishing a framework for international co-operation in research into and agreement on measures to protect the ozone layer. No attempt was made at this stage to set out a timetable for phasing out specific ozone-depleting substances. However, this step was taken two

---

232. For further details of the UK position in relation to climate change see *Royal Commission on Environmental Pollution: First Report* (Cmnd 4585), London: HMSO 1971; *This Common Inheritance: Britain's Environmental Strategy* (Cm 1200), London: HMSO 1990; *Sustainable Development*; *Report on United Kingdom National Programme for Limiting Carbon Dioxide Emissions: Report Submitted by the DoE to the EC Commission in 1992*, HMSO; *Climate Change: Our National Programme for $CO_2$ Emissions*, London: DoE 1992.
233. COM (92) 226 Final.
234. For further discussion of the Commission's proposals in this regard and national reactions to them see S. Turner and J. O'Shea, 'Taxes as tools of EC environmental policy: the case of the carbon/energy tax', Irish Journal of Taxation (forthcoming).

years later with the adoption of the Montreal Protocol on Substances that Deplete the Ozone Layer in 1987. The Montreal Protocol identified specific ozone-depleting substances and laid down a timetable for phasing out their production. This timetable has been tightened by subsequent agreement at meetings in London and Copenhagen in 1990 and 1992, respectively. As a party to these international agreements, the EC is obliged to implement their terms into EC law. Regulation 594/91/EEC,[235] as amended by Regulation 3952/92/EEC,[236] implements the Vienna Convention and the Montreal Protocol, as revised in London and in Copenhagen, and essentially regulates the import, export, production and consumption of specified ozone-depleting substances between the member states of the EC. The imposition of production limits has been employed as the principal mechanism of control. In effect, production limits apply to every producer of the controlled substances within the EC; the accelerated timetable now in force for the phasing out of their production is outlined below. Consumption of the controlled substances is regulated by controlling their supply. In essence, producers of controlled substances are obliged not to use or place controlled substances onto the market in quantities greater than those specified in Regulation 594/91/EEC, as amended. Regulation 594/91/EEC, as amended, also provides for some exceptions for 'essential uses', i.e. 'to satisfy the basic domestic needs of parties operating under Article 5 of the Protocol' and 'for the purpose of industrial rationalisation within the Member States concerned.' A further Regulation has been proposed which is designed to consolidate Regulations 594/91/EEC and 3952/92/EEC and to introduce a binding timetable for the reduction of halogenated chlorofluoro-carbons (HCFCs) and methylbromide.[237] The importing of such substances into the EC is controlled by means of the progressive reduction of quantitative limits.[238]

### Timetable for phasing out the production of ozone-depleting substances within the EC

Ozone-depleting substances are widely used in industry as propellants in aerosol spray cans, as refrigerants, as solvents, for blowing foam, and in air conditioning. The following production limits apply to each producer in the EC:[239]

- Chlorofluorocarbons (CFCs) and other fully halogenated CFCs (base year 1986): 85 per cent cut by 1 January 1994; ban by 1 January 1995
- Halons (base year 1986): ban by 1 January 1994
- Carbon tetrachloride (base year 1989): 85 per cent cut by 1 January 1994; ban by 1 January 1995

---

235. OJ L67, 14 Mar. 1991.
236. OJ L405, 31 Dec. 1992.
237. COM (93) 202.
238. See also Decision 91/359/EEC (OJ L193, 17 July 1991) concerning the allocation of import quotas and Regulation 2047/93/EEC (OJ L185, 28 July 1993) concerning the authorising of trade between EC members and states which are not parties to the Montreal Protocol.
239. The IRTU bulletin, *Point: Environmental News and Opportunities for Business* (no. 2, Feb. 1994), provides further information for those operating within Northern Ireland on how best to respond to the impact of the phasing out of substances controlled by EC Regulations.

- 1,1,1-trichloroethane (base 1989): 50 per cent cut by 1 April 1994; ban by 1 January 1996

## PART X FOREST DAMAGE CAUSED BY AIR POLLUTION

As a result of concern about damage to forests caused by acid rain and forest fires, the EC adopted Regulation EEC/3528/86,[240] which provides for the establishment of a periodic inventory of damage to forests and requires each member state to submit a periodic health report on their national forests. Further Regulations have been adopted by the EC which lay down detailed rules for the implementation of the inventory, including the use of a common method and format.[241] The Commission finances up to 50 per cent of the cost of collecting the data in each member state. Information collected concerning forests in the UK has been sent annually to the Commission since 1987.[242]

## PART XI INFORMATION CONCERNING AIR POLLUTION

Access to information concerning air pollution in Northern Ireland is currently controlled on a number of fronts. The principal points of control are as follows.

### Directive 90/313/EEC [243] on freedom of access to information on the environment

Directive 90/313/EEC confers a public right of access to 'environmental information' from all persons or bodies which carry out public functions or have public responsibilities that relate to the environment. Environmental information includes information concerning the state of the air, any activity or measure which is or is likely to have an adverse effect on the state of the air and any activity or measure (administrative or otherwise) designed to protect the state of the air. This Directive is implemented in Northern Ireland by the Environmental Information Regulations (NI) 1993.[244] The terms of this Directive and the Northern Ireland Regulations that implement it are discussed in detail in chapter 12.

---

240. OJ L326, 21 Nov. 1986. Regulations are binding from the date of their enactment (1 Jan. 1987) and therefore do not require implementation *via* national law. See: Haigh, supra, chap. 6.13, for further discussion as to the development of this Regulation and its requirements.
241. See Regulations EEC/526/87 (OJ L53, 21 Feb. 1987); EEC/1696/87 (OJ L161, 22 June 1987); EEC/1697/87 (OJ L161, 22 June 1987); EEC/1613/89 (OJ L165, 15 June 1989).
242. A copy of the Forest Service annual report on forests in Northern Ireland can be obtained from the Department of Agriculture for Northern Ireland, Dundonald House, Upper Newtownards Road, Belfast BT4 3SB.
243. OJ L158/56, 23 June 1990.
244. SR No. 45.

## Powers of district councils to provide and obtain information concerning air pollution

Articles 57–61 of the Pollution Control and Local Government (NI) Order 1978[245] empower Northern Ireland's district councils to disseminate and obtain information concerning air pollution. In this regard, district councils are specifically empowered to undertake or support investigation and research into the problem of air pollution, to arrange for the publication of information concerning air pollution and, under certain conditions, to obtain information about the emission of pollutants and other substances into the air from specific premises. Articles 57–9 govern the conditions under which district councils may obtain information concerning emissions from specific premises. However, it is important to note, that district councils do not have the power to obtain such information from private dwellings. In effect, article 57(2) provides that a district council may obtain information concerning the emission of pollutants and other substances into the air by three means:

1. Article 57(2)(a) provides that a district council may issue a notice under article 58 of the 1978 Order requiring the occupier of any premises in its district (other than a private dwelling) to supply, by periodical return or by other means, such estimates or other information as may be specified in the notice concerning the emission of pollutants and other substances into the air from the premises. The recipient of such a notice must comply within six weeks of the date of service or within such longer period as may be specified in the notice. Failure to comply with an article 58 notice without reasonable excuse is an offence under article 58(7); similarly, it is an offence to knowingly or recklessly make a statement in response to a notice which is false in a material particular. Article 58 lays down further rules governing the nature of such a notice and its effect in relation to works which are subject to the Alkali &c. Works Regulation Act 1906,[246] as amended (discussed in Part II, section 1, of this chapter). Article 59 provides that a person served with an article 58 notice, or any other person having an interest in the premises to which the notice relates, may appeal to the DoE(NI) on the grounds that: (i) giving the information requested to the district council or its disclosure to the public, in part or in full, would unreasonably prejudice some private interest by disclosing information about a trade secret or would be contrary to the public interest, or (ii) the information requested is not immediately available and cannot be readily collected or obtained without the recipient of the notice incurring undue expenditure for the purpose. If the DoE(NI) allows the appeal it has the power under article 59(2) to direct the district council to withdraw or to modify the notice or to take steps (specified by the DoE(NI)) to ensure that prejudicial information is not disclosed to the public. The district council is obliged to follow the DoE(NI)'s direction. The DoE(NI) is empowered under article 59(3) to make regulations governing the bringing of appeals under article 59. If a person is convicted of an offence under article 58(7), the district council cannot be prevented by the terms of article

---

245. SI 1978/1049.
246. c. 14.

57(3) (see below) from exercising its power to enter the premises and taking measurements and recording the emissions in question.

2. Article 57(2)(*b*) provides that a district council may enter any premises, whether by agreement or by exercising its compulsory powers under section 98 of the Local Government Act (NI) 1972, for the purpose of taking measurements and recording emissions of pollutants and other substances into the air. Article 57(3) provides that a district council may not exercise this power unless the council has given the occupier of the premises a notice which specifies the kind of emissions it intends to measure and record and the steps it intends to take on the premises for these purposes. In addition, the notice must state that the council intends to exercise its powers to enter the premises for the purpose of taking these measurements and recordings, unless the occupier makes a request to the council that an article 58 notice be served on him requiring him to provide the information himself (explained above). The council cannot exercise its power to enter a premises until a period of twenty-one days from the date on which the notice was served has expired. If during that period the occupier serves a notice on the council requesting that an article 58 notice be served on him, the council cannot exercise its power to enter for the purpose of measuring and recording emissions. Article 57(4) provides that the provisions of article 57 do not authorise a district council to use its powers to enter premises for the purpose of measuring and recording emissions or for the purpose of investigating any work which is subject to the Alkali &c. Works Regulation Act 1906 (addresed in Part II of this chapter). District councils can only obtain information concerning emissions of pollutants and other substances from such works by issuing an article 58 notice (see above) or by exercising their powers under article 57(1)(*a*) to undertake or contribute towards the cost of investigation and research relevant to the problem of air pollution. A district council may not enter such works even when exercising its powers under article 57(1)(*a*). Finally, it should be noted that when exercising its power to arrange for the publication of information concerning the problem of air pollution under article 57(2)(*b*), a district council must ensure that the material published concerning emissions does not disclose information relating to a trade secret, except with the written consent of a person authorised to give such consent.[247] Breach of this duty is actionable under article 57(6), but it would be a defence in civil or criminal proceedings to establish that the information relating to a trade secret was disclosed with consent. Article 57(6) will also apply in relation to any proceedings brought under article 36 of the Clean Air (NI) Order 1981 (unjustified disclosures of information, discussed in detail in Part I, section 9 of this chapter), which makes it an offence to disclose information relating to any trade secret.

3. A district council may also obtain information concerning emissions of pollutants and other substances into the air by entering into an agreement with the occupier of the premises under which the occupier would measure and record the emissions on behalf of the district council.

---

247. Art. 57(5) previously provided that the DoE(NI) could also consent to the disclosure of a trade secret. This provision has been repealed by art. 43, Sch. 5 to the Local Government (Miscellaneous Provisions) (NI) Order 1985.

As general matters concerning powers of district councils powers under article 57 and 58, it should be noted that when a district council is exercising its powers under article 57(2)(*a*), (*b*) or (*c*) it must consult, as appears to the council to be appropriate, any persons carrying on any trade or business in the council's district (or any organisations appearing to the council to represent such people) and any people who appear to the council to be conversant with problems of air pollution or to have an interest in local amenity, about: (i) the manner in which the council exercises its powers under articles 57 and 58 and (ii) the extent to which, and the manner in which, any information collected under those powers should be made available to the public. Such consultations must take place not less than twice in each financial year.

The DoE(NI) has the power under article 60 to prescribe, by means of regulations, the manner in which district councils are to perform their functions under articles 57 and 58. Article 60 contains a list of those persons who should be consulted before such regulations are made and also lists the particular purposes for which such regulations may be adopted.

Finally, it should be noted that article 61 empowers the DoE(NI) to direct a district council to make arrangements for the provision, installation, operation and maintenance of apparatus for measuring and recording air pollution and for transmitting information obtained to the DoE(NI). The DoE(NI) is obliged to pay the whole of the capital expenditure incurred by a district council in providing and installing the apparatus. It is obliged to consult the district council before making a direction under article 61, and the council is obliged to comply with any direction issued under article 61.

### Reporting obligations imposed on the UK

As a member of the EC, the UK has been required to furnish information annually to the Commission concerning the presence of smoke, sulphur dioxide, nitrogen oxides, carbon monoxide, ozone and suspended particulates of heavy metals in the air. While the legal obligation to exchange such information laid down in Decision 82/459/EEC[248] ceased in June 1989, information is still exchanged on an informal basis. It should also be noted that the UK is obliged under Directive 91/692/EEC to submit periodic reports concerning the implementation of specific EC Directives concerning air pollution; the UK's obligations in this regard are addressed in chapter 3 (Part II).

---

248. OJ L210, 19 July 1982.

# CHAPTER FIVE

# Water Pollution

## Introduction

As is the case throughout GB, water is regulated in Northern Ireland both as an environmental medium and as a resource. The purpose of this chapter is to examine the legal framework governing the prevention and control of water pollution and, therefore, only those provisions that relate to or impinge upon the protection of the aquatic environment will be addressed.

The law governing the prevention and control of water pollution is vast, but it can broadly be divided into two areas. On the one hand there is the law governing the pollution of inland, coastal and ground waters, while on the other hand, separate forms of control operate in relation to marine pollution, that is, pollution at sea. It is impossible within the confines of this chapter to address both aspects of water pollution law; instead, the intention is to focus exclusively on the legal framework governing the prevention and control of pollution of inland, coastal and ground waters, on the grounds that the law governing marine pollution is essentially common to the UK as a whole and is discussed in considerable detail in texts covering water pollution in Great Britain.[1]

## The legislative framework governing water pollution in NI

The DoE(NI) is responsible under section 1 of the Water Act (NI) 1972,[2] as amended,[3] for the conservation of water resources in Northern Ireland and for promoting the cleanliness of inland and coastal waters and of water in underground strata (ground water).[4] In carrying out its functions under the Water Act the Department is obliged under section 2 to have regard to the needs of industry and agriculture, the protection of fisheries, the protection of public health,

---

1. The Food and Environmental Protection Act 1985 (c. 48) governs marine pollution for the UK as a whole. The 1985 Act controls marine pollution via a system of licences which are issued for Northern Ireland purposes by the DoE(NI)'s Environment Service. The Deposits in the Sea (Exemptions) Order (NI) 1995 (SR No. 234) exempts specified operations carried on in UK waters adjacent to Northern Ireland from the licensing requirements laid down for Northern Ireland in Part II of the 1985 Act. The DoE(NI) is principally involved in issuing licences under the 1985 Act for disposing of sewage sludge and dredged material at sea and construction licences for engineering works which have an impact on the marine environment, e.g. as harbour developments. UK law governing marine pollution, which to a considerable extent implements standards set at international level, is dealt with in considerable detail by Leeson, *Environmental Law*, London: Pitman, 1995, p. 178–93.
2. c. 5.
3. The 1972 Act has been amended on a number of occasions, principally, for present purposes, by the Water and Sewerage Services (NI) Order 1973 (SI 1973/70), the Pollution Control and Local Government (NI) Order 1978 (SI 1978/1049), the Radioactive Substances Act 1993 (c. 12), and the Water and Sewerage Services (Amendment) (NI) Order 1993 (SI 1993/3165).
4. The 1972 Act refers to the Department of Development it should be noted that this is now the DoE(NI).

the preservation of amenity and the conservation of flora and fauna.[5] The DoE(NI) has the power under section 3 to prepare a water management programme for the water resources in any area in Northern Ireland, which, among other things, may contain an assessment of the quantity and quality of the water resources in a given area. In practice the DoE(NI)'s Environment Service exercises the Department's functions under the Water Act (NI) 1972 and is advised by the Northern Ireland Water Council, which was established under section 4 of the Act as the DoE(NI)'s statutory advisory body in this context.

Inland, coastal and ground waters in Northern Ireland are protected primarily by means of legislative provision, but the common law also plays a significant role. The legislative framework governing the prevention and control of pollution of coastal, inland and ground waters in Northern Ireland is complex in that it involves the interaction of numerous separate legislative provisions. The Water Act (NI) 1972, as amended, is the principal legislative provision governing the prevention and control of pollution in such waters. Two principal regulatory mechanisms are employed by the Act, namely, the discharge consent system, laid down under sections 7 and 8, as amended, which regulate the discharge of trade and sewage effluent and any other polluting matter into such waters, and the imposition of statutory water quality standards under sections 4B and 4C, as inserted by the Water and Sewerage Services (Amendment) (NI) Order 1993.[6] In effect, discharges of trade or sewage effluent or any other polluting matter can only lawfully be made to inland, coastal and ground waters with the DoE(NI)'s consent. The Department is empowered to grant a discharge consent subject to such conditions as it considers appropriate. However, when setting a discharge consent the Department must ensure compliance with a complex network of statutory standards, many of which are set at EC level, for example, emission standards for specific dangerous substances and mandatory water quality standards which have been set for specific physical, chemical and microbiological parameters according to the use to be made of the water. The protection afforded by the discharge consent system is reinforced under the Water Act (NI) 1972 by the creation of criminal offences. Not only is it an offence to discharge or deposit trade or sewage effluent or any other polluting matter into inland, coastal or ground water without the DoE(NI)'s consent, the Act also introduced a general pollution offence which applies when pollution is caused to such waters by the discharge or deposit of polluting matter. Although the discharge consent system can regulate specific or 'point' emissions, it is unable to provide effective protection against pollution from more diffuse sources, for example, the leaching of pesticides and organic fertilisers from agricultural land. The setting and enforcement of statutory water quality standards or objectives plays a vital role in tackling this more insidious but equally detrimental source of water pollution. In

5.  Art. 4A of the Water and Sewerage Services (Amendment) (NI) Order 1993 (SI 1993/3165) amends the 1972 Act by inserting a new s. 4A into Part II of the Act, which obliges the DoE(NI) to 'maintain maps showing what appear to the Department to be the fresh-water limits of every waterway.' In addition, the Department is obliged to make such maps available for public inspection at all reasonable times and free of charge. It should also be noted that the Department is empowered under s. 4A to provide, by order, that a specified waterway is to be treated as if it were not a waterway for the purposes of the Department's obligations under s. 4A.

6.  SI 1993/3165.

effect, whereas the discharge consent system operates to regulate point emissions, water quality objectives focus on the impact of pollutants from diffuse sources on the quality of the receiving waters. The DoE(NI) is empowered under sections 4B and 4C of the Water Act (NI) 1972 to set statutory water quality objectives for Northern Ireland waters, many of which implement water quality standards set at EC level; compliance with such standards is ensured by the Department itself through the discharge consent system and also through the continuous monitoring of water quality which is carried out by the Fisheries Conservancy Board and the Foyle Fisheries Commission. The 1972 Act further supports the controls exerted by the discharge consent system and the imposition of water quality objectives by conferring on the DoE(NI) a wide variety of preventive and administrative powers designed to facilitate the execution of the Department's functions in relation to water pollution. For example, the Department has extensive powers of entry, powers to obtain and remove samples, and the power to order the cessation of any activity which it considers likely to result in water pollution.

In addition to the various forms of regulatory mechanisms outlined thus far, it is important to note that a wide variety of other legislative provisions also operate to regulate specific sources of water pollution in Northern Ireland. The great majority of water pollution incidents in Northern Ireland are caused by agricultural processes. Until recently, the only form of regulation imposed on pollution from agricultural sources in Northern Ireland was the general offence contained in section 5 of the Water Act (NI) 1972. However, while the general offence addressed casual pollution from agricultural discharges, it became clear that more stringent and specific controls would have to be developed to tackle this source of water pollution, in particular, the complex process of water eutrophication[7] which is one of the most polluting consequences of contemporary intensive agricultural practices. In 1990 the Sludge (Use in Agriculture) Regulations (NI) 1990 were enacted to implement Directive 86/278/EEC, which regulates the application of sewage sludge on agricultural land. In addition, the DoE(NI) intends to introduce the proposed Nitrates Directive Regulations to implement Directive 91/676/EEC, which is designed to reduce and prevent water pollution caused by nitrates from agricultural sources, and the proposed Silage, Slurry and Agriculture Fuel Oil Regulations, which will prescribe standards for silos, slurry tanks and oil storage in agriculture.

The EC has also introduced a number of important Directives designed to control discharges of specific dangerous substances into the aquatic environment. These Directives have been implemented in Northern Ireland by various provisions which not only place the DoE(NI) under an obligation to take appropriate steps to reduce or eliminate water pollution from such substances but also make it an offence to make a discharge of any controlled substance without the DoE(NI)'s consent.

Discharges from sewerage systems and sewage treatment plants are another major source of water pollution in Northern Ireland. The DoE(NI)'s Water Executive is responsible under the Water and Sewerage Services (NI) Order

---

7. This phenomenon is explained in Part VIII of this chapter.

1973,[8] as amended, for the supply of water throughout Northern Ireland and also for the provision and maintenance of sewers and sewerage services. Although discharges into the DoE(NI)'s sewerage system and sewage treatment plants are discharges into an artificial environment, it is important to regulate such discharges in order to protect the surrounding environment from pollution from both the residues of sewage treatment works and direct discharges from the sewerage system by means, for example, of storm drains. In addition, there is the problem that most sewage treatment works themselves discharge into watercourses. Discharges of inadequately treated sewage sludge are a potent cause of water pollution, and it is therefore necessary to regulate discharges into and from sewers and sewage treatment works. The DoE(NI)'s Water Executive is empowered under Part V of the Water and Sewerage Services (NI) Order 1973, as amended, to control discharges of trade effluent into its sewerage system and sewage works by means of a discharge consent system; such consents are set by the Water Executive and are monitored and reviewed by the DoE(NI)'s Environment Service. As a Crown developer, discharges from the DoE(NI)'s sewerage system and works into receiving waters are not regulated under the discharge consent system provided for under the Water Act (NI) 1972. Instead, the Environment Service sets standards for such discharges and monitors them for compliance. The Department is not required to place these standards on a register which is available for public consultation.

Not surprisingly, one of the main criticisms levelled at the DoE(NI) is that it is both poacher and gamekeeper in operating sewage works and controlling water pollution in Northern Ireland. The House of Commons Environment Committee Report noted the views expressed by the British Field Sports Society to the effect that the DoE(NI) itself 'was probably the biggest single polluter in Northern Ireland'; and although the committee also noted that DoE(NI) figures for pollution incidents in Northern Ireland did not support this view, the report stated that:

> while a situation exists in which the Water [Executive] cannot be publicly held to account for water pollution incidents which it causes it is inevitable that enforcement by the DoE(NI) will be resented and regarded with suspicion. We have said many times in the past that it is unsatisfactory to have polluters controlling pollution . . .[9]

Although attempts have been made within the DoE(NI) to separate the Department's environmental protection role from its day-to-day responsibility for waste and sewage (e.g. the appointment of a Director of Environmental Services, who is a member of the Department's management board and, more recently, the establishment of 'Next Steps' agencies within the DoE(NI)), the poacher-gamekeeper criticism still holds true. There appear to be no immediate plans to remedy this situation. This stated, it should be noted that attempts have been made to strengthen provisions for public consultation in relation to water pollution control. For example, the DoE(NI) may require that an application for a discharge consent under the Water Act (NI) 1972 be advertised in local newspapers; it is obliged to advertise the setting and varying of water quality standards in Northern Ireland; and it is obliged under the recently enacted Urban Waste Water Treatment

8. SI 1973/70.
9. House of Commons Environment Committee First Report: *Environmental Issues in Northern Ireland,* HC 39 (1990), para. 78.

Regulations (NI) 1995 to publish a report every two years of its implementation of the Urban Waste Water Directive 91/271/EEC.

## Enforcement

In the event of a pollution incident, legal proceedings under the Water Act (NI) 1972 may only be instituted by the DoE(NI) or by, or with, the consent of the Attorney-General.[10] In this regard it should be noted that penalties for water pollution offences under the Act were recently raised from £2,000 to £20,000. However, even where prosecution is not warranted, polluters may be required to pay for the cost of clean up and also compensation for damages to fisheries. It should also be noted that the House of Commons Environment Committee reported that:

> the DoE(NI) has an impressive record on prosecutions for water pollution offences particularly when compared with the situation in Great Britain. In 1987 and 1988 there were 277 prosecutions in Northern Ireland compared with only 292 in England, 81 in Wales and 37 in Scotland. In 1987 we reported on the pollution of rivers and estuaries in England and were extremely critical of the poor prosecution record of the Water Authorities. At that time, prior to the establishment of the National Rivers Authority, less than two per cent of pollution incidents led to prosecution. We are pleased to record that in Northern Ireland the corresponding figure for 1988 was 18 per cent.[11]

Similar numbers of prosecutions under the Water Act (NI) 1972 are reported in the *Environment Service Report,* 1993–95[12] for the years 1989–94. The Environment Service employs a number of agents to assist it in the task of enforcing the legislation governing water pollution; these include the Fisheries Conservancy Board and the Foyle Fisheries Commission. It is also assisted in this regard by the DoE(NI)'s Environmental Health (Rivers) Officers.[13] The Fisheries Conservancy Board (FCB) is a non-departmental public body responsible for the application of fisheries legislation in Northern Ireland, apart from the Foyle Area, which is under the jurisdiction of the Foyle Fisheries Commission. It was established in 1966 as a result of the passing of the Fisheries Act (NI) 1966,[14] as amended, and is responsible for the conservation and protection of the salmon and inland fisheries of Northern Ireland. Section 47 of the Fisheries Act (NI) 1966 gives the FCB its role in water pollution control, the terms of which are quite similar to the general offence under section 5 of the Water Act (NI) 1972. Section 47 provides that 'if any person causes or knowingly permits any deleterious matter to enter any waters he shall be guilty of an offence and shall be liable on summary conviction . . .' Until the enactment of the Water Act (NI) in 1972 the FCB (along

---

10. The only exception to this concerns legal proceedings under s. 16(3) of the Water Act (NI) 1972, which empowers the DANI to regulate the way in which a waterway may be used for recreational purposes; in this context, the DANI and the AG have the sole right to bring legal proceedings. The provisions of the 1972 Act concerning recreational use are beyond the scope of this book.
11. Supra, note 9 at para. 74.
12. P. 36.
13. Appendix 1 of the *Environment Service Report,* 1993–95, p. 50, contains a list of the contact addresses and telephone numbers for Northern Ireland's Environmental Health (Rivers) Officers.
14. c. 17.

with the Foyle Fisheries Commission) was virtually the only body in Northern Ireland involved in water pollution control, and when the DoE(NI) was conferred with responsibility in this area, the Government and the FCB entered into arrangements to avoid duplication of activities. In effect the FCB is responsible for taking samples under the River Water Quality Monitoring Programme. It monitors compliance with discharge consents issued to industrial and other premises, it investigates pollution incidents and prepares reports concerning potential prosecutions and issues warning letters, and where fish kills occur, it prosecutes under section 47 of the Fisheries Act (NI) 1966. Any other pollution incidents are referred to the DoE(NI)'s Environment Service for prosecution under sections 5 or 7 of the Water Act (NI) 1972.[15]

The Foyle Fisheries Commission (FFC) was established in 1952 under section 11(1) of the Foyle Fisheries Act (NI) 1952[16] and section 11(1) of the corresponding legislation in the Republic, the Foyle Fisheries Act 1952. Section 11(2)(*b*) sets out the functions of the FFC, namely, 'the conservation, protection and improvement of the fisheries of the Foyle Area generally.' The FFC's powers under the Northern Ireland Act in relation to water pollution control have been gradually enhanced by the Foyle Fisheries (Amendment) Act (NI) 1962, the Fisheries Act (NI) 1966 and the Fisheries Amendment (NI) Order 1981. It should be noted that both the Northern Ireland Act and the Republic of Ireland Act are at present under review; it is expected that new legislation will be in place by the end of 1996. As with the FCB, arrangements were made to avoid duplication between government activities in relation to water pollution control and the activities of the FFC. The FFC's powers are essentially identical to those outlined in relation to the FCB above but only apply to the Foyle area; fish kills are prosecuted under section 41(1) of the Foyle Fisheries Act (NI) 1952.[17]

The Environment Service also provides a 24-hour emergency pollution response service[18] throughout Northern Ireland. In 1990 the DoE(NI) established a new Water Pollution Incident Response Procedures Plan, which covers inland pollution incidents and local clean-up operations following oil or chemical spills at sea or on the coast. This plan complements those established by the Department of Transport and Industry (Marine Pollution Control Unit) for dealing with oil or chemical spills at sea.

## The role of European Law

It is clear from the foregoing outline that the EC has exerted an enormous influence in developing and shaping the legislative landscape governing water pollution throughout the UK. Although the first EC measures concerning water

---

15. See also the FCB submission to House of Commons Environment Committee *First Report: Environmental Issues in Northern Ireland,* HC 39 (1990), p. 143 et seq., in which the FCB reports on its work in recent years in the context of different water pollution incidents. The FCB can be contacted at 1 Mahon Road, Portadown, Co. Armagh BT62 3EE; tel. (01762) 334666.

16. c. 5.

17. See also the FFC submission to the House of Commons Environment Committee, note 15, supra, p. 151 for a report of the Commission's recent activities in relation to water pollution. The FFC can be contacted at 8 Victoria Road, Derry BT47 2AB; tel. (01504) 42100.

18. Tel. (01232) 254754; outside office hours: (01232) 757414.

pollution were adopted in 1973–75, this sector is now the most fully developed area of EC environmental policy, with more than twenty-five Directives and Decisions now operating in this field. Broadly speaking, the EC has adopted two basic approaches to water pollution prevention and control, namely, the imposition of emission limit values or upper limits for discharges of specific substances (e.g. discharges of dangerous substances) and the imposition of mandatory water quality standards set according to the use to be made of the waters in question. Although the EC has regulated water pollution selectively, in that standards have not been adopted for all substances in relation to all waters, it has succeeded in bringing about significant changes in domestic approaches to water pollution control. In particular, the EC has been responsible for strengthening the protection afforded to ground waters; it has also required member states to introduce uniform and stringent emission limit values for discharges of specific dangerous substances to the aquatic environment, and it has been responsible for the introduction of a statutory system of water quality standards throughout the UK. In addition the EC has been responsible for the introduction of stringent controls on the use of organic and artificial fertilisers on agricultural land and on the collection, treatment and disposal of urban waste water.

## Reform of water pollution laws

At the time of writing, both national and EC approaches to water pollution control are in a state of flux. At the Northern Ireland level, two important changes are forthcoming. In December 1993 the DoE(NI) and DANI published the *Review of the Water Act (NI) 1972: A Consultation Paper,* which set out proposals designed to take account of scientific advances which have occurred since the adoption of the Water Act (NI) 1972 and the increase in public awareness of environmental issues and to implement the 'polluter pays' principle.[19] It is intended that the review process will culminate in the introduction of a new Order in Council in mid-1996. At the time of writing, the proposed Water (NI) Order 1996 has not been enacted, and copies of the new draft legislation will not be available until the end of 1996. As a result, it is only possible to elaborate on the proposals set out in the Consultation Paper. To avoid any confusion between existing controls and proposed changes, the proposals will be addressed separately at the end of each of the relevant sections. It should be emphasised that the new Order in Council may not embrace all these proposals and may indeed introduce changes which are not outlined in the Consultation Paper.[20]

The second major change in progress at national level is the forthcoming introduction of a system of integrated pollution control (IPC) for Northern Ireland. In March 1996 the DoE(NI) published the proposal for a draft Industrial Pollution Control (NI) Order 1996, which, when enacted, will establish a three-tier system of pollution control that incorporates a system of integrated pollution control for those industrial processes with the greatest capacity for generating pollution. In

---

19. This principle is also referred to in chap. 13.
20. Information on whether the new legislation has been enacted can be obtained from the DoE(NI)'s Environment Service (Legislation Section), Calvert House, 23 Castle Place, Belfast BT1 1FY; tel. (01232) 254754; fax (01232) 254700.

effect, enforcing authorities will be required to consider the total effect on all environmental media (land, water, and air) when deciding whether to authorise the carrying on of industrial processes with high pollution potential. The new control regime will require compliance in accordance with the 'best available techniques not entailing excessive cost' (BATNEEC) and in some instances will require consideration of the 'best practicable environmental option' (BPEO). The details of the proposed IPC system are outlined in chapter 4.

The EC's approach to water quality regulation is also changing from the adoption of individual, add-on or modified Directives to a more coherent, integrated framework structure designed to facilitate sustainable development and management of the EC's water resources. In 1994 the Commission published a draft Directive on the Ecological Quality of Water,[21] which, if adopted, will represent a distinct change of policy in this context. The draft Directive introduces two principal changes. First, it proposes to consolidate EC water quality Directives and thereby repeal the Freshwater and Shellfish Directives. Second, it proposes the introduction of a procedural framework which would govern action taken by member states as distinct from the establishment of precise standards, which has been the practice in this context thus far. Within this procedural framework, member states would be obliged to take the following action:

(i) Member states would be obliged to draw up an inventory of the various sources of pollution and other anthropogenic factors affecting the quality of water in order to decide on the measures needed to improve water quality (draft article 4). Technical specifications for this assessment would be drawn up by the Commission.

(ii) Member states would then be obliged by draft article 5 to define 'operational targets' for 'good ecological water quality' for all surface waters and for the territorial sea. A working definition of 'good ecological water quality' is provided in Annex I to the draft Directive, which provides that the ecological quality of water is defined by the state of the listed parameters that are relevant to the waters concerned (for example dissolved oxygen, concentrations of toxic or other harmful substances in water, sediment and biota, levels of disease in animal life, including fish, and in plant populations caused by anthropogenic influence, etc.).

(iii) Draft article 6 would oblige member states to adopt, publish and implement 'integrated programmes' designed to improve water quality, with the ultimate aim of reaching the operational targets adopted by each member state for the waters in question. Annex VI to the draft Directive would prescribe the specific elements that such integrated programmes would have to include; in particular Annex VI requires use of the 'best available techniques' (the EC formulation of BATNEEC) for point sources of pollution and the use of 'best environmental practices' for sources of diffuse pollution.

(iv) Draft articles 3 and 7 would require member states to establish measuring and monitoring systems (that comply with specified criteria) for determining the quality of water and to inform the public: (i) of their findings in this regard and (ii) of their findings as a result of the assessment of pollution sources under draft article 4 above.

---

21. COM (93) 680 Final. OJ 1994 C222/6, 10 Aug. 1994.

Ball and Bell point out that this approach to water quality control will, if adopted, confer considerable discretion on member states, which in turn will inevitably affect the uniformity of water quality standards throughout the EC and also the extent to which individuals and environmental groups can directly enforce the provisions of the Directive in national courts in the event that quality standards are breached.[22]

In response to requests from the Council and Parliament in 1995 to outline its views on the draft Directive, the Commission presented a communication in February 1996 in which it stated that much of the EC's legislation on water quality should be drawn together into a framework Directive on water resources which would replace the six water quality Directives adopted thus far.[23] In addition, the Commission stated that the proposed draft Directive on the Ecological Quality of Water would improve the coherence of water policy, maintain the high level of environmental protection already established, and ensure transparency and public accountability in the management of water resources. The Council of Ministers was scheduled to discuss the draft Directive further in March 1996.

## What is 'water pollution'?

Before embarking on a more detailed consideration of the laws governing the prevention and control of pollution of Northern Ireland's inland, coastal and ground waters it is necessary to clarify the meaning of the term 'water pollution'. The first point to make in this regard is that pure water, namely $H_2O$ absolutely free from any substances dissolved in it, does not exist outside the laboratory. Water in the natural state contains a wide variety of matter, ranging from dissolved gases, salts and fine particulate organic matter to minute organisms, to name but a few of its naturally occurring constituent elements.[24] As a result, difficulties can arise in identifying and assessing the existence and extent of water pollution. Against this background John Leeson points out that:

> [a]ccepting that as well as contamination from a variety of sources, both natural and man-made, natural waters have a range of self-cleansing and regenerative processes, the two essential features of pollution in the environmental context would seem to be that it is of human origin and excessive in quantity having regard to the toxicity of its contents and those naturally occurring powers of regeneration.[25]

In addition, it is important to stress that the use made of the waters in question will also be of considerable importance in determining whether water is polluted. As Professor Howarth put it, '[t]he pollution of water is characterised as the human modification of water which renders it less suitable for a particular use than that water would be in its original state.'[26]

There are three principal sources of inland, coastal and ground water pollution

---

22. Ball and Bell, *Environmental Law,* 3rd ed, London: Blackstone Press, 1995, p. 424.
23. Reported in *The Week in Europe* WE/7/96; available from the European Commission, Jean Monnet House, 8 Storey's Gate, London SW1P 3AT. See also, *Environmental Bulletin: Issue 29* (February 1996) (ENFO, Dublin), p. 12.
24. Briefing Sheet II: Water Pollution (ENFO).
25. Leeson, *Environmental Law,* London: Pitman, 1995, p. 157.
26. W. Howarth, *Water Pollution Law,* Dartford: 1988, p. 33.

in Northern Ireland, namely, pollution from agricultural practices, pollution from industrial processes, and pollution from water and sewage treatment. It is impossible in the present context to provide a comprehensive list of the different types of water pollution caused by these sources; suffice it for present purposes to identify the following as the principal categories. Discharges of certain substances such as pesticides, heavy metals or nitrate can, depending on the quantity of the discharge, be highly toxic to all forms of life in the receiving waters and can render the water completely unsuitable for any human use. Discharges of organic waste such as sewage sludge, silage, slurry and industrial wastes from food processing and dairy industries, farms or sewage treatment plants all have a deoxygenating effect on receiving waters, depleting the level of dissolved oxygen which is necessary to support fish populations and plant life and, in some cases, potentially affecting the suitability of receiving water for certain uses, for example, the abstracting of drinking water, which requires a certain amount of dissolved oxygen in order to be palatable. In addition, discharges of organic wastes and artificial fertilisers rich in nitrates and phosphates cause water eutrophication, stimulating an accelerated growth of scum, algal blooms and plant life, which in turn deoxygenates water and disrupts or destroys fish populations in receiving waters. Discharges of heated effluent can also contribute to the process of deoxygenation and can disrupt biological conditions in receiving water. Finally, releases of bacteria, the dumping of solids and the general disposal of refuse each contribute to water pollution by introducing disease, blocking out light, or damaging amenity.

## Chapter Structure

Although the legal framework governing the prevention and control of Northern Ireland's inland, coastal and ground waters involves the close interaction of numerous legislative provisions and also the operation of the common law, for the purposes of clarity, its constituent elements will be presented in this chapter as follows:

- Part I       General pollution offences
- Part II      Consents for discharges into inland, coastal and ground waters
- Part III     Preventive powers
- Part IV      Administrative powers
- Part V       Controlling, restricting or prohibiting water abstraction
- Part VI      Water quality control
- Part VII     Dangerous substances
- Part VIII    Control of pollution from agricultural sources
- Part IX      Discharges to and from sewers, sewerage systems, and sewage treatment works
- Part X       The common law and water pollution

## PART I GENERAL POLLUTION OFFENCES

### The nature of the offences

Section 5 of the Water Act (NI) 1972 (hereafter referred to as the WA) introduces a general pollution offence which essentially deals with casual discharges of polluting matter, normally of short duration (for example pollution from agricultural discharges), and operates to complement the more specific pollution offence of making a discharge without the DoE(NI)'s consent under sections 7–11 of the WA (considered in Part II of this chapter).

Section 5(1)(*a*)[27] of the WA provides that it is an offence 'whether knowingly or otherwise' to discharge or deposit 'poisonous, noxious or polluting matter' so that it enters a 'waterway'[28] or water contained in any 'underground strata'.[29] In addition, it is an offence under section 5(1)(*b*), whether knowingly or otherwise, to discharge or deposit 'any matter' in such a way that it enters a waterway or water contained in any underground strata and 'tends, either directly or in combination with similar acts (whether his own or another's), to impede the proper flow of the water' in such a way that it leads to or is likely to lead 'to pollution or a substantial aggravation of pollution due to other causes or of its consequences.' Section 5(6) provides that any reference to matter entering a waterway or water in any underground strata under section 5(1) includes matter which enters such water as a result of being carried into it.

The terms 'poisonous, noxious or polluting' are not defined by the WA. However, the Court of Appeal in *R. v. Dovermoss Ltd*[30] ruled that the term 'polluting', as used in similar provisions under the Water Resources Act 1991, which governs water pollution in England and Wales, did not require that actual harm be established; it was sufficient to establish that there was a likelihood or capability of harm being caused to those who use the water (including plants and animals).[31] Section 30(1) defines the term 'deposit' as including storing. The WA

---

27. S. 32(3) of the WA provides that s. 5 does not affect the operation of s. 448(2) of the Merchant Shipping Act 1894.
28. The term 'waterway' is defined in s. 30(1) of the WA as including any 'river, stream, watercourse, inland water (whether natural or artificial) or tidal waters.' It does not, however, include any sewer which is vested in a local authority. S. 30(2) provides that any reference to a waterway includes a reference to 'the channel or bed of a waterway which is for the time being dry.' 'Tidal waters' are defined as including 'the sea and the waters of any enclosed dock which adjoins tidal waters.'
29. S. 30(1) of the WA defines 'underground strata' as 'strata subjacent to the surface of any land, and any reference to water contained in any underground strata is a reference to water so contained otherwise than in a sewer, pipe, reservoir, tank or underground works contained in any such strata.' In effect the WA applies to what is known as 'ground water'. S. 30(3) provides that water contained for the time being in: (a) 'a well, borehole or similar work, including any adit or passage constructed in connection with it for facilitating the collection of water in the well, borehole or work' or (b) in 'any excavation into underground strata, where the level of water in the excavation depends wholly or mainly on water entering it from those strata,' will be treated as water 'contained in the underground strata into which the well, borehole or work was sunk, or the excavation was made, as the case may be'.
30. [1995] ELM 106.
31. For a more detailed discussion of the terms 'poisonous, noxious or polluting' as used in the Water Resources Act 1991 see Leeson, *Environmental Law*, London: Pitman, 1995, pp 164–6.

does not define the term 'discharge'. However, in *Smeaton v. Ilford Corporation* Upjohn J addressed the meaning of the term and ruled that a discharge is 'caused or permitted'.[32]

The phrase 'to knowingly or otherwise', on which the general offences are based, is not defined in the WA, nor have the Northern Ireland courts addressed its meaning. Assistance with the scope of this phrase may, however, be derived from the extensive case law concerning the phrase to 'cause or knowingly permit' the discharge or entry of polluting matter as used in legislative provisions governing the control of water pollution in England and Wales, including section 85 of the Water Resources Act 1991, which operates at present to create a similar offence to that contained in section 5 of the WA. In effect, the English courts have ruled that the phrase 'to cause or knowingly permit' creates two separate offences. The term 'cause' is regarded as creating an offence of strict liability, while the term 'knowingly' is deemed to create a more limited offence, in that knowledge must be established in order to secure a conviction. Although there is as yet no Northern Ireland case law relating to the meaning of the phrase 'to knowingly or otherwise', the English case law would suggest that the Water Act (NI) 1972 also creates two general offences. The first offence would clearly be based on knowledge, while the term 'or otherwise' arguably creates an offence of strict liability that is potentially even more strict than that created under similar English legislation, in that specific 'causation' need not be established.

The decision of the House of Lords in *Alphacell v. Woodward*[33] is the leading case on the nature of the liability inherent in the phrase to 'cause' a discharge. The court ruled that it was unnecessary to establish negligence or fault; Alphacell were deemed guilty of the general offence of causing pollution simply because they had conducted the activity which had caused the pollution in question, and as long as that activity was intentional, all that needed to be established was a causal link between their activity and the discharge causing the pollution. The court ruled furthermore that it was unnecessary to establish that the discharge had entered the controlled waters directly; it was sufficient in *Alphacell* that the polluting matter entered the river via a channel. The House of Lords' decision in *Alphacell* has been applied on many occasions, most recently by the House of Lords in *National Rivers Authority v. Yorkshire Water Services Ltd*,[34] where the court ruled that the question of causation is a question of fact to be decided in each case. It should be noted, however, that a court does not have total discretion in determining this question of fact; if its decision in this regard fails to satisfy the requirements laid down in *Jagendorf v. Secretary of State for the Environment*[35] it can be overturned. The final point to note concerning the English case law surrounding the offence of strict liability in this context is that two lines of case law have emerged which suggest two further limitations on the wide interpretation of the concept of causation laid down in *Alphacell*. One series of decisions addresses the position when a third party intervenes so as to interrupt the chain of causation, whereas the

---

32. [1954] 1 All ER 923 at 927.
33. [1972] AC 824.
34. [1995] 1 All ER 225.
35. [1987] JPL 771.

second concerns the position in which the defendant has been passive rather than active.[36]

The second general offence, 'to knowingly permit' a discharge, has also been considered by courts in England, though not as frequently as the offence of strict liability. In essence, the second offence is more limited, in that knowledge is required. One of the most important issues concerns the degree of knowledge required for conviction; in *Schulmans Incorporated Ltd v. National Rivers Authority*[37] the court ruled that constructive knowledge was sufficient.

## Defences

Section 5(3) provides that it is a defence to proceedings under section 5 of the WA to prove that the person making the discharge 'exercised all reasonable care to prevent the discharge or deposit of the matter in question.' Where a discharge of any effluent or any matter is made pursuant to a discharge consent[38] issued by the DoE(NI) under section 7 or 8 of the WA (addressed in Part II of this chapter), the discharge will not constitute an offence under, or a violation of, section 5 (section 11(1)). Finally, it should be noted that where matter to which section 5 applies is discharged into a sewer or sewage disposal works so that it enters a waterway or water contained in underground strata, section 5(2) provides that it will not be an offence under section 5 if the sewer or sewage disposal works are vested in a local authority and:

(i) the local authority is bound to receive the matter; or

(ii) the local authority has consented to receive the matter unconditionally; or

(iii) the local authority has consented to receive the matter subject to certain conditions, and the person making the discharge has observed those conditions.

## Penalties

Section 5(7) sets out the liability incurred for an offence under section 5. This provision has been amended by article 17 of the Water and Sewerage Services (Amendment) (NI) Order 1993,[39] which increases the fines for water pollution offences from £2,000 to £20,000 on summary conviction and removes the provision in section 5(7) concerning substantial repetitions of offences under section 5. In effect, a person found guilty of an offence under section 5 will be liable on conviction on indictment to imprisonment for a maximum term of two

---

36. Both lines of cases are discussed in detail in Ball and Bell, *Environmental Law*, 3rd ed., London: Blackstone Press, 1995, pp 432–3.
37. [1993] Env LR 1. The court did not elaborate on this point any further. For further discussion of this case see Wilkinson, 'Causing and knowingly permitting pollution offences: a review' (1993) Water Law 25. The general offence of 'knowingly permitting' pollution is also discussed further in Ball and Bell, ibid., pp 433–4.
38. A discharge consent in this context includes a consent which has been varied or substituted as a result of a review carried out by the DoE(NI) under s. 10 of the WA, but it does not cover a consent which was deemed to be granted by default under s. 9(4), that is, where the DoE(NI) fails to notify the applicant of their intended decision on the application for a discharge consent within the statutory period of three months from the date of receiving the application (s. 11(1) and (2)).
39. SI 1993/3165.

years or to an unlimited fine, or to both, and on summary conviction, to imprisonment for a maximum term of three months or to a maximum fine of £20,000, or to
both.

Section 5(4) empowers the court making the conviction under section 5 to
make an order directing the convicted person to take such measures as the court
considers necessary to 'remedy or nullify' any breach of section 5. The court's
power in this regard can only be invoked if the DoE(NI) has made an application
to that effect and the person charged has been given at least ten days notice of the
Department's application. Section 5(5), as amended by the Schedule to the Water
and Sewerage Services (Amendment) (NI) Order 1993,[40] provides that failure to
comply with the terms of an order made under section 5(4) is an offence under
section 5, the penalties for which are laid down in section 5(7).

### Preventing a breach of section 5

The DoE(NI) is empowered in certain circumstances to take action to prevent a
breach of section 5. These powers are outlined, together with the Department's
other preventive powers under the WA, in Part III of this chapter.

### Radioactive substances

Article 40 of the Radioactive Substances Act 1993,[41] which applies to the UK as a
whole, provides that 'no account can be taken of any radioactivity possessed by
any substance or article or by any part of any premises' for the purposes of
exercising or performing any statutory power or duty or in the enforcement of any
statutory provision under section 5 of the WA. In effect, the non-radioactive
elements of a discharge are governed by the WA, while the radioactive elements
are governed by the Radioactive Substances Act 1993.

### Proposals to expand the scope of water pollution offences

The pollution of rivers and watercourses by sullage water discharged from
domestic and industrial sources is one of the most difficult water quality problems
to emerge in Northern Ireland. In effect, sullage water is being discharged into
surface water drains rather than into foul sewers and is thereby reaching
watercourses. The *Review of the Water Act (NI) 1972: A Consultation Paper,*
issued by the DoE(NI) and the DANI in 1993, points out that because of the
extensive nature of drainage systems, the limited access that can be obtained to
them, and the sporadic nature of the discharges, tracing these discharges is a very
onerous task. Given the scale of the problem, both in its geographical spread and
in the potential sources of these discharges, the DoE(NI) has proposed that a
campaign be mounted which would ensure that the occupiers of premises would
undertake the necessary remedial works to ensure that sullage water is correctly
disposed of. This campaign would tackle the most serious sources of pollution first
and would continue for several years. To support this campaign, the Consultation
Paper proposes that it become an offence to discharge sullage water or sewage into

---

40. Ibid.
41. c. 12.

a surface water drain and, also, that the DoE(NI) be empowered to serve a notice on the occupiers of premises requiring them to have a connection made to a foul sewer. It is also suggested that failure to comply with such a notice would be an offence punishable by fine and that a right of appeal be granted to the magistrates' courts (paragraphs 10.1–10.4).

## PART II CONSENTS FOR DISCHARGES INTO INLAND, COASTAL AND GROUND WATERS

Before the adoption of the Water Act (NI) 1972 there was no system of control governing industrial, commercial or domestic discharges into inland, coastal or ground waters in Northern Ireland although it was an offence under Northern Ireland's fisheries legislation to pollute water. Sections 7–11 of the WA introduced the system of discharge consents which now controls such discharges in Northern Ireland. Sections 7 and 8 prohibit the discharge of either trade[42] or sewage[43] effluent, or any poisonous, noxious or polluting matter that is not trade or sewage effluent, into a waterway[44] or into any underground strata[45] without the DoE(NI)'s consent. It should be noted at the outset of this section that the discharge consent system contained in sections 7 and 8 does not apply to discharges into the DoE(NI)'s sewerage system or sewage treatment works; these are governed by a separate consent system under different legislation, which is discussed in Part IX of this chapter.

The DoE(NI) is empowered to issue consents for the discharge of trade or sewage effluent or for the discharge of poisonous, noxious or polluting matter; its consent may be issued subject to such conditions[46] as it thinks appropriate, and such conditions may have effect for specified periods.[47] Where consent is issued subject to a condition or conditions, these conditions will bind any person 'using any land or premises to which the consent relates' (section 7(2) and (3); section 8 (2) and (3)). A discharge consent will cease to have effect within three years; the

---

42. The term 'trade effluent' is defined in s. 30(1) as 'any liquid, either with or without particles of matter in suspension therein, which is discharged from premises used for carrying on any trade or industry, other than storm water or domestic sewage.'
43. The term 'sewage' is defined in s. 30(1) as including 'domestic sewage and domestic sewage and storm water if combined.'
44. The term 'waterway' for the purposes of the discharge consent system is defined at note 28, supra.
45. The term 'underground strata' is defined at note 29, supra.
46. References to 'conditions' in s. 9 include conditions that are either varied, imposed or substituted as a result of a consent being reviewed by the DoE(NI) under s. 10 of the WA.
47. It should be noted that a discharge of effluent or matter that is made in accordance with a discharge consent issued under s. 7 or 8 will not constitute an offence or a violation of s. 21–5 of the Gasworks Clauses Act 1847; s. 77 of the Public Health (Ireland) Act 1878; any regulations under s. 13 of the Foyle Fisheries Act (NI) 1952; s. 47 of the Fisheries Act (NI) 1966; or any bylaws under s. 26 of that Act or s. 5 of the WA. A discharge consent in this context includes a consent which has been varied or substituted as a result of a review carried out by the DoE(NI) under s. 10 of the WA, but it does not cover a consent that was deemed to be granted by default under s. 9 (4), that is, where the DoE(NI) fails to notify the applicant of their intended decision on the application for a discharge consent within the statutory period of three months from the date of receiving the application (s. 11(1) and (2)).

three-year period will be dated either from the date on which the consent was given if no discharge has been made pursuant to the consent, or, from the date on which the last discharge was made (section 9(8)). Provision is also made for the review of consents at three-year intervals or more regularly if requested. The position in this regard is set out below.

The penalties for making a discharge without the DoE(NI)'s consent or for making a discharge which breaches the terms of a condition attached to a consent have been increased considerably by the Water and Sewerage Services (Amendment) (NI) Order 1993 and are outlined below.

Where a person makes a discharge in violation of section 7 or 8 the Department may issue that person with a notice under section 9(2) imposing any such conditions as might have been imposed had an application been made for a discharge consent. This empowers the Department to issue a form of retrospective consent but does not provide immunity for offences committed before the consent was granted. In effect, section 9(2) enables the DoE(NI) to formalise the legal position concerning a particular discharge and to control the discharge by attaching appropriate conditions.

Schedule 3 to the Pollution Control and Local Government (NI) Order 1978[48] has inserted an additional provision into section 9(2) of the WA which empowers a person who has been served with a notice under section 9(2) to appeal the notice to the Water Appeals Commission for Northern Ireland. The appeal must be brought within twenty-eight days of the notice being served. It should also be noted that a person who makes a discharge in breach of sections 7 or 8 will not be regarded as having committed an offence under the WA until the Department makes a decision to either refuse or grant its consent (unconditionally or subject to conditions), provided the person making the discharge has made an application to the Department for a discharge consent under section 7 or 8 *and* the discharge made corresponds to the discharge specified in the application (section 9(11)).

### Application for a discharge consent

An application for a discharge consent must contain specified particulars concerning the nature of the discharge. The Department has specified the type of information required for particular applications and particular classes of application. In this regard, it should be noted, that it is an offence under section 22(*b*) to 'knowingly or recklessly' make a statement that is false in a material particular for the purpose of obtaining a discharge consent. The penalty incurred for an offence under section 22(*b*) is an unlimited fine or imprisonment for a maximum of two years, or both, if convicted on indictment or, alternatively, a maximum fine of £500 (level 2 on the standard scale) or imprisonment for a maximum of three months, or both, on summary conviction. The DoE(NI) may require the applicant to publish notices in specified newspapers that the application is being made, thereby introducing a level of public consultation where the Department deems it necessary.

Where an application is made to the Department for a discharge consent, section 9(4) of the WA, as amended by Schedule 3 to the Water and Sewerage

---

48. SI 1978/1049.

Services (NI) Order 1973,[49] provides that the Department must give notice of its decision on the application to the applicant and either to the Fisheries Conservancy Board for Northern Ireland, or the Foyle Fisheries Commission if the discharge is being made or is to be made in the Derry area. The applicant and the relevant board or commission may appeal that decision to the Water Appeals Commission for Northern Ireland within twenty-eight days of being given notice of the Department's decision. The Department is required under section 9(5) to give the applicant notice of its decision within three months of the date of receiving the application or within such period as is agreed in writing with the applicant; if the Department fails to do so, an unconditional consent will be deemed to have been granted.[50]

## Setting a discharge consent

As already stated, the DoE(NI) has the power to grant a discharge consent subject to such conditions it thinks fit. The *Environment Service Report* 1991–93 points out that in setting discharge conditions, the Department will have regard to the nature and volume of the discharge (in particular, the biochemical oxygen demand of the discharge and the levels of toxic or dangerous materials and suspended solids), the quality and quantity of the receiving waters (i.e. the dilution capacity of the receiving waters), the amenity value, and legitimate uses to which the receiving waters are put. The Department's objective is essentially to 'achieve an overall balance allowing effluent discharges to be made while preserving the uses and value of the receiving waters and ensuring that the water continues to meet its quality objectives.'[51]

It is also important to note that the DoE(NI) is obliged by statute to consider certain factors when setting a discharge consent. They are as follows:

1. When considering an application for a consent for a discharge of effluent or matter that is 'similar to an existing discharge' (i.e. where the discharge is similar 'in nature, composition and temperature to, and is of a similar volume and made at a similar rate to, a discharge of effluent or matter during any corresponding period within the [previous twelve-month period]') section 9(6) of the WA requires the Department to consider the following factors:

    (a) the length of time during which the effluent or matter has been discharged;

    (b) whether all reasonably practicable steps are being taken to prevent the effluent or matter causing pollution;

    (c) whether it is reasonably practicable to dispose of the effluent or matter in any other manner;

    (d) whether the discharge constitutes a significant threat to public health, fisheries or any persons using water.

2. The DoE(NI) must ensure that the discharge can be sustained by the receiving

---

49. SI 1973/70.
50. It should be noted that Sch. 4 to the Water and Sewerage Services (NI) Order 1973 repeals the word 'intended' in s. 9(5). As a result the DoE(NI) is now required to give notice of its decision within three months rather than notice of its 'intended' decision.
51. *Environment Service Report* 1991–93, p. 28.

water without breaching any of the water quality standards set in relation to specific physical, chemical and microbiological parameters at EC and national levels. The provisions operating in this regard are examined in detail in Part VI of this chapter together with the measures which implement these standards in Northern Ireland.

3. The DoE(NI) must also ensure compliance with EC standards governing discharges of certain specified dangerous substances to water, all of which are discussed in more detail in Part VII of this chapter.

4. The Urban Waste Water Treatment Regulations (NI) 1995[52] require that the DoE(NI) ensure that the standards laid down in the Regulations concerning the disposal of urban waste water to receiving waters are complied with by means of the discharge consent system laid down in the WA. The terms of the UWWT Regulations are set out in Part IX of this chapter.

5. Regulation 64 of the Conservation (Natural Habitats etc.) Regulations (NI) 1995[53] provides that in considering whether to grant a discharge consent under the WA the DoE(NI) must have regard to the impact of any 'plan or project' on a 'European site',[54] and in this regard regulations 43, 44 and 49 of the Habitats Regulations will govern the making of such an assessment[55] and the factors which must be taken into account.[56]

6. When exercising any of its functions under the WA, the Department is required to have regard to a number of interests when deciding whether to grant a discharge consent, namely, the needs of industry and agriculture, the protection of fisheries, the protection of public health, the preservation of amenity, and the conservation of flora and fauna (section 2(1)). In effect, the DoE(NI) could refuse to grant consent where it considers that the discharge in question would be detrimental to any of the interests listed in section 2(1).

The DoE(NI) will refuse to grant a discharge consent where the discharge in question would result in an unacceptable amount of pollution to receiving waters. However, where a consent is issued, the Department is obliged to monitor the discharge regularly to ensure compliance with the consent conditions. Finally, it should be noted that in 1990 the National Rivers Authority (which has general responsibility for water pollution in England and Wales under the Water Resources Act 1991) recommended the introduction of a more sophisticated test based on the toxicity of the discharge.[57] In the *Environment Service Corporate Plan, 1994–97* the Department stated that it would 'develop and implement (in conjunction with the National Rivers Authority) a consistent approach to the setting of toxicity-

---

52. SR No. 12.
53. SR No. 380.
54. A 'European site' is essentially a site designated under the Habitats Directive or Wild Birds Directive. The more precise meaning of this term and the protections afforded to such sites are discussed in chap. 7.
55. The nature of the environmental impact assessment is addressed in more detail in chap. 11.
56. It should be noted that although the DoE(NI) is required to take the preservation of amenity and the conservation of flora and fauna into consideration when deciding whether to grant a discharge consent, the protection afforded to European sites under the Conservation (Natural Habitats etc.) Regulations (NI) 1995 in this context is more stringent than that afforded to habitat sites of purely local interest. See chap. 7 for further discussion of the distinction between habitat sites protected under EC standards and those protected purely under national law.
57. *Discharge Consent and Compliance Policy: A Blueprint for the Future*, NRA 1990.

based discharge consents by the end of 1996', which would be used to set discharge consents for industrial effluent discharges, which frequently contain complex mixtures of chemicals.[58]

### Register of consents

The DoE(NI) is obliged to maintain a register of the consents and attached conditions that are currently in force, and this must be open to public inspection at all reasonable hours. In addition, the information contained in the register will be treated as conclusive evidence (in the defendant's favour) of the terms of any currently binding consent or condition.

### Review of consents

The DoE(NI) may review any consent that is granted under section 7 or 8 of the WA. However, it may only review discharge consents at intervals of not less than three years (section 10(1)). In this context the three-year period will be dated either from the date on which the consent was given or from the date on which the last consent review was conducted. It should be noted, however, that a review may be conducted at any time if the person making the discharge in question applies to the Department for a review. Where a review is conducted, the Department may vary[59] the consent or any of the conditions to which the consent is subject. The Department may not, however, vary the consent or its conditions unless it gives notice of the variation to the person to whom the consent was granted and to either the Fisheries Conservancy Board for Northern Ireland or, if the discharge is made in the Derry area, to the Foyle Fisheries Commission (section 10(2) and (3)).

In addition, section 10(3), as amended by Schedule 3 to the Water and Sewerage Services (NI) Order 1973, provides that the applicant and the relevant board or commission may appeal against the variation to the Water Appeals Commission for Northern Ireland; the appeal must be brought within twenty-eight days of the date on which notice of the variation was given to them. It should also be noted that it is also an offence under section 22(*b*) to 'knowingly or recklessly' make a statement that is false in a material particular for the purpose of obtaining a consent in the context of a review, the penalties for which are outlined in the discussion of the application procedure above.

### Penalties

Section 9(10), as amended by article 17(*b*) of the Water and Sewerage Services (Amendment) (NI) Order 1993, sets out the penalties for discharging matter without the DoE(NI)'s consent or for making a discharge that violates a condition attached to a consent. The 1993 Order increases the fine from £2,000 to £20,000 for summary conviction of an offence under section 7 or 8 and also removes the provision in section 9(10) concerning substantial repetition of such an offence. The position now is that a person who contravenes section 7 or 8, or any

---

58. P. 32.
59. S. 10(4) of the WA provides that the term 'vary' in this context includes the imposition of new conditions and the substitution of conditions.

conditions imposed on a consent issued under section 7 or 8, will be liable on conviction on indictment to imprisonment for a maximum term of two years or to an unlimited fine, or to both and, on summary conviction, to imprisonment for a maximum term of three months or to a maximum fine of £20,000, or to both. The penalties laid down in section 9(10) also apply to a breach of conditions attached to a retrospective discharge consent granted under section 9(2).

### Section 13 notices (emergency powers)

The DoE(NI) is empowered to issue a notice under section 13 of the WA prohibiting a discharge where it is in the public interest to do so. Such a notice can be issued regardless of the existence of a discharge consent and regardless of the conditions attached to that consent. The Department's powers under section 13 and the right to appeal a section 13 notice are discussed in Part III of this chapter, together with the DoE(NI)'s other powers to prevent water pollution.

### General DoE(NI) powers

The WA confers a wide range of administrative and preventive powers on the DoE(NI) to enable it to exercise its functions under the Act effectively. Because these powers can be used by the Department while exercising any of its functions in relation to the prevention and control of pollution in Northern Ireland's inland, coastal and ground waters, they are discussed separately in Parts III and IV of this chapter.

### Radioactive substances

Section 40 of the Radioactive Substances Act 1993,[60] which applies to the UK as a whole, provides that 'no account can be taken of any radioactivity possessed by any substance or article or by any part of any premises' for the purposes of exercising or performing any statutory power or duty or in the enforcement of any statutory provision under section 7 or 8 of the WA. In effect, this means that the non-radioactive elements of a discharge are governed by the WA, while the radioactive elements are dealt with under the Radioactive Substances Act 1993.

### Proposed changes to the consent discharge system

In 1993 the DoE(NI) and DANI issued a Consultation Paper[61] setting out proposals for a review of the Water Act with a view to introducing updated water pollution legislation in mid-1996. At the time of writing, the new legislation has not been enacted. However, the Consultation Paper sought views as to whether the following changes should be introduced to the discharge consent system that operates at present under the WA. Each will now be addressed in turn.

---

60. c. 12.
61. *Review of the Water Act (NI) 1972: A Consultation Paper,* Belfast: DoE(NI) and DANI 1993.

### Factors which may be considered when determining a consent application

Section 2(1) of the WA requires the DoE(NI) to have regard to specific interests when determining an application for consent, and the DoE(NI) may refuse to grant a consent where it considers that a discharge would be detrimental to any of the interests which section 2(1) seeks to protect. The Consultation Paper points out that situations can arise where the existence of a development, as opposed to a discharge, could pose a hazard to wildlife, which is one of the interests to be considered; the paper seeks views on whether the DoE(NI) should be empowered to consider the hazard posed by a development when considering an application for a discharge consent. In this regard, the paper was particularly concerned about the hazard posed by marine cages used for aquaculture, which are a potential hazard for fauna such as seals and cormorants. The paper also suggests that provision should be made to define 'premises' as including marine fish cages (paragraph 5.1.2 and 5.1.3).[62]

### Public consultation

The Consultation Paper points out that public interest in the control of water pollution has grown considerably in recent years, to the point where the DoE(NI) now requires all applications for discharge consents to be advertised in local newspapers (except for discharges from septic tanks serving single dwelling-houses). The paper points out that while some advertisements have generated large numbers of public representations, the WA does not empower the DoE(NI) to hold a public inquiry on a discharge application. Views are sought as to whether the DoE(NI) should be empowered to cause the Water Appeals Commission for Northern Ireland to hold a public inquiry to consider objections lodged in response to such an advertisement or to hold an inquiry where the proposed discharge is regarded as 'environmentally critical'. It is also proposed that an application for a discharge consent should be deemed legally invalid unless it has been advertised (with the exception of discharges from septic tanks serving single dwelling-houses), thereby reinforcing the importance of public consultation on water pollution issues.

The Consultation Paper also points to the fact that many discharge applications concern discharges from new developments, such as a new factory or landfill. Where the new development is controversial, the Planning Appeals Commission will hold a public inquiry into the application for planning permission, and in such a situation, if the DoE(NI) were given the power to hold a public inquiry, it is likely that the application for discharge consent would also result in a public inquiry. Given that water pollution is a material planning consideration, this would involve a considerable degree of duplication between the two inquiries; the Consultation Paper, therefore, seeks views as to whether the DoE(NI) should be

---

62. It should be noted that reg. 64 of the Conservation (Natural Habitats etc.) Regulations (NI) 1995 (SR No. 380) provides that in considering whether to grant a discharge consent under the WA, the DoE(NI) must have regard to the impact of any 'plan or project' on a 'European site'. This obligation extends only to areas designated as European sites and is explained in the context of the factors which must be taken into consideration when the DoE(NI) sets a discharge consent under s. 7 or 8.

empowered to direct that a joint public inquiry be held by the Planning and Water Appeals Commissions in such situations. The joint inquiry would include consideration of objections to the discharge consent and, in determining the consent application, the DoE(NI)'s Environment Service would be obliged to take the inquiry report into consideration.

The Consultation Paper also suggests that where a public inquiry has been held in relation to a consent application, the right of appeal to the Water Appeals Commission for Northern Ireland under section 9(4) should be extinguished, on the ground that it would be inappropriate to hold a second hearing into an appeal against the decision that was made in light of the inquiry. The paper suggests instead that the Foyle Fisheries Commission or the Fisheries Conservancy Board be given a statutory right to appear and be heard at any public inquiry held in relation to a discharge consent. Finally, the Consultation Paper recommends that provision be made for the advertisement of public inquiries into discharge consents and appeals of decisions concerning discharge consents (paragraph 5.2.1–5.2.7).

### Time limits on consent applications

The Consultation Paper proposes that the time limit for determining discharge applications under section 9(5) be extended from the present three months to four months. It is pointed out that the conditions which must now be imposed on discharge consents under national and EC water quality standards are much more complex than those envisaged when the WA was drafted in 1971, and, as a result, consent applications can seldom be dealt with within three months. It is proposed, however, that the present position concerning default consents be maintained, namely, that if a decision is not made within the statutory time limit, an unconditional consent is deemed to be granted (paragraph 5.3.1–5.3.2).

### Public registers of discharge consents

The present consent registers are only required to contain particulars of the consents issued and of consent conditions. The Consultation Paper suggests that public registers of discharge consents should be required to contain details of the applications for consents, the consents that have been issued, particulars of samples of water and effluent, analyses of these samples, and the steps which have been taken as a result of such monitoring. It is also suggested that the register would contain the standards that are set by the DoE(NI) for discharges from the Department's sewage and treatment works (paragraph 5.4.1). It should also be noted that the DoE(NI) intends to adopt the Discharge Consent Register Regulations in the near future pursuant to powers contained in the forthcoming Water Order.

### Review of consents

Section 10 of the WA empowers the Department to review any discharge consent after three years or more frequently at the request of the person making the discharge. Given that a review may result in the issue of a revised consent which significantly alters the conditions under which a discharge can be made, and given that the DoE(NI) has the power to require all applications for new consents to be advertised, the Consultation Paper states that the public should be informed of consent reviews and to this end proposes that the DoE(NI) be given the power to require that a consent review be advertised. It is also proposed that the period between reviews be increased from three to four years and that the period of a consent run from the date of any appeal decision. This proposal is designed to provide greater stability for dischargers, thus providing more security in investment and planning and thereby implementing the Government's deregulation policy. Finally, it is proposed that the DoE(NI) be empowered to serve notices that require existing discharges to be stopped in order to ensure compliance with new EC and international standards concerning the discharge of various substances to the aquatic environment (paragraph 5.5.1–5.5.4).

### Introduction of discharge consent fees

In line with the Government's commitment to the 'polluter pays' principle, fees are being introduced for all environmental controls and licences throughout the UK. It is proposed that fees be charged for discharge consents in Northern Ireland and also that powers be conferred on the DoE(NI) to recover the cost of granting and controlling consents issued under the WA. A further Consultation Paper will be issued on the latter proposal setting out specific proposals for the calculation of the charges; DoE(NI) proposals concerning discharge consent fees will be published in mid or late 1997. It should be noted that the DoE(NI) intends to adopt the Discharge Consent Fees Regulations in the near future pursuant to powers to be contained in the forthcoming Water Order.

## PART III PREVENTIVE POWERS

Although the main focus of the WA is on the control of discharges and on taking enforcement action where pollution has occurred, the WA also empowers the DoE(NI) to take various types of action to prevent the pollution of inland, coastal and ground waters. Each of these preventive powers will be outlined in turn.

### Section 13 notices (emergency power to control or prevent pollution)

The Department is empowered under section 13 to give any person a notice prohibiting him from depositing or discharging any specified matter on any land, into any waterway[63] or into any underground strata[64] that are specified in the notice. Such a notice may be issued where the Department is satisfied that it is in the public interest to do so. A notice issued under section 13 will have effect regardless of whether a discharge consent has been granted under section 7 or 8 (discussed in Part II of this chapter) and regardless of whether any conditions were imposed on that consent under section 9 or 10. In addition, the notice will continue in force until such time as:

(i) it is revoked by the DoE(NI),

---

63. The term 'waterway' is defined in note 28, supra.
64. The term 'underground strata' is defined in note 29, supra.

(ii) the DoE(NI) grants its consent to the discharge in question under section 7 or 8 in response to an application made by the person making the discharge; or

(iii) the person to whom the notice is given appeals the notice successfully.

Violation of a section 13 notice is an offence under section 13(5); the penalties incurred for conviction on indictment and summary conviction are identical to those incurred for violation of a discharge consent under section 9(10) of the WA, which are outlined in Part II of this chapter.

Section 13(3), as amended by Schedule 3 to the Water and Sewerage Services (NI) Order 1973, provides that a section 13 notice may be appealed to the Water Appeals Commission for Northern Ireland. However, the appeal must be brought within four weeks of the notice being served. The Commission is given the jurisdiction to quash or vary any provision contained in the notice which it considers to be unreasonable. Section 13(4), as amended by Schedule 3 to the 1973 Order, provides that where the person to whom the notice was served has complied with the terms of the notice *and* where the notice is subsequently varied or quashed on appeal, the Department is obliged to pay to that person an amount equal to the loss sustained or expenditure incurred by them in complying with the notice. Schedule 3 to the 1973 Order inserts a new paragraph 4A into section 13, which provides that any dispute as to the loss suffered or expenditure incurred will be determined by the Lands Tribunal.

## Works to prevent, remedy or mitigate pollution

Where the DoE(NI) considers that any poisonous, noxious or polluting matter is present in, or is likely to enter, a waterway or water contained in underground strata as a result of 'an accident or some other unforeseen act or event,' the Department is empowered under section 13(6) to carry out such operations as it considers necessary or expedient for the purposes of:

(i)   removing that matter from the water or land and disposing of it in any manner that the Department considers appropriate; and

(ii)  'remedying or mitigating any pollution' caused by the presence of the matter in the waterway or underground strata.

The Department may recover any expense incurred from any money received as a result of disposing of the material. However, in so far as they are not defrayed in this way, the Department's expenses are recoverable from the person in default as a contract debt due to the DoE(NI) (section 13(8)). Finally, it should be noted that section 13(7), which confined the DoE(NI)'s powers under section 13 to works of a temporary nature, has been repealed by Schedule 3 to the Pollution Control and Local Government (NI) Order 1978;[65] one should also note that the DoE(NI) possesses more general powers to carry out 'engineering or building operations' for the purposes of exercising any of its functions under the WA, these are discussed in Part IV of this chapter.

---

65. SI 1978/1049.

## The adoption of regulations

The DoE(NI) is empowered under section 12 to adopt regulations for various specified purposes, all designed to prevent pollution of inland and coastal waters. Schedule 2 to the WA, as amended by Schedule 3 to the Water and Sewerage Services (NI) Order 1973,[66] governs the adoption of regulations under section 12. The *Review of the Water Act (NI) 1972: A Consultation Paper* proposes that these powers be extended to enable the Department to adopt standards for agriculture and industry. The Department has exercised its powers under section 12 to adopt the Prevention of Pollution (Erne System) Regulations (NI) 1994,[67] which, in effect, provide that it is an offence for an owner or hirer[68] to keep or use, or to knowingly permit the keeping or use of, a vessel on the Erne System[69] that can discharge the contents of its sanitary appliances (toilets) directly into the water. Violation of the Regulations will be punishable on summary conviction by a maximum fine of £2,500.

## Section 6 notices (preventing a likely breach of section 5(1))

Where the DoE(NI) concludes that a breach of section 5(1) is likely to occur or that a repetition or continuation of an existing breach is likely to occur as a result of:

(i) the use or proposed use of 'a waterway or of land for the disposal of any matter'; or

(ii) the use or proposed use of 'any land for storing any matter'; or

(iii) the use or proposed use of 'a vessel or vehicle from which poisonous, noxious or polluting matter may enter a waterway or water in any underground strata',

the Department is empowered under section 6(1) to serve a notice which prohibits any of these proposed or actual uses, or which permits the use or proposed use subject to certain conditions. Notices under section 6(1) will be served either on the owner[70] of the land or on the person using or proposing to use the water, land, vehicle, or vessel. Such a notice may be appealed, within four weeks of the date of service, to the Water Appeals Commission for Northern Ireland; the Commission is empowered to quash the notice if it concludes that no violation of section 5(1) is likely to occur by reason of the use or proposed use complained of (section 6(7)).

A notice served under section 6(1) may require the removal of the matter complained of from the water, land, vehicle, or vessel, and in the event that such a requirement is not complied with, the Department itself may undertake the removal and disposal of such matter (section 6(3) and (4)). Any expenses incurred

---

66. SI 1973/70.
67. SR No. 20.
68. Reg. 2 defines a 'hirer' as 'any person to whom a vessel shall be on hire or any person in charge thereof by the appointment or with the permission of the owner.'
69. The 'Erne system' is defined as 'Upper and Lower Lough Erne and such portions of the River Erne and the tributaries of both of the Loughs as are in Northern Ireland and including all locks, quays, jetties, harbours and canals.'
70. S. 30(1) defines the terms 'owner' as a person 'who is for the time being receiving a rent of not less than two-thirds of the net annual value of any land whether on his own account or as agent or trustee for any person or who, if the land were let at such a rent, would receive it.'

by the Department in doing so may be recovered from any money received from its disposal, and, in so far as they are not fully defrayed, they will be recoverable as a contract debt due from the person in breach of the notice (section 6(6)).

The Department is obliged to provide particulars of any notices served under section 6 to any person who appears to the Department to be interested in any land whose use or proposed use is affected by the notice or where the notice is otherwise material to the use of the land. The Department's obligation in this regard will only be invoked if that person requests such particulars; these will be made available at that person's expense, and will be made available to any other person specified in the request. Finally, it should be noted that section 6(2) of the WA has been repealed by the Schedule to the Water and Sewerage Services (Amendment) (NI) Order 1993.

## Proposed changes to the system of preventive control

### *Section 6 notices preventing a likely breach of section 5(1)*

The Consultation Paper issued in 1993 concerning the WA points out that the DoE(NI)'s enforcement powers under section 6 are limited. Although an offender can be prosecuted where pollution occurs, the Consultation Paper points out that 'this sanction cannot, however, be used where pollution has not yet occurred but the occupier of the land fails to remove the material or to comply with conditions subject to which the disposal or storage is permitted, for example, the bunding of oil tanks or spoil heaps or the secure storage of chemicals.' Furthermore, the paper points out that while the DoE(NI) is empowered under section 6 to remove the material in question and to dispose of it where pollution has not actually occurred, such action can only be taken in exceptional circumstances.

Given the large numbers of premises in Northern Ireland in which potentially polluting substances are stored, the Consultation Paper points out that this is an impractical proposition. The paper seeks views on whether the DoE(NI) should be granted powers to prosecute for non-compliance with a section 6 notice even where pollution has not occurred (paragraph 6.1–6.6).

### *Expanding the DoE(NI)'s powers to adopt regulations to prevent pollution*

The Consultation Paper also points to the fact that even if the DoE(NI) was granted wider preventive powers under section 6, as outlined above, it would not be possible to serve section 6 notices in relation to every site in Northern Ireland where polluting material is based. The Consultation Paper states that it would be useful if standards could be prescribed by means of regulation in relation to bunds (embankments), holding tanks, secure enclosures, etc., thereby setting down clear standards for industry and agriculture as to the preventive measures which they would be obliged to take.

Although the DoE(NI) is empowered under section 12 to adopt regulations to prevent water pollution, these powers are limited. The Consultation Paper seeks views on whether the DoE(NI)'s powers to adopt such regulations should be extended. In particular, the proposal points to regulations adopted in Great Britain which lay down standards for silos, slurry tanks and oil storage in agriculture, and corresponding regulations which will be adopted for industry; it is suggested that the DoE(NI) be empowered to adopt parallel regulations for Northern Ireland (paragraph 6.7). In this regard it should be noted that the DoE(NI) intends to adopt the Silage, Slurry and Agriculture Fuel Oil Regulations in the near future pursuant to powers contained in the forthcoming Water Order.

## *Part IV* Administrative Powers

Sections 15–29 of the WA confer a wide variety of powers on the DoE(NI) which may be used by the Department in the exercise of its obligations or powers to prevent and control the pollution of Northern Ireland's inland, coastal and ground waters. These powers will each be addressed in turn.

### Acquisition and disposal of land

Section 17 of the WA grants the DoE(NI) the power to acquire land either by agreement or lease or compulsorily,[71] and also to dispose of such land, for any purposes in connection with the performance of its functions under the WA.[72]

### Engineering and building works

The Department has the power to carry out such engineering or building operations[73] as it considers necessary or expedient for the purposes of any of its functions under the WA. It also has the power to discharge water into any waterway or into any underground strata or onto land for these purposes, and may also vary the flow of water in a waterway or water in underground strata for these purposes (section 18(*a*)–(*c*)). The Department may adopt orders under section 19 which empower it to use such compulsory powers as it considers necessary for the purposes of exercising its powers under section 18; the functions for which such powers are being exercised must be specified in the order. Schedule 4 to the WA, as amended by Schedule 3 to the Water and Sewerage Services (NI) Order 1973, will apply to the making of such orders. This power has not been exercised to date.

### General power to collect information

The Department has the power to collect or commission the collection of such data and information as it considers necessary for the purposes of performing any of its functions under the WA, and, in addition, may carry out or commission research for the same purposes (section 20). The Department has discretion to decide

---

71. A vesting order will be made by the Department for the purpose of acquiring land compulsorily; s. 34(7) of and Sch. 5 to the Roads Act (NI) 1948 will apply (subject to the provisions contained in Sch. 3 to the WA) to the acquisition of land by vesting order under the WA.
72. S. 5 of the Stormont Regulation and Government Property Act (NI) 1933 will not affect the disposal or acquisition of land acquired by the DoE(NI) under s. 17 of the WA.
73. The DoE(NI)'s power to carry out 'engineering or building operations' includes (without prejudice to the generality of the expression) 'the construction, alteration, improvement or maintenance of any reservoir, waterway, dam, weir, well, borehole or other works, the closure or removal of any reservoir, waterway, dam, well, borehole or other works, the construction, alteration, improvement, maintenance or demolition of any building or structure, and the installation, modification or removal or any machinery or apparatus' (s. 30(1)).

whether to publish, or permit the publication of, any data or information collected by it, or the results of any research conducted or commissioned by it. The Department is, however, obliged under section 20(3) to provide 'reasonable facilities' for the public to inspect records of data or information collected by it or on its behalf. In addition, reasonable facilities must be provided for taking copies of and extracts from such records. It is important to note, that the Department is not obliged to provide facilities for public inspection etc. of the results of research conducted by or on behalf of the Department.

### Supply of information concerning abstraction or discharges

The DoE(NI) may direct any person who is abstracting[74] water from a waterway or any underground strata, or who is discharging effluent into such waterway or strata, to supply such information to the Department concerning the abstraction or discharge as is required by the Department; such information must be provided at the times and in the form specified in the direction (section 21(1)). Section 21(2), as amended by Schedule 3 to the Water and Sewerage Services (NI) Order 1973,[75] provides that the recipient of such a direction may appeal to the Water Appeals Commission for Northern Ireland to have the direction varied or quashed on the grounds that it would be 'unreasonable or unduly onerous' to comply with the terms of the direction. The appeal must be brought within four weeks of the date on which the direction was given to him. Failure to comply with a section 21 direction is an offence punishable on summary conviction by a maximum fine of £200 (level 1 on the standard scale). Similarly, where a person is required to provide information, it is an offence under section 22(a) to 'knowingly or recklessly' make a statement which is false in a material particular. The penalty incurred for an offence under this section is an unlimited fine or imprisonment for a maximum of two years, or both, if convicted on indictment, or, a maximum fine of £5,000 (level 5 on the standard scale) or imprisonment for a maximum of three months, or both, if convicted summarily.

### Powers of entry

A person authorised by the DoE(NI) may enter any land, vessel or vehicle at any reasonable time[76] for the purposes of performing any function conferred on the Department under the WA, whether it relates to that land, vehicle or vessel or not (section 23(1)(a) and (5)). Similarly, section 23(1)(b) provides that such a person may enter any land, vehicle or vessel at any reasonable time[77] to inspect or survey[78] the land, vehicle or vessel or to inspect any article contained therein in

---

74. S. 30(1) defines 'abstraction' as 'the doing of anything' whereby water is removed from coastal or inland waters or from underground strata.

75. SI 1973/70.

76. Admission onto land which is used for residential purposes or admission onto any other land with heavy equipment cannot be demanded under s. 23(1) unless seven days' notice in writing of the intended entry has been given to the occupier, except in cases of emergency.

77. As under s. 23(1)(a), admission onto land which is used for residential purposes or admission onto any other land with heavy equipment cannot be demanded under s. 23(1) unless seven days' notice in writing of the intended entry has been given to the occupier, except in cases of emergency.

78. S. 23(4) provides that the power to survey land in this context includes the power to sink boreholes.

order to determine whether, and if so in what manner, any of the Department's functions need to be performed on the land, vehicle or vessel and whether any provision of the WA has been complied with.[79]

A justice of the peace may, by warrant, authorise such a person to enter any land, vehicle or vessel, using force if necessary, if any of the circumstances specified in section 23(2) are established to the satisfaction of the justice on sworn information in writing *and* it is established that there are reasonable grounds for making the entry for the purposes for which the entry is required. The specified circumstances are:

(i) an authorised person has been refused admission to the land, or refusal is anticipated; or

(ii) the land is unoccupied or the occupier is temporarily absent; or

(iii) it is an urgent case; or

(iv) an application for admission would defeat the object of the entry.

A warrant issued under section 23(2) will remain in force until the purpose for which the entry was necessary is satisfied.

Section 24(1)–(8) sets out further provisions concerning the exercise of powers under section 23; they are as follows:

1. A person entering any land, vehicle or vessel under section 23 is obliged to produce evidence of their authority to enter before entering if such evidence is requested.

2. A person entering under section 23 may also take any such equipment as may be necessary with him.

3. An authorised person who enters any premises under section 23 which is unoccupied or whose occupier is temporarily absent must leave the premises as effectively secured against trespassers as he found them.

4. It is an offence to 'wilfully obstruct' an authorised person exercising powers under section 23; summary conviction for such an offence will incur a maximum fine of £1,000.

5. Where an authorised person under section 23 causes damage to land or chattels while exercising their powers, compensation will be payable by the DoE(NI) to any person with an interest in the damaged land or chattels. Similarly, any person whose enjoyment of any land or chattels is disturbed as a result of the exercise of such powers will also be entitled to compensation from the DoE(NI). Any dispute about the amount of compensation will be determined by the Lands Tribunal.

6. Finally, it is an offence for an authorised person who was admitted to a factory, workshop or work-place under section 23 to disclose any information obtained therein concerning a manufacturing process or trade secret, unless the disclosure was made in the performance of his duty. Such an offence is punishable on summary conviction by a maximum fine of £1,000 or by imprisonment for a maximum of three months, or both.

---

79. The power set out in s. 23(1)(*b*) is also exercisable for the purpose of inspecting any documents or statutory provision which are in the possession of any body and which relate to the functions of the body. In addition, the person carrying out any such inspection may take copies of, or extracts from, any such documents or provision (s. 23(6)).

## Repeal or amendment of inconsistent local or private Acts

The DoE(NI) is empowered under section 28(1) of the WA to adopt orders for the purpose of repealing, amending or adapting any local or private Acts[80] that were enacted before the enactment of the WA but which are inconsistent with any of its provisions, or with any regulations or orders adopted under the WA, or with anything done in the performance of any function under the WA. Thus far this power has not been exercised by the DoE(NI).

## Right to obtain and remove samples

Any person authorised by the DoE(NI) has the right to take samples of water from a waterway or underground strata and also to take samples of any effluent or matter that is 'passing or likely to pass from' any land, vessel or vehicle into a waterway or underground strata (section 25(1)). The right to take samples under section 25 includes the right to 'obtain and take away' samples. It is an offence, punishable by a maximum fine of £1,000 on summary conviction, to 'wilfully obstruct' a person in the exercise of a right conferred under section 25.

The Department may, after consultation with the occupier of any land or premises from which effluent is discharged, fix the points at which samples of effluent passing into any waterway or any underground strata are to be taken (section 25(3)). The Department is obliged under section 25(4) to maintain a register which contains the particulars of all sampling points fixed under section 25(3); this register must be open to public inspection at all reasonable hours. For the purpose of legal proceedings it will be presumed, until the contrary is established, that any sample of effluent which is taken at an inspection chamber, a manhole or any other place, in compliance with a condition imposed under the WA concerning any waterway or underground strata, is a sample of what was passing from the land or premises to that water or stratum (section 25(2)). Similarly it will be presumed, until the contrary is established, that any sample of effluent that is taken at a point fixed by the Department is a sample of what was passing from the land or premises to that water or those strata (section 25(3)).

Section 25(5) provides that where a sample taken under section 25 is analysed, the results of the analysis cannot be admitted as evidence in any legal proceedings concerning effluent passing from any land, vehicle or vessel unless the person taking the sample complies with the following steps:

(i) The person taking the sample must 'take all reasonable steps to notify the occupier[81] of the land or the owner or master of the vessel or owner of the vehicle of his intention to have it analysed.'

(ii) The person taking the sample must 'there and then' divide the sample taken into three parts and 'cause each part to be placed in a container which is sealed and marked.'

(iii) The person taking the sample must have one part of the sample analysed, must retain another part for future comparison, and must take all reasonable

---

80. The term 'Act' as used in s. 28(1) includes an Act of Parliament of the UK.
81. In legal proceedings concerning the passage of effluent from a local authority sewer into any waterway, s. 25(6) provides that s. 25(5) will have effect as if the reference to the occupier of the land were a reference to the authority by whom the sewer is maintained.

steps to deliver one part of the sample to either the occupier of the land,[82] the owner or master of the vessel, or the owner of the vehicle.

The Court of Appeal in *CPC (UK) v. NRA*[83] considered the sampling procedure laid down in section 209(1) of the Water Resources Act 1991, which, until its repeal under the Environmental Protection Act 1995, set out a sampling procedure for England and Wales identical to that which currently applies in Northern Ireland under section 25 of the WA. The court ruled that the sampling procedure is designed to protect both the defendant and the prosecuting authority against any subsequent arguments about the validity of the sample. Leeson also points out that it is important to note that the sampling procedure establishes a 'mandatory exclusionary rule', in that a 'failure to comply with this procedure will prohibit production of the sample in later legal proceedings'. However, the rule applies only to samples taken by the 'Authority', which in the Northern Ireland context is the DoE(NI). In other words, 'the products of routine sampling by the plant operator and the results would be admissible without satisfying these principles.'[84]

Leeson also points out that this sampling procedure is only obligatory 'where evidence is based on analysis of a sample.'[85] Section 25(8) of the WA defines the term 'analysis' very broadly; it states that any reference to an analysis in section 25 should be interpreted as including a reference 'to a test of whatever kind'.[86] The term 'sample' is not defined by the WA; however, the Court of Appeal in *CPC (UK) v. NRA* also considered the meaning of this term in the context of the Water Resources Act 1991. In the absence of a statutory definition the court relied on the *Oxford English Dictionary,* which stated that a sample is 'a small separated part of something . . .' The court ruled that the separation was essential to the nature of a sample, and in this regard stated:

> [T]his implies that the part must be separated physically from the whole, and in the case of water, that the part which becomes a sample must be isolated in some form of container. We do not consider that a 'sample' of the water comes into existence unless and until this is done.[87]

The court in *CPC* then concluded that readings of the pH (acidity) level taken from a static monitoring device which continuously diverted water from a river did not constitute a sample within the meaning of the Water Resources Act 1991. The court ruled that while 'the machine could be said to "sample" the flow of water in the same way as a hand-held probe could be said to do so, nevertheless the kind of machine which was used in this case [did] not . . . take a "sample" of water within the meaning of section 209.'

The recent decision of the Court of Appeal in *Attorney-General's Reference (No. 2 of 1994)* adopted a purposive interpretation of section 209. It ruled, firstly,

---

82. Ibid.
83. [1994] Crim Div, 15 July 1994. The ruling in this case is discussed in some detail in Leeson, *Environmental Law,* London: Pitman, 1995, p. 168.
84. Leeson, ibid., pp 168–9.
85. Ibid., p. 169.
86. The statutory definition of the term 'analysis' under s. 209 of the Water Resources Act 1991 is very similar to that contained in s. 25(8) of the WA. The 1991 Act defines an analysis as 'subjecting the sample to a test of any description'; in this regard Leeson argues that the term 'test' would appear to include 'ad hoc visual or olfactory examination', ibid., p. 169.
87. See: Leeson, supra note 83, p. 169.

that the owner did not necessarily have to be notified before the sample was taken and divided. The court stated that:

> there will be some latitude in the time surrounding the event of taking the sample, but not a great deal. In each case it will be a matter of degree as to whether that latitude is exceeded or not. Again, there may be cases where the need for surprise or some other reason may prompt the National Rivers Authority to notify the occupier immediately after taking the sample rather than beforehand; in other cases, trust, comity or other reasons may prompt the [National Rivers Authority] to notify the occupier in advance.[88]

The court went on to consider the meaning of the requirement that the sample be divided 'there and then' and ruled that it should be divided at a location 'at or proximate to' the site where the sample was taken.

### Proposals for the introduction of automatic composite sampling

The *Review of the Water Act (NI) 1972: A Consultation Paper* issued in 1993 raises the question whether composite sampling should be permitted in water pollution control and, also, whether automatic equipment should be permitted to provide composite samples. Composite sampling entails taking samples at hourly intervals over a 24-hour period, bulking the twenty-four samples, and then analysing the composite sample. EC Directive 91/271/EEC on the treatment of urban waste lays down monitoring requirements which involve taking composite samples; this technique is also being considered for other categories of discharge. Under the WA the results of sample analysis can only be admitted as evidence in legal proceedings where a 'spot sample' (or non-composite sample) has been taken by an authorised person and, where appropriate, the occupier of the premises is afforded an opportunity to witness the sampling. The Consultation Paper points out that were composite sampling of effluent discharges to be permitted, it would be very time-consuming and expensive for an individual officer to undertake. As a result, it suggests that the installation of an automatic sampler would be a more practical alternative. This equipment could be installed on the effluent discharge and programmed to take samples at set intervals and to place the sample in a sealed tank. The authorised officer would then divide the contents of the tanks into three parts, and, as is now required under section 25 of the WA, one part would be given to the occupier (paragraphs 7.1–7.2).

## PART V CONTROLLING, RESTRICTING OR PROHIBITING WATER ABSTRACTIONS

Section 14 of the WA empowers the DoE(NI) to adopt regulations for the purpose of making such provision as appears to it to be necessary to control, restrict or prohibit abstractions[89] of water from underground strata[90] or

---

88. [1995] 2 All ER 1000, at 1005.
89. S. 30(1) defines 'abstraction' as 'the doing of anything' whereby water is removed from coastal or inland waters or from underground strata.
90. The term 'underground strata' is defined at note 29, supra.

waterways,[91] excluding the sea. The Department also has the power to adopt regulations for the purpose of levying charges on the abstraction of water from such waters. Thus far, neither of these powers has been exercised. Although the abstraction of water from rivers and underground strata by means of boreholes and wells has been controlled in England and Wales for many years by means of a licensing system, the DoE(NI) has, thus far, not considered it necessary to control water abstraction in Northern Ireland, because of the ample rainfall.

### Proposed changes to the control of water abstraction

The *Review of the Water Act (NI) 1972: A Consultation Paper* issued in 1993 identified a number of factors that suggest that the current system of control governing water abstraction in Northern Ireland may need to be revised. They are:
  (i) Farmers and industrialists are now considering private sources of water supply as a result of charges levied for non-domestic supplies of water.
 (ii) The enactment of Directive 91/676/EEC, which attempts to reduce and prevent water pollution caused by nitrates from agricultural sources (discussed in Part VIII of this chapter), has focused attention on the need to protect underground aquifers from pollution; to this end the DoE(NI) has commissioned the British Geological Survey to carry out a baseline survey of Northern Ireland ground water, the purpose being, to identify hydrogeological units and to establish their resource potential in terms of the water balance and annual abstraction and, in addition, to establish a data-base of boreholes and wells and a water quality monitoring network.
(iii) The Government is introducing fees for all environmental controls and licences pursuant to the EC 'polluter pays' policy, to which the UK is committed.
   The Consultation Paper seeks views on whether, in the light of these facts, it is now necessary to introduce an abstraction licensing system in Northern Ireland, and if so, whether fees should also be charged for abstraction licences. It is also proposed that the DoE(NI) be granted powers to recover the cost of granting and controlling abstraction licences; a further consultation paper will be issued setting out proposals for the calculation of the charges (paragraphs 8.1–8.4 and 9).

## *Part VI* Water quality control

The setting and enforcement of water quality standards are of central concern to the supply of water in Northern Ireland in that public and private water supplies must comply with specific water quality standards. However, such standards also play an important role in the prevention and control of water pollution in Northern Ireland. In effect, whereas the discharge consent system (addressed in Part II of this chapter) operates to control specific or 'point' discharges of pollutants, the water quality approach focuses on the impact of pollutants from diffuse sources on the quality of receiving waters. Water quality standards are set for receiving waters in relation to specific physical, chemical and microbiological parameters.
   Leeson points out that the quality objective approach to pollution control serves

---

91. The term 'waterway' is defined at note 28, supra.

several functions.[92] First, it operates to identify changes in water quality; second, it assists in determining the conditions which should be attached to individual discharge consents; third, it assists in determining the uses (e.g. drinking water) for which particular waters may be suitable; and finally, where waters are used for a particular purpose, any deterioration or change in the quality of that water can be identified and remedied.

Although water quality objectives have been employed on an informal basis since the nineteen-seventies as a means of water pollution control throughout the UK, the introduction of statutory quality objectives is a recent innovation, which owes much to standards set at EC level. The introduction of statutory quality objectives throughout the UK began as a result of the enactment of Directive 76/464/EEC on Dangerous Substances in Water (discussed in more detail in Part VII of this chapter). During the debates leading to the enactment of Directive 76/464/EEC a fundamental difference in approach to water pollution control (and in particular to the control of dangerous substances) emerged between the UK and the European Commission. In effect, the Commission advocated the use of uniform emission limit values in order to control water pollution from dangerous substances; the UK, however, supported an approach based on compliance with water quality objectives for the receiving waters, which would then determine the setting of individualised discharge consent standards.[93]

Although both approaches were ultimately incorporated into the Directive by way of compromise, the Directive provides that member states may only use the quality objective approach if they can establish that the quality objectives are in fact being met. When Directive 76/464/EEC was enacted the UK did not have a formal system for setting water quality objectives. However, to implement the Dangerous Substances Directive by means of the quality objective approach, the UK had to introduce more explicit water quality objectives and ultimately was forced to introduce statutory quality objectives to comply with EC obligations. In 1978 the National Water Council developed a national system of water quality classification for river waters and estuaries.[94] This classification system was used by water authorities throughout the UK for setting what were then informal water quality objectives. It should be noted that this river classification system continues to be used throughout the UK; however, quality standards are now statutory requirements.

The classification system ranks freshwater in five categories determined according to the potential use of the water. They are:

- Good quality (1A): Water of high quality suitable for potable supply abstractions; supporting game or other high-class fisheries; high amenity value.
- Good quality (1B): Water of less high quality than class 1A but usable for substantially the same purposes.

92. Leeson, *Environmental Law,* London: Pitman, (1995) p. 130.
93. It is impossible within the confines of the present chapter to give a more detailed explanation of the differences in approach to pollution theory between the EC and the UK; this issue is considered in detail by Haigh, *Manual of Environmental Policy: The EC and Britain*, London, Longman, 1992, chap. 4.2, p. 6, and by Somsey, 'EC water Directives' (1990) Water Law 93.
94. *River Water Quality: the Next Stage,* National Water Council 1978.

- Fair quality (2): Water suitable for potable supply after advanced treatment; supporting reasonably good coarse fisheries; moderate amenity value.
- Poor quality (3): Water which is polluted to an extent that fish are absent or only sporadically present; may be used for low-grade industrial abstraction purposes; considerable potential for further use if cleaned up.
- Bad quality (4): Water which is grossly polluted and is likely to cause nuisance.

Although the Commission regarded the imposition of uniform emission standards as the most effective means of controlling water pollution by dangerous substances, the EC has employed the quality objective approach to water pollution control in several other contexts. To date six water quality Directives have been adopted. They are:

- Directive 75/440/EEC[95]: Quality of surface water intended for drinking
- Directive 79/869/EEC[96]: Sampling and analysis of surface water intended for drinking
- Directive 80/778/EEC[97]: Quality of water intended for human consumption.
- Directive 76/160/EEC[98]: Quality of bathing water
- Directive 78/659/EEC[99]: Quality of water for freshwater fish
- Directive 79/923/EEC[100]: Quality of water required for shellfish

Each Directive prescribes mandatory and guide quality objectives which are set according to the use to be made of the water. The EC has not adopted quality standards for all uses of water; instead Directives have been adopted concerning particular uses. However, where the EC has adopted objectives for particular water uses, the framework of control in each context follows the same essential pattern. This pattern was summarised by Ball and Bell as follows:

(a) water with particular uses must first be identified (this is usually left to the discretion of the Member States);

(b) the EC must establish a number of parameters: these are normally expressed either as Imperative (I) Values, which must be kept to, or Guide (G) Values, which Member States must try to achieve;

(c) environmental quality objectives must be set for the waters, having regard to the parameters;

(d) a competent national authority must be established for monitoring purposes and uniform sampling techniques are set by EC Directives . . .

(e) procedures are established for updating the I and G Values in light of new knowledge.[101]

The UK implemented each of these Directives initially by means of administrative action (in Northern Ireland within the framework of the Pollution Control and Local Government (NI) Order[102] and the Water Act (NI) 1972[103]). However, the European Court of Justice made it clear during the course of two

95.  OJ L194, 25 July 1975.
96.  OJ L271, 29 Oct. 1979.
97.  OJ L229, 30 Aug. 1980.
98.  OJ L31, 5 Feb. 1976.
99.  OJ L222, 14 Aug. 1978.
100. OJ L281, 10 Nov. 1979.
101. Ball and Bell, *Environmental Law,* 3rd ed. London: Blackstone Press, 1995, pp 420–1.
102. SI 1978/1049.
103. c. 5.

enforcement actions taken against the UK that formal legislation setting statutory quality objectives had to be introduced in order to implement these Directives correctly. Thus the UK was forced to transform its use of water quality objectives as a means of water pollution control from an informal system into a closely prescribed system of statutory control which largely implements standards set at EC level.

The Water and Sewerage Services (Amendment) (NI) Order 1993[104] amended the Water Act (NI) 1972 so as to confer power on the DoE(NI) to adopt statutory water quality standards for Northern Ireland. Article 16 of the 1993 Order inserted sections 4B and 4C into the Water Act (NI) 1972, which empower the Department, first, to adopt regulations for the purpose of prescribing a system of classifying the quality of any waters according to specific criteria and, second, to establish water quality objectives for any waters which are included in a classification system prescribed by the Department for the purpose of maintaining and improving the quality of such water. Section 4B(2) provides that the criteria specified in regulations adopted under section 4B in relation to any classification must consist of one or more of the following:

(a) general requirements as to the purposes for which the waters to which the classification is applied are to be suitable;

(b) specific requirements as to the substances that are to be present in or absent from the water and as to the concentrations of substances which are or are required to be present in the water;

(c) specific requirements as to other characteristics of those waters.

In addition, regulations adopted for the purpose of prescribing classification systems may provide that any question as to whether the prescribed requirements are satisfied may be determined by reference to such samples as may be prescribed. Section 4C(3) provides that where the Department wishes to establish water quality objectives for any waters included in a classification system prescribed by regulation under section 4B, it must comply with the procedure for public consultation laid down in section 4C(4). In essence, section 4C(4) provides that the DoE(NI) must give notice of its proposal to establish water quality objectives for any waters by publishing[105] a notice which sets out the proposal and that specifies the period within which representations or objections may be made concerning the proposal; in this regard, the Department may not specify a period of less than three months. Although the Department is required to consider any representations or objections that are submitted (and not withdrawn) before it makes its decision concerning the proposed water quality objectives, it is empowered to establish the quality objectives that were specified in the notice or to establish quality objectives that are appropriately modified in light of public representations or objections.

Having complied with the public consultation procedure, if the Department decides to establish water quality objectives for any waters it is obliged under section 4C(1) to publish a notice in one or more newspapers circulating in the area

---

104. SI 1993/3165.
105. Art. 4C(5) provides that the Department may publish the notice in 'such manner as the Department considers appropriate for bringing it to the attention of persons likely to be affected by it.'

in question that specifies: (i) the classification (or classifications) prescribed for the time being in relation to those waters and (ii) a date for each specified classification. The water quality objectives for waters to which the notice relates will essentially require that those waters, 'on and at all times after each date specified,' must satisfy the requirements which at the time of the notice were the requirements for the classification to which each date relates.

Section 4C(3) empowers the DoE(NI) to review water quality objectives established under section 4C(1) at not less than five-year intervals since the publication of the notice required under section 4C(1). Where such a review is conducted, the Department is prohibited from establishing water quality objectives by means of varying existing quality objectives, unless it complies once again with the public consultation procedure laid down in section 4C(4), outlined above. If, having conducted a review of the water quality objectives and having considered any representations or objections, the Department decides that water quality objectives should remain unchanged, it is required under section 4C(6) to publish a notice of its decision to that effect and to serve a copy of that notice on any person who submitted representations or objections during the review. The DoE(NI) is also empowered under section 4C(3) to further review its decision in this regard within a period of not less than five years from the date on which it published the notice under section 4C(6).

Section 4C(7) provides that where a person who has made representations or objections following such a review is dissatisfied with the Department's decision to leave the established water quality objectives unchanged, he may appeal against that decision to the Appeals Commission within twenty-eight days of the date on which notice of the Department's decision was served.

With the exception of the Freshwater Fish and Shellfish Directives, all the water quality standards laid down in the EC Water Quality Directives are now implemented in Northern Ireland. However, it is important to note that in each case the Northern Ireland implementing legislation was introduced long after the deadline for formal implementation had expired. Apart from the Bathing Water Directive, which was implemented in 1993 under general powers set out in the European Communities Act 1972,[106] the entire legislative framework governing water quality in Northern Ireland has been introduced since the enactment of the Water and Sewerage Services (Amendment) (NI) Order 1993, which confers power on the DoE(NI) to adopt statutory water quality objectives and thereby the power necessary to formally implement EC water quality Directives in Northern Ireland.

Although there have been long delays in the process of formally implementing the water quality Directives in Northern Ireland, the DoE(NI) has been applying the requirements contained in these Directives in practice since the early nineteen-nineties. In 1993 the DoE(NI)'s Environment Service published the most recent review of water quality in Northern Ireland, *River and Estuary Quality in Northern Ireland: Report of the 1991 Survey*.[107] The survey was carried out over a period of twelve months and was part of the continuing national five-year quality

---

106. c. 68.
107. London: HMSO 1993.

review.[108] It was intended that the Northern Ireland report would be published in 1990 together with reports published by the National Rivers Authority for England and Wales and the Environment Department of the Scottish Office. However, it was delayed until 1991 in order to include a more reliable classification of estuaries. The 1993 report provides a detailed account of the results of chemical and biological monitoring of Northern Ireland's principal rivers, based on the national classification system outlined above. Estuaries were classified into four ranks, rating water quality from good (class A) to bad (class D); the estuarine classification system is based on an assessment of the biological and aesthetic status of the water, together with the minimum dissolved oxygen content, as opposed to water use which forms the basis of the river classification system described above.[109] The findings of the 1991 survey were summerised as follows:

- The survey has shown that the waters of Northern Ireland continue to be of high quality with 89% of river length assessed as of Good or Fair Quality, chemically and biologically,[110] and 88% of estuary length assessed as of Good Quality.

- There was little overall change in river quality between 1985[111] and 1991, the percentage of river length in the various classes remaining fairly static, though some movement between classes did occur in a number of reaches.

- Present trends suggest little change in water quality over the next 5 years except for some improvements to Poor and Fair Quality waters.[112]

The *Environment Service Corporate Plan* 1994–97 sets out the following targets for the DoE(NI)'s Environment Service in relation to water quality for the period of the Corporate Plan:

- The DoE(NI)'s main objective is 'to manage river and estuarine systems so that water quality is at least Class 2 under the national classification schemes, with no downward movement between Classes, and to maintain or improve inland and coastal water quality as required by national policy, EC Directives and international agreements.'

- The strategy document states that the DoE(NI) will continue to carry out field trials throughout the period of the Corporate Plan to assess the potential use of new instrumentation technology, which provides continuous water quality monitoring.

---

108. It should be noted that while river quality has been monitored annually since 1973, Northern Ireland's estuaries have not been the subject of such intensive monitoring. However, a regular monitoring programme for Northern Ireland's major estuaries was established in 1991, and on the basis of the information collected these estuaries have been classified for 1991.

109. Full details of the classification systems used for rivers and estuaries in Northern Ireland are set out in Appendices I and II of the 1993 report and in Appendices 4–6 of the *Environment Service Report* 1991–93.

110. The *Environment Service Corporate Plan* 1994–97, 31, states that 'results for 1992 showed that 94% of the 2,397 km [of rivers] chemically monitored were of good or fair quality' under the national classification systems. In addition, 89 per cent of the 2,474 km biologically monitored were stated to be of good or moderate quality.

111. The 1985 survey was published in a report entitled *River Quality in Northern Ireland* 1985.

112. P. 7.

- The Department identifies the formulation of comprehensive water quality management plans for specific water catchments as being an important element in its efforts to maintain and enhance water quality. To this end the Department, in conjunction with the Department of the Environment in the Republic, is sponsoring the preparation of water quality management plans for the Foyle and Erne catchments under the INTERREG initiative. (This is an EC fund aimed at promoting the creation and development of networks of cross-border co-operation and, where relevant, the linking of these networks to wider community networks, in the context of the completion of the internal market of 1992. INTERREG is also aimed at providing assistance to eligible areas in overcoming the special development problems arising from their relative isolation within national economies and within the EC as a whole, in the interests of the local population and in a manner compatible with the protection of the environment.) In addition, it is intended that a management strategy be established for the Lough Neagh and Lagan catchment areas. Public consultation for the Erne, Foyle and Lagan plans is to be completed by the end of 1996, while a technical working group to develop the Lough Neagh plan will be established by the end of 1995. At the time of writing, none of these management strategy plans has been adopted by the DoE(NI)'s Environment Service.

- As has occurred in Great Britain, a Drinking Water Inspectorate will be established within the DoE(NI)'s Environment Service for the purpose of monitoring the Water Executive's compliance with the EC Drinking Water Directive on the quality of public and private drinking water supplies (discussed below).[113]

## Section 1. Quality of Surface Water Intended for the Abstraction of Drinking Water

Directive 75/440/EEC[114] is primarily designed to ensure that the quality of surface water which is abstracted for use as drinking water complies with certain standards and also that such water is subjected to adequate treatment before being made available for public supply. The Directive divides surface waters into three classifications or grades based on their existing quality, namely, A1, A2, and A3. Annex I of the Directive sets out the three methods of treatment which must be

---

113. See Haigh, supra, chap. 4.4, p. 6 and 10, for a discussion of the establishment of the Drinking Water Inspectorate in Great Britain. Initially the Government had intended to confer responsibility for regulating drinking water quality on the privatised water authorities. This proposal proved politically unacceptable and in addition would have rendered the UK liable to enforcement proceedings before the European Court of Justice on the grounds that the private water authorities did not constitute a 'competent body' to monitor compliance with Directive 80/778/EEC (the Drinking Water Directive). As a result a Drinking Water Inspectorate was established under s. 60 of the Water Act 1989.

114. OJ L194, 25 July 1975; formal compliance to be achieved by 18 June 1977; standards to be in place and achieved by the same date; improvements to be achieved 'over the next ten years,' i.e. by 18 June 1985.

used for water in each classification, ranging from simple physical treatment and disinfection in A1, to normal physical and chemical treatment and disinfection in A2, and then intensive physical and chemical treatment and disinfection in A3. The Directive provides that surface water whose quality falls below A3 cannot be abstracted for use as drinking water except in exceptional circumstances (Article 4).

The classification or grade ascribed to particular surface waters will depend on the concentrations of certain substances in the water. Annex II of the Directive sets out over forty physical, chemical and microbiological limits which define the quality of surface water in each of the three classifications. Some of these are listed as mandatory or imperative values (marked I), while others are simply guide values (marked G). No I or G values are laid down for some of the substances; however, these will be inserted at a later date. Where I or G values have been laid down, member states are required to establish values for sampling points where surface water is abstracted; national values must not be less stringent than I values, while G values must be respected as guide values. The Directive then provides that member states must ensure that 95 per cent of the samples comply with the I values and that 90 per cent of the samples comply with the other values.

The requirements of the Directive may be waived in certain circumstances, for example, in cases of flood or other natural disasters. Finally, the Directive requires member states to devise a timetabled national action plan for the improvement of surface waters to be abstracted for drinking water. These plans must be designed in particular to bring about 'considerable improvement' in the quality of A3 water within ten years (by 18 June 1985).

Directive 79/869/EEC[115] governs the methods of measurement and frequencies of sampling and analysis of surface waters intended for the abstraction of drinking water. This Directive governs the precision and accuracy with which the parameters laid down in Directive 75/440/EEC must be measured at the national level and also lays down non-mandatory reference methods for measuring these parameters (Annex I). While member states are entitled to determine the frequency with which samples are taken, Annex II dictates a minimum frequency for taking samples; in effect, as the quality category of the surface water in question decreases and the population supplied with the water increases, samples must be taken more frequently.

## Implementation in Northern Ireland

As was the case in Great Britain before the enactment of the Water Act 1989, Directives 75/440/EEC and 79/869/EEC were both initially implemented in Northern Ireland by administrative action within the framework of the Pollution Control and Local Government (NI) Order 1978[116] and the Water Act (NI) 1972.[117] In July 1980 the Commission issued a 'reasoned opinion' under Article 169 of the Treaty arguing that these administrative arrangements did not constitute proper implementation of the Directives. Infringement proceedings were not

---

115. OJ L271, 29 Oct. 1979; formal compliance to be achieved by 11 Oct. 1981.
116. SI 1978/1049.
117. c. 5.

taken; however, the UK introduced legislation which formally implemented the two Directives into national law.[118] The Water and Sewerage Services (Amendment) (NI) Order 1993[119] amended the Water Act (NI) 1972 so as to introduce the statutory powers necessary to formally implement Directive 75/440/EEC in Northern Ireland; these powers are outlined above at pages 192–3.

The Surface Waters (Classification) Regulations (NI) 1995[120] were adopted under section 4B of the Water Act (NI) Act 1972, as amended, for the purpose of giving effect to the requirements of Directive 75/440/EEC concerning the classification of surface water intended for use as drinking water. It should be noted, however, that Directive 79/869/EEC has not yet been formally implemented in Northern Ireland. The Surface Waters (Classification) Regulations (NI) 1995 set out classifications (DW1, DW2 and DW3) and criteria for determining the grade of waters in waterways[121] according to its suitability for abstraction by the DoE(NI) for supply as drinking water. It should be noted, however, that these Regulations only give effect to the mandatory or I values laid down in Annex II of Directive 75/440/EEC. Water quality objectives, which determine the type of treatment to which surface water should be subjected before it is put into public supply as drinking water, are then set on the basis of these classifications; water quality objectives are established under Part VI of the Water Quality Regulations (NI) 1994,[122] which is discussed below at page 207.

Part VI of the 1994 Regulations regulates the substances, processes and products which the DoE(NI) may use in connection with the supply of water. Regulation 22(1) of the 1994 Regulations prohibits the abstraction of surface waters for the supply of drinking water which falls below the A3 category as required by Directive 75/440/EEC. Regulation 22(3) then imposes requirements relating to the disinfection of water abstracted from any source which is intended for supply as drinking water and imposes such additional requirements for the treatment of 'surface water'[123] as are required to secure compliance with Directive 75/440/EEC.

Section 4C of the Water Act (NI) 1972, as amended by the Water and Sewerage Services (Amendment) (NI) Order 1993, governs the establishment and review of water quality objectives for waters classified under regulations adopted under section 4B of the 1972 Act and makes provision for public consultation in this context; the DoE(NI)'s powers under 4C are outlined above at page 192.

---

118. See Haigh, supra, chap. 4.3.
119. SI 1993/3165. The Amendment Order was enacted on 16 Dec. 1993; however, its provisions did not come into force until 17 Feb. 1994.
120. SR No. 11. The 1995 Regulations were enacted on 16 Jan. 1995; however, their provisions did not come into effect until 1 Mar. 1995.
121. The term 'waters' is defined by reg. 2 as 'surface fresh waters used or intended for use in the abstraction of drinking water.' The term 'waterway' (inland, coastal and ground waters) is defined by s. 30 of the Water Act (NI) 1972: see note 28, supra.
122. SR 1994 No. 221. The 1994 Regulations were enacted on 17 June 1994; however, their provisions did not come into effect until 1 Oct. 1994.
123. Part VI of the 1994 Regulations applies to 'surface water', defined by reg. 21 as 'including any river, stream, watercourse or inland water (whether natural or artificial) but does not include water from a spring.'

Finally, it should be noted that regulation 22(4) of the Water Quality Regulations (NI) 1994 provides that where surface water has been classified by the DoE(NI) as falling into one of the three classifications laid down in Directive 75/440/EEC before the Water Quality Regulations (NI) 1994 came into operation (on 1 October 1994), those waters will be treated as falling into that category for the purposes of setting quality objectives under the 1994 Regulations until the DoE(NI) publishes a notice under section 4C of the Water Act (NI) 1972 changing that classification.

## SECTION 2. QUALITY OF WATER INTENDED FOR HUMAN CONSUMPTION

Directive 80/778/EEC[124] lays down quality standards for all water intended for human consumption, whether as drinking water or for use in the manufacture of food and drink; both public and private water supplies are governed by the Directive, as is bottled water which is not recognised as natural mineral water or as medicinal water.[125] The purpose of the Directive is twofold, namely, the protection of human health and the protection of the environment itself.

Annex I of the Directive lays down over sixty parameters. These are listed either as guide levels (GLs), maximum admissible concentrations (MACs), or minimum required concentrations (MRCs). Member states have discretion in deciding whether to implement the parameters listed as GLs; however, where a parameter is listed as an MAC or an MRC, member states are obliged to set values which are as stringent as the MAC and MRC standards. In addition, they are obliged to ensure that water quality actually satisfies the MAC and MRC standards. It should also be noted that some of the parameters are not listed as either a GL, MAC, or MRC and, in such a situation, member states are on notice that a standard for that parameter will be included at a later date.

Member states may derogate from the requirements of Annex I in certain circumstances. However, in all cases they must inform the Commission. Annex II then lays down detailed monitoring requirements designed to ensure that the quality standards laid down in Annex I are complied with. Member states are given no discretion in this context; in other words, the monitoring requirements must be complied with in every detail.

Annex III governs the 'reference methods of analysis', and in this regard member states must comply with the parameters listed as far as is practicable; where national methods of analysis differ from those laid down in Annex III, member states must ensure that the results obtained by these methods are equivalent to, or comparable with, results obtained by the methods specified in Annex III. It should also be noted that in Case C-337/89 *Commission v. United Kingdom*[126] the European Court of Justice ruled that the obligations imposed by Directive 80/778/EEC are absolute. In other words, member states are not simply obliged to take all practicable steps to achieve compliance.

---

124. OJ L229, 30 Aug. 1980. Member states were required to complete formal implementation by 17 July 1982, while 17 July 1985 was the deadline for the achievement of the standards laid down by the Directive.

125. Water recognised as natural mineral water is governed by Directive 80/777/EEC OJ L229, 30 Aug. 1980.

126. [1992] 1 ECR 6103.

## Implementation in Northern Ireland

Article 4 of the Water and Sewerage Services (Amendment) (NI) Order 1993[127] inserted article 3A into the Water and Sewerage Services (NI) Order 1973[128] and thereby introduced the statutory means for implementing Directive 80/778/EEC in Northern Ireland. The Water and Sewerage Services (Amendment) (NI) Order 1993 revoked the duty imposed on the DoE(NI) to provide 'wholesome' water, as laid down in article 3(2) of the Water and Sewerage (NI) Order 1973, and replaced it with a new duty to provide wholesome water for domestic and food production purposes under article 3A of the 1993 Amendment Order. Before the introduction of article 3A the concept of wholesomeness was not defined in qualitative terms; it was simply understood to mean 'that water was to be clear, palatable and "safe" '.[129] However, in the wake of Directive 80/778/EEC this concept has now been defined according to mandatory water quality standards. The 1993 Amendment Order also places the Department under an obligation to keep informed of the wholesomeness and sufficiency of private water supplies, and enables the Department to require remedial action, where necessary, in respect of private supplies that are causing concern. Water quality standards for public supplies are now set for Northern Ireland under the Water Quality Regulations (NI) 1994,[130] while the provisions of Directive 80/778/EEC concerning private water supplies are implemented by the Private Water Supplies Regulations (NI) 1994.[131] The requirements laid down by the new provisions will be addressed in turn; however, given the technical nature of their provisions, it is only possible to do so in general terms.

Before discussing the terms of the implementing legislation in more detail, it is worth noting two cases concerning the implementation of Directive 80/778/EEC in the UK. The first concerned an enforcement action taken by the Commission against the UK before the European Court of Justice for failure to implement the Directive correctly and on time, while the second was a national action and concerned the legality of the Secretary of State's acceptance of undertakings from the ten water authorities in Great Britain as a means of ensuring compliance with the Directive within England and Wales. Each case will now be addressed in turn.

Member states were required to complete formal implementation of Directive 80/778/EEC by 17 July 1982 and, in addition, were required to ensure actual compliance with the terms of the Directive by 17 July 1985. As was the case with Directives 75/440/EEC and 79/869/EEC, concerning the quality of surface water intended for abstraction as drinking water, Directive 80/778/EEC was initially implemented throughout the UK by administrative means only. In 1987 the

---

127. SI 1993/3165.
128. SI 1973/70.
129. Haigh, supra, chap. 4.4, p. 5. See also Leeson, *Environmental Law,* London: Pitman, 1995, pp 150–51, for a discussion of Lord Upjohn's interpretation of the concept of 'pure water' in *Attorney-General of New Zealand v. Lower Hutt City Corporation* [1964] AC 1469, PC.
130. SR No. 221.
131. SR No. 237. In this regard it should also be noted that reg. 21 of the Private Water Supplies Regulations (NI) 1994 revokes reg. 8 of the Water Quality Regulations (NI) 1994, which concern private water supplies.

Commission informed the UK that it had failed to comply with its obligation to implement Directive 80/778/EEC. In particular, the Commission pointed to the fact that the administrative guidance given concerning the requirements imposed by the Directive did not give full effect to the Directive in that the standards laid down in the Directive were not being applied to water used for food production purposes. In addition, the Commission stated that the UK had failed to implement the Directive in practice in that it had failed to comply with the maximum admissible concentration of nitrate in some supply zones and, finally, that administrative action did not constitute adequate implementation of Directive 80/778/EEC; the introduction of formal legislation was required. It should also be noted that although the Water Supply (Water Quality) Regulations 1989[132] came into effect in England and Wales—thereby introducing quality standards that were as stringent as those imposed under the Directive—just months before the Commission took the case to the European Court of Justice, the Commission pointed to the fact that similar Regulations had not been enacted in Northern Ireland, and this formed part of the Commission's main case against the UK.

On 25 November 1992 the European Court of Justice ruled in Case C-337/89 *Commission v. UK* that the UK had failed to adequately implement the Directive into national law.[133] The UK argued that the Northern Ireland delay was due to the complicated legislative procedure governing the enactment of legislation for Northern Ireland. The European Court of Justice rejected this as a legitimate excuse. It ruled that the obligation to comply with the maximum admissible concentrations was an absolute one, thereby rejecting the UK's contention that member states were simply required to take all practicable steps to comply with these standards. The Court's ruling in this regard is important also in that it made it clear that non-compliance in practice would be treated as being equivalent to formal non-compliance. In other words, even if a member state has introduced legislation which implements an EC environment Directive formally in national law, a member state will be considered as having failed to comply with the obligation to implement a Directive if it fails to ensure adequate implementation in practice.

The national action relating to the implementation of Directive 80/778/EEC concerned an application for judicial review made by Friends of the Earth to quash the decision of the Secretary of State to accept certain undertakings from Britain's water companies as being sufficient to ensure compliance with the requirements laid down in the Drinking Water Directive. The Secretary of State was empowered under the Water Act 1989 (now replaced by the Water Industry Act 1991) to take such action as he considered necessary to ensure compliance by any water undertaker with any statutory requirement where he was satisfied that there was likely to be a continuing failure to meet such requirements. In effect, the Secretary of State could secure compliance either by means of an enforcement order or by accepting an 'undertaking' from the water company in question where he was of the opinion that the water company would pursue all such steps as appeared to him

---

132. SI 1989/1147, as amended by SI 1989/1384.
133. [1992] 1 ECR 6103. For further detail of the background to this case and the communications between the Commission and the UK see Haigh, supra, chap. 4.4, pp 4–8.

to be appropriate for the purposes of securing compliance with statutory requirements.

In 1989 Britain's ten water companies submitted action plans for ensuring compliance with the Drinking Water Directive. However, despite the fact that many of the action plans anticipated considerable delays in implementing some of the standards (particularly those concerning pesticides) required by the Directive, the Secretary of State decided to accept them as sufficient 'undertakings' to ensure conformity with the Directive. Friends of the Earth then took an action for judicial review against this decision, arguing that the Secretary of State's decision was insufficient to ensure compliance with the UK's 'primary obligation' to implement Directive 80/778/EEC correctly and its 'secondary obligation' to comply with the judgment of the European Court of Justice in Case C-337/89 *Commission v. UK* outlined above. The Secretary of State argued that while he accepted the ruling of the European Court of Justice in *Commission v. UK* and in particular the Court's ruling that member states were under an absolute duty to comply with the standards laid down in the Directive, he was of the opinion that acceptance of the undertakings was the most appropriate use of his enforcement powers in the circumstances, despite the lengthy delays faced in ensuring actual implementation.

In *R. v. Secretary of State for the Environment, ex parte Friends of the Earth* the Court of Appeal upheld the decision of Schiemann J in the High Court to dismiss the application for judicial review[134] and ruled that the Secretary of State's acceptance of the undertakings was an appropriate method of ensuring compliance with the UK's obligations. Although the Court of Appeal accepted the absolute nature of the 'primary' obligation, it appeared to take the view that the 'secondary' obligation to comply with the decision of the European Court of Justice could be qualified by considerations of what was practical in the circumstances. It is submitted that the distinction drawn by the Court of Appeal between a 'primary' and a 'secondary' obligation is artificial to say the least. There is no hierarchy within the EC Treaty between the obligation to implement a Directive correctly and the obligation to comply with the terms of a ruling by the European Court of Justice. In effect, the Court of Appeal's judgment in this case operates first to undermine the obligation to implement the Drinking Water Directive in absolute terms, and second to undermine the obligation to comply with the terms of the European Court's ruling in Case C-337/89. The ECJ's ruling in Case C-337/89 simply clarified the nature of the obligation contained in the Drinking Water Directive and can in no way be used to weaken it. Finally, it should also be noted that the Court of Appeal implicitly accepted that the provisions of the Drinking Water Directive are capable of being directly enforced by a private party before their national court, a point which was made clear in the European Court's ruling in Case C-337/89.

---

134. The judgment of the High Court delivered by Schiemann J is reported at [1995] 7 Admin. LR 26. The decision of the Court of Appeal is reported at [1995] ENDS report 44 and also in the *Times*, 8 June 1995, and the *Independent*, 7 June 1995.

### The Water and Sewerage Services (Amendment) (NI) Order 1993

As already stated, article 4 of the 1993 Amendment Order introduced the statutory means for implementing Directive 80/778/EEC in Northern Ireland. Article 4 inserted articles 3A-3F into the Water and Sewerage Services (NI) Order 1973 which, in effect, conferred new powers and imposed new obligations on the DoE(NI) concerning the quality of public and private water that is supplied for domestic and food production purposes in Northern Ireland. The new provisions governing both public and private water supplies will each be addressed in turn. However, before doing so, a number of points of definition should be clarified at the outset. The term 'domestic purposes' is defined by article 3[135] of the 1993 Amendment Order as meaning for the purposes of 'human consumption, cooking and washing necessary for human health or hygiene but does not include the purposes of the business of a laundry.' References to 'food production purposes' are defined by article 3(c)[136] of the 1993 Amendment Order as references to 'manufacturing, processing, preserving or marketing purposes with respect to food or drink for which water supplied to food production premises may be used.' The term 'food production premises' is defined by article 3 as premises which are used 'for the purposes of a business of preparing food or drink for consumption otherwise than on the premises.'

Regarding public water supplies—i.e. water supplied by the DoE(NI)—article 3A provides that, when supplying water to any premises for domestic or food production purposes, the DoE(NI) is obliged, first, to supply only water which is wholesome at the time of supply and, second, to ensure, as far as is reasonably practicable, that there is 'in general' no deterioration in the quality of the water supplied from each source or combination of sources. Water supplied by the Department will not be deemed to be unwholesome at the time of supply if it becomes unwholesome after leaving the Department's pipes. However, water that becomes unwholesome after leaving the Department's pipes will be deemed 'unwholesome at the time of supply' if it becomes unwholesome as a result of the Department's failure, while the water was in a pipe which was 'subject to water pressure from a main' (or would be so subject but for the closing of some valve), to take such steps as may be prescribed (for the purposes of eliminating or reducing to a minimum any prescribed risk that the water would cease to be wholesome after leaving the Department's pipes (article 3A(3)). Articles 3B and 3C essentially confer further powers on the DoE(NI) to adopt Regulations for the purposes of preserving the quality of water supplied to any premises for domestic or food production purposes and also for the purpose of prescribing standards of wholesomeness. The Water Quality Regulations (NI) 1994 have been adopted by the DoE(NI) pursuant to its powers under articles 3A, 3B and 3C; the requirements laid down by these Regulations will be discussed below.

Regarding private water supplies, articles 3D, 3E and 3F set out the DoE(NI)'s functions and powers concerning the quality of private water supplies. The term 'private supply' is defined in article 3 of the 1993 Amendment Order as a supply of

---

135. Art. 3 of the 1993 Amendment Order essentially inserts additional definitions into art. 2 of the Water and Sewerage Services (NI) Order 1973, as amended.
136. This definition is contained in para. (3) of art. 3(c) and is to be inserted into the Water and Sewerage Services (NI) Order 1973.

water 'provided otherwise than by the Department (including a supply provided for the purposes of the bottling of water).'[137] Article 3D(1) places the Department under an obligation to 'take all such steps as it considers appropriate for keeping itself informed about the wholesomeness and sufficiency of private supplies' and also 'to maintain a register of private supplies used for domestic or food production purposes.' Article 3D does not require the Department to make the register available for public consultation; however, such information may fall within the ambit of the Access to Environmental Information Directive (discussed in chapter 12). Where the DoE(NI) concludes that any private water supply used for domestic or food production purposes 'is, has been or is likely to become' either unwholesome or insufficient for domestic and sanitary purposes *and* that the unwholesomeness or insufficiency 'is, was or is likely to be such as to cause a danger to life or health,' the Department is obliged under article 3D(2) to notify the relevant district council and health and social services board. It should also be noted that the Department is empowered under article 3F to serve a notice on any person requiring them to furnish such information as is 'reasonably required' by the Department for the purposes of article 3D; the notice may require that the information requested be made available within a specified period or in a specified form and manner. Failure to comply with the terms of an article 3F notice ('without reasonable excuse') is an offence punishable on summary conviction by a maximum fine of £5,000 (level 5 five on the standard scale). Article 3D(3) also confers powers on the DoE(NI) to adopt regulations which supplement the provisions of article 3D and which the Department considers appropriate for the purpose of:

(i)  obtaining information about the quality and sufficiency of private water supplies, including information about the source of such supplies and the premises supplied by such supplies;

(ii)  regulating the performance of any function under article 3D; and

(iii)  prescribing the particulars concerning each private supply to be recorded in the private waters supply register.

Article 3D(4) goes on to identify further matters which may be prescribed by Regulations pursuant to these powers. However, these are without prejudice to the generality of the powers outlined in article 3D(3). Thus far the Private Water Supplies Regulations (NI) 1994[138] are the only Regulations adopted by the DoE(NI) pursuant to these powers; the requirements laid down by these Regulations will be discussed below.

Article 3E confers remedial powers on the DoE(NI) in relation to private water supplies which are causing concern. In effect, the Department is empowered to take remedial action in either of the following two situations:

(i)  where it is satisfied that any water which 'is being, has been or is likely to be supplied' by private means to any premises for domestic or food production purposes 'is not, was not, or . . . is likely not to be, wholesome'; or

---

137. Art. 3 of the 1993 Amendment Order essentially inserts additional definitions into art. 2 of the Water and Sewerage Services (NI) Order 1973, as amended. The definition of 'private supply' is subject to art. 2(4) of the 1973 Order, as amended, which defines a 'private water supply works' as 'a water works which is not vested in the [DoE(NI)].'
138. SR No. 237.

(ii) where it is satisfied that a private supply of water to any premises (where the water is used for domestic or food production purposes) 'is failing, has failed or is likely to fail to provide to any house on those premises' a supply of wholesome water which is sufficient for domestic and sanitary purposes as far as that house is concerned.

Where the Department is satisfied that either of these conditions is satisfied, it has the power to serve a notice on 'one or more of the relevant persons'[139] in relation to that private supply. A notice served under article 3E must give particulars of the reasons in respect of which the notice is served and must also specify the steps which the Department considers necessary to ensure that the premises in question are supplied with water which is both wholesome and, as far as any house on those premises is concerned, sufficient for domestic and sanitary purposes. Article 3E(2) provides that a person on whom an article 3E notice is served may appeal the notice to the Appeals Commission; the appeal must be brought within twenty-eight days of the date of service. An article 3E notice may require the person or persons on whom the notice is served to take one or more of the remedial steps specified in the notice. The notice may specify a reasonable period within which such action must be taken. Where appropriate, an article 3E notice may designate that some of the remedial steps be taken by the Department itself. The notice may require the person on whom the notice is served to reimburse the Department (or any other relevant person) for any expenses reasonably incurred in taking any of the remedial action specified in the notice; the notice may require such payments to be made at particular times. Similarly, the notice may provide that the Department itself will undertake to reimburse any relevant person for expenses reasonably incurred by them in taking any of the remedial steps specified in the notice. It should be noted, however, that the Water and Sewerage Services (Amendment) (NI) Order 1993 does not confer any right of action on any person in respect of any loss or damage sustained by that person as a result of a failure by any other person to carry out any remedial action required under the terms of an article 3E notice. However, any sum that is required to be paid to any person under an article 3E notice will be recoverable summarily as a civil debt by the person to whom it is owed from the person required to pay it (article 3E(6)).

In the event that a person required to take remedial action in relation to any premises under an article 3E notice fails to do so within the specified time, the Department is empowered to take that step under article 3E(4), and may recover any expenses reasonably incurred in so doing from the person who failed to take the action in question. Any sum paid to the Department in this regard will be deemed to be an expense incurred in the taking of the action in question by the person who failed to do it for the purposes of any requirement in the notice relating to the payment of money to that person by someone other than the DoE(NI) (article 3E(5)).

The DoE(NI) is also empowered under article 3E(7) to modify or revoke the effect, in relation to any person, of a notice served under article 3E. The

---

139. Art. 3E(8) defines 'relevant persons' in relation to a private supply to any premises as 'the owners and occupiers of those premises and the owners and occupiers of the premises where the source of that supply is situated and any other person who exercises powers of management or control in relation to that source.'

Department must, however, serve the person affected by the modification or revocation with a notice to this effect. Such a notice may be appealed by the person on whom it is served to the Appeals Commission within twenty-eight days of the date of service. However, a notice which either extends the period within which remedial action must be taken or which 'discharges, postpones or abates' any obligation imposed on that person to make a payment to the DoE(NI) cannot be appealed.

Finally, it should be noted that the Department is empowered under article 3F to serve a notice on any person requiring them to furnish such information as is 'reasonably required' by the Department for the purposes of article 3E. The provisions governing the nature and effect of an article 3F notice are identical to those applying for the purposes of article 3D above.

### The Water Quality Regulations (NI) 1994[140]

As already stated, water quality standards for public supplies of water to be used for domestic or food production purposes are set for Northern Ireland under the Water Quality Regulations (NI) 1994. The 1994 Regulations have been adopted by the DoE(NI) pursuant to its powers under articles 3A, 3B and 3C of the Water and Sewerage Services (NI) Order 1973 as amended by the Water and Sewerage Services (Amendment) (NI) Order 1993 (both of which are addressed above). In effect, the 1993 Order requires that water which is supplied by the DoE(NI) for human consumption (i.e. for domestic or food production purposes) must be 'wholesome'. Part II of the 1994 Regulations then defines the concept of wholesomeness for these purposes. Part II provides that such water is wholesome if it contains concentrations or values in respect of various properties, elements, organisms and substances that do not exceed the prescribed maximum or, as the case may be, the prescribed minimum concentrations or values. The majority of the prescribed maximum and minimum concentrations and values are listed in Schedule 1, Tables A–E; some are also listed in regulation 3. These concentrations and values give effect to the maximum and minimum concentrations and values specified in Annex I to Directive 80/778/EEC.

Part III of the Regulations empowers the DoE(NI) to relax the requirements contained in Part II concerning wholesomeness in certain specified circumstances (regulation 4). They are as follows:

1. The Department may authorise the relaxation of the requirements in Part II in the event of an emergency where it is necessary to maintain a supply of water for human consumption. However, such a relaxation may only be authorised in so far as it does not give rise to a risk to public health which is unacceptable in the opinion of the DoE(NI) after consultation with the Chief Medical Officer of the Department of Health and Social Services (regulation 4(*a*) and 5(*a*)). Article 10 of Directive 80/778/EEC also imposes an obligation on the member state authorising the relaxation to inform the Commission immediately and to specify the duration of the relaxation and the reasons.

2. The requirements as to wholesomeness may be relaxed in the event of 'exceptional meteorological conditions'. However, a relaxation in this situation

---

140. SR No. 221. These Regulations came into operation on 1 Oct. 1994.

must not give rise to a public health hazard, and the authorisation cannot relax the requirements concerning the parameters laid down in Table B or C or item 7 of Table D (toxic and microbiological parameters) (regulation 4(*b*) and 5(*b*), giving effect to Article 9 of the Directive).

3. The Department may authorise a relaxation of the standards laid down in Part II where it is necessary by reason of the nature and structure of the ground in the area from which the supply emanates. The restrictions imposed on the Department's powers to authorise a relaxation in this context are identical to those outlined in relation to exceptional meteorological conditions above (regulation 4(*c*) and 5(*b*)). In *Commission v. UK*[141] the European Court of Justice ruled that the UK was in breach of Article 9 of Directive 80/778/EEC as a result of granting authorisations to relax the requirements as to wholesomeness in relation to nitrate levels. The UK argued that the geological conditions in some areas made it difficult to comply with the nitrate parameters. However, the European Court of Justice ruled that this was an inaccurate interpretation of Article 9, because nitrate levels result from self-induced effects on the soil.

4. The Department may relax the requirements in Part II where the supply of water is used, or is to be used, solely for food production purposes, subject to the proviso, that the relaxation does not affect the fitness for human consumption of the food or drink in its final form (regulation 4(*d*) and 5(*c*)). It should also be noted that member states may not prevent or inhibit the marketing of foodstuffs on water quality grounds if the quality of the water used to produce the products complies with the requirements of Directive 80/778/EEC.

The Department is obliged under regulation 7(2) to revoke any authorisation granted under Part III 'as soon as the circumstances which gave rise to the authorisation cease to exist.' An authorisation to relax the requirements as to wholesomeness must specify (where relevant) the extent to which the concentration or value laid down in Part II of the Regulations may be breached. In addition, an authorisation issued in the case of an emergency or of exceptional meteorological conditions must specify the date on which the authorisation ceases to have effect. The DoE(NI) has a discretion as to whether to specify this date in the case of an authorisation issued by reason of the nature and structure of the ground in the area from which the supply emanates or where the water is used, or is to be used solely, for food production purposes (regulation 5(2) and (3)).

Regulation 6(1) provides that an authorisation issued under Part III may be limited to water supplied from a particular source or class of sources, or to water supplied for a particular food production purpose, or to a particular water supply zone,[142] or to parts of such zones or to zones of particular descriptions. In addition,

---

141. Case C-337/89 [1992] 1 ECR 6103.
142. The term 'water supply zone' is defined by reg. 2 of the 1994 Regulations for the purposes of these Regulations 'as an area in which, in the Department's estimation, not more than 50,000 people reside and in which all the premises supplied with water for domestic or food production purposes are normally supplied from the same source or combination or sources.'

the DoE(NI) has the power under regulation 6(2) to include conditions relating to the following matters in the authorisation:

(i) the quality of the water to which the authorisation applies;
(ii) the steps to be taken to improve the quality of that water;
(iii) monitoring the quality of the water in question;
(iv) the procedure governing notification of any matter relating to the water in question to any persons or body named in the authorisation.

Finally, the Department may also modify or revoke an authorisation granted under Part III or any condition attached to that authorisation at any time, regardless of the stated duration of the original authorisation. Regulation 6(1) and (2) will apply in the same way to any modification or revocation of an authorisation.

Parts IV and V of the 1994 Regulations set down the requirements concerning the monitoring of water supplies which must be satisfied in order to determine whether water quality complies with the requirements as to wholesomeness laid down in Part II or with relaxed requirements authorised under Part III. These monitoring requirements are prescribed by reference to the analysis of samples taken from consumers' taps and, in effect, implement the monitoring obligations laid down in Annex II to Directive 80/778/EEC. Regulation 11 requires the DoE(NI) to determine, in relation to areas which it must identify as 'water supply zones', such number and location of consumers' taps as will ensure that the samples taken are representative of the water quality within each zone. Regulation 12 prescribes the parameters in relation to which, and the circumstances in which, the Department may authorise samples to be taken from points other than from consumers' taps. Regulation 13 then governs the frequency of monitoring or what is referred to as the 'standard number' of samples which must be taken each year. The 'standard number' of samples for various parameters is specified in Schedule 2, Tables 1–6. In addition, regulation 13 also makes provision for taking samples where water quality within a water supply zone (or zones) may have been affected by changes in the DoE(NI)'s practices. Regulation 14 governs the sampling requirements where no standard number has been listed in relation to a particular parameter.

Regulations 15–20 set out additional provisions concerning monitoring. In particular, regulations 17 and 18 require that a standard number of samples be taken in respect of particular parameters at treatment works and at reservoirs which store treated water. Regulation 19 governs the sampling requirements for new sources of water or for sources which have not been in recent use (stand-by sources). Finally, regulation 20 governs the taking, handling, storage, transport and analysis of all samples taken under Parts IV and V of the Regulations.

Part VI of the 1994 Regulations governs the treatment of water and prescribes the substances, processes and products which may be used by the DoE(NI) in connection with the supply of water. As already stated, regulation 22 of Part VI also gives effect to the requirements of Directive 75/440/EEC on the quality required of surface water intended for the abstraction of drinking water (addressed in Part VI, section 1 of this chapter). It should also be noted that regulation 29 provides that it is an offence to 'wilfully or negligently' use a process, substance or product in connection with the preparation of water for domestic or food production purposes which breaches the provisions of regulations 24 and 25 which govern the substances, products and processes used in the treatment of such water. The penalty for an offence under regulation 29 is, on summary conviction, a fine not exceeding the statutory maximum and, on conviction on indictment, an unlimited fine. In addition, the DoE(NI) may recover any expenses from a person convicted under regulation 29 that were reasonably incurred by the Department in carrying out repair works or reinstatement necessitated by that person's action.

Part VII of the 1994 Regulations obliges the DoE(NI) to maintain records concerning the quality of water intended for human consumption in Northern Ireland and, also, to provide information to the public in this regard. In particular, regulation 26 provides that the Department must 'prepare and maintain' a record of the following information concerning each of its water supply zones:

(i) the name of the zone;

(ii) the name or names of any water treatment works from which water is supplied to premises within that zone (where the name or names of the treatment works do not include the name of the zone);

(iii) an estimate of the population of the zone;

(iv) the details of any authorisations issued by the Department to relax the requirements concerning wholesomeness laid down in Part II of the 1994 Regulations;

(v) the details of any action taken or required to be taken by the Department to comply with its duties under article 3A of the Water and Sewerage Services (NI) Order 1973, as amended by the Water and Sewerage Services (Amendment) (NI) Order 1993; the obligations imposed by article 3A are outlined above in the context of the 1993 Amendment Order (pages 199 and 202);

(vi) the results of any analysis of samples taken in accordance with the requirements laid down in Part IV of the 1994 Regulations or under regulations 15–18 in Part V;

(vii) information supplied by the Department annually to district councils under regulation 27(3) (the Department is obliged to provide each district council with information relating to the preceding year concerning the quality of the water supplied to premises in that council's area);[143]

(viii) any other particulars which the Department thinks are appropriate.

Regulation 26(2) goes on to prescribe the dates by which the above information must be entered in the Department's records. The Department is required to have made its 'initial entries' concerning matters identified in paragraphs (i) to (v) above before 1 October 1994. Any entries which relate to the results of the analysis of samples must be made within twenty-eight days of the day on which

---

143. Reg. 27(3) provides that such information must be made available to district councils by 30 June each year at the latest, beginning in 1996. The information should also include (as far as it is relevant to the council's area): (i) a summary of the samples taken in respect of each parameter regulated under the 1994 Regulations, (ii) the extent to which the DoE(NI) has complied with the requirements laid down in Parts II and IV concerning wholesomeness and monitoring, and (iii) information concerning the action taken by the DoE(NI) to comply with its obligations under art. 3A of the Water and Sewerage Services (NI) Order 1973, as inserted by the Water and Sewerage Services (Amendment) (NI) Order 1993. Any information to be supplied to district councils before 30 June 1996 must cover the fifteen-month period ending 31 Dec. 1995.

the result is first known to the DoE(NI). Finally, the Department is required to make its entries concerning the information which is supplied to district councils at the same time as it is complying with its obligation to make such information available to district councils under regulation 27(3). The DoE(NI) may dispose of records concerning matters identified in paragraphs (vi) or (vii) five years after the date on which the information was first entered in the record. Without prejudice to the provisions of regulation 26(2), the Department is obliged to review the record annually and to bring the information contained therein up to date. The DoE(NI) is obliged to make any record maintained under regulation 26 available for public inspection at all reasonable hours 'at such of its Water Executive Divisional Headquarters offices as are normally open to the public'. In addition, it must provide any person with a copy of any part of a record maintained under regulation 26 in relation to water quality on request; the Department may levy a reasonable charge for such service.

Regulation 28 requires the DoE(NI) to publish a report concerning the quality of water supplied by the Department for the period from 1 October 1994 to 31 December 1995 and for each year thereafter. In particular, the report must contain the following information:

(i) a summary of the quality of water supplied by the DoE(NI) for human consumption (i.e. for domestic and food production purposes);

(ii) a statement of the extent to which the quality of the water supplied by the Department has complied with the requirements as to wholesomeness laid down in Part II of the Regulations;[144]

(iii) details of any authorised relaxation in the requirements as to the wholesomeness of water supplied by the Department granted under Part III of the Regulations;

(iv) a statement of the action which the Department has taken, or a statement of the action that it is required to take and has not yet taken, to comply with its duties under article 3A of the Water and Sewerage Services (NI) Order 1973, as amended by the Water and Sewerage Services (Amendment) (NI) Order 1993, the terms of which are outlined in page 202;

(v) a statement that a person may inspect any record maintained in accordance with regulation 26, including particulars of the times and places at which the public may inspect such records;

(vi) any other information which the Department considers appropriate.

The first report (1 October 1994–31 December 1995) must be published by the Department on or before 30 June 1996. Subsequent annual reports containing the previous year's statistics will be required on or before 30 June each year. In addition, the Department must send copies of the report to every district council, every health and social services board, the Department of Health and Social Services, the DANI, the Northern Ireland Water Council, and the General Consumer Council for Northern Ireland.

Where an event occurs which gives rise to or is likely to give rise to a

---

144. Reg. 28(2) provides that the statement required in this regard must specify 'the microbiological and physio-chemical quality of water supplied by the Department and the number of the results of the analysis of samples which established a concentration or value in respect of any parameter which contravened the prescribed concentration or value.'

significant risk to the health of people living in an area as a result of its effect or likely effects on the water which is supplied by the DoE(NI), the Department is obliged under regulation 27(5) to notify the relevant district council and health and social services board 'as soon as may be after the occurrence of the event.' In the event that a council or board is notified of such an occurrence they may require the DoE(NI) to provide them with such information relating to the event and its consequences as they may reasonably need.

### *The Private Water Supplies Regulations (NI) 1994*[145]

The Private Water Supplies Regulations were adopted under articles 2, 3C and 3D(3) and (4) of the Water and Sewage Services (NI) Order 1973, as amended by the Water and Sewerage Services (Amendment) (NI) Order 1993, and operate to supplement the terms of articles 3C–3F of the 1973 Order as amended by the 1993 Amendment Order (outlined on pages 202–5). In essence, the Regulations are concerned with the quality of water supplied from private supplies (i.e. other than the DoE(NI)) for drinking, washing, cooking, or food production. These Regulations came into operation on 1 November 1994.

Part II (regulation 3 and Schedule 2) of the Regulations sets down the requirements for the quality or 'wholesomeness' of such water; as with public water supplies, quality is prescribed according to mandatory maximum and in some cases minimum concentrations and values for various parameters (i.e. properties, elements, organisms, and substances), thereby giving effect to the requirements laid down in Annex I to Directive 80/778/EEC. Part III of the Regulations empowers the DoE(NI) to authorise a relaxation in the quality requirements set out in Part II in certain circumstances (regulations 4–7).[146]

Quality requirements may be relaxed either in response to an application by a 'relevant person'[147] or on the Department's own initiative; the circumstances in which a relaxation may be authorised are identical to those governing the relaxation of public water supply quality under Part III of the Water Quality Regulations (NI) 1994 outlined at pages 202–6. Where the requirements concerning private water supply quality are relaxed, the DoE(NI) is obliged to send copies of the authorisation to the relevant district council. Where an application is submitted for an authorisation, the person making the application must serve notice of the application on all other relevant persons or must publish such a notice in one or more local newspapers 'at least once in each of 2 successive weeks.' It should also be noted that where an authorisation is granted in response to an application, the person making the application must inform the Department as soon as he becomes aware that the circumstances that gave rise to the application have ceased to exist; once the Department is so informed it must revoke the authorisation immediately (regulation 7(3)). As with public water supplies, a number of restrictions are placed on the DoE(NI)'s power to authorise

---

145. SR No. 237.
146. It should be noted that reg. 21 of the 1994 Regulations revokes reg. 8 of the Water Quality Regulations (NI) 1994, which previously governed the granting of authorisations to relax private water quality standards.
147. The term 'relevant person' is not defined in the 1994 Regulations; however, this term is used in the Water Quality Regulations (NI) 1994: see note 139 supra.

the relaxation of private water quality requirements (regulation 5); these limitations are identical to those applying to public water supplies, outlined at pages 205–6.

The Department is empowered by regulation 6 to attach conditions to any authorisation. With the exception of those concerning water sources and water supply zones, the conditions which may be attached to authorisations concerning public supplies are identical to those for private supplies addressed on page 207. Similarly, the Department has the power to modify or revoke an authorisation concerning private supplies (regulation 7). However, it must give at least six months' notice[148] of its intention to do either, unless it is of the opinion that immediate revocation or modification is necessary in the interests of public health.

Part IV of the Regulations prescribes the manner in which the quality of private water supplies must be monitored (regulations 8–18 and Schedules 1, 3, and 4). Private supplies must be classified as either Category 1 or Category 2 Supplies. Regulation 9 provides that a private supply is a Category 1 supply 'if any water from the supply is supplied for domestic purposes and the supply is not a Category 2 supply'. Regulation 10 provides that a private supply is a Category 2 supply 'if any water from the supply is supplied for food production purposes or is supplied for domestic purposes to premises' which are used for any of the following purposes:

(a)  as staff canteens or for the purposes of a business of preparing food or drink for consumption on the premises;

(b)  as hospitals, nursing homes, residential homes, hostels, boarding schools or similar institution; or

(c)  as camp sites or sites for touring caravans or for providing holiday or short term accommodation.

In certain circumstances, private supplies which are also used in connection with milk processing are classified as Category 1 or Category 2 supplies according to the volume of the water from the supply distributed or, if not distributed, used or consumed (regulation 10(2) and (3)).

The water supplies in each category are then divided into classes for the purposes of monitoring; classification depends on the estimated daily average volume of water distributed or, if not distributed, used or consumed from the supply. The estimated maximum number of people normally served by the supply on any one day is an additional consideration in relation to the classification of Category 1 supplies. It should also be noted that the Department is obliged to review the classification of all private water supplies at least once a year (regulation 12).

The taking and analysis of water samples from Category 1 and 2 supplies are governed by regulations 13–18 and Schedules 3 and 4. The frequency of sampling and the parameters to be analysed vary according to the category and classification of the water supply in question. Finally, Part V of the Regulations sets out the

---

148.  Notice must be given either by means of serving a notice of the Department's intentions on the person or persons who applied for the authorisation, or, by publishing a notice of the intended revocation or modification in such manner as the DoE(NI) considers appropriate for bringing the intended change to the attention of relevant persons (reg. 7(2)).

requirements governing the collection and handling of samples taken by the DoE(NI) and also makes provision for sampling and analysis by persons other than the DoE(NI).

## SECTION 3. QUALITY OF BATHING WATER

Directive 76/160/EEC[149] requires member states to take certain measures to reduce the pollution of bathing water and to protect such water against further deterioration for the purposes of protecting human health and for reasons of amenity.[150] The Annex to the Directive lists nineteen physical, chemical and microbiological parameters applicable to bathing water and requires member states to set, for all bathing areas or for each individual bathing area, the values applicable to bathing water for those parameters. Thirteen of the listed parameters are identified as being either imperative or mandatory values (marked I) or as guide values (marked G).

The Directive operates primarily to ensure that sewage is either not present in such waters or has been adequately treated, and as a result the most important parameters listed in the Annex are the coliform values. Member states must set values for the parameters which are no less stringent than the I values, while the G values must be observed as guide values. The term 'bathing water' is defined by Article 1.2 of the Directive as including 'all running or still fresh waters and parts thereof and sea water, in which bathing is explicitly authorised . . . or, bathing is not prohibited and is traditionally practised by a large number of bathers.' It should be noted that the Directive excludes water used for therapeutic purposes or in swimming pools and also that the Directive does not define the terms 'traditionally' or 'large numbers of bathers'. In effect, the Directive leaves it up to each member state to devise their own criteria in this regard.

The Directive goes on to lay down minimum sampling frequencies for the listed parameters and prescribes the means by which, and locations at which, samples should be taken. However, the Directive is silent as to the handling of samples before analysis and also as to the methods of analysis. It does, however, require that certain 'reference methods' be used, or comparable methods. As with other water quality Directives, member states may derogate from certain parameters, in this instance on the grounds of exceptional weather or geographical conditions or on the grounds of 'natural enrichment'. However, the Commission must be informed of the derogation, the reasons for it, and its expected duration. Directive 76/160/EEC also imposes an obligation on member states to provide the

---

149. OJ L31, 5 Feb. 1976. The Directive required formal implementation by 10 Dec. 1977 and actual implementation of its standards by 10 Dec. 1985.
150. In June 1995 the EC published its report on bathing water quality throughout the EC for the 1994 bathing season. The report stated that almost 90 per cent of coastal bathing areas identified in the EC met health limits under Directive 76/160/EEC. However, the position concerning inland bathing waters, which are generally more vulnerable to pollution than coastal waters, is less good, with only 65 per cent complying with the Directive. Insufficient samples had been taken at 23 per cent of the inland sites, and a further 12 per cent failed to comply with EC standards. The total number of bathing water sites identified by member states under the Directive has increased from 16,450 in 1993 to 17,172 in 1994 (*Week in Europe WE/23/95*).

Commission with comprehensive reports on the quality of national bathing waters; this report may be published with the member state's permission.

Member states were required to complete formal implementation of Directive 76/160/EEC by 10 December 1977. However, Article 4 of the Directive provides that member states were obliged to take all necessary steps to bring the water in all relevant areas into line with the standards laid down by the Directive within ten years of notification, namely by 10 December 1985. In 1980 the Commission issued a reasoned opinion against the UK for failing to implement the Directive formally in Scotland and Northern Ireland (formal implementing legislation was not introduced in Northern Ireland until 1993; this is discussed below).

By the end of 1985 the UK had only identified twenty-seven resorts as bathing waters, excluding Blackpool, Southport, and Formby. In 1986 the Commission informed the UK that the requisite standards had not been attained in these areas and also that the Directive should be applied to these areas. In 1988 the Commission issued a reasoned opinion to that effect; enforcement proceedings under Article 169 of the Treaty were instituted against the UK in 1990. In Case C-56/90 *Re the Bathing Water Directive: Commission v. United Kingdom*[151] the European Court of Justice ruled that the UK had failed to comply with its obligations to implement Directive 76/160/EEC in several respects. The three principal issues raised in the case concerned the UK's initial system for classifying bathing waters for the purposes of the Directive, the Commission's initial failure to object to this system, and the nature of the obligation imposed by the Directive. The UK argued that the definition of bathing water was too imprecise and therefore it had been forced to classify bathing water according to numerical thresholds, namely, the numbers of bathers. The Court ruled that the objectives of the Directive would not be achieved if the existence of facilities such as changing huts, toilets, markers indicating the bathing areas and supervision by lifeguards could be excluded by member states when assessing whether specific waters fell within the scope of the Directive. The UK argued that the action was inadmissible on the grounds that the Commission's failure to object to the UK's initial list of bathing waters, which identified only twenty-seven bathing waters, implied that the Commission approved of the UK's classification system. This argument was rejected by the Court, which stated that the Commission was not obliged to express its views on the initial list and that this omission could not preclude action before the Court under Article 169. Finally, the UK argued that Directive 76/160/EEC simply obliged member states to take all practicable steps to comply with the terms of the Directive; the UK argued that it had done so, but that such work was necessarily slow. The European Court of Justice ruled that the UK must take all necessary steps to ensure compliance with the Directive and that even assuming that absolute physical impossibility justified the UK's failure to implement the Directive, it had not established that this was the case.

Finally, it should be noted that the Commission submitted a new draft Bathing Water Directive[152] to the Council of Ministers in 1994, which, if adopted, would introduce a number of important changes to the system of control governing bathing water quality. In particular, the proposed Directive would introduce

---

151. [1994] 1 CMLR 769.
152. COM (94) 36 final-94/0006 (SYN), OJ C112 22 Apr. 1994.

considerable changes to the microbiological parameters; it would potentially have a direct impact on the cleanliness of beaches; it would affect sampling frequency; and it would introduce requirements concerning the identification of pollution sources. In addition, the member states' obligation to report to the Commission on implementation would be tightened, and the Commission would be obliged to publish these reports within four months of receiving national annual implementation reports.[153]

### Implementation in Northern Ireland

Directive 76/160/EEC is implemented in Northern Ireland by the Quality of Bathing Water Regulations (NI) 1993.[154] Regulation 3(1) imposes an obligation on the DoE(NI) to set values for bathing water (as defined in Article 2.1 of the Directive, above) in relation to each of the parameters listed in the Annex to the Directive.[155] In this regard, values for bathing water will be set for all bathing areas or for each individual bathing area.[156] When setting values, the Department is obliged to 'endeavour to observe' the G values as guidelines but must set values which are at least as stringent as the I values. Where the Annex to the Directive does not specify any value for a particular parameter, the Department may choose not to set a value until figures have been established at EC level.

Regulation 3(5) gives effect to the Schedule to the Regulations, which lays down the sampling requirements for bathing water. They are as follows:

1. The Department shall in each year throughout the period beginning on 30 April and ending on 30 September take samples of bathing water in accordance with the minimum frequency laid down in the Annex [to the Directive].

2. The Department shall take additional samples if the Department has grounds to suspect that the quality of the water is deteriorating for any reason or is likely to deteriorate as a result of any discharge or probable discharge of substances likely to lower the quality of water.

3. Samples shall be taken at places where the daily average density of bathers is at its highest and preferably 30 centimetres below the surface, except in the case of samples for testing for mineral oils, which shall be taken at surface level.

4. Where the Department uses methods of analysis and inspection other than those specified in the Annex, it shall ensure that the results obtained are equivalent or comparable to those specified in the Annex.

The Department is obliged to 'take all necessary measures' to ensure that the quality of bathing water satisfies the values set under regulation 3(1). However, it

---

153. See Leeson, *Environmental Law,* London: Pitman, 1995, pp 142–3, for further details of the nature of the proposed amendments to Directive 76/160/EEC.

154. SR No. 205. The 1993 Regulations were enacted on 26 Apr. 1993 and came into force on 1 June 1993. See Haigh, supra, chap. 4.5, pp 2–9, for a detailed discussion of the development of the Directive at EC level and its implementation in Great Britain.

155. It should be noted that the Bathing Water Regulations do not apply to water used for therapeutic purposes or to water in swimming pools (reg. 7).

156. A 'bathing area' is defined by regulation 2(1) as 'any place where bathing water is found.'

must also ensure that the implementation of measures taken pursuant to these Regulations does not lead 'directly or indirectly, to the deterioration of the current quality of bathing water' (regulation 3(6) and (7)). Regulation 3(8) requires the Department to carry out periodic local investigations in order to obtain 'geographical and topographical data and to determine the volume and nature of all polluting and potentially polluting discharges and their effects according to the distance from the bathing area.' In the case of fresh running water, such investigations must be 'of the conditions prevailing upstream,' and in the case of fresh still water and sea water the investigation must be of the 'ambient conditions'. Regulation 4 prescribes the conditions which must be fulfilled before bathing water can be deemed to conform to the values set by the Department. In effect, bathing water quality is deemed to be 'excellent' if the weekly sample meets the following G values:[157]

(i) 500 total coliforms per 100 ml of water and 100 faecal coliforms per 100 ml of water; and

(ii) annually 80 per cent of samples taken must meet these standards.

Bathing water quality is deemed to be 'good' if the weekly sample satisfies the following I values:

(i) 10,000 total coliforms per 100 ml of water and 2,000 faecal coliforms per 100 ml of water; and

(ii) annually 95 per cent of samples taken must meet these standards.

Poor bathing water quality indicates that the weekly samples have failed to meet the standards required for 'good' water quality.

Regulation 5 provides that the Department has the power to modify or not to apply the requirements of Directive 76/160/EEC in certain circumstances, namely:

(*a*) in the case of parameters marked (0) in the Annex, because of exceptional weather or geographical conditions; or

(*b*) when bathing water undergoes natural enrichment[158] in certain substances causing a deviation from the values prescribed in the Annex.

It is important to note, however, that the Department may not invoke its powers to modify or not to apply the standards laid down by the Directive where this would 'permit a risk to public health' (regulation 6).

Thus far, there are 458 identified bathing waters in the UK. Sixteen of these are in Northern Ireland; they are: Magilligan (Benone), Castlerock, Portstewart, Portrush (Mill Strand), Portrush (Curran Strand), Ballycastle, Brown's Bay, Helen's Bay, Crawfordsburn, Ballyholme, Groomsport, Millisle, Tyrella, Newcastle, Cranfield (Nicholson's Strand), and Cranfield Bay. When the weekly samples are taken by the DoE(NI), the results of analysis are sent to the district councils, who in turn display posters at or close to the relevant beaches containing the latest information on the quality of the bathing water. These posters list only the latest results for coliform counts as these are the most important parameters for assessing bathing water quality. However, a register containing a full set of results for all parameters is available for public consultation at the offices of the

---

157. DoE(NI), *Bathing Water Quality.*

158. Reg. 5(2) defines 'natural enrichment' as 'the process whereby, without human intervention, a given body of water receives from the soil certain substances contained therein.'

DoE(NI)'s Environment Service. The *Environment Service Corporate Strategy, 1994–97* states that all but one of Northern Ireland's sixteen coastal bathing water sites complied with the mandatory standards laid down in the Directive in 1993, representing a 94 per cent compliance rate, compared with the 80 per cent rate for the UK as a whole.[159] This compliance rate was repeated in 1994 and 1995. Only five of Northern Ireland's identified bathing waters have consistently complied with the more stringent guide values from 1988 to 1995, namely Magilligan (Benone), Portrush (Mill Strand), Portrush (Curran Strand), Tyrella, and Cranfield (Nicholson's Strand).

**Voluntary schemes for grading bathing water**

In addition to the mandatory system of bathing water quality control introduced by Directive 76/160/EEC, there are two informal systems in operation in Northern Ireland which grade bathing water and beach quality, both of which are administered by the Tidy Britain Group.[160] The first is the European Blue Flag Scheme, organised by the Federation of Environmental Education in Europe. A Blue Flag is awarded where bathing water complies with the G values laid down in Directive 76/160/EEC for microbiological parameters (total and faecal coliforms and faecal streptococci) of samples for the previous season. In addition, certain land-based criteria must be satisfied.

The second voluntary scheme is known as the Seaside Award Scheme and is also run by the Tidy Britain Group. This scheme complements the Blue Flag scheme, in that it is designed to recognise beaches and resorts which satisfy specific standards relating to the provision of facilities, beach or resort management, beach cleanliness, safety, information, and water quality. Blue Flag awards for 1996 were announced in March 1996; based on 1995 results, they have been awarded to Magilligan (Benone), Portstewart, Portrush (Mill Strand), Portrush (Curran Strand), and Cranfield (Nicholson's Strand). A Seaside Award has been awarded at Ballycastle, and a Rural Seaside Award was awarded at Crawfordsburn. Changes to annual results (available from the DoE(NI)'s Environment Service) depend on beach and water quality but also on whether the beach and bathing waters were entered for an award by the local authority.

SECTION 4. QUALITY OF WATER FOR FRESHWATER FISH

Directive 78/659/EEC[161] provides for 'the quality of fresh waters needing protection or improvement in order to support fish life.' Member states are required to designate such waters. The objective of the Directive is stated in Article 1.3 as being:

> to protect or improve the quality of those running or standing freshwaters which support or which, if pollution were reduced or eliminated, would become capable of supporting fish belonging to

159.  P. 31.
160.  The Tidy Britain Group is an independent registered charity and is partly funded by the DoE. It can be contacted at Seaside Award Office, Tidy Britain Group, Lion House, Muspole Street, Norwich NR3 1DJ; tel. (01603) 766076; fax (01603) 760580.
161.  OJ L222, 14 Aug. 1978.

— indigenous species offering a natural diversity, or

— species the presence of which is judged desirable for water management purposes by the competent authorities of the Member States.

The Directive identifies two categories of waters which must be designated, namely, waters which are suitable for salmonids (salmon, trout, grayling, and whitefish) and waters which are suitable for cyprinids (coarse fish such as pike, perch, and eel). Waters in natural or artificial fish ponds used for intensive fish-farming are excluded from the ambit of the Directive.

Annex I to the Directive sets out the physical and chemical parameters applicable to both categories of waters, some of which are listed as G values, while others are listed as I values. Member states are obliged to set values for each parameter and, in doing so, must set values which are no less stringent than the I values, and must endeavour to respect the G values. As with the other water quality Directives considered above, Directive 78/659/EEC sets specific sampling requirements governing the frequency and methods of analysis. Member states may derogate from the requirements laid down in the Directive in cases of exceptional weather conditions or special geographical conditions or for reasons of 'natural enrichment'. However, the Commission must be informed of all derogations. Member States are required to notify the Commission of the waters which have been designated pursuant to the Directive and must establish pollution reduction programmes for those waters. Member states are then required to ensure that designated waters actually satisfy the established values within five years of designation and must send a detailed report to the Commission on the state of those waters five years after designation.

## Implementation in Northern Ireland

Member states were required to introduce formal legislation to implement Directive 78/659/EEC by 20 July 1980 and were required to ensure compliance with the requirements of the Directive for designated waters by 20 July 1985. The Water and Sewerage Services (Amendment) (NI) Order 1993 introduced the necessary powers to implement Directive 78/659/EEC in Northern Ireland. However, thus far the Directive has not been formally implemented in Northern Ireland. The DoE(NI) intends to implement the Directive in 1996 by means of the proposed Freshwater Fish Directive Regulations.

Despite the lack of formal implementation, the DoE(NI) asserts that the requirements of the Directive are applied in practice; the *Environment Service Report* 1991–93 states that '1200 km of rivers have been designated as salmonid or cyprinid under the terms of the EC Freshwater Fish Directive . . . The most recent monitoring results available indicate that compliance with the Directive is generally good.'[162]

---

162. p. 26.

SECTION 5. QUALITY OF WATER REQUIRED FOR SHELLFISH

The purpose of Directive 79/923/EEC[163] is to ensure the existence of a suitable environment for the growth of shellfish (bivalve and gastropod molluscs), as distinct from the protection of shellfish consumers, which is addressed separately in Directive 91/492/EEC.[164] Directive 79/923/EEC applies to coastal and brackish (estuarine) waters which are in need of protection and improvement in order to support shellfish life and growth. Member states are required to designate such coastal or brackish waters and to revise these designations where appropriate.

The Directive lays down guide (G) and mandatory (I) values for various physical, chemical and bacteriological parameters, and member states must set values which are at least as stringent as the mandatory values and must endeavour to respect the guide values. The Directive also prescribes sampling frequencies. As is the case under the Freshwater Fish Directive, member states are required to notify the Commission of waters which have been designated under Directive 79/923/EEC and must establish pollution reduction programmes for those waters. Member states are then required to ensure that their designated waters actually satisfy the values set for those waters within six years of designation and must send a detailed report to the Commission as to the state of those waters six years after designation.

**Implementation in Northern Ireland**

As with the Freshwater Fish Directive (above), the Shellfish Directive has not been implemented formally in Northern Ireland to date. The powers to enable formal implementation were introduced by the Water and Sewerage Services (Amendment) (NI) Order 1993, and the DoE(NI) intends to enact formal implementing legislation in 1996 by means of the proposed Shellfish Water Directive Regulations. Despite the lack for formal implementation, the DoE(NI) asserts that the terms of the Directive have been applied in practice in Northern Ireland; the *Environment Service Report* 1991–93 notes that a '5 km² area of Strangford Lough is designated under the EC Shellfish Water Directive (79/923/EEC). The most recent monitoring results available (1991) indicate compliance with the Directive'.[165]

## PART VII DANGEROUS SUBSTANCES

In recent years the EC has adopted a number of important Directives that require member states to regulate the discharge of specific dangerous substances (selected on the basis of their toxicity, persistence, and bioaccumulation) into the aquatic environment. Legislation has been introduced to implement all of these Directives in Northern Ireland. The implementing legislation essentially requires the DoE(NI) to take appropriate steps to reduce or eliminate water pollution from such

---

163. OJ L281, 10 Nov. 1979.
164. OJ L268, 24 Oct. 1991. This Directive is primarily concerned with the quality of shellfish at the point of sale; however, it also addresses the conditions in which shellfish grow, and to this end chap. 1 of the Annex to the Directive prescribes the conditions for production areas by reference to the levels of contamination in the shellfish flesh.
165. P. 27.

substances and makes it an offence to discharge any controlled substance without the Department's written consent. The Department in turn must ensure that discharge consents for such substances comply with water quality objectives set for such substances. It should be noted that the *Environment Service Corporate Plan,* 1994–97 states that where necessary, the Environment Service will review existing discharge consents 'to ensure compliance with the EC Dangerous Substances Directive and its "daughter" Directives . . .'[166] It is intended that this review will be complete by the end of 1996. Each of these Directives will now be addressed in turn.

SECTION 1. DANGEROUS SUBSTANCES IN THE AQUATIC ENVIRONMENT

In 1976 the EC adopted Directive 76/464/EEC[167] on pollution caused by certain dangerous substances discharged into the aquatic environment of the Community. In effect, the Directive establishes a framework under which discharges of particularly dangerous substances into inland, coastal and territorial waters are eliminated or reduced. The Directive was also designed to ensure the co-ordinated or uniform implementation of a number of international conventions on water pollution throughout the Community in order to prevent the creation of unequal conditions in competition, which would interfere with the functioning of the common market.[168] Before addressing Directive 76/464/EEC any further, it should be noted that while the original text applied to discharges to ground water, these provisions have since been superseded by the terms of the Ground Water Directive 80/68/EEC addressed in section 2 below.

The Directive separates the controlled substances into two lists each of which is contained in the Annex to the Directive. List I (known as the 'Black List') identifies specific families and groups of substances which are considered to be particularly harmful. These substances are selected on the basis of their toxicity, persistence and bioaccumulation, with the exception of those which are biologically harmless or which are rapidly converted into substances which are biologically harmless. List I identifies the following families and groups of substances: (i) organohalogen compounds and substances which may form such compounds in the aquatic environment; (ii) organophosphorus compounds; (iii) organotin compounds; (iv) substances in respect of which it has been proved that they possess carcinogenic properties in or via the aquatic environment; (v) mercury and its compounds; (vi) cadmium and its compounds; (vii) persistent mineral oils and hydrocarbons of petroleum origin; (viii) (and for the purposes of certain provisions of the Directive) persistent synthetic substances which may float, remain in suspension or sink and which may interfere with any use of the waters. List II, which is referred to as the 'Grey List', identifies certain individual

---

166. P. 32,
167. OJ L129, 18 May 1976. See: Haigh, supra, chap.4.8, for a more detailed account of Directive 76/464/EEC
168. The international conventions in question are the Paris Convention for the Prevention of Marine Pollution from Land-Based Sources, the Convention for the Protection of the Rhine Against Chemical Pollution, and the Strasbourg Convention for the Protection of International Watercourses Against Pollution. For further details of international agreements concerning water pollution see Haigh, supra, chap. 13.1.

substances and categories of substances which belong to the following families and groups of substances: (i) twenty different metalloids and metals and their compounds; (ii) biocides and their derivatives not appearing on List I; (iii) substances which have a deleterious effect on the taste and/or smell of products for human consumption derived from the aquatic environment and compounds liable to give rise to such substances in water; (iv) toxic or persistent organic compounds of silicon and substances which may give rise to such compounds in water, excluding those which are biologically harmless or are rapidly converted in water into harmless substances; (v) inorganic compounds of phosphorous and elemental phosphorus; (vi) non-persistent mineral oils and hydrocarbons of petroleum origin; (vii) cyanides, flourides; (viii) substances which have an adverse effect on the oxygen balance, particularly ammonia and nitrites.

Directive 76/464/EEC requires member states to take the appropriate steps to 'eliminate pollution' of controlled waters by List I substances. Pollution in this context is defined as 'the discharge by man, directly or indirectly, of substances or energy into the aquatic environment, the results of which are such as to cause hazards to human health, harm to living resources and to aquatic ecosystems, damage to amenities or interference with other legitimate uses of water.' It is clear from this definition that the term 'eliminate' does not mean a zero-emission of List I substances; the term 'pollution' is defined for the purposes of the Directive by reference to the effect of the substance rather than by reference to its presence in the aquatic environment. Member states are required to take the appropriate steps to 'reduce pollution' of the controlled waters by List II substances. The Directive then provides that all discharges of List I and II substances must require prior authorisation by the competent national authority (Articles 3 and 7). An authorisation issued for a List I or II substance must lay down specific emission standards which must be satisfied by the discharger. It is important to note, however, that the basis for national emission standards for List I and II substances are different.

### List I substances

Directive 76/464/EEC provides that member states may choose between two alternative approaches to the control of List I substances. Under the first system of control the EC essentially imposes emission limit values (or upper limits) for specific List I substances through a series of 'daughter Directives'. National emission standards, on which prior authorisations for List I substances are based, must not exceed these EC limit values. Under the second system of control, national emission standards must be set in accordance with environmental quality objectives for the receiving waters, which are set by the EC itself through another series of daughter Directives. The quality objectives will be laid down on the basis of the toxicity, persistence and accumulation of the List I substance in question, as indicated by the latest conclusive scientific data, taking into account the different characteristics of salt-water and fresh water.

The choice between the two alternative regimes is essentially the product of disagreement between the European Commission and the UK as to the approach to be adopted to the control of water pollution generally and, particularly, in relation to discharges of dangerous substances. While all the other member states have opted to implement the first system of control based on EC emission limit values, which is the approach preferred by the Commission, the UK has opted to implement the system of control based on quality objectives. It is important to note, however, that the Directive only allows a member state to employ the quality objective approach in this context if it can prove to the Commission that the quality objectives set by the Community are actually being met and continuously maintained throughout the area which might be affected by the discharges. Such proof must be based on a monitoring procedure which is agreed between the Commission and the member state in question.

The confines of space do not allow for a more detailed explanation of the basis of the disagreement between the limit value and quality objective approaches to water pollution control;[169] suffice it to note Nigel Haigh's observation in relation to the impact of this conflict, namely, that the emergence of this 'so-called parallel' approach has 'undoubtedly weakened EC policy towards dangerous substances in water. It hindered the development of a more effective "combined" approach based on a more discriminating use of one or both methods and slowed agreement to daughter Directives, as member states argued over the equivalence of particular limit values and quality objectives.'[170]

Although the Community has identified a priority list of 129 potential Black List substances, thus far only 17 List I substances have been subject to control by means of a daughter Directive. It is important to emphasise that unless a daughter Directive has been adopted for a particular List I substance it will remain as a List II substance and will be regulated as such. The following is a list of the daughter Directives adopted thus far for List I substances; it should be noted that although these Directives set down both emission limit values and quality objectives, the list only identifies the compliance dates for the achievement of quality objectives as this is the control standard applied by the UK:

*Directive 82/176/EEC*[171]

Mercury discharges by the chloralkali electrolysis industry
Formal implementation date: 1 July 1983
Quality objectives to be met: 1 July 1986

*Directive 84/156/EEC*[172]

Mercury discharges from sectors other than the chloralkali electrolysis industry
Formal implementation date: 12 March 1986
Quality objectives to be met: 1 July 1989

---

169. For a full discussion of the disagreement between the UK and the Commission on the approach to dangerous substances in water see Haigh, supra, chap. 4.
170. Ibid., chap. 4.2, p. 1.
171. OJ L81, 27 Mar. 1982.
172. OJ L74, 17 Mar. 1984.

*Directive 83/513/EEC*[173]

Cadmium discharges
Formal compliance date: 28 September 1985
Quality objectives to be met: 1 January 1989

*Directive 84/491/EEC*[174]

Hexachlorocyclohexane
Formal compliance date: 1 April 1986
Quality objectives to be met: 1 October 1988

*Directive 86/280/EEC*[175]

DDT, carbon tetrachloride, and pentachlorophenol
Formal compliance date: 1 January 1988
Quality objectives to be met: 1 January 1991

*Directive 88/347/EEC*[176]

(i) Aldrin, dieldrin, endrin, and isodrin
(ii) Hexachlorobenzene, hexachlorobutadiene, and chloroform
Amends Directive 86/280/EEC by adding additional substances to List I
Formal compliance date: (i) 1 January 1989; (ii) 1 January 1990
Quality objectives to be met: as above

*Directive 90/415/EEC*[177]

1,2-dichloroethane, trichloroethane, perchloroethane, and trichlorobenzene
Further amends Directive 86/280/EEC by adding additional substances to List I
Formal compliance date: 1 January 1992
Quality objectives to be met: 1 January 1995

## Implementation of List I requirements in Northern Ireland

The requirements of framework Directive 76/464/EEC concerning List I substances and the environmental quality objectives laid down in each of the daughter Directives adopted thus far are implemented in Northern Ireland by the Pollution of Waters by Dangerous Substances Regulations (NI) 1990,[178] as amended by the Pollution of Waters by Dangerous Substances (Amendment) Regulations (NI) 1992.[179] Regulation 4 of the 1990 Regulations essentially places the DoE(NI) (as the competent national authority for NI) under an obligation to 'take the appropriate steps' to eliminate pollution of 'inland surface waters, territorial waters and internal coastal waters' by the dangerous substances in the families and groups of substances listed in List I of the Annex to Directive 76/464/EEC. As already stated, a substance will only be regarded as a List I substance if a daughter Directive has been adopted in relation to the substance. In addition, regulation 5 prohibits the discharge of List I substances into the waters controlled by the 1990 and 1992 Regulations without the Department's written

173. OJ L291, 24 Oct. 1983.
174. OJ L274, 17 Oct. 1984.
175. OJ L181, 4 July 1986.
176. OJ L158, 25 June 1988.
177. OJ L219, 14 Aug. 1990.
178. SR No. 38.
179. SR No. 401. The 1992 Amendment Regulations in effect take account of the quality objective standards laid down by Directive 90/415/EEC, which further amends Directive 86/280/EEC by extending its scope to include additional substances as List I substances: see pp 221–2.

consent. A discharge consent issued under regulation 5 must specify emission standards, conditions and limits that are in accordance with the terms of Directive 76/464/EEC, and in setting emission standards the DoE(NI) must comply with the environmental quality objectives laid down in Annex II of the various daughter Directives adopted in relation to those List I substances, outlined above.

It should be noted that all of the daughter Directives require that authorisations for List I discharges from new plant require use of the 'best technical means available for minimising pollution' from the substance in question, even where standards are based on environmental quality objectives, as is the case in the UK.[180] Where a discharge consent is given for new plant which does not require use of the best technical means, this decision has to be justified to the Commission; the Commission is required to provide its opinion on the authorisation within three months. It is an offence to breach the terms of regulation 5 or to make a discharge which violates the conditions or requirements attached to a discharge consent issued under regulation 5 (regulation 8); such an offence is punishable on summary conviction by a maximum fine of £5,000. Finally, it should be noted that the DoE(NI) is required by Article 11 of the Directive to draw up an inventory of discharges into inland and territorial waters which contain List I substances to which emission standards apply.

## List II substances

As already stated, Directive 76/464/EEC requires member states to take the appropriate steps to reduce pollution of inland, coastal and territorial waters caused by discharges of List II substances to such waters. As is the case in relation to List I substances, member states are also required to subject discharges of List II substances to such waters to prior authorisation by a competent national authority. Any prior authorisation granted in this regard would have to set down emission standards which comply with EC quality objectives. However, whereas quality objectives for List I substances are set down for specific substances in daughter Directives adopted under Directive 76/464/EEC, the emission standards for List II substances are required simply to comply with EC quality objectives laid down in any existing Directives. Article 7 of the Directive also requires member states to establish programmes for the reduction of pollution to controlled waters caused by List II substances. These programmes must be implemented by specific deadlines; each programme will identify its own completion date. Member states are required to communicate summaries of national programmes and the results of their implementation to the Commission who will in turn conduct regular comparisons of the various national programmes in order to ensure sufficient uniformity in their implementation.

## Implementation of List II requirements in Northern Ireland

The requirements concerning List II substances have not yet been implemented in Northern Ireland. However, it should be noted that the proposed Dangerous Substances in Water (List II) Directive Regulations will implement these

---

180. The concept of 'best technical means available for minimising pollution' is not defined in any of the daughter Directives.

requirements in the near future. The DoE(NI)'s submission to the House of Commons Environment Committee in 1990 notes that List II metals have been monitored in Northern Ireland waters. The results of monitoring established that 'all 54 monitoring stations complied with the Environmental Quality Standard for lead, nickel, chromium and arsenic but at seven stations in the Foyle catchment with very "soft" waters the average results for zinc and copper were marginally higher than the relevant [environmental quality standard] .'[181]

## SECTION 2. INTRODUCTION OF DANGEROUS SUBSTANCES TO GROUND
## WATER

The purpose of Directive 80/68/EEC[182] is to protect ground water throughout the Community from pollution, particularly pollution caused by certain toxic, persistent and bioaccumulable substances. Ground water is defined in Article 1.2(a) of the Directive as meaning 'all water which is below the surface of the ground in the saturation zone and in direct contact with the ground or subsoil'. As is the case in relation to Directive 76/464/EEC concerning the emission of dangerous substances to the aquatic environment (discussed in section 1 above), pollution is defined in Directive 80/68/EEC by reference to the effect of the substances in question instead of by reference to their presence. Article 1.2(d) defines pollution as meaning 'the discharge by man, directly or indirectly, of substances or energy into ground water, the results of which are such as to endanger human health or water supplies, harm living resources and the aquatic ecosystem or interfere with other legitimate uses of water'. As is the case under Directive 76/464/EEC, the Ground Water Directive contains a List I and a List II of families and groups of dangerous substances which are subject to control. Substances in List I are more dangerous than those contained in List II and, for this reason, more stringent controls are imposed on List I substances. It should be noted, however, that while the substances listed in the Ground Water Directive are similar to those listed in Directive 76/464/EEC, they are not identical. Article 2 of the Directive provides that the terms of the Directive will not apply to:

(a) discharges of domestic effluents from isolated dwellings not connected to a sewerage system and situated outside areas protected for the abstraction of water for human consumption;

(b) discharges which are found by the competent authority of the member state concerned to contain substances in Lists I or II in a quantity and concentration so small as to obviate any present or future danger of deterioration in the quality of the receiving ground waters;

(c) discharges of matter containing radioactive substances.

---

181. *House of Commons Environment Committee First Report: Environmental Issues in Northern Ireland,* HC 39 (1990) p. 49.
182. OJ L20, 26 Jan. 1980. Member states were required to implement the Directive (formal compliance) by 19 Dec. 1981, and actual control of new discharges was to be achieved by the same date; existing discharges were to be controlled by 19 Dec. 1985.

### List I substances

Article 3(a) of the Ground Water Directive provides that member states are obliged to take the necessary steps 'to prevent the introduction into ground water of substances in List I'. Article 4 of the Directive then goes on to set out more specifically what member states are required to do in order to comply with their obligations under Article 3(a). In relation to the obligation to prevent the introduction of List I substances into ground waters, Article 4.1 provides that member states:

— shall prohibit all direct discharges of substances in List I;

— shall subject to prior investigation any disposal or tipping for the purpose of disposal of these substances which might lead to indirect discharge. In the light of that investigation, Member States shall prohibit such activity or shall grant authorisation provided that all the technical precautions necessary to prevent such discharge are observed';

— shall take all appropriate measures they deem necessary to prevent any indirect discharge of substances in List I due to activities on or in the ground other than those mentioned in the second indent [i.e. above]. They shall notify such measures to the Commission, which in the light of this information, may submit proposals to the Council for revision of this Directive.

Although it might appear from a reading of the Directive that the prohibition of direct and indirect discharges of List I substances contained in Article 3(a) and the first and second indents of Article 4.1 is subject to the terms of Article 2(b), the European Court of Justice has made it clear that this is not the case. In Case C-131/88 *Commission v. Federal Republic of Germany*[183] the German Government argued that the prohibition imposed on direct and indirect discharges of List I substances in Directive 80/68/EEC was a relative rather than an absolute prohibition. In effect, Germany maintained that the prohibition must be read in conjunction with Article 2(b) of the Directive which, they argued, made provision for exceptions to the prohibition laid down in Articles 3(a) and 4.1 and thereby conferred a discretion on member states in the implementation of the provisions of the Ground Water Directive. The German Government had implemented the terms of the Ground Water Directive by introducing legislation under which authorisations to introduce List I substances into ground water could be granted but only if there was no reason to fear detrimental effects on ground water due to pollution or impairment of the properties of the ground water. The European Court of Justice completely rejected this interpretation of the Ground Water Directive and ruled that Germany had failed to implement the terms of the Directive correctly. In the Court's opinion, the obligation to prohibit all direct discharges of List I substances laid down in Article 4.1(first indent):

. . . is general and absolute and applies to discharges of substances in

---

183. [1991] 1 ECR 825. See also the ECJ's rulings in Case 291/84 *Commission v. The Netherlands* [1987] ECR 3483; Case 1/86 *Commission v. Belgium* [1987] ECR 2797; Case 6/11 *Commission v. Italy* [1987] 1 ECR 791. In addition, see the decision of Popplewell LJ in *R v. Vale of Glamorgan, ex parte James* Queens Bench Division, unreported, 10 August 1995.

List I without distinguishing between the substances themselves and solutions thereof. [Article 4.1] . . . does not empower the competent authorities of the member states to determine, on a case-by-case basis and having regard to the circumstances, whether or not discharges have a detrimental effect. That interpretation results, moreover, from a comparison between the wording of the first indent of Article 4.1 and the wording of Article 5 of the Directive, which does in fact introduce a system of authorisation for discharges of substances in List II. It also results from the ninth recital in the preamble to the Directive, according to which, with the exception of direct discharges of substances in List I, which are automatically prohibited, all discharges must be made subject to an authorisation scheme. Article 2(b) of the Directive must be interpreted having regard to the fact that it is to be found in an article that specifies the cases to which the Directive does not apply. Moreover, Article 2(b) of the Directive does not refer to discharges of substances in List I or II, whether or not in solution, but to discharges of other substances that contain substances in those two lists. Substances in Lists I or II contained in such discharges must be present in quantities sufficiently small as to obviate prima facie, without there even being a need for an evaluation, all risk of pollution of the ground water. That is why Article 2(b) of the Directive refers not to an evaluation by the competent authority of a member state but to a simple finding. Thus the meaning of that provision is that if the quantity of substances in List I (or II) contained in discharges of other substances is such that the risk of pollution cannot be automatically excluded, the Directive is applicable and, in that case, Article 2(b) cannot, contrary to what . . . [Germany] claims, be taken in conjunction with the other provisions of the Directive in order to interpret them. Consequently, it is not possible to refer to Article 2(b) of the Directive in order to call into question the foregoing interpretation according to which the prohibition laid down by the first indent of Article 4.1 is absolute. (paras. 14-18).

It is clear from this extract that the Court's ruling in Case C-131/88 considerably increases the protection afforded to ground water under the Directive. Whereas, on a literal interpretation of the Directive, it appeared that member states had the power to establish a discharge consent system for List I substances, under which a direct discharge of such substances would be prohibited only if the competent authority of the member state had reason to fear detrimental effects on the ground water as a result of pollution, or impairment of the properties of the ground water, the European Court has interpreted Directive 80/68/EEC so as to impose a complete ban on direct discharges of List I substances. In effect, the Court has interpreted the Directive by reference to the spirit and purpose of its provisions, rather than by reference to its literal meaning, an approach which characterises the entire spectrum of the Court's case law. As a result of the Court's decision, which is binding throughout the Community, Article 2(b) must be viewed as a separate provision serving a specific and separate function within the framework of the Directive. It cannot be regarded as a provision which qualifies the operation of Article 4 of the Directive. In effect, unless the amount of List I substances contained in a direct discharge is so small as to justify a finding to the effect that it is self-evident that their presence is irrelevant to the safety and quality of ground water, then the absolute prohibition will apply to the discharge. Article 2(b) will cease to have effect on the application of the Directive after that point.

Turning then to the nature of the prohibition imposed on indirect discharges of List I substances, the European Court of Justice ruled that the requirements laid down in Article 3(a) must be read in conjunction with those expressed in the second and third indents of Article 4.1 of the Directive. Read together, the Court stated that the following points could be made as to the requirements contained in Article 3(a) and Article 4.1 (second and third indents) concerning indirect discharges of List I substances:

1. As is the case in relation to direct discharges of List I substances, the Ground Water Directive imposes an absolute prohibition on any indirect discharges of List I substances. In effect, Article 2(b) of the Directive cannot be read in conjunction with Article 3(a) and the second and third indents of Article 4.1 to justify the establishment of a system of authorisations for indirect discharges of such substances. Article 2(b) operates in an identical manner in relation to direct and indirect discharges of List I substances.

2. As is the case in relation to direct discharge of List I substances, the prohibition on indirect discharges applies to all List I substances. This fact must be stated clearly in any implementing legislation.

3. Article 3(a) and the second indent of Article 4.1 apply to *any* disposal or tipping for the purposes of disposal capable of leading to an indirect discharge of List I substances. Although this fact must be stated clearly in any implementing legislation, it was not stated in the German implementing legislation. Article 3(a) and Article 4.1 (second indent) require member states to subject all such disposal and tipping for the purposes of disposal to a mandatory prior investigation (this fact must also be stated clearly in national implementing legislation; it is not sufficient that such prior investigations are conducted pursuant to national administrative practice even if it is an automatic practice). This investigation is carried out for the purposes of appraising the receiving environment and must be conducted with specific reference to the factors laid down in Article 7 of the Directive (i.e. it must include an examination of 'the hydrological conditions of the area concerned, the possible purifying powers of the soil and subsoil and the risk of pollution and alteration of the quality of the ground water from the discharge and shall establish whether the discharge of substances into ground water is a satisfactory solution from the point of view of the environment'). The investigation must, in all cases, result in either a prohibition or an authorisation. In this regard the Court ruled that the importance of the purpose of the Ground Water Directive required that an express measure, either prohibition or authorisation, must be adopted. An authorisation can only be granted, however, if all the technical precautions necessary to prevent all indirect discharges of List I substances are observed, a fact which must be stated clearly in the implementing legislation.

4. The purpose of Article 3(a) and the third indent of Article 4.1 is to prevent indirect discharges of List I substances resulting from any activity other than those referred to in the second indent of Article 4.1. Member states are obliged to take all appropriate measures to that end.

## List II substances

Article 3(b) provides that member states are under an obligation 'to limit the introduction into ground water of substances in List II so as to avoid pollution of this water by these substances'. Article 5.1 of the Ground Water Directive sets out more specifically what is required of member states in order to comply with their obligations under Article 3(b). In this regard, member states are obliged to conduct a prior investigation in relation to the following:

— all direct discharge of substances in List II, so as to limit such discharges;
— the disposal or tipping for the purpose of disposal of these substances which might lead to indirect discharge.'

Article 7 of the Ground Water Directive (outlined above on page 227) specifies the factors which must be examined in any such prior investigation. Having conducted the mandatory prior investigation, Article 5.1 provides that member states may only grant an authorisation provided that all technical precautions for preventing ground water pollution by List II substances are observed. Article 5.2 goes on to provide that, in complying with their obligations under Article 3(b), member states are also required to take the appropriate measures which they deem necessary to limit all indirect discharges of substances in List II due to activities on or in the ground other than those mentioned in Article 5.1.

In the course of its ruling in the *Commission v. Federal Republic of Germany,* the European Court of Justice also discussed the requirements laid down in the Ground Water Directive concerning direct and indirect discharges of List II substances. Although it is clear from the wording of the Directive that member states are under an obligation only to limit direct and indirect discharges of List II substances, the Court ruled that legislation introduced by the German Government which established an authorisation system for List I and II substances based on the provisions of Article 2(b) did not constitute a correct implementation of the Directive. As is outlined above in relation to List I substances, the Court ruled that the terms of Articles 4 and 5 could not be interpreted in light of Article 2(b). In addition, the Court pointed out that the German implementing legislation did not implement the requirements laid down in Article 5 with the precision and clarity necessary to satisfy the demands of legal certainty. In this regard the Court pointed to the fact that the national legislation in question did not make specific provision for the required mandatory prior investigation, nor did it stipulate that authorisations would be granted only if the necessary technical precautions were observed. Similarly, the legislation failed to state clearly that any disposal or tipping for the purposes of disposal and other activities on or in the grounds capable of leading to indirect discharges of List II are covered.

## Further requirements concerning ground water

1. Article 4.2 provides that where prior investigation reveals that the ground water into which List I substances are to be discharged is 'permanently unsuitable for other uses, especially domestic or agricultural', member states may authorise the discharge of such substances 'provided that their presence does not impede exploitation of ground resources'. Authorisations under Article 4.2 may be

issued only if all technical precautions have been taken to ensure that the List I substances cannot reach other aquatic systems or harm other ecosystems.

2. Article 4.3 of the Ground Water Directive provides that member states 'may, after prior investigation, authorise discharges due to re-injection into the same aquifer of water used for geothermal purposes, water pumped out of mines and quarries, or water pumped out for civil engineering works'.

3. Article 6 provides that, notwithstanding the requirements laid down in Articles 4 and 5, 'artificial recharges for the purpose of ground water management shall be subject to a special authorisation issued by member states on a case-by-case basis. Such authorisations shall be granted only if there is no risk of polluting the ground water'.

4. Member states are required under Article 15 of the Directive to maintain an inventory of the authorisations granted under: (a) Article 4 in relation to discharges of List I substances, (b) Article 5 in relation to direct discharges of List II substances and (c) under Article 6.

5. Article 16 empowers the Commission to require member states to provide specified information on a case-by-case basis concerning the implementation of the Directive; Article 16 also governs the publication of such information. In addition, it should be noted that Directive 91/692/EEC[184] introduced a reporting requirement for all member states in relation to action taken to implement the Ground Water Directive. The requirements laid down by this Directive are outlined in chapter 3.

6. Where member states intend to grant authorisations for discharges into transfrontier ground water, the competent national authorities are required to inform the other member states concerned before authorising the discharge. Any concerned member state may request that consultations be held with the Commission in this regard; such consultations will be held before the authorisation is granted.

## Procedural requirements contained in the Ground Water Directive

As already stated, Article 7 of the Ground Water Directive requires that any prior investigations referred to in Articles 4 or 5 must include examinations of specific factors. Articles 8–14 of the Ground Water Directive set out specific procedures and conditions governing the granting, monitoring and duration of authorisations under Articles 4, 5 and 6. During the course of its ruling in the *Commission v. Germany* the European Court of Justice ruled that the procedural provisions contained in the Ground Water Directive set down precise and detailed rules which are intended to create rights and obligations for individuals. As a result, the Court ruled that 'they must be incorporated into German law with the precision and clarity necessary in order to satisfy fully the requirement of legal certainty'. The Court went on to state, that 'mere administrative practices, which are alterable at the will of the administration and are not given adequate publicity, cannot be regarded as constituting adequate compliance with the obligations imposed on member states', to implement the terms of a Directive under Article 189 of the EC Treaty.

---

184. OJ L377/48, 31 Dec. 1991.

## Implementation of List I and II requirements in Northern Ireland

The requirements laid down by the Ground Water Directive in relation to List I and List II substances are implemented in Northern Ireland by the Pollution of Ground Water by Dangerous Substances Regulations (NI) 1994.[185] The Regulations place the DoE(NI) (as the competent authority for Northern Ireland) under an obligation to take the necessary steps, in accordance with the Ground Water Directive, to prevent the introduction of List I substances into ground water and to limit the introduction of List II substances into ground water so as to avoid pollution of this water by such substances (regulation 4). In addition regulation 5 prohibits the 'discharge or deposit' of List I or List II substances so as to allow their entry into ground water without obtaining the DoE(NI)'s written consent.

Violation of regulation 5 is an offence; it is similarly an offence to contravene any condition or requirement attached to a consent issued under regulation 5. Regulation 6 provides that a person who contravenes regulation 5 or any condition or requirement imposed under regulation 5 will be liable to a maximum fine of £5,000 on summary conviction and, on conviction on indictment, to a fine or imprisonment for a maximum term of two years, or to both.

Regulation 3 provides that the 1994 Regulations will not apply to those discharges listed in Article 2(a)–(c) of the Directive (outlined above). In this regard, regulation 3 repeats the exact wording of the Ground Water Directive.

Given the unequivocal nature of the European Court's ruling in *Commission v. Federal Republic of Germany* concerning: (i) the nature of the obligations laid down in the Ground Water Directive and (ii) the obligation imposed on member states to implement its terms with the precision and clarity necessary in order to fully satisfy the requirement of legal certainty, it would appear that not only were the Pollution of Ground Water by Dangerous Substances Regulations (NI) 1994 long overdue, but they also do not adequately implement the terms of the Ground Water Directive in Northern Ireland. In particular, the Regulations do not make clear the absolute nature of the prohibition on all direct and indirect discharges of List I substances and the role of the exceptions listed in regulation 3 which implements the provisions of Article 2 of the Directive (especially the exception listed in regulation 3(b)). Similarly, the 1994 Regulations fail to make clear the obligation imposed on the DoE(NI) to conduct a prior investigation, which examines specified factors, in relation to *any* disposal or tipping for the purpose of disposal which might lead to an indirect discharge of List I or II substances. The 1994 Regulations also fail to make clear that an authorisation can only be granted under the Directive if the DoE(NI) ensures that all the technical precautions necessary to prevent an indirect discharge of List I substances or for preventing ground water pollution by List II substances are observed. In addition, the Regulations fail to make clear the procedural requirements laid down in Articles 8–14 of the Ground Water Directive which set out specific procedures and conditions governing the granting, monitoring and duration of authorisations under Articles 4, 5 and 6. As already stated, the rulings of the European Court of Justice are binding throughout the Community; it would appear clear, therefore,

---

185.  SR No. 147. See Haigh, supra, at chap. 4.7, p. 3, for a full discussion of the implementation of the Ground Water Directive in Great Britain.

that the UK remains in breach of its obligation to implement the Ground Water Directive and, as such, is susceptible to enforcement proceedings under Article 169 of the EC Treaty. Indeed, it should also be noted that counsel for the Larne Borough Council has also submitted detailed arguments to the Magheramorne Landfill Public Inquiry to the effect that the 1994 Regulations fail to adequately implement the terms of the Ground Water Directive. At the time of writing, the outcome of the inquiry is unknown.

### EC Resolution on ground water protection

The pollution of ground water from agricultural activities (e.g. nitrates and pesticides) has emerged as one of the biggest water pollution problems facing the EC. On 20 February 1995 the Council of Ministers adopted a Resolution on Ground Water Protection[186] in which it emphasised the special significance of ground water 'as an essential component of the water cycle and ecosystems and as one of the most important resources in the provision of drinking water.' The Resolution also expresses the Council's concern that ground water resources in certain areas remain 'seriously endangered, both qualitatively and quantitatively.' In particular the Resolution reaffirms the priority given to the development of ground water management in the EC's Fifth Action Programme on the Environment, which highlighted 'maintaining the quality of unpolluted ground water, preventing further pollution [and] restoring, where appropriate, polluted water' as issues of particular importance.

In the light of this the Resolution calls on the Commission to tackle these issues and to draw up proposals in accordance with the principle of subsidiarity, which focus on the following:

(i)   the introduction of 'licensing systems and other instruments which could provide appropriate national management of ground water';
(ii)  the introduction of 'measures to provide for preventative, far-reaching ground water protection . . . in view of diffuse sources'; and
(iii) the introduction of 'general provisions to promote agricultural practices consistent with ground water protection.'

The Resolution also urges the Commission to consider the revision of Directive 80/68/EEC. Finally, the Council called for the submission of proposals concerning ground water management by the first half of 1995.

## Section 3. Discharge of Asbestos into the Aquatic Environment

Directive 87/217/EEC[187] governs the prevention and reduction of pollution by asbestos in all environmental media. The Directive imposes a general duty on all member states to ensure, as far as it is reasonably practicable, that emissions of asbestos are reduced at source and prevented. Limit values for emissions of asbestos into all environmental media are laid down in Directive 87/217/EEC.

---

186. OJ C49, 28 Feb. 1995. It should be noted that under Art. 189 of the EC Treaty, Resolutions do not have any legal effect.
187. OJ L85, 28 Mar. 1987.

**Implementation in Northern Ireland**

The requirements of the Directive concerning emissions of asbestos into the aquatic environment are implemented in Northern Ireland by the Control of Asbestos in Water Regulations (NI) 1995,[188] which provide that it is an offence to make a discharge of asbestos into the aquatic environment without the DoE(NI)'s written consent (regulation 4).

The term 'asbestos' is defined by Article 2.1 of the Directive, which is discussed in chapter 4. A consent granted under regulation 4 must specify emission standards, conditions and limits which are in accordance with Article 5 of Directive 87/217/EEC, and it is also an offence to breach any condition or requirement specified in the consent. An offence under the Regulations is punishable, on summary conviction, by a fine not exceeding level 5 on the standard scale (£5,000) or, on conviction on indictment, by imprisonment for a maximum of two years or a fine, or both. Regulation 3 provides that the DoE(NI) is obliged to take the necessary measures (in accordance with the terms of the Directive) to ensure that asbestos discharges into the aquatic environment are, 'as far as reasonably practicable, reduced at source and prevented.'

## PART VIII CONTROL OF POLLUTION FROM AGRICULTURAL SOURCES

Eighty per cent of the land in Northern Ireland is in agricultural use, and it is therefore not surprising that the great majority of water pollution incidents in Northern Ireland are caused by farming practices.[189] There are two principal sources of agricultural pollution, namely: (i) escapes of silage effluent, slurry, farmyard waste, sheep dip and pesticides from farmyards and (ii) the run-off and leaching of excess nutrients, especially nitrates and phosphates, from agricultural land. Until recently the general offence contained in section 5 of the Water Act (NI) 1972 (discussed in Part I of this chapter) was the only form of regulation imposed on pollution from agricultural sources in Northern Ireland. However, whereas section 5 addressed casual pollution from agricultural discharges, further measures were needed to tackle the complex process of water eutrophication, which is one of the most polluting consequences of contemporary intensive agricultural practices. Eutrophication is a phenomenon of over-enrichment of waters by so-called nutrients, principally nitrate and phosphate. When over-enrichment occurs it fertilises or stimulates the growth of attached plants below the waterline in rivers and of planktonic algae in lakes, leading to increased weed growth, an increased incidence of algal 'blooms' and scums in lakes, the blockage of channels, siltation, and in some cases deoxygenation, which in turn leads to

---

188. SR No. 93.
189. Statistics for reported pollution incidents investigated by the DoE(NI)'s Environment Service from 1989 to 1994 are set out in the *Environment Service Report, 1993–1995*, p. 36. See also the submissions of the Foyle Conservancy Board for Northern Ireland and the Foyle Fisheries Commission to *House of Commons Environment Committee First Report: Environmental Issues in Northern Ireland*, HC 39 (1990) pp 143–53.

serious disruptions in fish populations. Eutrophication of inland surface waters is principally caused by the presence of excess levels of phosphate, while the extent of eutrophication in estuarial and coastal (salt) waters is determined by the level of nitrate present. Nitrate and phosphates are both present in many forms of waste but particularly in sewage. In its submission to the House of Commons Environment Committee in 1990 the DoE(NI) stated that a survey of 1,690 lakes had been carried out and 370 of them had been sampled; the results established that 54 per cent of these lakes were either eutrophic or hypertrophic.[190]

The introduction of legislation to prevent and control water eutrophication has been stimulated primarily at EC level. The EC has addressed the problem of eutrophication in two ways. First, legislation has been enacted to control 'point' sources of pollution by restricting the volume of nutrient-bearing waste being discharged to receiving waters and also by imposing sewage treatment standards designed to remove nutrients from sewage sludge. Secondly, legislation has been introduced to tackle the diffuse leaching of nutrients to waters caused by the spreading of manure slurry on agricultural land and also by the use of artificial fertilisers in agriculture. Directive 91/271/EEC (the Urban Waste Water Directive) imposes specific treatment standards on urban waste water. It restricts its discharge to surface waters and requires that the practice of dumping sewage sludge at sea be stopped by 1998 in order to combat the eutrophication of coastal and inland waters. The obligations laid down by this Directive and its implementation in Northern Ireland are discussed in Part IX, section 2 of this chapter.

Two EC Directives have been adopted for the purposes of regulating the spreading of sewage sludge on agricultural land and the use of inorganic or artificial fertilisers, namely, Directive 86/278/EEC[191] and Directive 91/676/ EEC.[192] Directive 86/278/EEC has been implemented in Northern Ireland by the Sludge (Use in Agriculture) Regulations (NI) 1990,[193] while Directive 91/676/ EEC has not been implemented in Northern Ireland to date; however, the DoE(NI) intends to introduce the proposed Nitrates Directive Regulations for these purposes in the near future. It should also be noted that the DoE(NI) intends to introduce further legislation in relation to pollution from agricultural sources in the near future, namely, the Silage, Slurry and Agriculture Fuel Oil Regulations, which will prescribe standards for silos, slurry tanks and oil storage in agriculture; these Regulations will be adopted pursuant to powers contained in the forthcoming Water Order (discussed in Part III of this chapter).

Before discussing the specific requirements introduced by these measures, it is important to emphasise that the DoE(NI)'s Environment Service monitors pollution from agricultural sources intensively and, in addition, the Department of Agriculture (Northern Ireland) has undertaken a number of pollution prevention advisory campaigns, including the adoption of a Code of Good Agricultural Practice (copies of which are available free from Agriculture Development Centres). The DANI also provides free advice on pollution control and grant aid to

---

190. *House of Commons Environment Committee First Report: Environmental Issues in Northern Ireland,* ibid., p. 51. The Report also noted the long-standing problem of eutrophication in Lough Neagh (the UK's largest lake) and Lough Erne.
191. OJ L181/6, 12 June 1986.
192. OJ L375, 31 Dec. 1991; formal compliance required by 19 Dec. 1993.
193. SR No. 245. The Regulations came into operation on 30 July 1990.

improve effluent handling facilities. The *Environment Service Corporate Plan* 1994–97 reported a recent reduction in reported incidents of water pollution from agricultural sources and, also that the Department aims to make its submissions to the Director of Public Prosecutions within four and a half months of a water pollution incident.[194]

SECTION 1. REGULATING THE USE OF SEWAGE SLUDGE IN AGRICULTURE

The Sludge (Use in Agriculture) Regulations (NI) 1990 regulate the use of sludge and septic tank sludge on agricultural land, 'agriculture' being defined as 'the growing of all types of commercial food crops, including for stock-rearing purposes.' The 1990 Regulations implement the terms of Directive 86/278/EEC in Northern Ireland (see above).

Violation of any of the provisions of the Sludge Regulations is an offence, punishable, on summary conviction, by a maximum fine of £5,000. Regulation 3 provides that it is an offence to 'cause or knowingly permit' sludge to be used on agricultural land unless the requirements set out in regulation 3(2)–(7) are satisfied (regulation 3(2)–(7) sets out a series of technical requirements defined by reference to the terms of Schedules 1 and 2 to the Regulations). The term 'sludge' is defined in regulation 2 as 'residual sludge from sewage plants treating domestic or urban waste waters and from other sewage plants treating waste waters of a composition similar to domestic and urban waste waters.'

Regulation 4 makes it an offence for any person to supply sludge for use on agricultural land if he 'knows or has reason to believe' that the conditions laid down in regulation 3(6) will not be satisfied when the sludge is so used, the condition being that 'no fruit or vegetable crops, other than fruit trees, will be growing or being harvested in the soil at the time of the use.' Similarly, it is an offence for any person to supply sludge for use on agricultural land if he 'knows or has reason to believe' that the precautions set out in regulation 5 will not be complied with after the sludge is so used.

Regulation 5 sets out specific precautions that must be observed where any sludge or septic tank sludge has been used on agricultural land. It is an offence to 'cause or knowingly permit' non-compliance with these precautions. The term 'septic tank sludge' is defined in regulation 2 as 'residual sludge from septic tanks and other similar installations for the treatment of sewage.'

Regulations 6–8 impose a series of information supply obligations concerning the use of sludge on agricultural land. Regulation 6 provides that in the event that sludge is used on any agricultural land other than by or on behalf of a sludge producer (i.e. 'the DoE(NI) or any other person who manages a plant at which sludge is produced for disposal'), the occupier of the land in question must provide the following information to the sludge producer immediately:

(*a*)  the address and area of the agricultural unit[195] concerned;

(*b*)  the date on which the sludge was used;

(*c*)  the quantity of sludge so used; and

---

194. P. 32.
195. An 'agricultural unit' is defined by reg. 2 as 'an area of agricultural land used for a single agricultural purpose, not exceeding 5 hectares.'

(*d*) where the sludge was not supplied by the sludge producer, the name and address of the person who supplied that sludge, and the quantity of sludge so used which was supplied by that person.

All sludge producers are required under regulation 7 to prepare and maintain a register which contains the following information:

(*a*) the total quantity of sludge produced in any year;[196]

(*b*) in relation to sludge supplies for the purpose of use in agriculture in any year:

   (i) the total quantity of sludge supplied;

   (ii) the composition and properties of that sludge as determined in accordance with Schedule 1 [to the Regulations];

   (iii) the quantities of treated sludge supplied, and the type of treatment;

   (iv) the names and addresses of the person to whom the sludge was supplied; and

   (v) the address and area of each agricultural unit [defined above] on which sludge has been used, the quantity of sludge used thereon, and the amount of chromium and of each of the elements listed in the sludge table which has been added thereto;

(*c*) a copy of every analysis or assessment made under Schedule 2 [to the Regulations] relating to the soil of an agricultural unit on which sludge has been used.

Finally, regulation 8 imposes an obligation on all sludge producers (other than the DoE(NI) itself) to make the contents of this register available for inspection by the DoE(NI) at 'all reasonable times.' In addition, such sludge producers are obliged to provide the Department with any information or facilities as may reasonably be required by the Department in relation to the register for the purpose of verifying the information contained in the register, or for any other purpose relating to the sludge supplied by the sludge producer, and may include the provision of facilities for analysing representative samples of sludge or soil. All sludge producers (i.e. including the DoE(NI)) are obliged to provide all persons to whom they supply sludge with details of the analysis of sludge tests carried out in accordance with Schedule 1 to the Regulations as soon as is reasonably practicable.

## SECTION 2. POLLUTION OF WATERS CAUSED OR INDUCED BY NITRATES FROM AGRICULTURAL SOURCES

Nitrates from agricultural sources are the main cause of pollution from diffuse sources affecting the Community's waters. As a result, Directive 91/676/EEC,[197]

---

196. Reg. 7(2) defines 'year' in this context as 'the period from the operative date to 31st December 1990, and thereafter the period of 12 months from 31st December.'

197. OJ L375, 31 Dec. 1991; formal compliance required by 19 Dec. 1993. See: Haigh, supra, chap. 4.14, for a detailed treatment of the requirements of this Directive and its development.

known as the 'Nitrates Directive', has been adopted in order to reduce water pollution (i.e. eutrophication) caused or induced by the storage and application of artificial fertiliser and manure on farmland, and to prevent further such pollution. To this end the Directive is designed to protect human health, living resources and aquatic ecosystems, and to safeguard other legitimate uses of water.

The Directive first requires member states to identify those waters which are actually or potentially affected by pollution from nitrates. Pollution in this context is defined by Article 2(j) as the direct or indirect discharge of nitrogen compounds from agricultural sources, the results of which are such as to cause hazards to human health, harm to living resources and to aquatic ecosystems, damage to amenities or interference with other legitimate uses of water. Annex I to the Directive provides that these waters must be identified making use, amongst others, of the following criteria:

1. *surface freshwaters*, in particular those used or intended for the abstraction of drinking water, which contain or which could contain, if action pursuant to Article 5 of the Directive is not taken, more than the concentration of nitrates laid down in accordance with Directive 75/440/EEC on the quality of surface water intended for the abstraction of drinking (addressed in Part VI, section 1 of this chapter);

2. *ground waters*, which contain or could contain more than 50mg/l nitrates if action pursuant to Article 5 of the Directive is not taken;

3. *natural freshwater lakes, other freshwater bodies, estuaries, coastal waters and marine waters* which are found to be eutrophic or in the near future may become eutrophic if action under Article 5 of the Directive is not taken.

In applying the criteria listed above, Annex I requires member states to take account of: (i) the physical and environmental characteristics of the waters and land; (ii) the current understanding of the behaviour of nitrogen compounds in the environment (water and soil); (iii) and the current understanding of the impact of the action taken pursuant to Article 5 of the Directive.

Article 3 then goes on to provide that member states are required to designate as 'vulnerable zones' all known areas of land within their territories which drain into the waters identified as outlined above, and which contribute to pollution. Member states must complete the designation of their vulnerable zones by December 1993. The Commission must then be notified of the initial designation within six months. Member states are also required to review and, if necessary, make appropriate revisions or additions to the designation of vulnerable zones, every four years. Once again the Commission must be notified of any revision within six months. Article 6 of the Directive imposes specific monitoring and reporting obligations on member states for the purposes of designating and revising national vulnerable zones. The reference methods of measurements which must be used in this regard are set out in Annex IV of the Directive. It should be noted, however, that member states are exempt from the obligation to specify vulnerable zones if they establish and apply (throughout their territories) an action programme under Article 5 of the Directive.

Article 5 of the Directive provides that member states must establish action programmes in respect of the designated vulnerable zones for the purposes of realising the objectives of the Directive. National action programmes must be established by December 1995 and implemented by December 1999. A single action programme may relate to all of the vulnerable zones designated within a member state, or a separate programme may be established for each zone or parts of zones. Article 5.3 requires that the national programmes must take the following into account:

(i) available scientific and technical data; mainly with reference to respective nitrogen contributions originating from agricultural and other sources;
(ii) environmental conditions in the relevant regions of the member state concerned.

In addition, national action programmes must contain the mandatory measures laid down in Annex III to the Directive and those measures prescribed by member states in the codes of good agricultural practice which they are obliged to adopt by December 1993 (such codes of practice are to be implemented by farmers on a voluntary basis and should contain provisions covering at least the items listed in Annex II A to the Directive). If it becomes clear that the measures which must be contained in the national action programme are insufficient to realise the objectives of the Directive, the member state in question is obliged to take (within the framework of their national action programme) such additional measures or reinforced actions as they consider necessary. In selecting these additional measures, the state must take their effectiveness and their cost relative to other possible preventative measures into account. Member states are obliged to draw up and implement suitable monitoring programmes to assess the effectiveness of their national action programmes. Member States must also review and, if necessary, revise their action programmes at least every four years; the Commission must be informed of any changes made to the national programme(s). In addition, member states are under an obligation to submit a report to the Commission in every four year period (starting in June 1996) which contains the information specified in Annex V, namely:

(i) A statement of the preventative action taken under Article 4 of the Directive, i.e. the codes of good agricultural practice and a statement concerning their implementation.
(ii) A map which shows the waters identified by the state under Article 3 of the Directive as actually or potentially affected by pollution from nitrates from agricultural sources. In addition, the map must show the location of the designated vulnerable zones.
(iii) A summary of the monitoring results obtained pursuant to Article 6, including a statement of the considerations which led to the designation of each vulnerable zone and to any revision of or additions to designations of vulnerable zones.
(iv) A summary of the national action programmes established under Article 5 of the Directive and their implementation (in this regard the Annex lists specific information which must be included in the summary).

The Commission is then obliged to publish summary reports within six months of receiving these national reports (the first is scheduled for publication in December 1996); and in January 1998 the Commission will submit a report to the European Council concerning the implementation of the Nitrates Directive throughout the Community and, if necessary, will submit proposals for the revision of the Directive.

Finally, it should be noted that legislation has not yet been introduced to implement Directive 91/676/EEC in Northern Ireland. The DoE(NI) intends to implement the Directive by means of the proposed Nitrate Directive Regulations which are scheduled to be made in the near future.

## PART IX  DISCHARGES TO AND FROM SEWERS AND SEWAGE TREATMENT WORKS

The DoE(NI)'s Water Executive[198] is responsible under the Water and Sewerage Services (NI) Order 1973 (WSSO), as amended, [199] for the supply and distribution of water and the provision and maintenance of sewers and sewerage services for draining and dealing with domestic sewage and trade effluents in Northern Ireland.[200] As was explained at the beginning of this chapter, discharges from sewerage systems and sewage treatment works are one of the three most potent sources of water pollution in Northern Ireland. Although discharges into sewers and sewerage systems are discharges into an artificial environment, it is important to regulate such discharges in order to protect the surrounding environment from pollution from both the residues of sewage treatment works and direct discharges from the sewerage system by means, for example, of storm drains. In addition, there is the problem that most sewage works in Northern Ireland finally dispose of treated sewage sludge by discharging it into watercourses. Discharges of inadequately treated sewage sludge are a significant cause of water pollution in Northern Ireland and it has become increasingly important to regulate discharges to and from sewerage systems and sewage treatment works.

Part V of the WSSO, as amended, enables the DoE(NI)'s Water Executive to control discharges of trade effluent into its sewers and sewage treatment works by means of a statutory discharge consent system.[201] It is important to note that this system is entirely distinct from the discharge consent system established by the Water Act (NI) 1972 (discussed in Part II of this chapter). Discharge consents under the WSSO are set on an individual basis by the Water Executive but are monitored and reviewed by the Department's Environment Service. Part VII of the WSSO governs discharges of domestic waste to the sewerage system and sewage treatment works purely by making it an offence to pass, or permit to be passed, any substance which either alone or in combination with other matter or

---

198. The Northern Ireland Water Council acts as the DoE(NI)'s statutory advisory body on matters concerning the supply of water and sewerage services under the WSSO (art. 6 of the WSSO).
199. SI 1973/70. The WSSO is amended by the Water and Sewerage Services (Amendment) (NI) Order 1985 (SI 1985/756), the Water and Sewerage Services (Amendment) (NI) Order 1993 (SI 1993/3165), and the Urban Waste Water Treatment Regulations (NI) 1995 (SR No. 12).
200. A sewer is defined by article 2 of the WSSO as including 'all sewers, pipes or drains vested in the [Department] which are used for the drainage of buildings and yards appertaining to premises and includes any apparatus used in connection with such a sewer'. The sewerage system is used to carry sewage which is defined in article 2 of the WSSO as including 'domestic sewage, surface water and trade effluent'. Sewage treatment works are also defined in article 2 of the WSSO as meaning 'any works, apparatus, or plant used for the treatment or disposal of sewage and includes a septic tank'.
201. It should be noted, however, that the DoE(NI)'s Water Executive may extend the application of Part V to 'liquid or other matter of any description . . . which is discharged from any premises into the sewers or sewage treatment works of the [Department] . . .'

substances is likely to injure or interfere with the operation of the sewerage system or treatment works or is likely to be prejudicial to human health. Discharges of sewage sludge from sewers or sewage treatment works belonging to the Water Executive as a Crown developer are not subject to the discharge consent system laid down in the Water Act (NI) 1972; instead the DoE(NI)'s Environment Service sets standards for discharges from the Water Executive's sewage treatment works, but these are not placed on public registers. As already stated at the beginning of this chapter, one of the major criticisms levelled against the DoE(NI) is that it is both poacher and gamekeeper in operating sewage works and controlling water pollution in Northern Ireland. Although attempts have been made within the DoE(NI) to separate the Department's environmental protection role from its day-to-day responsibility for waste and sewage (e.g. the appointment of a Director of Environmental Services, who is a member of the Department's management board and more recently the establishment of 'Next Steps' agencies within the DoE(NI)), the poacher-gamekeeper criticism still holds true.

The recent enactment of the Urban Waste Water Treatment Regulations (NI) 1995 (UWWT) represents an important innovation in controlling and preventing water pollution from sewerage systems and sewage treatment works. The UWWT Regulations were introduced to implement Directive 91/271/EEC which essentially requires member states to considerably strengthen standards governing the collection and treatment of urban waste water (domestic and industrial waste and rain run-off) and also standards governing the disposal of treated urban waste water. In addition, the DoE(NI) is obliged to publish a 'situation report' every two years concerning the implementation of this Directive in Northern Ireland and also to report to the Commission in this regard. This obligation may introduce an element of public accountability into the DoE(NI)'s activities in the context of sewage disposal. The *Environment Service Corporate Plan, 1994–97* states that the DoE(NI)'s Environment Service is currently reviewing standards for the discharge of effluent from the Water Executive's water and sewage treatment works for the purposes of ensuring implementation of Directive 91/271/EEC. In addition, the report states that the Environment Service has made arrangements for monitoring discharges from Northern Ireland's major sewage treatment works, and monitoring will be extended to all other sewage treatment works in Northern Ireland. It is important to note that the Environment Service will not only expect the Water Executive to comply with the requirements laid down in the Directive by the end of 1996, it will also establish a public register of these standards by the same date.[202]

Finally, it should be noted that in order to ensure compliance with EC standards in relation to the emission of dangerous substances into the aquatic environment (discussed in Part III of this chapter) the UK introduced an additional form of control over the discharge of specific dangerous substances into sewers. In effect, HMIP is empowered to regulate discharges of substances or processes prescribed in Schedules 1 and 2 to the Trade Effluents (Prescribed Processes and Substances) Regulations 1989.[203] The prescribed substances are known as 'Red List'

202. P. 32.
203. SI 1989/1156, as amended by SI 1990/1629. For further reading on the Red List substances see Ball and Bell, *Environmental Law,* 3rd ed., London: Blackstone Press, 1995, at 465 and 297.

substances. At the time of writing, twenty-four prescribed substances have been listed in Schedule 1, and five processes have been listed in Schedule 2; the Red List also contains a number of substances that are not yet governed by EC Directives. Although the DoE(NI) has not made formal provision for the regulation of Red List substances in Northern Ireland, the Department stated in its submission to the House of Commons Environment Committee that it monitors Northern Ireland waters for Red List substances and has also drawn up an action plan to reduce the release of these substances.[204] The remainder of this Part will be divided into three sections. Section 1 will address the system of control established by the WSSO in relation to discharges of trade effluents into the DoE(NI)'s sewers and sewage treatment system. Section 2 will address the system of control introduced by Directive 91/271/EEC in relation to the treatment and discharge of urban waste water. Section 3 will identify other miscellaneous controls imposed on sewage sludge.

SECTION 1. CONSENTS FOR DISCHARGES OF TRADE EFFLUENT INTO SEWERS AND THE SEWAGE SYSTEM

Article 20(1) of the WSSO provides that the occupier [205] of any trade premises[206] may discharge any trade effluent[207] into the DoE(NI)'s sewers[208] or sewage treatment works.[209] This right is subject to article 20(2), which provides that it is an offence for the occupier of a trade premises to make such a discharge without the DoE(NI)'s consent where its consent was required under the WSSO. Similarly, it is an offence to make such a discharge in violation of any direction given or condition imposed by the DoE(NI) in relation to that discharge. A person found guilty of an offence under article 20 will be liable on conviction on indictment to an unlimited fine and on summary conviction to a maximum fine of £2,000. Where the court making the conviction is satisfied that the offence 'was substantially a

---

204. *House of Commons Environment Committee First Report: Environmental Issues in Northern Ireland*, HC 39 (1990) p. 49.

205. The term 'occupier' for the purposes of the WSSO is defined as 'the person in occupation or having the charge, management or control of premises either on his own account or as the agent of another person.'

206. The term 'trade premises' is defined by art. 2(2) of the WSSO as 'any premises used or intended to be used for carrying on any trade or industry.'

207. The term 'trade effluent' is defined by art. 2(2) of the WSSO as 'any liquid either with or without particles of matter in suspension therein which is wholly or in part produced in the course of any trade or industry carried out at trade premises, including trade waste waters or waters heated in the course of any trade or industry, and in relation to any trade premises means any such liquid which is produced in the course of any trade or industry carried on at those premises.'

208. The term 'sewer' is defined by art. 2(2) of the WSSO as including 'all sewers, pipes or drains vested in the [DoE(NI)] which are used for the drainage of buildings and yards appertaining to premises and includes any apparatus used in connection with such a sewer.' It should be noted, however, that the term 'drain' in this context does not include a drain or pipe that is used 'solely for or in connection with the drainage of one building or of any buildings or yards appurtenant to buildings with the same curtilage.'

209. The term 'sewage treatment works' is defined in art. 2(2) as 'any works, apparatus, or plant used for the treatment or disposal of sewage and includes a septic tank.'

repetition or continuation of an earlier offence by him after he had been convicted of the earlier offence' (whether under the WSSO or otherwise), he will be liable on conviction on indictment to imprisonment for a term not exceeding two years or to an unlimited fine, or to both, or on summary conviction, to the greater of either a fine not exceeding £2,000 or a fine not exceeding £40 for each day on which the offence is repeated or continued.

Part V of the WSSO distinguishes between 'new discharges' and 'existing discharges' for the purposes of the discharge consent system. The occupier or prospective occupier of a trade premises who wishes to make a 'new discharge' of trade effluent from those premises into the DoE(NI)'s sewers or sewage treatment works must obtain the DoE(NI)'s consent; that consent is then governed by article 23 of the WSSO, which sets out the application procedure for obtaining the discharge consent and the DoE(NI)'s powers in relation to such applications. Article 21 defines a 'new discharge' as meaning a discharge from trade premises where the discharge:

(i) has not previously been lawfully made into the DoE(NI)'s sewers or sewage treatment works or into the sewers or works of a local authority;

(ii) is not an 'existing discharge' within the meaning of article 28 and, whether begun before or after the WSSO came into effect (1 October 1973), has become 'substantially altered in nature or composition' or the 'temperature, volume or rate' of the discharge has been 'substantially increased' since the WSSO came into effect; or

(iii) has been discontinued for two years or more and is then resumed. However, the two-year period must either be wholly or partly after the date on which the WSSO came into effect (1 October 1973).

An 'existing discharge' is defined by article 28 as a discharge of trade effluent from trade premises into the sewers or sewage treatment works of a local authority that was lawfully made within the two-year period immediately before the commencement of the WSSO (i.e. ending on 1 October 1973). Article 28 goes on to provide that, where a local authority and the discharger have entered into an agreement before 1 October 1973 to the effect that the nature or composition of the discharge may be altered or that the temperature, volume or rate of discharge may be increased after 1 October 1973, then any discharge made in accordance with such an agreement will be treated as an 'existing discharge' for the purposes of Part V of the WSSO.

Finally, article 28 provides that any dispute between the DoE(NI)'s Water Executive and the discharger as to whether the discharge is an existing discharge within the meaning of article 28 will be determined by the county court; that court's decision will be final, except in relation to points of law. Whereas 'new discharges' can only be lawfully made with the DoE(NI)'s consent, an 'existing discharge' does not require the Department's consent and, except where otherwise agreed between the Department and the discharger, must be allowed to continue (article 29). Although article 29 does not empower the DoE(NI) to force the discharger of an existing discharge into an agreement, it is important to note that existing discharges, are not entirely beyond the control of the WSSO. Articles 30 and 31 empower the DoE(NI) to seek information concerning the nature and duration of existing discharges and also to review the making of existing discharges. In addition, the Department may impose such conditions on the discharge as it thinks fit.

Finally, before examining the controls exerted on new and existing discharges in more detail, it is important to note that Part V of the WSSO also empowers the DoE(NI) to enter into an agreement with the owner or occupier of any trade premises for the reception, treatment or disposal of any trade effluent produced on those premises. Once such an agreement is entered into, the discharger will not be required to obtain a discharge consent, nor will the discharge be reviewed by the DoE(NI).

### Applications for DoE(NI) consent to make a 'new discharge'

The procedure for obtaining a discharge consent under the WSSO is initiated by the serving of a 'trade effluent notice' on the DoE(NI)'s Water Executive. Article 23(2) of the WSSO provides that the trade effluent notice must state 'so far as is reasonably practicable':

   (a)  the nature, composition and temperature of the effluent;
   (b)  the maximum quantity of the effluent which it is proposed to discharge on any one day;
   (c)  the maximum hourly rate at which it is proposed to discharge the effluent.

In the event that the person applying for the discharge consent is not the owner[210] of the premises, the applicant must send a copy of the trade effluent notice to the owner at the same time as the notice is served on the DoE(NI), and in addition, the applicant must inform the owner that he may submit representations concerning the application to the Department within twenty-eight days of receiving his copy of the notice (article 23(3)). The DoE(NI) is obliged to take any representations made by the owner into account before making its decision on the application (article 23(4)). It should be noted, however, that unlike the discharge consent system contained in the Water Act (NI) 1972 which governs discharges of trade or sewage effluent or other noxious or polluting matter into inland, coastal or ground waters (explained in Part II of this chapter), the discharge consent system contained in the WSSO makes no provision for public consultation.

When an application for a discharge consent under the WSSO is submitted, the DoE(NI) is obliged under article 24 to make a decision on the application within three months of the date on which it was received. The Department may decide either to refuse its consent, grant its unconditional consent, or grant consent subject to such conditions as it thinks fit (including conditions as to charges). Where consent is granted, the Department may specify that the consent (and any conditions which are imposed) takes effect from a certain date or continues in force for a specified period (article 24(2)), or both. In addition, any decision made by the Department in relation to an application for a discharge consent will

---

210. Art. 2(2) of the WSSO defines 'owner' as 'a person who is for the time being receiving a rent of not less than two-thirds of the net annual value of any land whether on his own account or as agent or trustee for any other person or who, if the land were let at such a rent, would receive it.'

continue to have effect even where there has been a change of ownership or occupancy of the premises in question (article 24(3)). The DoE(NI) is obliged to inform[211] the owner and occupier, or prospective occupier, of the premises to which the application relates: (i) of its decision on the application for consent, (ii) the reasons for its decision, (iii) the effect of its decision under article 24, (iv) of their right to appeal the Department's decision to the Appeals Commission under article 26 and (v) of the Department's power to review a decision taken by it under article 27.

Article 26 of the WSSO, as amended by article 5(2) of the Water and Sewerage Services (Amendment) (NI) Order 1993, provides that where the applicant for a discharge consent under article 22 is aggrieved by the DoE(NI)'s decision, the applicant may appeal the decision to the Water Appeals Commission for Northern Ireland (except in so far as the decision relates to the imposition of charges); the appeal must be brought within twenty-eight days of receiving notice of the DoE(NI)'s decision.[212]

Article 27(1) of the WSSO, as amended by article 5(3) of the Water and Sewerage Services (Amendment) (NI) Order 1993, empowers the DoE(NI) to review a decision made by it in relation to an application for a discharge consent at intervals of not less than two years (the two years running from the giving of the decision in relation to the application or the date of the last review). The Department is, however, empowered to review its decision at any time if a review is requested by the person making the application for consent. When the Department decides to review a decision under article 27, it is obliged under article 27(2) to inform[213] the owner and occupier of the premises in question: (i) that it intends to do so, (ii) of the reasons for undertaking the review, and (iii) that they may make representations to the Department concerning the proposed review within twenty-eight days of being informed of the proposed review. Where any representations are made, the DoE(NI) is obliged under article 27(3) to take them into account before reviewing its decision. A review under article 27 will take effect from a date specified in the review; however, the review may not start to take effect within the three months following the date of the review (article 27(5)). Article 27(4) provides that the occupier of the premises to which the application relates may appeal the DoE(NI)'s decision on review (except in so far as the decision relates to the imposition of charges) to the Water Appeals Commission for Northern Ireland within twenty-eight days of the date of the review.[214]

Article 8 of the Water and Sewerage Services (Amendment) (NI) Order 1993 then inserts a new article 26A into the WSSO which provides that the DoE(NI) may require the owner or occupier of premises from which a new discharge is

---

211. It should be noted that art. 25 of the WSSO does not use the word 'inform'; instead it states that the DoE(NI) is obliged to 'intimate' its decision to the applicant. The Order is silent on the form in which the decision is to be intimated (i.e. whether oral or written); however, it is specific as to the matters that must be conveyed to the owner, occupier or prospective occupier of the trade premises in question.

212. The powers of the Appeals Commission are set out in art. 7 of the WSSO, as amended by art. 6 of the Water and Sewerage Services (Amendment) (NI) Order 1993.

213. As is the case under article 25, article 27 uses the word 'intimate' rather than 'inform'. See note 211, supra, concerning the use of the term 'intimate'.

214. See note 212, supra.

being made to provide the Department with such information (in writing) concerning the discharge as would be required in a trade effluent notice under article 23, outlined above. Failure to provide such information once requested, or to 'knowingly' make 'any misstatement' in the provision of such information, is an offence punishable on summary conviction by a fine not exceeding level 1 on the standard scale (£200).

The WSSO does not identify the criteria used to set discharges of trade effluent. In practice, discharge consents under the WSSO are set on an individual basis. The DoE(NI) considers each application for a discharge consent on its own merit, having regard to the polluting nature and/or the ability of the sewage treatment works both to receive and treat the proposed trade effluent discharge, the objective being that an attainable and environmentally acceptable set of conditions are attached to the discharger's consent to discharge. Although it is not actually relied on by the DoE(NI) in setting discharge consents under WSSO, the Water Authorities Association produced a booklet in 1986, *Trade Effluent Discharged to the Sewer*, which sets out the objectives of trade effluent control; these objectives are also reflected in the Urban Waste Water Treatment Regulations (NI) 1995, discussed below. It states that the objectives of trade effluent control are:

(i) to protect the sewerage system and the personnel who work in it;
(ii) to protect the sewage works and their efficient operation;
(iii) to protect the environment generally from the residues of the sewage treatment process or from direct discharges from parts of the system, such as storm drains; and
(iv) to ensure that dischargers pay a reasonable charge for the cost of the treatment.

**Control of 'existing discharges'**

As already stated, existing discharges within the meaning of article 28 (outlined above) do not need a discharge consent under article 22. However, existing discharges are not beyond the DoE(NI)'s control. Articles 30 and 31 of the WSSO confer various powers on the Department in relation to existing discharges. Article 30, as amended by article 8 of the Water and Sewerage Services (Amendment) (NI) Order 1993, provides that the DoE(NI) may require the owner or occupier of trade premises from which an existing discharge is being made to furnish in writing such information as an applicant for a discharge consent would be required to furnish in a trade effluent notice under article 23 (outlined above). In addition, such persons may be required to furnish written information concerning the duration of the discharge in question. Failure to provide such information is an offence; similarly, it is an offence to 'knowingly make any misstatement' in the provision of such information. A person found guilty, on summary conviction, of such an offence will be liable to a maximum fine of £200 (level 1 on the standard scale).

Article 31 of the WSSO confers powers of review on the DoE(NI) in relation to the making of existing discharges. In effect, article 31(1) provides that the DoE(NI) has a discretion to review the making of an existing discharge and may direct that any continuation of such a discharge be subject to such conditions (including conditions as to charge) as it thinks fit. Where the person making the existing discharge requests a review, the DoE(NI) is obliged to conduct one. If the Department makes a direction as a result of a review carried out under article 31, it may review that direction under article 31(2) at intervals of not less than two years (with time running from the date of the direction or from the date of the last review of the direction). The Department may, however, review a direction at any time if a review is requested by the discharger. Article 31(3) provides that before the DoE(NI) makes a direction under article 31(1), or before it undertakes a review of a direction issued under article 31(2), the Department must inform[215] the discharger in question: (i) that it proposes to do so, (ii) of the reasons for the direction or the review, and (iii) that they may make representations to the Department concerning their proposed action within twenty-eight days of being notified, and any representations made in this regard must be taken into account by the Department before either making the proposed direction or undertaking the proposed review.

Where the Department makes a direction under article 31(1) concerning an existing discharge or where it undertakes a review of a direction under article 31(2), article 31(5), as amended by article 5(4) of the Water and Sewerage Services (Amendment) (NI) Order 1993, provides that the discharger may appeal against the direction or the review to the Water Appeals Commission for Northern Ireland (except in so far as the direction or review relates to the imposition of discharge charges) within twenty-eight days of the date of the direction or the review.[216] A direction made under article 31(1) or a review under article 31(2) will take effect from a date specified therein. However, neither may take effect within three months of the date of the direction or the review.

## Agreements for the discharge of trade effluent

Part V of the WSSO makes provision for an alternative method of regulating discharges of trade effluent. Article 32 empowers the DoE(NI) and the owner or occupier or prospective occupier of any trade premises to enter into an agreement for the reception, treatment and disposal of any trade effluent produced on those premises. An agreement under article 32 includes an agreement to renew or vary an existing agreement, regardless of whether that agreement was entered into before or after the coming into force of the WSSO (1 October 1973). It should be noted, however, that the DoE(NI) may not force either the owner or occupier or prospective occupier of trade premises to enter into such an agreement.

Where the DoE(NI) proposes to enter into an article 32 agreement with an occupier (or prospective occupier) of trade premises who is not also the owner of those premises, the Department is obliged to inform the owner of the proposal; the owner may in turn submit representations to the Department concerning the proposed agreement within twenty-eight days of receipt of notification. In the event that representations are made, the Department is obliged under article 32(4) to take those representations into account before entering into the proposed agreement with the occupier or prospective occupier.

---

215. It should be noted that article 31 does not use the word 'inform', instead it states that the Department is obliged to 'intimate' its decision to the applicant. See note 211, supra, concerning the use of the term 'intimate' as used in art. 25.
216. See note 212, supra.

Once an agreement is entered into under article 32, a discharge of trade effluent made in accordance with the agreement will not require a discharge consent (as is otherwise the case for new discharges), nor will it be susceptible to review under article 31 (as is otherwise the case for existing discharges). As a result, articles 22–7 and 31 will not apply to such discharges. However, the DoE(NI) retains its power to seek information concerning the discharge, as is the case in relation to normal controls imposed on discharges of trade effluent. Where the agreement has not been renewed by the parties to the agreement on or before the date on which it expires, the Department has a discretion to direct that the making of the discharge be reviewed; where the owner, occupier or prospective occupier requests such a review, then the Department is obliged to hold one. Article 27(2)–(5) will apply to such a review (these provisions are outlined above in the context of the Department's powers to review a discharge consent for new discharges). Until such time as the agreement is reviewed by direction, the discharge may continue to be made in accordance with the agreement.

### Other relevant controls imposed by the WSSO

Parts VI and VII of the WSSO confer various powers on the DoE(NI)'s Water Executive to facilitate the exercise of its functions under the Order and also to create a number of criminal offences which are relevant to the issue of environmental protection. They are as follows:

1. It is an offence under article 34 of the WSSO to commit an act whereby water which either belongs to the Water Executive, or which it is authorised to take, is polluted. It is a defence to establish that all reasonable care was exercised to prevent the act which caused the pollution. Summary conviction for an offence under article 34 is punishable by a maximum fine of £2,000 and a further fine of £40 for every day during which the offence is continued after conviction; conviction on indictment is punishable by an unlimited fine.

2. Article 39 (Part VII) contains the only form of restriction imposed under the WSSO on discharges of domestic waste into Water Executive sewers or treatment works. Without prejudice to the terms of Part V of the WSSO (discussed above), article 39 provides that it is an offence 'to pass or permit to be passed into' the Department's sewers or sewage treatment works, or into a drain which connects with the Department's sewers or sewage treatment works, 'any matter or substance which, either alone or in combination with any matter or substance with which it is likely to come into contact while passing through any sewer or works, is likely to injure the sewer or works, or to interfere with the free flow of their contents, or to affect prejudicially the treatment or disposal of their contents or to be prejudicial to health.' It is a defence to prove that 'at the time he so passed or permitted to be passed the substance or matter in question, he did not know and could not reasonably be expected to know, that it would be likely to have the effects mentioned.' Conviction either summarily or on indictment is punishable as under article 34 (discussed at number 1 above).

3. Article 50 confers extensive powers of entry (at all reasonable hours) on authorised officers of the Water Executive for the purpose of carrying out and enforcing the terms of the WSSO; it is an offence to wilfully obstruct the

exercise of this power. Of particular importance for present purposes is the power to enter for the purpose of 'taking away for analysis samples of sewage or any other matter or substance which is passing from the premises into the sewers or sewage treatment works of the [DoE(NI)].' Article 51 governs the admissibility of the results of any samples taken under article 50 in any legal proceedings in respect of any discharge from any premises. The terms of article 51 are identical to those of article 25 of the Water Act (NI) 1972 (taking of samples) outlined in Part IV of this chapter, substituting references to the occupier of the premises or land for references to the owner, occupier or master of any land, vehicle, or vessel. Articles 46–9 of the WSSO confer various powers on the Water Executive to obtain information concerning the ownership of premises, maps of sewers and mains, and to conduct research and publicity, while article 52 governs the release of trade secrets or information concerning the manufacturing process by Water Executive officers.

SECTION 2. TREATMENT AND DISCHARGE OF URBAN WASTE WATER

Directive 91/271/EEC[217] is one of the most important water pollution Directives adopted thus far by the EC. This Directive addresses the pollution caused to inland and coastal waters by 'urban waste water' (i.e. domestic sewage, industrial waste water and run-off rain water). The Directive was adopted essentially in response to concern over the pollution of inland and coastal waters throughout the EC caused by discharges of inadequately treated sewage. In this regard the eutrophication (stimulated growth of algal and macrophyte blooms) of such waters caused by nitrate and phosphorus (contained in sewage) enrichment and the detriment to public health were of particular concern.[218]

The Directive requires member states to provide systems for the collection of urban waste waters ('collection systems') which are designed, constructed, operated and maintained to specific standards. In addition, it introduces minimum standards for the treatment of urban waste water entering these collecting systems and lays down timetables within which these treatment objectives must be achieved. The treatment standards and timetables vary according to the 'population equivalent' of the urban area ('agglomeration') in question; standards become more stringent as the size of the urban area increases. However, the essential objective is to ensure that secondary treatment for domestic waste water is the norm. The deadline for the achievement of this objective depends on the size of the urban area. However, all towns with a population equivalent of more than 15,000 must have a secondary treatment system operating by the end of the year 2000. More stringent treatment standards are imposed for sensitive areas (the criteria for which are set out in Annex II to the Directive). The Directive also introduces controls over the disposal of sewage sludge arising from waste water treatment; in particular, it requires the dumping of sludge at sea to be phased out

217. OJ L135, 30 May 1991; formal compliance is required by 30 June 1993.
218. It should be noted that eutrophication caused by the use of sewage sludge and artificial fertilisers on agricultural land is regulated under separate Directives, both of which are addressed in Part VIII of this chapter (Directives 86/278/EEC and 91/676/EEC). The water pollution caused by eutrophication is also explained in more detail in this context.

by the end of 1998, thereby implementing the agreement reached to that effect at the Conference for the Protection of the North Sea in 1990. Finally, the Directive requires that discharges of industrial waste water into sewerage systems and treatment plants be subject to prior regulation or specific authorisation by the end of 1993 and subjected to specified pre-treatments.

The UK is currently responsible for almost all the sewage sludge dumped at sea in the EC, and almost 90 per cent of it receives no secondary treatment at all.[219] At present, approximately 50 per cent of Northern Ireland's sewage sludge is disposed of at sea. Directive 91/271/EEC will therefore have a considerable impact on the disposal of sewage throughout the UK. Not only will the UK have to develop alternative methods for disposing of a dramatically increased volume of sewage once the ban on the dumping of sewage sludge at sea comes into effect in 1998 but the implementation of the Directive will also be extremely expensive. The UK's sustainable development strategy document, published in 1994,[220] estimated that it would cost as much as £10,000 million to implement the requirements of the Directive.

## Implementation in Northern Ireland

Although member states were required to complete formal implementation of Directive 91/271/EEC by 30 June 1993, the requirements of the Directive were not implemented in Northern Ireland until 1995 with the enactment of the Urban Waste Water Treatment Regulations (NI) 1995.[221] The Regulations came into effect on 1 March 1995.

Regulations 3–5 implement the requirements of the Directive concerning the establishment of collecting systems and the phased introduction of secondary treatment of urban waste water. The DoE(NI)'s Water Executive has drawn up plans for the implementation of the Directive. The deadlines for formal compliance with the treatment standards vary depending on the population equivalent of the area in question and the nature of the receiving waters; the earliest deadline is 31 December 1998, while the latest is 31 December 2005.

### *Identification of sensitive areas, less sensitive areas and estuaries*

Regulation 3 imposes an obligation on the DoE(NI) to review the identification of sensitive areas and less sensitive areas (referred to in the Regulations as areas of 'high natural dispersion') in accordance with the criteria set out in Schedule 1 by 31 December 1997 and thereafter at four-yearly intervals. Regulation 12 then obliges the DoE(NI) to keep maps of estuaries ('transitional area at the mouth of a river between fresh water and coastal waters, the outward (seaward) limits of which are shown on maps kept in accordance with regulation 12') and maps which show those areas identified as sensitive areas and high natural dispersion areas. These maps must be kept at Calvert House, 23 Castle Place, Belfast BT1 1FY, and must be made available for public inspection at all reasonable times and free of charge.

---

219. Haigh, supra, chap. 4.6, pp 4–7.
220. *Sustainable Development: The UK Strategy*, London: HMSO, p. 62.
221. SR No. 12.

## Establishment of collecting systems

Regulation 4 implements the obligation to establish systems for the collection of urban waste water;[222] this obligation is stated to supplement the DoE(NI)'s existing obligations under article 3(1)(*b*) and (*c*) of the Water and Sewerage Services (NI) Order 1973 to provide sewerage services (i.e. the obligation to: '(*b*) provide and maintain sewers for draining domestic sewage, surface water and trade effluent; and (*c*) to make provision for effectually dealing with the contents of its sewage'). In effect, regulation 4(2) and (3) of the 1995 Regulations provides that the DoE(NI) is obliged to provide collecting systems which satisfy the requirements laid down in Schedule 2, namely, that collecting systems must take waste water treatment standards into account and that their design, construction and maintenance be undertaken in accordance with the 'best technical knowledge not entailing excessive cost'. In this regard particular attention must be paid to the volume and characteristics of urban waste water, the prevention of leaks, and limiting the pollution of receiving waters caused by storm water overflows. Regulation 4(2) then sets out the timetable for the establishment of the requisite collecting systems, as follows:

1. Where the urban waste water discharges into receiving waters which are a sensitive area, the collecting system must be in place by 31 December 1998 for every urban area ('agglomeration') with a 'population equivalent'[223] of more than 10,000.

2. Without prejudice to the requirement at number 1 above, the DoE(NI) is obliged to provide the specified collecting system by 31 December 2000 for every urban area (agglomeration) with a population equivalent of more than 15,000 and by 31 December 2005 for every urban area with a population equivalent of between 2,000 and 15,000.

Regulation 4(3) creates an exception to the obligation to provide the specified collecting systems by the specified dates. The DoE(NI) will not be obliged to provide the collecting system where it is satisfied that the establishment of a collecting system is not justified because it would either 'produce no environmental benefit' or 'would involve excessive cost' and 'individual systems or other appropriate systems are provided that achieve the same level of environmental protection.'

Regulation 4(4) provides that the DoE(NI)'s obligation under article 3(1)(*c*) of the Water and Sewerage Services (NI) Order 1973 to 'make provision for effectually dealing with the contents of its sewers includes a duty to ensure that: (a) urban waste water entering these collecting systems is, before discharge, subject to the treatment standards laid down in regulation 5 and to ensure that (b): (i) the treatment plants which are built in order to comply with treatment

---

222. Art. 2(1) of the Regulations defines 'urban waste water' as 'any domestic waste water or the mixture of domestic waste water with industrial waste water and/or run-off rain water.'

223. The term 'population equivalent' is defined by reg. 2 as 'a measurement of organic biodegradable load, and a population equivalent of 1 (1 p.e.) is the organic biodegradable load having a five-day biochemical oxygen demand ($BOD_5$) of 60 g of oxygen per day (the load shall be calculated on the basis of the maximum average weekly load entering the treatment plant during the year, excluding unusual situations such as those due to heavy rain).'

standards laid down in regulation 5 are 'designed (account being taken of seasonal variations of the load), constructed, operated and maintained to ensure sufficient performance under all normal local climatic conditions';

(ii) that treated waste water and sludge which arise from the waste water treatment are 'reused whenever appropriate'; and

(iii) that disposal routes for treated waste water and sludge 'minimise the adverse effects on the environment.'

### Treatment works

Regulation 5(1)–(7) sets out the various treatment standards for urban waste water in Northern Ireland. Regulation 5(1) contains the normal treatment standard, i.e. the requirement that urban waste water should normally receive 'secondary treatment'[224] or an equivalent and, in addition, sets out the timetable for the introduction of secondary treatment standards according to the population equivalent of the area in question. Regulation 5(2)–(4) governs the situations in which more stringent treatment standards than those laid down in paragraph (1) must be applied, while regulation 5(5) governs the situations in which less stringent standards than those required in paragraph (1) may be applied. Regulation 5(6) then governs the treatment standards for smaller urban areas.

Regulation 5(1) provides that treatment plants which provide secondary treatment or an equivalent must be provided by the following deadlines:

1. All discharges of urban waste water from areas with a population equivalent of more than 15,000 must receive secondary treatment or the equivalent by 31 December 2000 or, in an exceptional case, by a later date (but not later than 31 December 2005), subject to the Commission's agreement pursuant to a request under Article 8.1 of the Urban Waste Water Treatment Directive.

2. All discharges of urban waste water from areas with a population equivalent of between 10,000 and 15,000 must receive secondary treatment or the equivalent by 31 December 2005.

3. All discharges to fresh waters and estuaries[225] from areas with a population equivalent of between 2,000 and 10,000 must receive secondary treatment or the equivalent by 31 December 2005.

Regulation 5(2)–(4) sets out the conditions in which more stringent treatment standards than those outlined in regulation 5(1) above must be applied. According to regulation 5(2) and (3) treatment plants which provide more stringent treatment than that described in regulation 5(1) must be provided by 31 December 1998 for all discharges from areas with a population equivalent of more than 10,000 into 'sensitive areas or into the catchment areas of sensitive areas where discharges contribute to the pollution of these areas'. The exact nature of the 'more stringent treatment' is not defined by the Regulations. It is important to note, however, that the obligation to provide more stringent treatment will not apply in relation to a

---

224. Reg. 2 defines 'secondary treatment' as 'the treatment of urban waste water by a process generally involving biological treatment with a secondary settlement or other process in which the requirements established in Table 1 in Schedule 3 are respected.'

225. Reg. 2 defines an estuary as 'the transitional area at the mouth of a river between fresh water and coastal waters, the outer (seaward) limits of which are shown on the maps kept in accordance with regulation 12.' The terms of regulation 12 are outlined p. 248.

sensitive area where the DoE(NI) 'is satisfied, as a result of monitoring, that the minimum percentage of reduction of the overall load entering all urban waste water treatment plants in that area, and all urban waste water treatment plants in the catchment of that area, the discharges from which contribute to the pollution of that area, is at least 75% for total phosphorus and at least 75% for total nitrogen.' Finally, it should be noted that where an area ceases to be identified as a high natural dispersion area (less sensitive area) or becomes identified as a sensitive area as a result of a review of waters under regulation 3 (outlined at page 248), the requirements contained in regulation 5(1) (normal areas) or 5(2) (sensitive areas) will have effect as if the relevant deadline specified in that paragraph were the 'seventh anniversary of the change of identification or, if later, the date so specified' (regulation 5(4).'

Regulation 5(5) provides that in certain circumstances less stringent treatment standards than those described in regulation 5(1) can be applied. These can be applied:

(i) to discharges of urban waste water from areas with a population equivalent of between 10,000 and 150,000 (or more than 150,000 in an exceptional case and with the Commission's agreement pursuant to a request under Article 8.5 of the Directive) to coastal waters that are in high natural dispersion areas, and

(ii) to discharges from areas with a population equivalent of between 2,000 and 10,000 into estuaries that are in high natural dispersion areas.

However, regulation 5(5) goes on to provide that less stringent treatment standards can only be used in the circumstances described at (i) and (ii) above if the discharges in question receive at least primary treatment[226] in accordance with the control procedures set out in Part II of Schedule 3 and the DoE(NI) is satisfied that 'comprehensive studies have indicated that such discharges will not adversely affect the environment.'

Finally, regulation 5(6) provides that urban waste water entering collecting systems must receive 'appropriate treatment'[227] by 31 December 2005 in respect of discharges to fresh waters and estuaries from areas with a population equivalent of less than 2,000 and discharges to coastal waters from areas with a population equivalent of less than 10,000.

## Case Law

Before moving on to consider the other forms of control introduced by the Urban Waste Water Treatment Regulations (NI) 1995, it is worth noting two recent judgments concerning the application of the equivalent Regulations in England.

---

226. Regulation 5(7)(b) defines the term primary treatment as 'treatment of urban waste water by a physical and/or chemical process involving settlement of suspended solids, or other processes in which the $BOD_5$ of the incoming waste water is reduced by at least 20% before discharge and the total suspended solids of the incoming waste water are reduced by at least 50%.'

227. Regulation 5(7)(a) defines the term appropriate treatment in this context as 'treatment of urban waste water by any process and/or disposal system which after discharge allows the receiving waters to meet the relevant quality objectives and the relevant provisions of the [UWWT] Directive and other Community Directives.'

The first judgment was delivered by the High Court in January 1996[228] in respect of two cases which were heard together, namely, *R. v. Secretary of State for the Environment, ex parte Kingston-upon-Hull City Council* and *R. v. Secretary of State for the Environment, ex parte Bristol City Council.* Both actions concerned applications for judicial review to quash decisions taken by the respondent city councils establishing the outer estuarine limits of the Humber and Severn Estuaries and designating high natural dispersion areas within those estuaries under the Urban Waste Water Treatment (England and Wales) Regulations 1994. In both cases the relevant discharges were from agglomerations with population equivalents greater than 15,000. If the receiving waters were identified as estuaries, then, under the terms of the UWWT Directive, the discharge of urban water to those waters would require secondary treatment, regardless of whether or not the receiving waters were in an area of high natural dispersion. Both city councils had established the outer estuarine limits in such a way that the receiving waters would be classified as coastal waters and, in addition, had identified the receiving waters as being in an area of high natural dispersion. In effect, the city councils sought to rely on the provisions in the Regulations which permitted discharges of urban waste water from areas with a population equivalent of between 10,000 and 150,000 to be subjected to primary treatment only, for example, where the receiving waters were coastal waters in an area of high natural dispersion. The equivalent provisions are contained in regulation 5(5) of the Northern Ireland Regulations.

The essential questions raised concerning the manner in which the outer limits of both estuaries had been established were: (i) whether the city councils had failed to comply with the Directive's definition of the terms 'estuary' and 'coastal waters' and (ii) whether the city councils had taken irrelevant considerations into account, namely, economic considerations concerning the cost of secondary treatment, and failed to take material considerations into account, namely, salinity and/or topographical characteristics of the receiving waters. The case turned on the approach taken to the definition of an estuary and, therefore, the court did not proceed to rule on the concept of an area of high natural dispersion.

Harrison J pointed first to the fact that Article 2.12 of the Urban Waste Water Treatment Directive did not specify any criteria which must be taken into account by member states when establishing an outer estuarine limit, and from this concluded that it was intended that member states have a discretion in deciding how to establish outer estuarine limits. The Court therefore rejected the applicants' argument that salinity or topography could be implied as the criteria that must be used in this assessment. While salinity and topography were deemed to be 'relevant considerations' to be taken into account when identifying 'the true limits of an estuary', the court ruled that there may be other relevant considerations depending on the circumstances and therefore that it would be incorrect to confine a member state to these criteria. The court concluded that:

> [t]he important point . . . is that there must be a genuine and rational assessment in each case of what actually constitutes the estuary having regard to all the relevant circumstances relating to the characteristics of

228. Unreported, Queen's Bench Division, 26 Jan. 1996; reported in the *Times,* 31 Jan. 1996, and the *Independent,* 8 Feb. 1996.

the area in question and having regard to the purpose of the Directive . . . the cost of the treatment of the waste water is not a relevant consideration in that exercise. An area of water either is or is not an estuary regardless of what it will cost to treat waste water discharged into it. The way in which the Directive has been framed is such that it is clear that discharges to estuaries from agglomerations of more than 10,000 p.e. must be the subject of secondary treatment regardless of whether or not those discharges are into LSAs or HNDAs [less sensitive areas or high natural dispersion areas]. It would be quite wrong to re-draw the boundary of what would otherwise have been genuinely assessed to be the estuary for the purpose of the Directive in order to escape that clear requirement of the Directive. If cost considerations were allowed to permit that to be done, the result would be the establishment of estuaries which were not really estuaries at all but areas of water defined in such a way as to avoid the obligations imposed by the Directive.[229]

Harrison J went on to say that the purpose of the Directive, namely, to prevent adverse environmental effects, could be taken into account to assist the decision-maker in considering what physical and other characteristics of the receiving waters should be taken into account when establishing the outer limits of an estuary. The court concluded that cost considerations had played a major role in the respondents' decisions when establishing the outer limits of the estuaries in these cases. In the court's opinion 'no explanation, consistent with a rational and genuine assessment of what constitutes an estuary' was given as to how the Humber and Severn road bridges came to be chosen as the outer limits in each case. The respondents' decisions were deemed to be pragmatic decisions based on the cost of providing secondary treatment and on their view that the environmental benefits of such treatment would be negligible; their decisions were therefore quashed.

It is clear from the *Hull City* and *Bristol City* cases that the courts will not permit economic considerations to be used to avoid the requirement to provide secondary treatment. However, in *R. v. National Rivers Authority, ex parte Moreton*,[230] Harrison J did not object to the National Rivers Authority's decision to identify receiving waters in the Tenby area as an area of high natural dispersion and to impose less stringent treatment standards, despite the fact that the NRA had not undertaken the 'comprehensive studies' required under the Urban Waste Water Treatment Regulations (England and Wales) 1994 to establish that such discharges would not adversely affect the environment. Harrison J ruled that he was reluctant to find that the absence of a mention of any comprehensive studies within the NRA's published position statement concerning sewage discharges into the Tenby area meant that the NRA had somehow misunderstood the Urban Waste Water Directive. The court pointed to the fact that the relevant requirement laid down in the Directive concerning the provision of secondary treatment does not come into force until the year 2000 and that it was persuaded that by this time the problems of the Tenby discharges might be resolved.

---

229. P. 19 of the Lexis transcript.
230. Unreported, Queen's Bench Division, 13 Sep. 1995.

### Discharges of treated urban waste water from treatment plants

Regulation 6(1) provides that all discharges of treated urban waste water from treatment plants described in regulation 5(1) and (2) or from any plant which provides treatment in accordance with regulation 5(5) must comply with the technical requirements and parameters (biochemical and chemical oxygen demand and total phosphorus and nitrogen concentrations) set out in Part I of Schedule 3 to the Regulations. The terms of regulation 6(1) do not apply to DoE(NI) treatment plants. The DoE(NI)'s Environment Service is then required under regulation 6(1) to ensure that discharges made from treatment plants (excluding those provided by the Department's Water Executive) comply with the following standards by means of its powers under the discharge consent system laid down in the Water Act (NI) 1972 (discussed in Part II of this chapter):

(i) the Department must ensure that discharges from treatment plants described in regulation 5(1), (2) or (5) satisfy the requirements laid down in regulation 6(1);

(ii) the Department must ensure that discharges described in regulation 5(5) and (6) satisfy the requirements laid down in regulation 5(5) or, as the case may be, regulation 5(6);

(iii) the Department must ensure that the pollution of receiving waters due to storm overflows is limited in respect of discharges from a collecting system described in regulation 4 or an urban waste water treatment plant described in regulation 5;

(iv) the Department must ensure that the discharge of sludge to surface waters is phased out by 31 December 1998 and that the 'total amount of toxic, persistent or bioaccumulable materials' in the sludge which may be discharged to surface waters under consents granted pursuant to Part II of the Water Act (NI) 1972 is controlled by such consents and is progressively reduced during the period ending on the 31 December 1998.

The DoE(NI) is required to review consents issued under the Water Act (NI) 1972 in relation to discharges from urban waste water treatment plants at regular intervals and, if necessary in order to ensure compliance with the UWWT Regulations, the DoE(NI) must modify or revoke any such discharge consent. In addition, nothing in section 10(1) of the Water Act (NI) 1972 (DoE(NI)'s power to review discharge consents issued under the Act) can restrict the Environment Service's power to modify or revoke a consent issued pursuant to the duty imposed by regulation 6 of the Urban Waste Water Treatment Regulations 1995. Although discharges from urban waste water treatment plants provided by the DoE(NI)'s Water Executive are not subject to control under the discharge consent system, regulation 6(3) provides that the DoE(NI) (Environment Service) must nevertheless ensure that all the discharge standards outlined at (i) to (iv) above are complied with by the Water Executive's treatment plants.

The taking of samples and the recording of information for the purposes of consents issued under regulation 6(2) (i.e. to plants not provided by the DoE(NI)'s Water Executive) are governed by regulation 10. Regulation 10 provides that where the operator of an urban waste water treatment plant, in respect of which a discharge consent has been issued under regulation 6(2), is required by a condition attached to the consent 'to provide any apparatus for the purpose of measuring or recording the volume, rate of flow, nature, composition or temperature of any waste water, or for the purpose of collecting samples of waste water, any such apparatus so provided shall be presumed to register accurately unless the contrary is shown.' In addition, any record that is produced by this apparatus or that is made by or on behalf of the operator in order to comply with the discharge condition, will be regarded as evidence of the matters appearing from the record and, in any proceedings brought under Part II of the Water Act (NI) 1972, any such record will be admissible in evidence against the operator (regulation 10(3)). Where a condition attached to a discharge consent in this context requires that an entry be made in any record concerning the observance of any condition of the consent, a failure to make the required entry will be admissible as evidence that the condition (or conditions) has not been observed. Where, in compliance with a discharge condition, a sample of waste water is collected by apparatus which is installed for the purpose of collecting such samples automatically, the sample will be treated as being taken (for the purposes of section 25(5) of the Water Act (NI) 1972[231]) only when it is removed from that apparatus. A sample of waste water which is taken and analysed by the operator of the plant in compliance with a condition attached to the consent will not be treated as being taken on behalf of the DoE(NI) for the purposes of section 25(5) of the Act.

## *Discharges of industrial waste water to collecting systems or treatment plants*

Regulation 7(1) imposes a duty on the DoE(NI)'s Water Executive to regulate discharges of industrial waste water[232] to collecting systems or treatment plants by means of the discharge consent system laid down in Part V of the Water and Sewerage Services (NI) Order 1973 (outlined at page 210 above) so as to ensure that such discharges comply with the requirements laid down in Schedule 4 to the Urban Waste Water Treatment Regulations (NI) 1995. Schedule 4 provides that:

industrial waste water entering collecting systems and urban waste water treatment plants shall be subject to such pre-treatment as is required in order to

— protect the health of staff working in collecting systems and treatment plants;

— ensure that collecting systems, waste water treatment plants and associated equipment are not damaged;

— ensure that the operation of the waste water treatment plant and the treatment of sludge are not impeded;

— ensure that discharges from the treatment plants do not adversely affect the environment, or prevent receiving water from complying with other Community Directives; and

— ensure that sludge can be disposed of safely in an environmentally acceptable manner.

---

231. The DoE(NI)'s powers to take samples under the Water Act (NI) 1972 are outlined in Part IV of this chapter.
232. The term 'industrial waste water' is defined widely in reg. 2(1) as 'any waste water which is discharged from premises used for carrying on any trade or industry, other than domestic waste water and run-off water.'

Regulation 7 provides that nothing in article 24(1) of the Water and Sewerage Services (NI) Order 1973 (concerning conditions of consent) will be construed as restricting the DoE(NI)'s power to impose any condition on any consent that is necessary to ensure compliance with the requirements laid down in Schedule 4. Similarly, regulation 7(3) provides that any agreement entered into between the Water Executive and the occupier of any trade premises will not be treated as a consent, direction or condition for the purposes of Part V of the 1973 Order, unless the agreement will ensure that any discharge covered by the agreement will comply with the terms of Schedule 4.

The DoE(NI) is obliged to review consents issued under Part V of the 1973 Order in relation to industrial waste water at 'regular intervals' and, if necessary, to modify those consents. In addition, the Department may vary any agreement under article 32 (page 245) of the 1973 Order which provides for the discharge of industrial waste water to an urban waste water treatment plant without first entering a public sewer. In addition, any such agreement will be unenforceable if, and to the extent to which, it permits any discharge of industrial waste water which does not comply with the requirements of Schedule 4 to the UWWT Regulations.

Finally, regulation 7(6) provides that nothing in Part V of the 1973 Order will operate to restrict the Department's powers to vary a consent, direction or condition which is designed to ensure that the Department's duty under regulation 7 is discharged. In addition, nothing in Part V of the 1973 Order will render the DoE(NI) liable to pay compensation as a consequence of any such variation made in pursuance of its duty under regulation 7.

## *Discharges of biodegradable industrial waste water to receiving waters*

From 31 December 2000 onwards the DoE(NI)'s Environment Service is obliged under regulation 8 of the UWWT Regulations to impose 'appropriate' conditions on all consents granted under the Water Act (NI) 1972 for direct discharges of biodegradable industrial waste water from plants that represent a population equivalent of 4,000 or more, which belong to the industrial sectors listed in Schedule 5[233] and which do not enter urban waste water treatment plants before being discharged into receiving waters. (The discharge consent system laid down under the Water Act (NI) 1972 is outlined in Part II of this chapter.) The obligation in this regard applies whether the Department is granting a new discharge consent or is reviewing an existing consent under section 10 of the Act. It should also be noted that the term 'appropriate' is stated in regulation 8 to mean a condition which is 'appropriate to the nature of the industry concerned for the discharge of such waste water.'

## *Dumping of sludge at sea*

The DoE(NI) is obliged under regulation 9 to exercise its functions as a licensing authority under sections 24 and 25(3) of the Food and Environmental Protection

---

233. The industrial sectors in question are: milk processing; manufacture of fruit and vegetable products; manufacture and bottling of soft drinks; potato processing; meat industry; breweries; production of alcohol and alcoholic beverages; manufacture of animal feed from plant products; manufacture of gelatine and of glue from hides, skin, and bones; malt-houses; fish processing.

Act 1985[234] to ensure that the dumping of sludge from ships to surface waters is phased out by 31 December 1998 and, also, that 'the total amount of toxic, persistent or bioaccumulable materials in sludge so disposed of is licensed for disposal and progressively reduced in the period ending on that date.' Similarly, the DoE(NI) is obliged to ensure that the same conditions are met in relation to sludge dumped at sea by the Department itself.

## Monitoring

In addition to the obligation to regulate discharges of urban waste waters by means of discharge consent, regulation 11 imposes extensive monitoring obligations on the DoE(NI) to ensure compliance with the various discharge standards laid down by the UWWT Regulations and also to ensure that the environment of the receiving waters is not being adversely affected. The DoE(NI) is also empowered to procure this monitoring obligation by a competent authority or an appropriate body.

### The provision of information concerning the implementation of Directive 91/271/EEC in Northern Ireland

The DoE(NI) is obliged under regulation 13 to publish a 'situation report' every two years on the disposal of urban waste water and sludge in Northern Ireland and, in addition, is required to 'establish, update and provide the Commission with information on a programme for the implementation of the Directive'.

## SECTION 3. OTHER CONTROLS IMPOSED ON SEWAGE SLUDGE

It should also be noted that the use of sewage sludge in agriculture is regulated by the Sludge (Use in Agriculture) Regulations (NI) 1990, while the Prevention of Pollution (Erne System) Regulations (NI) 1994 regulate discharges from the toilets of vessels using the Erne System. These provisions are discussed in Parts VIII and III (power to adopt regulations) of this chapter.

# PART X  THE COMMON LAW AND WATER POLLUTION

The common law, in its coverage of water pollution issues, offers a rather limited degree of protection to the environment as an incidental benefit of its primary function, the promotion of individual rights. Common law is, however, by its very nature likely to be of little utility in providing the precise and predictable levels of environmental protection mandated by modern statutory regimes. For example, the balance of conflicting interests that is the central feature of the main common law device concerning the environment, private nuisance, is based on the judge's view of the reasonableness of the defendant's activities and the plaintiff's expectations relative to the subsisting facts. Private law controls are reactive and unpredictable in their incidence, being triggered by the individual seeking protection for his rights, rather than proactive and offering continuing control like

234. c. 48. This 1985 Act applies to the UK as a whole.

statute law. Common law procedures tend to be lengthy and expensive, and the outcome of litigation is fraught with uncertainty; these factors tend to limit its appeal and utility in the area of environmental protection.

## SECTION 1.  GROUND WATER AND THE COMMON LAW

The relevance of common law, specifically the law of torts, to protecting ground water resources from pollution has been dealt with recently by the House of Lords in *Cambridge Water Co. Ltd v. Eastern Counties Leather PLC.*[235] The case involved the contamination of the chalk aquifer which supplied the Cambridge Water Company's borehole at Sawston Mill with water which was sold for domestic consumption. The contamination was traced to the spillage, over a period of many years, of the solvent perchloroethane at Eastern Counties Leather's tannery some 1.3 miles away, which had through time been carried by percolating water to the borehole. Cambridge Water's claim in respect of the damage that they had sustained was based on three heads: negligence, nuisance, and the rule in *Rylands v. Fletcher.*[236]

The company's claim was dismissed on all three counts by Kennedy J at first instance. The claims in negligence and nuisance were dismissed on the grounds that the damage was not reasonably foreseeable at the time the spillages occurred. The claim under *Rylands v. Fletcher* was dismissed on the grounds that the accumulation of solvents for tanning did not constitute a 'non-natural' use of land. The Court of Appeal allowed Cambridge Water's appeal, holding Eastern Counties Leather strictly liable for the contamination of ground water percolating under Cambridge Water's land under *Ballard v. Tomlinson.*[237] Damages of £1,064,886, along with interest of £642,885, were awarded. Eastern Counties Leather's appeal to the House of Lords was allowed. Lord Goff was of the opinion that the rule in *Ballard v. Tomlinson* was merely a particular application of the law of nuisance or the rule in *Rylands v. Fletcher* and therefore in any event there could be no liability on the facts of the present case in the absence of reasonable foreseeability of damage.

## SECTION 2.  SURFACE WATERS AND THE COMMON LAW

Water pollution can also be tackled by the common law through the special protection it offers to riparian rights through the law of private nuisance. This specific legal protection, while located within the broader law of private nuisance (particularly through its link with land ownership), tends to be of greater utility in practice.

Riparian rights accrue to those who own land adjoining watercourses, fisheries owners, etc. They are based on ownership of the river bed rather than ownership of the water itself, since the latter is a circulating resource. Landowners have a right to receive water in its natural state, although this is qualified by the right of those whose property is located upstream to put the water which flows through their land

---

235. [1994] 2 WLR 53. The strict liability aspects of this case are discussed in chap. 13.
236. [1868] LR 3 HL 530.
237. [1885] 29 Ch D 115.

to reasonable use. It is obvious that polluting activities by upstream users, whether by putting foreign substances into the water or by heating the water, thus affecting its dissolved oxygen content and its ability to support life, can adversely affect the use of water by those downstream. Likewise, excessive extraction of water upstream can have an adverse effect on those who rely on the resource downstream, both by reducing the quantity of water available and by causing pollutants to become more concentrated and thus more damaging in their impact.

To protect riparian interests, the law developed to categorise *any* interference with the natural quality or quantity of water as an actionable nuisance *(Young, and Co. v. Bankier Distillery Co*[238]*)*. There is no requirement that the plaintiff should prove damage; it is sufficient that the quality of the water is interfered with. There are no absolute quality standards under the common law; each watercourse is different, and the ability of water to 'self-clean' is affected by the physical characteristics of the water as well as by the quantity of the water and the pollutants that are discharged into it.

An action can be brought against any polluter, even if there are several contributors to the problem; see for example *Pride of Derby Angling Association v. British Celanese Ltd.*[239] Damages are available (in respect of past damage), as are injunctions (to prevent the continuance of the nuisance in future), though the latter may be suspended (as occurred in *Pride of Derby*) to allow polluters time to comply with the terms of the injunction in question. The suspension of injunctions appears to indicate that, while the social utility of the defendant's activity is irrelevant in determining whether his conduct constitutes a nuisance, it may be relevant to the question of providing a remedy. Acting within the terms of a statutory discharge consent does not act as a defence in a private nuisance action.

---

238. [1893] AC 698.
239. [1952] Ch 149.

# CHAPTER SIX

# Waste and Contaminated Land

## Introduction

The problem of waste disposal has always existed as a consequence of human activity. The difficulties associated with waste have, however, grown more acute in the context of modern urban living. In a developed society, such as that in Northern Ireland, waste is now being produced in greater quantities than ever before. The waste itself also features increasingly complex and toxic components, which adds another dimension to the already difficult problem of disposal.

Waste problems arise on two main fronts, both of which are intimately linked to the question of disposal. Firstly, the sheer quantity of waste generated threatens to outstrip society's capacity to dispose of it in the traditional manner, i.e. by landfill. Solutions to this aspect of the disposal problem can attempt to reduce the volume of waste for disposal in the first place, through waste minimisation strategies. One example of this approach is requiring manufacturers to reduce the quantity of packaging used in the marketing of their products. A second approach is to encourage the recycling and reuse of items which would otherwise be regarded as waste.

The disposal problem posed by increased volumes of waste, together with decreasing landfill capacity can also be tackled by attempting to find alternative methods of disposal—the most common is incineration—although these too can have adverse environmental consequences.

A second problem arising with waste is the disposal of harmful substances, which make up a sizable proportion of the total quantity of even domestic waste. The disposal of most types of material—metals, corrosive substances, and even some organic materials—in landfill sites will eventually, through the leaching of the contents into the soil and eventually ground water, cause chronic pollution problems.

The incineration of most types of waste will also raise air pollution issues, and the ash that is the end product of incineration raises further disposal issues.

While it is true to say that waste problems have reached a new level of prominence in the last two decades, the need to regulate the disposal of waste in order to prevent indiscriminate dumping has long been recognised. Initially public health laws[1] prevented the accumulation of waste from being allowed to become a hazard to human health and the human environment. It is perhaps surprising, though, that legislation introducing a specific regime for the licensing of waste disposal, treating disposal to land in a like manner to discharges to other environmental media, did not emerge in England and Wales until the passing of the Control of Pollution Act 1974 (COPA). Northern Ireland had to wait a further

---

1. For example the Public Health (Ireland) Act 1878.

four years for the Pollution Control and Local Government (NI) Order 1978 to introduce a parallel regime for the Province.

The 1978 Order continues to represent the current law of waste regulation applicable to Northern Ireland, though legislation to update the regime—the proposal for a Draft Order on Waste and Contaminated Land 1996 (see below)—will bring the law of Northern Ireland into line with that in the rest of the UK. The proposed Draft Order incorporates aspects of the Control of Pollution Amendment Act 1989, the Environmental Protection Act 1990 and the Environment Act 1995.

The chapter is divided into three parts.

- Part I    outlines action taken by the European Community in dealing with waste.
- Part II   deals with law and policy with regard to waste in Northern Ireland; section 1 deals with the regime for municipal waste provided by the Pollution Control and Local Government (NI) Order 1978[2] (as amended), while section 2 looks at the law governing 'special waste' under the Pollution Control (Special Waste) Regulations (NI) 1981.[3]
- Part III  examines key new initiatives in the law dealing with waste, notably the provisions of the proposal for a Draft Waste and Contaminated Land (NI) Order 1996, which is set to overhaul the law relating to waste in Northern Ireland.

## *PART I* THE EC DIMENSION OF WASTE REGULATION

EC policy on waste regulation is informed by three essential objectives, namely, to prevent waste at source by ensuring the proper design of products and processes, to recycle or reuse any waste and in particular to use waste as a source of energy, and to ensure that waste is disposed of in its country of origin. Although some commentators have argued that the EC has failed to achieve its overall aim, that is to ensure that an integrated approach to waste management throughout the region is established, EC waste legislation has had, and will continue to have, a considerable influence on the standards governing waste management in Northern Ireland.[4]

The EC's involvement in the regulation of waste began with the adoption of the Waste Framework Directive 75/442/EEC[5] in 1975, which has since been significantly amended by Directive 91/156/EEC.[6] Together these Directives define the concept of 'waste' (in Annexes which list categories of waste) and establish a general framework of control for waste management which requires member states to adopt measures which would: (i) ensure that the production of waste would be prevented or reduced, (ii) promote waste recovery, (iii) ensure the safe disposal of waste and (iv) establish an 'integrated and adequate' network of waste disposal facilities which uses the 'best available technology not entailing

2.  SI 1978/1049.
3.  SR No. 252.
4.  Krämer, *EC Treaty and Environmental Law,* 2nd ed., London: Sweet and Maxwell, 1995.
5.  OJ L194, 25 July 1975.
6.  OJ L78, 26 Mar. 1991.

excessive cost' (BATNEEC). In particular, the two Directives require that public agencies plan the disposal of waste properly and that a competent body regulates the licensing of waste disposal facilities; only certain categories of waste are permitted to be exempted from the licensing system, and exceptions may only be relied on if properly justified.

Member states were required to complete formal implementation of the standards laid down by Directive 91/156/EEC in April 1993. Directive 91/156/EEC will however only be implemented in Northern Ireland when the new proposal for a Draft Waste and Contaminated Land (NI) Order is enacted at the end of 1996.

Toxic and dangerous waste are regulated under Directive 78/319/EEC,[7] which essentially establishes a separate framework for controlling household and toxic wastes. Certain provisions of this Directive are implemented in Northern Ireland by the Pollution Control (Special Waste) Regulations (NI) 1981.[8] Directive 78/319/EEC has since been amended by the Hazardous Waste Directive 91/689/EEC,[9] which lays down more stringent requirements concerning hazardous wastes. The framework of control laid down in Directive 78/319/EEC and Directive 91/689/EEC is broadly similar to that applying to all waste under Directive 75/442/EEC, as amended. However, Directive 91/689/EEC lays down a common definition of 'hazardous waste' for the EC as a whole, which is based on generic features of the waste and the constituents and properties which render waste hazardous. The Directive required the Commission to draw up a list of hazardous wastes six months before the compliance date, which in effect meant that implementation of the Directive was conditional on the list being approved; it was finally agreed in December 1994, after lengthy debate. Member states were required to implement the Hazardous Waste Directive by 27 June 1995. To date its provisions have not been implemented in Northern Ireland; however, implementing regulations are scheduled to be introduced by the end of 1996.

Three Directives have been enacted governing the incineration of waste. Directives 89/369/EEC[10] and 89/429/EEC,[11] which require compliance in terms of the 'best available technology not entailing excessive cost', set down emission limit values for new and existing municipal waste incineration plants (MWIPs). MWIPs are defined as plants which only deal with domestic, commercial and trade waste. These Directives do not cover incinerators which handle sewage sludge, chemical waste, toxic waste, or hospital waste. Dust, heavy metals, traces of dioxins and acidic gases are among the emissions primarily associated with municipal waste incinerators.

Directive 89/429/EEC on existing MWIPs defines 'existing plants' as plants which were granted their first authorisation before 1 December 1990. A timetable is set out in the Directive stipulating the time frame within which existing plants must attain the standards laid down for new plants in Directive 89/369/EEC. Directive 89/369/EEC on new plants imposes emission limit values and also requires that from 1 December 1990 such limits be attached to the system of prior

7.   OJ L84, 31 Mar. 1978.
8.   SR No. 252.
9.   OJ L377, 31 Dec. 1991
10.  OJ L163, 14 June 1989.
11.  OJ L203, 15 July 1989.

authorisations required by the Air Framework Directive 84/360/EEC and the Waste Framework Directive 75/442/EEC. Member states were required to implement the terms of both Directives by 1 December 1990; thus far, neither has been formally implemented in Northern Ireland. It should be noted, however, that 'existing' MWIPs with a capacity of 1 tonne per hour or greater are controlled under the Alkali &c. Works Regulation Act 1906. There is only one such plant in Northern Ireland; the provisions of the Alkali Act are addressed in detail in chapter 4.

The Alkali &c. Works (Amendment) Order 1994[12] in effect brought all MWIPs under the system of control laid down in the 1906 Act, which means that in practice the emission limits imposed by the Directive are being complied with. The making of the proposed Draft Industrial Pollution Control (NI) Order in late 1996 will ensure the full implementation of both Directives in Northern Ireland. (The terms of the proposal for a Draft Order are outlined in chapter 4.) Directive 94/67/EEC[13] governs the incineration of hazardous waste. It imposes stringent emission limits based on the most up-to-date technology. This Directive will also be implemented in Northern Ireland by the making of the proposed Draft Industrial Pollution Control (NI) Order.

In 1992 in Case C-2/90 *Commission v. Belgium,*[14] the European Court of Justice ruled that waste must be treated as a 'good', the result being that waste must come within EC law governing the free movement of goods, and its movement throughout the EC must not be restricted. The Court went on to say, however, that the special nature of waste had to be considered. The Court's attitude towards waste broadly reflects that propounded by other Community institutions. In September 1989 the Commission published *A Community Strategy for Waste Management,* which, among other things, addressed waste management in the context of the single market, with particular reference to the movement of waste. The strategy document noted that 'in a Community without internal frontiers the flow of waste towards lower-cost disposal plants may become a flood'; and while the harmonisation of national disposal standards was agreed as an important priority, it was argued that 'the need to protect the environment may lead to a restriction of movements' in favour of disposing waste 'in the nearest suitable centres, making use of the most appropriate technologies to guarantee a high level of protection for the environment and public health.'

In 1990 the Council adopted a resolution on waste policy that expressed support for the Commission's views concerning the movement of waste. In essence, the EC has sought to implement what is known as the 'proximity principle',[15] whereby the movement of waste is kept to a minimum, both within the EC and also in shipments from the EC itself. Directive 84/631/EEC[16] on the transfrontier shipment of hazardous waste established a system for controlling the movement of hazardous waste within the EC and in and out of the EC. The

12. SR No. 104.
13. OJ L365 31 Dec. 94.
14. [1992] I ECR 4431.
15. For further reading on the EC's approach to the movement of waste see N. Haigh, *Manual of Environmental Policy, the EC and Britain,* London: Longman; 1992; K. Kummer, *International Management of Hazardous Wastes,* Oxford: Clarendon Press, 1995.
16. OJ L326, 13 Dec. 1984.

controls imposed by this Directive were unable to prevent illegal waste movement, and in 1994 it was replaced by Regulation EEC/259/93,[17] which now regulates such movements. Regulation EEC/259/93 also gives effect to the provisions of the Basel Convention on the Control of Transboundary Movements of Hazardous Wastes and the provisions of the fourth Lomé Convention (1990–95) which ban the export of hazardous waste to numerous African, Caribbean and Pacific countries. The Regulation is directly applicable in all member states and therefore does not require specific implementation. The Transfrontier Shipment of Waste Regulations 1994[18] make provision for the UK as a whole for the requirements of Regulation EEC/259/93 and the provisions of the Waste Framework Directive 75/442/EEC regarding the import and export of waste. In addition, Directive 92/3/Euratom[19] contains separate requirements for the supervision and control of shipments of radioactive waste between member states and into and out of the EC; this Directive is implemented for the UK as a whole by the Transfrontier Shipment of Radioactive Waste Regulations 1993.[20]

The framework EC legislation on waste is supplemented by a wide variety of other Directives on specific types of waste. Directive 75/439/EEC,[21] as amended by Directive 87/101/EEC[22] on the disposal of waste oils, is partly implemented in Northern Ireland by the Pollution Control (Special Waste) Regulations (NI) 1981[23] and the Waste Collection and Disposal Regulations (NI) 1992;[24] the proposal for a Draft Waste and Contaminated Land (NI) Order will ensure full implementation. Directive 86/278/EEC[25] on the use of sewage sludge in agriculture is implemented by the Sludge (Use in Agriculture) Regulations (NI) 1990[26]. None of the following Directives has yet been implemented in Northern Ireland: Directive 94/62/EEC[27] on the packaging and repackaging of waste; Directive 76/403/EEC[28] on the disposal of PCBs; Directive 85/339/EEC[29] on containers for liquids for human consumption; Directive 91/157/EEC[30] on batteries and accumulators containing certain dangerous substances; Directive 78/176/EEC[31] on waste from the titanium dioxide industry.

Finally, it should be noted that the EC is preparing Directives on landfills and on civil liability for damage caused by waste. The civil liability proposal, if adopted, would establish an extensive regime of strict liability for damage caused by waste; this proposal has been very controversial and, despite years of debate, has not yet been adopted. The proposal is discussed in more detail in chapter 13.

---

17. OJ L30, 6 Feb. 1993.
18. SI 1994/1137.
19. OJ L35/24, OJ L35, 12 Feb. 92.
20. SI 1993/3031.
21. OJ L194, 25 July 1975.
22. OJ L42, 12 Feb. 1987.
23. SR No. 252.
24. SR No. 254.
25. OJ L181, 4 July 1986.
26. SR No. 245.
27. OJ L 365, 31 Dec. 94.
28. OJ L108, 26 Apr. 1976.
29. OJ L176, 6 July 1985.
30. OJ L78, 26 Mar. 1991.
31. OJ L54, 25 Feb. 1978.

The landfill measure, if adopted, will harmonise national landfill standards by laying down specific requirements concerning almost every aspect of the design and operation of landfill sites.

## PART II WASTE IN NORTHERN IRELAND

### Waste policy

Each year Northern Ireland produces approximately 700,000 tonnes of household waste, 327,000 tonnes of commercial waste, 240,000 tonnes of industrial waste and over 1,000,000 tonnes of waste from the construction industry.[32] In Northern Ireland, as in the rest of the UK, landfill represents the most common form of waste disposal for much of this municipal waste; small quantities of clinical waste and special waste (see below) are incinerated.

The UK Government, partly motivated by the requirements of EC law but also by domestic policy imperatives, has been active in seeking a more environmentally sensitive disposal policy. The process of change in Northern Ireland was begun by a consultation exercise in 1993 instituted by the DoE(NI), based on Aspinwell and Company's *Review of Waste Disposal in Northern Ireland* (1990), which has helped in pushing the disposal debate forward. Recycling has been elevated to a policy priority, and district councils are now required to give priority to issuing and implementing recycling plans in addition to established waste disposal plans. This requirement is designed to support the Government's commitment to recycling 25 per cent of household waste by the year 2000.[33]

### *Managing waste*

The Environment Service within the DoE(NI)[34] is charged with responsibility for the legislative regime for waste management. It is therefore to the Environment Service that district councils submit their waste disposal plans (see below), and the Environment Service is the appellate body for licensing decisions taken by the councils on waste disposal site licences (see below). The Environment Service also provides the practical guidance that underpins the activities of local government and private site operators in this area, supplying professional advice on the collection and safe disposal of waste.

The Environment Service has, in its Corporate Plan,[35] set out a series of substantive aims and objectives in order to further its pursuit of strategic responsibilities in waste management. Its general aim is to encourage the efficient use of raw materials (and thus waste minimisation), reuse and recycling, and,

---

32. *Environment Service Report* 1991–93.
33. Ibid.
34. A new centralised waste regulatory inspectorate located within the ES will take over the tasks outlined, together with the additional functions envisaged under the proposal for a Draft Waste and Contaminated Land (NI) Order 1996: see the DoE's *Explanatory Document for a Proposal for a Draft Waste and Contaminated Land (Northern Ireland) Order: A Compliance Cost Assessment*, Feb. 1996.
35. The plan extends from 1994 to 1997.

where waste is unavoidable, its safe and efficient disposal. To this end waste minimisation, reuse and recycling will be actively encouraged, while at the same time the profligate use of resources will be discouraged by tightening regulatory standards and harnessing market mechanisms in order to curb waste generation. Research into alternative disposal routes is also promised.

The Environment Service originally envisaged a new statutory regime that would offer improved mechanisms for waste control being implemented by the end of 1994; this target was not met, though the new legislative machinery seems set to be established by the end of 1996 (for details see below).

## SECTION 1. THE POLLUTION CONTROL AND LOCAL GOVERNMENT (NI) ORDER 1978[36]

The 1978 Order is the relevant legislation currently applicable to most waste collection and removal and the licensing and execution of its final disposal. There is enhanced legislative provision for dealing with 'special waste' in the form of the Pollution Control (Special Waste) Regulations (NI) 1981,[37] made under powers contained in the 1978 Order, which will be examined in detail below.

District councils are the designated authorities for the collection and disposal of waste under the Order and for the licensing of private waste disposal sites and facilities.[38] In both these roles the councils are subject to the supervisory jurisdiction of the DoE(NI) Environment Service.

The fact that district councils have both operational and regulatory responsibilities for waste disposal creates the familiar poacher-gamekeeper problem, whereby the capacity for neutrality in operating the regulatory regime is eroded by a conflict of interest. The proposal for a Draft Order on Waste and Contaminated Land 1996 will solve this problem by placing the waste disposal licensing system in the hands of the DoE(NI). This will end the dual role of local authorities, replacing the rather loose controls which are available under the 1978 Order with highly visible regulatory controls.

### The definition of waste

'Waste' (specifically referred to in the Order as 'controlled waste') is defined by article 36 (1)[39] as including:

(a) any substance which constitutes a scrap metal or an effluent or other unwanted surplus substance arising from the application of any process; and

---

36. SI 1978/1049.
37. SR No. 252.
38. For the councils' general responsibilities see art. 3 of the 1978 Order.
39. The definition of 'waste' in the 1978 Order is fleshed out by the more detailed provisions of the Waste Collection and Disposal Regulations (NI) 1992 (SR 1992 No. 254). Explosives, as defined by the Explosives Acts 1875, 1924 and 1970 or covered by art. 3 of the Explosives (NI) Order 1972 (SI 1972/730), are explicitly excluded from this definition of waste.

(b) any substance or article which requires to be disposed of as being broken, worn out, contaminated or otherwise spoiled.[40]

The definition of waste is broken down into components by article 36(2); these are household waste, industrial waste, and commercial waste.

## Household waste

Household waste is defined by source in article 36(2)(*a*) of the 1978 Order as waste coming from private dwellings, residential homes, and premises that are part of a school, university or other educational establishment or part of a hospital or nursing home. This rather scant definition is fleshed out by regulations 3 and 4 and Schedule 1 to the Waste Collection and Disposal Regulations (NI) 1992.[41] Waste that is to be treated as household waste according to Schedule 1 includes waste from premises which do not count as private dwellings under the Rates (NI) Order 1977,[42] for example rooms let singly for residential purposes (paragraph 1), waste from premises exempt from rates, for example places of worship (paragraph 4), and waste that is closely connected to domestic usage, for example waste from garages or stores used wholly in connection with a private dwelling (paragraph 2). Waste from campsites (paragraph 6), residential hostels (paragraph 7) and penal institutions (paragraph 8) is also covered.

Regulation 4 specifically excludes waste consisting of any mineral or synthetic oil or grease, asbestos and clinical waste from being treated as household waste.

## Industrial waste

Industrial waste is defined by article 36(2)(*b*) as that coming from any factory[43] and from any nationalised industry.[44] This rather terse definition is expanded by regulation 6 and Schedule 3 to the 1992 Regulations. Included are:

- waste from premises that are used to maintain vehicles (paragraph 1);
- waste from workshops[45] that do not qualify as factories under the Factories Act (NI) 1965 (paragraph 2);
- waste from dredging, construction (including demolition), and tunnelling and excavation (paragraphs 5, 6 and 7, respectively);
- clinical waste (paragraph 9);
- waste and soil moved from previous deposit sites (paragraph 12);
- leachate from waste deposits (paragraph 13); and
- poisonous or noxious waste from trade or business premises concerned with mixing or selling paints; signwriting; laundering or dry cleaning; developing

---

40. Radioactive waste, as defined by the Radioactive Substances Act 1960, is subject to only limited control under the 1978 Order. Art. 36(4) provides that, although the general provisions of the Order do not apply to radioactive waste, regulations may be issued by the DoE(NI) subjecting such waste to a modified version of the Order's regime and amending the 1960 Act accordingly.
41. SR No. 254.
42. SI 1977/2157.
43. As defined by the Factories Act (NI) 1965.
44. Mine and quarry waste is excluded from art. 39(2)(*b*).
45. Computer operations and printing and lithographic activities are expressly excluded from para. 2.

film or making photographic prints; and selling petrol, diesel oil, etc. (paragraph 14).

It will be apparent from these examples that the definition of industrial waste is fairly exhaustive.

## Commercial waste

Commercial waste is that which, according to article 36(2)(c) of the 1978 Order, is constituted by materials and substances coming from premises used wholly or mainly for the purposes of trade or business, sport, recreation, or entertainment.[46] The 1992 Regulations (specifically regulation 7 and Schedule 4) further delineate commercial waste as including:

- waste from an office or showroom (paragraph 1);
- waste from clubs' and societies' premises (paragraph 4);
- waste from courts, government departments, district councils, bodies corporate or individuals discharging public functions (e.g. quangos), and bodies incorporated by royal charter[47] (paragraph 5); and
- waste from a fair or market (paragraph 7).

## Problems with the definition of waste

While the definition of the term 'waste' in the 1978 Order appears on first viewing to be fairly comprehensive, it is inadequate and incomplete in several respects.

First, by specifically omitting mine and quarry waste and waste from agricultural premises from coverage by the Order (relying for the control of these classes of refuse on the Town and Country Planning regime in the first case and the activities of DANI in the second) and thus narrowing the application of the new regime, inconsistencies in the disposal of waste are bound to arise.

Second, the definition of waste is unclear with respect to the recycling issue. The definition of 'controlled waste' adopted by article 36(1) of the Order is so broad that material accumulated for recycling will be classed as a deposit of waste—a failure to acknowledge that one person's waste is another's raw material. This problem arose under the identical provision in the equivalent legislation for England and Wales, COPA 1974. In the case of *Long v. Brook*[48] it was decided that whether or not an item would be defined as 'waste' was to be determined by the view of the person discarding it. The issue came to the fore once again in *Kent CC v. Queensborough Rolling Mill Co. Ltd*,[49] where a company was charged with committing an offence by disposing of waste on land without a licence. The company was using inert material being cleared from a disused site to shore up subsidence on its property. At first instance the magistrates decided that the material in the circumstances, because of its nature and the use to which it was being put, did not amount to waste. They also, however, sought the opinion of the

---

46. Art. 36(2)(c) specifically excludes: (i) household waste and (ii) mine and quarry waste and waste from agricultural premises (the latter are defined by the Agriculture Act (NI) 1949); and other waste prescribed in future under art. 36(2)(c).
47. If these do not fall under the household waste or industrial waste headings.
48. [1980] Crim LR 109.
49. [1990] JEL 257.

Divisional Court on the correctness of their initial view, and the decision was overturned on both counts; the Divisional Court decided that the material in question was in fact waste and that the final use to which it was put was irrelevant.

The same problem has arisen in EC law under the Framework Directive 75/442/EEC, and it was dealt with in much the same way by the European Court of Justice in the cases of *Vessoso*[50] and *Zanetti*.[51] The ECJ was of the opinion that material should be defined as waste even if it had the potential to be reused. While the court recognised that recycling was a valuable activity, a key purpose of EC waste law was to protect public health from the consequences of the accumulation of waste materials.

The view expressed by the ECJ gives the strongest justification for treating material collected for recycling in the same way as waste—though perhaps a better solution would be to operate an alternative, less onerous licensing system for the latter. A recycling licensing system should be designed to acknowledge that the temporary accumulation involved in recycling differs in the magnitude of the risks involved from permanent waste disposal.

## Waste collection

### Household waste

Article 14(1)(*a*) of the 1978 Order places each district council under a general obligation to 'arrange for the collection' of all household waste in its area. This responsibility is subject to the proviso that waste in very isolated areas, where collection costs would be 'unreasonably high', may be left in the hands of the person controlling the waste.[52] The collection of household waste is, except in prescribed cases,[53] to be carried out free of charge (paragraph (3)).

Councils are empowered to require occupiers of domestic premises (by a notice issued under article 15(1)) to place waste in specified receptacles[54] (i.e. dustbins). Failure to comply with such a notice will render the occupier liable to a fine of up to £1,000 (level 3 on the standard scale) on summary conviction (Criminal Justice (NI) Order 1994). The occupier may appeal against the requirements of a paragraph (1) notice to a court of summary jurisdiction within twenty-one days of

---

50. Case 206/88.
51. Case 207/88.
52. To leave waste in the hands of the person controlling it, the district council must be satisfied that adequate arrangements for its disposal have been made or can reasonably be expected to be made (art. 14 (1)(*a*)(ii)).
53. In prescribed cases a 'reasonable charge' may be made for waste collection (art. 14(3)(*b*)). The applicable charges are laid down in reg. 5 and Sch. 2 to the Waste Collection and Disposal Regulations 1992. Charges may be made in respect of waste which poses special difficulties (often because of its volume), for example by weighing more than 25 kg (para. 1), dead domestic pets (para. 5), waste from residential hostels, residential homes, premises forming part of a university, school etc. or waste from hospitals and nursing homes (para. 7), waste from caravans, tents etc. on sites not designated as suitable for year-round occupation (para.9(1)), and wastes from charitable or penal institutions (para. 10 and 12, respectively).
54. Art. 15(9) makes provision for regulations to be made concerning the size, construction and maintenance of receptacles, their position on premises, substances that may or may not be placed into them, etc.

the date for compliance specified in the notice.[55] Appeals will be entertained on the grounds stipulated in article 15(3); these are:
(i)   that the kind or number of receptacles specified is unreasonable, or
(ii)  that the receptacles already in use for the collection of household waste on the premises are adequate.

An appeal suspends the effect of the article 15(1) notice pending its determination (article 15(4)(*a*)). The court may dismiss the appeal, or it may quash or modify the notice (article 15(4)(*b*)).

The council may in its notice provide for the designated receptacles to be provided free of charge or subject to a single or periodic payment by the occupier (paragraph (2)(*a*)).

### *Commercial and industrial waste*

Article 14(1)(*b*) places councils under an additional responsibility for collecting commercial waste should this service be requested by the occupier of premises in its district. Councils may also undertake to arrange for the collection of industrial waste should this be requested by the occupier of premises in the area (article 14(2)). A reasonable charge may be imposed by the council for the collection of commercial[56] and industrial waste (paragraph (4)).

Councils may supply receptacles for the collection of both commercial and industrial waste at the request of an occupier who has asked the council to collect waste which falls into either of these classes. Charges may be made for these receptacles on the same basis as the collection charges referred to above (article 15(5)).

Councils have additional powers in respect of commercial and industrial waste under article 15(6), which allow them (by notice served on the occupier) to require that waste that is likely to either cause a nuisance or be detrimental to the amenities of the locality be stored in specified receptacles. As with household waste, failure to comply with such a notice will incur a fine of up to £1,000 on summary conviction. An appeal against such a notice within twenty-one days of the day on which it was served is provided for by article 15(7). Appeals may relate to the reasonableness of the type or number of receptacles specified (sub-paragraph (*a*)) or deny the council's view that the waste in question constitutes a nuisance or a danger to amenity (sub-paragraph (*b*)). An appeal under paragraph (7) has the same effect on the notice as under paragraph (4).

Once waste of any of the aforementioned classes has been collected it becomes the council's property and may be dealt with as the council sees fit (article 14(8)).

### Waste disposal

District councils, in addition to collecting waste, are also given responsibilities in the area of waste disposal at both an operational and a strategic level (see below). In addition to the powers contained in the 1978 Order dealing with disposal

---

55.  If no date is specified, the twenty-one day appeal period begins to run on the date on which the notice was served on the occupier (art. 15(3)).
56.  A council has the power to remove commercial waste free of charge where imposing a fee is deemed inappropriate (art. 14(4)).

activities, the Waste Control and Disposal Regulations (NI) 1992 have been made under the auspices of that Order in order to amplify some of the skeleton provisions contained in it.

The 1992 Regulations primarily concern themselves with delineating the contents of each of the classes of waste originally set out in the 1978 Order. Councils are required to make arrangements for the disposal of any waste that is collected within the area they control (article 21(2)). To this end councils may provide sites where waste can be deposited before transferral to a site for disposal (and processing), as well as sites for these purposes. Councils are also empowered to enter into agreements with others to provide waste disposal facilities and sites (article 21(5)) in order to satisfy the requirements of the Order.

Article 21(4) empowers councils to permit others to use facilities which they have provided for waste disposal. The council may make reasonable charges for the use of its facilities (sub-paragraph (*a*)).[57]

### Household waste disposal facilities

District councils are required to provide sites within their areas where household waste may be deposited by any person, at reasonable times and free of charge (article 22(1)).

### Recycling and reuse of waste, etc.

Councils have powers to provide plant and equipment for sorting and baling waste paper and for sorting and processing other waste (article 21(1) of the 1978 Order). Article 23 provides councils with additional (if somewhat vague) powers to do such things as they deem appropriate to enable waste to be reused or for substances to be reclaimed from it. Additional powers are given by article 23(*b*) enabling councils to purchase waste for reuse and recycling and by paragraph (*c*) to sell or otherwise dispose of waste or its by-products for these purposes.

Each of these powers, as one would perhaps expect of a legislative instrument of the vintage of the 1978 Order, is entirely permissive. It would appear, however, that changes in the policy background against which the Order operates have 'encouraged' greater use to be made of these powers; for example, the Environment Service in its Corporate Plan[58] projected a steady increase in the waste recycling disposal schemes that it would be required to assess, from four in 1994/95 to twenty-two in 1996/97.

Article 24(1) authorises councils to use waste for producing heat or electricity and to establish and operate the necessary facilities to carry out this purpose. Waste is not to be used to generate electricity without official consultation with electricity authorities and the approval of the relevant government department[59] (article 24(2)). Even where electricity production is authorised, power produced may only be used on the site (sub-paragraph (*a*)) or sold to Northern Ireland Electricity (sub-paragraph (*b*)). Alternative energy generation schemes have

---

57. No charges may, however, be made in respect of household waste (art. 21(4)(*b*)).
58. Supra.
59. Under the 1978 Order the Department of Commerce, now the Department of Economic Development.

gained ground in the last few years as part of a wider re-examination of energy policy and priorities, and these are discussed in chapter 10.

### Waste disposal plans

The 1978 Order placed district councils under an obligation, (contained in article 4), to prepare (and keep up to date) waste disposal plans for their areas. Article 4 powers are to be exercised at such times as directed by the DoE(NI) (article 4(7)).

Councils are first required to carry out an investigation to enable a decision to be arrived at concerning the present and future waste disposal needs of their area. Having determined what arrangements are necessary, the council must then compile a plan based on a statement of the arrangements proposed by the council itself and others concerned with waste disposal specified in the statement for the duration of the plan. The council is obliged to make periodic investigations in order to modify the plan.

Plans and modifications are to be made in consultation with the DoE(NI) (specifically the Environment Service) and with other district councils[60] (if any) affected by the contents of the plan in question and with any other persons the council deems appropriate from those involved in the waste disposal sector (article 4(3)(a)(i), (ii), and (iii), respectively).

Councils are also required (article 4(3)(b)) to publicise both plans and modifications[61] and to allow the public the opportunity to make representations. Any representations so made must be considered, and if changes in the plan are deemed to be appropriate these must be made.

Article 4(1) requires that councils will:

> have regard to the effect which the arrangements or modifications would be likely to have on the amenities of any relevant locality and to the likely cost to the council . . .

The minimum contents of the plan are stipulated by article 4(2) and include:

(i) the kinds and quantities of controlled waste the council expects to be generated in its area during the subsistence of the plan;

(ii) the kinds and quantities of waste the council expects to be brought into or sent out of its area during the subsistence of the plan;

(iii) the kinds and quantities of waste the council expects to dispose of itself during the subsistence of the plan;

(iv) the kinds and quantities of waste the council expects others to dispose of in the area during the subsistence of the plan;

(v) the methods the council thinks should be used to dispose of waste in its area, including waste reclamation, and priorities to be accorded to the different disposal options available;

(vi) the sites and equipment the council proposes to provide and that it expects others to provide during the subsistence of the plan; and

(vii) the estimated costs of the disposal methods mentioned in the plan.

---

60. If such an additional council refuses its consent to the final contents of the plan the DoE(NI) must give consent in its place art. 4(5)).

61. Art. 4(3)(b) qualifies the obligation to go through publicity and consultation procedures in respect of modifications that the council believes will not prejudice anyone.

Article 4(4) also requires the council to consider, in consultation with those it deems appropriate, and to include in the plan where appropriate, arrangements for reclaiming waste.

Once the final contents of the plan have been determined by the council, it must once again be publicised, and a copy must be sent to the DoE(NI) (article 4(6)).

## Scope of the 1978 Order: waste disposal offences

The 1978 Order, like COPA, deals with the disposal and deposit of controlled waste. The main offence under Part II of the Order is that contained in article 5(1), under which a person must not 'deposit . . . controlled waste on any land or cause or knowingly permit controlled waste to be deposited on any land'. Waste is additionally deemed to have been deposited in an 'aggravated' manner under sub-paragraph (*a*) if the conditions laid out in paragraph (3) are fulfilled, namely:

the waste in question is poisonous, noxious or polluting; and
its presence on the land is likely to give rise to an environmental hazard;[62] and
it is deposited in such circumstances or for such a period that the disposer may reasonably be assumed to have abandoned it or to have brought it to the site to be disposed of.

Breach of paragraph (3) is punishable on summary conviction by imprisonment for up to six months and a fine of up to £5,000 (level 5 on the standard scale, Criminal Justice (NI) Order 1994) or on indictment by imprisonment for up to five years or a fine, or both.

It is clear from the judgment in *R. v. Metropolitan Stipendiary Magistrate, ex parte London Waste Regulation Authority*[63] that deposit offences based on the COPA model cover both permanent and temporary deposits. This case cleared up the difficulties created by the judgment in the earlier case of *Leigh Land Reclamation Ltd. v. Walsall MBC*,[64] in which waste was deemed to have been deposited only when it had reached its final resting place on a site.

Returning to the main offence, article 5(1) further provides that a person shall not 'use any equipment, or cause or knowingly permit any plant or equipment to be used, for the purpose of disposing of controlled waste or of dealing in a prescribed manner with controlled waste.'

The waste-related activities under article 5(1)(*b*) which require a licence are delineated by regulation 8 and Schedule 5 to the Waste Collection and Disposal Regulations (NI) 1992. These are:

---

62. 'Environmental hazard' is defined by art. 6(5) as arising if the waste has been deposited in such a manner or quantity (whether by itself or cumulatively with other deposits) as to subject persons or animals to a material risk of death, injury or impairment of health or as to threaten pollution of any water supply (this covers both ground and surface water). The fact that the waste may be in containers is not necessarily sufficient to exclude risks that would exist if the waste was loose. Risk is measured in relation to art. 6(5) under the terms of art. 6(6), which allows any precautionary measures taken by the depositor of the waste to be taken into account, together with the likelihood of the waste or containers being tampered with.
63. [1993] 3 All ER 113.
64. [1991] 191 ENDS report 37.

   (i) baling, compacting, incinerating, pulverising, sorting or storing waste;

  (ii) processing or holding waste at a site designated to receive waste which is to be disposed of elsewhere;

 (iii) waste-shredding businesses;

 (iv) treating waste by pyrolysis;

  (v) using waste to generate fuel;

 (vi) using waste to make compost;

 (vii) processing or treating waste oil or solvent for reuse; and

(viii) using untreated waste to generate electricity.

Acting contrary to the general prohibitions contained in article 5(1)(*a*) and (*b*) constitutes an offence unless the activities in question are carried out under licence. Contravention of article 5(1) is punishable on summary conviction by a fine of £5,000 (article 5(2)(*a*)) or on indictment to a fine and/or up to two years' imprisonment (article 5(2)(*b*)).

## Defences

Article 5(4) provides for defences for those charged with offences under article 5(1)(*a*) and (*b*), (2) and (3). It is a defence under article 5(4)(*a*) for the person to prove that:

 (i) he took care to inform himself (from those who could provide such information) whether the deposit would be in contravention of paragraph (1), and

(ii) he had no reason to suppose that he had been given false or misleading information about the legal status of the waste in question.

A second defence is provided by article 5(4)(*b*), namely, that the person was acting under the instructions of his employer and that he had no reason to suppose that the deposit was in contravention of paragraph (1).

The third defence, contained in article 5(4)(*c*), relates specifically to making, causing or permitting a deposit of waste in contravention of the conditions of the applicable waste disposal licence and is made out if the person can prove that he took all reasonable steps to ensure that the licence requirements were complied with.

The final defence (article 5(4)(*d*)) covers emergency situations, where actions which would otherwise constitute an offence are excused if carried out in order to avoid danger to the public and particulars are furnished (as soon as reasonably practicable) to the district council in whose area the incident occurred.

## The household waste exclusion

Article 6(2) expressly excludes household waste that is deposited, disposed of or otherwise dealt with in the curtilage of the dwelling by the owner (or by another with his permission) from the remit of the article 5 offences.

## The licensing system

### Exceptions: council sites and the 1978 Order

While district councils are responsible under the 1978 Order for the creation and implementation of waste disposal plans and for running the licensing regime, council-run disposal sites and activities are not subject to the licensing provisions of the Order (article 13(1)).

Councils are not, however, given an entirely free hand on their own sites; they are obliged by article 13(2) to ensure that the land is used in accordance with conditions contained in a council resolution (article 13(2)(*b*)) designed to prevent danger to public health and serious detriment to the amenities of the locality (article 13(2)(*a*)).

Before council land (or land the council intends to occupy) is put to use for dealing with waste, the council must prepare a statement of the conditions[65] it intends to specify in its resolution (under article 13(3)(*d*)) covering that site (article 13(3)(*a*)). Both the proposal and the statement must be submitted to the DoE(NI) Environment Service (article 13(3)(*c*)).

A district council's resolution under article 13 is in many ways similar in its function to a waste disposal licence. Like a licence, it may be varied (it may also be rescinded) by a subsequent council resolution (article 13(4)(*a*)).

If it appears to a council that the continuation of activities being carried out under a subsisting resolution represents a danger to public health or a serious threat of detriment to local amenities (and this cannot be avoided by modification), then the activities must be discontinued and the resolution rescinded (article 13(6)). The DoE(NI) may direct a council to discontinue activities it is carrying out under an article 13 resolution (paragraph (7)).

## Applications

Any person or firm may also wish to undertake commercial waste disposal activities,[66] but they may only legally do so under a licence issued pursuant to the 1978 Order. An application for a waste disposal licence must be made in writing in the prescribed form to the district council responsible for the area where the site is located (article 7(1)).

Licences may only be issued, according to article 7(2), if the site in question has (if required) planning permission and/or a consent under the Water Act (NI) 1972 (as amended). (Provision is made for regulations to be issued to allow parallel consent proceedings, allowing a waste disposal licence application to be considered while the above-mentioned consents are pending.)

If an application is received for land, plant or equipment that holds the relevant permissions under paragraph (2), the district council, under article 7(3), may only reject the licence application if it is satisfied that this is necessary for the purpose of preventing danger to public health. This restricted power to reject licence applications is designed to reflect the fact that other specialised regimes exist to deal with amenity and water pollution issues and that such matters are better left in the hands of these experts.

---

65. These 'conditions' are likely in effect to be similar to those contained in a waste disposal licence under art. 8 (art. 13(3)(*b*)).
66. District councils may also support commercial waste disposal ventures by the provision and maintenance of plant or equipment (art. 14(7)).

### Licence contents

Subject to the relevant provisions[67] of the Waste Collection and Disposal Regulations (NI) 1992, article 8(2) lists the general areas regarded as suitable to be covered by conditions that may be imposed by the district council, should it think fit. The conditions listed in article 8(2) include:

(i) provision for the duration of the licence;

(ii) requirements for supervision of the activities authorised by the licence-holder;

(iii) stipulating the kinds and quantities of waste that may be dealt with during the subsistence of the licence, the methods sanctioned for dealing with the waste, and requiring that proper records be kept;

(iv) precautions to be taken on the land covered by the licence;

(v) any steps necessary to facilitate compliance with planning conditions and with water pollution consents;

(vi) the operating hours for the site; and

(vii) works to be carried out concerning the land, plant or machinery in question as a precondition of the granting of the licence or as a condition of its continuation.

Regulation 9 and Schedule 6 (paragraphs 1–16) to the 1992 Regulations exempt certain types of waste from the need for a waste disposal licence under the 1978 Order, for example:

- excavated material from peat working (paragraph 4);
- material extracted from mineral exploration boreholes[68] (paragraph 5);
- deposits of vegetable matter and waste soils in recreational grounds, churchyards, etc. (paragraph 7); and
- temporary deposits of waste on the site of origin for disposal (paragraph 13).

As a general rule, a waste disposal licence will not be required for trivial deposit or for activities authorised under other specific statutory controls.

The exemptions contained in Schedule 6 will not apply where the presence of the waste on land is likely to give rise to an environmental hazard,[69] and special waste is treated more strictly than ordinary controlled waste.[70]

A licence-holder may be obliged to carry out works or take other action under a licence condition, whether or not he is entitled as of right to take the action required.

The council is allowed two months,[71] dating from receipt of the application, to reach a determination on the licence in question. If no licence is issued during this period and no notice is given that the application has been rejected, the application will be deemed to have been refused (article 8(5)).

---

67. Reg. 9 and Sch. 6.
68. If such boreholes are not being used for petroleum exploration and if they are authorised under art. 13 of the Planning (NI) Order 1991 (SI 1991/1220).
69. Reg. 9(2).
70. Only para. 14 applies to special waste where a licence will not be required if the waste in question has been only temporarily deposited pending final disposal and is either: (i) in liquid form and of not more than 23,000 litres in volume and stored in secure containers, or (ii) non-liquid waste, of up to 80 cubic metres in volume and stored in secure containers, or (iii) non-liquid waste, of up to 50 cubic metres in volume and stored in a secure place.
71. A longer period may be agreed in writing with the applicant (art. 8(5)).

## Modification of licences

Once a licence is in force it may be altered either on the initiative of the district council or on application by the licence-holder. If the council chooses to exercise its discretionary powers to modify a licence it may only do so to the extent that it regards the change as desirable. The council may only require the licence-holder to undertake reasonable expenditure. Changes must be notified to the licence-holder (article 9(1)(*a*)(i)), together with the time from which any changes will take effect (article 9(4)).

A district council may be obliged to exercise its powers to modify a licence by article 9(1)(*b*) in order to ensure that the activities carried out under it do not cause danger to public health or become a serious threat to the amenities of the locality, in line with the provisions of article 11(1)(*a*).

A licence-holder may request a modification in his licence under article 9(1)(*a*)(ii). If the council accepts the changes, the licence-holder must be notified of these and of the time from which they will be effective (article 9(4)).

## Revocation of licences

If it appears to a council that the continuation of activities being carried out under a subsisting licence would cause danger to public health or be so seriously detrimental to the amenities of the locality (article 9(3)(*a*)) that they ought not to be allowed to continue, and that the danger cannot be avoided by modification of the licence (article 9(3)(*b*)), it must revoke the licence. The licence-holder must be notified of such a determination and of the time from which it takes effect (article 9(4)).

## Transfer of licences

A licence-holder may, on giving notice to the district council, transfer it on the day he has specified to a person whose name and address are recorded in the notice (article 10(1)). The council at this stage has no control over who may take over the works and sites covered by the licence; article 10(1), however, goes on to provide the council with a limited control mechanism in respect of transfers, in that the licence in question will cease to have effect ten weeks[72] from the date on which the council received the original notice if the council informs the transferee[73] that it will not accept him as the new licence-holder.

## Relinquishment of licences

If councils have few control powers in respect of the transfer of licences under the 1978 Order, the situation with regard to the relinquishment of licences is worse. According to article 10(4), a licence-holder can relinquish the licence simply by unilaterally delivering it to the relevant council and giving notice that he no longer requires it. The council has no control over the condition of the site at the time of surrender. Given the high probability of environmental pollution, particularly through leachate entering soil and ground water and through the generation of

---

72. The transferee will be deemed to be the holder of the licence within the ten-week period by virtue of art. 10(2).
73. By notice, within eight weeks of the council's original receipt of the notice of transfer.

methane gas, the problems posed by a unilateral cessation of a site licence are potentially extremely serious.

## Supervision of licences

In addition to the administration of the licensing regime, district councils are charged with responsibility for supervising subsisting licences in order to ensure that the terms of a given licence are being complied with (article 11(1)(*b*)) and to protect public health and local amenity (article 11(1)(*b*)). To these ends, council employees are empowered (with the council's written permission) to enter land covered by a licence and carry out necessary works to deal with an emergency (paragraph (2)). Where the council incurs costs under paragraph (2) these may be recovered from the licence-holder (or, if it has been revoked, from its last holder) unless he can show either that there was in fact no emergency or that the expenditure incurred was unreasonable (article 11(3)).

If the council is satisfied that a licence condition is being breached it can, without prejudice to the right to institute legal proceedings in respect of the breach, take action under article 11(4) by serving a notice on the holder requiring compliance with the condition within a given time (paragraph (*a*)). If he fails to comply with this notice his licence may be revoked (paragraph (*b*)).

## Registers of waste disposal licences

District councils are obliged by article 8(4) to keep a register containing all prescribed details of all the current waste disposal licences it has issued. The register must be open to inspection by the public at the council's principal office. Inspection must be free of charge, and the register should be available at all reasonable hours. The public must be allowed to obtain copies of entries at a reasonable charge.

Councils are also required to keep records of resolutions passed under article 13 in respect of their own waste disposal sites in the register of waste disposal licences.

## Offences connected with the licence system

In addition to the key offences created by article 5 of the 1978 Order, which are connected with the deposit or disposal of waste without a waste disposal licence (see above), there are several other offences that may be committed in respect of waste. The principal offences are dealt with below.

## Giving false information in a licence application

It is an offence under article 7(4) to knowingly or recklessly make statements that are false in any material respect as part of a licence application. This offence on summary conviction incurs a fine of up to £5,000 (level 5 on the standard scale, Criminal Justic (NI) Order 1994) and on indictment up to two years' imprisonment or a fine, or both. The same liability will attach to giving false information in respect of an application for a licence modification (article 9(2)).

## Contravention of a licence condition

It is an offence under article 8(3) for a licence-holder, without reasonable excuse, to contravene any licence condition (unless it is exempted from this paragraph by article 8(1)). The offence incurs a fine of up to £5,000 (level 5 on the standard scale, Criminal Justice (NI) Order 1994) on summary conviction. Proceedings may only be brought by or with the consent of the Director of Public Prosecutions for Northern Ireland or by the district council that issued the licence.

## Interference with refuse tips, dustbins, etc.

It is an offence under article 34 of the 1978 Order to 'sort over' or otherwise disturb rubbish on rubbish tips and that contained in receptacles, as defined in article 15(9), unless such activity is authorised[74] by the appropriate district council. Contravention of this provision will render the offender liable on summary conviction to a fine of up to £1,000 (level 3 on the standard scale, Criminal Justice (NI) Order 1994).

## Appeals in respect of licences

The DoE(NI), specifically the Environment Service, is the appellate authority in matters relating to waste disposal licences under the 1978 Order. If the Environment Service deems an appeal aptly made, district councils are obliged to give effect to its decision.

The matters which may be subject to appeal are outlined in article 12(1). Rejected applications for licences (or for the modification of licences), the conditions specified in a licence (and modifications of such conditions) and revocation of a licence may all be appealed. Appeals may be instituted by applicants, licence-holders, or the last holder of a revoked licence (article 12(1)).

Appeals must generally[75] be made within six months[76] of the decision that forms the basis of the appeal or the date of a deemed rejection of an application under article 8(5) of the 1978 Order.

The district council is required to be notified of the appeal and the grounds on which it is made[77] in the form[78] provided for by Schedule 7 to the Waste Collection and Disposal Regulations (NI) 1992. Appeals must be forwarded to the DoE(NI), along with two copies of the supporting documents, as stated in regulation 10(3) of the 1992 Regulations, namely:

(i) for appeals against a refusal of the application or against conditions contained in a licence—the application and any relevant plans, particulars, etc.;

(ii) for appeals against conditions, revocations and refusal to modify—a copy of the licence;

(iii) any other relevant consent, determination or notice given by the council;

---

74. Special provision is made in art. 34(1)(*b*) for those whose job involves emptying waste receptacles.
75. The DoE(NI) has discretion in determining whether to extend the six-month period.
76. According to reg. 10 of the Waste Collection and Disposal Regulations (NI) 1992.
77. Reg. 10(4) of the 1992 Regulations.
78. Reg. 10(2) of the 1992 Regulations.

(iv)  any relevant[79] planning permission that is in force;
 (v)  relevant consents under the Water Act (NI) 1972; and
(vi)  any other correspondence or relevant documents.

Appeals relating to the modification of licence conditions and licence revocations will render the initial decision ineffective pending the outcome of the appeal process (article 12(2)), unless the initial decision is stated by the council to have been made[80] in order to prevent danger to public health. The appellant can argue that a statement that the site or the activities carried out on it posed a danger to health was unreasonable. If the Environment Service upholds such a claim and the original appeal is still pending, the original determination will be rendered ineffective, since it will be included under article 12(2). In addition, the appellant will be entitled to recover compensation from the council for any loss he has sustained because of the council's statement (article 12(3)(*b*)).

## Removal of waste deposited in breach of the licensing system

### *Action against occupiers*

In addition to bringing proceedings or taking informal action with respect to licence infringements, district councils are also empowered by the 1978 Order to deal with the problems created by the flouting of statutory controls on the ground. If controlled waste is deposited on any land within the council's area in contravention of article 5(1), the council may serve a notice on the occupier of the land in question requiring him either to remove the waste within a specified period[81] (article 16(1)(*a*)) or to take specified action to eliminate or reduce the consequences of the deposit (article 16(1)(*b*)), or both. The person served with a notice under article 16(1) then has twenty-one days during which he may appeal to a court of summary jurisdiction against the notice. The notice will be quashed if the court is satisfied:

 (i)  that the appellant did not deposit the waste (or cause or knowingly permit the deposit) on the land (article 16(2)(*a*));
(ii)  that the service of the notice was not authorised by paragraph (1); or
(iii)  that the notice is defective in some material respect.

The court may also modify the notice or dismiss the appeal.

An article 16(1) notice will (under article 16(3)) be suspended pending the outcome of an appeal.

Failure to comply with an article 16(1) notice will constitute an offence, resulting in a fine of up to £5,000 (level 5 on the standard scale, Criminal Justice (NI) Order 1994) on summary conviction. Continued non-compliance following conviction will constitute a further offence under paragraph (4) and will incur on summary conviction a fine of up to £1,000 for each day on which the person has failed to act following his fist conviction (paragraph (5)).[82] The law, therefore, may not be flouted with impunity.

In addition, non-compliance with an article 16(1) notice will justify the council that served it in taking the steps specified therein. The council may then recover

---

79.  This should relate to the site and the use of relevant land, plant, or equipment.
80.  Under either art. 9 or art. 11(*b*).
81.  This period may not be less than twenty-one days.
82.  Time will run under art. 15(5) until the district council exercises its powers under art. 15(4)(*b*).

reasonable costs that it has incurred from the person served with the original notice (article 16(4)(*b*)).

### Action in other circumstances

Councils are empowered by article 16(6)(*a*) to take 'emergency' action to remove waste deposited contrary to article 5(1) from land (or take other steps) to prevent danger to public health.[83] The council may also exercise its powers to remove waste from land in two additional cases, namely, where the land in question has no occupier (paragraph (*b*)) or where the occupier of the affected land did not make or knowingly permit the deposit to be made (paragraph (*c*)) (i.e. he has been the victim of 'fly-tipping'; see below).

Costs incurred by the council in removing waste under article 16(6)(*a*) may be recovered from the occupier of the land in question according to article 16(7)(*a*). In any event, costs may be recovered from any person who deposited the waste (or caused or knowingly permitted the deposit to be made),[84] although—particularly in the case of 'fly-tipping'—it is often impossible to trace such persons. Any unlawfully deposited waste removed by the council under article 16 becomes the property of the council and may be dealt with accordingly (article 16(8)).

## SECTION 2. HAZARDOUS AND TOXIC (SPECIAL) WASTE

As one would expect, special statutory arrangements are available for dealing with the particular problems associated with hazardous and toxic wastes. The DoE(NI) Environment Service is closely involved in authorising the movement of such wastes, which are subject to strict administrative rules and the object of 'cradle-to-grave' surveillance.

Special wastes have been the subject of several EC Directives, which have been partially complied with in Northern Ireland by the Pollution Control (Special Waste) Regulations (NI) 1981 and which will be further pursued by the provisions of the proposal for a Draft Waste and Contaminated Land Order 1996.

Waste falling under enhanced control is divided into two categories: 'special waste'[85] (defined with reference to its physical or chemical characteristics) and 'hazardous waste' (as defined in the EC Directive on the Transfrontier Shipment of Hazardous Waste). The latter category of waste is subject to the Transfrontier Shipment of Waste Regulations 1994,[86] which are applicable throughout the UK.[87]

---

83. A threat to the local environment as represented by the protection of amenity will not justify direct action by the council under art. 16(6).
84. Art. 16(7)(*b*).
85. This class of waste must be in a form or concentration that renders it dangerous to life in order to be subject to special control.
86. SI 1994/1137.
87. There are also special provisions dealing with the transport of radioactive waste in the UK-wide Transfrontier Shipment of Radioactive Waste Regulations 1993 (SI 1993/3031), which implement Directive 92/3/Euratom on the Supervision and Control of Shipments of Radioactive Waste between member states and into and out of the EC.

In Northern Ireland only something in the region of 20,000 tonnes of special waste is generated each year.[88] Most of this is dealt with locally, although approximately 1,500 tonnes is transported to Great Britain for disposal in high-temperature incinerator facilities not at present available in the Province.[89]

## The Pollution Control (Special Waste) Regulations (NI) 1981

### Definition of 'special waste'

The 1981 Regulations, which were issued under article 17 of the 1978 Order, deal with special waste which was defined in regulation 3 as waste which:

(i)   consists of or contains substances that are listed in Part I of Schedule 1[90] and for that reason either: (*a*) represent a danger to life (as defined by Part II of Schedule 1)[91] or (*b*) have a flashpoint of 21° Celsius or less[92], or

(ii)   is a medicinal product[93] available only on prescription.

### Power to make direction as to the disposal of special waste

The 1981 Regulations reserve (regulation 16) to the DoE(NI) the power to make directions as to waste disposal sites which are covered by waste disposal licences (regulation 7) and sites referred to in regulation 13 resolutions under the 1978 Order. These directions may require specific conditions to be fulfilled (including the making of payments) with respect to the disposal of specified waste on a given site (regulation 16(2)). The Department is, except in emergencies, obliged to give at least twenty-eight days' notice[94] of its intention to invoke these powers.

### Dealing with special waste: the consignment note system

Part II of the Regulations institutes a system of administrative control for special waste with a regime based on consignment notes. The consignment note system works by placing each of those concerned with the waste chain, from its creation to its disposal, under specific duties to furnish specified information concerning the waste.

### Duties of waste producers

All special waste is required at all times to be accompanied by several[95] copies of

---

88.  *DoE Environment Service Report,* 1991–93.
89.  Ibid.
90.  These include acids and alkalis, compounds of several metals, arsenic compounds, biocides, certain classes of hydrocarbons and inorganic compounds, most organic halogen compounds, pharmaceutical and veterinary compounds, etc.
91.  Waste is regarded as dangerous to life pursuant to para. 1. of Sch. 1, Part II, either if a single dose of 5 cubic centimetres (or less) would be likely to cause death or serious tissue damage if ingested by a child of 20 kg body weight or if exposure for fifteen minutes (or less) would be likely to cause serious damage to human tissue by inhalation, skin contact, or eye contact.
92.  Flashpoints are to be established by apparatus determined by BS 3900.
93.  As defined by s. 130 of the Medicines Act 1968.
94.  Reg. 16(3).
95.  At least six in most cases (reg. 5(1)), though fewer may be supplied if the producer has reasonable grounds to suppose that fewer than six copies will be needed (art. 5(2)).

a consignment note provided by the producer of the waste. One copy of the consignment note must be sent to the district council for the area where the waste is to be disposed of. Consignment notes are designed to create a 'paper trail' that allows the district council to trace each movement of the waste in question from its initial production to its final disposal.

Consignment notes must follow the form laid down in Schedule 2 to the Regulations. The producer of the waste must fill out Parts A (the producer's certificate) and B (the description of the waste), which describe the person[96] to whom the waste is being transferred and the destination to which it is to be taken, and the waste itself, respectively. The waste should be identified by:

- a general physical description;
- its relevant chemical and biological components (and their maximum concentrations);
- the quantity, together with the size, type and number of containers; and
- details of the process which created the waste.

A copy of the consignment note must be sent[97] to the relevant district council within a specified period (ranging from a minimum of three days to a maximum of one month[98]) before the waste referred to in the note is to be removed from its site of origin (regulation 5(3)).

In addition to providing information to the district council, producers are also placed under a responsibility (by regulation 5(5)) to ensure that those transporting waste from the site (carriers) where it was produced to disposal sites sign Part C of the consignment note (the carrier's collection certificate) and are apprised of the appropriate precautionary measures to be taken concerning the waste (Part D—the producer's collection certificate).

Producers must keep a copy of the partially completed consignment note for themselves and, if the waste is to be disposed of outside the area in which the producer's premises are located, must furnish a copy of the information in their possession to their own district council (regulation 5(6)). All other copies of the consignment note are to be passed on to the carrier of the waste (regulation 5(7)).

## Duties of carriers of special waste

Carriers[99] are required to ensure that the final part of the consignment note (Part E—the disposer's certificate) is completed by the staff on the disposal site and to retain a copy of the completed paperwork, transmitting the other copies to the disposer (regulation 6(1)).

## Duties of disposers of special waste

The disposer of special waste is required (by regulation 7(1)) to supply the

---

96. The consignee of the waste should be identified by name, address, and telephone number. This information is to be accompanied by an estimated date for collection of the waste.
97. Posting will suffice if within the ordinary course of post the note would arrive with the district council within the time limit (reg. 5(4)).
98. Saturdays, Sundays and public holidays are not included in this reckoning.
99. District councils are exempted from compliance with reg. 6 if they are collecting and disposing of waste in their own district (reg. 6(2)).

information specified in Part E (on three of the remaining copies) of the consignment note, namely:

- the number of the waste disposal licence he holds, together with the name of the issuing authority;
- the name and address of the waste disposal facility;
- the registration number of the carrier's vehicle in which the waste was delivered;
- the name of the carrier;
- the date and time of delivery; and
- confirmation of instructions given concerning where the waste delivered should be taken.

The disposer should retain one copy of the note, furnish a copy to the district council in whose area the waste was produced, and provide a copy for the carrier.[100]

### Duties of importers and exporters of special waste

Importers of special waste are required to fulfil the same duties as producers of waste, treating the waste as if it had been produced at the point of entry to Northern Ireland (regulation 8(1)). Exporters of waste from Northern Ireland are placed under the regulation 7 duties of waste disposers (regulation 8(2)).

### Special rules for regular consignments of special waste

District councils are given a discretionary power by regulation 10, on the application of a waste producer located in their area (under regulation 12(1)), to direct in writing[101] that copies of his consignment notices be furnished to them (and to district councils in whose area his waste is being disposed of) at intervals not exceeding twelve months, rather than for each individual consignment. Directions of this nature are designed to deal with frequent consignments of waste of a similar composition to the same site (regulation 10(2)). If disposal is to be carried out outside the area of the council in whose district the waste producer's premises are situated, consultation with and the second council's agreement to the regulation 10(1) direction are required.

Disputes between councils are to be determined by the DoE(NI) (regulation 11). If a producer's application for a regulation 10(1) direction is refused he may, within six weeks,[102] appeal to the DoE(NI) under regulation 12(1). The council is obliged to make those alterations to its decision that the DoE(NI) deems necessary to give effect to its decision.

If the council has failed to reach a decision on a regulation 10(1) application within two months of receipt, the application is deemed to have been refused (regulation 12(2)).

Granting a regulation 10(1) direction does not mean that the administrative controls applicable to special waste have been entirely relaxed, since producers are

---

100. District councils need not comply with reg. 7 requirements if the waste in question is collected and disposed of within their district (reg. 7(3)).
101. Such a direction may be revoked in writing (reg. 10(3)).
102. Or a longer period if the DoE(NI) chooses to allow it (reg. 12(3)).

then obliged to make available to the council, at three-monthly intervals, a forecast of waste to be disposed of under the direction originating on their site (regulation 13(1)). If the waste to be disposed of within the three-month period differs materially from that covered by the forecast, the producer is obliged to provide the council with a notice of amendment (regulation 13(2)).

### Registers and records

Producers of waste are obliged by regulation 14(1) to keep at each of their sites a register containing copies of all consignment notes concerning special waste produced on that site.

Carriers are obliged by regulation 14(2) to keep copies of all consignment notes transferred to them for disposal. Producers and carriers are obliged to keep these documents for at least two years from the date of removal of the waste from the site where it was produced (regulation 14(4)).

Disposers are obliged by regulation 14(3) to keep a register at each of their sites of all consignment notes relating to special waste disposal on that site (unless the district council is obliged to keep such a register in its area). Disposers are obliged to keep copies of consignment notes until their disposal licence is surrendered or revoked and then to forward the register to the district council in whose area the site is located (regulation 14(5)). The potentially indefinite length of this obligation reflects the need to be able to account for waste on a disposal site in the long term; the keeping of site records performs a similar function.

Regulation 15 requires those who deposit waste to keep a record of the location of each deposit. Like registers of consignment notes, site records must be kept until the disposal licence covering the site is surrendered or revoked and then forwarded to the relevant district council. The form of these records is stipulated by regulation 15(2) as comprising either a plan marked with a grid or a site plan with transparent overlays marking out deposits relative to the contours of the site. Deposits are generally[103] to be described with reference to the register of consignment notes kept under regulation 14 (regulation 15(3)).

### Offences

The district council in whose area the waste is produced or imported is obliged to supervise the keeping of adequate records of consignment notes to ensure that this aspect of the regulations is complied with (regulation 18). Producers, carriers or disposers who fail to comply with any of the provisions of the Special Waste Regulations[104] will be liable on summary conviction to a fine of up to £5,000 (level 5 on the standard scale, Criminal Justice (NI) Order 1994) or on indictment to a fine or up to two years' imprisonment, or to both (regulation 17(1)).

### Defences

It is a defence to any charge under the 1981 Regulations for the defendant to prove

---

103. Waste disposed of by pipelines on site at a factory or other premises and waste disposed of by councils within their own districts are excluded from the operation of reg. 15(3).
104. Under reg. 16, where a fine on summary conviction will also be for £5,000, level 5 on the standard scale, Criminal Justice (NI) Order 1994—fines in relation to reg. 16 were originally set at a lower rate.

that he took all reasonable precautions and exercised all due diligence to avoid the commission of the offence by himself or by anyone under his control (regulation 17(3)).

For offences with respect to consignment notes under regulations 5, 6 or 7, it is a defence (under regulation 17(4)) for the person charged to prove that he was not, because of an emergency, reasonably able to comply with the regulations and that he took all reasonable steps to ensure that the necessary documents were completed and forwarded to the relevant parties as soon as practicable in the circumstances.

Where an offence is committed under the 1981 regulations because of the act or omission of another, action may be taken against the person who committed the offence, whether or not the other person's actions are the subject of proceedings (regulation 15(5)).

## Part III New Waste Initiatives

This year is set to see a revolution in the law dealing with waste as it applies to Northern Ireland. The key provisions of the proposal for a Draft Waste and Contaminated Land Order, which will be examined below, form the central thrust of a wider legislative initiative on waste. Another important element in the Government's new waste strategy involves fiscal change in the form of what is colloquially known as the 'landfill tax'. This tax will be instituted by the Finance Act 1996. Its purpose is to begin the process of making the economic cost of waste disposal more accurately reflect the environmental costs of landfilling. The tax will be levied at a differential rate; inert wastes (which by their nature have fewest environmental implications) will be taxed at a rate of £2.00/tonne, other wastes will face a tax fee of £7.00/tonne. It seems likely that the provisions of the Finance Act as they relate to landfill represent only the beginning of fiscal controls being applied to waste disposal issues.

The proposal for a Draft Waste and Contaminated Land (NI) Order, which is due to come into force, after a lengthy gestation period, in 1996, will substantially repeal and replace the existing law dealing with waste in Northern Ireland. Key elements of reform include an overhaul of the waste disposal licensing system, new controls over those who may hold a waste management licence, the introduction of a duty of care (and a supporting code of practice) applicable to each person involved in the waste stream, licensing controls for waste carriers, and provisions dealing with the vexed question of contaminated land.

### Enhanced waste licensing provisions

#### New regulators

While the basic licensing system remains similar to that under the 1978 Order, the whole climate within which the regime operates will be altered by the fact that it will be subject to the control of the planned Environment and Heritage Service Waste Inspectorate. The licensing system will thus be separated from operational waste disposal activities, with consequent gains in independence and objectivity.

## Waste management licences

Part I of the 1996 proposal for a Draft Order updates licensing provisions under the 1978 Order by replacing the archaic waste disposal licence with new, broader waste management licences. The new licences will cover not only the disposal of waste but also the treatment and keeping of waste,[105] so ending any surviving confusion generated by the former, more limited provision. Licensing provisions are expressly extended to cover the treatment, keeping and disposal of waste by mobile plant as well as on fixed sites.[106]

## A broader definition of waste

The definition of waste is expanded considerably by the detailed provisions of Schedule 1 to the proposal for a Draft Order. Waste will be divided into some fourteen specific and two 'catch-all' categories. Worn-out, adulterated, expired, contaminated, banned and substandard products, substances, materials and residues are all added to the customary class of discarded items by the new definition. The previous exceptions applicable to mine, quarry and agricultural waste under the 1978 Order will be removed; clause 32 of the proposal for a Draft Order empowers the Department to make regulations to cover these classes of waste. This provision ensures that a new, more comprehensive approach to waste will be possible in the future.

## Wider consultation

Additional arrangements are made in the proposal for a Draft Order to provide for greater consultation in respect of licence applications (clause 10) and certain licence variations (clause 14).

## The power to suspend licences

The range of control options for dealing with licence infringements which were created by the 1978 Order have been enhanced by an additional power under clause 13 to suspend licences if the holder ceases to be a 'fit and proper person' to hold a licence. A licence may also be suspended if the continuation of licensed activities would cause pollution, harm to human health, or serious detriment to the amenities of the locality.

## Surrender of licences

Licences under clause 14 of the 1996 proposal for a Draft Order may only be surrendered if the DoE(NI) accepts the surrender; an application to surrender the licence, supported by evidence, must be made to the Department before surrender can be accepted. The DoE(NI) is then under an obligation to inspect the land to which the licence relates before it reaches a decision on the application. If the Department is of the opinion that the land is unlikely to cause pollution or harm to human health it is obliged to accept the surrender; if it is not satisfied that this is the case, it must refuse the proposed surrender. The new provisions represent a considerable improvement on the previous law in this regard, the surrender of a licence being tightly controlled rather than unilateral.

---

105. Clause 7(1).
106. Clause 7(2).

### Transfer of licences

The 1996 proposal for a Draft Order also makes new provision for dealing with the transfer of licences. This will in future only be accomplished (under clause 15) on the acceptance of a joint application by the transferor and the proposed transferee to the Department. The transferee must fulfil the 'fit and proper person' requirement if a transfer application is to be acceptable.

### A wider primary waste disposal offence

Clause 5 of the proposal for a Draft Order outlines the primary offences concerning waste. Liability can be imposed on the person on three alternative grounds:

(i)   the depositing (or knowingly causing or permitting the deposit) of controlled waste in or on any land unless in accordance with the conditions of a waste management licence applicable to the site;

(ii)  the treating, keeping or disposal of controlled waste (or causing or knowingly permitting any of these activities) in or on any land, or by using mobile plant, unless the activities in question are covered by a waste management licence; or

(iii) the treating, keeping or disposal of controlled waste in a manner likely to cause pollution of the environment or harm to the human environment.

The new offences in the proposal for a Draft Order, in addition to widening the classes of activity that incur liability, also introduce for the first time in Northern Ireland waste disposal law, the idea that damage to the environment by itself can form the basis of liability.

The exception of household waste from the article 5(1) offence that exists in the 1978 Order is to be retained by its successor.

### 'Fit and proper persons'

The DoE(NI) will only be able, under clause 4 of the 1996 proposal for a Draft Order, to grant waste management licences (or allow authorised activities to continue) to those who qualify as 'fit and proper persons' for this purpose. A person's fitness to hold a waste management licence is to be judged by reference to the carrying on of the activities that are to be authorised and by his ability to comply with licence requirements.[107]

Factors which will militate against a person qualifying as a 'fit and proper person' are outlined in clause 4(3). These are:

(i)   a conviction (of the person in question or any other relevant person[108]) for a prescribed offence;[109]

(ii)  the management of (projected or subsisting) activities by a person who is not technically competent to do so;[110] or

---

107. Clause 4(2).
108. Under para. (6) this can include an employee acting in the course of his employment, a business partner, etc.
109. The Department is given the discretion by clause 4(4) to treat an individual as a 'fit and proper person' even if para. (3)(*a*) is applicable to him.
110. The Department is given the power to make regulations setting out the requirements of technical competence by para. (5).

(iii)  the failure or inability of the person holding (or to hold) the licence to make adequate financial provision to discharge licence obligations.

The 'fit and proper person' provision is designed to ensure that the waste disposal industry becomes more 'professional' in terms of the technical skills used in waste disposal and more financially sound—a particularly important provision given the question of liability for contamination caused by closed landfill sites.

## The new duty of care

The 1996 proposal for a Draft Order, following the lead of section 34 of the Environmental Protection Act 1990, will introduce a new duty of care, which is to be incumbent on all participants in the waste chain. The duty of care and the code of practice which will support it aim to ensure that waste is passed into proper hands and that it becomes the legal responsibility of each person who handles it, from its generation until its final disposal.

The duty of care is contained in clause 6 of the proposal for a Draft Order and is applicable (though not in the case of household waste: paragraph (2)) to producers, importers, carriers, brokers, and those who keep, treat, dispose of or otherwise exercise control over waste.

The duty requires members of each of these classes, as far as is reasonable in their capacity in the circumstances, to:

(i)  prevent others from committing an offence under article 5;
(ii)  prevent waste from escaping from their control or from that of any other person; and
(iii)  when waste is transferred, to ensure: (i) that it is transferred only to authorised persons (including carriers) and (ii) that transfers are accompanied by a written description that is adequate to enable those further along the waste chain to fulfil their duties under article 5 and to prevent waste from escaping.

The duty of care is designed to ensure that each link in the waste chain is forged in a responsible matter; the link to those further down the chain is based on ensuring that the person cannot absolve himself of his legal obligations under the proposal for a Draft Order by simply passing the waste to someone else, even a 'cowboy' operator. Fulfilling the duty of care will require those who are part of the waste chain to check the credentials of those with whom they are dealing as well as the documents and the packaging of the waste itself.

## Licences for waste carriers

The 1996 proposal for a Draft Order includes provisions (which will replicate those contained in the Control of Pollution (Amendment) Act 1989) for securing the registration of waste carriers. Under clause 39 it is an offence to transport controlled waste without a valid DoE(NI) registration. The Department will be empowered by clause 40 to make regulations providing both for the registration of carriers and to ensure the keeping of registers of information concerning carriers. Carriers must, under clause 43, be able to show valid authority to carry waste when stopped by constables or officers authorised by the Department.

The Department is to be given rather draconian powers under clause 44 to seize and destroy vehicles used for illegal waste disposal. These powers are designed, on a general level, to ensure that the carriage of waste is subject to the same level of control as other aspects of the waste chain and, on a specific level, to prevent the 'fly-tipping' of waste by 'cowboy' carriers.

## Contaminated land

An additional issue tackled by the 1996 proposal for a Draft Order, and one that is often closely related to waste issues,[111] is that of contaminated land. The question of legal liability for contaminated land has become a particularly vexed one in the UK in the last few years. Because of the substantial time lag between the law relating to waste in Great Britain and that in Northern Ireland, the first, seriously flawed, attempt to deal with contaminated land espoused by section 143 of the Environmental Protection Act 1990 has never been implemented in the Province.

The approach taken so disastrously by section 143 attempted to identify 'land which may have been subjected to contaminative use' (rather than land which was actually contaminated) by desk based survey.[112] The implications of section 143 registers, had they been implemented, would have been disastrous for the property market, causing widespread blight on brown-field sites. Attempts to amend the registers proved abortive, and in the end they were abandoned and replaced by the provisions of the Environment Act 1995 that are replicated in the 1996 proposal for a Draft Order.

Part III of the proposal for a Draft Order defines contaminated land (in clause 49) as land in such a condition (because of substances in or under it) that:

(i)   significant harm is being caused or there is a significant possibility of such harm being caused, or

(ii)  pollution of waterways or underground strata is being, or is likely to be, caused.

Contaminated land is in most cases to be the responsibility of district councils, though the DoE(NI) is given responsibility for 'special sites' designated under clause 51 or 52 of the proposal for a Draft Order.

Councils are required by clause 50 to inspect their area for contaminated and special sites (clause 51).[113] When such a site is identified the council is required to notify the DoE(NI), the owner of the land, the occupier of the land and others whom it deems 'appropriate' of this fact. The enforcing authority is required to ensure that a remediation notice is served in respect of contaminated sites, specifying what action is to be taken and the time for taking the required steps (clause 53).[114] An appeals mechanism against remediation notices is provided for by clause 58. A range of offences involving non-compliance with remediation notices is created by clause 59.

Enforcing authorities are empowered to carry out remediation themselves in order, among other things, to prevent imminent danger of serious harm or

---

111. Leachate from waste disposal sites is one major (though by no means the only) cause of contamination of both soil and ground water.

112. This strategy aimed to avoid the prohibitively expensive full scientific survey that would have been necessary to identify land which had actually been contaminated.

113. The Department can also designate special sites under clause 51(4); if it does so it must inform the district council in question.

114. This power is, however, subject to limitations under clause 56.

pollution of waterways or underground strata. The costs of such actions are recoverable under the terms of clause 61.

Clause 57 provides for liability in respect of contaminating substances that escape to other land; those who cause or knowingly permit substances to be in or on land are also taken to have caused or knowingly permitted any escape which occurs.

Registers[115] must be kept by enforcing authorities containing the following categories of information:

- details of remediation notices, appeals, and other relevant remediation information;
- details of appeals against charging notices served by the authority;
- details of special site designations, appeals against such designations, and notices terminating such designations;
- notifications of remediation notices, etc.;
- convictions under clause 59; and
- other matters prescribed by regulations under the proposal for a Draft Order.

The new contaminated land regime is much more sophisticated but also a good deal more ambitious and onerous than that envisaged in the 1990 Act. The problem of contaminated land is one that has reached legal maturity—admittedly of necessity—in a comparatively short time; we must hope that the more reasoned approach adopted in the 1996 proposal for a Draft Order will avoid the pitfalls encountered by the 1990 Act.

---

115. Registers are subject to certain exclusions for reasons of national security (clause 64) and commercial confidentiality (clause 65).

# CHAPTER SEVEN

# Nature Conservation

## Introduction

In recent decades the international community has witnessed dramatic losses in several species of wildlife and a continued reduction in natural and semi-natural habitats. The preservation of biological diversity and the maintenance of a balanced ecosystem have consequently emerged as important dimensions of environmental regulation at national, EC and international levels. Although Northern Ireland has not sustained the degree of damage experienced during the past half-century in Great Britain, certain habitat types, particularly peatlands, have been considerably reduced; there have also been dramatic losses in certain species, most notably the corncrake.

The legislative framework currently governing nature conservation in Northern Ireland essentially mirrors that operating in Great Britain; however, not only has the legislation been introduced into Northern Ireland very slowly, but the Province, despite its small size, has also lagged many years behind Great Britain in the implementation of these provisions.

It should be noted at the outset that while the issue of nature conservation is closely related to that of countryside protection, the present chapter will focus exclusively on the protection afforded to habitats and individual wildlife species; the 'human use' dimensions of countryside protection—concerning matters of landscape protection, amenity, and public access—are discussed separately in chapter 8.

As in Great Britain, habitats and species are protected in Northern Ireland primarily by statute. However, unlike the legislation governing countryside protection, which is almost entirely national in origin, the legislative framework governing nature conservation in Northern Ireland is driven very much by standards adopted at EC and international level. Two EC Directives have been particularly influential in this context, namely, Directive 79/409/EEC on the Conservation of Wild Birds[1] and Directive 92/43/EEC on the Conservation of Natural Habitats and of Wild Fauna and Flora.[2] These Directives have been given full legal effect in Northern Ireland by the combined operation of the three principal pieces of legislation currently governing nature conservation in Northern Ireland, namely, the Wildlife (NI) Order 1985,[3] as amended, the Nature

---

1. OJ L103, 25 Apr. 1979
2. OJ L206/7, 21 May 1992.
3. SI 1985/171. For further reading on the debates surrounding the adoption of this Order see NIA 131-I 1984, *Northern Ireland Assembly Report on the Proposal for a Draft Wildlife (NI) Order 1983*, London: HMSO, and NIA 131 and 132-II 1984, *Northern Ireland Assembly Report on the Proposals for a Draft Wildlife (NI) Order and a Draft Nature Conservation and Amenity Lands (NI) Order*, vol. II, London: HMSO.

Conservation and Amenity Lands (NI) Order 1985,[4] as amended, and the Conservation (Natural Habitats etc.) Regulations (NI) 1995.[5] In addition, these provisions give effect to the requirements of various international conventions on nature conservation to which the UK is a party, either as a member of the EC or as an individual state.

Northern Ireland's nature conservation legislation operates to protect wildlife and habitats in two principal ways; firstly, by affording special protection to the best examples of native habitat types, and secondly, by affording additional protection to threatened or vulnerable native species of wild animals and plants. This dual approach is necessary because many species of wildlife exist outside the boundaries of specially protected areas, with the result that additional conservation measures are necessary in order to protect certain species. The awarding of grants and the provision of incentives are also employed in Northern Ireland as a means of supporting and encouraging nature conservation. In this regard the DoE(NI) is empowered to award grants to individuals and approved bodies (such as district councils, the National Trust, and the RSPB) towards the costs of purchasing sites of high conservation value or to assist with the cost of conservation projects. There is also a growing network of grant schemes and incentives designed to encourage agricultural and forestry practices which are conducive to nature conservation. (While the DoE(NI)'s powers to award grants for the purposes of nature conservation to individuals and approved bodies will be discussed in this chapter, grants and incentives which relate to agricultural and forestry practices will be discussed separately in chapter 8.)

The DoE(NI) is responsible for the formulation of nature conservation policy in Northern Ireland and for the administration and enforcement of legislation operating in this area. In practice, the Countryside and Wildlife Branch within the Department's Environment Service exercises this function. It is advised by the Council for Nature Conservation and the Countryside (CNCC), which was established as the Department's statutory adviser in relation to conservation and countryside protection in 1989. It should be noted that the CNCC was established in response to the recommendations of the Balfour Report, *A New Look at the Northern Ireland Countryside* (1984), which called for wide-ranging improvements in the structure and organisation of countryside and nature conservation in Northern Ireland, and in particular for a stronger and more independent voice in this context. However, the House of Commons Environment Committee, in its First Report, *Environmental Issues in Northern Ireland*, voiced its concern that the level of staffing within the CNCC would not enable it to meet its objectives and therefore to meet the recommendations of the Balfour Report. It is also important to note the conclusions reached by Dr Kay Milton in *Our Countryside Our Concern* 1990 to the effect that the Balfour recommendations have not become a reality and that serious thought should be given to the establishment of an independent environment agency in Northern Ireland. This issue is discussed in more detail in chapter 2.

---

4. SI 1985/170. For further reading on the debates surrounding the adoption of this Order see *Northern Ireland Assembly Report on the Proposal for a Draft Nature Conservation and Amenity Lands (NI) Order 1983*, and NIA 131 and 132-II, 1984.
5. SR No. 380

This chapter is divided into three Parts.

Part I addresses the protection afforded to individual wildlife species in Northern Ireland. For the sake of clarity, Part I is further divided in two sections. Section 1 provides an overview of the legislative framework governing species protection in Northern Ireland. In this regard section 1 will provide an overview of the species requirements laid down at Community level and then an overview of the national measures which implement their terms in Northern Ireland. In addition, section 1 provides an overview of the role of the DoE(NI) and the CNCC in the enforcement of these provisions and also an overview of other species protection standards adopted by the EC which are binding on the UK as a whole. Section 2 then provides a detailed account of the principal legislative provisions governing species protection in Northern Ireland.

Part II addresses the protection afforded to habitats in Northern Ireland. Once again, for the sake of clarity, Part II is further divided into two sections. Section 1 provides an overview and then a detailed account of the national provisions currently governing habitat protection in Northern Ireland. Section 2 provides an overview of the EC standards concerning habitat protection and then a detailed account of the national measures which implement their provisions in Northern Ireland.

Part III addresses the international dimension of nature conservation. Because the majority of international conventions concerning nature conservation address both individual species protection and the protection of habitats, for the sake of clarity those international conventions concerning nature conservation to which the UK is a party will be addressed together in Part III.

## *PART I* PROTECTION OF INDIVIDUAL SPECIES

As in Great Britain, individual species of wild animals and plants in Northern Ireland are protected primarily by statute. Although the common law offers wildlife some protection via the exercise of property rights, it is a very limited form of protection and is essentially 'unsympathetic' to wildlife.[6] The principal national measures governing wildlife protection[7] in Northern Ireland are the Wildlife (NI) Order 1985,[8] as amended by the Wildlife (Amendment) (NI) Order 1995,[9] and the Conservation (Natural Habitats etc.) Regulations (NI) 1995.[10] The

---

6. Ball and Bell, *Environmental Law,* 3rd ed., London: Blackstone Press, 1995, pp 473–4.

7. There are numerous pieces of legislation relating to hunted species, for example game-birds, rabbits, and fish. However, as the protection of the individual animal in question is incidental to such legislation, it is not addressed in this book. Similarly, those provisions concerning animal welfare are beyond the scope of this book.

8. SI 1985/171. The Wildlife (NI) Order 1985 came into force on 15 Apr. 1985 under art. 2 of the Wildlife (1985 Order) (Commencement) Order (NI) 1985 (SI 1985/82 (c. 3)). The Wildlife (NI) Order 1985 repeals and replaces the Wild Birds Protection Acts (NI) 1931 (c. 14), 1950 (c. 26), and 1968 (c. 5), and the Grey Seals Protection Act (NI) 1933 (c. 11).

9. SI 1995/761. The Wildlife (1995 Order) (Commencement) Order (NI) 1995 (SR No. 322) governs the coming into force of the 1995 Amendment Order. Art. 3 came into force on 15 Aug. 1995, while art. 4 came into force on 15 Sep. 1995. The amendments made are addressed in Part I, section 2 of this chapter.

10. SR No. 380. These Regulations were enacted on 5 Oct. 1995 and came into force on 13 Nov. 1995.

Wildlife (NI) Order 1985 (hereafter referred to as the WO) was designed to implement the Berne Convention on the Conservation of European Wildlife and Natural Habitats (outlined in Part III of this chapter) and also implements the species requirements of Directive 79/409/EEC (the 'Wild Birds Directive'). Part III of the Conservation (Natural Habitats etc.) Regulations (NI) 1995 implements the species provisions of Directive 92/43/EEC ('the Habitats Directive').

## SECTION 1. THE NATIONAL AND EC DIMENSIONS: AN OVERVIEW

This section provides an overview of the legislative framework governing species protection in Northern Ireland and the role of the DoE(NI) in the enforcement of their provisions. For the sake of clarity the overview will be presented in the following order: (i) the species provisions of the Wild Birds Directive, (ii) the provisions of the WO which implement the species requirements of the Wild Birds Directive in Northern Ireland, (iii) the species provisions of the Habitats Directive, and (iv) Parts III and V of the Conservation (Natural Habitats etc.) Regulations (NI) 1995, which implement the species requirements of the Habitats Directive in Northern Ireland. In addition, this section provides an overview of other species standards adopted by the EC which are binding on the UK as a whole. Part I, section 2 then goes on to provide a detailed account of the WO and the Conservation (Natural Habitats etc.) Regulations (NI) 1995.

### The Wild Birds Directive

Directive 79/409/EEC represents the first major conservation initiative developed by the Community itself and gives effect to the terms of the Berne Convention (outlined in Part III of this chapter). The Directive was adopted in 1979 in response to public concern about the killing of migratory birds common in southern Europe and northern Africa. It establishes a system of protection for migratory wild birds and their habitats; however, it also imposes a general duty on member states to maintain the population of all 'species of naturally occurring birds in the wild state' within their countries 'at a level which corresponds in particular to ecological, scientific and cultural requirements, while taking account of economic and recreational requirements.' Member states are required to preserve, maintain or re-establish a sufficient diversity and area of habitats to ensure that the population of all such species is maintained. Subject to certain exceptions, they are required to prohibit the deliberate killing or capture of the species, the deliberate destruction of or damage to nests and eggs, the taking of eggs in the wild, deliberate disturbance during breeding and rearing, and the keeping of birds whose hunting and capture is prohibited. The Directive also controls the hunting and sale of wild birds.

Article 4 obliges member states to take special measures to conserve the habitat of two categories of birds, namely, particularly vulnerable or rare species and regularly occurring migratory species. In this regard Article 4 requires member states to designate the most suitable areas for these species as 'special protection areas' (SPAs), the objective being to protect the populations of these species by establishing a coherent network of protected habitats throughout the EC. The requirements laid down in the Directive concerning SPAs will be discussed in more detail in Part II, section 2 of this chapter in the context of habitat protection in Northern Ireland.

The species provisions of the Wild Birds Directive are implemented in Northern Ireland by the Wildlife (NI) Order 1985, as amended, while the habitat protection dimension of the Directive is implemented by the Nature Conservation and Amenity Lands (NI) Order 1985[11] (NCALO), as amended. An overview of the WO and the DoE(NI)'s role in the enforcement of the WO is provided below, while Part I, section 2 of this chapter contains a detailed explanation of the WO. The provisions of the NCALO are discussed in detail in Part II, section 1 of this chapter. It should also be noted that SPAs designated under the Wild Birds Directive now form part of the network of 'European sites' established by the Habitats Directive known as 'Natura 2000'. The Conservation (Natural Habitats etc.) Regulations (NI) 1995 implement the requirements of the Habitats Directive in Northern Ireland, and therefore these Regulations govern the protection and management of SPAs as part of Natura 2000. The requirements of the Habitats Directive and the Habitats Regulations in relation to habitat protection in Northern Ireland are addressed in Part II, section 2 of this chapter.

The Wild Birds Directive has generated a considerable body of case law from the European Court of Justice, the great majority of which has arisen from enforcement actions taken by the Commission under Article 169 of the EC Treaty against member states for non-compliance with the terms of the Directive.[12] Thus far, the European Court of Justice has held Germany, Ireland, France, Italy, Belgium and the Netherlands to be in breach of their obligations under the Directive. The most important decisions delivered by the European Court of Justice concerning the interpretation of the terms of the Directive itself were handed down in 1991 in Case C-57/89 *Commission v. Federal Republic of Germany*[13] and in 1993 in Case C-355/90 *Commission v. Spain*.[14] Both decisions concern the extent of the obligation imposed on member states to designate SPAs under the Wild Birds Directive and are discussed in Part II, section 2 of this chapter.

Finally, it should be noted that member states are required to submit a report to the Commission every three years on the implementation of the Wild Birds Directive within their own jurisdictions. The Commission is then required to produce a composite report. Member states are given an opportunity to verify that part of the draft report which relates to them; however, while member states are issued with a final version of the report, it is unclear as to whether this report is also available for public consultation.

---

11. SI 1985/170.
12. Case 236/85 *Commission v. Netherlands* [1987] ECR 3989; Case 247/85 *Commission v. Belgium* [1987] ECR 3029; Case 252/85 *Commission v. France* [1988] ECR 2243; Case 262/85 *Commission v. Italy* [1987] ECR 3073; Case 412/85 *Commission v. Germany* [1987] ECR 3503; Case 288/88 *Commission v. Germany* [1990] ECR I-2721. For information on the state of implementation of the Wild Birds Directive see H. Muntingh, 'Report on the implementation of the Directive on the conservation of wild birds in the EC', European Parliament Session Document A 2-0181/88. See also, A.M. Dodd, and D.E. Pritchard, (1993) *RSPB Planscape Northern Ireland: A Study of Development Plans in Northern Ireland*, RSPB, Sandy, Bedfordshire.
13. [1991] I-ECR 883.
14. [1993] Water Law 209.

## The Wildlife (NI) Order 1985

The WO creates blanket criminal offences for interfering with threatened native species of wild animals and plants, which are then followed by lists of exemptions and defences for permitted activities, many of which require a licence from the DoE(NI). Articles 4–9 of the WO set out the protection afforded to wild and captive birds, articles 10–13 set out the protection afforded to wild animals, while article 14 deals with the protection of wild plants. Article 15 governs the introduction of non-native wildlife species into Northern Ireland. Articles 19–23 control the killing and taking of deer and the sale and purchase of venison. Article 18 governs the DoE(NI)'s power to grant licences for the purpose of permitting activities in relation to wildlife that would otherwise be unlawful under the WO. Articles 16 and 17 empower the Department to declare wildlife refuges for the protection of some or all of the wildlife contained therein.

The greatest level of protection under the WO is accorded to wild birds. Unlike other forms of wildlife, wild birds are 'reverse-listed', in that the Order will apply to any bird that is 'ordinarily resident in or is a visitor to Northern Ireland in a wild state,' unless it is specifically exempted. Other forms of wildlife are only protected if they are specifically listed in the Schedules to the Order. The special protection afforded to wild birds is in part a result of the traditional influence exerted by voluntary bodies, notably the RSPB, throughout the UK; however, more recently it is a consequence of the standards set down in the Wild Birds Directive.

Thus far the WO protects all species of whales, dolphins, and porpoises, all species of bat, six other mammals, one species of reptile, one amphibian, and seven invertebrates, in addition to several species of plants. Regulations 33–41 and 67–70 of the Conservation (Natural Habitats etc.) Regulations (NI) 1995 set down slightly different and in some instances more stringent protections for those wildlife species protected by the Habitats Directive. These species are known as 'European protected species'; the relevant species are listed in the Schedules to the Regulations and do not include birds. Most of Northern Ireland's European protected species are also protected under the WO and therefore are subject to overlapping protection. This feature of overlapping national and EC protection is also a feature of habitat conservation, where many sites are protected under national and European provisions and, on occasion, by international standards also. However, it is important to note, that nothing in the provisions of Part III of the Conservation (Natural Habitats etc.) Regulations (NI) 1995 concerning animals or plants of a European protected species will be construed as excluding the application of the provisions of the Wildlife (NI) Order 1985, as amended (regulation 70).

The WO imposes a statutory duty on the DoE(NI) to protect those species of wildlife which have been listed in the Order. In practice, the Countryside and Wildlife Branch of the DoE(NI)'s Environment Service carries out this function. However, for the sake of brevity they will be referred to as the DoE(NI) throughout. The Wildlife Inspector oversees the implementation of the WO, controls by licence how certain species of wildlife may be caught or killed, regulates their sale, and also provides information to the public about the protection of rare species in Northern Ireland.

One of the most important powers conferred on the DoE(NI) in this context is that conferred by article 28 to vary the schedules to the WO. This power enables the DoE(NI) to ensure that the WO continues to respond to changes in Northern Ireland's wildlife population. In effect, the protection afforded by the WO can be extended to species which become vulnerable, while other species, that are no longer in danger, can be removed from its ambit. The effective monitoring of wildlife populations is, however, dependent on the existence of good biological records; the *Environment Service Corporate Plan* 1994–97, and the *Environment Service Reports* 1991–93 and 1993–95, outline the DoE(NI)'s recent work to ensure the efficient recording and dissemination of species information in Northern Ireland. It should be noted that while the DoE(NI)'s powers under article 28 have not been used thus far, the Department plans to review the schedules to the WO in the near future.

The CNCC now replaces the Committee for Nature Conservation as the statutory advisory body to the DoE(NI) under the WO. The CNCC was established under article 3 of the Nature Conservation and Amenity Lands (Amendment) (NI) Order 1989,[15] article 5 of which abolished its predecessor. The CNCC has the power to make representations to the DoE(NI) for the amendment of any of the schedules to the WO. However, the Department retains a discretion to decide whether or not to amend (article 28). The DoE(NI) is obliged under article 29(3) to consult the CNCC before making any order under the WO, including the declaration of wildlife refuges (discussed in Part I, section 2, page 323 of this chapter). In addition, the DoE(NI) is obliged to give any district council or any affected person an opportunity to submit objections or representations concerning the subject matter of a proposed order under the WO (article 29(3)(*b*)). Article 29(4) also obliges the DoE(NI) to 'give consideration' to any proposal submitted by a district council for the adoption of an order under the WO where the proposed order affects an area within that council's district. If the DoE(NI) thinks fit it may also cause a public inquiry to be held to examine the content of a proposed order under the WO (article 29(3)(*c*)).

Articles 25–7 of the WO set out police powers of entry, search, seizure and arrest for the purpose of enforcing the terms of the WO, the time limits within which summary proceedings must be brought under the WO, the conferring of jurisdiction under the WO, and the court's power to order the forfeiture of the wild animal or bird in respect of which the offence was committed and any vehicle, animal, weapon or other thing that was used to commit the offence.

**The Habitats Directive**

The Habitats Directive was adopted in May 1992 after years of intense debate and represents the most important conservation measure adopted thus far at Community level. Article 2 describes the objective of the Habitats Directive as being 'to contribute towards ensuring bio-diversity through the conservation of

---

15. SI 1989/492. For further reading on the reasons for the establishment of the CNCC and the success of its operation to date see: *A New Look at the Northern Ireland Countryside* (the Balfour Report); NIA 191 1985, *Northern Ireland Assembly Report on the Balfour Proposals: a New Look at the Northern Ireland Countryside,* London: HMSO; *House of Commons Environment Committee, First Report: Environmental Issues in Northern Ireland,* HC 39(1990), para. 109–18; K. Milton, *Our Countryside Our Concern,* Belfast: NI Environment Link 1990.

natural habitats of wild fauna and flora' throughout the EC. Measures taken pursuant to the Directive must be designed to 'maintain or restore, at favourable conservation status, natural habitats and species of wild fauna and flora of Community interest' and must take account of 'economic, social and cultural requirements and regional and local characteristics.' The Habitats Directive gives full legal force, at EC level, to the more precise obligations laid down by the Berne Convention on the Conservation of European Wildlife and Natural Habitats and the Bonn Convention on the Conservation of Migratory Species of Wild Animals (outlined in Part III of this chapter). Although it contains provisions for the protection of specific species of wild animals and plants, the Habitats Directive is primarily concerned with the general issue of habitat protection and the creation of a network of European protected sites known as 'Natura 2000'.

Articles 12–16 of the Habitats Directive contain the species provisions of the Directive. The Directive does not extend any protection to wild birds but for the first time extends EC protection to individual species of wild flora. Those species of wild animals protected by the Directive are listed in Annex IV($a$) and V($a$) to the Directive, while the protected plant species are listed in Annex IV($b$). The Habitats Directive also extends more stringent protection to those species threatened with extinction (identified as 'priority species'). However, none of these species occurs within Northern Ireland. Articles 12–16 follow the species provisions of the Berne Convention particularly closely and, as a result, the Wildlife (NI) Order 1985 (WO), which was itself designed to implement the provisions of the Berne Convention, broadly conforms to the standards laid down by the Habitats Directive. However, to give full legal effect to the species provisions of the Directive it was necessary to introduce a variety of additional and in some instances more stringent provisions for the protection of those species protected by the Directive. These provisions were introduced by Parts III and V of the Conservation (Natural Habitats etc.) Regulations (NI) 1995[16] ('Habitats Regulations'). The protection afforded by Parts III and V of the Habitats Regulations extends only to those species of animals and plants listed in Annex IV($a$) and ($b$) and V($a$) to the Habitats Directive whose natural range includes any area in Northern Ireland. The relevant species are listed in the schedules to the Habitats Regulations and are referred to in the Regulations as 'European protected species'; most of Northern Ireland's European protected species are also afforded protection under the WO and are therefore subject to overlapping protection.

Article 17 imposes an obligation both on the Commission and on member states to provide periodic information concerning the implementation of the Habitats Directive. This information is to be made available to the public. The requirements laid down in this regard are discussed in Part II, section 2 (page 370) of this chapter.

---

16. SR No. 380. A Consultation Paper entitled *Proposals to Implement the Habitats Directive in Northern Ireland* was issued by the DoE(NI) in December 1993 outlining the background to the Habitats Directive and the Government's proposals for implementing the Directive in Northern Ireland. In March 1995 a Guidance Note was also issued by the DoE(NI) outlining the main changes introduced by the Conservation (Natural Habitats etc.) Regulations (NI) 1995.

## The Conservation (Natural Habitats etc.) Regulations (NI) 1995

Parts III and V of the Habitats Regulations implement the species requirements laid down by the Habitats Directive. These Regulations:

(i) afford a greater level of protection to European protected species than that afforded to species protected under the WO;

(ii) empower the DoE(NI) to grant licences in relation to European protected species which in effect suspend the protection normally afforded by the Regulations, but controls are also imposed on the Department's powers to grant such licences;

(iii) control the introduction of European protected species into Northern Ireland via the licensing system introduced by the Regulations;

(iv) set out a list of prohibited means of killing and taking European protected species (this list differs slightly from the list of prohibited means of killing and taking species protected under the WO) and

(v) essentially replicate the enforcement system in place under the WO.

The Habitats Regulations require the DoE(NI) to exercise its functions under Northern Ireland nature conservation legislation (including the WO and the Habitats Regulations) 'so as to secure compliance' with the requirements of the Habitats Directive. Although neither the CNCC nor district councils play any specific advisory role under the Habitats Regulations, it is important to note that regulation 3(4) of the Habitats Regulations requires that 'every competent authority in the exercise of any of its functions shall have regard to the requirements of the Habitats Directive so far as they may be affected by the exercise of those functions.' The term 'competent authority' is defined by regulation 5 of the Habitats Regulations as including 'Government departments, district councils and statutory undertakers, and any trustees, commissioners, board or other persons who, as a public body and not for their own profit, act under any statutory provision for the improvement of any place or the production or supply of any commodity or service.' In this regard, the CNCC must have regard to the provisions of both the Habitats Regulations and the Habitats Directive in the exercise of its statutory functions under the WO.

As is the case under the WO, the DoE(NI) has the power to cause a public inquiry to be held under the Habitats Regulations. However, in this context the Department's power is in relation to 'any matter arising under these Regulations' (regulation 71(1)). The Department is empowered to make procedural rules which must be followed when a public inquiry is being held by or on behalf of the Department under regulation 71.[17] Where a public inquiry is to be held in relation to some matter arising out of the Habitats Regulations and another public inquiry is also to be held either in relation to another matter arising out of the Habitats Regulations or in relation to some other statutory provision, the DoE(NI) may direct that the two public inquiries be held concurrently or combined as one inquiry where the 'Department concerned' is of the view that the matters 'are so far cognate that they should be considered together.' In this instance the 'Department concerned' is either the DoE(NI) itself or, where the second inquiry is

---

17. These rules are without prejudice to s. 23 of the Interpretation Act (NI) 1954 (c. 33). To date, the Department has not adopted any procedural rules in this regard.

being held by another Government department, then the 'Department concerned' is the DoE(NI) and that other Department acting jointly.

The powers conferred on the police and courts under regulations 67–9 to enforce the species provisions of the Habitats Regulations are essentially identical to those conferred on the police and courts under the WO.

Although it is not specified in the Habitats Regulations, member states are required by Article 11 of the Habitats Directive to 'undertake surveillance' of the conservation status of the natural habitats and native species within their territory. They are required to pay particular attention to the position of 'priority' habitat types and species. However, none of the priority species occurs within Northern Ireland. Article 14 of the Directive provides that if the result of the surveillance makes it necessary, member states must take measures 'to ensure that the taking in the wild of specimens of [European protected species] listed in Annex V, as well as their exploitation, is compatible with their being maintained at a favourable conservation status.' A list of the measures which may be adopted in this regard is then set out in Article 14.2. Member states may derogate from this obligation provided that there is 'no satisfactory alternative' and 'the derogation is not detrimental to the maintenance of the populations of the species concerned at a favourable conservation status in their natural range' (Article 16.1). Article 16.1(a)–(e) sets out the purposes for which such derogations may be made, while Article 16.2 requires member states to report to the Commission every two years on any derogations made. The contents of this report and the procedures surrounding the report are set out in Part I, section 2 of this chapter in the context of the DoE(NI)'s powers to grant licences in relation to European protected species.

The requirements of the Habitats Regulations concerning species protection are set out in detail at the relevant junctures in Part I, section 2 of this chapter. The requirements of the Habitats Directive concerning habitat protection are implemented by Parts II and V of the Habitats Regulations; these provisions are outlined in detail in Part II, section 2 of this chapter.

### Other species standards adopted by the EC

Broadly speaking, the EC has adopted two types of measure in the context of nature conservation. On the one hand, the Community has become a party to various international nature conservation conventions and has adopted EC legislation to implement their terms within the Community legal order. On the other hand, the EC itself has generated a number of important nature conservation measures which impose more stringent standards than those adopted at international and national levels and, as with the Habitats Directive, introduce innovative approaches to the problem of nature conservation. The Wild Birds Directive and the Habitats Directive represent the two most significant pieces of nature conservation legislation adopted by the EC to date, and their provisions are addressed in detail in this chapter. The following is a summary of the other species protection standards adopted by the EC which are relevant to Northern Ireland.[18]

---

18. A more comprehensive list of all EC species protection standards can be found in L. Krämer, *EC Treaty and Environmental Law,* 2nd ed., London: Sweet & Maxwell, 1995, pp 18–20; N. Haigh, *Manual of Environmental Policy: The EC and Britain,* London: Longman, 1992, chaps 9 and 13; *European Community Environment Legislation, vol. 4: Nature,* Commission Publication 1992.

The EC prohibits the importing of skins from harp and hooded seal pups and also articles made from them under Directive 83/129/EEC.[19] Similarly it prohibits the use of leghold traps within the EC and also the importing of pelts and other manufactured goods from certain animals caught in leghold traps under Regulation EEC/3254/91.[20] The EC also bans the importing of raw and worked ivory from the African elephant under Regulation EEC/2496/89.[21]

In 1982 the Community adopted Decision 82/72/EEC[22] and Decision 82/461/EEC[23] for the purpose of approving the Convention on European Wildlife and Habitats (the Berne Convention) and the Convention on Migratory Species (the Bonn Convention), respectively. A decade later the Community adopted Decision 93/626/EC,[24] which approved the Convention on Biological Diversity within the Community legal order. Although the EC has been unable to become a party to the 1973 Convention on International Trade in Endangered Species of Wild Fauna and Flora (CITES) because, thus far, the Convention is open to ratification only by states, it has adopted a number of measures designed to implement the terms of CITES within the Community legal order. Regulation EEC/3626/82[25] in effect ensures the uniform application of CITES throughout the EC and, in some instances, goes further than the Convention itself in that it prohibits trade in certain species not protected by CITES. The Regulation also empowers member states to take even more stringent measures to control trade in protected species than those required by CITES, provided they are consistent with the terms of the EC Treaty itself. In 1992 a fundamental revision of Regulation EEC/3626/82 was proposed;[26] however, at the time of writing, no progress has been made in this regard. Regulation EEC/3418/83[27] sets out the requirements for a uniform system of permits and certification for the control of imports, exports and re-exports of specimens protected under CITES.

All these conventions have been ratified by the UK in its capacity as an individual state, and as a result they are binding within Northern Ireland both as a consequence of membership of the EC and as an international commitment undertaken by the UK itself. The terms of these international nature conservation conventions are considered in more detail in Part III of this chapter.

---

19. OJ L91/30, 28 Mar. 1983. The provisions of this Directive have been implemented for the UK as a whole by the Endangered Species (Import and Export) Act 1976 (Modification) Order 1983 (SI 1983/1609), which modifies Sch. 3 to the Endangered Species (Import and Export) Act 1976. The 1983 Order came into force in Nov. 1983 for an initial period of two years; this period was later extended in 1985 by SI 1985/1502; no expiry date was specified.

20. OJ L308/1, 4 Nov. 1991. The species protected by the Regulation are beaver, otter, coyote, wolf, lynx, bobcat, sable, racoon, musk rat, fisher, badger, marten, and ermine. The EC ban on imports of fur from animals caught in leghold traps was due to come into force on 1 Jan. 1996; however, the Commission has postponed the ban for a further year on the grounds that it is necessary to bring EC trading regulation into line with GATT trade requirements. The European Parliament has been very critical of this decision; see European Parliament, *This Week,* 11–15 Dec. 1995, final edition, p. 2.

21. OJ L240/5, 2 Aug. 1989. EC Regulations are binding on all member states from the moment of enactment and do not require any formal implementation into national law.

22. OJ L38/1, 10 Feb. 1982.

23. OJ L210/10, 19 July 1982.

24. OJ L309/1, 13 Dec. 1993.

25. OJ L384/1, 3 Dec. 1982.

26. OJ C26/1.

27. OJ L344/1, 28 Nov. 1983.

## SECTION 2. THE WILDLIFE (NI) ORDER 1985 AND THE CONSERVATION (NATURAL HABITATS ETC.) REGULATIONS (NI) 1995

This section provides a detailed explanation of the terms of the Wildlife (NI) Order 1985 (hereafter referred to as the WO) and the Conservation (National Habitats etc.) Regulations (NI) 1995 (hereafter referred to as the Habitat Regulations). Any reference to an 'article' of legislation in the remainder of this section should be read as referring to an article of the WO unless otherwise stated. Provisions of the Habitats Regulations are inserted at the relevant junctures throughout this section. See Part I, section 1 above for a list of those areas of species protection affected by the Habitats Regulations.

### The protection of birds

#### *Protection of wild birds, their nests and eggs*

Article 4 provides a wide-ranging protection to 'wild birds', their nests and eggs. The term 'wild birds' is defined by article 2(2) of the WO as 'any bird of a kind which is ordinarily resident in or is a visitor to Northern Ireland in a wild state but does not include poultry.' 'Poultry' is defined in article 2(2) as 'domestic fowls, turkeys, geese, ducks, guinea-fowls, pigeons and quails.' For the purposes of article 4 the term 'wild bird' does not include 'game-birds', defined by article 2(2) as 'any pheasant, partridge (including chukar partridge and red-legged partridge), woodcock, snipe or red grouse.'[28] Finally, it is important to note that while other species of wild animals and plants are protected by the provisions of the WO only if they are specifically listed in the schedules to the WO, birds are 'reverse-listed'. In other words, all native species of wild birds are protected by the WO unless specifically excluded; some particularly vulnerable or rare species of wild birds are afforded an even greater level of protection.

#### *Offences under article 4*

Article 4(1) provides that any person who intentionally:
  (a) kills, injures or takes any wild bird; or
  (b) takes, damages or destroys the nest of any wild bird while that nest is in use or being built; or
  (c) takes or destroys an egg[29] of any wild bird;

will be guilty of an offence. It is also an offence under article 4(2) to have 'possession or control' of:
  (a) any live or dead wild bird or any part of, or anything derived from, such a bird; or
  (b) an egg of a wild bird or any part of such an egg.

---

28. The definition of a 'wild bird' is subject to the provisions of art. 2(4), which provides that only references to wild birds in arts 6, 16, 17, 18 and Part IV of the WO will include a reference to a 'game bird'.
29. The term 'destroy' when used in relation to an egg is defined by art. 2(2) as including 'doing anything to the egg which is calculated to prevent it from hatching.'

Similarly, article 4(6) provides that a person who intentionally:

  (*a*) disturbs any wild bird ... while it is building a nest or is in, on or near a nest containing eggs or young;[30] or

  (*b*) disturbs dependent young of such a bird,

is guilty of an offence.

### Defences to offences under article 4(2)

Article 4(3) states that a person will not be deemed guilty of an offence under article 4(2) if they can prove that:

  (*a*) the bird or egg had not been killed or taken, or had been killed or taken otherwise than in contravention of the relevant provisions;[31] or

  (*b*) the bird, egg or other thing in his possession or control had been sold (whether to him or any other person) otherwise than in contravention of those provisions.

### Penalties for offences under article 4

In essence, a bird is deemed to be a 'wild bird' unless the contrary is proved. However, the WO provides special protection for rarer birds. Birds listed in Schedule 1 are afforded special protection by means of the imposition of a 'special penalty'. References to birds in Schedule 1 will always involve references to birds listed in Part I of Schedule 1; such birds are subject to special protection at all times. However, references to birds in Schedule 1 will also include birds listed in Part II of Schedule 1 during the close season[32] for the bird in question.

Article 4(5) provides that a person found guilty of an offence under article 4(1) or (2) in relation to a bird listed in Schedule 1 to the Order (or in relation to any part of, or anything derived from such a bird, or the nest or egg or part of the egg of such a bird) will be liable on summary conviction to a 'special penalty'. Similarly, a person found guilty of an offence under article 4(6) in relation to a bird listed in Schedule 1 will be liable on summary conviction to a 'special penalty'.

Article 27(1)(*a*) defines a special penalty for the purposes of article 4 as a fine not exceeding level 5 on the standard scale (£5,000). Article 27(1)(*b*) provides that a person found guilty on summary conviction of offences under article 4 in relation to birds not listed in Schedule 1 will be liable to a fine not exceeding level 3 on the standard scale (£1,000). Article 27(7) provides that where an offence is committed in relation to more than one bird, egg or nest 'the maximum fine which may be imposed ... shall be determined as if the person convicted had been convicted of a separate offence in respect of each bird, nest or egg.'

---

30. Art. 4(1) of the Wildlife (Amendment) (NI) Order 1995 (SI 1995/761) repeals the exemption contained in art. 4(6)(*a*) of the WO in relation to birds included in Part II of Sch. 2.

31. The term 'relevant provisions' is defined by art. 4(4) as including the provisions of this Part of the Order, i.e. Part II of the Wildlife (NI) Order 1985, and any orders made pursuant to the WO.

32. The 'close season' is defined in art. 4(8) as 'the period in any year commencing with 1st February and ending with 31st August.' Art. 4(9)–(12) confers powers on the DoE(NI) to vary the close season for any wild bird specified in the WO for the whole or any part of Northern Ireland.

### *DoE(NI)'s power to vary the close season or to extend protection to wild birds outside their close season*

Article 4(9)–(12) confers power on the DoE(NI) to vary, by order, the close season for any wild bird specified in the WO for the whole or any part[33] of Northern Ireland.[34] In addition, the DoE(NI) may declare any period outside the close season (not exceeding fourteen days) as a period of special protection for any wild bird listed in Part II of Schedule 1 or Part I of Schedule 2 where it appears expedient to do so. The order may apply to the whole or any part of Northern Ireland. In the event that such a period of special protection is declared, articles 4 and 5 will apply as though the period of special protection formed part of the close season for those birds. Before making the declaration of special protection the DoE(NI) is required to consult a representative of persons interested in shooting those birds which it proposes to subject to such special protection.[35] Neither of these powers has been exercised to date.

### *DoE(NI)'s power to issue licences which suspend the operation of article 4*

Article 18 empowers the DoE(NI) to grant licences which suspend the operation of article 4 for specified purposes, for example, ringing and educational purposes. The terms of article 18 are considered in more detail below, page 326.

### *Exceptions to article 4*

Article 5 sets down the following exceptions to the prohibitions contained in article 4:

1. Article 5(1) provides that a person will not be deemed guilty of an offence under article 4 for killing, taking or injuring a bird listed in Part I of Schedule 2 outside the 'close season'[36] for that bird.[37]

2. Article 5(4) provides that the provisions of article 4 will not render unlawful any action taken pursuant to a requirement by the Department of Agriculture (Northern Ireland) under any scheme made under section 6 of the Agriculture

---

33. Art. 2(5) provides that a reference to 'any part of Northern Ireland' includes, 'unless the context otherwise requires, a reference to the territorial waters adjacent to that part.'
34. Art. 29(3) and (5) requires the DoE(NI) to satisfy certain requirements when making an order under the WO. Art. 29(3) states that before making any order the DoE(NI) must: (i) consult the CNCC and (ii) give any district council or other person affected an opportunity (by such means as it considers appropriate) to submit objections or representations with respect to the subject-matter of the order. In addition, the Department may, if it thinks fit, cause a public inquiry to be held. Art. 29(5) requires the making of an order to be published by the DoE(NI) in the *Belfast Gazette*.
35. This obligation does not affect the further requirements imposed on the DoE(NI) under art. 29(3) of the WO outlined above.
36. The definition of 'close season' and details of the DoE(NI)'s powers to vary the close season are outlined at note 32, supra.
37. Art. 5(3), as amended by art. 4(2) of the Wildlife (Amendment) (NI) Order 1995 (SI 1995/761), provides that art. 5(1) will not apply 'on Sundays or during the period commencing one hour after sunset on any day and ending one hour before sunrise on the next day.' Art. 4 of the Amendment Order comes into force on 15 Sep. 1995 under the Wildlife (1995 Order) (Commencement) Order (NI) 1995 (SR No. 322). Art. 5(2) has been repealed by art. 4(1)(b) of the Wildlife (Amendment) (NI) Order 1995.

Act (NI) 1949, section 2 of the Agriculture (Miscellaneous Provisions) Act (NI) 1959, or the Drainage (NI) Order 1973.

3. Notwithstanding the provisions of article 4, article 5(5) provides that a person will not be deemed guilty of an offence under article 4 for any of the following:

   (a) taking a wild bird where it can be proved: (*a*) 'that the bird was disabled otherwise than by his unlawful act' and (*b*) that the bird was only taken 'for the purposes of tending it and releasing it when no longer disabled';

   (b) killing a wild bird where it can be proved: (*a*) that the bird was 'seriously disabled otherwise than by his unlawful act' and (*b*) that the bird was so seriously disabled that 'there was no reasonable chance of its recovering'; or

   (c) 'any act made unlawful by [article 4] if he shows that the act was the incidental result of a lawful operation and could not reasonably have been avoided.'

4. Article 5(6) provides that notwithstanding the provisions of article 4, an 'authorised person'[38] will not be deemed guilty of an offence under article 4 as a result of 'killing or injuring' a wild bird (other than birds listed in Schedule 1) if the following conditions are satisfied:

   (*a*) if he shows that his action was necessary for the purposes of—

      (i) preserving public health or public or air safety,

      (ii) preventing the spread of disease, or

      (iii) preventing serious damage to livestock,[39] foodstuffs for livestock, crops, vegetables, fruit, growing timber, pasture or fisheries; and

   (*b*) he notifies the (DoE(NI)) immediately after taking such action.

### General licences to kill wild birds

Article 4(1)(*e*) of the Wildlife (Amendment) (NI) Order 1995[40] repeals Part II of Schedule 2 to the WO, thus removing the notion of a list of 'pest birds' which could be taken or killed (including the destruction of their nests and eggs) at any time by authorised persons. Article 4(1)(*b*) of the 1995 Amendment Order also repeals article 5(2) of the WO, which specifically exempted the killing and taking of such birds (including the taking and destruction of their nests and eggs) from the general prohibition contained in article 4. This system has been replaced (as in Great Britain) by the introduction of a general licence to kill wild birds inserted

---

38. 'Authorised person' is defined in art. 3(1) of the WO as the owner or occupier of the land on which the authorised action takes place (including a person authorised by the owner or occupier of the land) or a person authorised by the DoE(NI). The authorisation of a person for the purposes of the WO does not confer any right of entry on any land.

39. 'Livestock' is defined in art. 3(1)(*b*) of the WO as including any animal which is kept: (a) for the provision of food, wool, skins or fur; (b) for the purpose of its use in the carrying on of any agricultural activity; or (c) for rearing and release into the wild for the provision or improvement of shooting or fishing, or for the purposes of nature conservation.

40. SI 1995/761.

into article 18 (see page 326), and in practice the position is very similar. These amendments in effect implement the requirements of Directive 79/409/EEC on the Conservation of Wild Birds, which outlaws the concept of a list of 'pest birds'. The Wildlife (1995 Order) (Commencement) Order (NI) 1995[41] provides that article 4 of the 1995 Amendment Order comes into force on 15 September 1995.

## Prohibition of certain methods of killing or taking wild birds

Article 6(1) of the WO provides that it is an offence to use certain methods of killing and taking wild birds; those methods are specified in article 6(1)(*a*)–(*e*). The list of such methods may be varied by the DoE(NI) by order under article 6(2); thus far, however, this power has not been exercised.[42] For the purposes of article 6 the definition of 'wild birds' includes 'game-birds', which are defined in article 2(2) of the WO as 'any pheasant, partridge (including chukar partridge and red-legged partridge), woodcock, snipe or red grouse.' In addition, article 6(5) provides that any occupier[43] of land or any person 'concerned in the management of any land' who 'permits or suffers' another person to violate the provisions of article 6(1)(*a*)–(*e*) on that land will be guilty of an offence. Similarly, any person who 'sells, offers or exposes for sale,[44] any self-locking snare with a view to its being used for a purpose which is unlawful under article 6(1)(*a*) or (*b*)' will be guilty of an offence under article 6(6).

## Exemptions from article 6(1)

Article 6(4) provides that the prohibition contained in article 6(1) will not render unlawful 'the use of a cage-trap or net for the purpose of taking any game-bird, if it is shown that the taking of the bird is solely for the purpose of breeding.' However, article 6(4) does not make it lawful to use 'any net for taking birds in flight' or to use any net 'which is projected or propelled otherwise than by hand' to take birds on the ground. See below the amendments made to article 6.

## Defence to proceedings under article 6(1)(a)

Article 6(1)(*a*) provides that it is an offence to set in position 'any springe, trap, gin, snare, hook and line, any electrical device for killing, stunning or frightening or any poisonous, poisoned or stupefying substance or muscle-relaxing agent' which is 'of such a nature and is so placed as to be calculated to cause bodily injury to any wild bird coming into contact therewith.' Article 6(3) provides that in proceedings for violation of article 6(1)(*a*) it is a defence to prove that the article in question was set in position for the purpose of killing or taking those wild animals which could lawfully be killed or taken by those means 'in the

---

41. SR No. 322.
42. Art. 29(2), (3) and (5) requires the DoE(NI) to follow certain procedures when making an order under art. 6; the requirements laid down by para. (3) and (5) are outlined at note 34, supra. Art. 29(2) requires that an order made under art. 6 be subject to affirmative resolution.
43. 'Occupier' is defined in art. 3(1) of the WO as including 'any person having any right of hunting, shooting, fishing or taking game or fish.'
44. 'Sale' is defined in art. 2(2) of the WO as including 'barter and exchange, and any other transaction by which anything is disposed of for value.'

interests of public health, agriculture, forestry, fisheries or nature conservation' and that 'all reasonable precautions' were taken by the accused to prevent injury to wild birds.

### Penalties for offences under article 6

A person found guilty of using a method of killing or taking wild birds that is prohibited under article 6(1) will be liable on summary conviction to a special penalty, defined by article 27(1) as a fine not exceeding level 5 on the standard scale (£5,000). A person found guilty of an offence under article 6(5) or (6), outlined above, is not liable to a special penalty; they are liable instead under article 27(1)(*b*) to a fine not exceeding level 3 on the standard scale (£1,000). As with an offence under article 4, article 27(7) provides that where an offence under article 6 is committed in respect of more than one bird, 'the maximum fine which may be imposed . . . shall be determined as if the person convicted had been convicted of a separate offence in respect of each bird.'

### DoE(NI)'s power to grant licences which suspend the operation of article 6

Article 18 empowers the DoE(NI) to issue licences which suspend the terms of article 6 for specific purposes. The terms of article 18 are outlined below at page 326.

### Amendments to article 6

Article 4(1) of the Wildlife (Amendment) (NI) Order 1995[45] repeals article 6(4)(*a*) of the WO, which contained a further exception to the terms of article 6(1). The Wildlife (1995 Order) (Commencement) Order (NI) 1995[46] provides that article 4 of the 1995 Amendment Order comes into force on 15 September 1995.

### Sale etc. of live or dead wild birds, eggs, etc.[47]

### (a) Sale etc. of live wild birds by 'any person'

Article 7(1)(*a*) provides that it is an offence if 'any person sells, offers or exposes for sale,[48] or has in his possession or transports or causes to be transported for the purpose of sale at any premises: (i) any live wild bird or an egg of a wild bird or any part of such an egg, or (ii) any live bird one of whose parents was such a wild bird, or an egg of such a bird or any part of such an egg . . .' Similarly, it is an offence to publish or cause to be published 'any advertisement likely to be understood as conveying that [one] buys or sells, or intends to buy or sell,' any of the above.

---

45. SI 1995/761.
46. SR No. 322.
47. The term 'wild bird' as used in art. 7 does not include a reference to 'game-birds', defined by art. 2(2) of the WO as 'any pheasant, partridge (including chukar partridge and red-legged partridge), woodcock, snipe or red grouse.'
48. Note 44, supra.

### (b) Sale etc. of dead wild birds by 'unregistered persons'

Article 7(2) creates an identical offence in relation to the sale etc. of any dead wild bird or any part of, or anything derived from, dead wild birds by unregistered persons.[49] It should be noted, however, that birds listed in Schedule 3 to the WO are not covered by article 7(2). Schedule 3 identifies those birds which may be sold dead at all times; woodpigeon is currently the only bird listed in Schedule 3.

### Inspection of premises where wild birds are kept by registered persons

Article 7(6) provides that an 'authorised'[50] person may enter and inspect any premises where wild birds are kept by a registered person, 'at any reasonable time,' in order to determine whether the provisions of article 7 are being or have been violated. The person authorised to enter and inspect must produce evidence of authorisation where it is requested. It is an offence under article 7(7) to 'intentionally obstruct' an authorised person from exercising their power of entry and inspection under article 7(6).

### Penalties for offences under article 7

Article 7(3) provides that a person found guilty on summary conviction of an offence under article 7 in respect of a wild bird listed in Schedule 1 will be liable to a special penalty, defined under article 27(1)(a) as a fine not exceeding level 5 on the standard scale (£5,000). A special penalty will also be imposed for offences in relation to 'any part of, or anything derived from' a Schedule 1 wild bird, including the egg or any part of the egg of such a bird. Article 27(1)(b) provides that conviction for offences under article 7 in relation to any other birds or for any other offences under article 7 will be punishable by a fine not exceeding level 3 on the standard scale (£1,000). As with articles 4 and 6, article 27(7) provides that where an offence under article 7 is committed in respect of more than one bird or

---

49. Art. 7(2) confers powers on the DoE(NI) to adopt regulations under which individuals may be registered to sell dead wild birds and anything derived therefrom; the Dead Wild Birds and Animals (Registration to Sell etc.) Regulations (NI) 1985 (SR No. 285) have been adopted pursuant to these powers. Art. 7(4)(a) provides that this power includes the power to impose requirements governing the carrying out of any act by registered persons that, 'apart from the registration,' would be an offence under art. 7. Art. 7(4)(b) also empowers the DoE(NI) to make it an offence to violate the provisions of these regulations. Art. 7(5)(a) and (b) provides that persons having been convicted of offences under Part II of the WO concerning the protection of wild birds will not be permitted under the Regulations to be registered to sell dead wild birds within three or five years of the conviction, depending on the nature of the offence. However, for these purposes no account can be taken of a conviction that has become spent under the Rehabilitation of Offenders (NI) Order 1978 (SI 1978/1908). Art. 24 provides that it is an offence for any person who is applying for such registration either on their own behalf or on behalf of another to knowingly or recklessly make a false statement or representation or furnish a document that is false in a material particular. A person found guilty of violating this provision will be liable on summary conviction to a fine not exceeding level 4 on the standard scale (£2,500) (art. 27(4)). Where an offence is committed in respect of more than one of the above 'the maximum fine which may be imposed . . . shall be determined as if the person convicted had been convicted of a separate offence in respect of each [of the above]' (art. 27(7)). Note also that under the terms of article 7 these provisions and the Registration Regulations also apply to registration in relation to wild animals under art. 13(2).
50. Such a person must be authorised 'in writing' by the DoE(NI) (art. 7(6)).

egg, 'the maximum fine . . . shall be determined as if the person convicted had been convicted of a separate offence in respect of each bird or egg.'

## Shows, competitions, etc.[51]

### (a) Showing or causing or permitting the showing of birds for competition

Article 8(1) provides that it is an offence to show or to cause or permit to be shown any wild bird or any live bird 'one of whose parents was such a wild bird' either: (i) 'in any premises in which a competition is being held' or (ii) 'for the purposes of any competition.' Article 8(1)(*a*) excludes from this prohibition any wild bird listed in Schedule 4 to the WO which has been 'bred in captivity'[52] and which has been 'ringed under a licence granted by the DoE(NI) in accordance with article 18(2)(*d*)' (outlined on page 326 *et seq*).

### (b) Promoting public exhibitions or competitions of Schedule 4 birds

Article 8(2) requires any person who promotes public exhibitions or competitions of birds listed in Schedule 4 to notify the DoE(NI) 'in writing at least 7 days before the date upon which the event is to take place.' Failure to do so is an offence.

### Penalties under article 8

Article 27(3) provides that a person found guilty on summary conviction of an offence under article 8(1) will be liable to a fine not exceeding level 4 on the standard scale (£2,500). Article 27(5) provides that a person found guilty on summary conviction of failing to notify the DoE(NI) as required of a public exhibition or competition of Schedule 4 birds will be liable to a fine not exceeding level 3 on the standard scale (£1,000). Article 27(7) also provides that where an offence has been committed under article 8 in respect of more than one bird 'the maximum fine which may be imposed . . . shall be determined as if the person convicted had been convicted of a separate offence in respect of each bird.'

### DoE(NI)'s power to grant licences suspending the operation of article 8

Article 18 empowers the DoE(NI) to grant licences which provide that the terms of article 8 will not apply to activities carried out for specified purposes. The terms of article 18 are outlined in more detail below (see page 326).

## Protection of captive birds[53]

Article 9(1) provides that it is an offence to confine 'any bird whatsoever' in a

---

51. References to 'wild birds' in art. 8 do not include references to 'game-birds', which are defined at note 47, *supra*.
52. Art. 3(2) of the WO provides that 'a bird shall not be treated as bred in captivity for the purposes of this Part [of the WO] unless its parents were lawfully in captivity when the egg was laid.'
53. References in art. 9 to 'wild birds' do not include references to 'game-birds', which are defined at note 47, *supra*.

'cage or other receptacle' which is of insufficient 'height, length or breadth to permit the bird to stretch its wings freely.'

### Exceptions to article 9(1)

Article 9(2)(*a*)–(*d*) sets out a series of exceptions to the prohibition contained in article 9(1). Article 9(1) does not apply to:

(i) 'poultry', defined in article 2(2) of the WO as 'domestic fowls, turkeys, geese, ducks, guinea-fowls, pigeons and quails';

(ii) the 'keeping or confining of any bird' that is in the process of being conveyed 'by whatever means';

(iii) the 'keeping or confining of any bird' that is in the process of being shown for public exhibition or competition, provided the bird is not so confined for an aggregate period of more than seventy-two hours;

(iv) the 'keeping or confining' of a bird while it is being examined or treated by a veterinary surgeon or veterinary practitioner;

(v) the temporary 'keeping or confining' of a bird in a 'birdbag or keeping cage as part of a ringing exercise' being carried out pursuant to a licence issued under article 18(2)(*a*) of the WO; the exercise must also be carried out in accordance with the terms of the licence.

### Liberation of captive birds for the purpose of being shot or hunted immediately following liberation

Article 9(3) provides that any person who 'promotes, arranges, conducts, assists in, receives money for, or takes part in, any event whatsoever' during which captive birds are liberated for the 'purpose of being shot' or 'hunted by trained birds of prey immediately after their liberation' will be guilty of an offence. Similarly, an owner or occupier of land who permits such land to be used for these purposes will be guilty of an offence.

### Penalties for offences under article 9

A person found guilty of an offence under article 9(1) or (3) is liable to a special penalty, defined in article 27(1)(*a*) as a fine not exceeding level 5 on the standard scale (£5,000). Article 27(7) provides that where an offence under article 9 has been committed in respect of more than one bird, the 'maximum fine which may be imposed . . . shall be determined as if the person convicted had been convicted of a separate offence in respect of each bird.'

### DoE(NI)'s power to issue licences that suspend the operation of article 9

Article 18 empowers the DoE(NI) to issue licences which suspend the terms of article 9 for specified purposes; the terms of the licensing system established under article 18 are outlined at page 326.

**Protection of animals other than birds**

Article 10 extends protection to those wild animals[54] listed in Schedule 5 to the
WO, namely, badgers, all species of bats, seven species of butterflies, all species of
whales, porpoises, and dolphins, the common lizard, the pine marten, the common
newt, the common otter, the common and grey seal, and the red squirrel. Several
statutory offences are created by article 10; however, these are subject to the
exceptions and defences laid down in article 10 itself and by article 11. It should
also be noted that all species of 'typical' bats, all species of dolphins, porpoises
and whales and the common otter are also protected as 'European protected
species' under the Conservation (Natural Habitats etc.) Regulations (NI) 1995,[55]
also discussed in this section.

*Offences under article 10*

The terms of article 10 broadly reflect the protection afforded to wild birds by
article 4 of the WO. Article 10(1) provides that it is an offence to 'intentionally
kill, injure or take' any wild animal listed in Schedule 5 to the WO. Similarly
article 10(2) provides that it is an offence to have 'possession or control' of any
live or dead wild animal listed in Schedule 5 or 'any part of, or anything derived
from,' such animals. Article 10(5) provides that in proceedings for offences under
article 10(1) and (2) the animal in question will be 'presumed to have been a wild
animal unless the contrary is shown.' In addition, any person who intentionally:

- (a) damages or destroys, or obstructs access to, any structure or place
  which any wild animal included in Schedule 5 uses for shelter or
  protection;
- (b) damages or destroys anything which conceals or protects any such
  structure; or
- (c) disturbs any such animal while it is occupying a structure or place
  which it uses for shelter or protection

will be guilty of an offence under article 10(4) of the WO.

*Defences to proceedings concerning 'possession or control'*

Article 10(3) provides that it is a defence in proceedings concerning possession or
control of live or dead wild animals under article 10(2) to prove that:

- (a) the animal had not been killed or taken, or had been killed or taken
  otherwise than in contravention of the provisions of [the WO]; or
- (b) the animal or other thing in his possession or control had been sold

---

54. 'Wild animal' is defined in art. 2(2) of the WO as 'any animal (other than a bird) which is or
    (before it was killed or taken) was living wild.' This definition is subject to the terms of art. 2(3),
    which provides that references to wild animals in arts 12, 16, 17, 18 and Part IV will include
    references to 'game'. 'Game' is defined by arts 2(2) of the WO as 'any hare or game-bird and
    includes deer.' 'Game-bird' is defined by art. 2(2) as 'any pheasant, partridge (including chukar
    partridge and red-legged partridge), woodcock, snipe or red grouse.' Art. 2(6) of the WO also
    provides that any reference 'to an animal of any kind includes, unless the context otherwise
    requires, a reference to an egg, larva, pupa, or other immature stage of an animal of the kind.'
55. SR No. 380.

(whether to him or any other person) otherwise than in contravention of the provisions of [the WO].'

## *Penalties for offences under article 10*

Although article 10 does not specifically impose a 'special penalty' for a violation of its terms, article 27(2) provides that a person found guilty on summary conviction of an offence under article 10 will be liable to a fine which is, in effect, equivalent to the special penalty imposed for certain offences in relation to wild birds, namely, a fine not exceeding level 5 on the standard scale (£5,000). In addition, article 27(7) provides that where an offence has been committed in respect of more than one animal, 'the maximum fine which may be imposed . . . shall be determined as if the person convicted had been convicted of a separate offence in respect of each animal.'

## *DoE(NI)'s power to issue licences which suspend the operation of article 10(1), (2), and (4)*

Article 18 empowers the DoE(NI) to issue licences which suspend the application of article 10(1), (2) and (4) for specified purposes. The terms of article 18 are outlined at page 326.

## *Exceptions to article 10*

Article 11 sets out a series of exceptions to the provisions of article 10. These exceptions reflect to a considerable degree the exceptions to article 4 concerning wild birds laid down by article 5. They are as follows:

1. The exceptions laid down in article 5(4) and (5) (concerning birds, outlined above) also apply to article 10. However, references to article 10 should be substituted for references to article 4, and references to wild animals should be substituted for references to wild birds (article 11(1)).
2. A person cannot rely on the provisions of article 5(5)(*c*) (i.e. that the act in question was 'the incidental result of a lawful operation and could not reasonably have been avoided') as a defence to 'anything done in relation to a bat . . . unless he had notified the DoE(NI) of the proposed action or operation and allowed them a reasonable time to advise him as to whether it should be carried out and, if so, the method to be used.' This provision does not apply to action taken in relation to bats in the 'living area of a dwelling house' (article 11(4)(*a*)). Bats are afforded the most stringent level of protection of any mammal under the WO; they are also European protected species under the Habitats Regulations, outlined on page 316.
3. Article 11(2) provides that the prohibition laid down in article 10(4) concerning the destruction or obstruction of places and structures used by wild animals for shelter will not render unlawful actions carried out 'within a dwelling house'. However, this exception is itself subject to the terms of article 11(4)(*b*). Article 11(4)(*b*) provides that a person cannot rely on the above exception in relation to anything done to a bat unless the DoE(NI) has been notified of the intended operation, allowing them a reasonable time to advise whether the action should be carried out and, if so, the method to be used. Article 11(4)(*b*) does not,

however, apply to actions taken in relation to bats within the 'living area of a dwelling house'.

4. Article 11(3) provides that the exception laid down in relation to birds in article 5(6)(*a*)(iii) and (*b*) (i.e. 'prevention of serious damage to livestock, foodstuffs for livestock, crops, vegetables, fruit, growing timber, pasture or fisheries') also applies to article 10; once again references to wild animals should be substituted for references to wild birds.[56] However, article 11(5) provides that an authorised person cannot rely on the defence provided by article 11(3) in relation to 'any action taken at any time' if it had already become apparent that the action in question would be necessary to prevent 'serious damage to livestock, foodstuffs for livestock, crops, vegetables, fruit, growing timber, pasture or fisheries' and either:

(*a*) a licence under article 18 authorising that action had not been applied for as soon as reasonably practicable after that fact had become apparent; or

(*b*) an application for such a licence had been determined.

## Prohibition of certain methods of killing or taking wild animals

Article 12 prohibits the use of specified methods of killing and taking wild animals,[57] and once again its terms reflect to a large extent the terms of article 6 concerning the killing and taking of wild birds. While article 10 extends protection to those animals listed in Schedule 5 to the WO, article 12 provides general protection for all wild animals in relation to certain methods of killing or taking; article 12(2) provides specific protection for those animals listed in Schedule 6. Schedule 6 extends protection to badgers, all species of bats, fallow, red and sika deer, the brown and Irish hare, the hedgehog, the common lizard, the pine marten, the common newt, the common otter, the common and grey seal, and the red squirrel.

### *Offences under article 12*

Article 12(1)(*a*)–(*c*) and article 12(2)(*a*)–(*d*) prohibit the use of various methods of killing and taking wild animals and provide that violation of the prohibition is an offence.[58] Article 12(4) provides that in proceedings concerning offences under article 12(1)(*b*) or (*c*) or under article 12(2)(*b*) – (*d*) the animal in question will be presumed to be wild unless the contrary is proved. Like article 6(5) (birds), article

---

56. The exception laid down in art. 5(6) of the WO can only be invoked by an 'authorised person'. This term has the same meaning in the context of art. 11 as it has in the context of art. 5(6); see note 38, supra.

57. Art. 2(3) of the WO provides that the definition of a 'wild animal' will include 'game' for the purposes of art. 12. 'Game' is defined by art. 2(2) as 'any hare or game-bird and includes deer.' 'Game-bird' is defined by art. 2(2) as 'any pheasant, partridge (including chukar partridge and red-legged partridge), woodcock, snipe or red grouse.' Art. 2(6) provides that any reference to an animal of any kind in the WO includes, 'unless the context otherwise requires, a reference to an egg, larva, pupa, or other immature stage of an animal of the kind.'

58. Art. 12(3) confers powers on the DoE(NI) to amend the provisions of art. 12(1) and (2) in relation to the species of wild animals protected by art. 12 or the methods of killing or taking prohibited by art. 12; this power has not been exercised to date.

12(6) provides that a person 'concerned in the management of land' or the 'occupier of land'[59] will be guilty of an offence if he 'permits or suffers another person to commit an offence' under article 12(1) or (2) on that land. Article 12(7) creates an identical offence to that laid down in article 6(6) concerning the sale or the offer or exposure for sale of 'any self-locking snare, with a view to its being used for a purpose which is unlawful' under article 12(1)(*a*) or (*b*).

### *DoE(NI)'s power to issue licences that suspend the operation of article 12(1) and (2)*

Article 18 empowers the DoE(NI) to issue licences which suspend the application of article 12(1) and (2) for specified purposes. The terms of article 18 are outlined on page 326.

### *Defence to proceedings under article 12(2)(a)*

Article 12(5) provides a defence to proceedings under article 12(1)(*a*), which is expressed in terms almost identical to the defence provided in article 6(3) (outlined above), the only difference being that 'forestry and fisheries', which are included in the list in article 6(3), are not listed as grounds of defence in article 12(5). For the reference to wild birds in article 6(3) a reference to wild animals should be substituted for the purposes of article 12(5).

### *Penalties incurred under article 12*

Article 27(2) provides that a person found guilty on summary conviction of an offence under article 12(1) or (2) will be liable to a fine not exceeding level 5 on the standard scale (£5,000). Article 27(1) provides that a person found guilty on summary conviction of an offence under article 12(6) or (7) will be liable to a fine not exceeding level 3 on the standard scale (£1,000). Article 27(7) provides that where an offence has been committed under article 12 in respect of more than one animal, 'the maximum fine which may be imposed . . . shall be determined as if the person convicted had been convicted of a separate offence in respect of each animal.'

### Sale etc. of live or dead wild animals

Article 13 governs the sale of live and dead wild animals in terms identical to the protection afforded to wild birds under article 7(1), (2), and (4)–(7) outlined above. It should be noted, however, that article 13 extends protection only to those wild animals listed in Schedule 7 to the WO. Article 13(1) prohibits the sale etc. of 'live wild animals' listed in Schedule 7 by any person in terms identical to the protection afforded to wild birds under article 7(1). Article 13(4) provides that in proceedings under article 13(1) the animal in question will be presumed to be wild unless the contrary is proved. Article 13(2) prohibits the sale etc. of 'dead wild animals' listed in Schedule 7 'or any part, or anything derived from, such a wild

---

59. 'Occupier' includes 'any person having any right of hunting, shooting, fishing or taking game or fish' (art. 3(1)).

animal' by unregistered persons in terms identical to the protection afforded to wild birds under article 7(2), considered above.[60]

As in proceedings under article 13(1), the animal in question in proceedings under article 13(2) will be presumed to be wild unless the contrary is proved (article 13(4)). Article 13(3) provides that article 7(6) and (7), which governs the DoE(NI)'s powers to enter and inspect premises where wild birds are kept by registered persons, will also apply in the context of wild animals. Similarly, it is an offence to 'intentionally obstruct' the exercise of this power.

### Penalties for offences under article 13

Article 27(2) provides that a person found guilty on summary conviction of an offence under article 13(1) or (2) will be liable to a fine not exceeding level 5 on the standard scale (£5,000). Note also that under article 27(1) a person found guilty of an offence under article 13(3), i.e. intentionally obstructing an exercise of the power of entry and inspection conferred by Article 7(6), is liable to a fine not exceeding level 3 on the standard scale (£1,000). Article 27(7) provides that where a person is found guilty of an offence under article 13 in respect of more than one animal, the 'maximum fine which may be imposed . . . shall be determined as if the person convicted had been convicted of a separate offence in respect of each animal.'

### 'European protected species'

Part III (regulations 33–6) of the Conservation (Natural Habitats etc.) Regulations (NI) 1995[61] introduces the necessary additional provisions for the protection of those species of wild animals protected by Directive 92/43/EEC on the conservation of natural habitats and of wild fauna and flora (the Habitats Directive, discussed in Part I of this chapter). The species of wild animals protected by the Habitats Directive are listed in Annex IV(*a*) and V(*a*) to the Directive; it is important to note, however, that birds are not protected by the Habitats Directive. The species listed in Annex V(a) are less vulnerable than those listed in Annex IV(a). In effect, the species listed in group V(a) may be taken or exploited (Article 14 of the Habitats Directive) provided this is compatible with their maintenance at a favourable conservation status.

The Habitats Regulations implement the requirements of the Directive in relation to those species whose natural range includes any area of Northern Ireland. The relevant species from Annex IV (*a*) for Northern Ireland are listed in Schedule 2 to the Habitats Regulations, while the relevant species from Annex V(a) are listed in Schedule 3.

Overall, the Habitats Directive adopts a traditional approach to the issue of species protection. Animals listed in Schedule 2 are afforded the greatest level of

---

60. Art. 13(3) provides that art. 7(4) and (5), which governs the DoE(NI)'s powers to adopt regulations concerning the registration of persons permitted to sell etc. dead wild birds, also applies to wild animals. The Dead Wild Birds and Animals (Registration to Sell etc.) Regulations (NI) 1985 (SR No. 285) govern the registration of persons to sell dead wild birds and animals. In this regard see note 49, supra.

61. SR No. 380.

protection under the Habitats Regulations. They are all species of bats, all species of dolphins, porpoises, and whales, and the common otter. Those animals listed in Schedule 3 are protected by the Habitats Regulations only in so far as certain methods may not be used as a means of taking or killing such species. They are mountain hare, river lamprey, pine marten, Atlantic salmon, the common and grey seal, and the allis and twaite shad. Although all Schedule 2 species are already protected under the provisions of the WO, and also some Schedule 3 species (pine marten, mountain hare, and both species of seal), it was necessary to enact additional provisions to fully implement the slightly different and in some instances more comprehensive protection afforded to European protected species under the Directive. For the sake of clarity, the provisions of the Habitats Regulations will be set out in full; differences between the level of protection provided will then be highlighted. It is important to note at the outset that while there are differences between the species protection provisions of the WO and the Habitats Regulations, the differences are, for the most part, technical rather than practical, to ensure compliance with the requirements of the Habitats Directive.

Regulation 34(1) provides that it is an offence, at all stages of the life of the animal:

    (a) deliberately to take or kill a wild animal of a European protected species;

    (b) deliberately to disturb any such animal;

    (c) deliberately to take or destroy[62] the eggs of such an animal; or

    (d) to damage or destroy a breeding site or resting place of such an animal.

The WO and the Habitats Regulations both prohibit the killing and taking of protected species of wild animals. Regulation 34(1) does not make it an offence to injure an animal of a European protected species, as is the case under article 10(1) in relation animals protected under the WO. However, European protected species are afforded comprehensive protection from being disturbed. The Habitats Regulations make it an offence to deliberately disturb an animal of a protected species; the WO, however, makes it an offence only to disturb a protected animal while it is occupying a structure or place that it uses for shelter or protection. It is interesting to note that while Article 12.1(b) of the Habitats Directive requires that disturbance of a protected species of animal be prohibited, particularly during its period of breeding, rearing, hibernation, and migration, regulation 34(1), which implements this provision, does not impose different levels of penalty depending on when the animal in question is disturbed.

The Habitats Regulations make it an offence to 'deliberately take or destroy the eggs' of European protected species. Although the WO does not explicitly outlaw the destruction or taking of animals' eggs, as is the case in relation to wild birds under article 4, article 2(2) of the WO defines the term 'wild animal' for the purposes of the Order as including the egg, larva, pupa or other immature stage of an animal protected under the Order. In effect, therefore, the WO also makes it an offence to intentionally kill, injure or take the eggs etc. of protected animals.

---

62. Reg. 2(1) of the Habitats Regulations provides that the term 'destroy' in relation to an egg includes 'doing anything to the egg which is calculated to prevent it from hatching.'

The WO makes it an offence to damage or destroy any structure or place that a protected wild animal uses for 'shelter or protection'. However, the Habitats Regulations appear to provide a greater level of protection in this regard, in that they explicitly protect the animal's 'resting place and breeding site'. The prohibitions laid down in regulation 34(1) explicitly apply to all stages of the life of the animals in question; the protection afforded to listed animals under the WO also applies to the immature stages of the animals in question by means of the definition of a 'wild animal' laid down in article 2(2) above.

Regulation 34(2) goes on to make it an offence to 'keep, transport, sell or exchange, or offer for sale or exchange, any live or dead wild animals of a European protected species, or any part of, or anything derived from such an animal.' Regulation 34(2) in effect reflects the provisions contained in article 10(2) of the WO (concerning the unlawful possession and control of dead or live animals) and article 13(1) of the WO (concerning the sale etc. of live or dead animals), the principal differences being: (i) that regulation 34(2) does not appear to provide the extensive degree of control over the sale of species protected under the Habitats Regulations as is provided for listed animals under the WO and (ii) that regulation 34(2) makes it an offence to 'exchange' or 'offer for exchange' a dead or live European protected species of animal, a protection that is not afforded either to wild birds or listed animals under the WO. As in proceedings concerning wild animals protected under the WO, an animal is presumed to be wild for the purposes of an offence under regulation 34 unless the contrary is proved. Anyone found guilty of an offence under regulation 34 will be liable, under regulation 34(6), on summary conviction to a fine not exceeding level 5 on the standard scale (£5,000)—an identical penalty to that imposed for offences under articles 10 and 13(1).

Regulations 34(4) and 35 set out various exceptions to the offences created by regulation 34. Subject to minor differences, these are framed in terms almost identical to the equivalent exceptions laid down in the WO in relation to wild birds and listed animals. They are as follows:

1. A person will not be deemed guilty of an offence under regulation 34(2) if he can establish that the animal in question either was not taken or killed or was taken or killed without violating regulations 34–6 of the Habitats Regulations or Part II of the WO, as amended, i.e. articles 10–13. Alternatively, a person will not be deemed liable for an offence under regulation 34(2) if he can establish that the animal or thing in question was sold, either to him or to another person, without violating regulations 34–6 of the Habitats Regulations or articles 10–13 of the WO, as amended (regulation 34(4)). In effect, regulation 34(2) mirrors the exceptions created in relation to wild birds and animals under articles 4(3) and 10(3) of the WO, subject to the reference to the provisions of the Habitats Regulations.

2. Regulation 35(1) mirrors the exception laid down in article 5(4) of the WO in relation to birds (which also operates under article 11(1) to wild animals) substituting a reference to the provisions of regulation 34 for the reference to article 4.

3. Regulation 35(3) mirrors the exception provided in article 5(5) of the WO in relation to birds (which also applies to wild animals under article 11(1)) substituting a reference to the provisions of regulation 34 for the reference to

article 4 and references to a wild animal of a European protected species for references to wild birds.

4. Regulation 35(2) provides that regulation 34(1) will not render it unlawful to deliberately disturb an animal of a European protected species or to damage or destroy a breeding site or resting place of such an animal where the action in question is done within a dwelling house. However, regulation 35(4) repeats the protection afforded to bats contained in article 11(4) of the WO. In effect, regulation 35(4) provides that one cannot rely on the exception contained in regulation 35(2) (concerning acts done within a dwelling house) or that provided under regulation 35(3)(c) (exempting acts done during the course of a lawful operation that could not reasonably be avoided) to excuse anything done in relation to a bat outside 'the living area of a dwelling house', unless one had first notified the DoE(NI) of the proposed action and allowed the Department a reasonable time within which to give advice on whether the action should be carried out and, if so, the best method to be used.

5. Regulation 35(5) almost mirrors the exception provided in relation to wild animals under article 11(3)(a) and (b) of the WO substituting references to regulation 34 for references to article 10. However, whereas article 11(3) exempts the 'killing or injuring' of scheduled wild animals by an authorised person under the circumstances specified in (a) and (b), regulation 35(5) exempts the 'killing or disturbing' of an animal of the European protected species by an authorised person[63] in identical circumstances. Regulation 35(6) also mirrors the provisions of article 11(5) of the WO, which prevents an authorised person from relying on the exception in regulation 35(5) in certain circumstances; however, substitute references to regulation 35(5) for the references to article 11(3) and references to licences under regulation 39 of the Habitats Regulations for the reference to licences under article 18 of the WO.

As with article 12 of the WO, the Habitats Regulations prohibit the use of certain methods of killing or taking animals protected under the Regulations. Article 15 of the Habitats Directive requires that member states prohibit 'the use of all indiscriminate means capable of causing local disappearance of, or serious disturbance to, populations of such species,' and in particular those methods listed in Annex VI(a), and modes of transport listed in Annex IV(b) to the Directive. Regulation 36 implements this requirement and sets out a list of methods that are prohibited as methods for killing or taking those animals of a European protected species (listed above). Where the Habitats Regulations permit the killing or taking of species listed in Schedule 2, they may not be killed or taken by the means prohibited in regulations 36; in addition, the Regulations extend this protection to species listed in Schedule 3 that are not otherwise protected by the Habitats Regulations. The list of prohibited methods in regulation 36 is broadly similar, but not identical, to that in article 12 in relation to listed animals under the WO. As with article 12 of the WO, it is an offence to violate the terms of regulation 36; a person found guilty on summary conviction of an offence under regulation 36 will be liable to a fine not exceeding level 5 on the standard scale (£5,000).

---

63. References to an 'authorised person' under reg. 35 of the Habitats Regulations have the same meaning as under art. 3(1) of the WO: see note 38, *supra*.

As with the WO, the DoE(NI) is empowered under regulations 39 and 40 of the Habitats Regulations to grant licences which permit activities that would otherwise be an offence under regulations 34 and 36. The Department's powers in this regard are outlined in the context of the Department's general powers to grant licences under the WO, below at page 326.

Finally, it should be noted that Article 12.4 of the Habitats Directive obliges member states to 'establish a system to monitor the incidental capture and killing' of animals listed in Annex IV(*a*) to the Directive. Member states are then required to use the information gathered to inform further research or conservation measures which they are obliged to adopt for the purpose of ensuring that such incidental capture and killing does not have 'a significant negative impact' on the species concerned. In the Consultation Paper[64] issued to outline the DoE(NI)'s proposals for the implementation of the Habitats Directive in Northern Ireland, the Department pointed to the proposed marine mammal stranding schemes as being among key programmes that would ensure compliance with the terms of article 12(4). In addition, the DANI (Fisheries Division) have established a voluntary reporting scheme for the bye-catch of cetaceans.

## Protection of wild plants

### *Destruction of wild plants*

Article 14(1)(*a*) makes it an offence to 'intentionally pick,[65] remove, uproot or destroy' any of the fifty-five rarer wild plant[66] species listed in Part I of Schedule 8 to the WO. In addition, article 14(1)(*b*) makes it an offence for anyone, other than an 'authorised person',[67] to 'intentionally uproot[68] or destroy any wild plant not included in that Part of the Schedule'—in effect the primrose, which is listed in Part II of Schedule 8. Article 14(3) states that it is a defence to proceedings under article 14(1) to prove that the act in question 'was an incidental result of a lawful operation and could not reasonably have been avoided.'

### *Sale etc. of live and dead wild plants*

Article 14(2)(*a*) and (*b*) makes it an offence to sell etc. 'any live or dead wild plants' listed in Part I or II of Schedule 8 'or any part of, or anything derived from, such a plant.' The offence is expressed in terms identical to those used in article 7(1) and (2) in the context of wild birds (outlined above). Article 14(4) provides that in proceedings for an offence under article 14(2)(*a*), concerning the sale or transport for sale of live or dead wild plants, the plant in question will be presumed to be wild unless the contrary is proved.

---

64. *Proposals to Implement the Habitats Directive in Northern Ireland:* DoE(NI) 1993.
65. To 'pick' is defined in art. 2(2) as to 'gather or pluck any part of the plant without uprooting it.'
66. 'Wild plant' is defined by art. 2(2) as 'any plant which is or (before it was picked, removed, uprooted or destroyed) was growing wild and is of a kind which ordinarily grows in Northern Ireland in a wild state.'
67. An 'authorised person' is the owner or occupier of land or anyone authorised by them or any person authorised by the DoE(NI) (art. 2(3)).
68. To 'uproot' in relation to a plant is defined in art. 2(2) of the WO as to 'dig up or otherwise remove the plant with its roots from the land on which it is growing.'

### Penalties for offences under article 14

Article 27(3) provides that a person found guilty on summary conviction of an offence under article 14 will be liable to a fine not exceeding level 4 on the standard scale (£2,500). Article 27(7) provides that where an offence under article 14 has been committed in respect of more than one plant, 'the maximum fine which may be imposed . . . shall be determined as if the person convicted had been convicted of a separate offence in relation to each plant.'

### *DoE(NI)'s power to issue licences which suspend the operation of article 14(1)*

Article 18 empowers the DoE(NI) to issue licences that suspend the application of article 14(1) for certain specified activities. The terms of article 18 are outlined on page 326.

### *'European protected species'*

Regulations 37 and 38 of the Conservation (Natural Habitats etc.) Regulations (NI) 1995[69] implement the species requirements concerning plants laid down in the Habitats Directive (also discussed in Part I, section 1 of this chapter). In effect, the Habitats Regulations provide protection for those species of plants listed in Annex IV(*b*) to the Directive whose natural range includes Northern Ireland. The relevant plant species for Northern Ireland are listed in Schedule 4 to the Regulations and are referred to as 'European protected species'; they are the Killarney fern and the yellow marsh saxifrage. Both of the European protected species of plant are already protected under the WO; however, it was necessary to extend additional protection to these species to implement the terms of the Habitats Directive fully in Northern Ireland. As with wild animal protection, the Habitats Directive adopts a traditional approach to the protection of wild flora.

Regulation 38(1) implements the requirements of Article 13.1(*a*) of the Habitats Directive and makes it an offence to 'deliberately . . . pick, collect, cut, uproot or destroy a wild plant of a European protected species.' Although this provision is similar to that laid down in Article 14(1) of the WO, it provides more extensive protection for European protected plant species, in that it is also unlawful to 'deliberately cut' a plant species protected by the Regulations. The term 'remove' used in the WO is replaced by the term 'collect' in the Regulations, and the term 'intentionally' used in the WO to define the offence is replaced by the term 'deliberately' in the Regulations. Regulation 38(2) makes it an offence to 'keep, transport, sell or exchange, or offer for sale or exchange, any live or dead wild plant of the European protected species, or any part of, or anything derived from, such a plant,' in effect implementing the requirements of Article 13.1(*b*) of the Habitats Directive. Although the terms of regulation 38(2) do not appear to provide the same level of control over the sale of protected species as is afforded to listed animals under article 14(2) of the WO, the Habitats Regulations appear to provide more extensive protection to European protected species, in that it is also an offence to deliberately exchange such species or to offer them for exchange, neither of which is explicitly prohibited under the WO.

---

69. SR No. 380.

As with animals of a European protected species, the protection afforded to plants under the Habitats Regulations extends to 'all stages of the biological cycle of the plants to which they apply' (regulation 38(3)). Regulation 38 sets out two defences to proceedings under regulation 38(1) and (2). The first, set out in regulation 38(4), provides a defence to the offence created by regulation 38(1) and is framed in terms identical to the defence laid down in relation to wild plants protected under article 14(3) of the WO. The second, laid down in regulation 38(5), provides that a person will not be deemed guilty of an offence under regulation 38(2) if he can establish that the plant or other thing in question was sold either to him or to another person without violating regulations 37 and 38 of the Habitats Regulations or Part II of the WO. Identical penalties are imposed for offences in relation to protected plant species under the WO and the Habitats Regulations.

Finally, it should be noted that the Habitats Regulations empower the DoE(NI) to grant licences which permit activities that would otherwise be an offence under regulation 38. The Department's powers in this regard are outlined below (page 326) in the context of the DoE(NI)'s general powers to grant licences under the WO.

### The introduction of new species to Northern Ireland

Both the WO and the Habitats Directive require member states to regulate the introduction of non-native plant and animal species into the wild. Article 22 of the Habitats Directive requires member states 'to ensure that the deliberate introduction into the wild of any species which is not native to their territory is regulated so as not to prejudice natural habitats within their natural range or the wild native fauna and flora, and if they consider it necessary, prohibit such introduction.' This requirement is essentially implemented by article 15 of the WO, which prohibits the introduction of foreign plant and animal species into the wild in Northern Ireland, the intention being to prevent further instances of the ecological damage caused by the introduction of foreign species such as the grey squirrel and giant hogweed.

Article 22 of the Directive also requires member states to study the desirability of reintroducing native animals and plants of a European protected species where it might contribute to the conservation of such species. However, member states should only undertake the reintroduction of such species if the results of the study establish that such reintroduction 'contributes effectively to re-establishing these species at a favourable conservation status.' In this regard, member states are required to take experiences in other member states or elsewhere into account and also to undertake 'proper consultation of the public concerned'. Thus far the Conservation (Natural Habitats etc.) Regulations (NI) 1995[70] control the introduction of native plants and animals of a European protected species into areas of Northern Ireland by means of the licensing system set out in regulation 39, the terms of which are outlined at page 326 in the context of the DoE(NI)'s general powers to issue licences under the WO.

---

70. Ibid.

### Animal species

Article 15(1) makes it an offence to 'release or allow to escape into the wild' any animal that: (i) is not 'ordinarily resident in and is not a regular visitor to Northern Ireland in a wild state' or (ii) is listed in Part I of Schedule 9 to the WO.

### Plant species

Article 15(2) provides that if any person 'plants or otherwise causes to grow in the wild' any plant listed in Part II of Schedule 9 they will be guilty of an offence.

### Defence to proceedings under article 15(1) and (2)

Article 15(3) and (4) governs the types of defences which may be relied on in proceedings for offences concerning the introduction of foreign plant or animal species into the wild in Northern Ireland. Article 15(3) provides that it is a defence to prove that the accused 'took all reasonable steps and exercised all due diligence to avoid committing the offence.' Article 15(4) provides that it is not permissible to assert in one's defence that the offence was committed 'due to the act or default of another person' unless the accused has given the prosecutor seven days' notice (before the hearing) of any information in his possession concerning the identity of the other person. Article 15(4) empowers the court to give leave to avoid these provisions.

### DoE(NI)'s power to enter land

A person authorised (in writing) by the DoE(NI) may enter any land for the purpose of determining whether an offence under article 15(1) or (2) 'is being or has been committed on that land.' The authorised person may only enter the land at a reasonable time and, if required to, must produce evidence of authorisation. Authorisation to enter land for these purposes does not confer a right to enter any dwelling. It is an offence to intentionally obstruct the exercise of this power.

### Penalties under article 15

Article 27(6) provides that a person found guilty of an offence under article 15 will be liable on summary conviction to a fine not exceeding the statutory maximum or, if convicted on indictment, to an unlimited fine. The statutory maximum is detailed in the Criminal Justice (NI) Order 1994.

## Wildlife refuges

In addition to protecting individual species of wild birds, plants and animals in Northern Ireland, article 16 of the WO also empowers the DoE(NI) to adopt orders which essentially turn specified areas of Northern Ireland into wildlife refuges, which protect either all or specified species of the wild animals,[71] birds[72] or plants

---

71. Art. 2(3) of the WO provides that a reference to a 'wild animal' in art. 16 will include a reference to 'game' for the purposes of this article. 'Game' is defined in art. 2(2) as 'any hare or game-bird and includes deer.' 'Game-bird' is defined in art. 2(2) as including 'any pheasant, partridge (including chukar partridge and red-legged partridge), woodcock, snipe or red grouse.'
72. Art. 2(4) of the WO provides that any reference to a 'wild bird' in art. 16 will include a reference to 'game-birds', as defined in art. 2(2) of the Order. The definition of 'game-bird' in this context is provided ibid.

within that area. The concept of a wildlife refuge is essentially a disturbance-based designation, and although the DoE(NI) is given the power to make arrangements for the management of a wildlife refuge, its scope in this regard is not as great as in the context of the national and European site designations considered in Part II, sections 1 and 2 of this chapter. There are as yet no wildlife refuges in Northern Ireland. However, negotiations for a refuge at Lough Shark in County Armagh are being conducted.

An order under article 16 can:

(i) make it an offence to intentionally do some or all of the acts described below, either at all times or during specified periods, and/or

(ii) make it an offence for any person, except as may be provided in the order, to enter the area (or any part of it) at any time or during certain specified periods.

The acts which may be prohibited by an order under article 16(1) essentially mirror those acts which are already prohibited by the WO in respect of individual wild animal, plant and bird species for Northern Ireland as a whole. More specifically, article 16(1) provides that such an order may provide that any person who does any of the following within the area protected by the order is guilty of an offence:

(i) kills, injures or takes any wild bird or wild animal or any wild bird or wild animal so specified,

(ii) takes, damages or destroys any nest or any structure or place which such a bird or animal uses for shelter or protection while that nest or structure is in use or being built or while that place is in use,

(iii) takes, damages or destroys anything which conceals or protects any such nest, structure or place;

(iv) takes or destroys an egg of such a bird or the egg, larva, pupa or any such immature stage of such an animal,

(v) disturbs such a bird or animal while it is building a nest or structure for shelter or protection or while it is in, on or near such a nest or structure containing the egg of such a bird or the egg, larva, pupa or any such immature stage of such an animal,

(vi) disturbs the dependent young of such a bird or animal, or

(vii) picks, removes, uproots or destroys any wild plant or wild plant so specified...

### Enforcement of orders adopted under article 16(1)

Where an authorised person[73] 'suspects with reasonable cause that any person is committing or has committed an offence' under an order adopted pursuant to article 16(1), he may require that person to provide their full name and address and also to leave the area immediately. A refusal to comply with either request is an offence under article 16(3).

---

73. 'Authorised person' is defined by art. 3(1) of the WO as the owner or occupier of land (or someone authorised by them) or a person authorised by the DoE(NI). Authorisation does not confer any right of entry upon any land.

### Penalties for offences under article 16

Article 16(1)(*c*) provides that a person found guilty of any offence (within the protected area) under Part II of the WO, or any offence under Part II of the WO as may be specified in the order, will be liable to a special penalty. Article 27(1)(*a*) defines a special penalty under article 16 as a fine not exceeding level 5 on the standard scale (£5,000). A person found guilty on summary conviction of an offence under article 16(3) will be liable to a fine not exceeding level 3 on the standard scale (£1,000). Article 27(7) also provides that where an offence under article 16 is committed in respect of more than one animal, bird, plant, egg, nest, or thing, 'the maximum fine which may be imposed . . . shall be determined as if the person convicted had been convicted of a separate offence in respect of each bird, nest, egg, animal, plant or thing.'

### Obligations imposed on the DoE(NI) when making an order under article 16(1)

Before making an order under article 16(1), the DoE(NI) is obliged to consult any district council within whose district the area in question is situated. In addition, the DoE(NI) must give written notification of the proposed order to every owner and occupier of any land that is to be included in the protected area. Where the Department considers it impracticable to give such notice, it must advertise the particulars of the intended order in a newspaper 'circulating in the locality in which the area is situated' (article 16(5)(*a*) and (*b*)). The Department cannot make an order under article 16(1) unless all owners and occupiers of any land affected by the order have either consented to the order or have not objected to the order within three months of the date of the notice or advertisement or unless such persons have withdrawn their objections to the order (article 16(6)).

### Effect of an order under article 16 on rights to land

Article 16(4) provides that an order under article 16 will 'not affect the exercise by any person of any right vested in him, whether as owner, lessee or occupier of any land in that area or by virtue of a licence or agreement.'

### DoE(NI)'s power to issue licences which suspend the operation of orders made under article 16

Article 18 empowers the DoE(NI) to issue licences which provide that orders made under article 16 will not apply to activities carried out for certain specified purposes. The terms of article 18 are outlined at page 326.

### Amendments to article 16

Article 16(2) of the WO exempted the killing of wild birds (and their nests, eggs and young) listed in Schedule 2 to the WO from the protection afforded by an article 16(1) order. Article 4(1)(*c*) of the Wildlife (Amendment) (NI) Order 1995[74] has repealed this exemption. Article 4 of the Amendment Order came into force on

---

74. SI 1995/761.

15 September 1995 under the Wildlife (1995 Order) (Commencement) Order (NI) 1995.[75]

### Exceptions to article 16

Article 17 provides that the exceptions contained in articles 5, 11 and 14(3) to offences concerning wild animals,[76] birds[77] and plants laid down in articles 4, 10 and 14(1) will apply to the protection afforded to animals, plants and birds by orders made under article 16(1), as follows:

1. The exceptions contained in article 5(4) and (5) of the WO in relation to wild birds will apply to offences under article 16(1) in the same way as they apply to offences under article 4. References to an order adopted under article 16 should be substituted for references to article 4, and any reference to a wild bird should include a reference to a wild animal.
2. The exception contained in article 5(6) of the WO to offences concerning any wild bird and their nests and eggs will apply to corresponding offences relating to wild birds under article 16(1) in the same way as they apply to offences under article 4.
3. The exception contained in article 11(3) of the WO to offences concerning wild animals and their shelter will apply to corresponding offences under article 16(1) in the same way as they apply to article 10.
4. The exception contained in article 14(3) of the WO to offences concerning wild plants will apply to corresponding offences under article 16(1) in the same way as they apply to article 14(1).

### DoE(NI)'s power to grant licences

This section will address the DoE(NI)'s powers to grant licences in relation to wildlife species protected under the WO and the Conservation (Natural Habitats etc.) Regulations (NI) 1995.[78]

### (a) Licences under the WO

Article 18 of the WO empowers the DoE(NI) to issue licences which allow the suspension of articles 4, 6, 8, 9, 10 and 12 of the WO and orders adopted under article 16 of the WO for certain specified purposes. In effect, the system of licences creates a further series of exceptions to the protection afforded to wild animals,[79] birds,[80] and plants. However, article 18(1)–(3) provides that a licence will only operate to exempt the licensee from the provisions of the WO in question

---

75. SR No. 322.
76. Art. 2(3) of the WO provides that a reference to a wild animal in art. 17 will include a reference to 'game'. The definition of this term is provided at note 71, supra.
77. Art. 2(4) of the WO provides that any reference to wild birds in art. 17 will include a reference to 'game-birds'; this term is defined at note 71, supra.
78. SR No. 380.
79. Art. 2(3) of the WO provides that a reference to 'wild animals' will include a reference to 'game' for the purposes of art. 18. This term is defined at note 71, supra.
80. Art. 2(4) provides that a reference to 'wild birds' in art. 18 will include a reference to 'game-birds'. This term is defined at note 71, supra.

if the activities carried out are carried out in accordance with the terms of the licence.

It is also important to note that article 3 of the Wildlife (Amendment) (NI) Order 1995[81] amends article 18(6) so as to introduce a power to issue general licences to kill wild birds. This power in effect replaces the concept of a list of 'pest birds' which could be killed or taken at any time by an authorised person, which was declared illegal under Directive 79/409/EEC on the Conservation of Wild Birds (the Wild Birds Directive). Finally, it should be noted that none of the following articles of the WO applies to anything done under, and in accordance with, the terms of a licence granted by the DoE(NI): articles 7(1) and (2) (sale of live and dead wild birds), 13(1) and (2) (sale of live and dead wild animals), 14(1)(*a*) and (2) (destruction and sale of live or dead wild plants), and 15 (new species).

Article 18, as amended, empowers the DoE(NI) to issue licences in relation to wild birds, animals and plants for the following purposes:

1. A licence may be granted which provides that the terms of articles 4, 6, 8, 9, 10(1), (2) and (4), 12(1) and (2) and 14(1) and orders under article 16 will not apply to actions carried out for the purpose of education, photography, preventing the spread of disease, preservation of public health and safety or air safety (article 18(1)).
2. A licence may be granted which provides that the terms of articles 4, 6, 8 and 9 and orders under article 16 will not apply to activities carried out for the purpose of ringing or examining the ring, marking or examining the mark on wild birds or their eggs, conservation of wild birds, protection of any collection of wild birds, falconry, or aviculture,[82] public exhibition or competition, taxidermy, or the prevention of serious damage to livestock,[83] foodstuffs for livestock, crops, vegetables, fruit, growing timber, pasture, or fisheries (article 18(2)).
3. A licence may be granted which provides that the terms of articles 10(1), (2) and (4), 12(1) and (2) and 14(1) and orders under article 16 will not apply to anything done for the purpose of ringing and marking wild animals or for the purpose of examining any ring or mark on wild animals, the conservation of wild plants or animals or introducing them into particular areas, the protection of any zoological or botanical collection, or the prevention of serious damage to livestock etc. as listed at number 2 above with the addition, in this context, of anything done to prevent serious damage to any other form of property (article 18(3)).

*General provisions concerning the granting of licences under the WO*

A licence granted under article 18 may be 'general or specific' in nature, it may be

---

81. SI 1995/761.
82. 'Aviculture' is defined in art. 3(1) of the WO as 'the breeding and rearing of birds in captivity.'
83. 'Livestock' is defined in art. 3(1) of the WO as including 'any animal which is kept: (*a*) for the purposes of food, wool, skins or fur; (*b*) for the purposes of its use in the carrying on of any agricultural activity; or (*c*) for rearing and release into the wild for the provision or improvement of shooting or fishing, or for the purposes of nature conservation.'

granted to an individual person or to a class of persons,[84] it may be granted subject to certain conditions, it will be valid for the period stated in the licence, and it may be 'modified or revoked at any time' by the DoE(NI). The Department is empowered to charge 'such reasonable sum as it may determine' for the licence (article 18(5)).

### Power to issue general licences to kill wild birds

Article 18(6) has been amended by article 3 of the Wildlife (Amendment) (NI) Order 1995[85] to introduce a power to issue a general licence to kill wild birds, which replaces the now abolished list of 'pest birds' which could be killed at any time by an authorised person (at page 306). Article 18(6) now provides that a licence to kill wild birds issued under article 18 must specify the species of wild birds which may be killed, the area within which such birds may be killed, and the methods by which they may be killed. The licence is no longer required to specify the persons authorised to kill such wild birds, as was required under article 18(6). A licence to kill wild birds will be valid for the period laid down in the licence; however, this period must not exceed a maximum of two years. This is subject to the DoE(NI)'s power under article 18(5) to modify or revoke, at any time, any licence issued under article 18. The Wildlife (1995 Order) (Commencement) Order (NI) 1995[86] provides that article 3 comes into effect on 15 August 1995.

### Power to issue licences to kill wild animals

Article 3 of the Wildlife (Amendment) (NI) Order 1995 introduces paragraph 6A to article 18 which, in effect, maintains the original position in relation to licences to kill wild animals, namely, that a general licence cannot be issued. Article 18(6A) provides that a licence issued under article 18 which authorises the killing of wild animals must specify the species of wild animal which may be killed, the person who is authorised to do so, the area within which they may be killed, and the methods that may be used to kill such wild animals. As with wild birds, a licence to kill wild animals will be valid for the period specified in the licence, but this must not exceed two years. The DoE(NI) retains the power in this context to revoke or modify, at any time, a licence issued under article 18. The Wildlife (1995 Order) (Commencement) Order (NI) 1995 provides that article 3 comes into effect on 15 August 1995.

### False statements made for the purpose of obtaining a licence

It is an offence for any person who is applying for a licence either on their own behalf or on behalf of another to either knowingly or recklessly make a false statement or representation or to furnish a document which is false in a material particular (article 24). A person found guilty on summary conviction of an offence

---

84. Art. 18(7) provides that for the purposes of a licence granted under art. 18, the 'definition of a class of persons may be framed by reference to any circumstances whatever including, in particular, their being authorised by any other person.'
85. SI 1995/761.
86. SR No. 322.

under article 24 will be liable to a fine not exceeding level 4 on the standard scale (£2,500) (article 27(3)). Where an offence has been committed in respect of more than one of the above, article 27(7) provides that the 'maximum fine which may be imposed . . . shall be determined as if the person convicted had been convicted of a separate offence in respect of each [of the above].'

*Licences granted in relation to deer*

The DoE(NI) is also empowered to grant licences in relation to deer. These powers are set out in article 21, Part III, of the WO, which is discussed separately on page 333.

### (b) Licences granted in relation to European protected species

As with article 18 of the WO, regulation 39 empowers the DoE(NI) to grant licences for specific purposes, which in effect suspend the operation of regulations 34, 36, and 38, provided the activity in question is carried out in accordance with the terms of the licence. A licence may be granted by the DoE(NI) under regulation 39 in relation to a European protected species of plant or animal for the following purposes:

(*a*) scientific or educational purposes;

(*b*) ringing or marking, or examining any ring or mark on, wild animals;

(*c*) conserving wild animals or wild plants or introducing them to particular areas;

(*d*) protecting any zoological or botanical collection;

(*e*) preserving public health or public safety or other imperative reasons of overriding public interest including those of a social or economic nature and beneficial consequences of primary importance for the environment;

(*f*) preventing the spread of disease; or

(*g*) preventing serious damage to livestock, crops, vegetables, fruit, growing timber, pasture or any other form of property or to fisheries.

In effect, regulation 39 implements the terms of Article 16.1 of the Habitats Directive, which essentially creates further exceptions to the protection afforded to European protected species by permitting member states to derogate from the provisions of Articles 12 and 15 (animals) and article 13 (plants) of the Directive. The provisions of articles 12, 15 and 13 of the Directive are implemented by regulations 34, 36, and 38, respectively, of the Habitats Regulations (outlined at pages 316 and 321). It is important to note the following points concerning these exceptions:

1. Although the list of specific purposes for which a licence under regulation 39 may be granted is not as extensive as that contained in article 18 of the WO, the terms of regulation 39(*e*) have the potential to be interpreted broadly, thereby widening the range of possible exceptions to the protection afforded to European protected species. Regulation 39(*e*) essentially reflects the circumstances in which the DoE(NI) may consent to damaging operations being conducted on a site protected as a European site that would otherwise be

prohibited (regulation 16 and 17 of the Habitats Regulations, outlined in Part II, section 2 of this chapter). The scope of regulation 39(*e*) will depend on the manner in which the concepts of economic and social interests are interpreted by the DoE(NI), national courts, and the European Court of Justice.

2. Unlike the position under article 18 of the WO, the DoE(NI)'s power to grant a licence, for any purpose, is controlled by the Habitats Regulations in two ways. The first requires the DoE(NI) itself to refuse a licence unless certain criteria are satisfied; the second is a control exerted by the Commission at Community level. Regulation 39 prohibits the DoE(NI) from granting a licence for any of the listed purposes unless it is satisfied that there is 'no satisfactory alternative' and 'that the action authorised will not be detrimental to the maintenance of the population of the species concerned at a favourable conservation status in their natural range.' The extent of the control exerted will once again depend on the manner in which it is interpreted in future years. Article 16.2 of the Habitats Directive imposes the second (Community) level control on a member state's freedom to interpret these derogations. Article 16.2 requires that member states send a report to the Commission every two years detailing any derogation from the protection afforded to those plants and animal species covered by the Directive—in effect, a report of the licences granted in Northern Ireland under regulation 39. In addition, the report must specify:

   (i)   the species which are subject to the derogations, the reasons for the derogation, including the nature of the risk, with, if appropriate, a reference to alternatives rejected and scientific data used;
   (ii)  the means, devices or methods authorised for the capture or killing of animal species and the reasons for their use;
   (iii) the circumstances of when and where such derogations are granted;
   (iv)  the authority empowered to declare and check that the required conditions obtain and to decide what means, devices or methods may be used, within what limits and by what agencies, and which persons are to carry out the task.

The Commission is required by Article 16.2 to give its opinion on these derogations within twelve months of receiving the report and to give an account to the committee established under Article 20 of the Directive. This committee consists of representatives from each member state, chaired by a representative of the Commission, and votes by majority decision in accordance with Article 148(2) of the EC Treaty. In effect, the Commission may propose that certain measures be taken, but it may only adopt the proposed measures if the committee agrees. However, where the committee does not agree with the Commission, or the committee delivers no opinion on the matter, the proposals may be submitted to the Council as a matter of urgency. The Commission may adopt the measures if the Council supports the proposed measures by a qualified majority within three months of the date of referral.

   Although it is not stated explicitly in the Directive, it would appear that the Commission is not only empowered to comment on the manner in which these derogations are being interpreted by member states but may also, with the consent of the committee or Council, compel member states to alter their practices where they do not comply with the objectives of the Directive.

3. Regulation 40 sets out the general provisions governing the nature and duration

of licences issued under regulation 39. They are identical to those applying under article 18(5) of the WO (above), with one exception. Whereas the DoE(NI) is expressly granted the power to charge a reasonable sum for licences issued under article 18, regulation 40 is silent in this regard. The provisions of regulation 40 concerning the DoE(NI)'s power to issue a licence to kill an animal of a European protected species (i.e. relating to the nature and duration of the licence) are identical to those set out in relation to animals, other than birds, under the WO, as amended by the 1995 Amendment Order (pages 327 and 328).

4. Finally, identical provisions are also laid down under article 24 of the WO and regulation 41 of the Habitats Regulations concerning the giving of false information when applying for a licence under either measure; identical penalties are also imposed (page 328).

## Protection of deer

Articles 12 and 19–23 of the WO make provision for the protection of deer in terms similar to that afforded to other wild animals, birds, and plants. Unless otherwise provided, the term 'deer' in this context includes 'deer of any species and their hybrids, and includes those on enclosed land where deer not in the wild state are usually kept' (article 2(2)). Nothing in articles 19, 20 or 21 will affect 'any requirement under any statutory provision which applies to game' (article 19(6)).

### Killing, injuring or taking of deer

Article 19(1) provides that any person who 'intentionally kills, injures or takes any deer of a species and description mentioned in Schedule 10 during the close season prescribed by that Schedule' will be guilty of an offence. Schedule 10 lists fallow, red and sika deer. Each species and each type of deer within a species has a specific close season; these are specified in Schedule 10. The DoE(NI) has the power to alter the close season for any species of deer in relation to any part of Northern Ireland under article 19(5); thus far this power has not been exercised. However, notwithstanding the provisions of article 19(1), article 19(2) provides that any person who 'intentionally kills, injures or takes' any deer 'between the expiration of the first hour after sunset and the commencement of the last hour before sunrise' will be guilty of an offence.

### Prohibited methods of killing deer

In addition to the provisions of article 12 (considered above), which prohibit certain methods of killing or taking wild animals (including deer in general and those species listed in Schedule 6, namely red, sika and fallow deer), article 19(3)(*a*) provides that it is an offence to kill or injure 'any deer' by using any of the firearms or forms of ammunition listed in Schedule 11. Article 19(3)(*b*) provides that any person who 'discharges any firearm' or who 'projects any missile from any mechanically propelled vehicle' at any deer will be guilty of an offence.

### Interference with live deer

Article 19(4) provides that any person who:

    (a) takes and removes any live deer;

    (b) marks, or attaches any tag, ring, collar or other device to, any live deer; or

    (c) uses any aircraft for the purpose of transporting any live deer other than in the interior of the aircraft

will be guilty of an offence.

### Penalties for offences under article 19

A person found guilty of an offence under article 19 will be liable under article 27(4) to a fine not exceeding level 4 on the standard scale (£2,500) or to a term of imprisonment not exceeding three months, or to both. Article 27(7) provides that where an offence is committed in respect of more than one deer, 'the maximum fine which may be imposed . . . shall be determined as if the person convicted had been convicted of a separate offence in respect of each deer.'

### Exceptions to articles 12 and 19

Article 20 of the WO sets out the following exceptions to the provisions of articles 12 and 19:

1. The occupier of any enclosed land where deer 'not in the wild state are usually kept' (or any person authorised[87] by the occupier of such land) will not be caught by the provisions of articles 12(2)(*d*) and 19(3)(*b*), which normally prohibit the use of certain forms of killing or taking deer, so long as the action is taken in relation to such deer on that land.

2. Articles 12 and 19 do not apply to anything done by a veterinary surgeon or veterinary practitioner for the purpose of treating a deer.

3. Any act which would normally be an offence under article 12(2)(*c*)(iii) or (iv), article 12(2)(*d*) or article 19(1), (3)(*b*) or (4)(*a*) or (*b*) will not be an offence where it is done by a person who 'keeps and breeds deer for the purposes of a trade or business' if:

    (i) the act is done 'in the course of that trade or business' and the DANI has certified, for the purpose of this provision, that such a person is indeed carrying on such a trade or business, or

    (ii) if the act is done 'for the purposes of protecting any person immediately endangered by a deer on any enclosed land on which deer not in the wild state are usually kept, where that act is reasonable in the circumstances.'

---

87. 'Authorised person' in the context of art. 20 (which contains the exceptions to art. 19) is defined by art. 20(9) as: '(*a*) the occupier of the land on which the action is taken; (*b*) any member of the occupier's household normally resident on the occupier's land, acting with the written authority of the occupier; (*c*) any person in the ordinary service of the occupier on the occupier's land, acting with the written authority of the occupier; or (*d*) any person having the right to take or kill deer on the land on which the action is taken, or any person acting with the written authority of a person having that right.'

4. A person who uses or sets in position 'any trap or net' in order to 'prevent suffering by an injured or diseased deer' will not be guilty of an offence under article 12(2)(*a*) or (*b*). Similarly, any person who does any act for such a purpose will not be guilty of an offence under article 19(1) or (2).

5. Any action taken by the DANI under section 2 of the Agriculture (Miscellaneous Provisions) Act (NI) 1959[88] will not be rendered unlawful by article 19(1).

6. Article 20(6) provides that a person who takes, injures or kills by shooting any deer 'on cultivated land, enclosed pasture, enclosed woodland or garden grounds' will not be guilty of an offence under article 19(1) if that person can satisfy the court hearing the action:

   (*a*) that he was an authorised person,[89] and

   (*b*) that he had reasonable grounds for believing that deer of the same species were causing, or had caused, serious damage to crops, pasture, vegetables, fruit, growing timber or any other form of property on that land, pasture, woodland or those grounds, and

   (*c*) that there was a likelihood of further serious damage and that such action was likely to be serious, and

   (*d*) that his action was necessary for the purpose of preventing any further damage.

7. Article 19(7) provides that a person will not be guilty of any offence under article 19(3)(*a*) for either:

   (i) the killing or injuring of any deer on any land by using one of the two types of 'smooth bore guns' specified in article 19(7)(*a*) if the person in question can satisfy the court hearing the action of the conditions described in article 20(*b*)(*a*)–(*d*) above, or

   (ii) the killing of any deer by using 'any smooth bore gun' if the person in question can establish that the deer 'had been so seriously injured, otherwise than by his unlawful act, or was in such a condition, that to kill it was an act of mercy.' The DoE(NI) has the power to alter the terms of this exception or to repeal it; thus far, this power has not been exercised.

### DoE(NI)'s power to grant licences in relation to deer

The DoE(NI) is empowered by article 21 to grant licences for specific purposes which, in effect, suspend the operation of article 19. Licences may be granted for scientific and educational purposes and for the purpose of 'removing deer from one area to another.' However, article 21(1) provides that a licence will only operate to suspend the effect of article 19 if the terms of the licence are complied with. Article 18(5)–(7) of the WO governs the scope and duration of a licence granted under article 21, and also sets out specific provisions concerning the granting of a licence to kill deer. Article 24, which governs the making of false statements when applying for a licence under article 18, also applies to applications for licences under article 21. The terms of article 18(5)–(7) and article 24 are addressed above at pages 327–9.

---

88. c. 2.

89. The definition of an 'authorised person' for the purposes of art. 20 is provided at note 87, supra.

### Poaching deer

It is an offence to enter any land without the consent of the owner or occupier or without any 'other lawful authority' for the purpose of searching for or pursuing any deer with the intention of killing, injuring or taking it (article 22(1)). Similarly, any person who commits any of the following acts without such consent or lawful authority 'while on any land' will be guilty of an offence under article 22(2):

    (a) intentionally kills, injures or takes any deer;

    (b) searches for or pursues any deer with the intention of killing, injuring or taking it; or

    (c) removes the carcass of any deer or any part thereof.

A person will not be guilty of an offence under article 22(1) or (2) where the action in question was 'done in the reasonable belief' that either: (i) the owner or occupier of the land would have given their consent had they known that the person in question was taking such action and of the circumstances in which it was being done or (ii) he had the lawful authority to do so (article 22(3)). An 'authorised person'[90] is empowered under article 22(5) to request any person to leave any land, giving their full name and address, where they suspect, 'with reasonable cause,' that the person in question is either in the process of committing an offence or has committed an offence under article 22(1) or (2) on that land. Failure to comply with such a request is an offence under article 22(5).

### Penalties for offences under article 22

A person found guilty of an offence under article 22 will be liable on summary conviction to a fine not exceeding level 4 on the standard scale (£2,500) or to a maximum of three months imprisonment, or to both (article 27(4)). Article 27(7) provides that where an offence under article 22(1), (2) or (5) is committed in respect of more than one deer 'or other thing . . . the maximum penalty which may be imposed . . . shall be determined as if the person convicted had been convicted of a separate offence in respect of each deer or thing.' Article 22(4) in effect reiterates the terms of article 27(7) in relation to offences under article 22(2).

### Sales and purchases etc. of venison

#### (i) Sale by unlicensed game dealers

It is an offence for an unlicensed game dealer to sell or to offer or expose for sale any venison[91] to a person who is not a licensed game dealer. This prohibition applies at all times (article 23(1)). It is also an offence under article 23(1) for an unlicensed game dealer to sell or to offer or expose for sale, have in his possession, transport or cause to be transported for the purposes of sale at any premises any venison at any time during 'the prohibited period'. The concept of a prohibited period is defined by article 23 in relation to those deer for which a close

---

90. The term 'authorised person' for the purposes of art. 22 is defined by art. 22(6) as 'the owner or occupier or any person authorised by the owner or occupier of the land, and includes any person having the right to take or kill deer on the land.'

91. 'Venison' is defined by art. 23(3) as 'the carcass, or any edible part of the carcass, of a deer, and includes imported venison, but not canned or cooked venison.'

season is prescribed in Schedule 10. This provision covers all deer except those kept or bred for the purpose of a trade or business (article 20(2)). The term 'prohibited period' means 'the period beginning with the expiration of the tenth day, ending with the expiration of the last day, of that season' (article 23(3)).

*(ii) Sale, purchase or receiving of venison from deer killed or taken in violation of the WO*

Article 23(2) provides that it is an offence for 'any person' to knowingly[92] sell or offer or expose for sale, possess, transport or cause to be transported for sale at any premises, purchase, offer to purchase or receive any venison which comes from a deer that was killed or taken in circumstances that violate the terms of the WO.

### Penalties for offences under article 23

A person found guilty of an offence under article 23(1) will be liable on summary conviction to a fine not exceeding level 3 on the standard scale (£1,000) (article 27(5)). A person found guilty of an offence under article 23(2) will be liable on summary conviction to a fine not exceeding level 4 on the standard scale (£2,500) or a maximum of three months' imprisonment, or to both (article 27(4)). Where an offence has been committed under article 23(1) or (2) in relation to more than one venison, article 27(7) provides that 'the maximum fine which may be imposed . . . shall be determined as if the person convicted had been convicted of a separate offence in respect of each [venison].'

## PART II HABITAT PROTECTION

The protection and management of the most important sites for wild flora and fauna and geological and physiographical features is the cornerstone of conservation practice throughout the world. As in Great Britain, the legislative framework governing site protection in Northern Ireland essentially comprises two systems of protection. On the one hand, sites may be protected under national designations laid down in the Nature Conservation and Amenity Lands (NI) Order 1985,[93] as amended. On the other hand, a site may also be protected as a 'European site' under Directive 92/43/EEC on the Conservation of Natural Habitats and of Wild Fauna and Flora (Habitats Directive), as implemented in Northern Ireland by the Conservation (Natural Habitats etc.) Regulations (NI) 1995.[94] Sites of purely local interest will be protected under national designation only; however, sites of Community interest will be protected under both the national and European systems. Although there is a certain degree of overlap between their provisions, the EC system of site protection is more stringent. The UK is also bound by a number of international nature conservation conventions as a state and, also, almost invariably, because the EC itself has also become a party

---

92. In other words, where the person in question 'knows or has reason to believe' that the venison comes from deer killed in violation of the WO (art. 23(2)(*b*)).
93. SI 1985/170.
94. SR No. 380.

to the agreement. The standards laid down in these international agreements are reflected in both the national and EC systems of control.

For the sake of clarity, the national and EC dimensions of site protection are addressed separately in this chapter. Part II, section 1 outlines the national system of protection, while Part II, section 2 addresses the EC dimension. Areas of overlap are highlighted at the appropriate places, and the implementation of international standards within both spheres of control is indicated where relevant.

## SECTION 1. THE NATIONAL DIMENSION

The Nature Conservation and Amenity Lands (NI) Order 1985 (NCALO), as amended by the Nature Conservation and Amenity Lands (Amendment) (NI) Order 1989[95] (the '1989 Amendment Order'), is the principal piece of national legislation governing the protection and management of wildlife sites and important areas of geological and physiographical importance in Northern Ireland. The NCALO repeals and replaces the earlier legislation governing this issue in Northern Ireland, namely the Amenity Lands Act (NI) 1965.[96] In effect, the NCALO affords protection to such sites by means of a web of protective designations, namely, 'areas of special scientific interest' (ASSI), 'national nature reserves' (NNR), 'nature reserves' (NR), 'marine nature reserves' (MNR), and 'areas of outstanding natural beauty' (AONB).

As in Great Britain, the ASSI[97] and the NR/NNR designations are used to protect the most important sites in Northern Ireland. There are two principal differences between NRs and NNRs on the one hand and ASSIs on the other hand. First, reserves are almost invariably in public ownership and, as a result, are all actively managed and controlled by the DoE(NI) or other public bodies. ASSIs, on the other hand, are almost all privately owned; however, restrictions are placed on land use. Second, while the DoE(NI) has a discretion to declare an area as an NR or NNR, the Department is obliged to declare an area an ASSI where it meets objective scientific criteria. In practice the ASSI designation is reserved for the most important sites in Northern Ireland; an NR or NNR will only be declared where positive management or public access to the site is required.

As is the case in relation to SSSIs in Great Britain, the approach to the management of ASSIs in Northern Ireland rests on a policy of voluntary co-operation between the DoE(NI) and owners and occupiers of land. Owners and occupiers of land are perceived as having the primary responsibility for site protection, and therefore compulsory controls will only be used as a last resort.

It is important to note that an area can be protected by several overlapping designations, including the EC and international designations discussed below in Part II, section 2 and Part III. For example, an area might be declared an NR but might also be declared an ASSI where the scientific criteria are satisfied. In

---

95. SI 1989/492. For further reading on the debates surrounding the adoption of this Order see: *Northern Ireland Assembly Report on the Proposal for a Draft Nature Conservation and Amenity Lands (NI) Order 1983,* and *Northern Ireland Assembly Report on the Proposal for a Draft Wildlife (NI) Order and a Draft Nature Conservation and Amenity Lands (NI) Order,* vol. II.

96. c. 9.

97. The 'site of special scientific interest' (SSSI) is the British equivalent of the Northern Ireland ASSI designation.

addition, the area might be listed as a candidate for 'special area of conservation' status under the Habitats Directive and as a 'special protection area' under the Wild Birds Directive; it might also be declared an AONB.

## Enforcement of the NCALO

Article 3 of the NCALO obliges the DoE(NI) to formulate and implement policies for nature conservation. In particular, Part II of the NCALO sets out the Department's powers to conduct research, provide information, make grants and loans to the National Trust, carry out works, and provide facilities. Part V empowers the DoE(NI) to establish and maintain nature reserves and national nature reserves; Part VI imposes an obligation on the Department to designate certain areas as ASSIs; while Parts III and VIII contain various general powers and obligations to support the DoE(NI)'s overall work in this context, including the provision of financial assistance and the adoption and enforcement of bylaws. The Secretary of State is empowered to declare marine nature reserves under Part V.

Article 4 of the NCALO provides that public bodies[98] which exercise statutory functions relating to land are required 'to have regard to the need to conserve the natural beauty and amenity of the countryside and the need to protect (so far as reasonably practicable) flora, fauna and geological and physiographical features of the countryside from any harmful effects which might result from the exercise of such functions.' In addition, article 32 provides that the CNCC (considered below) and any other body having functions under the NCALO have a duty to have 'due regard to the needs of agriculture, forestry and fisheries' in the exercise of these functions. The DoE(NI) itself is required to have 'due regard to any representations made to it by the Department of Agriculture (Northern Ireland) on behalf of persons engaged in agriculture, forestry or fisheries.' In addition, it should be noted that regulation 3(2) of the Conservation (Natural Habitats etc.) Regulations (NI) 1995 requires the DoE(NI) to exercise its functions under Northern Ireland nature conservation legislation (including Parts V and VI of the NCALO concerning the declaration of NNR or NRs and ASSIs) so as to secure compliance with the requirements of Directive 92/43/EEC on the conservation of natural habitats and of wild fauna and flora (Habitats Directive). Regulation 3(4) also provides that 'every competent authority in the exercise of any of its functions shall have regard to the requirements of the Habitats Directive so far as they may be affected by the exercise of those functions.'[99] (The habitat protection requirements laid down by the Habitats Directive are discussed in detail in Part II, section 2 of this chapter.)

## The Council for Nature Conservation and the Countryside

Article 5(1) of the Nature Conservation and Amenity Lands (Amendment) (NI)

---

98. Art. 4(2) of the NCALO defines the term 'public body' as including 'Government departments, district councils, statutory undertakers, and any trustees, commissioners, board or other persons who, as a public body and not for their own profit, act under any statutory provision for the improvement of any place or the production or supply of any commodity or service.'
99. The term 'competent authority' is defined by reg. 5 of the Habitats Regulations in identical terms to the definition of a public body under article 4(2) of the NCALO, provided note 98, supra.

Order 1989[100] (1989 Amendment Order) abolished both the Committee for Nature Conservation and the Ulster Countryside Committee, while article 3 of the Amendment Order established the Council for Nature Conservation and the Countryside (CNCC) to replace them as the statutory advisory body to the DoE(NI) on matters concerning nature conservation and the countryside under the NCALO.[101] Article 4 provides that the functions previously conferred on the Committee for Nature Conservation and the Ulster Countryside Committee by the NCALO are to be transferred to the CNCC. Thus far, the CNCC has produced three reports of its work since 1989, the most recent covering the period 1992–93. A more substantial full-term report covering the period up to May 1995 is due to be published shortly.

The CNCC's functions in relation to habitat protection are as follows.[102] It is required to advise the DoE(NI) on the establishment and management of nature reserves and to advise the Secretary of State on the establishment and management of marine nature reserves, while district councils must consult the CNCC about the declaration of district council nature reserves. The DoE(NI) is required to consult the CNCC about the provision of facilities on nature reserves and before making nature reserve bylaws; similarly, the Secretary of State is required to consult the CNCC on the adoption of marine nature reserve bylaws. In addition, the DoE(NI) is obliged to consult the CNCC about the declaration and denotification of ASSIs. The CNCC may be heard at any inquiry held under any statutory provision where matters concerning nature conservation are involved.[103] It may advise the DoE(NI) on the payment of grants to voluntary bodies and on promotional and educational activities. Article 32 of the NCALO provides that the CNCC, and any other body having functions under the NCALO, have a duty to have 'due regard to the needs of agriculture, forestry and fisheries' in the exercise of their functions. Regulation 23 of the Conservation (Natural Habitats etc.) Regulations (NI) 1995[104] also requires the DoE(NI) to consult the CNCC before making bylaws for the protection of a European site (outlined in Part II, section 2 of this chapter). Finally, it should be noted that Northern Ireland is represented on the Joint Nature Conservation Committee, which co-ordinates the work of

---

100. SI 1989/492.
101. The Schedule to the Amendment Order sets out the constitution of the CNCC and supplementary provisions as to the remuneration and procedure of the council. The CNCC is empowered to create committees on specialist subjects which may be serviced by persons who represent a specific interest but who are not members of the CNCC. For further reading on the reasons for the establishment of the CNCC and the success of its operation to date see: *A New Look at the Northern Ireland Countryside* (the Balfour Report); *Northern Ireland Assembly Report on the Balfour Proposals: a New Look at the Northern Ireland Countryside*; *House of Commons Environment Committee First Report: Environmental Issues in Northern Ireland,* HC 39(1990) pp 109–18; K. Milton, *Our Countryside Our Concern.*
102. The CNCC's functions in relation to wildlife protection are outlined in Part I, section 1 of this chapter, while its functions in relation to countryside protection are outlined in chap. 8.
103. Art. 4(5) of the Nature Conservation and Amenity Lands (Amendment) (NI) Order 1989 provides that the DoE(NI) will defray any costs incurred by the CNCC in obtaining DoE(NI) approved legal representation for the purposes of such inquiries. However, the amount paid cannot exceed the amount agreed with the DoE(NI) and approved by the Department of Finance and Personnel (art. 4(6)).
104. SR No. 380.

conservation agencies in England, Scotland, and Wales, by the Chairman of the CNCC and the Director of Conservation within the DoE(NI).

## Research and information concerning nature conservation

Article 3(2)(*a*) of the NCALO empowers the DoE(NI) to carry out, commission, finance or support by other means any 'inquiries, investigations, or researches' that it considers necessary or expedient, while article 3(2)(*b*) provides that the Department may also 'provide advice and disseminate knowledge about nature conservation and the conservation and enhancement of the natural beauty and amenity of the countryside.' Article 4(3)(*b*) of the Nature Conservation and Amenity Lands (Amendment) (NI) Order 1989 provides that the CNCC must advise the DoE(NI) on promotional and educational activities conducted in relation to the conservation of nature.

## Areas of special scientific interest (ASSIs)

The ASSI designation, introduced by the NCALO in 1985, has been the principal tool employed by the DoE(NI) for the purposes of protecting the most important biological and geological sites in Northern Ireland. An ASSI is declared by the DoE(NI) where it is satisfied (after consultation with the CNCC) 'that an area of land is of special scientific interest, by reason of its flora, fauna or geological, physiographical or other features, and accordingly needs to be specially protected' (article 24(1)). It is important to note that whereas the DoE(NI) previously had a discretion to declare ASSIs under the NCALO, article 10(1) of the Nature Conservation and Amenity Lands (Amendment) (NI) Order 1989 now imposes a statutory duty on the Department to declare an area of land as an ASSI where the land is of special scientific interest (according to the criteria laid down in article 24(1)) and therefore needs special protection.

Before considering the ASSI concept in any further detail, it is important to distinguish between 'areas of scientific interest' (ASIs) and ASSIs. While they frequently overlap, ASIs and ASSIs are quite distinct. ASIs were notified under section 15 the Amenity Lands Act (NI) 1965 (now repealed by the NCALO), and a total of forty-eight were established between 1965 and 1984. Once an area was declared an ASI it meant that planning applications were checked for their potential impact on nature conservation; much stricter controls are imposed on land use within an area declared as an ASSI under the NCALO. Article 24 of the NCALO provides: (i) that section 15 of the 1965 Act ceases to have effect and (ii) that any notification made under section 15 in relation to any land will take effect as though it were an ASSI declaration under article 24. In addition, article 24 provides that the DoE(NI) is obliged to notify affected district councils and every owner and occupier of such land that redeclaration is taking place and also of the terms of the declaration. However, the Department's obligation to consider objections to and representations concerning ASSI designations under article 24(5) (considered below) will not apply to the redeclaration of ASIs under article 24. To date, no ASIs have been redeclared under the NCALO. ASIs remain in effect as if current ASSIs. ASI owners do not, however, have a list of notifiable operations (addressed below) and, therefore, the provisions of the NCALO concerning such operations do not apply.

An area is selected for declaration as an ASSI on the basis of objective scientific criteria, with only those areas of the highest degree of scientific value being finally designated. However, it should be noted that in *Sweet v. Secretary of State and Nature Conservancy Council,*[105] which concerned the boundaries of 'sites of special scientific interest' (the equivalent in Great Britain to ASSIs) under section 29 of the Wildlife and Countryside Act 1981, the court held that land of lesser scientific interest could be included within an SSSI notification where such land formed part of the same environmental unit as the land which was of special interest.

In assessing the nature conservation interest of a site, the DoE(NI) has relied heavily on the *Guidelines for Selection of Biological SSSIs,* published by the Nature Conservancy Council (GB) in 1989. ASSIs can broadly be divided into three categories, namely habitat sites, earth science sites and species sites. The selection of habitat sites has formed the bulk of the ASSI work in Northern Ireland.[106] The principal criteria used in assessing the nature conservation importance within each habitat type are 'size, diversity, naturalness and rarity.'[107] Other criteria, however, such as 'fragility, recorded history and intrinsic appeal,' will also be used where appropriate.[108] The criteria for earth science sites are different, the principal objective being to 'have a network of protected sites which collectively represent the geological and geomorphological evolution of Northern Ireland, including contemporary processes.'[109] The criteria for species sites are less well developed, because the information needed to determine the individual requirements for site protection is still in the process of being gathered and collated, particularly for species occurring in highly specialised niches, species that are highly dependent on habitat mosaics, and those species of high tropic status. In this regard the production of Red Data Books[110] is an extremely important vehicle for identifying and reviewing threatened plant and animal species, as are site-specific computer records being placed on the Recorder computer system. It should be noted that the DoE(NI) intends to publish a report during 1996, which will explain in more detail the application of the criteria used for site selection.

In 1993 the Government identified the protection of peatland as 'one of the top objectives for nature conservation in Northern Ireland,'[111] in particular raised and blanket bogs. As discussed in Part III of this chapter, peatland sites are listed as

---

105. [1989] JEL 245.
106. *Target 2001,* DoE(NI) 1993, Table 1, p. 10, provides a list of the basis habitat types used for ASSI selection in Northern Ireland. See: L.E. Davidson, and C. Mellon, *Safe and Sound?—A health check of Northern Ireland's Areas of Special Scientific Interest.* 1996 RSPB, for a detailed examination of the DoE(NI)'s implementation of its obligations in relation to ASSIs. Copies of this document can be obtained from: RSPB (Northern Ireland Office), Belvoir Forest Park, Belfast BT8 4QT.
107. *Target 2001,* Ibid., p. 11.
108. Ibid.
109. Ibid., p. 12.
110. 'Red Data Books' are published by HMSO, London.
111. *Conserving Peatland in Northern Ireland: a Statement of Policy* (1993). This statement was based on the CNCC's Peatland Strategy (1992). In Aug. 1993 the RSPB issued a written response to the Government's strategy document. The issue of peatland protection is also discussed further in Part III of this chapter.

habitats of international and EC importance, and the UK is specifically required under Community and international law to protect such habitats. Although it is not required under EC or international law, the Government has decided as a matter of policy that the ASSI designation will form the 'cornerstone of Government policy towards protecting peatland sites of recognised nature conservation value in Northern Ireland.'[112] In effect, peatlands of international significance must be declared as ASSIs before they are designated as European sites under the Wild Birds and/or Habitats Directive (Part II, section 2 of this chapter) or as Ramsar sites (Part III).[113]

There is no fixed size for an ASSI. Protected sites range from a small lowland grassland-fen meadow of 1 hectare with a single owner, to Lough Neagh, which is currently the largest ASSI in Northern Ireland, covering 39,800 hectares, with 460 owners and occupiers. The boundaries of an ASSI may not coincide with the boundaries of ownership; instead they will follow natural features such as obvious changes in vegetation.

Unlike NRs, which are mainly owned by the DoE(NI) or other public bodies, the great majority of ASSIs are privately owned. Although restraints are placed on the use of land declared as an ASSI so as to ensure that damaging activities do not occur (considered below), the policy underlying the protection of ASSIs is to achieve conservation by working in partnership with owners and occupiers of land so that the area can be protected through voluntary effort. Rights of access are unaffected by ASSI declaration—in fact there is usually no noticeable change wrought as a result of the declaration. Indeed, the DoE(NI) has stated that 'the ideal future management is almost always the same as past practice.'[114]

In 1990 the House of Commons Select Committee report, *Environmental Issues in Northern Ireland,*[115] highlighted the fact that Northern Ireland has lagged far behind Great Britain in nature conservation and emphasised in particular that the rate of ASSI declaration would have to be substantially increased for the ASSI programme, requiring the establishment of a comprehensive network of ASSIs covering all site types, to be completed. The Government's response a year later[116] was to pledge to complete the ASSI programme by the year 2001. A principal scientific officer was appointed to take charge of this programme and to develop a strategy of action.

In 1993 the DoE(NI) published *Target 2001,* which formally set out the Department's programme for the scientific survey, declaration and monitoring of areas of special nature conservation interest within Northern Ireland, the objective

---

112. Ibid., at p. 2.
113. It is important to note that non-governmental bodies have disagreed with the Government's approach to the selection of which peatland sites qualify for protection in Northern Ireland. In this regard the RSPB has been particularly critical of the DoE(NI)'s selection of candidate sites: see the RSPB's response to the Government's peatland strategy, published in August 1993; the Irish Peatland Conservation Council's *Policy Statement and Action Plan, 1992–1997*; A. Dodd and D. Pritchard, *RSPB Planscan Northern Ireland: a Study of Development Plans in Northern Ireland,* RSPB, 1993; and also Davidson and Mellon, supra, note 106.
114. *An Introduction to Areas of Special Scientific Interest,* Belfast: DoE(NI), 7.
115. HC 39 (1990).
116. *The Government's Response to the First Report from the House of Commons Select Committee on the Environment (Environmental Issues in Northern Ireland),* DoE(NI) London: HMSO (Cm 1484).

being the establishment of an ASSI network comparable with that operating in Great Britain by the year 2001. In essence, the programme aims to 'set in place a network of sites which are sufficient in number and size to guarantee the survival of Northern Ireland's habitats and wildlife and examples of its physical features.' To achieve this target, approximately 8 per cent of the area of Northern Ireland will have to be protected by ASSI declarations—approximately 110,000 hectares. Since the initiation of *Target 2001* the rate of ASSI declaration has increased considerably. In March 1993 there were forty ASSIs; during the period of the most recent *Environment Service Report* 1993–95, thirty-two new ASSIs were declared, involving consultations with over 1,300 owners and occupiers. At the time of writing, a total of 87 ASSIs have been declared under the NCALO, accounting for 5.35 per cent of the area of Northern Ireland.

The logical progression of ASSI declaration in Northern Ireland has been substantially disrupted by the obligation to implement the requirements of Directive 92/43/EEC on the Conservation of Natural Habitats and of Wild Fauna and Flora (the Habitats Directive), adopted by the EC in May 1992. As part of the preparation towards developing 'Natura 2000', the Directive requires that a list of prospective 'special areas of conservation' (SACs) (considered further in Part II, section 2) be submitted to the Commission by June 1995. However, the Government decided that before a site could be listed as a candidate SAC, it would have to be protected by an ASSI designation (or SSSI in Great Britain) by 31 March 1995. As a result, candidate SAC sites have had to take priority in the ASSI programme, at the expense of sites of purely local interest.

The final issue which should be noted at this point is the question of monitoring ASSI sites once they have been declared. *Target 2001* notes that post-declaration activities on ASSIs have been predominately reactive in nature, with the DoE(NI) mainly reacting to requests for consents to carry out notifiable operations (see below). *Target 2001* states that 'for the most part, [the Environment Service] do not know the extent of any damage or other significant changes occurring on ASSIs'[117] and acknowledges that the current management of ASSIs is insufficient to ensure that the scientific interest of these sites is protected. The report concludes that 'there is an imperative requirement to monitor sites proactively'[118] and states that a programme of 'proactive site integrity monitoring' will be initiated in the near future and will feature a timetable of visits to each ASSI based on the fragility of, and likelihood of change in, individual sites.

The *Environment Service Corporate Plan* 1994–97 confirms the need for adequate monitoring of ASSIs and makes the following commitment for the period of the plan:

> As we proceed with our designation programme we intend to put in place a system of monitoring to ensure that the scientific interest of ASSIs and [nature reserves] is maintained. We aim to have site management plans

---

117. Para. 3.7.1, p. 20; para. 3.7.2, p. 21. *Target 2001* notes that approximately eleven ad hoc reports have been submitted, mostly by third parties, concerning damage to ASSIs. It should be noted, however, that the RSPB (NI Branch) have recently published Davidson and Mellon (1996), *Safe and Sound?—A health check of Northern Ireland's Areas of Special Scientific Interest*, which provides a detailed analysis of the issue of monitoring NI's ASSIs. The report includes the findings of the monitoring pilot study commissioned by the DoE(NI).
118. Ibid.

completed by March 1995 for those ASSIs which will be SACs, by March 1996 for those ASSIs which will be SPAs and by March 1997 for the remaining existing ASSIs. We also aim to complete the software design for an ASSI database for site-specific monitoring by March 1995.[119]

Draft management plants for candidate SPAs and SACs have been completed.

## Procedure governing declaration of an ASSI

Article 24(1)–(5) of the NCALO sets down the procedures which must be followed by the DoE(NI) when declaring an area to be an ASSI. The Department is required to consult with the CNCC before making the declaration (article 24(1)). Where an ASSI is declared, the declaration itself must specify 'the flora, fauna or geological, physiographical or other features' which make the land of special scientific interest and also 'any operations and activities appearing to the Department to be likely to damage that flora or fauna or those features' (article 24(2)). The DoE(NI)'s *Introduction to ASSIs* points out that, in practice, the Department has drawn up a master list of operations and activities which might be damaging to any form of wildlife or natural feature. However, only those activities and operations which are relevant to a particular ASSI are listed in the declaration for that ASSI.

The court in *Sweet v. Secretary of State and Nature Conservancy Council* made it clear in relation to SSSIs under section 29 of the Wildlife and Countryside Act 1981 (governing Great Britain) that the concept of a notifiable operation would be interpreted widely and would include:

cultivation, including ploughing, rotavation, harrowing and reseeding; grazing; mowing or other methods of cutting vegetation; application of manure, fertilisers and lime; burning; the release into the site of any wild feral or domestic animal, reptile, amphibian, bird, fish or invertebrate, or any plant or seed; the storage of materials; the use of materials; the use of vehicles or craft likely to cause damage or disturb features of interest.[120]

Once included in the declaration, these are then termed the 'notifiable operations'[121] for that ASSI. When selecting the notifiable operations for a particular ASSI, the DoE(NI) 'takes into account the nature of the scientific interest, the variety of habitats found in the ASSI, and the range of possible land use options.'[122] There is a single list of notifiable operations for each ASSI in Northern Ireland; however, the DoE(NI) endeavours to keep the list as short as possible. Once the declaration is made, the DoE(NI) is required to notify the

---

119. *Environment Service Corporate Plan,* 1994–97, pp 8–9.
120. [1989] JEL 245. See also Appendix 2 of Davidson and Mellon, supra note 117, which contains the standardised coding system for notifiable operations in NI produced by MarEnCo, the Environmental Consultants commissioned by the DoE(NI) to undertake a monitoring pilot study of ASSIs. It should be noted that these notifiable operations codes were based on English Nature's *SSSI LCST Information System—Phase 2* which introduced a standardised coding system throughout the monitoring procedure for SSSIs.
121. These activities or operations are termed 'notifiable operations' because owners and occupiers of land within the ASSI are then required to notify the DoE(NI) of any proposal to carry out any such activity or operation. The procedure governing notification is outlined pp. 346–9.
122. *Introduction to Areas of Special Scientific Interest,* DoE(NI), 14.

declaration to all affected district councils[123] and every owner[124] or occupier of the land in question. Statutory bodies, such as Northern Ireland Electricity, will also be informed of all ASSIs within their operating areas. The notification must set out the terms of the declaration and the period within which and the manner in which representations and objections to the declaration can be made. In this regard the notification may not specify a period of less than three months from the date of the notification.

The DoE(NI) is obliged to consider any representation or objection to the declaration which is submitted within the time stated in the notification and must either confirm (with or without modifications) or rescind the declaration within three months of the representation or objection being made. The Department must give notice of its decision in this regard to all affected district councils and to every owner and occupier of the land in question. It should be noted, however, that an unconfirmed ASSI has the same status as a confirmed ASSI, which means that landowners cannot lawfully carry out damaging operations once the site has been declared an ASSI.

The complex nature of the legislative provisions governing the creation and management of ASSIs resulted in considerable hostility towards early designations. However, the *Environment Service Report* 1991–93 points out that the DoE(NI) now invests more resources in liaison with owners and occupiers of ASSI land to ensure that the consequences of designation are fully explained before the declaration is made. An effort is made to visit the majority of owners and occupiers twice, explaining the situation in some detail. For larger ASSIs meetings are held with groups of owners, interest groups, and district councils. In the event that an ASSI declaration is confirmed, the DoE(NI) may be obliged to compensate any person with an estate in the land in question for loss sustained as a result of the declaration. (See page 350 below.)

### ASSI management agreements

Where an ASSI has been declared, the DoE(NI) has the power to enter into an agreement with any owner or occupier of land in the area to ensure that their land is managed as an area of special scientific interest (article 24(8)(*a*)). Article 17(2)–(6) of the NCALO will apply to management agreements concerning ASSIs in the same way as they apply to agreements entered into under article 17(1) concerning nature reserves (article 24(9)). The DoE(NI) does not have the power to force an owner or occupier of land within an ASSI to enter into a management agreement. However, where such a person agrees to do so, the agreement may impose any restrictions on the exercise of rights over the land which may be necessary for the purposes of the agreement (article 17(2)).

The management agreement may make provision for compensation to be paid to the owner or occupier for the effect of any such restrictions (article 17(3)(*c*)). In

---

123. A district council is affected where the land in question lies either wholly or partly within the district of the council.
124. Art. 2(2) of the NCALO defines an 'owner' as 'any person (other than a mortgagee not in possession) who is the holder of or who is for the time being entitled to sell or otherwise dispose of the fee simple (including a fee farm grant) of the land or any person entitled to possession of the land by virtue of any estate in the land other than a mere licence.'

addition, the agreement may make provision for the positive management of the land by specifying that the land be managed in a particular manner, or that work be carried out on the land, or that any 'other things' as might be necessary for the purposes of the agreement be done (article 17(3)(*a*)). The agreement may make provision for the execution of any of the above[125] and also for the defrayment of any costs incurred in so doing either by the DoE(NI) or by the owner or occupier or by both (article 17(3)(*b*)). A management agreement will bind any person who derives title to the land by reason of a grant, or an agreement to grant a right in the land. In addition, a management agreement will bind a successor in title to such land in the same way as it affected the owner or occupier of the land (article 17(4)).

Article 17(5) provides that a management agreement may be made irrevocably or subject to specified provisions for revocation or variation of the agreement. The DoE(NI) has the power to waive, either temporarily or permanently, any condition or covenant included in a management agreement concerning an ASSI which is either inconsistent with the provision of a development plan or a development order under the Planning (NI) Order 1991 (article 17(6)).[126] Finally, the DoE(NI) may also make loans or grants (in addition to payments made under management agreements) to assist owners and occupiers of land within ASSIs to improve or conserve their land. In addition, various tax concessions and exemptions may be available in relation to land within ASSIs. An ASSI will usually be exempt from inheritance tax where satisfactory conservation measures have been agreed with the DoE(NI), usually under a management agreement. Where land within an ASSI is sold to an approved conservation body the sale may qualify for capital gains tax concessions, and further tax concessions may be made if a trust fund is established for the maintenance of the land.[127]

### Registration obligations concerning ASSIs

Article 33 of the NCALO provides that 'any declaration made and confirmed under article 24, that an area of land is an area of special scientific interest' must be registered in the Statutory Charges Register. Similarly, article 33 provides that any management agreement entered into under article 24(8)(*a*) for the management of an ASSI, and any waiver of the agreement, must be registered in the Statutory Charges Register.

### Acquisition of land within an ASSI or for the purpose of providing access

Article 24(8)(*b*) of the NCALO empowers the DoE(NI) to enter into an agreement

---

125. Note that art. 17(3)(*b*) has been amended by art. 8 of the Nature Conservation and Amenity Lands (Amendment) (NI) Order 1989, which requires that a reference to 'sub-paragraph (*a*)' be substituted for the reference to 'paragraph (2)'.

126. Art. 17(6) refers to the Planning (NI) Order 1972; however, this Order has since been replaced by the Planning (NI) Order 1991 (SI 1991/1220), which is now the principal legislative provision governing planning in Northern Ireland. The terms of the 1991 Order are beyond the scope of this book; they are addressed in detail by A. Dowling, *Northern Ireland Planning Law,* Dublin: Gill & Macmillan, 1995.

127. *Introduction to Areas of Special Scientific Interest,* DoE(NI), 20.

with any owner[128] or occupier of land within an area which has been declared an ASSI for the acquisition of his estate in that land. Where the DoE(NI) does acquire land within an ASSI it may also acquire land for the purpose of providing access to that area, or for the purpose of providing public facilities to be used in or in relation to that area (article 24(10)).

Article 6(4)–(6) governs the DoE(NI)'s power to transfer such land.[129] Article 6(4) of the NCALO, as amended by article 7(*a*) and (*b*) of the Nature Conservation and Amenity Lands (Amendment) (NI) Order 1989, provides that the DoE(NI) may transfer such land to 'any person' where it considers that the land in question would be more 'expediently or efficiently managed or conserved in the public interest' by such a person. The land may be transferred on whatever terms and conditions the DoE(NI) thinks fit. In addition, the Department may impose such restrictions on the use of the land as it thinks necessary and may grant or reserve such rights over the land as it thinks fit. Finally, without prejudice to the foregoing powers, the DoE(NI) also has the power to dispose of any land which it no longer requires as amenity land or for providing public access to such land, subject to whatever terms and conditions the Department thinks fit.[130]

### Obligations imposed on owners and occupiers of land within ASSIs

Once an ASSI has been declared and notified, article 25(1) of the NCALO, as amended by article 10(2) of the Nature Conservation and Amenity Lands (Amendment) (NI) Order 1989, imposes certain duties on owners[131] and occupiers of land within the area in question. As long as the ASSI declaration remains in force, owners and occupiers of land within the ASSI may not 'carry out or cause or permit to be carried out on that land' any notifiable operation (explained above) listed in the ASSI declaration itself without first notifying the DoE(NI) and satisfying the relevant consent procedure laid down in article 25, as amended. This article sets out different consent procedures, depending on the nature of the proposed activity or operation. Before outlining the details of these consent procedures it should first be noted that failure to comply with the terms of article 25(1) is an offence under article 25(6). A person found guilty of such an offence will be liable to a fine not exceeding level 5 on the standard scale (£5,000).

---

128. 'Owner' is defined in art. 4(2) of the NCALO as 'any person (other than a mortgagee not in possession) who is the holder of or who is for the time being entitled to sell or otherwise dispose of the fee simple (including a fee farm grant) of the land or any person entitled to possession of the land by virtue of any estate in the land other than a mere licence.'

129. Art. 6(6) provides that nothing in s. 5 of the Stormont Regulation and Government Property Act (NI) 1933 (c. 6 ), concerning the taking and disposal of land for the public services, will affect the DoE(NI)'s power to dispose of land under art. 6.

130. In this regard art. 6(5) specifically states that the DoE(NI) may dispose of land where it no longer requires the land for the purposes laid down in art. 6(1), namely, conserving any area of natural beauty or amenity, establishing a nature reserve, providing a means of access to such land, providing a national park or public facilities in or in relation to such a park, or for the purpose of restoring or improving the appearance of a derelict site or the amenities of the neighbourhood of the site.

131. The term 'owner' is defined at note 124, supra.

However, it appears that only an owner or occupier[132] of land within an ASSI may commit such an offence. Article 25(6) provides that it is a defence to prove that one had a 'reasonable excuse' for carrying out the notifiable operation without first satisfying the terms of article 25(1). The term 'reasonable excuse' is defined in article 25(7), as amended by article 10(2)(d) of the Amendment Order 1989, as meaning either that:

(a) the operation was authorised by a planning permission granted on an application under [articles 25 and 29 of the Planning (NI) Order 1991]; or

(b) the operation was an emergency operation particulars of which (including details of the emergency) were notified to the Department as soon as practicable after the commencement of the operation.

*(i) Consent procedure for notifiable operations which will not cause damage to the ASSI*

Where an owner or occupier of land within an ASSI wishes to carry out, or cause or permit to be carried out, a notifiable operation which would not, in the DoE(NI)'s opinion, cause any damage to the scientific interest of the area,[133] he may only do so if:

(i) he has given notice of his proposed action to the DoE(NI) either orally or in writing,[134]

(ii) the DoE(NI) has given its written consent to the operation or activity in question, and

(iii) he has not been served with notice of the DoE(NI)'s intention to purchase the land compulsorily[135] (article 25(1)(a)(i)–(iii), as amended by article 10 of the 1989 Amendment Order).

Statutory bodies operating within the area will also be expected to comply with this requirement.

---

132. In *Southern Water Authority v. Nature Conservancy Council* [1992] 3 All ER 481 the House of Lords considered the meaning of the term 'occupier' as used in s. 28 of the Wildlife and Countryside Act 1981 (equivalent legislation operating in England and Wales). The court ruled that someone is an occupier within the meaning of s. 28 if they have some form of stable relationship with the land in question. The House of Lords concluded that the water authority which was carrying out temporary drainage works on the SSSI did not commit an offence under s. 28, despite the fact that it knew that the works in question were potentially damaging operations and were in fact described by the House of Lords as 'ecological vandalism'. See also Withrington and Jones, 'The enforcement of conservation legislation' in Howarth and Rodgers (eds.), *Agriculture, Conservation and Land Use,* Cardiff: University of Wales Press, 1992; and Ball and Bell, *Environmental Law,* 3rd ed., Blackstone: London, p. 481.

133. Some long-standing or traditional practices come within the scope of notifiable operations; however, they may not normally cause damage to the scientific interest of the area, for example where the operation is carried out at a particular time of the year or in certain parts of the ASSI.

134. The DoE(NI) will provide a form on which written notice can be given.

135. Note that s. 97(2) and (3) of, and Sch. 6 to, the Local Government Act (NI) 1972 will apply, subject to the modifications specified in Sch. 2 to the NCALO, for the purpose of making a vesting order under art. 25.

*(ii)  Consent procedure for all other notifiable operations*

Where an owner or occupier of land within an ASSI (or a statutory body operating within the area) wishes to carry out, or cause or permit to be carried out, a potentially damaging notifiable operation or activity, they may only do so if the following three conditions laid down in article 25(1)(*b*)(i)–(iii) (as amended by article 10 of the 1989 Amendment Order) are satisfied:

1. The owner or occupier must give the DoE(NI) written notice of the proposal to carry out the operation or activity, giving details of the nature of the operation and specifying the land on which it is proposed that the operation be carried out.
2. One of the conditions set out in article 25(2)(*a*)–(*c*) must be satisfied, namely: (i) the DoE(NI) gives written consent to the proposed operation or activity, (ii) the operation is carried out in accordance with the terms of a management agreement entered into under article 24(8)(*a*) (explained above), or (iii) the DoE(NI) has, within three months of receiving the notice,[136] offered either to enter into a management agreement with the person giving notice, or, to acquire[137] that person's interest in the land;[138] however, this three-month period has now expired, as has any 'further period' of negotiation declared by the DoE(NI) (being a period not exceeding six months from the expiry of the initial three-month period).
3. The person giving notice has not been served with a notice of the DoE(NI)'s intention to acquire the land compulsorily.

In effect, where the DoE(NI) makes an offer either to acquire the interest in the land or to enter into a management agreement within the initial three-month period after notification, the owner or occupier who has given notification can simply refuse both offers and wait for the maximum statutory negotiating period of nine months to elapse (i.e. the initial three months together with a maximum 'further period' of six months) before proceeding unimpeded with a damaging notifiable operation. This is subject, however, to the Department's power to acquire the interest in the land compulsorily by means of a vesting order made under article 25(4), which may be used in the event that the Department considers either the wildlife or nature features of the area to be in danger of destruction. Article 25(4) provides that this power may be exercised by the DoE(NI) where it comes to the

---

136. These three months constitute the 'initial period' referred to in art. 25(2)(*c*), defined in art. 25(10). In effect, these three months provide the DoE(NI) with a formal statutory period of negotiation within which attempts can be made to discuss how best the features of the area can be safeguarded. Provided the DoE(NI) has either offered to enter into a management agreement with such a person or offered to acquire their interest in the land, the DoE(NI) is empowered to extend the period of negotiation by a maximum of six months from the day on which the initial three-month period expired—referred to as the 'further period' in art. 25. The DoE(NI) must, however, notify every owner and occupier of the land in question of its intention to extend the period of negotiations in this way.

137. Art. 25(5) provides that art. 24(10) and (11) will apply to the acquisition of land under art. 25 in the same way as it applies to the acquisition of land under art. 24. See p. 345.

138. Thereby exercising the DoE(NI)'s powers under art. 25(3) (to offer to enter into an acquisition agreement or a management agreement with a person who gives notice of their wish to carry out a notifiable operation that is likely to harm the ASSI within three months of the DoE(NI)'s receipt of the written notice), as is required by art. 25(2)(*c*).

conclusion during the periods of statutory negotiation: (i) that, having offered to do so within the initial period of three months from receiving the notice, it will be unable to enter into either a management agreement with the person who submitted the notice under article 25(1)(*b*) or an agreement to acquire that person's interest in the land within either the initial or further periods of negotiation, and (ii) that the land should be acquired by the DoE(NI) compulsorily in order to protect 'the flora, fauna or geological, physiographical or other feature by reason of which the land is of special scientific interest.'

In practice the DoE(NI) will only exercise its powers of compulsory purchase in exceptional circumstances. Where the Department decides not to exercise this power, the owner or occupier of the land may carry out the operation in question without the Department's consent once the formal periods of negotiation have expired, but not before.[139]

## *The enforcement of article 25*

The DoE(NI) has the power to enforce the provisions of article 25 (article 25(8)), and proceedings under article 25 may not be brought by anyone other than the DoE(NI) unless with the consent of the DPP for Northern Ireland (article 25(9)).

## *Restoration of damage caused to an ASSI*

Article 27(1) provides that where an owner or occupier of land within an ASSI has been found guilty of an offence under article 25 (i.e. carrying out, or causing to be carried out or permitting, any notifiable operation within an ASSI without first satisfying the relevant consent procedure laid down in article 25(1)), *and* the operation in respect of which proceedings were instituted results in damage to or destruction of any feature of scientific interest on the land, the court convicting that person under article 25 has jurisdiction under article 27 to make an order 'requiring him to carry out, within such period as may be specified in the order, such operations for the purpose of restoring the land to its former condition as may be so specified.' Article 27(2)(*a*) provides that the specified period within which the restoration must be completed will not begin until the statutory limitation period for giving notice of appeal against a decision of a court of summary jurisdiction has expired. Where notice of appeal is submitted within the statutory limitation period, the restoration period cannot begin until the appeal has been determined (article 27(2)(*b*)).

Failure to comply with the restoration order within the time specified is an offence under article 27(4). A person found guilty of such an offence will be liable on summary conviction to a fine not exceeding level 5 on the standard scale (£5,000), and in the case of a continuing offence, to a further fine not exceeding £500 for each day during which the offence continues after conviction. It is a defence to establish that one had a 'reasonable excuse' for failing to comply with the restoration order within the specified period. However, the term 'reasonable excuse' is not defined by the NCALO.

---

139. For further details of the operation of this consent procedure, see: Davidson and Mellon, (1996), supra note 106, pp 15–18.

Finally, where the restoration order has not been fully complied with within the specified period, the DoE(NI) may authorise (in writing) a person to enter the land and carry out any specified operations still not completed and to recover from the person against whom the order was made any reasonable expenses incurred by the Department in doing so (article 27(5)).

The court making the restoration order also has the jurisdiction, at the request of the person against whom it was made, to discharge or vary the order at any time before the restoration process has been completed where it appears to the court that 'a change in the circumstances has made compliance or full compliance with the order impracticable or unnecessary' (article 27(3)).

### Compensation for loss sustained as a result of an ASSI declaration

Article 26 of the NCALO, as amended by article 11 of the Nature Conservation and Amenity Lands (Amendment) (NI) Order 1989, obliges the DoE(NI) to pay compensation to any person having an estate in land which has been declared as an ASSI in the following circumstances:

1. Where a person who has an estate in land located within an agricultural unit[140] receives a notification[141] in respect of the land, the DoE(NI) must compensate such a person where he can prove that 'the value of his estate in that land is less than it would have been if a declaration had not been made in relation to that land' (article 26(1)(a) and (b)). The amount of the compensation 'shall be equal to the difference between the two values.'[142] Article 26(7) provides that a claim for compensation under article 26(1) cannot be made in respect of any ASSI declaration unless the DoE(NI) has given notice of its decision under article 24(5) to either confirm, rescind or modify the ASSI declaration in the light of any objections to or representations concerning the ASSI declaration. Without prejudice to article 26(5)(a) (which requires that an estate in land be valued at the time when the declaration is made) the decision taken by the Department in response to such representations and objections must be taken into account when assessing the compensation payable in respect of the ASSI declaration.

2. Article 26(2) provides that compensation must be paid when a loss is sustained as a result of a DoE(NI) decision to extend the initial negotiating period beyond three months where it has received notice from an owner or an occupier under article 25(1)(b)(i) of a proposal to carry out a potentially damaging notifiable

---

140. Art. 26(1), as amended by art. 11 of the 1989 Amendment Order, provides that the term 'agricultural unit' is used within the meaning provided by art. 2(2) of the Planning Blight (Compensation) (NI) Order 1981.

141. 'Notification' in this context means notification by the DoE(NI) under art. 24(3) that the land has been declared an ASSI.

142. Art. 26(5)(a)–(c) of the NCALO sets down various rules governing the date on which the estate in the land will be valued for these purposes, the position in the event that the claimant has more than one estate in such land, and the application of art. 13 of the Land Acquisition and Compensation (NI) Order 1973 concerning mortgages, trusts for sale and settlements to this situation. It should also be noted that art. 11(1)(c) of the Nature Conservation and Amenity Lands (Amendment) (NI) Order 1989 has amended art. 26(6) to the effect that the rules laid down in art. 6 of the Land Compensation (NI) Order 1982 will now apply to the assessment of compensation under art. 26(1), rather than under art. 26(2), as was previously the case.

operation on land within an ASSI (explained above).[143] In this regard, the DoE(NI) is obliged to compensate 'any person' who had an estate in the land to which the article 25(1)(*b*)(i) notice relates, at the time the notice was submitted to the Department, if that person can establish either:

(*a*) that he has reasonably incurred expenditure which has been rendered abortive, or expenditure in carrying out work which has been rendered abortive by reason of the extension of the initial period; or

(*b*) that he has incurred loss or damage which is directly attributable to the extension of the initial period.

It is important to note, however, that article 26(2) will not entitle any person to compensation 'in respect of any reduction in the value of his estate in the land in respect of which the notification was given'.

The Nature Conservation (Claims for Compensation under Article 26) Regulations (NI) 1985,[144] adopted by the DoE(NI) under article 26(4), prescribe the times within which and the manner in which applications for compensation under article 26(1) and (2) must be made. Except in so far as is provided by regulations made by the DoE(NI) under article 26, any disputes concerning compensation will be determined by the Lands Tribunal.

### *DoE(NI)'s powers to carry out works or provide facilities on an ASSI*

Article 10 of the NCALO, as amended by article 9 of the Nature Conservation and Amenity Lands (Amendment) (NI) Order 1989, confers power on the DoE(NI) to carry out such works and other things on land acquired under articles 24 or 25 of the NCALO as it thinks necessary or expedient for the proper management and use of the land for the purpose for which that land was acquired. The Department's powers under article 10(4) to provide or to arrange for the provision of facilities on or in relation to land acquired under articles 24 or 25 (where the Department considers that the facilities on or in relation to such land are inadequate or unsatisfactory) are identical to those conferred on the DoE(NI) in relation to nature reserves. Similarly, the Department's powers under article 10(4) will apply in relation to land which is subject to a management agreement entered into by the Department under article 17 in the same way as it applies to land acquired under articles 24 or 25; the application of article 10(4) to such land is subject to the same conditions as those applying to nature reserves. The provisions of article 10 as they apply to nature reserves are outlined at page 357.

---

143. Art. 26(6) of the NCALO, as amended by art. 11(1)(*c*) of the 1989 Amendment Order, provides that the rules set out in art. 6 of the Land Compensation (NI) Order 1982 will apply to the assessment of compensation payable under art. 26(1) (subject to any necessary modifications) in the same way as they apply to the assessment of compensation where land has been acquired compulsorily. In effect art. 6 of the 1982 Order no longer applies to the assessment of compensation under art. 26(2). However, art. 11(2) of the 1989 Amendment Order provides that nothing in art. 11(1)(*c*) of the 1989 Amendment Order will affect the assessment of compensation under art. 26(2) of the NCALO 'for any claim made before art. 11(1)(*c*) comes into operation.'
144. SR No. 240.

### Land no longer considered to be of special scientific interest

Although an ASSI declaration lasts indefinitely, it is possible that the scientific interest of the area may diminish, either because of changes to the site or because improved knowledge reveals that the site is not as important as previously thought. Where the DoE(NI) concludes that an area of land is no longer of special scientific interest it is obliged to immediately inform every affected district council and every owner and occupier of the land in question that the land is to be denotified and that the ASSI designation no longer applies. The Department is also obliged to immediately terminate any management agreement which might have been entered into in relation to that land (article 24(6)).

### Bylaws concerning land acquired as an ASSI or land which is being managed as an ASSI

Article 30 of the NCALO, as amended by article 12 of the Nature Conservation and Amenity Lands (Amendment) (NI) Order 1989, confers general powers on the DoE(NI) or, as the case may be, district councils to adopt bylaws for the protection of land acquired under articles 24 and 25 of the NCALO. Similarly, bylaws may be adopted in relation to land that is subject to a management agreement entered into under article 17 of the NCALO. The DoE(NI) also has the power to enforce these bylaws under article 31.

### Planning Control and ASSIs

The DoE(NI)'s *Introduction to ASSIs*[145] points out that operations which require planning permission are not normally included in the list of notifiable operations for an ASSI and consequently are not subject to the consent procedures outlined above. A person seeking to carry out an operation which requires planning permission is advised to simply submit the application in the normal way to their Divisional Planning Office. However, it is worth noting that the Department would 'welcome the opportunity to discuss any planning proposal on an ASSI' on an informal basis before the application is submitted. Given that a Divisional Planning Office will consult the DoE(NI)'s Environment Service in any event on any application that affects an ASSI, the Department points out that such informal discussion may be advantageous.[146]

### Nature Reserves and National Nature Reserves

Articles 3, 6–8 and 15–18 of the NCALO empower the DoE(NI) to establish, manage and maintain nature reserves (NRs) and national nature reserves (NNRs) in Northern Ireland; NRs are sites of local importance, while NNRs are sites of national importance. Provision is also made under the NCALO for the declaration

---

145. *Introduction to Areas of Special Scientific Interest*, DoE(NI) 18.
146. For a more detailed discussion of the role of planning control in the protection of ASSIs see: A. Dowling, *Northern Ireland Planning Law* (1995), Dublin: Gill & Macmillan, chap. 6, p. 39. See also *R. v. Poole BC, ex parte Beebee* [1991] JPL 643, in which the Secretary of State revoked planning permission which had been granted by Poole BC to itself for housing on Canford Heath, which is an SSSI within the town's boundaries.

of district council nature reserves and marine nature reserves; these provisions will be addressed separately below. Article 2(2) of the NCALO defines a 'nature reserve' as any area reserved, managed and used for the purpose of:

(a) conserving flora, fauna, or features of geological, physiographical or other scientific or special interest therein; or

(b) providing, under suitable conditions and control, special opportunities for the study of, and research into, matters relating to flora and fauna and the physical conditions in which they live, or for the study of features of geological, physiographical or other scientific or special interest therein;

or for both of those purposes.

Article 18(1) provides that the DoE(NI) may declare any land that:

(a) is being managed as a nature reserve under an agreement entered into with the DoE(NI);

(b) is held by the DoE(NI) and is being managed by it as a nature reserve; or

(c) is held by an approved body[147] and is managed by that body as a nature reserve

to be a national nature reserve where the Department is satisfied that the nature reserve in question is of national importance.

In effect, a nature reserve is declared where positive management of the site is required in order to ensure that the nature conservation interest is protected, or where it is necessary to provide access to the site for educational or research purposes, or for the purposes of facilitating public enjoyment of the site. To declare an area as a nature reserve the DoE(NI) must have control of the area in question so that it can be managed as a nature reserve. As a result, while areas designated as ASSIs normally remain in private ownership, nearly all areas designated as nature reserves in Northern Ireland are owned either by public bodies, namely, the DoE(NI) and the DANI's Forest Service, or by voluntary bodies, namely, the Royal Society for the Protection of Birds (RSPB), the National Trust and the Ulster Wildlife Trust (UWT). It should be noted, however, that as with ASSIs, the principle of voluntary co-operation underlies the Department's approach to the declaration and management of Northern Ireland's nature reserves; the Department's compulsory powers in this context will only be used as a last resort.

At the time of writing there are forty-five statutory nature reserves in Northern Ireland, the substantial majority of these being within coastal regions.[148] Thirty-nine of these were declared under the Amenity Lands Act 1965,[149] while the other six sites have been declared under NCALO. The six reserves under the NCALO

---

147. 'Approved body' is defined by art. 18(3) of the NCALO as a body that is approved by the DoE(NI) for the purposes of art. 18.

148. *National Nature Reserves in Northern Ireland* (DoE(NI)) provides a brief overview of the location, grid reference and area (in hectares) of all nature reserves in Northern Ireland and a brief scientific description of the special features of each reserve. Each of these reserves is managed by a warden; the DoE(NI) *Environment Service Report, 1993–95,* Appendix 1, p. 48, contains a comprehensive list of telephone numbers and addresses at which these wardens can be contacted.

149. c. 9. The Amenity Lands Act (NI) 1965 was repealed by the NCALO.

have all been declared as national nature reserves. In 1992 the DoE(NI) completed a review of all existing and proposed nature reserves in NI in order to ensure that the Department's policies concerning the selection and management of sites were relevant to current needs. In particular, the review was concerned to ensure that the network of reserves included 'good representative examples of all the major semi-natural habitats in Northern Ireland'.[150] The *Environment Service Corporate Plan 1994–97* notes that the survey indicated that several of the pre-NCALO nature reserves need to be redesignated as national nature reserves under NCALO. It is anticipated that thirty-two of the pre-NCALO reserves will be redesignated as national nature reserves under NCALO, while seven will remain as nature reserves of local importance.

As with ASSIs, the DoE(NI) perceives the management and monitoring of site quality as being of vital importance. The *Environment Service Corporate Plan 1994–97* makes the following commitments in this regard:

> The management and maintenance of our estate, both Nature Reserves and Country Parks, will continue and management plans for each will be completed by December 1994 and integrated into the computerised Countryside Management System. . . . A programme of site quality monitoring will be enshrined in each management plan, tailored to the character and requirements of each site. The operational aspects of each management plan . . . will reflect priority requirements and the availability of resources. Where we manage Nature Reserves in partnership with other bodies, we will continue our liaison work and attendance at management committee meetings, etc. We will also continue to work closely with graziers and neighbouring landowners. Environmental audits of each of our management units will be conducted at the rate of two each year. These audits will be reviewed every two years . . . we propose to market test the management and maintenance of our properties'.[151]

The Department is expected to have management plans in place for all nature reserves by June 1996; these plans will include site monitoring programmes.

### Declaring a nature reserve

Before a nature reserve can be declared, the NCALO requires that specific consultations be conducted concerning the proposed reserve. Article 15(2) provides that the DoE(NI) is obliged to consult all affected district councils[152] before either acquiring land or entering into a management agreement or covenant for the purpose of establishing a nature reserve. In addition, the CNCC is obliged under article 15(1) to advise the DoE(NI) on the establishment and management of nature reserves.

Article 16(1), as amended by article 8 of the Nature Conservation and Amenity Lands (Amendment) (NI) Order 1989, then governs the categories of land that

---

150. *Environment Service Report,* 1991–93, p. 6.
151. P. 16. The Countryside Management System referred to in this extract is a database system for planning and reporting on the management of nature conservation sites, such as nature reserves. It is essentially a computerised form of management plan.
152. A district council is affected if the DoE(NI) proposes to establish a nature reserve on land that is either wholly or partly within the district of the council.

may be declared as a nature reserve under the NCALO. Before listing these categories of land, it should be noted that any declaration made by the Department under article 16(1) that land 'is established and is being managed as a nature reserve' must be considered as being conclusive evidence of the facts contained therein and, in addition, the Department is obliged under article 16(4) to give notice of any declaration made under article 16(1) by whatever means the Department considers best suited for informing the persons concerned.

In essence, the Department may declare that any of the following land 'is established and is being managed as a nature reserve':

1. Any land which has been acquired by the Department under article 6 of the NCALO. Article 6 empowers the DoE(NI) to acquire any land (either by agreement or compulsorily) which it considers expedient to acquire for the purposes of conserving any area of natural beauty or amenity, establishing a nature reserve, providing a means of access to either of these, providing facilities in or in relation to a National Park, or restoring or improving the appearance of a derelict site or improving the amenities of the neighbourhood of a derelict site. Where such land is acquired by agreement, the Department may do so by way of purchase, lease or exchange. Where such land is acquired compulsorily, the Department will do so by means of a vesting order adopted under article 6(2).[153]

2. Any land acquired by the Department under articles 24 or 25 of the NCALO concerning the acquisition of land within an ASSI; these powers are addressed in the context of ASSIs above (page 345).

3. Any land acquired by the Department under section 1 of the Amenity Lands Act (NI) 1965 (which is broadly equivalent to article 6 of the NCALO).

4. Any land in relation to which an agreement or covenant has been entered into under article 8 or 17 of the NCALO or under section 2 or 2A of the Amenity Lands Act (NI) 1965. Article 8 empowers the Department to enter into an agreement or covenant with the owner of land of natural beauty or amenity restricting the use or development of that land and this is addressed in detail in the context of AONBs in chapter 8. Article 17 empowers the DoE(NI) to enter into management agreements for land declared as a nature reserve or as an ASSI and is addressed in Part II, section 1 of this chapter (page 344). Sections 2 and 2A of the 1965 Act were broadly equivalent to the powers described under articles 8 and 17 of the NCALO.

## *DoE(NI)'s power to transfer land acquired for a nature reserve*

Article 6(4), as amended by article 7 of the Nature Conservation and Amenity Lands (Amendment) (NI) Order 1989, provides that the DoE(NI) has the power to transfer any land acquired (either by agreement or compulsorily) under article 6 to 'any person' where the Department is of the opinion that the land would be 'more expediently or efficiently managed or conserved in the public interest' by that person. The land may be conveyed for value or otherwise and on such terms and

---

153. Art. 6(3) of the NCALO provides that s. 97(2) and (3) of, and Sch. 6 to, the Local Government Act (NI) 1972 will apply, subject to the modifications specified in Sch. 2 to the NCALO, for the purpose of the making of vesting orders under art. 6.

conditions as the DoE(NI) thinks fit. In addition, and without prejudice to the powers laid down in article 6(4), the DoE(NI) has the power to dispose of any land acquired under article 6 that it no longer requires for the purposes of a nature reserve or for the purpose of providing access to that reserve (article 6(5)). Once again the DoE(NI) may dispose of the land on such terms and conditions, and subject to such restrictions, as it thinks fit. Nothing in section 5 of the Stormont Regulation and Government Property Act (NI) 1933 (concerning the taking and disposal of land for the public services) will affect the disposal of land acquired under article 6.

### *DoE(NI)'s power to grant loans for the purposes of establishing a nature reserve*

In addition to the Department's general power to make grants and loans under article 29 of the NCALO (addressed on page 361), the DoE(NI) is also conferred with a specific power under article 7 to make grants (either by endorsement or otherwise) or loans to the National Trust. Grants and loans under article 7 may be made either: (i) towards the cost of acquiring land for the purpose of establishing a nature reserve and/or 'providing means of access' to a nature reserve or (ii) for the purpose of 'improving, maintaining or managing any land so acquired.' Grants and loans under this provision must be approved by the Department of Finance and Personnel and will be made subject to such terms and conditions as the DoE(NI) thinks fit.

### *Management agreements for nature reserves*

The DoE(NI) may enter into an agreement with any person having an estate in land which, in the Department's opinion, should be managed as a nature reserve, to ensure that the land is managed as a nature reserve (article 17(1)). Article 17(2)–(6), as amended by article 8 of the 1989 Amendment Order, governs the making of such an agreement and the granting of compensation for any restrictions contained in the agreement. The details of these provisions are outlined in the context of management agreements for ASSIs at page 344. It should also be noted that, as with ASSIs, the principle of voluntary co-operation underlies the Department's approach to the management of nature reserves in Northern Ireland.

### *Nature reserve covenants*

As already stated, the DoE(NI) may declare and manage any area of land that is subject to an agreement or covenant under article 8 of the NCALO as a nature reserve. In effect, article 8 empowers the DoE(NI) to accept a covenant from the owner of land which, in the Department's opinion, is of 'natural beauty or amenity', restricting the 'use or development' of the land, or any part thereof, in any manner. Similarly, the DoE(NI) may enter into an agreement with such a person to the same effect. The agreement or covenant may be permanent or for a specified period and may be made for consideration or otherwise. The DoE(NI) may waive either permanently or temporarily any condition contained in such an agreement or covenant that is inconsistent with any provision of a development plan or development order under the Planning (NI) Order 1991.[154]

Where the owner of land making the agreement or covenant has the power to make the agreement or covenant binding on his successors in title and does so, article 8(2) provides that the DoE(NI) will have the power to enforce the agreement or covenant against the owner's successors in title 'in the like manner and to the like extent as if the DoE(NI) were possessed of or entitled to or interested in adjacent land and as if the agreement or covenant had been expressed to be entered into for the benefit of the adjacent land.'

### Land which ceases to be a nature reserve

Where the DoE(NI) is satisfied that any land which had been declared a nature reserve has ceased to be managed as a nature reserve, or is satisfied that any agreement or covenant concluded in relation to the land (either under article 8 or 17 of the NCALO, or under sections 2 or 2A of the Amenity Lands Act (NI) 1965) has ceased to have effect, it must declare that the land is no longer being managed as a nature reserve (article 16(2)). Any such declaration will be conclusive evidence of the matters contained therein. The DoE(NI) is required to give notice of such a declaration 'in such manner as appears to the DoE(NI) best suited for informing persons concerned' (article 16(4)).

### Registration requirements concerning nature reserves

Article 33 of the NCALO requires that any agreement or covenant entered into under article 8(1), and any agreement entered into under article 17 for the management of a nature reserve, must be registered in the Statutory Charges Register. Similarly, a waiver in the conditions of a covenant or agreement entered into under articles 8 or 17 must be registered.

### DoE(NI)'s power to carry out works and provide facilities

Article 10 of the NCALO sets out the Department's powers to carry out works and provide facilities on land which has been acquired by the Department under article 6, or in relation to which the Department has entered into a covenant or an agreement under articles 8 or 17. In this regard, article 10(1) empowers the Department to carry out such works or other things on land acquired under article 6 as it thinks necessary or expedient for the proper management and use of that land for the purpose for which that land was acquired. In addition, where the Department is of the opinion that the facilities on or in relation to a nature reserve are inadequate or unsatisfactory, it may, under powers conferred by article 10(4), provide or arrange for the provision of accommodation, parking places and other such facilities as it thinks fit (having consulted with the CNCC) for the purposes of the reserve. Article 10(4) will also apply to land which is subject to a covenant or agreement entered into under article 8 or 17 of the NCALO in the same way as it applies to land acquired under article 6, if the agreement or covenant so provides, or if the owner of the land consents to the Department 'carrying out works, doing

---

154. The Planning (NI) Order 1991 (SI 1991/1220) repeals and replaces the Planning (NI) Order 1972.

other things, or providing or arranging for the provision of facilities'. Finally, it should be noted that the DoE(NI) may impose charges (which are reasonable in the Department's opinion) for facilities provided under article 10. However, the Department is obliged to ensure that any charges imposed for facilities provided under an arrangement made by the DoE(NI) under article 10 are subject to the Department's approval.

### Bylaws concerning nature reserves

Article 19(1) confers on the DoE(NI) a general power to adopt bylaws for the protection of any nature reserve or national nature reserve (other than a district council nature reserve under article 22, below) declared under articles 16(1) or 18(1). Article 19(2) contains an extensive list of the purposes for which such bylaws might be adopted. However, this list is stated to be without prejudice to the general power conferred on the DoE(NI).

A bylaw adopted under article 19 will not interfere with the exercise of rights vested in the owner, lessee or occupier of land within a nature reserve, nor will it affect the exercise of any public right of way or any statutory functions of any local or public authority[155] in relation to such land. Where such bylaws do 'prevent or hinder' the exercise of rights vested in an owner, lessee or occupier by reason of being entitled to an estate in the land, article 19(6) provides that such persons are entitled to compensation from the DoE(NI). The compensation will be calculated by reference to the depreciation of the value of their estate in the land in question. Any disputes concerning compensation will be determined by the Lands Tribunal. Finally, the DoE(NI) is obliged to consult the CNCC before making any bylaw under article 19; and where a national nature reserve is being managed by a body approved by the DoE(NI) for those purposes, the Department cannot adopt a bylaw in relation to that reserve except at the request of that body (article 19(3) and (4)).

It should also be noted that, in addition to its specific powers under article 19, the DoE(NI) is granted general powers under article 30 to adopt bylaws in relation to land that has been acquired: (i) under articles 6, 24 and 25, (ii) under section 1 of the Amenity Lands Act (NI) 1965, (iii) in relation to land that is subject to an agreement or covenant under articles 8 and 17, or (iv) under sections 2 or 2A of the 1965 Act. Article 31 also grants the DoE(NI) the power to enforce bylaws adopted under articles 19 and 30.

### District council nature reserves

Article 22(1) of the NCALO empowers district councils to 'provide'[156] nature reserves on land within their district where the council considers it expedient that the land be managed as a nature reserve. However, it is important to note that the

---

155. Art. 2(2) of the NCALO, as amended by art. 6 of the Nature Conservation and Amenity Lands (Amendment) (NI) Order 1989, defines a 'local or public authority' as 'including any authority or body specified in Schedule 1 to the Financial Provisions (NI) Order 1983 as an authority or body to whom government loans may be made by the Department of Finance and Personnel under Article 8 of that Order.'

156. Art. 22(5) provides that the term 'provide' should be construed in accordance with s. 147(*a*) of the Local Government Act (NI) 1972.

council may not provide a nature reserve on land that is already established and managed as a nature reserve or national nature reserve by the DoE(NI) (explained above). In additon, the district council must consult the CNCC when exercising this power. District councils may acquire land by agreement (but not compulsorily) for the purpose of providing a nature reserve and may also adopt bylaws for the protection of such a reserve. Article 19(2) and (3) will apply to the district council's power to adopt bylaws in the same way as it applies to the DoE(NI)'s power to adopt bylaws in relation to nature reserves and national nature reserves.[157]

## Marine nature reserves

Articles 20 and 21 of the NCALO govern the establishment and management of marine nature reserves. Unlike nature reserves and national nature reserves, which are established by the DoE(NI), marine nature reserves are designated by the Secretary of State. However, once again the CNCC is obliged to advise on the establishment and management of marine nature reserves. Article 20(1) provides that the Secretary of State may designate 'any land covered (continuously or intermittently) by tidal waters or part of the sea in or adjacent to Northern Ireland up to the seaward limits of territorial waters' as a marine nature reserve where it appears to the Secretary of State that the land and the waters covering the land should be managed by him for one or both of the following purposes:

(a) conserving marine flora, fauna or features of geological, physio- graphical or other scientific or special interest in the area; or

(b) providing, under suitable conditions and control, special opportunities for the study of, and research into, matters relating to marine flora and fauna and the physical conditions in which they live, or for the study of features of geological, physiological or other scientific or special interest in the area.

The *Environment Service Corporate Plan, 1994–97* points out that 'marine nature conservation has lagged behind that of terrestrial habitats'. At the time of writing only one marine nature reserve has been declared in Northern Ireland, namely Strangford Lough, which was designated in 1995. It is important to note that the MNR designation affords very little, if any, practical protection to marine sites. One of the principal weaknesses of the NCALO is that it empowers the Secretary of State to designate only tidal and coastal waters; marine habitats below low-water mark are not afforded any protection either by statute or by planning control regulations. In this regard, it is worth noting the recent observations made by Davidson and Mellon of the RSPB (NI Branch) that this gap in the protection afforded to marine sites 'can cause ecological anomalies and the potential for non-compliance with EC Directives'.[158]

In addition to the general obligation imposed on the DoE(NI) and other competent authorities to exercise their functions under Parts V and VI of the NCALO so as to ensure compliance with the Habitats Directive (outlined on page

---

157. Art. 2(3) provides that references to a district council should be substituted for references to the DoE(NI) in art. 19(2) and (3) of the NCALO for these purposes.

158. Supra, note 106.

337 in the context of the enforcement of national legislation concerning habitat protection), regulation 3(3) of the Conservation (Natural Habitats etc.) Regulations (NI) 1995[159] requires 'any competent authority having functions relevant to marine conservation' to exercise those functions so as to secure compliance with the requirements of the Habitats Directive.[160] This obligation applies in particular to functions exercised under, among others, articles 20 and 21 of the NCALO concerning marine nature reserves.

### Procedure governing the designation of a marine nature reserve

The procedure governing the designation of a marine nature reserve is a lengthy one; Parts I and II of Schedule 3 to the NCALO set out the rules governing this procedure. Article 20(3) provides that where a marine nature reserve is designated, the Secretary of State's powers to manage the reserve will include the power to 'install markers indicating the existence and extent of the reserve.' As with nature reserves and national nature reserves, the designation of a marine nature reserve or the adoption of bylaws concerning the reserve will not interfere with the exercise of any rights vested in any person or with the exercise of any statutory functions by any 'relevant body'.[161]

### Adoption of bylaws in relation to a marine nature reserve

Article 21(1) confers a general power on the Secretary of State, in consultation with the CNCC, to adopt bylaws in relation to areas which have been designated as a marine nature reserve. Article 21(2) lists various purposes for which such bylaws may be adopted. However, this is without prejudice to the general nature of the Secretary of State's power in this context. It is important to note that the following restrictions are placed on bylaws adopted under article 21:

1. A bylaw may not prohibit or restrict a vessel's[162] right of passage through the marine nature reserve. However, bylaws may prohibit a pleasure boat's right of passage at particular times of the year in relation to certain parts of the reserve (article 21(4)(*a*) and (*b*)).
2. A bylaw may not render unlawful anything done for the purpose of 'securing the safety of any vessel',[163] 'preventing damage to any vessel or cargo,' or 'saving life,' or for the purpose of discharging 'any substance from a vessel' (article 21(5)). Similarly, marine nature reserve bylaws may not render unlawful anything done 'more than 30 metres below the sea bed'.

---

159. SR No. 380.
160. In the context of marine areas, the relevant authorities are 'such of the following as have functions in relation to land or waters within or adjacent to' a marine area or European marine site: a district council, the Commissioners of Irish Lights, a harbour authority as defined by the Harbours Act (NI) 1970 (s. 38), the Fisheries Conservancy Board for Northern Ireland, the Foyle Fisheries Commission, and a pilotage authority within the meaning of the Pilotage Act 1983 (reg. 4).
161. Art. 20(6) defines a 'relevant body' as 'the Commissioners of Irish Lights, a district council, a harbour authority as defined by the Harbours Act (NI) 1970, the Fisheries Conservancy Board, the Foyle Fisheries Commission, and a pilotage authority within the meaning of the Pilotage Act 1913'.
162. Art. 21(6) provides that the term 'vessel' will be interpreted as including a 'hovercraft and any aircraft capable of landing on water and "pleasure boat" will be construed accordingly.'
163. Ibid.

Note also the provisions of article 31, outlined below, concerning the enforcement of bylaws adopted under article 21.

## General DoE(NI) powers to make nature conservation grants and loans

In addition to its specific power to make grants or loans to the National Trust in relation to nature reserves under article 7 (outlined at page 356), the DoE(NI) is also given a general discretion under Part VIII of the NCALO to make grants to non-profit-making bodies which have wildlife and countryside conservation among their objectives (article 29(1)(*a*)). Similarly the DoE(NI) may give financial assistance by way of grants or loans (or partly in one way or the other) to any person in respect of expenditure incurred by that person for doing anything that the DoE(NI) considers conducive to the attainment of the objectives of the NCALO, i.e. nature conservation and the conservation and enhancement of the natural beauty and amenity of the countryside (article 29(1)(*b*)).

All loans and grants must be made with the approval of the Department of Finance and Personnel, and any grant or loan to an individual person may be made subject to whatever conditions the DoE(NI) thinks fit, including repayment conditions in the case of a loan. Article 4(3) of the Nature Conservation and Amenity Lands (Amendment) (NI) Order 1989 provides that the CNCC must advise the DoE(NI) on the payment of grants under article 29(1)(*a*).

## General DoE(NI) power to adopt bylaws under NCALO

Without prejudice to its specific power to adopt bylaws under article 19 concerning nature reserves and national nature reserves (considered at page 358), the DoE(NI) is also granted a general power under article 30 to adopt bylaws in relation to land acquired under articles 6, 24 and 25 of the NCALO and land acquired under section 1 of the Amenity Lands Act (NI) 1965. Similarly, the DoE(NI) may adopt bylaws in relation to land which is subject to a management agreement, or a covenant entered into under articles 8 or 17, where the agreement or covenant so provides, and in relation to land managed as a nature reserve under section 2 or 2A of the 1965 Act. In this context the DoE(NI) may adopt bylaws for the purpose of preventing damage to the land in question and also for ensuring that people behave themselves on the land in such a way as 'to avoid undue interference with the enjoyment of the land by other persons' (article 30(1)).

In the event that such land has been conveyed to a district council under article 6(4), as amended, the district council is empowered to adopt bylaws in relation to that land for the purposes outlined above (article 30(2)). Article 30(3) identifies a number of purposes for which the DoE(NI) or district councils may adopt bylaws in this context; it is important to note, however, that this list is without prejudice to the general power conferred by article 30(1) and (2).[164]

---

164. The following are listed as possible purposes of such bylaws: controlling the use of land, either by traffic or otherwise; controlling the use of mechanically propelled vessels on watercourses in, or whose shores lie within, any such land; controlling the lighting of fires on the land; controlling the use of any camping site, caravan park or parking place provided under art. 10 of the NCALO; and controlling the removal of soil, turf, sand or minerals of any description from the land. In this context 'watercourse' is defined as including 'tidal and coastal waters, rivers, canals, lakes and reservoirs'.

The DoE(NI) or, as the case may be, the district council is required to consult the CNCC concerning the adoption of any bylaw which might affect either the natural beauty and amenity of the land or matters relating to nature conservation (article 30(4), as amended by article 4 of the Nature Conservation and Amenity Lands (Amendment) (NI) Order 1989). Finally, as with bylaws adopted under article 19, bylaws adopted under article 30 will not affect the exercise of rights vested in any person as an owner, lessee or occupier of land to which article 30 applies, nor will they interfere with the exercise of any public right of way or of any statutory function exercised by a local or public authority in relation to such land.[165]

### Enforcement of bylaws adopted under the NCALO

Article 31(1) empowers the DoE(NI) or, as the case may be, the Secretary of State to authorise persons (appointed or employed) to enforce bylaws adopted pursuant to articles 19, 21 or 30 of the NCALO and may also authorise them 'to take all steps and do all acts and things, necessary for that purpose.' In particular, article 31(2) empowers such authorised persons to 'remove or exclude' a person from any land affected by bylaws adopted under articles 19, 21 or 30 'who commits, or whom he reasonably suspects of committing, an offence against any such bylaw.' This power can only be exercised after the authorised person has given the person in question 'due warning'. A person who 'commits an offence against any bylaw' adopted under articles 19, 21 or 30 or who obstructs any person authorised to enforce such bylaws will be guilty of an offence and will be liable on summary conviction to a fine not exceeding level 2 on the standard scale (£500).

### Areas of outstanding natural beauty

The designation of an area as an 'area of outstanding natural beauty' (AONB) is primarily a means of protecting particularly scenic landscapes. However, it does have a nature conservation element. Given its central role in countryside conservation and management, it is considered in greater detail in chapter 8.

## SECTION 2. THE EUROPEAN DIMENSION

In recent years the EC has played an important role in the development of standards concerning nature conservation; however, its influence has been particularly evident in the context of habitat protection. As was explained in Part I, section 1 of this chapter, Community measures concerning nature conservation fall, broadly speaking, into two categories. The EC has become a party to various international conventions concerning nature conservation and has adopted a number of measures to approve these international standards within the Community legal order, the most important of which are outlined in Part I, section 1. In addition to the assimilation of international standards on nature conservation, the EC has adopted a number of its own initiatives concerning habitat protection, the most important of which are Directive 79/409/EEC[166] on

---

165. The definition of a local or public authority in this context is provided at note 155, supra.
166. OJ L103, 25 Apr. 1979.

the Conservation of Wild Birds (the 'Wild Birds Directive') and Directive 92/43/EEC[167] on the Conservation of Natural Habitats and of Wild Fauna and Flora (the 'Habitats Directive').

The Wild Birds Directive was the EC's first major conservation measure and focuses exclusively on the protection of wild birds and their habitats. The more general Habitats Directive builds on the experience of the Wild Birds Directive and represents the most significant measure concerning habitat protection adopted by the EC thus far. In effect, the Habitats Directive attempts to provide a comprehensive system of protection for vulnerable species of flora and fauna (other than birds) and seriously threatened habitat types. The Habitats Directive also gives full legal force, at EC level, to the more precise obligations laid down by the Berne and Bonn Conventions and should strengthen their implementation throughout the territories of the member states. (The requirements laid down in both Conventions are outlined in Part III of this chapter.) Both of these Directives relate to individual species and habitats protection. Part I, section 1 of this chapter addresses the species requirements of both Directives; the present section will address their requirements in relation to habitat protection. To this end this section begins by providing a broad outline of the objectives and requirements laid down by each Directive in relation to habitat protection and then moves on to provide a detailed outline of the national legislation which has been introduced to implement their terms in Northern Ireland.

### The Wild Birds Directive

The Wild Birds Directive imposes a general duty on member states to maintain the population of all 'species of naturally occurring birds in the wild state' within their territory 'at a level which corresponds in particular to ecological, scientific and cultural requirements, while taking account of economic and recreational requirements.' Member states are required to preserve, maintain or re-establish a sufficient diversity and area of habitats so as to ensure that the population of all species is maintained. The species requirements laid down by the Wild Birds Directive have already been outlined in Part I, section 1; the present section will address the provisions of the Directive concerning the protection of bird habitats.

Article 4 of the Wild Birds Directive obliges member states to take special measures to conserve the habitat of two categories of birds, namely, particularly vulnerable or rare species and regularly occurring migratory species. In this regard Article 4 requires member states to designate the most suitable areas for these species as 'special protection areas' (SPAs), the objective being to protect the populations of these species by establishing a coherent network of protected habitats throughout the EC. The Directive requires that particular attention be paid to the protection of wetlands, especially those of international importance.[168]

In Case C-355/90 *Commission v. Spain,*[169] the European Court of Justice considered the scope of the obligation laid down in Article 4. It held that the

---

167. OJ L206/7, 21 May 1992.
168. This requirement gives effect to the requirements of the Ramsar Convention concerning wetlands of international importance, outlined in Part III of this chapter.
169. [1993] Water Law 209.

Spanish Government was in breach of Article 4 because it had failed to designate an important wetland area as an SPA. In effect the Court made it clear that member states are under a duty to designate an area as an SPA and therefore to protect it if it satisfies the ornithological criteria laid down in the Directive. At the time of writing, the ruling of the European Court of Justice is awaited on Case C-44/95 *R. v. Secretary of State for the Environment, ex parte the RSPB,* which concerns a case taken by the RSPB challenging the Government's failure to designate an area known as Lappel Bank within the Medway Estuary and Marshes as an SPA under the Directive. The argument focuses on whether it is permissible to take economic factors into account in deciding whether or not, and over what area, to designate an SPA. The RSPB has relied on the European Court of Justice's ruling in *Commission v. Spain* in support of the argument that only ornithological criteria can be taken into consideration at this stage. The Court of Appeal decided in the Government's favour. However, the House of Lords has referred the question to the European Court of Justice for an authoritative ruling; it should be noted that the House of Lords refused to grant interim relief.

Article 4.4 provides that once an SPA has been designated, member states must take appropriate measures to avoid significant pollution or deterioration of the habitats contained therein or disturbance of the birds within it. In 1991 in Case C-57/89 *Commission v. Germany,*[170] the European Court of Justice ruled that a reduction in the area of an SPA was justifiable only on very limited grounds, such as where the works were necessary for reasons of public health or safety. Although the Court ruled that the works should be permitted on the grounds of a superior general interest (in this instance the need to prevent flooding), it stated that such works could not be permitted for economic or recreational reasons. This ruling was later confirmed in *Commission v. Spain* (above), in which the Court went on to suggest that Article 4.4 might be capable of direct enforcement.

However, the very strong protection afforded to SPAs by the Court's decisions in these cases has since been reduced by the Habitats Directive. Article 7 of the Habitats Directive amends Article 4.4 of the Wild Birds Directive in that it requires the less protective regime which applies to European sites that do not contain priority species or habitats (set out in Article 6.2–4 of the Habitats Directive, discussed in Part II, section 2 of this chapter) to be applied to SPAs designated under the Wild Birds Directive. In effect, Article 6.4 provides that social or economic considerations may be taken into account in determining whether or not to allow a plan or project that may have a negative effect to proceed within an SPA. Article 6.4 does, however, retain the more stringent protection afforded by the European Court of Justice in *Commission v. Germany* in relation to sites which contain priority species or habitats. However, as Ball and Bell have pointed out, given that there are no priority bird species, 'the stronger controls applicable to priority sites cannot apply to SPAs designated under the Wild Birds Directive'. [171]

The SPA designation programme is to be completed by 1998. However, it is important to note that all member states have encountered difficulties in bringing

---

170. [1991] ECR I-883.
171. This issue is discussed further at page 368–9. See also Ball and Bell, supra, p. 493.

about full implementation of the Directive. Krämer identifies the main problems in this regard as being:

> . . . the impairment of bird habitats as a result of anthropogenic activity, in particular agriculture and tourism, and the failure to adopt suitable measures for their protection; also in 1993, fewer than half the approximately 1,600 habitats falling within the Directive's field of application had been designated and therefore hunting continued of bird species protected by the Directive, including the hunting and trapping practices.[172]

Although it is not required by the Directive, the Government requires that candidate SPA sites within the UK be designated as ASSIs (or SSSIs) or as NRs or NNRs under national legislation before they can be designated as SPAs. Thus far, Northern Ireland has lagged substantially behind Great Britain in its SPA designation programme. Whereas over ninety SPAs have been designated in Great Britain, only two have been designated in Northern Ireland to date. Swan Island, a small NR and RSPB reserve in Larne Lough, supporting an important tern colony, including the roseate tern which is endangered at the European level, was designated in March 1992. Sheep Island, an ASSI on the north Antrim coast, supporting the second-largest colony of breeding cormorants in the British Isles, was designated in December 1992. In 1993 a review of sites which might qualify for SPA status throughout Ireland (commissioned by the DoE(NI) in co-operation with the National Parks and Wildlife Service in Dublin) was completed. The *Environment Service Corporate Plan 1994–97* now estimates that 'about 10 of our existing ASSIs, together with a further 15 sites still to be declared as ASSIs, are likely to merit SPA, SAC and/or Ramsar designation.'[173] It is anticipated that a further eleven SPA sites will be designated in addition to the two already classified. The *Environment Service Report, 1993–95* states that the DoE(NI)'s Environment Service 'has already begun the process of identifying precise boundaries for these sites and will complete their declaration as ASSIs in time for them to be designated [as SPAs] by 1998'.[174] Management plans for these sites were completed by the March 1996 deadline set down in the *Environment Service Corporate Plan 1994–97*.[175] Finally, it should be noted that the Government has decided as a matter of planning policy that where a site meets the criteria for designation as an SPA, that site should be treated as having been formally designated.[176]

The requirements in the Wild Birds Directive concerning habitat protection have been implemented in Northern Ireland by the Nature Conservation and Amenity Lands (NI) Order 1985,[177] as amended by the Nature Conservation and

---

172. L. Krämer, *EC Treaty and Environmental Law,* 2nd ed., London: Sweet & Maxwell, 1995, p. 18.
173. P. 8. The reference to 'Ramsar' designation is a reference to the Government's obligations to designate wetland habitats under the Ramsar Convention, outlined in Part III of this chapter.
174. P. 5.
175. P. 9.
176. In Great Britain this policy has now been enshrined in *Nature Conservation* (Planning Policy Guidance Note 9), Oct. 1994. *PPS2 Planning and Nature Conservation* is the equivalent NI document. It was published in draft form in October 1995, copies are available from the Planning Service Headquarters in Belfast.
177. SI 1985/170.

Amenity Lands (Amendment) (NI) Order 1989.[178] As already stated, the provisions of the Wild Birds Directive have been amended by the Habitats Directive. However, as will be explained below, the provisions of the two Directives are also interrelated, in that SPAs designated under the Wild Birds Directive constitute one category of European site which makes up the EC network of specially protected sites known as 'Natura 2000'. The implementation of the Habitats Directive will be discussed below.

## The Habitats Directive

After several years of intense debate, the EC adopted its next major conservation initiative, the Habitats Directive, in May 1992. The overall objective of the Habitats Directive is expressed in Article 2 as being 'to contribute towards ensuring bio-diversity through the conservation of natural habitats of wild fauna and flora' throughout the EC; measures taken pursuant to the Directive must be designed to 'maintain or restore, at favourable conservation status, natural habitats and species of wild fauna and flora of Community interest' and must take account of 'economic, social and cultural requirements and regional and local characteristics'.

Although it contains general provisions for the protection of listed animal and plant species, the Directive is primarily concerned with the issue of habitat protection. In this regard the principal initiative in the Habitats Directive is the creation of a coherent EC-wide network, on both land and sea, of specially protected sites to be known as 'Natura 2000', consisting of SPAs designated under the Wild Birds Directive (outlined above) and 'special areas of conservation' (SACs) designated under the Habitats Directive. Annex I to the Habitats Directive lists 168 habitat types whose conservation requires designation as an SAC. These are grouped into the following categories: coastal and halophytic habitats, coastal sand dunes and continental dunes, freshwater habitats, temperate heath and scrub, sclerophyllous scrub (matorral), natural and semi-natural grassland formations, raised bogs and mires and fens, rocky habitats and caves, and forests. Some of these habitat types are identified as 'priority' habitat types, because, in European terms, they are at the greatest risk of disappearing altogether.[179]

The EC is divided into five 'biogeographical' regions for the purpose of selecting candidate SACs, namely Alpine, Atlantic, Continental, Macronesian, and Mediterranean. The UK forms part of the Atlantic biogeographical region, and the importance of candidate sites will be assessed in the context of that region. In effect, the Government is obliged to ensure that 'together the sites proposed are

---

178. SI 1989/492.

179. Priority habitat types are defined in Art. 1(*d*) of the Directive and are identified in Annex I by an asterisk. It is important to note that active raised and blanket bogs are listed as priority habitats in the Habitats Directive. The protection of peatlands of recognised nature conservation value is now one of the government's primary objectives for nature conservation in Northern Ireland. Such peatlands are first protected, as a matter of policy, under the NCALO as ASSIs before they are designated as European sites or as Ramsar sites under the Ramsar Convention. The concept of ASSI designation is discussed in Part II, section 1 of this chapter, while the requirements of the Ramsar Convention are discussed in Part III.

those which would contribute the most to the maintenance or restoration of the habitat types and species within the Atlantic region.'[180]

The Habitats Directive also establishes a list of species (contained in Annex II) (other than birds) whose habitats must be protected in order to ensure their survival. Annex II lists 632 types of animals and plants whose conservation requires the SAC designation. As with habitat types in particular danger, species in danger of extinction are given 'priority' status. However, none of these species occurs in Northern Ireland. In effect, Natura 2000 will consist of SAC sites containing the habitat types listed in Annex I and the habitats of the species listed in Annex II, and will incorporate the SPAs designated under the Wild Birds Directive.

Article 4 sets out complex procedures which the Government and the Commission must follow in selecting and designating SACs.[181] The first stage of compliance requires each member state to submit a list to the Commission by June 1995 of those areas which it believes will qualify as SACs. The list must be drawn up by reference to the criteria laid down in Annex III (stage 1) of the Directive and 'relevant scientific criteria'. Member states may propose modifications to their lists at a later date where the results of habitat and species surveillance renders such modification appropriate (Article 11).

Although it is not required by the Directive, the Government has decided that all candidate sites must first be designated under national legislation; in this context the site must be designated as an ASSI or SSSI by 31 March 1995. The *Environment Service Report,* 1993–95 states that the programme to declare all candidate SACs within Northern Ireland as ASSIs has been completed and covers the best examples of eleven of the habitat types listed in the Directive; the Northern Ireland list of candidate sites has been sent to the Commission as part of the UK's submission—17 candidate SAC sites were included in Northern Ireland's submission under the Directive.

The Commission is now obliged under Article 4.2 of the Directive to compile a draft list of 'sites of Community importance', taking account of the criteria listed in Annex III (stage 2) of the Directive. A final agreed list is then produced by the Commission after consultation with a committee of independent scientific experts. In addition, the Commission is required to produce a separate list of 'priority sites' which identifies those sites that contain one or more of the priority habitat types or species. The Commission's work in this regard must be completed by June 1998.

The Commission may not include a site on either list without the member state's consent. Article 5 of the Directive makes provision for a bilateral

---

180. *Consultation Paper: Proposals to Implement the Habitats Directive in Northern Ireland,* Belfast: DoE(NI) 1993, 5. In March 1995 a Guidance Note on the Conservation (Natural Habitats etc.) Regulations (NI) 1995 was issued by the DoE(NI) outlining the changes introduced by the new Regulations. A Planning Policy Statement was published in draft form in October 1995: *PPS2 Planning and Nature Conservation.* Copies are available from the Planning Service Headquarters in Belfast.

181. The Consultation Paper issued by the DoE(NI) concerning the implementation of the Habitats Directive pointed out that the names of the habitat types listed in Annex I of the Directive did not coincide with the vegetation classification system normally used in Northern Ireland. However, the paper stated that the Northern Ireland contribution to the UK initial list of candidate SACs would be selected using the scientific information contained in Annex I, 'the best available scientific information on marine habitats and any necessary additional interpretative work on the Habitats Directive's listings' (p. 5).

consultation process between the Commission and a member state in the event of disagreement about whether a particular priority site should be included on the list. However, the site can only be included on the list with the unanimous agreement of the Council of Ministers. A site which is subject to the consultation procedure, or in relation to which a decision is pending from the Council under Article 5, will be afforded a certain level of protection under the Directive. The actual designation of SACs can only begin following approval from the Commission, which might not be forthcoming until 1998. Member states are required to complete the process of SAC designation as soon as possible after approval is given and within six years at the latest (Article 4.4). The selection and designation programme of SPAs under the Wild Birds Directive (outlined above) will continue in parallel to the selection of SACs under the Habitats Directive. However, as already stated, the programme of SPA designation must be completed by 1998.

Now that Northern Ireland's list of candidate sites has been drawn up, consultation with owners and occupiers of the affected sites and other affected interests will be conducted in order to explain the implications of designation as a European site. In this regard it is important to note that human activity is not excluded from a site simply because the site has been listed as a site of Community importance, or has been designated as an SPA, or is subject to the Article 5 consultation procedure, or is ultimately designated an SAC. In the Environment Service's words, the Habitats Directive 'does not seek to create totally protected "no entry" zones.'[182] Sustainable management is one of the key principles underlying the Directive, meaning that activities carried out on European sites must be done in such as way as not to harm or threaten the nature conservation interest. However, it is important to note that European sites are afforded a greater level of protection than sites designated as ASSIs or NRs under the NCALO (addressed in Part II, section 1 of this chapter).

Articles 10 and 11 of the Habitats Directive set down general conservation duties requiring member states to encourage the management of certain landscape features which are 'of major importance for wild fauna and flora' (Article 10) and to monitor the conservation status of all natural habitats and species, particularly priority species and habitat types (Article 11). However, in addition to these more general duties the Directive imposes specific conservation obligations in relation to SACs (once designated), sites identified by the Commission as sites of Community importance, SPAs designated under the Wild Birds Directive, and sites subject to the consultation procedure referred to above. They are as follows:

1. Once an SAC is designated, Article 6.1 obliges member states to establish the 'necessary conservation measures', including, where necessary, appropriate management plans and 'appropriate statutory, administrative or contractual measures.'

2. Article 6.2 provides that member states are obliged to take appropriate steps to avoid the deterioration of natural habitats and the habitats of species as well as significant disturbance of the species for which the following sites have been adopted by the Commission: SACs, sites included on the Commission's list as

---

182. Consultation Paper, p. 3; note 180, supra.

sites of Community importance, SPAs designated under the Wild Birds Directive and sites subject to the consultation procedure laid down in Article 5.

3. Article 6.3 provides that any plan or project (not directly connected with or necessary to the management of the site) that is likely to have a significant effect on an SAC, a site included on the Commission's list of sites of Community importance or sites designated as SPAs must be assessed to determine whether the nature conservation interest would be damaged. If the plan or project receives a negative assessment it may only proceed if there is no alternative and it is necessary for 'imperative reasons of overriding public interest, including those of a social or economic nature.' In such a case the member state is obliged to take 'all compensatory measures necessary to ensure that the overall coherence of Natura 2000 is protected.' It must also inform the Commission of the measures taken in this regard. More strict criteria are applied where the site contains priority habitat types or species. The only considerations which may be raised to justify proceeding with such a plan or project in a site which contains a priority habitat type or species are those relating to: (i) beneficial consequences of primary importance to the environment, (ii) human health or public safety, (iii) other imperative reasons of overriding public interest, or (iv) where the Commission is of the opinion that there are considerations of overriding public interest (Article 6.3–4).

As already stated in the context of the Wild Birds Directive, it is important to note that there are no priority bird species covered by the Habitats Directive, and therefore the more stringent controls applicable under Article 6.4 to priority sites cannot apply to SPAs designated under the Wild Birds Directive. Finally, it should be noted that Article 6.2–4 is drafted in similar terms to Article 4.4 of the Wild Birds Directive. Given the suggestion in *Commission v. Spain* that Article 4.4 was capable of direct enforcement, it is likely that Article 6.2–4 will also satisfy the test for direct effects.

## Implementation of the Wild Birds and Habitats Directives in Northern Ireland

The provisions of the Wild Birds Directive concerning habitat protection have been implemented in Northern Ireland by the Nature Conservation and Amenity Lands (NI) Order 1985, as amended (its provisions are set out in Part II, section 1 of this chapter). Although the NCALO also broadly implements the requirements laid down by the Habitats Directive concerning habitat protection, the Directive requires member states to have specific legal powers to protect European sites and, as a result, it was necessary to introduce additional legislation to strengthen certain aspects of existing Northern Ireland legislation concerning habitat conservation. In October 1995 the Conservation (Natural Habitats etc.) Regulations (NI) 1995[183] ('Habitats Regulations') were enacted to effect full legal implementation of the Habitats Directive. These Regulations came into force on 13 November 1995.

---

183. SR No. 380. A Guidance Note on the Conservation (Natural Habitats etc.) Regulations (NI) 1995 was issued by the DoE(NI) outlining the changes introduced by the new Regulations. A Planning Policy Statement was published in draft form in October 1995, *PPS2 Planning and Nature Conservation,* is available from Planning Service Headquarters in Belfast.

The new Regulations do not attempt to redesign Northern Ireland law on nature conservation; instead, as in Great Britain, the Government has adopted a 'minimalist approach', simply grafting the new Regulations onto the existing framework of planning and other legislative controls operating to protect habitats in Northern Ireland.[184] In effect, the system of protection laid down by the Habitats Regulations for European sites is very similar to, but more stringent than, that provided by the NCALO for ASSIs and NRs declared under articles 24 and 17 of the NCALO.

Regulation 3(3) of the Habitats Regulations obliges the DoE(NI) to exercise its functions under Northern Ireland nature conservation legislation so as to secure compliance with the requirements of the Habitats Directive. Similarly, any competent authority[185] having functions relevant to marine conservation must exercise its functions so as to secure compliance with the requirements of the Habitats Directive.[186] More generally, regulation 3(4) provides that 'every competent authority'[187] must have regard to the requirements of the Habitats Directive so far as the requirements of the Directive may be affected by the exercise of the authority's functions. The DoE(NI) is also empowered to cause a public inquiry to be held in relation to any matter arising under the Habitats Regulations. These powers are outlined in Part I, section 1 (at pages 300–301).

### Information concerning the implementation of the Habitats Directive

Article 17 of the Habitats Directive imposes specific obligations on both member states and the Commission to report on the implementation of the Habitats Directive. It is important to note that the information generated in this context must be made available to the public. Member states are obliged to submit a report to the Commission every six years from the date on which the Directive was notified to the member states (May 1992) on the implementation of the Habitats Directive within their own jurisdictions. The report must include information concerning the conservation measures which member states are required to take under Article 6.1 of the Directive in relation to SACs designated under the Directive (explained above). In addition, the report must provide an evaluation of

---

184. For comment on the equivalent legislation in Great Britain see Ball and Bell, supra, pp 492–6; M. Fry, *A Manual of Nature Conservation Law*, Oxford: Clarendon Press, 1995.

185. In the context of marine conservation the relevant authorities 'are such of the following as have functions in relation to land or waters within or adjacent to' a marine area or European marine site: a district council, the Commissioners of Irish Lights, a harbour authority as defined by the Harbours Act (NI) 1970 (s. 38), the Fisheries Conservancy Board for Northern Ireland, the Foyle Fisheries Commission, and a pilotage authority within the meaning of the Pilotage Act 1983 (reg. 4).

186. Reg. 3(3) provides that this applies in particular to functions under the following provisions: Foyle Fisheries Act (NI) 1952; Fisheries Act (NI) 1966 ; s. 2(2) of the Military Lands Act 1900 (these powers were extended by s. 7 of the Land Powers (Defence) Act 1958); Harbours Act (NI) 1970; art. 20 and 21 of NCALO (marine nature reserves); Water Act (NI) 1972; Water and Sewerage Services (NI) Order 1973; Drainage (NI) Order 1973; and Conservation (Natural Habitats etc.) Regulations (NI) 1995.

187. In this regard the term 'competent authority' includes 'Government departments, district councils and statutory undertakers, and any trustees, commissioners, board or other persons who, as a public body and not for their own profit, act under any statutory provision for the improvement of any place or the production or supply of any commodity or service' (reg. 5).

the impact which measures adopted under Article 6.1 have had on the conservation status of the natural habitat types listed in Annex I and the species listed in Annex II (species whose habitats must be protected).

Article 11 of the Habitats Directive requires that member states also 'undertake surveillance' of the conservation status of the natural habitats and species within their territory, the main results of which must be included in the report that member states are obliged to submit to the Commission under Article 17. This surveillance must pay particular attention to the status of priority habitat types. The Commission is then required to produce a composite report based on the various national reports, which must include an 'appropriate evaluation' of the progress achieved and, in particular, of the contribution of Natura 2000 to the achievement of the objectives of the Directive. Member states must be given an opportunity to verify the contents of the Commission's report, and, after submission to the committee established under Article 20 of the Directive (containing representatives from each member state), the final version of the report must be published within two years of the receipt of the national reports.

### Scope of the Habitats Regulations

The protection afforded by the Habitats Regulations will only apply to sites that come within the meaning of a 'European site' as defined by regulation 9. They are as follows:

### (i) An SAC once designated

The Regulations simply reproduce the provisions of Article 4 of the Habitats Directive concerning the selection of candidate SACs (outlined above). Regulation 6 obliges the DoE(NI) to compile the Northern Ireland list of sites; the list was submitted as part of the UK submission by the June 1995 deadline laid down by Article 4 of the Directive. It is important to note that although the Habitats Regulations came into force in November 1995, the DoE(NI) cannot designate a site as an SAC until the UK Government and the Commission agree that the site is a site of Community importance and that it should be designated as an SAC. As explained above, this decision will be made at some point before June 1998.

### (ii) A 'site of Community importance'

A 'site of Community importance' is a site which has been included on the Commission's list (explained above) under Article 4.2 of the Habitats Directive. Regulation 7(1) provides that once a site has been adopted by the Commission as a site of Community importance, the DoE(NI) is obliged to designate that site as an SAC 'as soon as possible and within six years at most.' In this regard the Habitats Regulations require the DoE(NI) to establish priorities for the designation of SACs in the light of: (i) 'the importance of the sites for the maintenance or restoration at a favourable conservation status of a natural habitat type listed in Annex I to the Habitats Directive [above] or a species listed in Annex II to the Directive [above] and for the coherence of Natura 2000 [above]' and (ii) 'the threats of degradation to which those sites are exposed.' Where a site is a marine site, references to the Secretary of State should be substituted for references to the DoE(NI).

### (iii) A site subject to the consultation procedure provided for in Article 5 of the Habitats Directive

The consultation procedure can only be invoked in relation to sites which contain priority habitats or priority species, and a site will remain 'subject to the consultation procedure' pending discussions between the member state and the Commission or pending a decision by the Council (see above). Regulation 9(2) provides that this category of European site will not be covered by regulations 17 and 23, which govern the approval of certain types of plans and projects on European sites. However, this exclusion does not affect their protection under other regulations. This limitation of the protection afforded to sites subject to the consultation procedure mirrors the limitation imposed by Article 6.3 of the Habitats Directive itself (outlined above). A site which is subject to this consultation process can only be added to the Northern Ireland list of candidate SACs if the DoE(NI) agrees that it should be, or if the Council of the European Union, acting on a proposal from the Commission, so decides. However, Article 5 of the Habitats Directive requires the Council's decision to be unanimous.

### (iv) An SPA designated under the Wild Birds Directive

Although the DoE(NI) cannot designate a site as an SAC until it receives Commission approval, the Department has been empowered to designate sites as SPAs since the Wild Birds Directive came into force in 1979. The Habitats Regulations will apply to existing SPAs and to new SPAs as soon as they are designated. The process of SPA designation is to be completed by 1998. To date two SPAs have been designated in Northern Ireland (above); it is anticipated that a further eleven SPAs will be designated by 1998.

As a general point it should be noted that the Habitats and Wild Birds Directives apply to the European territory of member states; as a result, the implementation of the Directives will extend to the limits of the territorial sea.[188] Provisions governing European sites must cover the marine environment, and special supplementary provisions have been incorporated into the Habitats Regulations to ensure full compliance with the requirements of the Habitats Directive in this context. The selection of marine SACs and SPAs will be carried out by the DoE(NI) in conjunction with the Department of Agriculture (NI), which is responsible, among other things, for the management, conservation and protection of fisheries in Northern Ireland.

---

188. For the purpose of the Habitats Regulations, reg. 2(4) provides that the territorial waters of the UK adjacent to Northern Ireland will be treated as part of Northern Ireland, and reference to Northern Ireland will be interpreted as including the adjacent territorial waters. Territorial waters include 'any waters landward of the baselines from which the breadth of the territorial sea is measured.'

### DoE(NI) register of public information concerning European sites in Northern Ireland

Regulation 10 obliges the DoE(NI) to 'compile and maintain in such form as it thinks fit' a register of European sites in Northern Ireland. A copy of the register must be available for public inspection at 'all reasonable hours and free of charge.' The register must list:

(i) SACs as soon as they are designated;

(ii) sites of Community importance as soon as they are placed on the Commission's list;

(iii) any site which is subject to the consultation procedure under Article 5 of the Habitats Directive (above) or in relation to which a decision is pending from the Council;

(iv) SPAs as soon as they are designated; if an SPA has already been designated before the enactment of the Habitats Regulations, the SPA must be listed 'as soon as practicable' after the Regulations come into force (13 November 1995).

The Department may amend an entry in the register where it is appropriate to do so and is required to remove an entry if an SAC ceases to be an SAC as a result of declassification by the Commission under Article 9 of the Habitats Directive[189] or if a site ceases to fall within any of the categories of European sites listed above.

Regulation 11 requires the DoE(NI) to notify every owner and occupier of land within the site, each district council in whose district the site (or part of the site) is located and any other persons or bodies the Department thinks fit, that the site has been included in, or removed from, the DoE(NI)'s register, or, that the entry in the register concerning the site has been amended. Notification must be given as soon as is practicable and must be accompanied by a copy of so much of the relevant register as relates to the land which concerns the person or body being notified. An entry in the DoE(NI)'s register under regulation 10 concerning a European site must also be registered in the Statutory Charges Register (regulation 12).

### Management of European sites

Regulations 13 and 14 govern the DoE(NI)'s power to enter into agreements for the management of European sites. These provisions are identical to the terms of article 17 of the NCALO, as amended, which govern management agreements for NRs and ASSIs. The terms of article 17, as amended, are discussed in detail in Part II, section 1 of this chapter. As with management agreements for ASSIs and NRs, management agreements under regulation 13 must be registered in the Statutory Charges Register.

Regulation 14 provides that any management agreement entered into under article 17 of the NCALO concerning a nature reserve, or under article 24(8) of the

---

189. Art. 9 requires the Commission to conduct periodic reviews of the contribution of Natura 2000 to the objectives of the Habitats Directive, and in this regard a site may be declassified where this is warranted by 'natural developments noted as a result of the surveillance which Member States are required to carry out under Article 11 of habitats and species within their territory.'

NCALO concerning an ASSI, which on or after the commencement of the Habitats Regulations becomes land within or adjacent to a European site, will have effect as if it were entered into under regulation 13. Similarly, anything done or deemed to have been done under any provision of Parts V (NRs), VI (ASSIs) or VIII (general provisions concerning bylaws, financial assistance, enforcement of bylaws, etc.) of the NCALO in respect of any land before it becomes land within or adjacent to a European site, will continue to have effect as if it were done under the corresponding provisions of the Habitats Regulations. Finally, any reference in any enactment not contained in or made under the NCALO to a nature reserve within the meaning of article 2(2) of the NCALO will be construed as including a European site (regulation 14(3)).

As a matter of general policy, the DoE(NI) is required by regulation 32 to endeavour, where necessary, to encourage the management of landscape features which are of major importance for wild flora and fauna in its land use planning and development policies. Regulation 32 defines these features as those which 'by virtue of their linear and continuous structure (such as rivers with their banks or the traditional systems for marking field boundaries) or their function as stepping stones (such as ponds or small woods), are essential for the migration, dispersal and genetic exchange of wild species.'

### Control of potentially damaging operations on European sites

One of the most important differences between the protection afforded to ASSIs under article 24 of the NCALO and European sites under the Habitat Regulations is that the Habitats Regulations impose more stringent control over the carrying out of potentially damaging operations on European sites.

As explained in Part II, section 1 above, when an ASSI is declared under article 24 of the NCALO, the declaration will specify the nature of the scientific interest of the land in question and also those operations which must be notified to the DoE(NI) before they can be carried out on that land, i.e. 'notifiable operations'. Regulation 15(1) of the Habitats Regulations provides that any declaration issued under article 24 of the NCALO in respect of land which is also part of a European site will continue to have effect for the purposes of the Habitats Regulations. As already explained above, the UK Government decided as a matter of policy that all candidate SACs and SPAs must be protected under national nature conservation legislation before they can be designated as an SPA or SAC. All candidate SAC sites in Northern Ireland have been designated as ASSIs, while one of the two Northern Ireland SPAs has been designated an NR and the other an ASSI.

Unlike the position under the NCALO, regulation 15(2) of the Habitats Regulations empowers the DoE(NI) to amend the declaration, at any time, in terms of its statement of the scientific interest of a European site and/or its statement of the notifiable operations for that site. Such an amendment can be made for the purpose of securing compliance with the requirements of the Habitats Directive. The DoE(NI) is obliged to notify any owner or occupier of any land within the European site who may, in the Department's opinion, be affected by the amendment and any district council in whose district the site is wholly or partly located. The Guidance Note issued by the DoE(NI) in March 1995 explaining the terms and application of the Habitats Regulations, states that an ASSI declaration will only be amended after full consultation. It is important to note that the amendment will only come into force in relation to the owner or occupier 'upon the notice being given to him' (regulation 15(3)) and also that regulation 15(4) requires that the amendment of the declaration be registered in the Statutory Charges Register.

The most important distinction between the control of potentially damaging operations within ASSIs which do not contain European sites and ASSIs which do contain such sites lies in the DoE(NI)'s powers to prevent an owner or occupier from carrying out potentially damaging operations within a European site without the Department's consent. As with ASSIs designated under the NCALO, owners and occupiers of land within a European site may not carry out, or cause to be carried out, any of the notifiable operations listed in the ASSI declaration in force in relation to the site, unless the DoE(NI) has been notified (regulation 16). Like article 25(1) of the NCALO, regulation 16(1) of the Habitats Regulations sets out two separate consent procedures which must be satisfied, depending on whether or not the proposed operation is likely to cause damage to the scientific interest of the site. The consent procedure for notifiable operations which, in the DoE(NI)'s opinion, are not likely to damage the scientific interest of the site is laid down in regulation 16(1)(*a*) and is identical to that laid down in article 25(1)(*a*) of the NCALO, as amended by article 10 of the Nature Conservation and Amenity Lands (Amendment) (NI) Order 1989[190] (discussed at page 347). However, the control of notifiable operations on European sites which are potentially damaging is more stringent than that applying under the NCALO to ASSIs which do not contain European sites, in that the DoE(NI)'s consent must be obtained by an owner or occupier before they can lawfully carry out, or cause or permit to be carried out, such an operation within a European site. As was explained in the context of ASSIs, an owner or occupier of land within an ASSI could in effect wait for the nine-month period of statutory negotiation to expire and then carry out a potentially damaging notifiable operation without obstruction, subject to the DoE(NI)'s power of compulsory purchase, which in practice is rarely used. This option is now removed in the case of land within a European site. In effect, regulation 16(1)(*b*) requires that a potentially damaging notifiable operation can only be carried out on a European site where:

(i) the owner or occupier has given the DoE(NI) written notice of the proposal to carry out the operation, specifying its nature and the land on which it is proposed to carry it out;

(ii) either the DoE(NI) has given its written consent to the operation or the operation is carried out in accordance with the terms of a management agreement, and

(iii) the DoE(NI) has not served on the owner or occupier notice of its intention to acquire the land compulsorily.

The Guidance Note issued by the DoE(NI) in March 1995 concerning the terms and application of the Habitats Regulations notes that where the Department is unable to give its consent under regulation 16 it will examine other methods of resolving the situation. Like the position under the NCALO in relation to ASSIs,

---

190. SI 1989/492.

the DoE(NI) has the power to enter into management agreements concerning European sites and also has the power to acquire the land in question compulsorily. However, the guidance note states that, as with ASSIs, this power is likely to be used in exceptional circumstances only.

Regulation 16(3)–(6) lays down almost identical provisions to those of article 25(6)–(9) of the NCALO, as amended, concerning the offence of violating the procedures governing notifiable operations, available defences, penalties and the enforcement of these provisions, the only difference being that although the Habitats Regulations and the NCALO both list a grant of planning permission as being a 'reasonable excuse' and therefore a defence to prosecution, the Habitats Regulations require the effect of any plan or project on a European site to be considered before a grant of planning permission can be made (regulations 43, 44 and 49). In addition, the Habitats Regulations provide that planning permissions granted before the date on which the site becomes a European site (or, if later, on the commencement of the Habitats Regulations) must be reviewed, and in certain circumstances revoked, where the integrity of the site would be adversely affected (regulations 45, 46, and 50–3).

It should also be noted that regulation 18(1) provides that any notices previously submitted to the DoE(NI) under article 25(1) of the NCALO, notifying the Department of a proposal to carry out either potentially damaging or non-damaging notifiable operations on land within an ASSI which on or before the commencement of the Habitats Regulations, became a European site, will have effect as if given under regulation 16 and will thereby be subject to the more stringent controls applying under the Habitat Regulations. Similarly, regulation 18(1) provides that any consent previously given by the DoE(NI) under article 25 of the NCALO in relation to land which became a European site either before, or on the commencement of the Habitats Regulations, will have effect as though it were given under regulation 16 and will thereby be subject to more stringent control.

The DoE(NI) is obliged to review any consent issued under article 25(1) in relation to an ASSI which on or after the commencement of the Habitats Regulations became a European site (regulation 18(2)). The consent will be reviewed in the light of its 'compatibility with the conservation objectives of the site', and the Department may modify or withdraw the consent. Where it decides to modify or withdraw the consent it must give notice of the modification or withdrawal to every owner or occupier of land within the site who, in the Department's opinion, might be affected by such a change. The modification or withdrawal of the consent will only take effect in relation to an owner or occupier 'upon such notice being given to him', and the modification or withdrawal of a consent will not affect anything done in reliance on a consent before the notice takes effect.

Finally, regulation 18(5) provides that, to the extent that a notifiable operation ceases to be covered by a consent because it has been withdrawn or modified, article 16(1) will apply from the moment notice of the change takes effect. This means that an owner or occupier of land would have to reapply under article 16(1) to the DoE(NI) for permission to carry out the operation in question to the extent to which it was not covered by a consent; the Department's power to grant the consent will then be subject to the controls imposed by regulation 17, outlined below.

### Controls on the DoE(NI)'s powers to consent to potentially damaging operations within a European site

In addition to requiring that the DoE(NI) give written consent to the carrying out of any potentially damaging operation on a European site (or that the operation be undertaken in accordance with a management agreement), the Habitats Regulations impose controls on the Department's power to consent to the carrying out of such an operation on a European site. These controls are laid down in regulation 17, which essentially reproduces the requirements laid down in Article 6.3 and 6.4 of the Habitats Directive. It should be noted at the outset, however, that these controls do not apply to sites which come within the definition of a European site by reason of the fact that they are subject to the consultation procedure under Article 5.1 of the Habitats Directive (explained at pages 367–8) nor do these controls apply to sites in relation to which a decision from the Council under Article 5.3 is pending (also explained at pages 367–8). The protection afforded by regulation 17 applies therefore only to sites adopted by the Commission as sites of Community importance, sites designated as SPAs under the Wild Birds Directive, and sites ultimately designated as SACs under the Habitats Directive.

In effect, regulation 17(1) provides that where an owner or occupier of land within a European site makes an application to the DoE(NI) under regulation 16 for permission to carry out a potentially damaging notifiable operation within the site, the Department is obliged to make an 'appropriate assessment of the implications for the site in view of that site's conservation objectives' where the operation in question appears to form part of a plan or project which is 'not directly connected with or necessary to the management of the site and is likely to have a significant effect on the site (either alone or in combination with other plans or projects).' The Department may give consent to the operation only if the assessment shows that the plan or project will 'not adversely effect the integrity of the site.'

However, regulation 17(3) and (4) makes provision for two exceptions to this general position. They are as follows:

1. Regulation 17(3) provides that the Department may grant consent to the operation, despite a negative assessment of the plan or project, if it is satisfied that there are 'no alternative solutions' and that the plan or project 'must be carried out for imperative reasons of overriding public interest.' It is important to note that these reasons may include reasons of an economic or social nature. As explained above, by including economic and social factors as possible justifications for granting consent to damaging operations, Article 6 of the Habitats Directive in effect reduced the protection afforded by the earlier decision of the European Court of Justice in *Commission v. Germany* to SPAs designated under the Wild Birds Directive, and potentially to all European sites, in that the Court decided that economic and social considerations could not justify a reduction in the area of an SPA.

2. The second exception is laid down by regulation 17(4), which goes on to retain the more stringent control laid down by the European Court of Justice in

relation to European sites containing priority habitats or species listed in Annex I or II of the Habitats Directive.[191] Regulation 17(4) provides that the DoE(NI) may grant consent in this context only where there is no alternative solution and where the plan or project must be carried out for imperative reasons of overriding public interest. However, the only considerations which may be raised in this regard are those relating to:

(i) human health or public safety, or

(ii) 'beneficial consequences of primary importance to the environment' or

(iii) 'other reasons which in the opinion of the European Commission are imperative reasons of overriding public interest'.

The level of protection afforded by the controls set down by regulation 17 will clearly depend on the DoE(NI)'s willingness to refuse consent where appropriate. In this regard, the outcome of the public inquiry currently being conducted into the establishment of a landfill site at Magheramorne quarry (Larne Lough) will provide a significant indication of the manner in which these controls will be applied in practice. The Department's Environment Service and the Northern Ireland Branch of the RSPB have both argued that there is a significant risk that the proposed landfill site would threaten the important tern colony on Swan Island (which has been designated as an SPA and an NNR) because of the additional gulls which it would attract to the area. At the time of writing, the public inquiry is on-going.

It should be noted that where the DoE(NI) does grant its consent to a damaging operation within a European site, whether it contains priority habitat types and species or not, the Department is obliged to secure that 'such compensatory measures are taken as are necessary to ensure that the overall coherence of Natura 2000 is protected' (regulation 17(5)). (The concept of Natura 2000 is explained above.) Article 6.4 of the Habitats Directive requires that the Commission be informed of the compensatory measures adopted.

### Duties of the Department of Agriculture (NI) in relation to European sites

Regulation 65(1) of the Habitats Regulations provides that where an application for a farm capital grant is made under article 16(1) and (2) of the Agriculture and Fisheries (Financial Assistance) (NI) Order 1987[192] in relation to expenditure incurred, or to be incurred, for the purpose of activities on land within a European site, the Department of Agriculture (NI) must exercise its functions under the 1987 Order to 'further the conservation of the flora or fauna or geological or physiographical features by reason of which the land is a European site' so far as may be consistent with the purpose of the grant provisions.

### Obligation to restore land where a notifiable operation is carried out in violation of regulation 16

Regulation 22 sets out the obligation to restore land which may be imposed on an

---

191. 'Priority' habitats and species are highlighted by an asterisk. It should be noted, however, that none of the priority species occurs within Northern Ireland, and, as birds are not covered by the Habitats Directive, there are no priority bird species.

192. SI 1987/166.

owner or occupier of land within a European site who is convicted of an offence under regulation 16 (i.e. who carries out, or causes or permits to be carried out, any notifiable operation on that land without the DoE(NI)'s consent and without reasonable excuse). The jurisdiction of the court to impose the obligation to restore under regulation 22 is identical to its jurisdiction under article 27(1)(*a*) and (2)–(5) of the NCALO (outlined at page 349). It should be noted that whereas article 27(1)(*b*) requires: (i) that the owner or occupier be convicted of an offence under article 24 of the NCALO (which corresponds to regulation 16 of the Habitats Regulations) and (ii) that the scientific interest of the land is actually damaged as a result of the operation before the obligation to restore can be imposed, regulation 22 of the Habitats Regulations simply requires that the owner or occupier be convicted of an offence under regulation 16.

## *Compensation*

As under article 26 of the NCALO, the Habitats Regulations make provision for the payment of compensation, in certain circumstances, to persons detrimentally affected by reason of the fact that their land, which is within a European site, has been declared as an ASSI. As already stated at page 374, an ASSI declaration which contains a European site will continue to have effect for the purposes of the Habitats Regulations under regulation 15(1), subject to the additional controls imposed under the Habitats Regulations explained above. Regulations 19 and 20, which are both based on article 26 of the NCALO, set out the rules which govern entitlement to, and calculation of, compensation for the purposes of the Habitats Regulations.

With regard to entitlement to compensation, regulation 19 provides that any person who has an estate in land which is part of an 'agricultural unit'[193] and which is also within a European site affected by an ASSI declaration under regulation 15(1) will be entitled to compensation from the DoE(NI) where they can establish that the value of their estate in the land is less than it would have been if the ASSI declaration had not applied to that land. Regulation 21 of the Habitats Regulations provides that regulations adopted under article 26 of the NCALO, governing the making of claims for compensation, will have effect for the purposes of regulations 19 and 20. The Nature Conservation (Claims for Compensation under Article 26) Regulations (NI) 1985,[194] adopted by the DoE(NI) under article 26(4), prescribe the times within which, and the manner in which, applications for compensation under article 26 and regulations 19 and 20 must be made.

Where entitlement to compensation is established, regulation 20 provides that the amount of compensation will be the difference between the value of the estate in the land and what it would have been had an ASSI declaration not been applied to the land under regulation 15. Regulation 20(3), (4) and (5) governs the assessment of the compensation in terms which are identical to the provisions of article 26(5)(*a*)–(*c*) and (6) of the NCALO (outlined in Part II, section 1 above),

---

193. Reg. 19 provides that the term 'agricultural unit' must be understood as being within the meaning of art. 2(2) of the Planning Blight (Compensation) (NI) Order 1981.

194. SR No. 240.

subject to the modification that the time at which the land will be valued is the time at which the ASSI declaration is applied to the land by virtue of regulation 15 —not the time at which the declaration was made, as is the case under article 26(5) of the NCALO.[195] Finally, it should be noted that any disputes concerning compensation will be determined by the Lands Tribunal unless alternative provisions are made under regulations adopted by the DoE(NI).

### *DoE(NI)'s power to acquire and dispose of land*

Regulation 27 sets out the DoE(NI)'s powers to acquire and convey land within a European site. In essence, the Department is empowered under regulation 27(1) to acquire land, either by agreement (whether by way of purchase, lease or exchange) or compulsorily, where it is satisfied:

    (a)  that it is unable to enter into a management agreement with any person having estate in any land within a European site, on terms appearing to it to be reasonable; and

    (b)  that it is expedient for the purposes of conserving land within a European site.

Where the Department decides to acquire land by exercising its compulsory powers, it is empowered to make an order vesting that land in the Department and section 97(2) and (3) of, and Schedule 6 to, the Local Government Act (NI) 1972[196] will apply, subject to the modifications specified in Schedule 1 to the Habitats Regulations, to the making of such an order. The Department's powers to transfer land acquired under regulation 27 are identical to its powers in this regard under article 6(4) of the NCALO, as amended, which are outlined on page 355 in the context of nature reserves. Finally, it should be noted that the Department is also empowered to dispose of any land acquired under regulation 27 which it no longer requires for any of the purposes referred to in regulation 27(1)(*a*) and (*b*). The disposal of such land may be subject to any terms and conditions the Department thinks fit. In addition, the DoE(NI) may attach restrictions and grant or reserve rights in relation to the land being disposed of. Nothing in section 5 of the Stormont Regulation and Government Property Act (NI) 1933 will affect the disposal of land which was acquired by the Department under regulation 27.

### *DoE(NI)'s power to adopt bylaws*

Regulation 23 provides that the DoE(NI)'s general power to make bylaws to protect nature reserves under article 19 of the NCALO (outlined at page 358) may also be used to make bylaws for the protection of a European site (excluding European marine sites, which are protected by bylaws adopted under regulation 31). As is the case under article 19, the DoE(NI) must consult the CNCC before adopting bylaws under regulation 23. Like article 19, regulation 23 goes on to list

---

195. Article 13 of the Land Acquisition and Compensation (NI) Order 1973 (SI 1973/1896) will apply in relation to compensation under regulation 19 as it applies to compensation under Part II of that Order. Article 6 of the Land Compensation (NI) Order 1982 (SI 1982/719) will govern the assessment of compensation payable under regulation 19 (subject to necessary modifications) in the same way as it governs compensation for compulsory land purchases.

196. c. 9.

various purposes for which bylaws may be made in this context, but, as with article 19, the list is without prejudice to the DoE(NI)'s general power to adopt bylaws. This list is similar to that laid down in article 19 itself but with two main differences: firstly, the protection afforded to birds under article 19(2)(*c*) is not listed in regulation 23 as a purpose for which bylaws might be adopted, and secondly, regulation 23 empowers the DoE(NI) to adopt bylaws that affect areas surrounding and adjacent to a European site; such bylaws may protect the whole or part of any European site and different provisions may be made to protect different parts of the site. Subject to minor adjustments for the European site context, regulations 24 and 25(1) and (2) repeat the provisions of article 19(5)–(7) concerning the limitations on the effects of bylaws adopted under regulation 23, compensation for the effects of bylaws and the adjudication of disputes concerning such compensation.

Regulation 26 provides that any bylaws previously adopted under article 19 of the NCALO in relation to land which on or after the commencement of the Habitats Regulations became land within or adjacent to a European site, will have effect as if made under article 19 as it applies by virtue of regulation 23. Such bylaws will be interpreted as though they were originally made under article 19 as it applies to European sites by virtue of regulation 23.

### Enforcement of bylaws

Regulation 66 lays down identical provisions to those applying under article 31 of the NCALO concerning the enforcement of bylaws adopted under articles 19 and 21 of the NCALO. In the context of European sites, these powers are described as applying in relation to the enforcement of bylaws adopted under articles 19 and 21 of the NCALO as they apply by virtue of regulations 23 and 31.

### Special provisions concerning European marine sites

Marine sites are protected under articles 20 and 21 of the NCALO as 'marine nature reserves'. As already stated, this designation affords very little protection to marine sites in practice. Terrestrial sites are afforded a far greater level of protection under the NCALO than marine sites. The Habitats Directive, however, extends much more stringent protection to European marine sites than marine sites protected purely by the NCALO, and as a result, the provisions of articles 20 and 21 did not provide an adequate basis for meeting the requirements of the Habitats Directive in this regard.

The Habitats Regulations contain supplementary provisions which, in effect, introduce a new approach to the conservation of marine sites within European sites. Regulation 28 provides that as soon as a site becomes a European marine site[197] the Secretary of State is obliged to advise 'the relevant authorities'[198] as to

---

197. A 'European marine site' is defined by reg. 2(1) as a European site that 'consists of, or so far as it consists of, marine sites.'

198. In the context of marine conservation the relevant authorities 'are such of the following as have functions in relation to land or waters within or adjacent to' a marine area or European marine site: a district council, the Commissioners of Irish Lights, a harbour authority as defined by the Harbours Act (NI) 1970 (s. 38), the Fisheries Conservancy Board for Northern Ireland, the Foyle Fisheries Commission, and a pilotage authority within the meaning of the Pilotage Act 1983 (reg. 4).

the conservation objectives for that site and also of any operations which may cause deterioration of natural habitats or the habitats of individual species or the disturbance of species for which the site was designated. The Secretary of State may also install markers for the purpose of indicating the existence and extent of a European marine site.

As already stated, regulation 3(3) provides that any competent authority having functions relevant to marine conservation[199] must exercise its functions so as to secure compliance with the requirements of the Habitats Directive. Regulation 29 empowers the DoE(NI) and any relevant authority to establish a management scheme for a European marine site under which their functions in relation to the marine site would be exercised so as to ensure that the requirements of the Habitats Directive are complied with for that site. However, only one management scheme may be made for each European marine site. The Secretary of State, or persons authorised on his behalf, is granted various powers to control the establishment of such management schemes and to require that they be amended. In particular, the Secretary of State may:

(i) require specific conservation measures to be included in the scheme;
(ii) appoint one of the relevant authorities to co-ordinate the establishment of the scheme;
(iii) set limits within which any steps are to be taken;
(iv) require that the Secretary of State's approval is necessary before a scheme can be established; and
(v) require that any relevant authority supplies specified information to the Secretary of State concerning the establishment of the scheme (regulation 30(1) and (2)).

Regulation 29(3) empowers the relevant authorities to amend the management scheme from time to time and also empowers the Secretary of State (or authorised persons) to issue general or specific directions concerning the amendment of a management scheme. All directions under regulation 30 must be in writing and may be varied or revoked at a later date. As soon as a management scheme is established or amended, regulation 29(4) requires that a copy of the scheme be sent by the relevant authority (or authorities) to the Secretary of State. Finally, it should be noted that regulation 31 confers on the Secretary of State the power to make bylaws for the protection of European marine sites under article 21 of the NCALO (substituting references to European marine sites for the references to marine nature reserves). However, nothing in bylaws made by virtue of regulation 31 will interfere with the exercise of any functions of a relevant authority, any statutory function or any right of any person, regardless of when those rights were vested in that person. Regulation 66 governs the enforcement of bylaws adopted under both regulation 23 and regulation 31. The DoE(NI)'s powers under regulation 66 are set out above in the context of the enforcement of bylaws adopted under regulation 23.

---

199. Reg. 3(3) provides that this applies in particular to functions under the following provisions: Foyle Fisheries Act (NI) 1952; Fisheries Act (NI) 1966; s. 2 (2) of the Military Lands Act 1900 (these powers were extended by s. 7 of the Land Powers (Defence) Act 1958); Harbours Act (NI) 1970; art. 20 and 21 of NCALO (marine nature reserves); Water Act (NI) 1972; Water and Sewerage Services (NI) Order 1973; Drainage (NI) Order 1973; and the Habitats Regulations.

In effect, the Habitats Regulations afford a more stringent level of protection to marine sites which are designated as European sites. Unlike the position in relation to marine nature reserves under the NCALO, the provisions of the Habitats Regulations require that the activities of all bodies operating in relation to the European marine site be properly co-ordinated. However, it is important to note that because the criteria laid down in the Habitats Directive for the selection of candidate SACs are so cumbersome, only one marine site has been listed for designation within Northern Ireland, namely Strangford Lough. Important marine sites, such as Rathlin Island, could not be included as candidate sites.[200]

### *Impact of the Habitats Regulations on planning controls in Northern Ireland*

Part IV of the Habitats Regulations introduces a wide range of important adaptations to planning and other regulatory systems which reinforce the protection afforded to European sites in Northern Ireland. A detailed explanation of these provisions is beyond the scope of this chapter; in brief they are as follows:

1. Planning permission must be obtained for any development within an SAC or an SPA, and the DoE(NI)'s Planning Service will take the nature conservation interest of the SPA or SAC fully into account when determining a planning application. Regulations 43, 44 and 49 require that the effect on a European site be assessed before planning permission can be granted and also require, subject to certain exceptions, that the grant of planning permission be restricted where the integrity of a European site would be adversely affected. The terms of regulations 43 and 44 substantially mirror those of regulation 17, which controls the DoE(NI)'s powers to consent to the carrying out of certain notifiable operations within a European site. A planning policy statement *(PPS2 Planning and Nature Conservation)* was published in draft form in October 1995 by the DoE(NI)'s Planning Service concerning planning policy in relation to SPAs and SACs; the DoE(NI)'s Guidance Note (1995) concerning the application of the Habitats Regulations provides a general overview of the controls imposed in relation to planning applications in this context.

2. Regulations 45, 46 and 50–53 require that planning permission granted in relation to the site before the date on which it became a European site (or, if later, on the date when these Regulations commence) be reviewed and in certain circumstances revoked where the integrity of the site would be adversely affected.

3. Regulation 54 limits claims for compensation under the Land Development Values (Compensation) Act (NI) 1965 where the DoE(NI) makes a decision not to confirm a provisional order under article 38 (revocation or modification of planning permission) or article 39 (discontinuance of a use etc.) of the Planning (NI) Order 1991. Compensation is essentially limited to loss or damage directly attributable to the temporary modification, suspension, or imposition of conditions. Regulations 62–4 set out equivalent provisions (i.e. the requirement to consider the effect on a European site and the obligation to review consents) in relation to roads under the Roads (NI) Order 1993, waste disposal licences

---

200. In this regard, see: Davidson and Mellon, p. 32, supra note 106.

etc. under the Pollution Control and Local Government (NI) Order 1978, and discharge consents under the Water Act (NI) 1972.

4. Finally, regulations 55–60 lay down special provisions in relation to general development orders, special development orders, simplified planning zones, and enterprise zones.

## PART III THE INTERNATIONAL DIMENSION: SPECIES AND HABITAT PROTECTION

The UK is bound by a number of international agreements concerning nature conservation as a member of the EC or as a result of ratification as an individual state, or both. The standards laid down in these conventions now underlie the legislative framework currently governing nature conservation in the UK. It is impossible within the confines of this chapter to outline the individual provisions of these international agreements in any detail; instead it is intended to provide a brief outline of the obligations laid down by the principal nature conservation conventions signed by the UK. However, particular attention will be devoted to the Ramsar Convention, given the international importance of peatlands in Ireland, both North and South, as wetland habitats.

### The Ramsar Convention

The Convention on the Conservation of Wetlands of International Importance, Especially as Waterfowl Habitat (the Ramsar Convention) was adopted in Ramsar, Iran, in 1971 and came into force in 1975. The UK signed the Convention in 1973 and ratified it in 1976. The purpose of the Ramsar Convention is essentially threefold:

  (i)   to stem the progressive encroachment on and loss of wetlands now and in the future, recognising the fundamental ecological functions of wetlands and their economic, cultural, scientific and recreational value;
  (ii)  to encourage the 'wise use' of the world's wetland resources;
  (iii) to co-ordinate international efforts for this purpose.[201]

A wetland is defined very widely by the Convention to include an area of marsh, fen and peatland or water, whether natural or artificial, permanent or temporary, with water that is static or flowing, fresh, brackish, or salt, including areas of marine water whose depth at low tide does not exceed six metres. Wetlands may also include adjacent areas of land, such as coasts, river banks, and islands. It is estimated that almost two-thirds of Europe's wetlands have almost disappeared as a result of drainage, land reclamation, pollution, the over-exploitation of wetland species, and planning processes that have not taken the functions and needs of wetland areas adequately into account.[202] Although the EC is not a party to the Convention, the protection of wetlands of international importance is a priority under the Wild Birds Directive, while active raised and

---

201. *Green Globe Yearbook,* 1995, Fridtjof Nansen Institute, p. 19.
202. *Wetland Conservation: Actions Committed by the European Community,* DG XI, Environment, Nuclear Safety and Civil Protection, p. 1.

blanket bogs are listed as priority habitats by the Habitats Directive (both of which are discussed in Part II, section 2 of this chapter).

To protect these vital habitats, the Ramsar Convention requires parties to designate at least one national wetland for inclusion in a 'List of Wetlands of International Importance'. In addition, the Convention requires parties to formulate and implement their planning so as to promote the conservation of the wetlands included in the list and, as far as possible, to ensure the 'wise use' of wetlands within their territory. Finally, the Ramsar Convention requires parties to establish wetland nature reserves, co-operate in the exchange of information, train personnel for wetland management, and co-operate in the management of shared wetlands and shared wetland species.

The protection of peatland habitats is of particular importance in Northern Ireland, and in recent years a number of governmental and non-governmental policy statements have been published. In 1992 the CNCC published its *Peatland Conservation Strategy*,[203] and a year later the Government published its strategy document concerning peatland protection, *Conserving Peatland in Northern Ireland: a Statement of Policy*. The RSPB (Northern Ireland Branch) published its response in August 1993. The Government identified the protection of peatland, particularly in the form of raised and blanket bogs, as 'one of the top objectives for nature conservation in Northern Ireland.' The DoE(NI) also endorsed the obligations and principles laid down in the Ramsar Convention in its policy document *Nature Conservation and Planning*, published in 1990, and more recently in *A Planning Strategy for Rural Northern Ireland*, published in 1993.

Thus far, Northern Ireland has only one Ramsar listed site, namely, Lough Neagh together with Lough Beg. Although it is not a requirement under the Convention (or under EC law), in practice the UK Government will only add sites to the UK list of Ramsar sites if they are first protected under national designation under the NCALO. The Northern Ireland Ramsar site is currently protected as an ASSI. The *Environment Service Corporate Strategy, 1994–97*[204] states that approximately ten of Northern Ireland's existing ASSIs, together with a further fifteen sites yet to be declared ASSIs, are likely to merit designation as Ramsar sites and/or as special protection areas or special areas of conservation under the EC Habitat and Wild Birds Directives (Part II, section 2).

## Further information

Further information may be obtained from the Ramsar Convention Bureau, Rue Mauverney 28, 1196 Gland, Switzerland. Information officer: Ms Mireille Katz. Telephone: +41 22 9990170; fax: +41 22 9990169; e-mail: ramsar@hq.iucn.ch.

---

203. Available from CNCC Secretariat, Commonwealth House, 35 Castle Street, Belfast BT1 1GU; tel. (01232) 251477; fax (01232) 315717. See also the *Report of the Plantlife Commission of Enquiry into Peat and Peatlands* (1992), which covered lowland raised bogs throughout the UK; the recommendations of the Plantlife Commission were similar to those put forward by the CNCC.
204. P. 8. For further discussion of the implementation of the Ramsar Convention in Northern Ireland, see: Davidson and Mellon, note 106, supra, p. 21.

## The World Heritage Convention

The Convention Concerning the Protection of the World's Cultural and National Heritage was adopted in Paris in 1972 and came into force in 1975. Its objectives are to 'establish an effective system of collective protection of the cultural and national heritage of outstanding universal value, organised on a permanent basis and in accordance with modern scientific methods and to provide both emergency and long-term protection for [animal habitats].'[205] The Giant's Causeway has been designated a World Heritage Site under this Convention.

## CITES

The Convention on International Trade in Endangered Species of Wild Fauna and Flora (CITES) was adopted in Washington in 1973 and came into force in 1975. Its essential objectives are 'to ensure, through international co-operation, that the international trade in species of wild fauna and flora does not threaten the conservation of the species concerned and to protect certain endangered species from over-exploitation by means of a system of import/export permits issued by a management authority under the control of a scientific authority.'[206] The provisions of CITES were implemented in the UK under the Endangered Species (Import and Export) Act 1976.

   The EC has thus far been unable to sign CITES, as it is only open to ratification by states. Although the terms of the Convention have been amended to enable the EC to become a member, the amendment is subject to ratification by existing CITES members. It is important to note, however, that the EC has implemented the requirements laid down in CITES by means of various Regulations, outlined in Part I, section 1 of this chapter.

## The Berne Convention

The Berne Convention on the Conservation of European Wildlife and Natural Habitats was negotiated under the auspices of the Council of Europe in September 1979 and came into force in June 1982. Its objectives are 'to conserve wild flora and fauna, to promote co-operation between states and to give particular attention to endangered and vulnerable species including migratory species.'[207] It applies to all species and their habitats, regardless of their scarcity, and applies to visiting migratory species that are not confined to Europe and also to European species of flora and fauna found outside the European continent. To give effect to the Convention, Article 2 requires the parties 'to maintain the population of wild flora

---

205. *Green Globe Yearbook, 1995*; supra, note 201, p. 182.
206. Ibid., p. 188.
207. Phillippe Sands, *Principles of International Environmental Law, vol. 1: Frameworks, Standards and Implementation,* Manchester: Manchester University Press, 1995, chap. 10, 395. See also *Implementation of the Bern Convention: An IUCN Overview with Recommendations,* Gland: International Union for the Conservation of Nature and Natural Resources, 1986; S. Lyster, *International Wildlife Law,* Grotius, 1985; S. Lyster, *European Wildlife Convention: Report on Problems in the UK,* London: Wildlife Link, 1985; H. Muntingh, 'Report on the Implementation of the Bern Convention and the Bonn Convention', European Parliament Session Document A 2-0179/88.

and fauna at, or adapt it to, a level which corresponds in particular to ecological, scientific and cultural requirements while taking account of economic and recreational requirement needs and the needs of sub-species, varieties or forms at risk locally.' The UK signed the Berne Convention as a state. However, as the EC is also a party to this Convention, the UK is also bound in its capacity as a member of the EC.[208] (For national and EC implementation of this Convention see Part I and Part II, sections 1 and 2 of this chapter.)

### The Bonn Convention

The Convention on the Conservation of Migratory Species of Wild Animals (the Bonn Convention) was adopted in 1979 and came into force in 1983. Its objective is to conserve those species of wild animals which migrate across or outside national boundaries by developing and implementing co-operative agreements, prohibiting the taking of endangered species listed in Appendix I, conserving the habitats of such species, eliminating, preventing or minimising other impediments to their migration, and preventing, reducing or controlling factors which endanger such species. The UK signed the Bonn Convention as a state. However, as the EC is also a party to this Convention,[209] the UK is also bound in its capacity as a member of the EC. (For national and EC implementation of this Convention see Part I and Part II, sections 1 and 2 of this chapter.)

### The Convention on Biological Diversity

This Convention was adopted in Rio de Janeiro in 1992 and came into force in 1993. Its objectives are 'to ensure the conservation of biological diversity and the sustainable use of its components and to promote a fair and equitable sharing of the benefits arising out of the utilisation of genetic resources, including appropriate access to genetic resources, and by appropriate transfer of relevant technologies (taking into account all rights over those resources and to technologies), and by appropriate funding.'[210] Both the UK and the EC are parties to this Convention, which came into effect within the EC in 1993.[211]

### The Small Cetacean Convention (ASCOBANS)

The Agreement on the Conservation of Small Cetaceans in the Baltic and North Seas (ASCOBANS) was signed and adopted as an agreement under the Bonn Convention in 1992 and was subsequently ratified by the UK in July 1993.[212] The EC is not a party. The agreement was adopted in response to the dramatic reduction in the population of small cetaceans throughout the North and Baltic

---

208. Decision 82/72/EEC OJ L38, 10 Feb. 1982, approved the terms of the Berne Convention within the EC legal order.
209. Decision 82/461/EEC OJ L210, 19 July 1982, approved the terms of the Bonn Convention within the EC legal order. See Muntingh, supra, note 207.
210. *Green Globe Yearbook,* 1995, 184.
211. Decision 93/626/EC OJ L309, 13 Dec. 1993, approved the terms of the Convention within the EC legal order.
212. For further information concerning ASCOBANS see P. Sands, supra, note 207, p. 436.

Seas and is designed to achieve a 'favourable conservation status' for such species by means of a framework for co-operation between the signatory states. Parties are required to implement the conservation, research and management measures within the limits of their national jurisdiction, set out in the 'Conservation and Management Plan' contained in the Annex to the agreement. More specifically, the plan addresses the issues of habitat conservation and management, surveys and research, the use of by-catches and stranding, legislation, information, and education. Small cetaceans are defined by Article 2.1 and 2.2 of the agreement as 'any species, subspecies or population of toothed whales *Odontocet,* except the sperm whale *Physter macrocephalus'.* The provisions of the agreement do not affect the rights and duties assumed by a party under other international conventions.

At the time of writing, the Government is considering whether the provisions of this Convention can be extended to cover Northern Ireland waters and boats. Contact has recently been made with the Irish Government with a view to extending this agreement to the Republic of Ireland. Northern Ireland nature conservation legislation already extends protection to all species of small cetaceans under the Wildlife (NI) Order 1985 and the Conservation (Natural Habitats etc.) Regulations (NI) (addressed in Part I, section 1 and Part II, section 2 of this chapter). In addition to the work of the DoE(NI) in enforcing the terms of these national provisions, voluntary bodies, such as the Irish Whale and Dolphin Society, provide assistance to the DoE(NI) and undertake their own species protection work in relation to species of small cetaceans.

# CHAPTER EIGHT

# Countryside Conservation, Management and Public Access

## Introduction

The regulation of the countryside from the perspective of environmental protection can be divided into two broad areas. First, there is the issue of nature conservation, which involves the protection of natural and semi-natural habitat types and the individual species which exist throughout the countryside. Second, there is the more 'human use' dimension of countryside regulation, which itself can be divided into two areas, namely: (i) the conservation and management of the countryside itself and (ii) the provision of public access to the countryside. Although both dimensions are closely related in practice, in that conservation of the countryside and its wildlife requires effective action in both contexts, they are examined in separate chapters for the sake of clarity. Chapter 7 examines the legislative framework governing nature conservation in Northern Ireland, while the present chapter examines the conservation and management of the Northern Ireland countryside and the provision of public access to it.

The present chapter is divided into two parts. Part I addresses the conservation and management of the Northern Ireland countryside. Part II addresses the issue of public access to the Northern Ireland countryside as provided for under the Access to the Countryside (NI) Order 1983.

Before proceeding with either part of this chapter, it is important to note that while European and international standards have exerted a considerable influence on the legislative framework governing nature conservation in Northern Ireland, this is not the case in the present context. With the exception of coastal zone management policies and the introduction of various financial incentives under EC agricultural policy designed to encourage agricultural practices which promote countryside conservation, the legislative provisions governing countryside conservation and management are entirely national in origin. The legislation governing the provision of public access to the countryside is also entirely national in origin; however, it should be said that EC agri-environment measures may begin to play an important role in encouraging farmers in Northern Ireland to provide public access to privately owned land.

## PART I CONSERVATION AND MANAGEMENT OF THE COUNTRYSIDE

The Northern Ireland countryside is conserved and managed by a wide variety of interrelated means. The principal approaches are as follows:

### Statutory designations

The Nature Conservation and Amenity Lands (NI) Order 1985,[1] as amended, makes provision for two forms of statutory designation, namely, the 'area of outstanding natural beauty' (AONB) designation and the 'national park' designation. Both designations provide statutory recognition of areas of countryside with unique qualities of landscape, heritage and wildlife and of the need to ensure their conservation through sensitive policies. In addition, the AONB and national park designations operate to promote public enjoyment of, and access to, such areas. It should also be noted that the 1985 Order makes provision for other forms of designation designed to protect habitats; these are addressed separately in Chapter 7.

### Coastal zone management

One of the most important emerging areas of countryside protection is that of coastal zone management. Coastal zones throughout the EC, and indeed throughout the world, have sustained considerable damage in recent years through increasing urbanisation and pollution. As a result, there is mounting pressure at both EC and international levels to develop sustainable strategies for the management of coastal zones. The DoE(NI) is currently devising a management strategy designed to protect Northern Ireland's extensive coastline.

### Grant aid

The provision of grant aid plays an important role in the conservation and management of Northern Ireland's countryside. Broadly speaking, financial assistance operates in two ways. Firstly, grants can be awarded for the purpose of defraying costs incurred by individuals, local authorities or certain other bodies in carrying out activities that promote countryside conservation, and secondly, grants can provide financial incentives to encourage agricultural practices which promote countryside conservation.

### Town and country planning

Northern Ireland's town and country planning legislation operates to regulate development not only in urban areas but also in the countryside and thereby plays a vital role in countryside conservation.

### Agriculture and the environment

Contemporary agricultural practices have not only emerged as a potent source of pollutants but have also wreaked considerable damage on Northern Ireland's countryside. Although the EC's Common Agricultural Policy has traditionally supported intensive and environmentally 'unfriendly' farming practices, the EC has recently sought to integrate consideration for the environment into the formulation and operation of agriculture policy. To this end the EC and the Government have introduced a number of financial mechanisms and other

---

1. SI 1985/170.

initiatives, most notably the concept of 'environmentally sensitive areas', the 'set-aside' programme, and habitat protection initiatives, in an effort to encourage farmers to adopt more environmentally sensitive agricultural practices.

### Derelict sites

The Nature Conservation and Amenity Lands (NI) Order 1985 makes provision for the restoration or improvement of derelict sites throughout Northern Ireland.

### Role of the DoE(NI) in countryside conservation and management

As with nature conservation, the DoE(NI) is primarily responsible for countryside conservation and management in Northern Ireland. This function is carried out by the Department's Environment Service, in consultation with the Council for Nature Conservation and the Countryside. Article 3(1) of the Nature Conservation and Amenity Lands (NI) Order 1985[2] (NCALO) obliges the DoE(NI) to formulate and implement policies for nature conservation and the conservation and enhancement of the natural beauty and amenity of the countryside. In carrying out its functions in this regard, the DoE(NI) is granted power by article 3(2) to conduct, commission or finance research, to provide information concerning nature conservation and the conservation and enhancement of the natural beauty and amenity of the countryside and information concerning places of particular interest therein, and to take steps to enhance public facilities for the enjoyment of the countryside and open-air recreation in the countryside. However, the Department is obliged to ensure that 'suitable methods of publicity are used for the prevention of damage in the countryside and for encouraging a proper standard of behaviour on the part of persons resorting to the countryside' (article 3(3)).

Article 30 provides that the DoE(NI), in carrying out its functions under the NCALO, must have 'due regard' to any representations submitted to the Department by the DANI on behalf of persons engaged in agriculture, forestry, or fisheries. More specifically, the DoE(NI) is responsible under the NCALO for the declaration and management of 'areas of outstanding natural beauty' and national parks and for managing the restoration of derelict sites in Northern Ireland. In addition, the DoE(NI) is empowered under the NCALO to provide financial assistance to individuals and bodies as a means of contributing towards the cost of activities carried out for the purpose of countryside conservation, and at present it is in the process of consulting on the formulation of a strategy for coastal zone management in Northern Ireland. The DoE(NI)'s Planning Service is responsible for implementing Northern Ireland's town and country legislation, which also affords protection to the Northern Ireland countryside by regulating development in such areas, while the Department's Environment Service monitors planning applications from the point of view of their potential impact on the countryside.

### The DANI and the environment

The role played by the DANI in the administration of various initiatives at present operating to encourage environmentally sound agricultural practices is detailed

---

2. Ibid.

separately in the specific context of agriculture and the environment, discussed in Part I, section 6 of this chapter.

## Council for Nature Conservation and the Countryside

As in the context of nature conservation, the CNCC, established under the Nature Conservation and Amenity Lands (Amendment) (NI) Order 1989[3] is the DoE(NI)'s statutory adviser in relation to the protection of the Northern Ireland countryside.[4] Article 4 of the 1989 Order transferred the functions previously exercised by the Ulster Countryside Committee and the Committee for Nature Conservation to the CNCC. The CNCC's powers in relation to countryside protection can be summarised as follows:

(i) The council is obliged to enquire into and report on matters affecting the natural beauty or amenity of any area or place in Northern Ireland.

(ii) The council must advise the DoE(NI) on the establishment and management of national parks. The Department must consult the council before formulating proposals in relation to national parks, and in certain circumstances the Department may consult the council before designating a national park where representations or objections are received concerning the proposed designation.

(iii) The Department must consult the council about proposals to designate AONBs and must also consult it before formulating proposals for the conservation or enhancement of the natural beauty or amenity of an AONB.

(iv) The Department must consult the council in relation to the provision of facilities on land which has been acquired for amenity purposes and in certain circumstances must consult the council about bylaws in relation to such land.

Article 32 of the NCALO imposes a statutory duty on the CNCC, and any other body having functions under the NCALO, to have 'due regard to the needs of agriculture, forestry and fisheries' in the exercise of its functions under the NCALO. It should also be noted that the CNCC is empowered to create committees on specialist subjects, which may include people who represent a specific interest but who are not members of the council itself. At the time of writing, the CNCC Secretariat is located with the Environment Service's Countryside and Wildlife Branch at Commonwealth House, 35 Castle Street, Belfast BT1 1GH; however, this may change in the near future with the establishment of 'Next Steps' agencies in April 1996.

---

3. SI 1989/492.
4. The CNCC has published three reports on its activities since it was established in 1989. The most recent report covers the period 1992–93; however, a report that will cover the period up to May 1995 is forthcoming. The CNCC was established in response to the recommendations in the Balfour Report that greater status be accorded to nature conservation and countryside protection and that an independent body be established in this context. For further reading on the reasons for establishing the CNCC and concerns that it might not be able to fulfil those purposes see: J. Balfour, *A New Look at the Northern Ireland Countryside*, HMSO, Belfast; *NIA* 191 1985, *Northern Ireland Assembly Report on the Balfour Proposals: A New Look at the Northern Ireland Countryside*, HMSO, Belfast; *House of Commons Environment Committee First Report: Environmental Issues in Northern Ireland*, HC 39 (1990), 109–18; K. Milton, *Our Countryside Our Concern*, NIEL, Belfast. This issue is also addressed in chap. 7.

## Duty imposed on public bodies in relation to land

Article 4 of the NCALO imposes a general duty on all public bodies[5] exercising any statutory function in relation to land to have 'regard to the need to conserve the natural beauty and amenity of the countryside and the need to protect (so far as reasonably practicable) flora, fauna and geological and physiographical features of the countryside from any harmful effects which might result from the exercise of such functions.'

## SECTION 1. AREAS OF OUTSTANDING NATURAL BEAUTY

Article 14(1) of the NCALO empowers the DoE(NI) to designate an area (not being an area within a national park) as an area of outstanding natural beauty (AONB) where the area is of such 'outstanding natural beauty' that it is desirable that it be subject to the provisions of the NCALO. The AONB designation is the principal method used in Northern Ireland to conserve 'particularly fine landscapes of high scenic quality'.[6] The *Environment Service Report* 1991–1993 describes the designation as operating to give statutory recognition to both the distinctive character and special scenic quality of the landscape and the need to ensure its conservation through sensitive policies, and, in addition to promote public enjoyment of and access to the area in question. At present AONBs cover 2,796 sq km, or approximately 20 per cent of Northern Ireland.[7] Over 70 per cent of the coastline falls within AONBs.[8] Thus far four AONBs have been designated under the NCALO, namely Mourne (1987), Antrim Coast and Glens (1988), Causeway Coast (1989) and the Ring of Gullion (1991); consultations are currently being conducted for the designation of two new AONBs in Fermanagh.[9]

The Amenity Lands Act (NI) 1965[10] provided the original legislative basis for the designation of AONBs in Northern Ireland. However, it is important to note that under the 1965 Act the AONB designation simply operated as an additional form of planning control, in that the designation recognised the special quality of the landscape in question by guiding appropriate forms of development within the area. The role of the AONB designation was considerably enhanced under the

---

5. The term 'public bodies' is defined in art. 4(2) as including 'government departments, district councils and statutory undertakers, and any trustees, commissioners, board or other persons who, as a public body and not for their own profit, act under any statutory provision for the improvement of any place or the production or supply of any commodity or service.'

6. *Environment Service, Corporate Plan, 1994–97*, p. 11. See also NIA 64 *Northern Ireland Assembly Report on a Consultation Paper issued by the DoE for Northern Ireland, 'Areas of Special Control and Outstanding Natural Beauty'*, London: HMSO, 1983.

7. *Environment Service Report,* 1991–93, pp 10–11.

8. Ibid. See also *Delivering Coastal Zone Management in Northern Ireland: A Consultation Paper,* Belfast: DoE(NI)1995.

9. Erne Lakeland and Fermanagh Caveland. See *Environment Service Report,* 1993–95, p. 8, for further details on progress thus far in this regard. See also the booklets published by the Environment Service explaining the scope and effect of these proposed designations. In addition, *Environment Matters: Areas of Outstanding Natural Beauty in Northern Ireland* (Fact Sheet no. 29), Belfast: Environment Service, 1995, provides more specific details of the main features of the existing AONBs (both designated under the NCALO and the Amenity Lands Act (NI) 1965).

10. c. 9.

NCALO, in that, for the first time, provision was made for the positive management of designated areas. Five areas were designated under the Amenity Lands Act (NI) 1965, namely, Lagan Valley (1965), Lecale Coast (1967), North Derry (1966), Sperrin (1968), and Strangford Lough (1972). However, the changed role of the AONB designation has meant that the DoE(NI) has had to review the position concerning these AONBs to assess whether and how these areas should be designated as AONBs under the NCALO. At the time of writing, consultation is in progress concerning the 'redesignation' of Strangford Lough, while the remaining AONBs designated under the 1965 Act are scheduled for review and designation under the NCALO within the next few years.[11]

The House of Commons Environment Committee First Report, *Environmental Issues in Northern Ireland,* published in 1990, noted the view expressed by the Ulster Society for the Preservation of the Countryside that the process of redesignating AONBs has been 'unduly slow'.[12] The Environment Service, for its part, points to the nature of the designation process itself, which requires extensive consultation to generate the necessary support within affected communities for the proposed designation, as being the cause of slow progress. Finally, it should be noted that although the NCALO repealed the Amenity Lands Act (NI) 1965, AONBs designated under the Act technically continue to operate under the 1965 Act until the area is designated under the NCALO. However, in practice, the Environment Service treats an AONB designated under the 1965 Act as an AONB designated under the NCALO.

## Procedure governing the designation of an AONB

The procedure which must be followed before the designation of an area as an AONB is set out in article 14(2)–(4) of the NCALO. It is broadly similar to, but not as detailed as, the procedure governing the designation of a national park. The DoE(NI) is first obliged to consult the CNCC and affected district councils about the proposed designation. It must then inform the public by publishing the proposed designation order in the *Belfast Gazette* and in two newspapers circulating in the areas of the affected district councils. The notice must indicate that the DoE(NI) proposes to make the designation and the effect of the designation. It must also specify the period within which the public may make representations to the DoE(NI) concerning the designation and the procedure which must be followed when doing so.

Although the DoE(NI) is obliged 'to consider any representation' made to it concerning a proposal to designate an area an AONB, it is not possible to formally appeal against the proposal. Having said this, it should be noted that although the NCALO makes the above provision for consultation with the CNCC and affected district councils and for public notification of the proposal, in practice, the DoE(NI) conducts a much more extensive consultation and notification process than is formally required. Given that the great majority of areas designated as

---

11. See *Environment Service Report* 1993–95, pp 8–9, and *Environment Service Corporate Plan* 1994–97, 11–13, for further details concerning DoE(NI) activity, thus far, in this regard.
12. *House of Commons Environment Committee First Report: Environmental Issues in Northern Ireland,* HC 39 (1990), para. 46.

AONBs are in private ownership, and given that the DoE(NI) does not have the power to force owners or occupiers to enter into management agreements, it is essential that AONB designations are supported by the local community in order to ensure that the objectives of the designation are achieved in practice. As a result, the DoE(NI)'s Environment Service consults extensively with organisations and interest groups involved with the countryside in question. Both the *Environment Service Report* 1991–93 and the *Environment Service Corporate Plan* 1994–97 emphasise that this process of consultation addresses not only the boundaries of the proposed AONB but also, increasingly, the proposed plans for the management of the area, the intention being to foster 'a greater understanding of the principles behind designation and [to ensure] more widespread support for the designation within the local community'.[13]

Following consultation with all interested parties and groups, the DoE(NI) produces a brief 'guide to designation', which essentially states the agreed policies for the activities of public bodies in relation to the proposed AONB and the management proposals agreed by Government departments, affected district councils and other interested organisations. In addition, the Department advertises the proposed designation in the *Belfast Telegraph* and in a representative selection of the regional newspapers. When the designation is made, the DoE(NI) is obliged to ensure that copies of the designation order are available for public consultation at all reasonable times at the offices of affected district councils and at any other place in or near the designated area as the Department may determine.

Finally, it should be noted that the AONB designation does not affect ownership or occupation of land within the area in any way, nor does the designation affect the duty or role of the district council in the administration of the area. Although the NCALO confers various powers on the DoE(NI) to promote the conservation and management of AONBs, the principle of voluntary co-operation underlies the use of each of these powers.

## The management of AONBs

Conservation is the primary objective of the AONB designation. However, it is important to note that this does not imply the suspension of all changes within the designated area. Instead, it means that the designation seeks to ensure that the distinctive character and special scenic quality of the landscape are conserved for future generations. Although the DoE(NI)'s Environment Service is responsible for the designation of AONBs, the management of a designated area is shared among many groups and individuals on the basis of voluntary co-operation and is achieved by several different means, namely management agreements, management plans, restrictive covenants and agreements, powers of land acquisition and disposal, provision of public facilities, adoption and enforcement of bylaws, the Environmentally Sensitive Areas scheme, planning controls, and grant aid. Each will be considered in turn.

---

13. *Environment Service Report,* 1991–93, p. 11.

### (a) Management agreements

Article 9 of the NCALO empowers the DoE(NI) to enter into management agreements for the purpose of 'conserving or enhancing the natural beauty or amenity of any land or promoting its enjoyment by the public.' A management agreement may be entered into with any person who has an estate in such land and may be entered into either for a specified period or for an indefinite period. In this regard it is important to note that article 9 does not empower the DoE(NI) to require or force owners or occupiers to enter into management agreements.

A management agreement may impose restrictions on the methods used to cultivate the land and on the agricultural purposes for which it may be used. In addition, the agreement may restrict the exercise of rights over the land and may also require the owner of the land (with whom the agreement is entered into) to carry out specific work on the land or specific agricultural or forestry operations on the land. A management agreement entered into under article 9 may also contain such 'incidental and consequential' provisions as the DoE(NI) considers necessary or expedient for the purposes of the agreement (such conditions may include arrangements for payment by the Department). None of these specific powers will affect the general nature of the Department's power to enter into a management agreement. Finally, it should be noted that a management agreement will, unless otherwise agreed, bind persons deriving title to the land from the person who entered into the agreement with the DoE(NI). The Department has the power to enforce the terms of the agreement against such persons. Article 33(*b*) of the NCALO requires that any management agreement entered into under article 9 be registered in the Statutory Charges Register.

### (b) Management plans

Article 14(5) and (6) of the NCALO provides that once an AONB has been designated, the DoE(NI) may proceed, in consultation with affected district councils and the CNCC, to formulate proposals for the enhancement and conservation of the natural beauty of the area, the conservation of wildlife, historic objects or natural phenomena within the area, the promotion of public enjoyment of the area, and the provision or maintenance of public access to the area. In 1990 the House of Commons report was critical of the DoE(NI) for focusing entirely on the 'negative or restrictive aspects of conservation' and stated that at the time, 'none of the more positive measures such as . . . management plans' had been attempted in Northern Ireland.[14] The report recommended that a more positive approach be taken to countryside conservation.

Since the publication of the report the DoE(NI) appears to have made progress in this regard. The *Environment Service Corporate Plan, 1994–97* states that where the effective management of an AONB requires that the activities of a number of bodies be co-ordinated, the Environment Service may establish a management structure which involves all relevant bodies for that area.[15] A management structure may adopt any one of a number of models and may be serviced by staff from the DoE(NI)'s Environment Service or by staff specially

---

14. Supra, note 12, at para. 124.
15. P. 11.

employed for these purposes. At the time of writing, management structures have been established for the Mourne, Strangford Lough, Causeway Coast and Lagan Valley AONBs. In addition, the DoE(NI) has published detailed management plans for the Causeway Coast and Mourne AONBs. Where formal management structures are not required informal arrangements will exist particularly between district councils whose districts are affected by the designation.

### (c) Restrictive covenants and agreements

The DoE(NI) is empowered under article 8 of the NCALO to enter into an agreement or a covenant with an owner of land of natural beauty or amenity which restricts (either permanently or for a specified period) the manner in which the land may be developed or the purposes for which the land may be used. The DoE(NI) may not force the owner of such land to enter into such an agreement or covenant; the arrangement may affect the whole or any part of the land; and such an agreement or covenant may be made for consideration or otherwise (article 8(1)).

Article 8(2) and (3) goes on to govern the extent to which such an arrangement can bind successors in title and the position in the event of inconsistencies with the Planning (NI) Order 1991 (their respective provisions are outlined in the context of covenants concerning nature reserves addressed in chapter 7). Any agreement or covenant entered into under article 8 of the NCALO must be registered in the Statutory Charges Register (article 33(*a*)). Similarly, any waiver relating to the agreement must also be registered.

### (d) Powers to acquire and dispose of land

Article 6 of the NCALO empowers the DoE(NI) to acquire land for the purposes of:

(i) conserving any area of natural beauty or amenity;
(ii) providing a means of access to any such area;
(iii) providing, in or in relation to any such area or any National Park, facilities for the use of that area or Park by the public;
(iv) restoring or improving the appearance of a derelict site or, of improving the amenities of the neighbourhood of a derelict site.

Such land may be acquired by agreement, either by way of purchase, lease, or exchange. Any arrangements to acquire land in this context must be approved by the Department of Finance and Personnel. However, the DoE(NI) also has the power to acquire land for these purposes compulsorily by means of a vesting order under article 6(2). In this regard, section 97(2) and (3) of, and Schedule 6 to, the Local Government Act (NI) 1972,[16] subject to the modifications contained in Schedule 2 to the NCALO, will govern the making of such a vesting order. Given that the principle of voluntary co-operation underlies the DoE(NI)'s approach to the designation and management of AONBs, the Department will only use its powers of compulsory acquisition as a last resort. Article 6(4) of the NCALO empowers the DoE(NI) to transfer land acquired for the purposes set out above where the Department is of the opinion that the land would be 'more expediently

---

16. c. 9.

or efficiently managed or conserved in the public interest' by another person or body. The rules which govern the DoE(NI)'s discretion in this regard are outlined in chapter 7 in the context of nature reserves.

### (e) DoE(NI)'s power to carry out works and provide facilities

Article 10(1) of the NCALO, as amended by article 9 of the Nature Conservation and Amenity Lands (Amendment) (NI) Order 1989,[17] confers power on the DoE(NI) to carry out such works or other things on land which has been acquired under article 6 as it considers necessary or expedient for the proper management and use of that land, for the purpose for which that land was acquired. In addition, article 10(2) provides that where the Department is of the opinion that the facilities on or in relation to such land are inadequate or unsatisfactory, it may provide or arrange for the provision of accommodation, meals and refreshments, camping sites and caravan parks and parking places on or in relation to such land. The Department is also conferred with a general power under article 10(2) to provide or arrange for the provision of such other facilities for persons using the land as it thinks fit (having consulted with the CNCC). Where any land acquired under article 6 is covered by water, the Department may, under powers conferred by article 10(3), provide or arrange for the provision of facilities for the use of the water by the public for recreational purposes. The Department's powers under article 10(2) and (3) will also apply in relation to land which is subject to a covenant or an agreement under articles 8 and 9 in the same way as they apply to land acquired under article 6, provided that the agreement or covenant so provides, or the owner of the land in question consents to the Department 'carrying out works, doing other things, or providing or arranging for the provision of facilities'. Finally, it should be noted that the DoE(NI) may impose such charges (as it thinks reasonable) for the provision of facilities under article 10. However, the Department is obliged to ensure that any charges levied for facilities provided under an arrangement made by the Department under article 10 are subject to the Department's approval.

### (f) The adoption and enforcement of bylaws

Article 30 of the NCALO empowers the DoE(NI) to adopt bylaws in relation to land which is acquired under article 6, or in relation to land which is subject to a management agreement under article 9, or a restrictive agreement or covenant under article 8, where the agreement or covenant so provides. The DoE(NI)'s powers in this regard are identical to the general powers conferred on the Department in relation to land designated under the NCALO for the purposes of nature conservation (these powers are outlined in chapter 7). In addition, article 31 empowers the Department to authorise appointed or employed persons to enforce such bylaws and also to take whatever steps and to carry out whatever acts are necessary to enforce those bylaws. The powers of enforcement conferred on such persons are outlined in chapter 7.

---

17.  SI 1989/492.

### (g) Environmentally sensitive areas

The ESA scheme essentially provides financial incentives to farmers to encourage the adoption of agricultural practices which are sensitive to the environment. Although ESAs will be discussed in more detail in Part I, section 6 of this chapter, it is important to note that this scheme plays a vital role in ensuring the conservation of areas of the countryside in which the landscape, wildlife or historic interest are of particular significance. The ESA scheme is administered by the DANI; however, there is close consultation with the DoE(NI)'s Environment Service about the location and boundaries of ESAs. At the time of writing, the five designated ESAs[18] in Northern Ireland correspond to a considerable degree with the boundaries of existing or proposed AONBs.

### (h) Planning controls

The DoE(NI)'s Planning Service is responsible for administering the statutory planning system, which controls the development and use of land in Northern Ireland. It is impossible within the confines of this book to provide a detailed examination of the role played by planning controls in countryside management. However, this issue is discussed in detail in Dowling, *Northern Ireland Planning Law.*[19] For present purposes, suffice it to refer to the Department's *Fact Sheet Number 29, Environment Matters,* which points out that where areas of landscape within AONBs are identified as coming under threat from excessive or inappropriate development pressures, they will be designated as Countryside Policy Areas or will be included within 'Green Belts', the policy being to minimise further development within such areas. In exceptional instances a special policy will be drawn up for the purpose of protecting a unique landscape, such as the High Mournes, which will prohibit any development within the area unless it is in the public interest. The DoE(NI)'s Planning Service provides advice and guidance on the design principles to be applied within AONBs, and to this end it has published *A Design Guide for Rural Northern Ireland* in 1994, which applies generally to development within the Northern Ireland countryside and, thus far, two local design guides, for the Antrim Coast and Glens and Mourne.

### (i) Grant aid

Various provisions of the NCALO confer power on the DoE(NI)'s Environment Service to provide grants to groups and individuals for the purpose of promoting countryside conservation and management. The DoE(NI)'s specific powers in this regard are outlined separately in Part I, section 4 of this chapter. However, it is important to note that the provision of grants plays an important role in the management of AONBs.

## SECTION 2. NATIONAL PARKS

The DoE(NI) is empowered by article 12(1) of the NCALO, as amended, to

---

18. They are Antrim Coast, Glens and Rathlin, Mournes and Slieve Croob, West Fermanagh and Erne Lakeland, Slieve Gullion and the Sperrins.
19. Dublin: Gill and Macmillan, 1995.

designate 'extensive areas of countryside' as national parks where it considers that such designation is desirable for the purpose of:

(a)  conserving or enhancing the natural beauty or amenities of that area;

(b)  conserving wildlife, historic objects or natural phenomena therein;

(c)  promoting the enjoyment by the public of the area; and

(d)  providing or maintaining public access to the area.

Before addressing the procedure governing the designation of national parks under the NCALO, it is important to note that, despite the existence of statutory powers to do so, no national parks have been designated in Northern Ireland thus far. Although this approach was criticised in submissions made by environmental groups to the House of Commons Environment Committee, which reported on environmental issues in Northern Ireland in 1990,[20] the DoE(NI)'s Environment Service has, in effect, used its very broad powers under article 14 of the NCALO to fulfil all the objectives listed in article 12 above. Article 14, which governs the AONB designation, essentially mirrors the provisions of article 12 and, as a result, the Department has not found it necessary to designate any national parks.

The CNCC is required to advise the DoE(NI) on the establishment and management of national parks, and in addition, article 12(4) obliges the DoE(NI) to consult any district council whose area is affected by the establishment of a national park before the designation is made. Part I of Schedule 3 to the NCALO sets down the detailed procedure which must be followed before an area may be designated a national park. In effect, the DoE(NI) is required to publicise the proposal and to consult extensively and also may be required to conduct a local inquiry.

Once the designation has been made, the DoE(NI) is required to publish a notice in the *Belfast Gazette* and in two further newspapers circulating in the area affected by the designation informing the public that a designation order has been made, explaining the effect of the designation, and naming a place where a copy of the order can be consulted at all reasonable times. It should also be noted that, unlike an AONB designation, a proposed national park designation can be appealed under Part 1 of Schedule 3 to the NCALO. The DoE(NI) is also empowered to formulate proposals, in consultation with the CNCC and affected district councils, for the achievement of the purposes for which the designation was made (article 13(1) and (2)). The NCALO also makes almost identical provision to that applying in relation to AONBs for the acquisition and disposal of amenity land for the purpose of national parks, the adoption and enforcement of bylaws governing national parks, the establishment of management agreements and restrictive covenants for the management of land within national parks, the carrying out of works and the provision of public facilities within national parks, and the provision of financial assistance to defray the costs of activities carried out for the purpose of ensuring the conservation of an area within a national park. These powers are outlined in detail in the context of AONBs above.

---

20. *House of Commons Environment Committee First Report, Environmental Issues in Northern Ireland,* HC 39(1990).

## Country and regional parks

It is important at this juncture to distinguish between the national parks designation under article 12 of the NCALO and Northern Ireland's system of country and regional parks. Country and regional parks are established in areas which are attractive by virtue of their landscape and wildlife; however, they are not statutory designations. Nine country parks have been established; seven have been established on land which is owned and managed by the DoE(NI) (Castle Archdale, Ness Wood, Roe Valley, Redburn, Peatlands Park, Crawfordsburn, and Scrabo), while two others (at Delamont and Carnfunnock) are owned by district councils (purchased with the assistance of DoE(NI) grants) and managed with assistance from the DoE(NI).

The regional park concept is specifically designed to protect and enhance open spaces located on urban fringes; thus far, only one has been established in Northern Ireland, namely, the Lagan Valley Regional Park, which serves the Belfast urban area. Approximately one-third of the Lagan Valley Regional Park is in public ownership. The Lagan Valley park was originally part of the Lagan Valley AONB, which was the first AONB designated under the Amenity Lands Act (NI) 1965, and essentially arose from a Planning Service allocation of land use under an Area Plan. The DoE(NI) has published a Local Plan for the Lagan Valley and has established an advisory committee for the area which includes representatives of local interest groups; a detailed management strategy for the Lagan Valley park is at present being prepared. It should also be noted that the DoE(NI) has proposed the Belfast Hills as the site for a second regional park and is currently preparing a Local Plan for this area.

The principal purpose of the country and regional parks system is to promote public enjoyment and understanding of the countryside and also to provide and maintain public access to areas of the countryside. With the exception of Redwood and Ness Wood parks, all the country parks have countryside centres, which provide visitors with information aimed at enhancing understanding and enjoyment of the countryside in question and also the environmental issues relevant to each locality. Some of the country parks also have specialised functions, for example, Peatlands Park illustrates increasingly vulnerable peatland habitats and also the type of management which is required to conserve such areas.

The DoE(NI) has published leaflets concerning all its country parks, and the contact telephone numbers and addresses for park wardens are provided in Appendix I to the *Environment Service Report, 1993–95*.

## SECTION 3. COASTAL ZONE MANAGEMENT

One of the most important questions arising in the context of countryside conservation and management concerns the protection of coastal zones, namely, coastal waters, intertidal areas, and maritime land. Coastal zones are highly complex and dynamic systems which support many of the richest and most sensitive ecological areas.[21] However, because they are also of considerable social and economic importance, they are subject to many demands and uses. In recent years coastal environments throughout the EC have sustained considerable damage as a result of increasing urbanisation and pollution; and although the coastal environment is afforded protection under various legislative provisions (ranging from planning legislation, water pollution and waste disposal controls and provisions concerning wildlife, to landscape conservation and legislation controlling fishing and aquaculture), there is growing support, at both EC and national levels, for a strategy which can effectively co-ordinate the diverse activities occurring within coastal areas while ensuring that the coastal zone is managed in a sustainable manner.

The issue of coastal zone management (CZM) has been the subject of considerable discussion at international,[22] EC[23] and national[24] levels and at each level there is general agreement that the formulation of policy concerning coastal areas should be co-ordinated by a single institution and also that data collection and analysis concerning the natural systems within coastal zones should be increased. The Fifth Environmental Action Programme, which sets out the EC's environmental policy from 1993 to 2000, identifies the sustainable management of coastal zones as a key issue in the EC's transition towards sustainable development and, to this end, recommends that an operational framework for the development of integrated planning and management of coastal zones should be in place by 1998.

Almost three-quarters of the Northern Ireland coastline lies within one or more of the designations provided for under the Nature Conservation and Amenity Lands (NI) Order 1985[25] for nature conservation or countryside protection, namely nature reserves, areas of special scientific interest, and areas of outstanding natural beauty.[26] Several documents have been published recently concerning coastal zone management in Northern Ireland. The CNCC opened the

---

21. S. Mullard, 'Towards an EU strategy for integrated coastal zone management' (1995) EEL Rev. 16. The coastline of the European Community, which extends over 58,000 km, contains more than 50 per cent of the EC's most important natural sites.

22. Agenda 21, agreed at the United Nations 'Earth Summit' in 1992, calls for the 'integrated management and sustainable development of coastal areas.' Similar proposals are made by the Organisation for Economic Co-operation and Development in *Coastal Zone Management Integrated Policies,* OECD 1983.

23. *Towards Sustainability: Fifth Environmental Action Programme,* European Commission, COM (92) 23, 27 Mar. 1992; L. Brinkhorst, 'Prospects for a Community strategy' (1991) 67 Naturopa; G. Steeley, Council of European Municipalities and Regions, *Draft Proposition for a Green Paper on the Planning and Management of Coastal Zones,* June 1994; European Coastal Charter, *Conference of Peripheral Maritime Regions of the EEC,* 1981; *Europe's Environment: The Dobřiš Assessment,* European Environment Agency: Copenhagen (1995), chap 35.

24. *House of Commons Environment Committee, Second Report, Coastal Zone Protection and Planning* HC 1 (1992); Council for Nature Conservation and the Countryside Proposal Document 1994; DoE(NI), *Delivering Coastal Zone Management in Northern Ireland: A Consultation Paper,* 1995; RSPB Responses to DoE(NI) Consultation Paper were submitted in 1995.

25. SI 1985/170.

26. DoE(NI) *Delivering Coastal Zone Management in Northern Ireland: a Consultation Paper* (1995), para. 2.1, p. 3. Further details of the exact proportions of coastline included in each category of designation are provided in paras 2.3–2.20 of the consultation paper. Those designations employed for the purposes of nature conservation are discussed in chap. 7, while the countryside protection designations are addressed in the present chapter in Part I, sections 1 and 2.

debate in 1994 with the publication of their proposals for CZM; the Government then responded a year later in *Delivering Coastal Zone Management in Northern Ireland: A Consultation Paper.* Part 1 of the Consultation Paper outlines the major governmental controls, or 'components of CZM', currently operating in Northern Ireland for the purpose of maintaining the environmental quality of, and regulating development within, coastal areas.[27] Part 2 then sets out the Government's proposals for a strategy of sustainable CZM. In this regard, the paper states that the principles underlying the UK's Strategy for Sustainable Development[28] are equally applicable in the coastal context, and identifies the following as being the key issues for sustainable coastal zone management:

- to protect the coast for its landscape, wildlife, cultural, recreational and natural resource value;
- to maintain or improve water quality standards through continuing to control inputs into the sea;
- to understand and work with coastal processes, and
- to manage the fishing industry to prevent over-exploitation of fish stocks.[29]

The Government states that it is satisfied that the current system of coastal management operating in Northern Ireland, which is based on the sectoral approach, is the best system and notes that all the component mechanisms for planning and managing the coastal zone in Northern Ireland are in place. However, while the Government remains convinced of the merits of the sectoral approach to coastal management, it acknowledges that the formulation of coastal policy must be co-ordinated at national and local levels in order to ensure the long-term sustainability of coastal resources and also that there is a need for greater openness and liaison in the decision-making process concerning the Northern Ireland coastline. To this end the paper makes three essential proposals. First, it is proposed that a 'Coastal Zone Forum' be established to bring together the principal interests concerned with coastal zone management and to provide a forum in which the principal issues concerning coastal policy could be discussed by decision-makers.[30] Second, it is proposed that where a coastal area is subject to conflicting and multiple uses, local consultation and co-ordination arrangements may be needed.[31] In areas such as these, the paper states that local integrated

---

27. Part 1 of the consultation document addresses the following components of coastal zone management in Northern Ireland: landscape, nature and heritage conservation; planning and development controls operating in relation to development on coastal land; the regulation of development on the seabed; water quality controls; controls on fisheries; coastal defence; and recreation and tourism.

28. *Sustainable Development: The UK Strategy* London: HMSO, (Cm 2426 1994).

29. Para. 9.3, p. 23.

30. Para. 10.1 and 10.2, p. 24.

31. In this context the paper refers to the local management structures operating in relation to Belfast Harbour and Strangford Lough. In addition the paper notes that the proposed designation of Lough Foyle and Carlingford Lough as 'European sites' will require the governments of Northern Ireland and the Republic to prepare and agree management plans for these areas in order to satisfy the requirements of the Habitats Directive (the European sites designation and the Habitats Directive are both discussed in detail in chap. 7). To achieve this, local advisory forums will be established to address the needs of each area.

management plans can provide 'a structured means at the local level of bringing together different interests and agreeing priorities.'[32] Third, the paper recommends that the gathering and analysis of information concerning coastal zones should continue to be a high priority within government research programmes in order to ensure that coastal policy can be based on the best available scientific information; in this regard, the JNCC's Coastal Directories Project is noted as a particularly important source of data on the coastal zone.[33]

The RSPB has recently submitted a response to the DoE(NI)'s Consultation Paper which is critical of the Government's proposed approach to coastal zone management in Northern Ireland, both in relation to its assessment of the existing component elements of coastal management, and in relation to the Government's proposals for reform in this area. In relation to the latter, the society expressed particular concern at the lack of discussion in the Consultation Paper of the actual mechanisms that would ensure effective co-ordination of coastal policy between the numerous bodies concerned and also that the proposed Coastal Zone Forum would simply operate as a 'talking shop'. The deadline for responding to the Government's Consultation Paper was June 1995; at the time of writing, no further action has been taken.

Finally, it should be noted that in December 1995 the European Council of Environment Ministers held an open discussion on the question of the integrated management of coastal zones, as a result of which Council conclusions were adopted. The conclusions: (i) emphasise the importance of coastal zones and the difficulties involved in managing them in an integrated manner, (ii) acknowledge the analysis carried out by the Commission of the causes for the environmental degradation sustained by many coastal zones throughout the EC, and (iii) emphasise that there should be greater co-ordination between the different tiers of responsibility in developing and implementing sustainable development policies for coastal zones. The Commission has proposed that a 'demonstration programme' be conducted as a joint learning process to make the best use of the available experience in coastal zone management; to this end it was recommended that a number of cases throughout the EC be selected to participate in the study, and a three-year timetable was proposed. A parallel initiative is currently being developed in Ireland.

## SECTION 4. GRANT AID

The provision of financial assistance plays an important role in countryside conservation and management in Northern Ireland. Financial assistance in this regard can operate either to defray costs incurred by individuals, local authorities or certain bodies in carrying out activities which are designed to conserve the countryside or to provide financial incentives to encourage countryside conservation. The DANI is empowered under various EC agriculture schemes to

---

32. Para. 11.1, p. 24.
33. The Coastal Directories Project is a UK-wide inventory of data sets concerning coastal zones; most of the information gathered in this context will be put onto a geographical information system called UKDMAP. For further information on this project see paras 12.3–12.6 of the Consultation Paper.

provide farmers with financial incentives to adopt agricultural practices which are sensitive to the environment.

The present section will set out the DoE(NI)'s powers under articles 7, 28 and 29 of the NCALO to contribute towards costs incurred by individuals, district councils and voluntary bodies while carrying out activities which protect the Northern Ireland countryside; exact details of the amount of grant aid awarded by the DoE(NI) in recent years and the purposes for which it has been granted are provided in the *Environment Service Reports,* 1991–93 and 1993–95. The DANI's powers to provide financial incentives to farmers for the purpose of encouraging practices which promote countryside conservation are discussed separately in section 6 below.

## DoE(NI) power to make grants and loans to the National Trust

As with nature reserves, the DoE(NI) is empowered under article 7 of the NCALO to make grants and loans to the National Trust towards the costs of acquiring land for the purpose of conserving any area of natural beauty or amenity, for providing access to such an area, or towards the cost of improving, maintaining or managing any land acquired for these purposes. Any grants or loans made under article 7 may be subject to such terms and conditions as the DoE(NI) thinks fit. In addition, any such arrangements must be made with the approval of the Department of Finance and Personnel.

## Financial assistance for the restoration or improvement of derelict sites

Article 28 of the NCALO makes provision for the restoration or improvement of derelict sites. In effect, the DoE(NI) is empowered to assist either the owner of such a site, voluntary bodies or district councils in the restoration or improvement of derelict sites. The specific nature of these powers is discussed below in section 7.

## General DoE(NI) powers to provide financial assistance

Article 29 confers on the DoE(NI) the general power to make grants to non-profit-making bodies whose objectives include wildlife and countryside conservation. It also has the power to give financial assistance by way of grants or loans in respect of expenditure incurred by any person in doing something that, in the DoE(NI)'s opinion, 'is conducive to the attainment of any of the purposes, of the NCALO'. Financial assistance granted under article 29 may be subject to such conditions as the DoE(NI) thinks fit and must also be made with the approval of the Department of Finance and Personnel.

## SECTION 5. PLANNING CONTROL

The Northern Ireland planning system was established by the Planning (NI) Order 1972; subsequent amendments of the 1972 Order led to the adoption of the Planning (NI) Order 1991 which consolidates the legislative provisions governing planning control in Northern Ireland. Planning in Northern Ireland is dealt with by the DoE(NI)'s Planning Service. In essence, the Planning Service has two functions, namely, strategic planning and the control of development. Strategic planning is achieved by means of the preparation of 'development plans', which in turn guide the controls exercised over development, that is, the individual decisions which are made on applications for planning permission.

The Northern Ireland system of planning control affords an important form of protection to the countryside. However, a detailed outline of the nature of the protection provided is beyond the scope of this book. It should be noted that in his book *Northern Ireland Planning Law* Alan Dowling addresses the role of planning control as a form of countryside protection in some detail. Strategic planning guidance for development in the countryside is provided by *A Planning Strategy for Rural Northern Ireland,* published by the DoE(NI) in 1994. This document essentially revised the strategic guidance provided by the DoE(NI)'s *Regional Physical Development Strategy,* 1975–95, to take account of developments in environmental policy at international, EC and national level. The 1994 strategy document was preceded by a discussion leaflet entitled *What Kind of Countryside Do You Want?: Options for a New Rural Strategy for Rural Northern Ireland,* which attracted extensive public response, including representations from environmental groups, politicians, farmers' unions, and district councils.[34]

## Section 6. Agriculture and the environment

The scale and importance of the environmental impact of agricultural activities on the countryside are now readily appreciated even by the lay person, but this has not always been so. Early EC agricultural policy, culminating in the vast programme of subsidy and support that constituted the Common Agricultural Policy (CAP), was shaped by the horrors of shortage and rationing induced by the Second World War and the need to ensure that agriculture moved forward to meet the needs of the new Europe. The vast costs, endemic corruption and unconscionable surpluses engendered by the CAP were legendary and led to radical reform of the system, principally through the courageous and politically unpopular efforts of Ray McSharry, then the Commissioner for Agriculture. While we are not concerned within the limits of this text with the CAP in itself, its effect in facilitating and promoting the emergence of agriculture as an industry is of central importance to the environment.

### Agriculture and pollution

Until the second half of this century, agriculture was basically an organic activity, using only limited quantities of machinery (and therefore fossil fuels) and virtually no chemicals; pesticides and inorganic fertilisers came into their own only after the Second World War. Farming was essentially viewed as an 'environmentally friendly' activity and the farmer as the custodian of the natural environment and landscape. This romanticised view lived on long after it bore any relation to reality. The use of the new fertilisers and pesticides served to boost agricultural

---

34. For further reading on the role of planning control as a form of countryside protection in Northern Ireland see Dodd and Pritchard, *RSPB Planscan Northern Ireland: A Study of Development in Northern Ireland* (RSPB 355/5.93), 1993.

production and were thus encouraged throughout the world. Ironically, it was concern about the environmental effects of new agricultural practices which spurred scientific concerns about environmental pollution issues on a much larger scale; many commentators trace the emergence of modern environmental debate to the publication of *Silent Spring* by Rachel Carson in 1963,[35] a book documenting the impact of DDT-based chemicals on the animal food chain and fertility.

It became widely recognised that agricultural pollution represented a serious threat both to the soil and to surface and ground water, and these issues quickly found a place on the international (and more specifically the EC) policy agenda. The laws which eventually began to emerge at EC and then national level to tackle agricultural pollution did not, however, adopt a 'polluter pays' perspective; rather they concentrated on paying farmers not to pollute. The reasons for this are partly moral, partly political, and partly practical. It would appear to be unjust to make farmers pay for pollution which was the result of policies actively promoted by central government. On a political level the farming lobby is in an immensely strong position, holding control over food production. Finally, on a practical level, the agricultural industry is so geographically dispersed that its regulation relies heavily on the co-operation of farmers, and should they be sufficiently alienated to withdraw their co-operation the regulatory regime would in effect grind to a halt.

The EC, recognising these circumstances, in 1985 issued Regulation EEC/797/85,[36] as amended, on improving the efficiency of agricultural structures, geared towards making financial provision[37] for supporting environmentally sound farming practices. This Regulation changed the face of the CAP as far as the environment was concerned, providing a new framework for all EC agricultural funding. Article 19 of the Regulation authorised member states to set up schemes to support environmentally sound farming practices, which the EC would in turn support. In the UK particular emphasis has been placed on the strategy of designating 'environmentally sensitive areas' (paying farmers in these threatened zones to adopt less intensive and polluting production methods) promoted in the Regulations.

In addition to financing 'clean' farming methods in areas which are subject to particularly severe environmental pressures, the EC also in effect pays farmers to 'produce' countryside through the 'set-aside' initiative. Set-aside is designed with the prime aim of reducing the EC's agricultural production by 20 per cent, but it incidentally produces positive environmental effects; land taken out of agricultural production may be used for tree-planting schemes or left fallow—in any event this creates pockets of habitat which will go some way to replacing that which has been lost in the last fifty years. In practice the set-aside and clean farming strategies overlap, both on the ground and in the law, though for convenience sake we will examine separately the main domestic provisions applicable to each.

---

35. London: Hamish Hamilton, 1963.
36. OJ L 93, 30 Mar. 1985. The text was reissued, taking into account the many amendments made to it, as Regulation EEC/2328/91, OJ L1 218, 6 Aug. 1991. The process begun by Regulation EEC/797/85 has been continued, for example by Regulation EEC/2078/92, which also promotes aid for environmentally sensitive farming practices.
37. The EC pays at least 25 per cent of the costs of environmental measures covered by the Directive.

### The protection of agriculture for social and economic ends

The UK, and Northern Ireland in particular, is the subject of enhanced intervention in respect of the agricultural environment, as much of its agricultural land falls into the category of 'less favoured areas' in Regulation 797/85 itself and Directive 75/268/EEC,[38] as amended, on mountain and hill farming and farming in less favoured areas. The latter law, while producing positive environmental effects, gives priority to the support of farming activities in areas where their viability[39] is in question, preventing rural depopulation and as a result conserving the countryside from a social and economic as well as an environmental perspective; the latter aim is a subsidiary one.[40]

### The DANI and the environment

The DANI is a department with a long history and a well-established role in the control and promotion of agriculture. Its functions, therefore, while they have a direct and considerable environmental impact, are primarily economic. The Department is given responsibility pursuant to section 2(2) of the European Communities Act 1972[41] for dealing with the CAP and, under the powers conferred on it, has developed environmental policy and law in Northern Ireland.

The degree of financial control which the DANI exercises is enormous. It is responsible, under the Sub-Programme for Agriculture and Rural Development Regulations (Northern Ireland) 1994[42] for administering EC funds and is authorised to formulate the conditions on which grant payments will be made (regulation 4) and to designate the information required to support applications and the manner and form which payments will take (regulation 3). The DANI has the power to retrieve grant payments if any conditions it has placed on payments have been breached, or if false information was supplied in support of the application for funding (regulation 6(*a*) and (*b*), respectively). Anyone who knowingly or recklessly makes a false statement in support of an application for grant aid (whether by himself or another) under the regulations will be liable on summary conviction to a fine of up to £2,000 (regulation 7). The DANI is authorised to send its own personnel (or others, if necessary)[43] onto land belonging to anyone applying for a grant, in order to inspect the property, premises or machinery, plant or other equipment to verify claims or the use of funds already paid (regulation 8).

### Environmentally sensitive areas

Regulation EEC/797/85 introduced specific environmental protection measures in the form of environmentally sensitive areas (ESAs) into the agricultural funding

---

38. OJ L 128, 19 May 1975, amended by 80/666/EEC, 82/786/EEC, and 3808/89/EEC.
39. Through compensatory payments to balance natural disadvantages; in the UK this covers payments in respect of sheep and cattle.
40. See Commission answer to a question posed in the European Parliament OJ C287, 4 Nov. 1982, for confirmation of the subsidiary role given to environmental protection in the context of Directive 75/268/EEC.
41. SI 1972/1811.
42. SI 1994/ 413.
43. Evidence of the entrant's appointment or authority should be produced in order to gain access to the property in question (reg. 8).

mechanism of the CAP. ESAs are provided for generally in Northern Ireland law by the Agriculture (Environmental Areas) (Northern Ireland) Order 1987,[44] as amended by the Agriculture (Environmental Areas) (Amendment) Regulations (Northern Ireland) 1994.[45] The DANI is empowered by these pieces of legislation to designate as ESAs areas in which it is particularly desirable to conserve, enhance or protect environmental features by the adoption of particular agricultural techniques. Article 3(2) of the 1987 Order introduces the principal mechanism for implementing ESAs by authorising the DANI to enter into management agreements (under article 3(2) of the 1987 Order) (to facilitate the conservation of environmental features) with those holding an estate in farmland[46] in designated areas. Management agreements operate by making environmentally sound farming practices, methods, operations and equipment the subject of payments at agreed rates.

The DANI has made rapid and wide use of its designation powers, and each ESA is covered by its own specifically tailored designation order. The first ESA designated in Northern Ireland covered the Mournes and Slieve Croob;[47] this was followed by the Antrim Coast, Glens, and Rathlin,[48] the Sperrins,[49] Slieve Gullion,[50], and west Fermanagh and Erne lakeland.[51] By 1994 more than 20 per cent of Northern Ireland was covered by an ESA designation.[52]

### (a) The Designation Order

The Environmentally Sensitive Areas (Mourne Mountains and Slieve Croob) Designation Order (Northern Ireland) 1993, as amended (hereafter referred to as the Designation Order), provides a typical example of the specific operation of the ESA system, the core approach adopted being common to each of the designated areas. The purposes of a Designation Order, in compliance with article 3(1) of the 1987 Order, are listed in the introduction to the Order as follows:

(i) to conserve and enhance the natural beauty of the area referred to in article 3 of the Designation Order;

(ii) to conserve the flora and fauna and geographical and physiological features of that area; and

(iii) to protect buildings and other objects of archaeological, architectural or historic interest in that area.

A Designation Order is to be made (under article 3(1) and 3(3) of the 1987 Order) if it appears to the DANI that these features will be conserved, enhanced

---

44. SI 1987/ 458.
45. SI 1994/ 419. These Regulations implement Regulation EEC/ 2078/92, OJ L215, 30 July 1992, in respect of agricultural methods promoting environmental protection and the maintenance of the countryside for public access by allowing the DANI to include access agreements within wider management agreements.
46. As defined by art. 3(6).
47. SI 1993/ 178, as amended by SR 1994/ 375.
48. SI 1993/179 covered the Glens; this was extended to the Coast and Rathlin by SR 1994/ 376.
49. SI 1994/ 213, as amended by SR 1995/179.
50. SI 1994 212
51. SI 1993/180.
52. See *This Common Inheritance: UK Annual Report, 1995,* Cm 2822, HMSO: London, chap. 33, para. 569, for progress of the ESA policy to date.

and protected by the adoption and maintenance of agricultural methods specified in the schedules to such an Order. The environment is viewed holistically; both its natural and its human-made characteristics are set to benefit from an ESA designation.

### (b) The designated area

Article 3 of the Designation Order delineates the land to be covered by the ESA by referring to the area marked in green on a map signed and sealed by the Permanent Secretary of the DANI. The map is available for inspection at the Department's head office in Belfast and in the relevant County Agricultural Development Office during normal office hours.

### (c) Contents of management agreements

The schedules to the Designation Order provide a list of practices, methods, operations and equipment which may, under article 4, form part of the substance of a management agreement. Compliance with Schedules 1 and 2 is mandatory, while compliance with the provisions dealt with by Schedule 3 is optional.

Schedule 1 provides for the general requirements of an agreement which include:
- provisions prohibiting the increase of the density of livestock on land (paragraph (2))
- prohibitions on the increase of the use of fertiliser (paragraph (3))
- prohibitions on tree planting and construction projects (paragraph (8))
- limitations on the use of herbicides (paragraph (9)), and
- the prevention of the escape of polluting substances from silage effluent, sheep dip, etc. (paragraph (10))

to name but a few of the panoply of controls available in some twenty paragraphs. Schedule 2 makes specific provision for woodland and scrubland (Part I), heather moorland (Part II), and archaeological, architectural or historic features (Part (IV)). Schedule 3 makes provision for additional conservation provisions (Part I) and enhancement provisions, such as restoring hedgerows and dry-stone walls (Part II), which are geared particularly to the protection of wildlife. There is more specific provision for wildlife protection in the Habitat Improvement Regulations (Northern Ireland) 1995[53] (see below); and the fact that this is available explains why protection for wildlife is not an integral feature of the ESA scheme.

### (d) Rates of payment

Article 6 sets out a flat rate of payment for each type of activity (or indeed inactivity) outlined in Schedule 1 (article 6(1)(a)(b) and (c)) and (at higher rates) in Schedule 2 (article 6(2)). Payments under Schedule 3, Part I, for conservation provision are laid out in article 7. Schedule 3, Part II, payments for wildlife enhancement provisions are dealt with by article 8, which authorises additional payments of £100 per hectare per year or £2,000 per year (whichever is less). The range of payments—which are all based on hectares of land designated for a

---

53. SI 1995/134.

particular use—range in the Mourne Mountains ESA from £10 per year for rough moorland grazing affected by Schedule 1 (article 6(1)(*c*)) to £200 per year for improved land which is subject to controls under Schedule 3 (article 7(*b*)).

### (e) Breach of the terms of a management agreement

It is provided within the structure of management agreements themselves that breach of the terms specified for the particular agreement under article 4 will allow the DANI (having first given written notice to the farmer in question) to terminate the agreement and reclaim all or part of the money advanced (article 5(*a*)). The question whether or not a breach has occurred is to be determined by an arbitrator agreed by the parties[54] (article 5(*b*)).

### Set-aside

While the set-aside initiative does share some common features with the ESA scheme in terms of deintensification of agriculture, its aims are not primarily environmental but rather the reduction of surplus production. The side effects of set-aside can be very positive for the environment, since set-aside leads incidentally to a diversification of habitats which would not occur naturally in the homogeneous countryside which is the result of modern industrialised agricultural practices.

The set-aside initiative was introduced in Northern Ireland by the Set Aside Regulations (Northern Ireland) 1988,[55] as amended by the Set Aside (Amendment) Regulations (Northern Ireland) 1989.[56] Set-aside is, like the ESA system, the responsibility of the DANI. The scheme takes the form of a grant system administered by the DANI, and the Department's personnel (and other persons it has authorised) have powers of entry and inspection in respect of land covered by a set-aside agreement (article 15(1)).

The set-aside system is in many ways similar to, but less complex than, that of ESAs, concentrating on the withdrawal of agricultural land from production. Set-aside schemes run for a period of five years, after which time the operation of the scheme in particular cases will be reviewed.

### (a) The extent and duration of set-aside agreements

Set-aside is applicable to arable land (as defined in Schedule 1), and the DANI may make payments to farmers who give undertakings to adopt set-aside in respect of at least 20 per cent of such land in their holdings for a period of five years (article 3(1)(*a*)). (This is subject to the proviso that the area set aside should amount to at least 1 hectare, contained in either a single field (article 4(1)(*a*)) or adjacent fields (article 4(1)(*b*)). Set-aside strips of land should be at least 15 metres wide (article 4(2)). After three years the farmer may, subject to the requirement that he give the DANI three months' written notice (supported by

---

54. If no agreement on an arbitrator is reached, art. 5(*b*) provides that the task is to be undertaken by the Northern Ireland chairman of the Royal Institution of Chartered Surveyors, under the rules set out by the Arbitration Act (NI) 1973.
55. SI 1988/ 279.
56. SI 1989/ 239.

such information as the DANI may specify), opt to terminate his set-aside undertaking (article 10). Should the person terminate his agreement with the DANI, the Department may not accept a new aid application from him in respect of the same land within the next two years. This provision aims to prevent aid beneficiaries from attempting to 'play the system' to achieve more favourable rates by terminating one agreement simply to enter another.

### (b)  The use of set-aside land

The DANI may, after three years, allow a farmer to add to the area of land included in the original agreement for the remainder of its duration. Set-aside land can (under article 3(*b*)) be used in the following ways:
  * permanent fallow
  * rotational fallow
  * woodland
  * non-agricultural purposes.[57]

The specific practical implications of each variety of set-aside are included in the provisions of Schedule 2. The DANI may, after three years of an agreement have run, allow any permitted additional set-aside land to be used for the purposes referred to above (article 3(2)(*b*)). Beneficiaries may change the use to which particular set-aside land is used (except for woodland) but must first provide the DANI with written notification of the proposed change (article 11(2)), and the change must be approved by the DANI. Any differences in funding which result will be dealt with by the DANI, which may withhold or reclaim payments as appropriate (article 11(4)).

### (c)  Applications for aid

The DANI has a high degree of control over the initial operation of the set-aside scheme and its extension. This includes the capacity to determine the timing and content of applications, subject to the provisions of article 5, which require that the application be supported by a map indicating the extent of the set-aside proposal (article 5(1)(*a*)) and details of production for each field, both at the time of application and for the duration of the proposed undertaking (article 5(1)(*b*)), together with like information in respect of the land to be covered by set-aside (article 5(1)(*c*)). Should the DANI so require it, documentary evidence of the applicant's interest in the property must be provided (article 5(1)(*d*)).

The DANI's power to enter into agreements in respect of set-aside is qualified in several important ways. Generally speaking, owner-occupiers have more freedom in entering into set-aside agreements than tenants, who are generally required: (i) to satisfy the Department that they have obtained their landlord's consent to agreements to put land to use as woodland or for non-agricultural

---

57. There are limits on qualifying non-agricultural purposes in regard to set-aside: those expressly excluded are covered by art. 9(2)(*a*) and (*b*) of the Order and include mining; industrial processes; retail and housing or office uses (special provision is made in art. 9(3) excluding building works that fall within the provisions of the Farm Business Specification Order (NI) 1987 (SR No. 448) from the ambit of art. 9(2)). The aim of these exclusions is to prevent the applicant from making a double profit from his land at the state's expense.

purposes (article 6(1)) and (ii) to notify landlords of the intention to make an application in respect of using land for permanent or rotational fallow (article 6(2)). Applications in respect of land in a designated ASSI cannot be accepted by the DANI unless the applicant has notified the DoE(NI) in writing of his intentions (article 6(3)). The DANI may also refuse applications that would frustrate the purposes of previous EC funding or which would duplicate other EC assistance (article 6(5)).

### (d) Payments

Five payments are to be made (in arrears) annually in respect of approved set-aside schemes (article 13(1)). The rates of payment are specified in Schedule 3 to the Order. Payments made under the Agriculture (Environmental Areas) (Northern Ireland) Order 1987 (noted above) may be deducted from payments under the set-aside regime (article 13(5)); this is to enable the DANI to prevent duplication of funding in respect of land covered.

### (e) Breach of set-aside obligations

Should the Department discover that false or misleading information has been supplied (by the beneficiary or others) in respect of an application for set-aside aid, it may set about recovering all or part of the money already paid (article 16(1)). The making (whether knowingly or recklessly) of false statements in respect of set-aside payments is also an offence, liable on summary conviction to a fine of up to £2,000. Should the beneficiary fail to comply with either the substantive or (without reasonable excuse) the procedural[58] requirements of the Order, aid may also be recovered, in whole or in part, as the DANI deems appropriate (article 16(2)). In either case, if the DANI recovers from the beneficiary, the whole sum granted, it may also require the payment of interest (at a rate determined annually by the Department) for the appropriate period (article 16(4)).

### Agriculture and habitat protection

The Habitat Improvement Regulations (Northern Ireland) 1995[59] introduce a new long-term[60] approach to reconciling agricultural methods and behaviour with the needs of the natural environment and the species which inhabit it. The long-term approach espoused by the Regulations represents a new maturing of environmental aid provision at both EC and domestic levels, in attempting to tailor the aid package to a time scale which will allow progress 'on the ground'. Aid covers both the improvement of existing habitats and the creation of new ones (regulation 3(1)). Aid may be offered by the DANI to applicants who undertake to either:

(a) withdraw land from agricultural production for 20 consecutive years to establish or improve waterside or grassland wildlife habitats; or

---

58. For example supplying information to the DANI and/or, if relevant, a landlord.
59. SR 1995 No. 134.
60. Habitat Protection Agreements under the 1995 Regulations can be for either twenty or ten-year periods in fulfilment of Regulation 2078/92/EEC OJ L215, 30 July 1992, art. 2(1)(f) and 2(1)(d), respectively.

(*b*) to use farming practices compatible with environmental protection for 10 consecutive years, using the land in question to establish or improve waterside, or grassland or woodland wildlife habitats.

The designation of sites is subject to geographical, administrative and practical limitations. These are outlined in respect of each habitat type and for both of the time options available in Part I of the Schedule to the Regulations. The most important qualification is that the habitat in question may not fall within what has previously been designated as an environmentally sensitive area; the Regulations are designed to extend habitat protection, not to duplicate existing arrangements.[61] Applicants are also required to undertake to observe the management requirements set out for the relevant class of habitat in Part II of the Schedule to the Regulations (regulation 3(2)(*a*)) and to manage the habitat site in accordance with the management plan agreed in writing with the Department (regulation 3(2)(*b*)). The management requirements outlined in Part II of the Schedule are exacting; for example, the use of the site for agricultural production (including raising livestock) must be entirely abandoned (paragraph 1); the treatment of the land with fertilisers (both organic and inorganic), pesticides etc. must be undertaken only with the DANI's agreement (paragraph 3); and beneficiaries are forbidden to damage or destroy features of landscape, wildlife or historic importance, both on the designated habitat site itself and bordering it.

### (a) Eligibility

Regulation 4 allows owners or tenants (for the previous twelve months) to apply for aid in respect of sites fulfilling the criteria relevant to the habitat listed in Part I of the Schedule to the Regulations, provided the site in question is at least 1 hectare in extent (regulation 4(2)).

### (b) Application procedure

Once again the DANI controls the applications, being empowered by regulation 5 to determine the timing and content of the procedure, subject to the necessary elements detailed in that regulation. These include a map of the applicant's farm showing the relevant habitat site (or sites) and features of landscape, wildlife and/or historic interest, a statement of the area of each habitat site, a description of how the site has been used in the previous twelve months, a management plan, and (if the DANI requires it) evidence of the applicant's estate in the land.

### (c) Successors in title and the protection of habitat sites

The Regulations, because of the unusual length of the designation periods available, also make express provision for the problem of changes in occupation of farms containing habitat sites subject to management agreements. The provisions designed to allow the continuation of this scheme are, like the original agreements themselves, typical in their approach to the environmental regulation of agriculture, stressing voluntary compliance with aid schemes rather than

---

61. Waterside habitats are subject to a particular requirement that they be immediately adjacent to those watercourses listed in Sch. 6 of the Regulations.

command and control regulation. The Regulations do, however, adopt a rather novel approach in order to 'encourage' continuation of habitat schemes, since if, within three months of the new occupier taking over, no undertaking to continue the scheme has been given, the DANI may withhold payments from the original beneficiary or recover payments already made (regulation 7(6)).[62]

Beneficiaries are required to notify the DANI (in writing) of any change of occupation (regulation 7(1)(*a*)). It is then open to the new occupier[63] to undertake[64] with the DANI to continue to comply with the (relevant[65]) obligations undertaken by his predecessor in title for the remainder of the agreed period (regulation 7(1)(*b*)). The undertaking takes effect from the date on which the DANI accepts it; this could potentially represent a loophole in the legal protection offered to habitat sites should the DANI fail to act swiftly.

The DANI's power to grant aid applications is not unqualified. Regulation 6 provides for both general and particular conditions which must be met in respect of applications. Firstly, the Department is under a general obligation, having regard to the condition of the site itself and the surrounding area, together with the proposals contained in the application, to accept only those applications which will provide 'significant benefit to the environment' (regulation 6(1)). Secondly, applications made by tenants will be accepted only if the DANI is satisfied that the owner of the land has been notified of his intentions by the tenant who is applying for the grant (reg. 6(2)). Thirdly, the DANI may refuse applications where granting them would conflict with or duplicate other agricultural grant schemes under either national or EC law (regulation 6(3)(*a*) and (*b*), respectively).

### (d) Rates of payment

Regulation 8 determines the amount of grant aid to be claimed (annually in arrears) (paragraph (1)) in respect of habitat sites. The initial rates (which can be altered in regulations issued by the DANI under regulation 8(2)) range; for undertakings under regulation 3(1)(*a*)[66] on waterside and grassland habitats, from £125 per hectare for grazed marshland or rough moorland to £325 per hectare for improved land; and for undertakings under regulation 3(1)(*b*)[67] from £50 per hectare for grazed marshland or rough moorland to £260 per hectare for improved land. The scale of payments reflects the lost production value of the land, both in respect of its own characteristics and with regard to the duration of the agreement entered into.

---

62. The power to recover money under reg. 7(6) is qualified in that it is not applicable in respect of compulsory purchase and in cases where the beneficiary was a tenant farmer whose death led to the termination of the lease on the property (reg. 7(7)(*a*) and (*b*), respectively).
63. Subject to the new occupier satisfying the DANI that he has a valid title to the property or is acting as the personal representative of the beneficiary (reg. 7(3)).
64. A new occupier who gives such an undertaking will supply the DANI with such information in such time as the Department will specify after he takes up occupation to support his undertaking (reg. 7(4)).
65. Changes in occupation may refer to the whole of the site or only part of it, and it is for the DANI to determine which obligations are relevant to the successor in title in any given situation (reg. 7(2)).
66. The twenty-year option.
67. The ten-year option.

## *(e) Regulating the system*

The DANI is given, as is usual in respect of agricultural aid packages, power to enter and inspect land in order to verify compliance with the terms of a subsisting management agreement. Regulation 9(1)(*a*) empowers the DANI (and anyone it should choose to authorise) to examine the applicant's documentary or other records (or those of his successor in title, where relevant), and regulation 9(1)(*b*) gives a more general power to ascertain whether undertakings given have been complied with. Both applicants and beneficiaries are obliged to render 'all reasonable assistance' to authorised persons carrying out such enquiries (regulation 9(2)); this includes the production of documents and records (including computer records) and allowing them to be copied, and taking the DANI personnel to examine the property.

Information furnished which is false or materially misleading will justify the DANI in both withholding money payable under the Regulations and recovering (in whole or in part) sums already paid (regulation 10(1)). The furnishing (whether knowingly or recklessly) of false information is also an offence (regulation 11(1)); those found guilty will be liable to a maximum fine, on summary conviction, of £5,000 (level 5 on the standard scale) (regulation 11(2)). Proceedings in respect of this offence must be instituted within six months of the date on which the DANI had sufficient evidence to justify proceedings (regulation 11(3)); evidence of the date takes the form of a certificate signed on behalf of the Department (regulation 11(4)). In addition, failure (without reasonable excuse) to comply with obligations imposed by the Regulations or failure to permit entry or inspection by authorised personnel may result in the same penalties being imposed (regulation 10(2)). The DANI is obliged (by regulation 10(3)), before using its punitive powers, to afford the beneficiary a written explanation for its proposed actions (paragraph (*a*)) and to allow the beneficiary an opportunity to be heard[68] (paragraph (*b*)). The DANI must consider a report based on the hearing and furnish the beneficiary with a copy before taking action (paragraph (3)).

## SECTION 7. DERELICT SITES

Article 28 of the NCALO makes provision for the restoration or improvement of derelict sites. In effect, the DoE(NI) is empowered to aid the owner of such a site, voluntary bodies or district councils in the restoration or improvement of derelict sites in Northern Ireland. A derelict site in this context is defined by article 2(2) of the NCALO as:

> land which the DoE(NI), after consultation with the district council within whose district the land is situated, considers as detracting from the amenity of the area by reason of any unsightly, dilapidated or neglected structure or works or unsightly vegetation, refuse or waste material on the land.

In relation to the owner of such a site, the Department is empowered to pay (at most) half the cost of restoring the site or improving the appearance of the site.

---

68. The hearing will take place before a person appointed by the Department.

Any arrangements entered into by the DoE(NI) in this regard must be approved by the Department of Finance and Personnel, and any cost incurred by the owner in this regard must first be approved by the DoE(NI) in order to invoke its power to contribute to the costs incurred. It should also be noted that the DoE(NI) may arrange, with the consent of the owner, that a voluntary body assist the owner in the restoration or improvement of the site. Where a voluntary body does provide assistance, the DoE(NI) may contribute towards any expenses incurred by the body in question, and once again the Department of Finance and Personnel must approve any such payments. No upper limit is imposed on such contributions.

Where the DoE(NI) acquires a derelict site under article 6 of the NCALO pursuant to its general powers (outlined below), it may enter into an agreement with the district council in whose district the site is located, that the council carry out whatever works are regarded by the Department as being necessary to restore or improve the appearance of the site, and any costs incurred by the council in executing such work will be paid by the DoE(NI). Finally, it should be noted that the NCALO also makes provision for the acquisition and disposal of derelict sites and for the adoption and enforcement of bylaws governing such land. These powers are almost identical to those applying in relation to AONBs and are therefore outlined in that context at pages 397–8.

## *PART II* ACCESS TO THE COUNTRYSIDE

As in England, the public in Northern Ireland do not have a general right to roam in the open countryside or on the foreshore.[69] A person is deemed to be a trespasser on private land unless they are legally entitled to enter such land. Legal rights of access to private land can be conferred either on a specific individual[70] or on the general public. Historically, public rights of access to privately owned land could be created by virtue of a 'public right of way' (public footpaths, bridleways and byways) established in accordance with the common law principles of 'dedication and acceptance.' In effect, a public right of way was created when public use of the route in question was so 'extensive and continuous that it raised the presumption that the owner of the land in question must have "dedicated" the

---

69. The issue of a public 'right to roam' has been the subject of intense controversy throughout the UK in recent years. For an overview of the arguments raised during this debate see M. Shoard, *This Land is Our Land,* London: Paladin 1987; M. Ewing MP, Freedom to Roam (Access to the Countryside) Bill, introduced in the House of Commons on 22 Mar. 1994, 240 HC *Hansard* (6th series), col. 137–9; D. Hughes, *Environmental Law* (2nd ed.), London: Butterworths 1992, 179–82. See also the following Countryside Commission reports on this issue: *Recreation 2000: Policies for Enjoying the Countryside* (CCP234), 1987; *Recreation 2000: Enjoying the Countryside: Policies for Action* (CCP266), 1989; *Paths, Routes and Trails: Policies and Priorities* (CCP266), 1989; *Managing Rights of Way: An Agenda for Action* (CCP273), 1989; *Rights of Way: An Action Guide* (CCP375), 1992; *National Target for Rights of Way* (CCP436), 1993; K. Milton, *Our Countryside Our Concern,* Northern Ireland Environment Link, 1994. The American courts have been more prepared to infer a general right to roam; in this regard see Gray, *Elements of Land Law,* 1987, p. 641.
70. For example by means of a licence or an easement. The issue of access to the countryside concerns only the extent to which the general public have rights of access to the countryside; as a result, rights of access conferred on specific individuals will not be developed further in this chapter.

route to the public for their use, and that the public had "accepted" it by using it'.[71] It should be noted, however, that the principles of dedication and acceptance have since been supplemented and to a large extent replaced by legislative provision.[72] In addition, the public can be granted a right of access to private land in Northern Ireland by virtue of 'public paths' and 'long-distance routes' or by means of 'access agreements or orders', all of which are created under statutory provision.

Although the legislative framework governing access to the countryside in Great Britain has been evolving since 1949,[73] there was no equivalent legislation in operation in Northern Ireland until the introduction of the Access to the Countryside (NI) Order 1983 (hereafter referred to as the ACO).[74] Part I of the ACO contains introductory provisions. Part II is intended to ensure the effective exercise, enforcement and maintenance of public rights of way and, in addition, makes provision for the creation, diversion, closure and maintenance etc., of public paths and for the establishment of long-distance routes. Part III makes provision for public access to 'open country'[75] for recreational purposes by means of access orders and agreements or land acquisition, while Part IV contains supplementary provisions.

Although a considerable body of case law has developed concerning the common law principles and legislative provisions governing access in Great Britain, this is not the case in Northern Ireland. There are as yet no decisions from the courts in Northern Ireland concerning public rights of way and other common law access principles which could be regarded as having set a legal precedent in this context. Similarly, there are as yet no reported or unreported judgments from the Northern Ireland judiciary concerning the provisions of the ACO which could assist in clarifying the scope and application of its provisions. Although the courts in Northern Ireland are not obliged to follow the decisions of courts in England and Wales, their judgments would undoubtedly be persuasive in relation to disputes concerning the application of common law access principles. However,

---

71. F. Barker and N. Parry, 'Private Property, public access and occupiers' liability' (1995) 15 Legal Studies 335 p. 340. For further detail on the concepts of dedication and acceptance see also S. Sauvin, *Highway Law,* London: Sweet and Maxwell, 1989, pp 24–43, and T. Bonyhady, *The Law of the Countryside: The Rights of the Public,* Abingdon: Professional Books, 1987, pp 29–39.

72. F. Barker and N. Parry, ibid. Barker and Parry also point out that 'the use made of the public rights of way network has shifted from being for essential communication and transport to being for recreation.'

73. National Parks and Access to the Countryside Act 1949. The complete framework of legislation currently governing access in Great Britain is listed at note 76, infra.

74. SI 1983/1895. The ACO has been amended by the Access to the Countryside Regulations (NI) 1984 (SR No. 342) and the Access to the Countryside (Amendment) Regulations (NI) 1985 (SR No. 152). While the ACO is the primary legislative provision governing access in Northern Ireland, it should be noted that the following measures also have an impact on access to the countryside: Public Parks (Ireland) Act 1869 (the creation of public parks by district councils); Open Spaces Act 1906 (empowers district councils to accept gifts or transfers of land that constitute 'open space' under the Act); Recreation and Youth Services (NI) Order 1986 (obliges district councils to secure facilities for recreational, social, physical and cultural activities); Nature Conservation and Amenity Lands (NI) Order 1985 (imposes an obligation on the DoE(NI) to formulate and implement policies for nature conservation and the conservation and enhancement of the natural beauty and amenity of the countryside). See also *NIA 40, Northern Ireland Assembly Report on the Proposal for a Draft Access to the Countryside (NI) Order.*

75. Open country is defined in art. 25 as land that is 'wholly or predominantly mountain, moor, heath, hill, woodland, cliff, foreshore, marsh, bog or waterway'.

while the terms of the ACO are broadly similar to the equivalent legislation operating in England and Wales,[76] they are not as extensive or as closely prescribed and, as a result, the case law surrounding these provisions is of limited value in defining the scope of the ACO.[77]

Northern Ireland's twenty-six district councils are primarily responsible for the implementation of the ACO. Before outlining their responsibilities in this regard, it should be noted that when exercising their functions under the ACO, district councils are required to have regard to the needs of agriculture and forestry and to the need to conserve the natural beauty and amenity of the countryside, including its wildlife and natural (geological and physiographical) features.[78] District councils are under a statutory duty to assert, protect, maintain and record public rights of way and to assess the measures which are necessary in order to ensure public access to open country for the purpose of open-air recreation. In addition, district councils are granted several other discretionary powers which may be used in carrying out these statutory duties; these include the power to create, divert and close public paths, to signpost and maintain public paths, to propose long-distance routes, to enter into access agreements or to make access orders for the purpose of ensuring public access to open country, to adopt bylaws for the prevention of damage to land which is subject to public access, to appoint rangers, and to provide financial assistance to any persons or bodies who assist the council in carrying out general maintenance work on public-access land.

Although the DoE(NI) has a direct remit for informal countryside recreation in Northern Ireland, the Department's formal function under the ACO is limited to a reserve role. In essence, the DoE(NI) performs quasi-judicial, consultative and enabling functions, all of which are exercised by the Department's Environment Service in consultation with the CNCC. In relation to its quasi-judicial role, the Department is required to determine whether a public path should be created, diverted or closed in the event that it is opposed, it must confirm all district council access orders, and must determine all representations made to the Department to exclude land used or intended for agriculture and forestry from the ambit of access orders. In its consultative role,[79] the DoE(NI) must be consulted by district

---

76. National Parks and Access to the Countryside Act 1949; Highways Act 1959; Countryside Act 1968; Highways Act 1980; Wildlife and Countryside Act 1981; and the Rights of Way Act 1990.

77. The legislation operating in England and Wales was rejected as a model for Northern Ireland on the grounds that it was too complex for the Northern Ireland context; it was also regarded as being too confrontational and therefore unlikely to achieve the objective of encouraging agreement among the numerous parties involved in the provision of access to the countryside. It was decided instead to base the ACO on the equivalent Scottish legislation, the Countryside (Scotland) Act 1967, which was regarded as providing a legislative framework better suited to the scale and population density of Northern Ireland. However, given the lack of Northern Ireland precedent on the scope and application of the ACO, it is important to note that the proximity between the Northern Ireland and Scottish access legislation may lead to confusion as to whether Northern Ireland courts should follow Scottish or English judicial precedents. In this regard see *Access to the Northern Ireland Countryside: Summary Report*, London: HMSO 1994, 13; NIA 40, *Northern Ireland Assembly Report on the Proposal for a Draft Access to the Countryside (NI) Order.*

78. Art. 44.

79. When the ACO was enacted, the DoE(NI) issued six circulars to district councils giving guidance on the implementation of the ACO. CD 1/84–6/84 remain in operation and provide the only detailed advice issued thus far by the Department. For further details of the impact and contents of the circulars see note 95, infra.

councils when considering the extent of open country within their districts and what action should be taken to ensure public access thereto. Similarly, councils are required to consult the Department concerning proposals for long-distance routes and in relation to applications for the temporary closure or diversion of public paths which the council wishes to refuse. The Department's enabling or executive functions include contributing towards the expenses incurred by district councils in exercising their powers under the ACO or expenses incurred by any other body or person who assists in the implementation of a proposal approved by the DoE(NI) for a long-distance route; the confirmation of bylaws made by councils in relation to open country; default powers to make bylaws concerning public rights of way, public paths, land subject to access orders and agreements, and long-distance routes; determining proposals submitted by district councils concerning long-distance routes; and acquiring land on its own behalf for the purpose of providing access. The DoE(NI) may decide to conduct a public local inquiry in relation to any of its own functions under the ACO;[80] however, the Department does not have the power to direct a district council to exercise its powers to provide public access, nor, with the exception of its power to acquire land for the purpose of providing public access, does it have the power to adopt public path orders or access orders or agreements where a district council fails to act.

The first comprehensive study of public access to the Northern Ireland countryside was commissioned in 1993 jointly by the Environment Service, the Northern Ireland Tourist Board and the Sports Council for Northern Ireland; a summary of the final report was published in 1994.[81] The study addressed a wide range of issues concerning access in Northern Ireland, including the key influences on countryside accessibility throughout the Province, the development and promotion of access as a tourist product, the administration and management of countryside access, access in practice, key themes and issues arising in the context of access to the Northern Ireland countryside, strategic choices and direction for the future, and a programme of action to bring about an effective access system.

Sections 1–3 provide a summary of the principal findings relevant to the system of legal control governing access in Northern Ireland:

## SECTION 1. THE CURRENT EXTENT OF PUBLIC ACCESS

The report found that public opportunities for recreational access to the countryside are 'severely restricted in comparison to the network of public rights of way in England and Wales or traditional access "freedoms" in Scotland'.[82] In addition, the report noted that 'many traditional routes which satisfy the criteria for public rights of way have not been asserted'.[83] Only a limited number of paths

---

80. Art. 54. The DoE(NI) may also adopt rules for the purpose of regulating the procedures followed during an inquiry conducted under the ACO, but this power is without prejudice to s. 23 of the Interpretation Act (NI) 1954.
81. *Access to the Northern Ireland Countryside: Summary Report*, London: HMSO 1994. The full report, which was not published, is entitled *Access to the Countryside in Northern Ireland: Full Report 1994*. References to the report in this chapter should be read as references to the summary report unless otherwise stated.
82. Para. 2.3, p. 3 of the summary report; p. 14–18 of the full report.
83. Para. 6.1, p. 25 of the summary report.

are available for recreational access, and these are primarily in popular coastal, mountain and urban fringe areas. There is no 'formally recognised or assured' access to open country in Northern Ireland, although there is a tradition of open access in some areas.[84] Apart from country roads, assured public access was found to be confined largely to 'honeypot' sites, namely, country, regional and forest parks, National Trust properties, and land in public ownership.[85] The report identified traditional patterns of land ownership and use[86] and a 'turbulent history of property ownership, the closeness of farming families to the land and traditional protectiveness over ownership rights'[87] as having had a direct influence on the current position on access in Northern Ireland.[88]

## SECTION 2. IMPLEMENTATION OF THE ACO

The report opened by noting that the provision of public access to the countryside depended 'on complex and dynamic interrelationships between a wide range of interest groups',[89] including landowners, recreational users, conservationists, community interests, government bodies and district councils; however, one of the key issues raised by the report was that, while the range of organisations with an interest in access has increased, access 'remains a low priority for most public bodies, including district councils'.[90]

### District councils

Important information on the role of district councils in the administration and management of access was derived from the study on which the summary report is based. A questionnaire survey, to which twenty councils responded, and interviews with sixteen councils, showed that approximately two-thirds of Northern Ireland's district councils have failed to discharge their statutory obligations under the ACO (in particular in relation to the assertion, protection and maintenance of public rights of way) and have also failed to make effective use of the discretionary

---

84. *Access to the Countryside in Northern Ireland: Full Report* (1994), p. 17, notes that areas such as the Mourne Mountains, parts of Fermanagh, Antrim Hills and Sperrins have a tradition of open access. Further details of the location and extent of access to the open countryside are provided at p. 17 of the full report.

85. It should be noted that Northern Ireland's country and regional parks are entirely distinct from the statutory 'national parks' designation discussed in Part I, section 2 of this chapter. There is no statutory basis for the establishment of country and regional parks, and their primary function is to promote public enjoyment and understanding of the countryside and to provide free public access to countryside areas. The role played by these parks is discussed in Part I, section 8 of this chapter.

86. The summary report (p. 2) points out that the pattern of land ownership and use in Northern Ireland differs markedly from that in Great Britain. Over three-quarters of the land in Northern Ireland is in agricultural use, over half of agricultural holdings are unlikely to provide full-time employment, and almost three-quarters of agricultural land has been conferred with less favoured status within the EC, most of which is classified as 'severely disadvantaged'.

87. Summary report, p. 2. The full report provides a more detailed explanation of the historical context of land ownership in Northern Ireland, pp 9–10.

88. A map of the principal areas subject to public access in Northern Ireland is provided in the summary report.

89. Para. 1.2, p. 1.

90. Para. 6.1, p. 24.

powers conferred by the ACO concerning the provision of public access.[91] Five main factors were identified as combining to give rise to this situation.

First, the report addresses the effects of the 'fundamental contradiction' which underlies the provision of public access to the countryside, namely, that on the one hand there is a need to protect and promote public rights of access to the countryside, while on the other hand there is a belief in the inviolability of private property rights. The report stated that an important factor underlying a district council's willingness to implement the ACO was the degree to which each council supported the provision of public access to the countryside and their view of the legitimacy of their role in this process. Many district councils:

(i) were found to doubt the legitimacy of providing public access to the wider countryside and of the need for councils to intervene on behalf of the public;

(ii) were found to be willing to defer to the wishes of the farming community (which is generally hostile to the establishment of formal access rights over private land), either because elected members of the council were themselves farmers or because they feared losing votes from the farming community;

(iii) were either unaware or refused to accept that councils were under a statutory obligation to take specific steps to ensure public access; and

(iv) held the view that the subject of access is 'controversial and technically difficult, and would involve the unproductive and unjustified use of staff and resources.'[92]

Second, the report found that most district councils refused to use any of their compulsory powers, showing instead a strong preference for achieving public access by means of negotiation with the landowner, despite the fact that when the provision of public access is opposed, negotiations can be very protracted and tend to achieve no more than 'insecure, permissive agreements'.[93]

Third, the report identified 'shortfalls in the legislation', which meant that 'many important legal issues remain unresolved or have to be decided case by case on the assumed application of common law principles.'[94]

Fourth, the report noted that most district councils are too small to have specialist staff with the practical and legal expertise necessary to implement the ACO effectively. Finally, the report pointed out that the six circulars[95] issued by the DoE(NI) to district councils concerning their duties and powers under the ACO placed a strong emphasis on the provision of public access by means of conciliation and negotiation, while de-emphasising the important compulsory and discretionary powers conferred on councils in this regard.

---

91. Para. 4.4, p. 15–19, and para. 6.1, p. 25.

92. Factors (i)–(iv) are addressed at p. 17 of the summary report. However, these issues are discussed more generally at p. 16–19 and p. 27–31 of the summary report.

93. Para, 6.1, p. 25, and para. 4.4, p. 16.

94. Para. 6.1, p. 25. It should be noted in this regard that the decision by the Lisburn Magistrates' Court not to confirm a disputed assertion of a public right of way, although an isolated case, has also had an influence on district councils: *Court for the Division of Ards: Lisburn Borough Council v. Agnes Anne Jennifer Adgey and Lisburn B.B. v. Trevor George,* undated transcript from Lisburn B.C.

95. CD 1/84 (public rights of way, public paths, and access to open country); CD 2/84 (financial assistance from the DoE(NI)); CD 3/84 (the assertion and protection of rights of way); CD 4/84 (strategy and objectives concerning the creation of public rights of way); CD 5/84 (consultation with interested parties); and CD 6/84 (the use of volunteers).

## Government departments

The report found that the DoE(NI)'s involvement in the provision of public access to the countryside was characterised by 'a low-key, reactive' approach.[96] In this regard, the report identified the following factors as contributing to this approach:[97]

1. The DoE(NI) has not developed a corporate strategy concerning access to the countryside.
2. The nature of its circulars to district councils (explained above) has resulted in a low level of activity among councils, with the result that the DoE(NI) is 'seldom . . . required to exercise its formal, statutory functions' under the ACO.[98]
3. There are gaps in the DoE(NI)'s powers under the ACO; for example it does not have the power under the ACO to take action to ensure public access where a district council failed to do so, nor is it empowered to direct a district council to take the necessary action.
4. The DoE(NI)'s Environment Service was found to lack the level of staffing and resources necessary to oversee and monitor the ACO effectively or to provide the necessary 'overall leadership, co-ordination, expertise and guidance' required to administer the access system.
5. The Environment Service had accorded a low priority to the provision of public access to the countryside in comparison with nature conservation and the management of areas of outstanding natural beauty under the Nature Conservation and Amenity Lands (NI) Order 1985.[99]

The report stated that the Water Executive, which had extensive land holdings and possessed the power to regulate access to such land, was 'cautious' about providing access for purposes other than fishing because of concerns about liability, vandalism, and interference with water quality. Finally, the report noted that other than its Forest Service, which is a major provider of public access, the DANI does not view access as a priority issue.[100]

## Other interest groups

In relation to landowners' interest groups, the report noted that neither of the two farmers' unions has developed a formal policy on public access to the countryside. The Ulster Farmers' Union (mainly full-time farmers) objected strenuously to the adoption of the ACO; ten years after its enactment its members continue to

---

96. Para. 4.3, p. 15.
97. All are outlined in more detail in para. 4.3, p. 15, and para. 6.1, p. 24–5, of the summary report.
98. Para. 4.3, p. 15, of the summary report. *Access to the Countryside in Northern Ireland: Full Report*, p. 55, goes on to state that 'only one opposed public path order is known to have been made, and the Department does not have the established administrative procedures or policy framework to deal with appeals and other matters that it could be called upon to determine in significant numbers, if the provisions of the [ACO] were fully applied.'
99. SI 1985/170.
100. Para. 2.4, p. 6.

perceive public access to the countryside as a threat[101] and remain concerned about occupiers' liability in the event that public access is established.[102] Members of the Northern Ireland Agricultural Producers' Association (mainly family and part-time farmers) take the view that they would respond positively to the provision of public access where an economic incentive existed for the landowner. Recreational organisations[103] all regard the improvement of public access as an important issue. However, the report found that they had not to date lobbied for improvements in this context, that there was very little co-ordination in their activities, and that some were unaware that district councils were responsible for the provision of public access. Conservation organisations all support managed public access to the countryside,[104] while an increasing interest in the provision of access was noted amongst community groups and local development associations. The report also noted that the Rural Development Council supported the need to provide guidance to community development associations in relation to undertaking access projects.

## SECTION 3. REFORM OF THE ACCESS SYSTEM

The report set out an extensive series of recommendations for reform dealing with almost every aspect of the Northern Ireland access system; each will now be addressed in turn.

### Developing the basis for a planned policy framework

The 'key starting point' in the reform process was identified as the immediate assertion and protection of all known traditional public rights of way throughout Northern Ireland, thereby establishing a basic framework on which to develop a planned policy framework for a more extensive network of areas subject to public access.[105]

### Reform of the practical administration and management of the access system

In this context the report noted that while reform should develop existing organisational partnerships within the Northern Ireland access system, the paucity

---

101. In this regard the report points towards the DoE(NI)'s confirmation of the controversial public path creation order in north Down in 1992 (Ballysallagh Road to Clandeboye Avenue) as contributing towards this attitude.
102. In this regard it is worth noting that the summary report found 'no firm evidence to show that significant numbers of liability claims are being made against private landowners as a result of the public's use of the countryside for recreation, nor of any increase in the cost of landowners' insurance premiums to reflect their potential liability' (para. 4.2, p. 14).
103. The organisations noted were the Ulster Federation of Rambling Clubs, the Mountaineering Council of Ireland, the Cyclists' Touring Club, the Northern Ireland Cycling Federation, the British Horse Society, and the Ulster Rural Riders' Association. Details of membership of each interest group are provided in para 2.4, p. 6, of the summary report.
104. The attitudes of the National Trust, the RSPB, the Ulster Wildlife Trust, the NI Environment Link and the Conservation Volunteers (NI) were each addressed in this report at para. 2.4, p. 7.
105. Para. 7.1, p. 27. In this regard the report went on to make further recommendations for the development of a range of access opportunities throughout the wider countryside in Northern Ireland.

of district council action made it clear that the present arrangements for the administration of the access system were 'unsustainable'. The report emphasised that the Environment Service should 'take overall, strategic responsibility for countryside access' as a matter of immediate importance.[106] In the medium and long term, the report recommended that the following changes be introduced:

1. Changes should be made to departmental structures; for example, an 'independent access directorate' should be established within the Environment Service, regional officers should be appointed, and interdepartmental working arrangements should be improved.

2. A separate 'countryside agency' should be established in Northern Ireland to parallel the role played in Great Britain by the Countryside Commission, the Countryside Council for Wales, and Scottish Natural Heritage.

3. Formal regional arrangements should be established to ensure effective co-ordination between groups of district councils, and semi-independent Countryside Trusts should be sponsored by local and central government that would work in partnership with a wide range of bodies and groups interested in access in Northern Ireland.

4. The ACO should be amended in three regards.[107] Firstly, the Government should amend the ACO so that the responsibility for providing access could be shared between the district councils and the DoE(NI) so that, for example, certain categories of access cases could be referred to the Department, or empower the DoE(NI) to compel a district council to act in certain circumstances. Secondly, members of the public should be empowered to submit formal applications to district councils requesting action or to require that action be taken in certain situations, for example, to assert or protect a right of way. Thirdly, it was recommended that certain specialist functions relating to the assertion of public rights of way be transferred to the DoE(NI) from the magistrates' courts.

## Reform of the approach to access negotiations

The report acknowledged the desirability of providing access by means of negotiation and agreement. However, it went on to emphasise that it was essential to address the fact that considerable political pressure could be exerted on district councils by farmers and landowners who strongly resisted the prospect of greater

---

106. Para. 7.1, p. 28. The report goes on to make several more detailed recommendations on the immediate reforms that should be made in relation to the manner in which the Environment Service approaches its role in the provision of access in Northern Ireland. In particular, the report recommended that a higher priority be afforded to access in the overall work of the Environment Service, that it should secure greater funding for the provision of access; that it should define and develop a national and local strategy or framework for the provision of access; and that it should promote liaison between, and co-ordinate action by, the various groups and bodies interested in the issue of access in Northern Ireland. The report then recommended that in undertaking these 'key roles' the Environment Service should develop its promotional and advisory functions in a variety of specified ways.

107. Para. 7.1, p. 29.

public access to the countryside.[108] Indeed the report pointed out that a decision on this issue would 'be crucial in determining the extent and type of access opportunities that can be provided in the Northern Ireland countryside and the rate and cost at which progress can be made.'[109] More specifically, the report concluded that 'substantial progress' could only be made if district councils were ultimately willing to use their compulsory powers under the ACO in any access negotiation. In this regard the report stressed that any approach to the provision of access that rejected the use of legal or compulsory powers 'in any circumstance' could not provide secure public access and would require a 'prohibitively high input of staff time.' The report concluded that while each district council must decide for itself how best to proceed in individual cases, it is important that the DoE(NI) emphasise to councils: (i) that they must act 'in the interests of the community as a whole,' (ii) that they have a statutory duty to assert all public rights of way, and (iii) that the only way to achieve a full debate and an independent decision in a given situation on whether or not there is a need for greater public access is to make a public path creation order, which, as an opposed order, would have to be referred to the DoE(NI) for determination under the ACO.[110] Finally, the report pointed out that the conflict between those seeking to protect private property rights and those seeking greater public access might be resolved, to some extent, if some means could be found of surmounting landowners' 'fundamental objections' to public access. In this regard the report noted that scope for the provision of financial incentives in exchange for the provision of public access now exists under EC agri-environment regulations and recommended that the DANI and the Environment Service 'give early consideration to the development of a voluntary scheme which offers market-level payments to secure additional access opportunities in priority areas for access developments, in Environmentally Sensitive Areas,[111] or generally throughout Northern Ireland.'[112] However, the report states that the basic criteria for any such scheme should be that the access provided would be 'sufficiently long-term to justify public investment and enable it to be promoted, and that farmers should not be subject to any increased legal liability.'[113]

---

108. In this regard it should also be noted that the report points out the imbalance in the influence exerted by those who seek to protect private property rights and those who seek to ensure greater public access to the countryside. Landowners and farmers, who are professionally represented, exert considerable influence, while those who support public access are largely voluntary groups, whose actions are un-co-ordinated and which lack awareness of the access system operating in Northern Ireland. The report also pointed out that these imbalances in the representation of interests are 'reinforced by the approach of the Environment Service, DANI and most district councils.' Para. 6.1, p. 24.
109. Para. 7.1, p. 29.
110. Ibid.
111. The concept of environmentally sensitive area is addressed in Part I, section 6 of this chapter.
112. Para. 7.1, p. 29.
113. Ibid.

## SECTION 4. PUBLIC RIGHTS OF WAY

### Duty to assert, protect, and maintain

The ACO places district councils under a statutory obligation to 'assert'[114] public rights of way[115] and, in addition, to 'protect and keep open and free from obstruction or encroachment any public right of way' (article 3(1)). To this end, a district council is empowered to institute proceedings in its own name. The ACO does not make clear what evidence the council requires before taking action to assert or protect a right of way. However, in the context of an action concerning section 116 of the Highways Act 1959 (which operates in England but contains similar provisions to those operating in Northern Ireland) it was held that the duty to act is not invoked unless the district council is satisfied that it is beyond serious dispute that the road or path in question is a public right of way.[116] Furthermore, article 3(2) provides that district councils may maintain any public right of way but must first consult the landowner[117] concerned; this provision does not,

---

114. The term 'assert' is not defined by the ACO. However, in *Re Guyer's application* [1980] 2 All ER 520 at 528, Ackner LJ considered the meaning of this term in the context of s. 116 of the Highways Act 1959. He stated that 'I take this word "assert" in the context of this subsection to mean in essence to claim that there exists. It may well involve action which falls short of the normally accepted use of the word "protect". Let me give a simple example. If I find what I consider to be a public footpath obstructed, and go to the council and provide it with information which seems to suggest that it is a footpath, it may well be prepared to write a letter to the person obstructing it, saying: "From enquiries we have made to date, we think that this is a public footpath." That seems to me to be a mere assertion and may fall short of an obligation, if an obligation exists, to protect.' The ACO does impose such an obligation and provides that legal proceedings may be instituted by a district council in its own name in order to execute this obligation.

115. The ACO does not define the concept of a 'public right of way' except to state that it does not include a 'way or any other road which is maintained by a government department' (art. 2). Put simply, a public right of way is regarded as including public footpaths, bridleways and byways and is sometimes known as a 'highway'. The *Access to the Northern Ireland Countryside: Summary Report*, p. 13, provides a fuller explanation of the meaning of this concept. It states that 'a public right of way is a highway which any member of the public may use; not a privilege granted by the landowner; [it] may be created specifically or through "deemed dedication", i.e. by the public openly using the path for a period of time (in some circumstances, for as little as a few years) with the knowledge of the landowner; [it] may be limited to certain types of user, e.g. walkers only or walkers and horse riders; [it] is a permanent legal entity and remains in existence unless and until the path is extinguished or diverted by due legal process.' The legal maxim is 'once a highway, always a highway.' The summary report also notes that a public right to wander over land 'cannot arise through a tradition of use, albeit that customary access to unenclosed land may be a *de facto* reality or that people may have used land for centuries in the belief that they do so as of right.' In addition, the report notes that a right to use land for 'lawful sports and pastimes may be acquired by tradition by local inhabitants, but not by the public at large' (para. 14.1, p. 13). Finally, the report points out that trespass occurs 'when a person is on land without legal entitlement, or exceeds their rights of passage on a right of way. Trespass is nearly always a civil wrong rather than a criminal offence' (para. 14.1, p. 13). For a fuller exposition of the creation and nature of public rights of way see J. Wylie, *Irish Land Law* (2nd ed.) Professional Books, 1986, para. 6.041, and Megarry and Wade, *The Law of Real Property* (5th ed.), 1984, 844.

116. *Re Guyers' application* [1980] 2 All ER 520.

117. The term 'owner' is defined by art. 2 of the ACO as 'a person who is for the time being receiving a rent of not less than two-thirds of the net annual value of any land whether on his own account or as agent or trustee of any other person or who, if the land were let at such a rent, would receive it.'

however, relieve 'any person from any liability to maintain a public right of way.'[118] District councils are obliged to 'compile and preserve maps and other records of public rights of way in its district' (article 3(3)).[119]

## Signposts

In addition to their statutory obligation to assert, protect and maintain public rights of way, district councils are also empowered to erect and maintain signposts or similar works after due consultation with the landowner.[120] However, when exercising their aforementioned power, district councils are obliged to erect such signposts or similar works as the council considers necessary to assist someone who is unfamiliar with the locality to follow the course of the right of way (article 4(1) and (2)).

## Stiles

Article 5 imposes a statutory duty on the owner[121] of land which is crossed by a public right of way to maintain 'any stile, gate or other similar structure across a public right of way' in a 'safe condition' and to the standard of repair necessary to 'prevent unreasonable interference' with the rights of persons using the right of way. This obligation does not apply in certain circumstances to land that is being used for the purpose of agriculture or forestry and that is governed by article 6 (considered below), nor does it apply where the district council is liable, pursuant to a written agreement, for the maintenance of stiles etc. The district council is

---

118. One of the most important issues arising during negotiations relating to the assertion of a public right of way concerns the occupier's liability towards users of the right of way. The legislative framework operating in Northern Ireland concerning liability for injury or damage caused to persons on the land of another by reason of the state of the land itself is contained in the Occupiers' Liability Act (NI) 1957 and the Occupiers' Liability (NI) Order 1987. An exposition of the extent of this liability is beyond the scope of this chapter; reference should be made to the standard works on this subject, for example J. Wylie, *Irish Land Law* (2nd ed.) Professional Books, 1986. The *Access to the Northern Ireland Countryside: Summary Report*, 14, also provides a very useful summary of the legal position in this regard. It should be noted that the Law Reform Advisory Committee for Northern Ireland in April 1993 published a discussion paper on whether specific legislation is required in relation to public rights of way: *Discussion Paper no. 4: Injuries on Unadopted Public Rights of Way*, para. 6.3.2 and 6.5. The paper notes that 'it should be obvious to users of rural rights of way that the paths have not been made up and that they therefore cannot reasonably expect that degree of maintenance that would be appropriate for a properly constructed urban road or footpath.' As a result, the advisory committee proposed that any new statutory liability be limited to urban housing developments; it did not support any move towards making the owners of land which is crossed by public rights of way liable for nonfeasance, nor did it support the imposition of responsibility for all rights of way on the DoE(NI). See also: F. Barker and N. Parry, 'Private property, public access and occupiers' liability' (1995) 15 Legal Studies 335; McMillan, 'An outdated immunity?' (1991) 42 NILQ 138; and *Brady v. Northern Ireland Housing Executive* [1990] 5 NIJB 9 at 60.
119. It is important to note that the provisions of the ACO concerning the provision and maintenance of maps are much less extensive than those applying under equivalent legislation in England and Wales. See, for example, Pearlman, 'Definitive map amendment orders under the Wildlife and Countryside Act 1981' [1986] JPL 176; Chesman, 'Local authorities and the review of the definitive map under the Wildlife and Countryside Act 1981' [1991] JPL 611.
120. The definition of 'owner' for the purposes of the ACO is provided at note 117, supra.
121. Ibid.

obliged to contribute at least a quarter of the expenses reasonably incurred by the landowner in this regard, or more if it considers it reasonable in the circumstances. Where a landowner has failed to comply with this duty, the district council may take all necessary steps to repair the stile etc. and may recover all or part of the expenses incurred in this regard from the landowner. The council must give the owner or occupier of the land fourteen days notice of its intention to carry out such works.

Article 6 provides that the owner, lessee or occupier of land which is being used, or is about to be used, for the purpose of agriculture or forestry may request that the district council permit the erection of stiles, gates or other similar structures on a public right of way which crosses such land for the purpose of preventing the entry or exit of animals. Where such a request is made, the district council is empowered to authorise the erection of stiles etc. However, the council is also empowered to impose conditions concerning the maintenance of the structures and conditions that ensure that the right of way may be exercised without undue inconvenience to the public. Where the council authorises the erection of such structures on a public right of way, the right of way will be deemed to be subject to a condition that such stiles etc. are erected and maintained in accordance with the conditions set down by the council.

### Right to plough a public right of way

Articles 7 and 8 of the ACO make provision for the ploughing of a public right of way which crosses land which is being used for the purpose of agriculture or forestry and, also, for the temporary diversion of the public right of way while the land is being ploughed. The right to plough a public right of way is subject to a number of conditions (including conditions concerning the reinstatement of the right of way), violation of which is an offence under the ACO. The temporary diversion of a public right of way on account of ploughing must be authorised by the district council. Specific provisions are set down governing the factors which may be taken into account by the council in making a decision in this regard, the period during which the council may divert a public right of way, the procedure which must be followed in diverting the way, and the effect of such a diversion.

### Pasturing of bulls on land crossed by a public right of way

It is an offence to permit a bull to be at large in a field or enclosure which is crossed by a public right of way. Only the occupier of the field or enclosure will be held liable for such an offence; such a person will be liable on summary conviction to a fine not exceeding £1,000 (article 9). Article 9 does not apply to bulls under ten months of age or to bulls which are not of a recognised dairy breed and which are at large in any field or enclosure in which cows and heifers are also at large.

### Notice deterring a public right of way

It is an offence to place or maintain a notice on or near a public right of way which contains 'any false of misleading statement likely to deter the public from using the [right of] way' (article 10). A person found guilty of an offence under article 10 will be held liable on summary conviction to a fine not exceeding £200.

**Supplementary provisions concerning public rights of way**

1. The powers conferred on district councils in relation to public paths under articles 11 and 12 (outlined in section 5, below) will also apply where the council wishes to widen an existing public right of way; in such situations references to public paths will be read as references to public rights of way (article 18(2)).

2. Articles 14–16 and article 19 (outlined in section 5, below) of the ACO, which concern the permanent and temporary closure and diversion of public paths by district councils and the DoE(NI), will apply in relation to public rights of way created before or after the commencement of the ACO (22 March 1984) in the same way as they apply to public paths (article 18(3)). Articles 14–16 and 19 will not prejudice any power conferred by any other statutory provision to close or divert a road and will not affect the operation of any statutory provision relating to the closure, suspension, diversion or variation of rights of way (article 18(4)).

3. District councils are granted a general power to adopt bylaws under article 46 in relation to land which is crossed by a public right of way for the purposes of preventing damage to, and ensuring public order on, such land; the council may recover any expenses incurred in repairing damage caused by a person found guilty of breaching a bylaw adopted under article 46.[122] The council may also appoint rangers to enforce such bylaws and carry out any other duties that the council may determine (article 48).

4. A district council may provide parking places for the purpose of facilitating the use of public rights of way and may acquire land compulsorily for these purposes (article 45).

5. A district council may appoint rangers under article 48(1).

6. The DoE(NI) may provide financial assistance to district councils in connection with the exercise of their powers under the ACO (article 50).

## SECTION 5. PUBLIC PATHS

**Creation of a public path (by agreement or compulsorily)**

District councils have a discretion under article 11 of the ACO to decide whether or not to create a public path.[123] A public path may be created either pursuant to a 'public path creation agreement' under article 11, or compulsorily pursuant to a

---

122. The DoE(NI) has the power to adopt bylaws in relation to land crossed by a public right of way in default of the district council under art. 47; such bylaws have effect as if adopted by the district council.

123. A 'public path' is defined by art. 2 of the ACO as 'a way over which the public have by virtue of Article 11, 12, 15 or 16 (but subject to any conditions, limitations, orders or bye-laws) a right of way on foot, on horseback and (by virtue of Article 20) on a pedal cycle, but not using a motor vehicle.' The term 'pedal cycle' is defined in art. 2 as 'a bicycle or tricycle which is designed and constructed for propulsion solely by the physical exertions of a person or persons seated thereon.' The term 'motor vehicle' is defined by art. 2 as including a motorbicycle.

124. It is important to note that art. 53 of the ACO makes special provision for public access to land owned by the Crown, that is, land that belongs to a Government department or that is held in trust for Her Majesty for the purposes of a Government department.

'public path creation order' made under article 12.[124] Where a public path is created by agreement, the district council may enter into the agreement with any person who possesses the power to do so; the path creation agreement may subject public use of the path to agreed conditions or limitations and may contain terms as to payment.

In the event that a district council considers that the creation of a public path is both necessary and expedient, and that it would be impracticable to create the path by agreement, it may create a public path compulsorily by means of a public path creation order.[125] It is important to note that in deciding whether or not the creation of a public path would be expedient, the district council must have regard:

(i) to the extent to which the path would add to the convenience or enjoyment of a substantial section of the public, or to the convenience of persons residing in the district, and

(ii) to the effect which the creation of the path would have on the rights of persons interested[126] in the land, account being taken of the provisions as to compensation contained in Article 17 [considered below].

Article 18(1) provides that where a district council is considering making a public path creation order or entering into a public path creation agreement it must consult the DoE(NI) and any other body which appears to the council to be representative of those likely to be affected by the agreement or order. The district council must submit a public path creation order to the DoE(NI) for confirmation where it is opposed; the council is only empowered to confirm the order itself where the order is unopposed.

Schedule 1 to the ACO sets out the procedures that must be followed by the district council when making a public path creation order. Regulation 3 and Schedule 1 to the Access to the Countryside Regulations (NI) 1984[127] set out the required contents of, and format for, public path creation orders. Regulation 6 sets out the procedures which must be followed by district councils when submitting an opposed public path creation order to the DoE(NI) for confirmation and the notification requirements which must be satisfied once an opposed order has been confirmed by the DoE(NI) or when district councils are themselves confirming an unopposed order. Schedule 3 to the 1984 Regulations contains the form for a notice confirming a public path order. Finally, article 56 and Schedule 3 to the ACO provide that public path creation orders and agreements must be registered in the Statutory Charges Register under Schedule 11 to the Lands Registration Act (NI) 1970.

## Closure of a public path

A district council may close a public path on the grounds that it is not needed for

---

125. A right of way created compulsorily may be unconditional or subject to such conditions or limitations as may be specified in the public path creation order (art. 12(2)).

126. The term 'interest' in relation to land is defined by art. 2 of the ACO as including 'any right over land, whether the right is exercisable by virtue of the ownership of an interest in land or by virtue of a licence or agreement, and in particular includes sporting and fishing rights.'

127. SR No. 342.

public use. In such an event the council will issue a 'public path extinguishment order' (article 14(1)).[128] Where the order is opposed, it must be submitted to the DoE(NI) for confirmation, otherwise it may be confirmed by the council itself. Article 14(2) provides that an extinguishment order may not be confirmed by either the DoE(NI) or a district council unless they are satisfied that it is expedient to close the public path, having regard to: (i) the extent to which the path is likely to be used by the public[129] and (ii) the likely effect of the closure on land that is served by the path; in both instances the provisions for compensation (laid down in article 17, below) must also be taken into account by the council. Article 14(6) provides that any 'temporary circumstances' which 'prevent or diminish' the public's capacity to use the path should be disregarded for these purposes.

Article 18(1) provides that before making a public path extinguishment order a district council must consult the DoE(NI) and any other body which appears to the council to be representative of those likely to be affected by the order. Schedule 1 to the ACO governs the procedure which must be followed by the district council when making a public path extinguishment order. Regulation 3 of the Access to the Countryside Regulations (NI) 1984[130] and the form in Part I of the Schedule to the Access to the Countryside (Amendment) Regulations (NI) 1985[131] govern the content of, and format for, an extinguishment order. Regulation 6 of the 1984 Regulations governs the procedure which must be followed by a district council when submitting an opposed order to the DoE(NI) for confirmation and the notification requirements which must be satisfied once the opposed order has been confirmed by the DoE(NI) or when the district council is itself confirming an unopposed order. Schedule 3 to the 1984 Regulations contains the form for a notice confirming a public path order. Preliminary proceedings for the confirmation of an extinguishment order may be held concurrently with proceedings for the confirmation of a public path creation or diversion order and, in such a situation, the district council or DoE(NI) may consider the extent to which the new or diverted path would provide an alternative path when assessing whether the path is needed for public use and the extent to which the path is likely to be used by the public.

Article 14 of the ACO will not prejudice any power conferred by any other statutory provision to close or divert a road and will not affect the operation of any statutory provision relating to the closure, suspension, diversion or variation of rights of way (article 18(4)). The DoE(NI) itself may make a public path extinguishment order under article 16 of the ACO where it is satisfied that it is necessary to do so to enable either: (i) development in accordance with planning

---

128. Art. 19 and art. 18(4) of the ACO make provision for the temporary closure of public paths in the interests of good farming or forestry or otherwise. It is important to note that art. 53 of the ACO makes special provision for public access to land that is owned by the Crown, that is, land that belongs to a government department or that is held in trust for Her Majesty for the purposes of a Government department.

129. In this regard see the following cases concerning similar provisions of the Highways Act 1980 (s. 116, 118, and 119) which applies in England and Wales: *R. v. Secretary of State for the Environment, ex parte Stewart* [1980] JPL 175; *Ramblers' Association v. Kent CC* [1991] JPL 530; *R. v. Secretary of State for the Environment, ex parte Cheshire CC* [1991] JPL 537.

130. SR No. 324.

131. SR No. 152.

permission or (ii) development by a Government department, to be carried out. With the exception of article 14(1), (2) and (6), the provisions of article 14 outlined above in relation to district council path extinguishment orders will apply to the making of a DoE(NI) path extinguishment order under article 16. The provisions of Schedule 1 to the ACO, regulation 3 of the Access to the Countryside Regulations (NI) 1984[132] and the form in Part I of the Schedule to the Access to the Countryside (Amendment) Regulations (NI) 1985[133] govern the procedures, format and content of a DoE(NI) path extinguishment order in an identical manner to that explained above in relation to district council path extinguishment orders under article 14. Similarly, regulation 6 and Schedule 3 to the 1984 Regulations, respectively, govern the notification requirements which must be satisfied once the DoE(NI) has made an order and the form which the notice making the order must take.

Finally, article 56 and Schedule 3 to the ACO provide that all public path extinguishment orders must be registered in the Statutory Charges Register under Schedule 11 to the Land Registration Act (NI) 1970.

### Diversion of a public path

A district council may divert the line of a public path, or part of the line, by means of a 'public path diversion order' where the council considers that it is in the interests of the owner, lessee or occupier of the land that is crossed by the path. In doing so, the path may be diverted onto the land of the same person or onto land owned by another person (article 15).[134]

The path diversion order may create any new path, or extinguish any existing path, as is necessary to effect the diversion. The use of the new path may be conditional or unconditional; it does not matter whether use of the extinguished path was conditional or unconditional. As with path creation and extinguishment orders, the diversion order must be confirmed by the DoE(NI) where the order is opposed, or by the council itself where the order is unopposed. Article 15(2) provides that the district council may carry out such work as appears to it to be necessary to facilitate the convenient use of the new path; the old path may be extinguished some time after the new path is created in order to enable work on the new path to be completed.

Where an owner, lessee or occupier of land requests that a path diversion order be made, the district council may require him to make an agreed contribution towards the compensation payable under article 17 (considered below) or to the expenses incurred by the council in bringing the new path to a state fit for public use. Article 15(5) provides that neither the district council nor the DoE(NI) can confirm a path diversion order unless they are satisfied:
  (i)  that the diversion is expedient in the interests of the lessee, owner or occupier of the land in question;

---

132. SR No. 324.
133. SR No. 152.
134. Art. 19 and art. 18(4) of the ACO make provision for the temporary diversion of public paths in the interests of good farming or forestry or otherwise. It is important to note that art. 53 of the ACO makes special provision for public access to land that is owned by the Crown, that is, land that belongs to a Government department or that is held in trust for Her Majesty for the purposes of a Government department.

(ii) that the path will not be rendered 'substantially less convenient' to the public as a result of the diversion; and

(iii) that it is expedient to confirm the diversion, having regard to: (*a*) the effect the diversion would have on 'public enjoyment of the path as a whole or of any other path,' (*b*) the effect the diversion order would have on other land which is served by the existing right of way, and (*c*) the effect any new right of way created by the diversion order would have on the land crossed by the new right and on any land held with that land. When considering the factors listed in (*b*) and (*c*) above the district council or DoE(NI) is required to take the provisions of article 17 concerning compensation into account.

Article 18(1) provides that before making a public path diversion order a district council must consult the DoE(NI) and any other body which appears to the council to be representative of those likely to be affected by the order. Schedule 1 to the ACO governs the procedures which the district council must satisfy when making a path diversion order. Regulation 3 and Schedule 1 (form number 3) to the Access to the Countryside Regulations (NI) 1984[135] govern the form and content of a diversion order. Regulation 6 sets out the procedure which must be followed by the district council when submitting an opposed diversion order to the DoE(NI) for confirmation and the notification requirements which must be satisfied once the order has been confirmed by the DoE(NI) or by the district council if it is unopposed. Schedule 3 to the 1984 Regulations contains the form for a notice confirming a public path order.

As with the closure of public paths, the DoE(NI) may make a path diversion order under article 16 of the ACO where it considers that it is necessary to do so in order to allow development to be carried out either pursuant to planning permission or by a Government department. The provisions of article 15, as outlined above in relation to district council diversion orders, apply to diversion orders made by the DoE(NI) under article 16, with the exception of the requirements laid down in article 15(5) which require certain factors to be considered by a district council before such an order is confirmed. As is the case in relation to district council diversion orders under article 15, Schedule 1 to the ACO, regulation 3 and Schedule 1 (form number 3) to the Access to the Countryside Regulations (NI) 1984[136] govern the procedures, format and content of a DoE(NI) path diversion order. Similarly, regulation 6 and Schedule 3 to the 1984 Regulations, respectively, govern the notification requirements which must be satisfied when a DoE(NI) path diversion is made and the form which the notice making the order must take.

Articles 15 and 16 will not prejudice any power conferred by any other statutory provision to close or divert a road and will not affect the operation of any statutory provision relating to the closure, suspension, diversion or variation of rights of way (article 18(4)). Finally, it should be noted that article 56 and Schedule 3 to the ACO provide that all public path diversion orders must be registered in the Statutory Charges Register under Schedule 11 to the Land Registration Act (NI) 1970.

---

135. SR No. 342.
136. Ibid.

## Maintenance of a public path

Once a public path has been created, either by agreement or compulsorily, or where the district council has made a public path diversion order, the council is obliged to carry out such work as is necessary to bring the path to a state which is fit for public use in conformity with the terms and conditions laid down in the path creation order or agreement; the council is also obliged to maintain the path in such a state (article 13).

## Bylaws

District councils are granted a general power to adopt bylaws under article 46 in relation to land which is crossed by a public path for the purposes of preventing damage to, and ensuring public order on, such land. The council may recover any expenses incurred in repairing damage caused by a person found guilty of breaching a bylaw adopted under article 46.[137] The council may also appoint rangers to enforce such bylaws and carry out any other duties which the council may determine (article 48).

## Compensation

Where a public path creation, diversion or extinguishment order depreciates the value of an interest in land, or where it causes any person to suffer damage as a result of being disturbed in his enjoyment of land, article 17 of the ACO provides that compensation may be payable to such a person. Compensation will be equal to the amount of the depreciation or damage and will be paid by the body making the order in question, i.e. either the district council or the DoE(NI). Article 17(3), however, goes on to provide that a person cannot claim a right to compensation under this provision unless the right of way created as a result of the creation or diversion order 'would have been actionable at [the suit of the claimant] if it had been effected otherwise than in the exercise of statutory powers.' Article 17(2)(a)–(c) sets out the procedure which must be followed when making a claim for compensation.

## Statutory undertakers and public paths

Neither the district council nor the DoE(NI) may make or confirm a public path creation, extinguishment or diversion order relating to a right of way 'over land under, in, upon, over, along or across which there is an apparatus belonging to or used by any statutory undertakers[138] for the purpose of their undertaking' unless the statutory undertakers have consented to the making or confirmation of the order (article 18(7)). Such consent may be given subject to the condition that the order include such provisions for the protection of the statutory undertaker as they

---

137. The DoE(NI) has the power to adopt bylaws in relation to land crossed by a public path in default of the district council under art. 47; such bylaws have effect as if adopted by the district council.
138. A 'statutory undertaker' is defined in art. 2 of the ACO as 'any persons authorised by any statutory provision to carry on any railway, canal, inland navigation, dock, harbour, gas, electricity, or other public undertaking and includes the Post Office and British Telecommunications.'

may reasonably require. Article 18(8), however, goes on to provide that a statutory undertaker may not withhold its consent unreasonably; any dispute arising as to: (i) whether the withholding of consent is unreasonable or (ii) whether any request is reasonable, must be determined by arbitration. Finally, article 18(9) makes provision for the situation where a British Telecom telegraphic line lies under, in, upon, over, along or across a public path which is the subject of a public path extinguishment or diversion order.

### Cyclists and public paths

Article 20 provides that any member of the public has, as a right of way, the right to ride a pedal cycle on any public path, but in exercising that right, cyclists must give way to pedestrians and persons on horseback. This provision will have effect subject to any orders or bylaws made by district councils. Article 20 does not impose an obligation on district councils to facilitate the use of paths by cyclists.

### Parking facilities

A district council may provide parking places to facilitate the use of public paths and to this end may acquire land compulsorily (article 45).

### Financial assistance for district councils

The DoE(NI) may provide financial assistance to a district council in relation to expenditure incurred in exercising its powers under the ACO (article 50). The amount of the grants awarded by the DoE(NI) in recent years for the purpose of ensuring access to the countryside is listed in the *Environment Service Reports, 1991–93* and *1993–95* and the *Environment Service Corporate Plan, 1994–97*. Article 18(5) and (6) make provision for the defrayment (as between district councils) of expenses incurred, and the maintenance of public paths, where a public path creation, diversion or extinguishment order affects the district of more than one district council.

## SECTION 6. LONG-DISTANCE ROUTES

Articles 21–24 make provision for the creation of long-distance routes[139] where it appears to the district council that the public should be enabled to make 'extensive journeys on foot, on pedal cycles or on horseback along such a route,' and also for the provision of ferries, meals, accommodation and refreshments for the purpose of long-distance routes.[140]

Where a district council wishes to create a long-distance route it must prepare and submit a report of its proposals to the DoE(NI); detailed requirements governing the contents of the report are laid down in article 21. Once the proposal is approved, the district council is under a duty to ensure that the proposal is

---

139. Art. 21(1) defines a long-distance route as a route 'which for the whole or greater part of its length does not pass along roads mainly used by vehicles.'

140. District councils are also given compulsory purchase powers for land needed in connection with the provision of such facilities: see art. 23(3) (ferries) and 24(5) (accommodation etc.).

implemented (article 22(2)). However, the DoE(NI) may provide financial assistance to the council in relation to expenses incurred by the council in exercising its powers under the ACO and to any body or person who assists in the implementation of an approved proposal for a long-distance route (article 50). District councils are also granted a general power to adopt bylaws under article 46 in relation to land which is crossed by a long-distance route for the purpose of preventing damage to, and ensuring public order on, such land; the council may recover any expenses incurred in repairing damage caused by a person found guilty of breaching a bylaw adopted under article 46.[141] Thus far, there is only one long-distance route in Northern Ireland, namely, the 'Ulster Way'. The *Access to the Northern Ireland Countryside: Summary Report* (1994) noted that a detailed assessment of the route found that 'despite the quality of much of the scenery through which it passes, the Ulster Way has significant deficiencies and is unable to meet the high standards expected of a "national trail".'[142]

## SECTION 7. ACCESS TO OPEN COUNTRY

Part III (articles 25–42) of the ACO regulates the provision of public access to 'open country'[143] for the purpose of open-air recreation.[144] Article 25(2) provides that Part III of the ACO applies to either:

(i)   land which 'is, or which gives or forms part of access to open country' and is land to which article 26 applies by reason of an access agreement or an access order; or

(ii)  land which was acquired by a district council or the DoE(NI) under articles 39 and 40, respectively, for the purpose of providing public access.

In effect, Part III of the ACO empowers district councils, in consultation with the DoE(NI) and other interested bodies,[145] to identify land which falls within the definition of 'open country' and to assess what action should be taken to secure public access to open country for the purpose of open-air recreation (i.e. whether it is necessary to ensure public access by means of an access agreement or compulsorily by means of an access order, or whether it is necessary to acquire the land in order to secure public access). In considering what action should be taken to ensure public access to open country, article 27(2) provides that the district

---

141. The DoE(NI) has the power to adopt bylaws in relation to land crossed by a long-distance route in default of the district council under art. 47; such bylaws have effect as if adopted by the district council.

142. London: HMSO, para. 5.2, p. 20. The report details the nature of the deficiencies and, at para. 8.1, p. 34, makes a number of recommendations for reform in this context.

143. In this context 'open country' is defined by art. 25(2) as any land which consists 'wholly or predominantly of mountain, moor, heath, hill, woodland, cliff, foreshore, marsh, bog or waterway.' The term 'waterway' is defined in art. 2 of the ACO as 'any lough, river, reservoir, canal or tidal or coastal waters, being (in any case) water suitable, or which can reasonably be rendered suitable, for sailing, boating, bathing, fishing or other water sport or recreation.'

144. The term 'open air recreation' is not defined by the ACO. However, it is worth noting that s. 114(1) of the National Parks and Access to the Countryside Act 1949, which forms part of the legislative framework operating in Great Britain, provides that open-air recreation does not include organised games.

145. Art. 27(1) requires that district councils consult 'such bodies as appear to the district council to be representative of owners and occupiers of land . . .'

council must have regard to all the 'relevant circumstances', including, as a matter of general concern, 'the extent to which there is a need for greater facilities in the district for such access, whether for persons living in the district or for other persons,' and in relation to particular land, 'the extent to which public access to open country for the purpose of open-air recreation is likely to be available without such action being taken' by the district council.

Once an access order or access agreement has been made in respect of an area of open country, article 26(1) provides that a person who is on such land or enters such land for the purpose of open-air recreation, without causing damage, will not be treated as a trespasser on that land nor will they incur any other liability as a result of having entered the land or being on the land. However, it is important to note that article 26(2), (3) and (4) imposes the following limitations on the operation of article 26(1):

(i) Article 26(1) will not apply to 'excepted land'[146] unless the access agreement provides that article 26(1) does apply (article 26(2)(*a*)).

(ii) Article 26(1) will not entitle a person to enter, or to be on any land, or to do anything on that land which is in violation of any prohibition contained in, or which has effect under, any statutory provision (article 26(2)(*b*)).

(iii) An access agreement or order may contain provisions that restrict public access to the land in question; such provisions may include restrictions which exclude the public's right of access for certain periods. Article 26(1) will not apply to any person who enters the land or who is on the land in violation of restrictions contained in an access agreement or order (article 26(3)).

(iv) Article 26(1) will have effect subject to the provisions of Schedule 2 to the ACO, which contains a general list of activities that are always prohibited in open country (article 26(4)).

The following sections outline the more specific provisions of the ACO relating to access agreements and orders, compensation, the enforcement and suspension of such orders and agreements, the issue of safe and sufficient access, the acquisition of land for public access, maps and boundaries.

---

146. Art. 26(5) defines 'excepted land' as 'land which for the time being is of any of the descriptions contained in Schedule 3.' Sch. 3 to the ACO has been amended by Sch. 4 to the Nature Conservation and Amenity Lands (NI) Order 1985 (SI 1985/170). Sch. 3, as amended, lists eight types of land; briefly they are: (i) land used for agriculture, (ii) land comprised in a declaration under art. 16 of the Nature Conservation and Amenity Lands (NI) Order 1985 (declaration of land as a Nature Reserve) where a bylaw prohibits entry to the Reserve (see chap. 7), (iii) land covered by buildings or the curtilage of such land, (iv) land already used for the purposes of a park, garden, or pleasure ground at the date when the relevant access agreement or order was made, (v) land used for the purposes of a railway, golf course, sports ground, playing field or aerodrome or for getting minerals by surface working, (vi) land that does not fall into earlier categories but which is covered by works used for the purposes of a statutory undertaking or the curtilage of such land (definition of 'statutory undertaking', supra, n. 138), (vii) land excepted from art. 26 under art. 30 (agricultural land), and (viii) land on which development is in progress as a result of which it will become land falling into categories iii, v, or vi. However, art. 26(5) goes on to say that land which is comprised in an access agreement or order will not be regarded as 'excepted land' by reason of any development that is carried out on the land if the development is one which requires planning permission but either the planning permission has not been granted, or any condition subject to which it has been granted has been violated.

## Access agreements

Article 28 governs the powers of district councils to enter into access agreements. Access agreements may be entered into with any person who has an interest in the land in question;[147] the agreement may contain agreed provisions concerning revocation or variation of the agreement and may make provision for the district council to make payment in consideration for the agreement[148] and/or to make contributions to any expense incurred by the person making the agreement as a result of entering into the agreement. Where an access agreement is entered into with one or some, but not all, of the people with interests[149] in the land in question, article 28(5) provides that Part III of the ACO will not operate so as to prejudice a non-party's rights in relation to that interest, nor will Part III impose any restriction on a non-party or confer any right against such a person. In addition, the district council is obliged to serve a copy of the agreement on every person who has an interest in the land in question but who is not a party to the agreement as soon as may be after it has been concluded. An access agreement may also contain various provisions for the purpose of securing safe and sufficient public access to the land in question; more specific district council powers in this regard are outlined below.

Finally, article 56 and Schedule 3 to the ACO provide that an access agreement must be registered in the Statutory Charges Register under Schedule 11 to the Land Registration Act (NI) 1970; similarly, any instrument or order that varies or revokes an access agreement must also be registered. District council and DoE(NI) powers to vary or revoke access agreements are outlined below.

## Access orders

In the event that there is no effective access agreement in operation in relation to an area of open country and it appears to the district council that it would be 'impracticable' to enter into an access agreement, article 29 provides that the council may secure public access to the land for the purpose of open-air recreation compulsorily by making an access order.[150] The district council is always obliged to submit the order to the DoE(NI) for confirmation (regardless of whether the order is opposed or not); the Department itself cannot confirm an access order

---

147. Any person who has the powers of a tenant for life may enter into such an agreement in relation to the settled land or any part of the land either for consideration or gratuitously (art. 28(4)). It is important to note that art. 53 of the ACO makes special provision for public access to land which is owned by the Crown, that is, land which belongs to a Government department or which is held in trust for Her Majesty for the purposes of a Government department.
148. Art. 28(2) provides that payments of this nature must be made 'on the basis of an assessment of the capital value of the land arrived at in accordance with the provisions of Schedule 4 [to the ACO]'.
149. The term 'interest' in this context is defined by art. 2 of the ACO as including 'any right over land, whether the right is exercisable by virtue of the ownership of an interest in land or by virtue of a licence or agreement, and in particular includes sporting and fishing rights.'
150. In the context of compulsory powers, it is important to note that art. 53 of the ACO makes special provision for public access to land which is owned by the Crown, see supra, note 147.

before bylaws have been adopted and confirmed under article 46 of the ACO or adopted under article 47 (default powers in relation to bylaws).

Schedule 1 to the ACO governs the procedure which must be followed by the district council before submitting an access order to the DoE(NI) for confirmation; regulations 4 and 5 of the Access to the Countryside Regulations (NI) 1984[151] and the form contained in Part II of the Schedule to the Access to the Countryside (Amendment) Regulations (NI) 1985[152] govern the content and form of an access order. Regulation 6 of the 1984 Regulations governs the procedure which must be followed by the district council when submitting an access order to the DoE(NI) for confirmation and also the notification requirements which must be satisfied once an order has been confirmed by the DoE(NI). Part III of the 1985 Regulations contains the amended form for a notice confirming an access order. An access order may also contain provisions for the purpose of securing safe and sufficient public access to the land in question; more specific district council powers in this regard are outlined below.

Article 56 and Schedule 3 to the ACO provide that an access order must be registered in the Statutory Charges Register under Schedule 11 to the Land Registration Act (NI) 1970; similarly, any instrument or order which varies or revokes an access order must also be registered. District council and DoE(NI) powers to vary or revoke access orders are outlined below.

### Effect of an access agreement or order on the rights and liabilities of persons with interests in the land in question[153]

Article 31(1) of the ACO provides that a person with an interest[154] in land which is the subject of an access agreement or order is prohibited from carrying out any work on that land which would substantially reduce the area to which the public have access under the agreement or order; this provision does not, however, affect activities on land whereby the land becomes 'excepted land' under article 26(5).[155] Article 31(2) provides that any restriction arising under a covenant or otherwise, concerning the use of land which is the subject of an access order or agreement, will have effect subject to the terms of Part III of the ACO; any liability of a person 'with an interest in such land in respect of such a restriction shall be limited accordingly'. Finally, public use of land in accordance with an access order or agreement will be disregarded for the purpose of presuming the grant of an

---

151. SR No. 342.

152. SR No. 152.

153. As already stated, the issue of occupiers' liability is beyond the scope of this book. See note 118, supra, for further details of standard works on this issue.

154. The definition of 'interest' in this context is provided at note 126, supra.

155. The term 'excepted land' is defined at note 146, supra. Art. 33(1) provides that where a person violates the terms of art. 31(1) (or art. 32(1) concerning the provision of safe and secure access) the district council has the power to serve that person with a notice requiring him to carry out such work as the council considers necessary to remedy the breach; the notice will specify the required works and the time within which it should be completed. If the person on whom the notice is served fails to carry out the required work within the time specified in the notice, the district council is then empowered to take all necessary steps to carry out the work and to recover expenses reasonably incurred in doing so (art. 31(2)). Art. 33(3) makes provision for appealing against such a notice and also sets out the powers of the court hearing the appeal.

easement or a right of way under any rule of law or statutory provision (article 31(3)).[156]

### Compensation for access orders

Where the adoption of an access order results either in the value of a person's interest in land being depreciated or in a person suffering damage as a result of their enjoyment of the land being disturbed, article 35(1) provides that the district council must pay compensation to that person equal to the amount of the damage or depreciation. However, article 35(2) goes on to provide that article 35(1) will not entitle a person to compensation for disturbance or depreciation if the land in which that person has an interest is not subject to the access order, or if the land in question is excepted land under article 26(5) (explained above).

There are, however, two exceptions to the exception created by article 35(2) namely, compensation will be payable if:

(i)   the depreciated land, or land whose enjoyment has been disturbed, is held with land which is not excepted land and which is subject to the access order, or

(ii)  the failure to exclude the public from land which is subject to the access order or any part of that land would have been actionable at the suit of the person seeking compensation if the access order had not been adopted.

Article 36 provides that compensation cannot be claimed or paid under article 35 until a period of five years has expired from the date on which the access order giving rise to the claim for compensation came into operation, the rationale being, to enable compensation payable under article 35 to be assessed in the light of experience gained of the actual effect which public access has had on the land. It should be noted, however, that article 38 makes provision for the payment of compensation 'on account' within the five-year period on the grounds of 'special circumstances'.[157] Article 36(2), (3) and (4) then sets out the criteria which must be considered when calculating the compensation payable at the end of the five-year period; the position concerning compensation should the access order be varied or revoked during the five-year period; and the position concerning the assessment of compensation should two or more adjacent or contiguous areas of land become subject to access orders at different stages within the five-year period. Article 37 sets out the procedure which must be followed by a person when actually making a claim for compensation and interest under article 35. Finally, article 49 contains various supplementary provisions concerning applications for, and disputes concerning, compensation under the ACO.

---

156. It should also be noted that art. 52 of the ACO provides that the following provision should be added to the end of s. 1 of the Occupiers' Liability Act (NI) 1957 (c. 25): 'A person entering any premises in exercise of rights conferred by virtue of an access agreement or order under the Access to the Countryside (NI) Order 1983 is not, for the purposes of this Act, a visitor of the occupier of those premises.'

157. The term 'special circumstances' is not defined by the ACO. However, art. 38 provides that a person may appeal a district council's refusal to make a payment on account, and where the council agrees to make a certain payment on account, a person may appeal the council's assessment of the amount which should be paid.

## Arrangements for land used for agricultural purposes

Article 30(1), (2) and (4) provides that where a representation is made to the DoE(NI) to the effect that land:

(i)  is being used, or being brought into use, for agriculture or forestry and that public access would prejudice that use or proposed use of the land, or

(ii) is being used to grow trees for the purpose of providing a valuable neighbourhood amenity and that public access to the area would prejudice the growth or regeneration of the trees

the DoE(NI) has the power to do any of the following:

(*a*)  the Department may refuse to confirm a proposed access order; or

(*b*)  it may vary an access order so as to exclude land from public access;[158] or

(*c*)  it may request that a district council vary an existing access agreement so as to exclude land from public access.[159]

Article 30 imposes a variety of conditions which must be satisfied by the Department before it exercises any of its power in this regard. Before outlining these conditions, it should be noted that the conditions vary according to which power the Department proposes to use (i.e. in *(a)*, *(b)* or *(c)*). The conditions are as follows:

1. Article 30(1), (2) and (4) requires that in all situations (i.e. regardless of whether the Department intends to use its power in *(a)*, *(b)*, or *(c)*) the Department must be satisfied that the conditions listed in *(i)* and *(ii)* above are fulfilled and also that they 'outweigh the benefit arising from the increased facilities for public access'.

2. Article 30(5) provides that the DoE(NI) may not reach a conclusion concerning a request to vary an existing access agreement or order unless it has either held a local inquiry into the issue, or has afforded both the district council in question and the person making the request an opportunity to be heard by a person appointed by the Department and, in either case, has considered the report submitted by the person holding the inquiry or hearing the two parties. It should be noted that references to varying an access agreement or order, so as to exclude land from public access, include references to varying an agreement or order by the imposition of such restrictions under article 26(3) of the ACO as are regarded as necessary by the DoE(NI) for the purposes of article 30. The terms of article 26(3) are outlined below in number 3.

3. Article 30(6) provides that when determining whether the conditions listed in *(i)* and *(ii)* above are satisfied in the context of any proposed access order, the

---

158. Where the DoE(NI) decides to vary an existing access order for the reasons stated in art. 30, so as to exclude land from public access under art. 26, the variation will be made by an order adopted by the DoE(NI) (art. 30(4)).

159. Where the DoE(NI) decides that an access agreement should be varied for the reasons laid down in art. 30, so as to exclude land from public access, the DoE(NI) will notify the district council that entered into the agreement of its decision, and the council itself will make the variation (art. 30(2)). The fact that the access agreement was expressed to be irrevocable will not prevent the variation of the agreement in this context (art. 30(3)(*a*)); in the event that the district council cannot obtain the agreement concerning the variation from all parties to the agreement (or their successors in title), the council is empowered to vary the agreement by order, with the approval of the DoE(NI) (art. 30(3)(*b*)).

Department must have regard to the terms of article 26(3) of the ACO. Article 26(3) provides that an access order may contain provisions which restrict public access to the land in question, including restrictions on access for certain periods.

## Provisions concerning safe and sufficient access

Articles 32, 34 and 42 all concern issues of safety on land which is subject to an access order or agreement; article 32 also makes provision for ensuring sufficient access to such land.

Article 32(1) provides than an access agreement or order may make such provision as is expedient for the purposes of securing safe and sufficient access for the public, and lists a number of provisions which may be included in an agreement or order in this regard. To the extent to which these provisions require the carrying on of works, article 32(4), (5) and (6) governs agreements between district councils and owners and occupiers of the land as to who will carry out the work, payment for such work, the position in the event that the agreed work is not completed, and the position in the event that a district council is unable to make an agreement to have such work carried out.

Article 33 sets out the enforcement powers conferred on district councils in the event that a person violates any restriction imposed under article 32(1) on the doing of any thing which would detrimentally affect any means of access to land which is subject to an access order or agreement.[160] Similarly, article 33 governs district councils' enforcement powers in the event that any person violates the terms of article 31(1) (see page 440).

Article 34 empowers the district council to exclude public access to land which is subject to an access agreement or order, or any part of that land, where the council is satisfied that the prevailing weather conditions are likely to result in fires occurring on that land.

Article 42 provides that a district council may, in consultation with the owner and occupier of the land, delimit certain areas of land which are subject to an access agreement or order where the council considers it necessary to avoid danger to the public or to persons employed on the land. To this end, the district council may vary an agreement or order so as to exclude such land from public access (either by order or by agreement); in addition, it may carry out such works as appear necessary to protect the public from any source of danger on the land or adjoining land.[161] Article 42(6) also governs the application of article 26 to land which contains 'any factory, magazine, store or premises' established before or after the commencement of the ACO and whether such land can be regarded as an 'open place of resort for the public, or a public place' under the Explosives Acts (NI) 1875–1970 or any order made or licence granted under those Acts.

---

160. The district council's powers under art. 33 are set out in note 155, supra.
161. Art. 42(4) provides that the district council's power to carry out such works applies both in relation to land that is subject to an access agreement or order, or, to land which is held by the district council and which was acquired by the council under art. 39 for the purposes of providing public access. Art. 42(5) also confers identical powers on the DoE(NI) in relation to land which is held by the DoE(NI) and which was purchased by the Department for the purpose of providing public access under art. 40 of the ACO.

### Acquisition of land by district councils for the purpose of public access

District councils are empowered to acquire land by agreement and compulsorily for the purpose of providing public access where the land 'gives or forms part of access to open country' (article 39(1)). The district council's powers in this regard may only be used where the council concludes that it is necessary that the public should have access to that open country for open-air recreation and that it is expedient to acquire the land in the circumstances; its powers of compulsory acquisition can only be used where it appears to the council to be impracticable to obtain public access by means of an access order or agreement or by acquiring the land by agreement.

Once land has been acquired for these purposes (whether by agreement or compulsorily), the district council is then empowered to carry out such work on that land as the council considers necessary for the purpose of providing a convenient means of access to the land, or any other work which is necessary for the provision of public access to the land for the purpose of open-air recreation. However, the council is obliged (for the duration of the period during which the land is held by the council for the purpose of providing public access) to manage the land so as to ensure that as much of the land as is practicable[162] is available for public access for the purpose of open-air recreation. Finally, a district council may provide parking places to facilitate the use of land which is subject to public access, and to this end may acquire land compulsorily (article 45).

### Acquisition of land by the DoE(NI) for the purpose of public access

Article 40 of the ACO, as amended by Schedule 4 to the Nature Conservation and Amenity Lands (NI) Order 1985,[163] confers powers of acquisition on the DoE(NI) which are equivalent to those conferred on district councils under article 39 of the ACO (above). In effect, the DoE(NI) is empowered (subject to the approval of the Department of Finance and Personnel) to acquire land either by agreement, by way of purchase, lease, exchange, or compulsorily, in accordance with articles 6 and 10 of the Nature Conservation and Amenity Lands (NI) Order 1985.[164] As with district council powers, the DoE(NI) may only use its powers of acquisition in relation to land which 'is or which forms part of access to open country' and where the Department concludes that it is necessary that the public should have

---

162. In determining what is 'practicable' the district council must have regard to the following factors: (i) the nature of the various parts of the land in question; (ii) whether anything done on the land will expose the public or people working on the land to danger unless public access to the land or to adjoining land is restricted; and (iii) all other relevant circumstances (art. 39(3)). It should also be noted that the district council's powers in relation to safety on land which is subject to an access order or agreement also apply in relation to land acquired by a district council under art. 39. These powers are outlined under the general heading 'Provisions concerning safe and sufficient access', p. 443.
163. SI 1985/170.
164. Art. 6 of the Nature Conservation and Amenity Lands (NI) Order 1985 relates to the acquisition and disposal of amenity lands. Art. 10 sets out the DoE(NI)'s powers to carry out works and provide facilities on land acquired under art. 6 of the 1985 Order. The terms of arts 6 and 10 are outlined in Part I, section 1 of this chapter.

access to that open country for open-air recreation and that it is expedient to acquire the land in the circumstances.

### District council obligations to prepare and maintain maps of land subject to public access

Article 41 imposes an obligation on district councils to prepare and update a map[165] which defines[166] the following areas of land:

(i) any land within the council's district which is subject to an access agreement or an access order and any land therein which is excepted land,[167] and

(ii) any land which has been acquired either by the district council or the DoE(NI) under articles 39 or 40 (outlined above) which is, for the time being, held for the purpose of providing public access; the map must also define any areas within such land from which the public are excluded for the purpose of avoiding danger or for other purposes.

Once the map has been prepared, the district council is under two further obligations:

(i) it must place copies of the map (on an appropriate scale) and notices which specify: (*a*) any restrictions which have been imposed on access to the land or any part of the land and (*b*) whether the restrictions have effect by virtue of the ACO or any other provisions, at such places as it thinks fit, including places where the public obtain access to the land in question;

(ii) it must make copies of the map and of the above notices available for inspection by the public at such places as the council may determine.

Finally, district councils have the power to erect and maintain notices or other markers for the purpose of indicating the boundaries of the land which is subject to an access agreement or order and the boundaries of excepted land (article 43).[168]

### Bylaws

District councils are granted a general power to adopt bylaws under article 46 in relation to land which is either the subject of an access order or agreement, or is land to which the public has access as a result of being acquired (under Part III of the ACO) by the DoE(NI) or the district council. Such bylaws must be adopted for the purpose of providing public access to the land ·and for the purpose of preventing damage to, and ensuring public order on, such land. The council may recover any expenses incurred in repairing damage caused by a person found guilty of breaching a bylaw adopted under article 46.[169] The council may also appoint rangers to enforce such bylaws, and may carry out any other duties that the council may determine (article 48).

---

165. The precise scale of these maps is prescribed in the Access to the Countryside Regulations (NI) 1984 (SR No. 342).

166. The manner in which such areas are to be defined is prescribed under the Access to the Countryside Regulations (NI) 1984 (SR No. 342).

167. The term 'excepted land' is defined at note 146, supra.

168. Ibid.

169. The DoE(NI) has the power to adopt bylaws in relation to public access land in default of the district council under art. 47; such bylaws have effect as if adopted by the district council.

**Financial assistance from the DoE(NI)**

As is the case in relation to district council powers throughout the ACO, the DoE(NI) may provide financial assistance to councils in relation to expenditure incurred in the exercise of their powers concerning the provision of public access to open country (article 50). The amount of grants awarded by the Department in recent years for the purpose of ensuring access to the countryside is listed in the *Environment Service Reports,* 1991–93 and 1993–95 and the *Environment Service Corporate Plan,* 1994–97.

# CHAPTER NINE

# Noise

## Introduction

Noise is an age-old problem which has, through the passage of time, grown in scale and complexity. The law has shown itself able to adapt to some extent to novel developments concerning noise—although legal progress tends inevitably to lag behind changes in society. Since noise is the inevitable by-product of just about every human activity, the law cannot offer a solution to every problem which may arise, and instead in many cases it attempts only to offer a workable compromise between conflicting social interests.

## What is noise?

The task of finding a working legal definition of noise is fraught with difficulty, in that it contains both subjective and objective elements. The EC in its Second Environmental Action Programme (1977–81) provided a definition characterising noise as:

> a number of tonal components disagreeable to man and intolerable to him because of the discomfort, fatigue, agitation and, in some cases, pain it causes.

The problem is that, although an objective definition of noise is possible, it is not very useful in practice, since what is 'disagreeable' or even 'intolerable' is a subjective issue depending not only on the circumstances but also on the individual exposed to the noise. To this end a system has been worked out to provide a means of measuring noise; the decibel scale. The decibel scale begins with the hearing threshold 0 dB = 20 millionths of a pascal. The pain threshold is between 130 and 140 dB.

## The effects of noise

Noise represents a serious problem which can manifest itself in one or more of several ways. Excessive or prolonged exposure to noise can have a variety of effects on human health, some obvious, some less so. These include deafness (both temporary and permanent, and most commonly manifesting itself in the work-place), effects on the cardiovascular system (blood vessels constrict, adrenalin flow is accelerated, and fatigue and headaches can result), and interference with sleep patterns and quality, with associated side effects. Noise can also induce stress, which has a host of physical and practical effects.

Noise also affects other areas of human activity; for example, in the work-place excessive noise can impede effective communication; this can be a problem in itself and can cause (or aggravate the effects of) accidents. Noise can also have a more generalised effect on the smooth running of the work-place. Unexpected noise can impede efficiency; noise louder than 90 dB is equated with a significant increase in errors made in employment requiring concentration. One important side effect of noise is vibration, which can cause nausea in those exposed to it.

This chapter is divided into the following Parts. Part I, on noise and the common law, contains a brief overview of the law of nuisance (both private and public) and of negligence as they touch on noise problems. Part II, on noise and statute law, deals with general statutory noise nuisance provisions, as contained in Part III of the Pollution Control and Local Government Order (Northern Ireland) 1978.[1] The chapter then proceeds to examine the specific problem of occupational noise, as dealt with by Directive 86/188/ EEC on the protection of workers from risks related to exposure to noise at work and its implementation by the Noise at Work Regulations (Northern Ireland) 1990.[2]

## PART I  NOISE AND THE COMMON LAW

### Noise and negligence

Since noise can cause physical damage, most notably in the form of hearing loss, it is no surprise that it can form the factual basis for an action in negligence. A case in point is *Baxter v. Harland and Wolff PLC*.[3] Mr Baxter worked as an electrical fitter (a job involving constant exposure to some of the noisiest processes in the yard) at Harland and Wolff between 1937 and 1944 and between 1946 and 1962. He was not provided with ear defenders or other safety equipment. Several of Mr Baxter's co-workers complained that their hearing had been damaged by exposure to the noise levels which prevailed in the yard. When Mr Baxter ceased to work in the yard he became aware that his hearing too had been permanently impaired and that he needed to wear a hearing aid. He sued for negligence; his case was dismissed as out of time by the Recorder of Belfast, but he succeeded in the Court of Appeal in showing that his employers had indeed been negligent towards him.

The basis of the court's decision on this point was the fact that Harland and Wolff knew at the time in question that noise in the yard was causing deafness in the work force but (like other shipyard owners) failed to do anything about it or even to consider or take advice about whether action might be necessary.

Noise has, however, more commonly been tackled as an 'environmental issue' by the common law than as primarily focused on health and safety issues.

### Private nuisance

The law first tackled the impact of noise on the human environment through the common law of nuisance, which is designed to deal with damage or interference with the enjoyment of the property of a person through the unreasonable activities of his neighbour. The dominant branch of the law of nuisance is that known as private nuisance, which involves the unlawful interference by another with a

---

1. SI 1978/1049.
2. SI 1990/147.
3. [1990] IRLR 516. The case also involved liability under s. 27 of the Factories Act (NI) 1938 (as amended).

person's use or enjoyment of land or some right over or in connection with it. The law of tort, of which nuisance forms a part, is not concerned specifically with environmental protection, although this can be one of the by-products of its operation. The law of nuisance is much older than modern environmental values, concerning itself with protecting the individual's ancient right to enjoy his property free from undue molestation by his neighbours.

## What is covered by private nuisance?

The law of nuisance allows an affected person to make a claim against those who cause physical damage to his property (this would include damage caused by vibration); and, as discussed in some detail in the decision in *St Helen's Smelting Company v. Tipping*,[4] claims may also be made for intangible interference with the 'use and enjoyment' of property (for example through noise). Cases involving interference with the use and enjoyment of property require the courts to exercise special care in balancing the conflicting interests of neighbours.

The subjective nature of interference with the use and enjoyment of property because of noise provides a case in point; it would not do to allow an oversensitive person to persecute his neighbours through a nuisance action, but at the same time it is not only physical damage which can ruin the enjoyment of property. The courts have therefore ensured that claims in respect of this latter class of damage are qualified by a two-part objective test, which involves both comparing the alleged misconduct with the typical standards of comfort and freedom from interference generally to be expected in the locality in question and also looking at what an affected person can reasonably expect of his neighbours in the circumstances. The person's legally enforceable expectations are identified, courtesy of *Walter v. Selfe*,[5]

> not merely according to elegant or dainty modes of living, but according to plain and simple notions among English people.

The application of these objective elements to a noise-based nuisance has resulted in the courts developing a situation-based approach to nuisance claims, which aims to provide a rational and balanced solution to inevitable conflict. As a result it has clearly emerged from case law that those who live in an urban location cannot expect the same standard of quiet as those who live in the countryside. This does not mean, however, that those who live in towns and cities have waived their right to protection under the law of nuisance, since even in an urban area, certain reasonable expectations of the conduct between neighbours are acknowledged by the courts. One example is found in the decision in *Rushmer v. Polsue & Alfieri Ltd*,[6] where the plaintiff was a milkman who lived with his family in Fleet Street, then the centre of newspaper production in London. The defendant had recently introduced a new printing-press onto its neighbouring premises, which operated at night. The court held that despite the urban location and the considerable

---

4.  [1865] 11 HL Cas 642.
5.  [1851] 4 De G. and Sm. 315.
6.  [1905] 51 S.J. 324 HL.

background noise which prevailed in the area, the noise made by the printing-press represented a serious source of discomfort to the plaintiff and was therefore unreasonable and a nuisance. This case illustrates a general rule; noise which would be acceptable during daylight hours will be more likely to be found to be a nuisance at night.

Noise need not be constant to constitute a nuisance; this will be a question to be determined on the facts of each case, and therefore even intermittent noise may be covered, as for example in *Kennaway v. Thompson*.[7] The protection offered by the law of nuisance does not normally extend, however, to temporary noise; for example, reasonably executed building works do not constitute a nuisance, as held in *Andrae v. Selfridge*.[8]

### Whose interests are protected by private nuisance?

Traditionally the law of private nuisance has required the complainant to have a proprietary interest in the property affected by the alleged nuisance in order to gain redress; see, for example, *Malone v. Laskey*,[9] in which relief was denied to the wife of a tenant injured by a nuisance. This view may perhaps be changing following the decision in *Khorasandjian v. Bush*[10] to grant relief to a plaintiff without such an interest, in respect of harassment by phone calls made by the defendant to her parental home.

### Some additional factors the courts may consider in deciding whether a nuisance exists

The social utility of the defendant's conduct will be one of the factors weighed in the balance in deciding whether or not a nuisance exists; the more useful the defendant's conduct is to society as a whole, the less likely it is that his actions will be found to be unreasonable. This factor will not, however, be decisive in itself, as illustrated in the Irish (public nuisance) case of *Bellew v. Cement Co.*,[11] in which the only cement works in the country, providing essential material for industry and employing considerable numbers, was temporarily closed when an interlocutory injunction was granted in respect of the noise nuisance caused to its neighbours by blasting work at the quarry that supplied the works with its raw materials.

### Who may be held liable in private nuisance?

Liability generally lies with the creator of the nuisance, whether or not it originates on his property, as in the case of the noise nuisance created by lorries on the highway when turning in to the defendant's plant in *Halsey v. Esso Petroleum*.[12] An occupier may also be liable for damage resulting from allowing the continuation of a nuisance created by another, as was the case in *Sedleigh*

---

7.    [1981] QB 88.
8.    [1937] 3 All ER 255.
9.    [1907] 2 KB 141.
10.   [1993] QB 727.
11.   [1948] IrR 61.
12.   [1961] 2 All ER 145.

*Denfield v. O'Callaghan*.[13] The crucial factor importing liability for a nuisance created by another lies in control of the property. The courts have in the past displayed a tendency to adopt a broad definition of 'control'; for example, the occupier may be found to have constructive knowledge of a nuisance created by another on his land. This was the case in *R. v. Shorrock (Peter)*,[14] where the defendant let a field on his farm to three people for the weekend (while he himself went away), who then held an illegal 'rave'. The party lasted fifteen hours and was the subject of 275 complaints from people living as far as four miles away. The landowner was held liable for the noise nuisance, and his appeal based on a lack of knowledge failed, the court being of the opinion that he should have been aware of the risk of a nuisance of this type materialising.

If a landlord authorises a nuisance he may be held liable for it although not physically responsible for its creation, as for example in *Tetley v. Chitty*,[15] where a local authority was found liable for the noise nuisance resulting from its decision to authorise a go-kart track in a residential area.

## Defences

There are several specific defences (in addition to the general defences available under the law of torts) in nuisance proceedings; they are, however, of varying strength and utility.

One of the most valuable defences is that of statutory authorisation. This is a complete defence, covering activities authorised by any act of Parliament, whether public or—as in the leading case in this area, *Allen v. Gulf Oil Refining Ltd*[16]— private. The House of Lords in this case held that the inevitable environmental side effects of operating an oil refinery provided for in legislation (oil smuts and noise) were authorised, although not explicitly mentioned in the text of the Act. The decision was reached on the basis of a straightforward construction of the Act; if Parliament had authorised the building and operation of the refinery then it had also necessarily authorised its inevitable side effects. The defendant will be expected to act to mitigate the effects of his activities if possible; statutory authorisation does not give a defendant carte blanche to disturb his neighbours. The application of the statutory authorisation defence is, however, strictly confined; the courts refused to extend it to cover a grant of planning permission by a local authority in the case of *Gillingham B.C. v. Medway (Chatham) Docks Co. Ltd*.[17]

A second possible defence, though one that will rarely be proved in practice, is prescription. Essentially, to make out this defence the defendant must show that the nuisance has subsisted and has been acquiesced to by the plaintiff for twenty years. In practice this defence most usually arises in respect of noise nuisance. It is not a valid defence, however, to show that the nuisance predated the plaintiff's presence and that he in effect 'came to the nuisance'. This point is well illustrated in *Webster v. Lord Advocate*,[18] where the pursuer bought a flat adjacent to

13. [1940] 3 All ER 349.
14. [1994] QB 279.
15. [1986] 1 All ER 663.
16. [1981] AC 1001.
17. [1992] 3 WLR 449
18. [1985] S.L.T. 36.

Edinburgh Castle, knowing that she would encounter the noise generated by the annual military tattoo; her foreknowledge of the noise problem did not, however, absolve the defenders from liability.

## Remedies

When a nuisance is committed, the law provides a remedy for the aggrieved person in the form of damages (to provide redress for past injury) or an injunction (to prevent the continuation of an injurious state of affairs or activity in the future).[19] The remedies offered in nuisance in respect of both noise and vibration are well illustrated in the case of *Halsey v. Esso Petroleum*.[20] The plaintiff lived in a street across the road from a petrol-processing plant operated by the defendants. The plant had recently begun round-the-clock operations, and the resulting traffic and plant noise was disturbing the sleep of residents in the street, most notably the plaintiff, who lived opposite the gates of the plant. The court intervened to grant relief to the plaintiff, limiting the hours of the plant's operation because of the noise.

The law has, however, become more complex in the intervening years, with a claim in public nuisance (see below) involving noise, pollution and traffic congestion consequent on the authorised (under the planning system) conversion of a former naval dockyard to commercial use, being denied in *Gillingham B.C. v. Medway (Chatham) Dock Co. Ltd and Others*.[21] The grant of planning permission was deemed by the court to have changed the character of the locality in question, thus altering the conditions that residents could reasonably expect to enjoy in the locality.

The decision in the *Gillingham* case, however, does not appear to have been conclusive in determining the effect of planning permission in all cases. See, for example, the case of *Wheeler v. Saunders*,[22] in which the court was of the opinion that a planning decision relating to adding a single unit to a pig farm (which then caused a nuisance to its neighbours) did not alter the character of the locality in question and thus a remedy was available.

## Public nuisance

There is a second, related area of the law of nuisance which can affect environmental standards with regard to noise, namely, the law of public nuisance, breach of which can constitute a tort or, more usually, a criminal offence.

### What is covered by public nuisance?

Public nuisance involves the defendant's actions causing undue interference with

---

19. Abatement or self-help is a historical remedy for nuisance which remains technically available, though it is heavily discouraged by the courts, as external control ensuring that the action taken is proportionate to the nuisance in question is impossible in such circumstances. The courts have commented extremely negatively on abatement in *Lagan Navigation Co. v. Lambeg Bleaching, Dyeing and Finishing Co* [1927] AC 226.
20. Supra, note 12.
21. Supra, note 17.
22. [1995] 2 All ER 697.

the comfort and convenience of life of a 'class of Her Majesty's citizens.' What amounts to an appropriate 'class' for action will be a matter of fact in each case, as determined by Lord Denning in *A.G. v. P.Y.A. Quarries Ltd*,[23] a case involving public nuisance in the form of noise and vibration. The question the court asks is whether the nuisance is of such an extent that it would be unfair to expect a single person to take legal action to put an end to it and that action therefore should be taken on behalf of the public at large.

An important class of public nuisance involves obstruction of the highway. In public nuisance the location of the disturbance may be all-important; for example, in *Halsey v. Esso Petroleum*[24] damage caused to the plaintiff's washing in his garden by smuts from a neighbouring oil-processing plant was held to be a private nuisance, but damage from the same source by the same means to the plaintiff's car parked on the highway was held to be a public nuisance.

## Who may bring an action?

Public nuisance may be classed as either a crime (actionable by the state through the Attorney-General, or local authorities or by an aggrieved individual who has been authorised to act in the public interest by the Attorney-General granting his fiat) or a tort, actionable again by the Attorney-General, a local authority or an individual who has sustained a measure of damage over and above that typical of the class of which he forms a part.

## PART II NOISE AND STATUTE LAW

While the common law of nuisance, particularly private nuisance, provides primarily for the protection of the person whose comfort is adversely affected by the unreasonable conduct of his neighbour, a by-product of the operation of the law may be a limited improvement in the quality of the local environment. The potential impact of the law of nuisance on the noise problem both for individuals and wider society is, however, curtailed by the nature of the proceedings, the limited class of people who may claim relief, and the fact that a fresh action must be taken for each new incidence of the nuisance in question. Legal action under the common law remains both cumbersome and expensive; its limitations were, however, recognised fairly early on, and this led Parliament to introduce an abbreviated statutory approach to dealing with nuisance.

### General statutory nuisance

Statutory nuisance owes much of its shape and content to the common law of nuisance; the main difference between them (bar of course their legal form) is the procedure by which the nuisance is brought to an end. The current law of statutory nuisance in Northern Ireland is to be found in Part III of the Pollution Control and Local Government (Northern Ireland) Order 1978. This Order followed the

---

23. [1957] 1 All ER 894.
24. Supra, note 12.

provisions of Part III of the Control of Pollution Act 1974 for England and Wales; the provisions applicable in the latter jurisdiction have been replaced by Part III of the Environmental Protection Act 1990[25] and the specific Noise and Statutory Nuisance Act 1993.[26]

The impetus for giving a new, more comprehensive statutory treatment to noise nuisance lay in the work of the Scott Committee, culminating in its report *Neighbourhood Noise.*[27] Despite pressure from the Confederation of British Industry, the report favoured the view that noise was a local issue, best handled by local authority personnel, rather than an area so technical as to require central government control. It has since been suggested by the Royal Commission on Environmental Pollution[28] that this approach be modified in Great Britain by the inclusion of noise within the responsibilities of a centralised environmental inspectorate, but this idea has not come to fruition, although the inspectorate itself has.

Noise,[29] therefore (and vibration, which is included in the remit of the 1978 Order by virtue of article 53(1)), for the most part remains a local issue, subject to control as an environmental health issue. Noise control is therefore one of the few areas of environmental control in Northern Ireland which remains substantially within the remit of local government, specifically the environmental health departments within district councils.

This does not mean, however, that district councils have an entirely free hand in dealing with noise nuisance. The DoE(NI) plays an important role in the statutory nuisance system, both by dealing with appeals from the decisions of councils and through the power to make regulations under the 1978 Order. The DoE(NI) also holds the power to issue and approve codes of practice for minimising noise under article 51 of the Order.[30] The Department therefore exercises an important role in directing and guiding district councils in the exercise of their powers to deal with noise nuisance.

## Civil aviation

The most important exception to local responsibility for noise nuisance is found in respect of aviation noise. The need for a national approach to this problem, securing a level playing-field for all airports in attracting custom, is clear; in addition, the size and complexity of the issue, together with the shared core of the problem regardless of the location, also support a nationwide system of control.

The Civil Aviation Act 1982 alters considerably the normal operation of the law of nuisance (both common law and statutory) for noise nuisance caused by aircraft in flight (section 76) and at aerodromes (section 77). The regulation of noise and

---

25. Suggestions that the provisions of the 1990 Act be extended to Northern Ireland have been dismissed by the Government as 'low priority'.
26. Certain provisions of the 1993 Act apply to Scotland, but it does not extend to Northern Ireland.
27. Noise Advisory Council, *Neighbourhood Noise,* London: HMSO, 1971.
28. RCEP, *Fifth Report: Air Pollution Control: an Integrated Approach* (Cmnd 6371), London: HMSO, 1976.
29. Note that the 1978 Order, although wide in its remit, does not cover noise from aircraft (with the exception of models) (art. 53 (4)).
30. Codes to date cover audible intruder and burglar alarms, ice cream van chimes, and model aircraft.

vibration from aircraft is placed in the hands of central government; the Act authorises the Secretary of State for Transport to make Air Navigation Orders and to issue statutory notices dealing with noise controls. These provide for the maximum number and frequency of take-offs or landings of planes of certain classes and for particular times for these activities for individual airports, in line with internationally agreed norms. An operator of aircraft will only be held liable for nuisance if he is also in breach of the relevant Air Navigation Order (section 77 (2)); therefore by implication such an order can authorise a level of noise that would otherwise constitute a nuisance.

The Airports (Northern Ireland) Order 1994[31] represents a deviation from the previous 'nationalised' approach to the problem of noise pollution generated by civil aviation. It gives the DoE(NI)[32] powers to instruct those who run airports to take such measures as it considers fit to deal with noise and vibration (article 21). The DoE(NI) may also adopt schemes requiring airports to make grants contributing to the installation of insulation in properties affected by their activities (article 22).

Complaints in respect of airport nuisance should be channelled to the airport operator. The DoE(NI) can of course intervene and invoke its powers under the 1994 Order should the need arise.

## District councils and statutory nuisance

The 1978 Order makes a two-pronged attack on the noise question, utilising both a reactive and a preventive approach.[33]

### *General reactive powers*

The 1978 Order places a district council under a duty (article 37) to inspect its area[34] for noise nuisances that ought to be dealt with under its powers to take summary proceedings (article 38) and to consider the creation of preventive noise abatement zones. A district council will of course be expected to respond to complaints from those living in its area and to consider whether or not to exercise its powers under article 38.

### *Preliminary investigation*

A preliminary investigation by an environmental health officer of reported or other noise represents the first step in assessing and deciding on appropriate action in respect of an alleged nuisance.[35] If the council is satisfied that a nuisance does

---

31. SR No. 194.
32. Specifically its Environmental Protection Division.
33. The Town and Country Planning system also offers the potential for proactive control over noise through the use of planning conditions: see A. Dowling, *Northern Ireland Planning Law*, Dublin: Gill & Macmillan, 1995.
34. The area of those districts bounded by or seaward of the high water mark of mean tides is deemed to include the territorial sea outside the district seaward of the high water mark in the district (art. 53 (2)); for this reason noise from vessels is included within the remit of the 1978 Order. The DoE(NI) is given power to determine whether a place is within the area of a given council (art. 53 (2) (*a*).
35. For an outline of law and procedure designed to explain the 1978 Order to the public see *Bothered by Noise: a Guide to Noise Complaints Procedure*, DoE Environment Service.

exist it will normally attempt to make informal contact with the person responsible in an attempt to achieve a quick and cheap solution to the problem.

## The role of the common law

The common law of nuisance remains relevant in establishing whether or not the noise in question represents an undue interference with the use and enjoyment of land, although, unlike the common law, statutory nuisance does not require any person to actually have had his interests interfered with by the noise. This was demonstrated in the English cases of *A. Lambert Flat Management Ltd v. Lomas*,[36] *Cooke v. Adatia and Others*,[37] and *Wellingborough Borough Council v. Gordon*[38] (these cases deal with the noise nuisance offence created by the Control of Pollution Act 1974, which is almost identical to that created by the 1978 Order).

The powers of district councils under the Order are not strictly confined to their own areas. Article 38(7) allows a council, when a nuisance exists or has occurred affecting its area but which appears to wholly or partly originate outside the district, to take action as if the nuisance was located within its own area. The only substantial difference from a straightforward case is that appeals are to be heard by a court of summary jurisdiction in the area where the alleged nuisance is located.

## The abatement notice

The procedure laid down in article 38 is as follows. Once satisfied that a noise amounting to a nuisance exists or is likely to occur or recur in its area, a council must (informal action to address the problem having failed) serve a notice (under article 38(1)) on the person responsible (article 38(2)). If that person cannot be found, or the nuisance has yet to occur, the notice may be served on the owner or occupier of the premises from which the noise is being or would be emitted.

Notices under article 38 are colloquially known as abatement notices. A notice issued under article 38(1) can impose any or all of the following requirements:

(a) the abatement of the nuisance or prohibiting or restricting its occurrence or recurrence;

(b) the execution of such works, and the taking of such other steps, as may be necessary for the purpose of the notice or as may be specified in the notice.

The notice, in addition to specifying what action is required, must also specify the time allowed for compliance with its terms.

## The content of an abatement notice

Article 38 of the 1978 Order (which in this respect is identical to section 59 of COPA 1974) gives the local authority considerable discretion with regard to the

---

36. [1981] 2 All ER 280. Thus the fact that in this case no-one affected would have been able to establish a claim at common law was irrelevant.
37. [1988] 153 JP 129. The expert evidence (consisting of a noise measurement in decibels) of an environmental health officer can be sufficient of itself to justify a local council in exercising its powers to deal with statutory nuisance.
38. [1991] JPL 874. An inference drawn from the evidence of police officers investigating loud music emanating from a house where a party was in progress, although no complaints were received from neighbours, was sufficient to support a case in statutory nuisance.

content of any notice issued. This legal approach is in sharp contrast to previous relevant legislation, originating with the Public Health Act 1875, in which noise nuisance is treated merely as a species of wider statutory nuisance, an approach which also prevails in the new statutory nuisance regime introduced for England and Wales in the Environmental Protection Act 1990.[39]

The difference between the two approaches is illustrated in the judgment of McCullough J in *Sterling Homes (Midlands) Limited v. Birmingham City Council*,[40] a case involving a notice issued in respect of statutory nuisance under sections 79 and 80 of the Environmental Protection Act 1990. The relevant part of section 80 reads:

(1) Where a local authority is satisfied that a statutory nuisance exists, or is likely to occur or recur, in the area . . . [it] shall serve a notice imposing all or any of the following requirements:

   (a) requiring the abatement of the nuisance or prohibiting or restricting its occurrence or recurrence;

   (b) requiring the execution of such works, and the taking of such other steps as may be necessary for any of those purposes . . .

Under the 1978 Order the notice *may* specify the works which should be undertaken in order to abate the nuisance, although a notice stating that 'such works as are necessary to abate the nuisance' must be undertaken would be equally legally valid. In contrast, under the 1990 Act it is necessary to specify the action required; thus in *Sterling Homes (Midlands) Ltd v. Birmingham City Council*,[41] an abatement notice issued under section 80 of the 1990 Act which failed to specify the works to be undertaken in order to comply with the law was held to be invalid.

The 1978 Order therefore gives councils a higher degree of latitude in the wording of notices. This of course will make the council's job easier, in that it need only specify the end to be achieved and can leave the question of means to the creator of the nuisance—a rudimentary application of the 'polluter pays' principle.

Contravention of a section 38 notice, or of any of its individual requirements, without reasonable excuse constitutes an offence (article 38(4)). Once again decided cases covering the provisions COPA 1974 are relevant, the 'reasonable excuse' proviso also applying to section 58. In *A. Lambert Flat Management Ltd v. Lomas*[42] the managers of a block of flats failed to show that the fact that their tenants had signed leases assenting to noise from the lift in their building (such consent would amount to a defence at proceedings in common law) meant that the COPA should not apply to their situation. They were unable to show that they had in fact a reasonable excuse for failing to comply with an abatement notice issued under section 58 of the COPA. They had failed to avail themselves of the appeal mechanism provided by COPA and also failed to show that they had good reason for this failure.

---

39. The unique problems of noise nuisance have, however, been the subject of the Noise and Statutory Nuisance Act 1993.
40. Lexis transcript by John Larking, hearing date 5 July 1995.
41. Ibid.
42. Supra, note 36.

The reasonable excuse proviso also failed to absolve the respondent from liability in *Wellingborough Borough Council v. Gordon,*[43] in which, although the defendant took considerable precautions and avoided any complaints by his neighbours with regard to loud music played at a birthday party, liability still accrued. (Precautions will, however, serve as a mitigating factor in the punishment of offences.)

*Appeal against an abatement notice*

The person who has been served with an abatement notice has twenty-one days from the date of service to appeal to a court of summary jurisdiction (article 38(3)). It would appear, based on the approach adopted on the COPA provisions, that the question whether or not a notice should be upheld is to be determined with reference to the facts as they subsist at the date of the court hearing and not as they were when the notice was served (*Johnsons News of London v. Ealing London Borough Council*[44]).

*Defences to article 38(4) proceedings*

A defence is available (under article 38(5)) to an offence under article 39(4) for noise nuisances arising in the course of a business if the defendant can show that he has used the best practicable means to prevent or ameliorate the effect of the noise. The concept of 'best practicable means' has been a feature of environmental statutes in the UK since the Alkali Act 1879, though it has to a degree been surpassed by the 'BATNEEC'[45] standard as the best means of ensuring environmentally sound business practice. The best practicable means standard, as indeed is the case with its successor, essentially represents a compromise between the often exacting demands placed on business by environmental protection and economic reality.

The 1978 Order contains its own definition (which is also applicable to any codes of practice issued under the Order) of 'best practicable means' in article 52. 'Best' is not an absolute requirement; it is qualified by compatibility with other legal duties, particularly those imposed on statutory undertakers—i.e. those authorised by statute to run railways, road transport, docks, harbours, the post office, and energy supply (paragraph 4).

'Practicable' is defined in paragraph 2 as 'reasonably practicable having regard among other things to local conditions and circumstances, to the current state of technical knowledge and to financial implications.'

'Means' for the purposes of the 1978 Order include 'design, installation, maintenance and manner and periods of operation of plant and machinery, and the design, construction and maintenance of buildings and acoustic structures' (paragraph 3).

---

43. Supra, note 38.
44. [1989] 153 LGR 1014.
45. BATNEEC (best available techniques not entailing excessive cost) is a central feature of the system of integrated pollution control introduced by Part I of the Environmental Protection Act 1990. It is broader than the traditional 'best practicable means' approach, in that it extends beyond the use of appropriate technologies to issues of optimum plant design, staff training, etc.

The whole 'best practicable means' test, which aims to address the practical and technical limitations of what can be expected of defendants, is applicable only as far as it is compatible with safety and safe working conditions (paragraph 5).

Article 38(6) provides for more widely available defences, the first being that the alleged offence had in fact been authorised by an article 40 notice or an article 41 or 45 consent (see below). Secondly, it is a defence to show that the premises were, at the relevant time, operating under an article 46 notice and that the level of noise did not exceed the level stipulated in that notice. Thirdly, it is also a defence to show that a fixed noise level under article 47 (as opposed to an article 46 notice) is applicable to the premises and that the stipulated noise level has not been exceeded. The latter two defences are available to defendants regardless of whether the article 46 or 47 instruments were the subject of an appeal at the time when the alleged article 38 offence was committed.

### High Court proceedings

A district council is also empowered (by article 38(8)) in exceptional situations to institute proceedings in the High Court in respect of a noise nuisance where it is of the opinion that proceeding by article 38(4) would not provide an adequate remedy. Proceedings in the High Court may be used to secure the abatement, prohibition or restriction of the nuisance. There is no requirement that the councils have suffered damage as a result of the nuisance. The defendant[46] will be able to make out a defence to an article 38(8) action by showing that the noise in question was authorised under an article 40 notice or an article 41 consent (see below).

### Penalties for noise nuisance

Under Part III of the 1978 Order, fines on summary conviction can amount to £5,000 (level 5 on the standard scale, Criminal Justice (NI) Order 1994). In addition, if a second (or further) conviction under the same article of the Order follows within a year of the first conviction an additional fine of £1,000 per day (level 3 on the standard scale, Criminal Justice (NI) Order 1994) from the date of the second contravention is payable (article 54(1)).

An infringement of wider statutory nuisance provisions under section 114 of the Public Health Act 1878 may also be deemed to constitute a second offence under the 1978 Order (article 54(2)).

## Action by aggrieved occupiers

The law of statutory nuisance may offer a more attractive legal option than the common law to the individual who suffers as the result of the activities of their neighbours.[47] Most plaintiffs in going to court hope that the magistrates will grant them an injunction to prevent the continuation of the state of affairs that is deemed to be a nuisance. Damages will only deal with the past impact of the nuisance on

---

46. Where more than one person is responsible for noise, action in statutory nuisance under the 1978 Order is applicable to all the contributors, whether or not the noise generated by any individual would in itself amount to an actionable nuisance (art. 53(3)).

47. The DoE(NI) Environment Service in its pamphlet *Bothered by Noise: a Guide to Noise Complaints Procedure* suggests that legal action is a last resort, encouraging informal action as the most positive approach to the problem.

their property; the injunction, however, looks to the future. While damages are not available in statutory nuisance, the relatively swift and simple procedure can result in an order being issued that will have a positive impact on the defendant's future conduct.

Article 39 of the Order allows a court of summary jurisdiction to act on a complaint by the occupier of any premises bothered by noise amounting to a nuisance. Those wishing to proceed with a statutory nuisance action are advised to attempt an informal resolution to the problem in the first instance, by writing (and keeping a copy of) a dated letter to the person responsible for the noise. Should this fail, the individual may then approach the local Petty Sessions Office, informing them that a complaint is to be made under article 39 of the 1978 Order. A summons will then be issued to the person alleged to be responsible for the noise, stating the date and time for the court hearing.

### The court order

To exercise its jurisdiction, the court must be satisfied (under article 39(2)) that a nuisance either exists or, if abated, is likely to recur on the same premises. Once this condition is satisfied, the court must then make an order for either or both of the following purposes:

(i) requiring the defendant to abate the nuisance, within a time specified in the order, and to execute any works necessary for that purpose;

(ii) prohibiting the recurrence of the nuisance, and requiring the defendant within a time specified in the order to execute any works necessary to prevent the recurrence.

According to paragraph (4), anyone who contravenes any part of an order issued under paragraph (2) commits an offence, although once again the 'best practicable means' defence applies to business premises (paragraph (5)).

Proceedings may, under article 39(2), be brought against the author of the nuisance or, if he cannot be found, against the owner or occupier of the premises from which the noise is being or would be emitted.

The 1978 Order contains a safeguard against the author of the nuisance being unwilling to act to abate the nuisance. Once a person has been convicted of an offence under paragraph (4), the court of summary jurisdiction may, after hearing the district council in whose area the nuisance is situated, direct the council to do any of the things originally required of the author of the nuisance by the original order.

## District councils and the 1978 Order: general proactive powers

### Noise abatement zones

The 1978 Order gives district councils wider proactive powers to tackle the problem of noise through the creation of noise abatement zones. These can be created under article 43 and can cover all or part of the district. Any order made to establish a noise abatement zone must specify the class of premises to which it is applicable (paragraph (2)).

The procedure for making an order creating a noise abatement zone and for bringing it into operation was originally found in Schedule 1 to the 1978 Order; these provisions have now been replaced by Schedule 3 to the Local Government

(Miscellaneous Provisions) (NI) Order 1985.[48] These powers have not yet been used in Northern Ireland, though, should the need arise, they could of course be employed.

### Publicity

The district council is required to publicise its actions. The minimum criterion to satisfy the publicity requirement is fulfilled by placing a notice (as required by Schedule 3 to the 1985 Order) in the *Belfast Gazette* and in one or more newspaper circulating in the district for two successive weeks.

The notice should contain the following particulars:
  (i) a statement that an order is to be made and the general effects of the proposed order;
 (ii) details of the place in the district where a copy of the order and any attached maps or plans will be available for consultation, free of charge, for at least six weeks from the date on which the notice is last published; and
(iii) notice that within the six week period any person who will be affected by the order may make his objections known to the council.

In addition to publicity in the press Schedule 3 requires that the council take action to draw the proposed order to the attention of those people within the district who will be affected by its terms.

### Making the Order

Schedule 3 to the 1985 Order obliges the council to consider any objections duly made within the six week period before proceeding with making the order. The council may then proceed with the order in its original form, amend its proposal or decide to abandon its proposal.

It is no longer necessary for the DoE(NI) to confirm the order (as was originally the case under the 1978 Order).

### Objections

Originally, if any duly made objection to an order remained unresolved, the DoE(NI) could give the objector and the council an opportunity to be heard before an adjudicator appointed by the Department. The Department's powers in this regard were removed by the provisions of Schedule 3 to the 1985 Order, as part of the more general move to liberate this area of district council responsibility from such stringent central control.

### Bringing the Order into effect

Once an order has been agreed and made by a district council it must generally come into effect on the date specified within it. The council does however retain the power under Schedule 3 to the 1985 Order to postpone the coming into effect of the order by passing a resolution to that effect. Schedule 3 requires that a postponement resolution fulfil certain publicity requirements in order to be valid. A notice that a postponement resolution has been made must be published (at least once in two successive weeks) in one or more newspaper circulating in the affected area.

---

48. SI 1985/1206.

### Operation of a noise abatement zone

#### Measurements and registers of noise levels

Once a noise abatement zone has been designated, the district council must measure the noise emanating from premises of the class covered by the order in the area in which it operates (article 43(1)). The measurements attained under paragraph (1) are made at a time determined by the council (paragraph (7)) and are then required to be recorded in an official 'noise level register' kept by the council. The register is to be open to the public, at no charge, at all reasonable hours, and copies of entries are to be made available for a reasonable fee (paragraph (7)).

When the council records a noise level in the register it is also required to serve a copy of the record on the owner and/or occupier of the premises concerned. Those upon whom the record is served then have twenty-eight days to appeal to the DoE(NI) against the record (paragraph (4)). The Department may then give such directions to the council as it deems fit with regard to the record in question (paragraph (4)).

The appeal mechanism outlined above constitutes the only method (except judicial review) by which the validity or accuracy of an entry on the noise level register may be questioned (paragraph (5)).

The Order provides for the making of regulations determining, or allowing the DoE(NI) to determine, the methods by which noise is to be measured and calculated for all purposes relating to noise abatement zones (paragraph (8)).

#### Consent to exceed recorded noise levels

Once the noise level for any affected premises is recorded it may not be exceeded without the written consent of the council (article 45, paragraph (1)). If given, this consent (which must be applied for) may be subject to conditions relating to the size of the increase and the period (or periods) for which the increase is permitted. A consent under article 45(2) is not a defence to an action in respect of general statutory nuisance under article 39.

Particulars of any such consent are to be recorded by the council in the noise level register (paragraph (2)).

#### Appeals in respect of consents to exceed recorded noise levels

The council has two months to reach a decision (unless the applicant agrees in writing to a longer period) on an application to exceed the noise level recorded in the noise level register. If the applicant receives no word from the council within this period, his application is deemed to have been refused (paragraph (3)). The applicant then has three months from the date of notification (or the end of the period referred to in paragraph (3)) to appeal to the DoE(NI) against the council's decision (paragraph (4)). The council must abide by the Department's decision.

#### Contravention of a consent to exceed a recorded noise level

Contravention of a consent (or of any of its individual terms) under article 45 is an offence. If an individual is convicted by a court of summary jurisdiction, that court may, if it is satisfied that the offence is likely to continue or recur, make an order requiring the carrying out of any works necessary to prevent this. The contravention of such a court order without reasonable excuse is also an offence (paragraph (6)).

The court may also (under paragraph (7)), after allowing the council in question the opportunity to be heard, order the council to do anything that the court has required the person convicted to do under paragraph (6). This order may be used in addition to, or as an alternative to an order under paragraph (6).

### Reduction of noise levels

According to article 46, the district council may, if it appears that the noise level emanating from a building which is covered by a noise abatement order is unacceptable (given the purposes the order is supposed to fulfil and that a reduction in the noise generated is practicable at a reasonable cost), serve a noise reduction notice on the person responsible for the noise. The council's capacity to intervene is limited by the financial resources of the person responsible for the noise.

### Noise reduction notices

The noise reduction notice issued will require the person responsible for the noise to reduce the noise to a specified level and to prevent any subsequent increase in noise levels (unless the council gives its consent) and will specify the steps to achieve these ends (paragraph (2)). The notice may specify times or days during which the noise level is to be reduced; these may vary (paragraph (4)). The notice will also specify a time (not less than six months from the serving of the notice) within which the noise reduction is to be attained (paragraph (3)). The council must record details of a noise reduction notice in the noise level register (paragraph (6)).

A noise reduction notice takes precedence over a consent to breach usual noise levels given under article 45. This in effect forms a safety net, allowing immediate action if the consequences of an article 45 consent prove to be more severe than originally expected. A person served with a noise reduction notice has three months from the date on which it is served to appeal to a court of summary jurisdiction (paragraph (7)).

Contravention of a noise reduction notice is an offence (paragraph (8)), although the 'best practicable means' defence is available in respect of noise generated in the course of a trade or business (paragraph (9)).

### New sources of noise

The district council's continuing responsibility to monitor its area for noise nuisance under the 1978 Order can enable it to anticipate certain problems before they arise. Article 47(1) of the Order details two of the most common ways in which this may arise where a building is to be constructed to which a noise abatement order will apply on its completion, and the alteration of premises in such a way as to become subject to such an order. In such circumstances the council may, on application by the owner or occupier (or anyone who can satisfy the council that he is negotiating to acquire an interest in the premises in question), or indeed on its own initiative, determine the noise emanation level which will be acceptable from the premises.

If the council fails to respond to an application under paragraph 1 within two months (or a longer period agreed in writing with the applicant) it will be deemed to have given notice that it has decided against making a determination on this application. This then allows the applicant to set the appeal process in motion (paragraph (4)). Otherwise the noise level deemed appropriate by the council must be recorded in the noise level register (paragraph (2)).

The council's decision must also be notified to the applicant (or, when it has acted on its own initiative, to the owner or occupier). The recipient of such notification then has three months from the date of notification within which to appeal to the DoE(NI); the council is bound to abide by the Department's decision (paragraph 3).

If a building is being erected or altered so that it will fall under an operative noise abatement order and the council has not taken any action under article 47, then article 46 will apply to it, subject to the following alterations:
  (i) the proviso that reduction of the noise to an appropriate level be practicable at reasonable cost contained in article 46(1)(b) is removed; and
  (ii) the six month minimum period specified for noise reduction applicable under article 46(3) is replaced by a three month minimum; and
  (iii) the best practicable means defence open to those operating a trade or business under article 46(9) is not available.

It is wise, therefore, particularly if one operates a trade or business which will be located in premises being built or altered in an area where they will be subject to a noise abatement order, to take the precaution of making an application to the council under article 47, since even a determination requiring considerable effort to achieve compliance on the part of the applicant will still be less onerous than the unusually stringent requirements of article 47(5).

### Specific sources of statutory noise nuisance in the 1978 Order

In addition to the general provisions mentioned above allowing district councils and aggrieved occupiers to bring the law of statutory nuisance into play through the use of a council notice or a court order in respect of a broad range of nuisances, the Order also makes provision for specific classes of nuisance.

#### Noise and Construction Sites

The works covered by article 40 of the Order are defined comprehensively as:
  (i) the erection, construction, alteration, repair or maintenance of buildings structures or roads;
  (ii) breaking up, opening or boring under any road or adjacent land in connection with the construction, inspection, maintenance or removal of works;
  (iii) demolition or dredging work; and
  (iv) any work of engineering construction.

It is of considerable importance, however, particularly in Northern Ireland, where the role of the state is so wide in all sectors of construction activity, that works by Government departments are explicitly excluded from the remit of article 40.

## Notices covering construction works

Article 40 places the onus of action on the district council to ascertain whether works (as outlined above) are being or are going to be carried out on premises in their area and to decide whether it wishes to exercise its power to serve a notice directing the manner in which the works are to be carried out. The council is allowed to publish these requirements in such a way as it thinks fit.

The Order specifies (in paragraph (3)) the types of requirements that may be included in an article 40 notice. These include:

 (i) the plant or machinery which is or is not to be used;
 (ii) the hours during which the noise may subsist; and
 (iii) the level of noise which may be emitted from the premises (or any specified part of them) or the levels which may be emitted during specified hours.

The notice may also provide for any change in circumstances. The district council receives further guidance in the exercise of its article 40 powers in paragraph (4), which requires it to have regard to the following factors:

 (i) relevant provisions of any Code of Practice issued under Part II of the Order;
 (ii) the need to ensure the promotion of the best practicable means to minimise noise;
 (iii) before specifying methods or plant whether it would be desirable to allow the recipients of the notice to suggest alternatives which would be as effective in dealing with the noise but also more acceptable to them;
 (iv) the need to protect any persons in the locality from the effects of noise.

The notice may specify the time allowed for compliance with its requirements, together with the steps necessary to attain the purpose of the notice (the steps may themselves be specified) (paragraph (6)).

## Contravention of a notice covering construction works

Contravention of any part of the notice without reasonable excuse is an offence (paragraph (8)). The notice is served on the person who appears to the council to be carrying out or going to carry out the works and to such other persons as appear to the council to be responsible for or to control the carrying out of the works (paragraph (5)).

The potential class of defendants under article 40 is therefore wider than that under articles 38 and 39. The reason for this is simple; in the case of noise nuisance created in the context of construction, responsibility should not be attributed solely to the contractor but also to the person whose interests are being forwarded by the work which has resulted in the nuisance.

## Appeals against a notice covering construction works

The person served with the notice then has twenty-one days from the date of service to appeal against it to a court of summary jurisdiction (paragraph (7)).

## Consent for construction works

It is possible to avoid the danger of being exposed to statutory nuisance proceedings in respect of a construction site by applying in advance for the district council's consent to activities that would otherwise incur liability under article 40 (8). The procedure for obtaining consent is laid down in article 41.

Where the works in question, in addition to falling within article 40, also require approval under the Building Regulations (Northern Ireland) Order 1972,[48a] an application under article 41 must be made at the same time or later than the application for approval under the Building Regulations.

### Applications for a construction works consent

The applicant is required (by article 41(3)) to provide particulars of:
(i)   the works themselves and the method by which they are to be carried out; and
(ii)  the proposed measures to be taken to minimise the noise impact of the works.

### The granting of a construction works consent

If, on receipt of such an application,[49] the district council is satisfied that the information contained is sufficient to show that the noise nuisance will in fact be minimised to the extent that, if carried out in the manner indicated, it would not be the subject of an article 40 notice, it must give its consent (paragraph (4)). The district council does, however, have the power under paragraph 5 to:
 (i) attach any condition to the consent; and
 (ii) limit or qualify consents to allow for changes in circumstances; and
(iii) limit the duration of the consent.

The council is required to notify the applicant of its decision, and if it gives its consent it may, if it thinks it fit, publish notice of this in any manner it deems appropriate (paragraph (6)).

### Appeals concerning construction consents

If the council has failed to inform the applicant of its decision within the twenty-eight days (or the period otherwise agreed) or has refused its consent, or gives qualified consent to the application, the applicant can appeal to a court of summary jurisdiction within twenty-one days of the end of the original time limit (paragraph (7)).

While a consent issued under article 41(4) and (5) will be a defence against article 40 proceedings, it does not offer any protection against proceedings under the more general nuisance offence in article 39 (paragraph (9)).

### Contravention of a construction works consent

It is an offence for any person to knowingly permit or carry out the works in contravention of any term of the consent issued under paragraph (5). As under article 40, the law here takes into account the fact that one actor may commit a nuisance in furthering the interests of another; and so in article 41(10), where a consent is given for construction works which are to be carried out by someone other than the applicant, he must take all reasonable steps to ensure that the

---

48a. SI 1972/1996.
49.  The council has twenty-eight days (or longer if the applicant agrees to this in writing) to reach a decision on an application for a construction works consent (para. (7)).

consent and its terms are brought to the notice of that other. Failure to comply with paragraph (10) is in itself an offence.

## Noise in the streets

The 1978 Order makes specific provision to deal with nuisances in the street.[50] Article 42 deals with noise generated by loudspeakers. Article 42(1) places a general prohibition on the use of loudspeakers between the hours of nine in the evening and eight the following morning for any purpose, and at any other time for advertising any entertainment, trade, or business. Article 42(2) then lists seven categories of exception to this rule; these are:

  (i) loudspeakers being used for 'official' purposes; this category includes, as one would expect, noise generated by the police, fire brigade and ambulance services. The provision, however, also extends beyond this to cover noise made by the DoE(NI) (currently through the Water Executive) in the exercise of its functions under the Water Act (Northern Ireland) 1972 (as amended), and the Water and Sewerage Services (Northern Ireland) Order 1973 (as amended), as amended, for example in announcing interruption to the water supply. Noise by district councils within their districts is also included within this category of excepted loudspeaker noise;

 (ii) loudspeakers being used to communicate with people on a vessel to direct its (or any other vessel's) movements (for example by river pilots);

(iii) loudspeakers which form part of a public telephone;

(iv) loudspeakers in or fixed to a vehicle and used solely for the entertainment of or communication with drivers or passengers (for example a taxi radio) or where the loudspeaker operates solely to act as a warning to other vehicles (i.e. it acts as a horn) and is operated in such a way as not to give reasonable cause for annoyance to those in the vicinity;

 (v) the use of loudspeakers (otherwise than on the road) on public transport by staff to communicate with passengers or prospective passengers or other employees (for example railway public address systems);

(vi) the use of loudspeakers by travelling showmen for funfairs; and

(vii) the use of loudspeakers in emergencies.

Each of the above categories (with the notable exception of (vi)) involves necessary communication, whether for purposes of efficiency or safety, or both. The exception in category (vi) has more in common with the final exception to the general prohibition on the use of loudspeakers found in article 42(3), which allows the use of loudspeakers between noon and seven in the evening when attached to a vehicle used for the conveyance of perishable goods for human consumption and used solely to advertise that a product is for sale—for example the chimes of an ice cream van. This exception is subject to the proviso that the loudspeaker be

---

50. This is one area in which the 1978 Order differs from the COPA, which dealt only with noise from premises, noise from mobile loudspeakers not being expressly included within its remit: *London Borough of Tower Hamlets v. Manzoni and Another* [1984] JPL 437. This omission was finally remedied in Great Britain by the Noise and Statutory Nuisance Act 1993—which incidentally also covers noise from another scourge of modern life, the audible intruder alarm; this is not yet specifically covered in Northern Ireland.

operated in such a way as not to give reasonable cause for annoyance to persons in the vicinity.

### Noise and the work environment

The 1978 Order makes special provision (in article 48) for noise from plant and machinery, over and above its application to noise emanating from premises. These powers, although having a fairly broad ambit, are not permitted to derogate from the other, more general noise nuisance provisions of the 1978 Order (article 48(5)).

The Order provides for the creation of regulations requiring the application of noise abatement technologies and strategies to plant and machinery (article 48(1)(*a*)). Additional powers exist for limiting the permitted level of noise emission from plant and machinery used in works covered by article 40 and noise levels outside factories[51] caused by machinery falling under article 48(1)(*b*).

Regulations made under article 48(1)(*a*) and (*b*) are explicitly allowed to apply 'standards, specifications, descriptions or tests' contained in documents which do not themselves form part of the regulations. This allows, among other things, for flexibility and the following of EC standards on noise.

Regulations made under article 48 will be subject to the DoE(NI) carrying out consultation with the users and producers of plant and machinery who will be affected by them. This requirement, contained in article 48(2), is designed specifically to ensure that any regulations issued would not, in the DoE(NI)'s opinion, be 'impracticable' or 'involve unreasonable expense'.

The contravention of regulations (which includes causing or permitting another to do so) under article 48 is an offence—though it will be a defence in connection with regulations under paragraph (1)(*a*) concerning technologies or strategies to reduce noise from plant or machinery to prove that means alternative to, but not less effective than, those specified in the regulations were used. While the contents of the regulations are important in themselves, the focus under the 1978 Order is clearly on the ends to be achieved rather than on the means used.

The DoE(NI) is empowered (if it should so wish) to make different regulations applicable to different areas, and district councils are required to enforce the regulations relevant to their areas (article 48(4)).

### Works carried out by district councils and noise nuisance

If a person fails to carry out all or any works which he is directed to do under article 38, a noise reduction order, or a court order pursuant to articles 39(2) or 45(6), the council may, under article 49(1), carry out the works included in the order or notice in question (paragraph (2)).

If the works in question fall under article 39(6) or 45(7) or article 49 itself, the council can recover the cost of executing the works from the defaulter. (The latter can, however, limit his financial liability in respect of those parts of the expenditure that he can show to have been unnecessary (paragraph (3)).

If events go so far that the council has to carry out the works specified and then seeks to recover its expenses, it is not open to the defaulter to raise those issues

---

51. As defined by the Factories Act (NI) 1965.

which he could have raised in an appeal against the original notice (paragraph 4). In those circumstances the defendant has in effect waived this right by his continued failure to respond to the terms of the order or notice which refers to him or to set the appeals mechanism in motion to end any dispute about its contents.

## Appeals under the 1978 Order

Article 50 of the 1978 Order provides for regulations governing appeals in respect of noise nuisance proceedings to both the DoE(NI) and courts of summary jurisdiction. Such regulations concern the technical aspects of the appeals process, including whether notices are to be regarded as having been suspended pending an appeal decision. In addition, regulations can be used to prescribe the form to be taken by appeal notices and details of how they should be served and with what accompanying information.

Apart from any specific regulations, there is a general rule applicable to both the Department and the courts, which are required to take into account claims by the appellants that they are performing a legal duty in the course of activities which cause the noise emissions (article 50(3)).

## Noise and the work environment: specific statutory provision

In addition the provisions of the 1978 Order, which deal with general and specific classes of what could be termed 'environmental noise', there is specific provision in Northern Ireland law for the impact of noise on people in the work-place. We owe the existence of this specific provision, contained in the Noise at Work Regulations (Northern Ireland) 1990,[52] to Directive 86/188/EEC[53] on the protection of workers from risks related to exposure to noise at work. Noise levels which are lower than those covered by the 1990 Order but which still represent a problem can be dealt with under the Health and Safety at Work (Northern Ireland) Order 1978, by virtue of the general duty it imposes on employers to ensure the health, safety and welfare of their employees and others who may be affected by activities associated with the work.[54]

## Directive 86/188/EEC

The Directive's stated aim[55] is to harmonise procedures for the protection of workers exposed to noise. It also aims to protect health and promote safety. The

---

52. SR No. 147. The Regulations were made on 12 Apr. 1990 and came into operation on 11 June 1990; the equivalent Regulations for the rest of the United Kingdom, the Noise at Work Regulations 1990, came into force on 1 Jan. of that year. The Regulations applicable in Northern Ireland should be read in conjunction with the Health and Safety at Work (NI) Order 1978 (SI 1978/1039) and the Safety Representatives and Safety Committees Regulations (NI) 1979 (SR No. 437).

53. OJ No. L137, 24 May 1986, p. 28. The specific, up-to-date and detailed provisions of Directive 86/188 followed earlier, less comprehensive action on noise in the Directive on the Protection of Workers from the Risks Related to Exposure to Chemical, Physical and Biological Agents at Work.

54. Health and Safety at Work legislation is enforced by environmental health officers employed by district councils or the Health and Safety Inspectorate of the DED.

55. See the preamble to the Directive.

Directive concentrates on two main means of improving noise control; noise prevention in building design and working procedures and the provision of ear defenders as a complementary measure (and indeed where noise cannot be avoided by other means). The Directive, in the light of the paucity of scientific knowledge on the health implications of occupational noise, other than hearing impairment, concentrates on the latter type of impact. The Directive does not succeed in setting out an agreed noise exposure level below which there is no risk to the health of workers; the EC accepts that economic realities mean that some threat to the hearing of workers is inevitable.

### *The Regulations*

#### *Creation and implementation*

The Noise at Work Regulations in Northern Ireland are the product of joint responsibility in this area of the DANI, the DED, the DoE(NI), and the DHSS, all of which deal with workers and working conditions to some extent. The DED is, however, given prime responsibility for the outworking of the Regulations.

#### *Applicability of the regulations*

Duties under the Regulations are imposed on employers[56] and are applicable to employees, self-employed persons, and (as far as is reasonably practicable) any other persons at work who may be affected by the work carried out (regulation 2 (2)(*a*) and (*b*)). Seagoing vessels and aircraft or hovercraft (regulation 3(*a*) and (*b*), respectively) are specifically excluded from the remit of the Regulations.

### *Requirements placed on employers by the regulations*

#### *Assessment of exposure*

Employers whose workers are likely to be exposed to a 'daily personal noise exposure' level of more than 85 dB(A)[57] (the first action level) or to the peak action level of 200 pascals are required to have a noise assessment of their operations carried out by a competent person. The assessment must firstly be of a sufficient standard to enable employees who suffer exposure above the first action level to be identified (regulation 4(1)(*a*)). Secondly, employers are obliged to provide the necessary information with regard to the noise to enable the obligation to take practical action (under regulation 4(1)(*b*)) to be fulfilled. Practical action includes steps to:
- reduce noise exposure (regulation 7);
- provide ear protection (regulation 8);
- establish ear protection zones (regulation 9); and
- provide information to employees (regulation 11).

---

56. Under reg. 2(3))(*a*) and (*b*) the definition of 'employer' includes mine managers as defined by s. 156 of the Mines Act (NI) 1969 and owners, occupiers and agents in control of quarries as defined by art. 2 of the Quarries (NI) Order 1983 (SI 1983/150).

57. dB(A) is a technical term, 'A' describing the frequency weighting given by noise-measuring equipment, indicating the logarithmic progression which represents the ear's response to sound.

The daily personal noise exposure of employees is calculated by a mathematical formula contained in Part I of the Schedule to the Regulations, which calculates the extent and intensity of the individual's personal exposure to sound over a period of eight hours.

The noise assessment is kept strictly under review. If there is any reason to suspect that it is no longer valid or that there has been a significant change in the work to which the assessment relates, changes must be introduced to ensure that the assessment reflects actual conditions in the work-place and is not only a hollow administrative exercise (regulation 4(2)).

Both noise assessments themselves and any subsequent review carried out must be adequately recorded (regulation 5).

## Practical obligations

### Reduction of the risk of hearing damage

Employers are placed under a general obligation to reduce the risk of hearing damage to their employees to the lowest level reasonably practicable (regulation 6). The requirement of reasonable practicability imports a familiar element of cost-benefit analysis to the noise abatement equation.

### Reduction of noise exposure

If an employee is likely to be subject to a daily personal noise exposure level of 90 dB(A) (the second action level) or the peak action level of 200 pascals, his employer must take action,[58] once again subject to the requirement of reasonable practicality, to reduce that employee's exposure.

### Ear protection

Employers are obliged by regulation 8(1) to ensure that workers who are exposed to a daily personal noise exposure level of more than 85dB(A) and less than 90 dB(A), and who request ear protection, are provided with 'suitable and efficient' ear defenders.

If an employee is likely to be exposed to a noise level of 90 dB(A) or more, or to the peak action level of 200 pascals, his employer is obliged to ensure (subject to the reasonable practicality proviso) that the employee is provided with suitable personal ear protectors. The equipment provided should, when properly worn, be such that it can be reasonably expected to offer protection against hearing damage by reducing exposure below the levels mentioned above. The employer is obliged by article 10(1) to ensure, as far as it is reasonably practicable, that any equipment he provides to facilitate his compliance with the regulations is fully and properly used. The only exception to this duty involves personal ear defenders; the Regulations are not paternalistic in this respect, and the proper use of personal ear safety equipment is the personal and indeed the legal responsibility (subject to the requirement that it be practicable) of employees (regulation 10(2)). The same

---

58. This refers to action other than the provision of ear defenders (reg. 7).

provision places employees under a duty to report any defects they discover to their employers.

Employers are also obliged, by regulation 10(1)(*b*), to maintain (subject to the reasonable practicality proviso) any equipment that they provide—including ear defenders—in an efficient state, in working order and good repair.

*Ear protection zones*

Employers are obliged (as far as it is reasonably practicable) to signpost[59] the premises they control in order to demarcate ear protection zones. These are areas where employees will be likely to be exposed to noise levels greater than 90 dB (A) or 200 pascals (regulation 9(2)). Signs should indicate that the area is an ear protection zone and that employees need to wear personal ear defenders (regulation 9(1)(*a*) and (*b*)).

*Provision of information to employees*

Employers are obliged to provide adequate information, instruction and training to employees exposed to noise levels of 85 dB(A) or more or 200 pascals or more for the following purposes:
   (i)   to apprise them of the risk of damage to their hearing through the noise exposure in question;
  (ii)   to show them what steps can be taken to minimise the risk;
 (iii)   to show them the steps they can take to obtain personal ear protectors; and
 (iv)   to show them their legal obligations under the regulations.

*Exceptions and exemptions*

Special provision is made for fairground equipment (regulation 12). The DED also has powers under regulation 13 to grant exemption certificates (these may be conditional or subject to time limits and are subject to written revocation at any time) to employers in respect of:
   (i)   the noise reduction obligation in regulation 7, if the noise exposure level of the relevant employee when averaged over a week is less than 90 dB(A), calculated using the formula provided by Part II of the Schedule to the Regulations; for an exemption to be granted there must be adequate arrangements in place to ensure that the qualifying average noise level is not exceeded;
  (ii)   the obligation under regulation 8(2) to provide ear protectors where the following conditions are fulfilled:
        (*a*)   the daily personal noise exposure level averaged over a week is less than 90 dB(A) and adequate arrangements exist to ensure that this is not exceeded,
        (*b*)   the full and proper use of ear defenders would create health and safety problems for the user, or
        (*c*)   it is not reasonably practicable for ear defenders to be employed even

---

59. Such signs are required to fulfil the conditions specified in A.3.3 of Appendix A to Part I of BS 5378.

though they would normally represent the optimum means of protection against hearing risks.

The power to grant exemptions (and to attach conditions to them) is designed to be used sparingly. It is qualified by the need to take into account other statutory requirements applicable to the operation in question and by an overriding consideration that the health and safety of those whose employer gains an exemption will not be prejudiced as a result.

In addition to the DED's general competence to grant exemptions from the Regulations, the Ministry of Defence may, by virtue of regulation 14, by providing a written certificate, exempt Her Majesty's forces and/or visiting forces[60] from any requirement imposed by the Regulations. Such an exemption is subject to the same limitations as the general exemptions granted by the DED. The Secretary of State for Defence, before granting a regulation 14 exemption, must satisfy himself that suitable arrangements have been made to assess the health risks posed by the noise to be subject to the exemption and to adequately control the noise exposure levels of those covered by the exemption.

Dealing with noise in the work-place, therefore, involves not only complex issues of the balance of responsibilities between employers and employees but also social and economic factors and even national security. It is thus a question of compromise and fitting general controls to specific circumstances rather than attempting to find a single absolute standard applicable to all cases.

### Noise and road traffic

The Motor Vehicles (Construction and Use) Regulations (NI) 1989[61] prohibit excessive noise from the running of motor vehicles and their horns. Breach of these regulations will result in a fine under the Road Traffic (Northern Ireland) Order 1981.[62] The Highway Code for Northern Ireland states that horns should not be used in built-up areas between half past eleven at night and seven o'clock in the morning. Complaints in respect of car horn noise and noisy vehicles should be addressed to the RUC; complaints in respect of general traffic noise based on routing problems should be addressed to the relevant local office of the DoE(NI) Roads Service.

---

60. These are defined by part 1 of the Visiting Forces Act 1952.
61. SR No. 299.
62. SI 1991/154.

# CHAPTER TEN

# Energy and the Environment

## Introduction

This chapter seeks to identify the major issues connected with the generation and use of energy which will shape policy and action in this area into the new millennium. Coverage is focused on the dual environmental problems which are inextricably linked to the energy question; the use of finite resources in generating power, and energy conservation. The pollution implications of the energy sector, while touched on here, are examined in detail in chapter 4.

This chapter is divided into three parts. Part I sets the scene for consideration of the law relating to energy in Northern Ireland by looking at global and regional perspectives on energy issues; Part II focuses on questions of energy generation, with particular reference to the Electricity (Northern Ireland) Order 1992,[1] the Electricity (Non-Fossil Fuel Sources) Order (Northern Ireland) 1994,[2] and the Gas (Northern Ireland) Order 1977;[3] and Part III examines energy conservation issues, concentrating on grant-based initiatives under the Energy Efficiency Grants Regulations (Northern Ireland) 1994[4] and on appliance labelling schemes instituted under the auspices of the EC.

## PART I ENERGY PROBLEMS

The production and use of energy is an extremely sensitive political issue, tied as it is to the securing of a country's industrial progress and prosperity and the domestic comfort of its inhabitants. The central problem is that the advantages alluded to must be bought at a price.

Firstly, the overwhelming proportion of power used in the modern world (and the UK is no exception in this[5]) is generated by using finite natural resources, the fossil fuels, including oil, coal, and natural gas. The continued use of fossil fuels in the prodigal fashion which has characterised human behaviour, particularly since the industrial revolution, is not sustainable. Put simply, we are depleting the resources which stand to be inherited by future generations.

Secondly, in addition to resource issues, the use of fossil fuels to generate energy also creates severe and complex pollution problems, particularly through the production of the so-called 'greenhouse gases' most notably carbon dioxide.

---

1. SI 1992/231.
2. SR No. 132.
3. SI 1977/596.
4. SI 1994/306.
5. The current breakdown of UK energy production by source is (approximately) as follows: fossil fuels 78 per cent, nuclear power 20 per cent, renewable sources 2 per cent.

## International pollution and energy: initiatives

Scientists have long been aware that the production of energy can lead to adverse effects on the environment. As long ago as 1850 a Scottish chemist, Robert Angus Smith, identified the phenomenon which is now widely known as acid rain, and attributed primarily to the emissions of power stations.[6] Because emissions from the burning of fossil fuels can be both airborne and precipitation-borne, acid deposition, while it can occur within national boundaries, also creates international problems. Environmental damage can, it was eventually discovered, be caused by one state 'exporting' its polluting discharges to other states.

International action to deal with this large-scale problem, however, was slow to say the least. The idea of legal action, although supported by those states bearing the burden of pollution generated by others—for example the Scandinavian countries and West Germany—was strongly opposed by states which were net exporters of emissions, notably the UK. Emission controls required the adoption of new technologies, for example flue gas desulphurisation equipment, which would prove costly, so that instead of taking advantage of the status quo and letting the damage lie where it fell, polluters would be forced to bear at least some of the cost of their polluting emissions.

In the end the considerable weight of scientific opinion in respect of the cause and effect of acid rain carried the day. Legal intervention was finally taken in Europe under the framework provided by the Long-Range Transboundary Air Pollution (LRTAP) Convention, which was agreed in 1979, and its subsequent substantive protocols.[7]

While the negotiations which led to the LRTAP agreement and its protocols were extremely lengthy and complex, they at least had the advantage of being supported by fairly conclusive and widely agreed scientific information. The same cannot be said for the next pollution issue intimately connected with energy production, namely, global warming.

The science underlying the debate on global warming is comparatively new, originating with the work of Stolarski and Cicerone and of Molina and Rowland in the early nineteen-seventies, and it is also a controversial area. Estimates of the potential temperature increase due to the proliferation of greenhouse gases vary considerably. The issue is not merely national or even regional (as was the case with acid rain) but global. Some of the range of projected results of global warming will affect everyone to at least some extent; these include (and this list is by no means exhaustive):

- the possibility of low-lying states being engulfed by rising sea levels;
- desertification;
- mass migration;
- variations in agricultural production patterns;
- adverse effects on human health (particularly through the proliferation of skin cancers).

---

6. He also coined the term 'acid rain' itself in his book *Air and Rain: The Beginnings of a Chemical Climatology*, London: Longmans Green 1872.
7. Sulphur dioxide, 1985; nitrogen oxides, 1988; and volatile organic compounds, 1991.

It was widely recognised at a fairly early stage that despite the lack of scientific certainty on the future scale and impact of the problem, the need for action was imperative. The precautionary principle which was to dominate measures to tackle the global warming issue, had already met with success in dealing with the global pollution problem, and acted as the motive force behind the Montreal Protocol on Substances which Deplete the Ozone Layer in 1987. Global warming, however, on both a scientific and political level, presented altogether more complex and controversial problems.

### UN Framework Convention on Climate Change, 1992

The UN Conference on Environment and Development (UNCED) (the 'Earth Summit'), held at Rio de Janeiro in 1992, was a landmark in international environmental affairs. The agenda which will lead us into the next millennium in our dealings with the environment was set at this massive meeting of 178 governments and over 500 non-governmental organisations.

Much of what emerged as a result was not law but, as in the non-binding Rio Declaration on Environment and Development and Agenda 21, took the form of statements of principle and plans for action. The deep divisions between the countries of the industrialised north and the less industrialised southern countries were clear throughout the conference and especially so in the documents mentioned above. Yet Rio did generate some substantive law, where agreement was reached despite formidable political obstacles, and the UN Framework Convention on Climate Change emerged from the conference.

The Climate Change Convention came into being as the result of several years of discussion, firstly scientific (it being widely agreed among scientists by as early as 1985 that global warming was at least a potentially serious issue) and later political. After some preparatory investigation by the UN Environment Programme (UNEP), the General Assembly took over responsibility for negotiating an agreement dealing with climate change, and talks commenced in Washington in 1991 to come up with a complete text for debate in time for the Earth Summit in June the following year. This period of preparation was to prove central to the Convention's success by providing the groundwork which would make it possible to thrash out a compromise between hugely divergent views.[8] The Convention does, however, bear all the hallmarks of a compromise, limiting itself to a commitment to objectives and principles rather than definite targets for the reduction of emissions of greenhouse gases.

The agreed objective of the Convention, as expressed by Article 2:

is to achieve . . . the stabilisation of greenhouse gas concentrations in the atmosphere at a level which would prevent dangerous anthropogenic interference with the climate system. Such a level should be achieved within a time frame sufficient to allow ecosystems to adapt naturally to climate change . . . and to enable economic development to proceed in a sustainable manner.

---

8. For a discussion of some of the divergent negotiation positions adopted see M. Grubb et al., *The Earth Summit Agreements: a Guide and Assessment,* London: Earthscan 1993.

The principles nominated in Article 3 to guide action are largely aspirational, ranging from a conventional commitment to the precautionary principle, through the idea that industrialised countries[9] should take a lead in tackling global warming, to the right of all parties to sustainable development.

The commitments to action enshrined in Article 4[10] are of a purely procedural nature. They include undertaking national inventories of emission sources and carbon sinks;[11] the development and publication of programmes for mitigating climate change; technology transfer to help less industrialised countries to deal with emissions; resource protection plans; and reporting back to the Conference of Parties on action taken. It is in this last requirement that an indication of one of the strengths of the Convention is found.

While the Convention itself is complex and riddled with ambiguity and compromise, it contains within itself the means of ensuring future progress in the substantive law on climate change; Article 7 provides for the creation of the Conference of Parties, which acts as the engine for future action. The Conference of Parties is charged with the responsibility to:

> keep under review the implementation of the Convention and any related legal instruments . . . and [to] make, within its mandate, the decisions necessary to promote the implementation of the Convention.

Article 7 also lays down specific tasks, the most important being to review the obligations contained in the Convention with a view to determining whether they continue to be adequate in the light of developing scientific knowledge. The Convention is therefore provided with a rolling review element which will allow it to keep pace with events. In addition, the Convention may be amended by a three-fourths majority of signatories, should agreement not be possible by consensus.

The Framework Convention adopted the goal of achieving a return to 1990 emission levels by the year 2000. It should be noted, however, that while this target represents some progress on the global warming issue, it will not be sufficient to reverse or even halt the process. Historical emissions are already present in the atmosphere in sufficient quantities to cause a considerable rise in global temperature. Recent research on global warming quoted by Pearce et al., in *Blue Print 3: Measuring Sustainable Development*[12] suggests that a 'business as usual' scenario would lead to an increase in global mean temperature of 2.7°C by 2100. If industrialised countries acted radically to virtually abandon fossil fuels, temperatures would still rise by 2.2°C by 2100. Even if all countries cut their greenhouse emissions by half, the temperature would still rise by 1.7°C.

## Energy policy in the UK

The UK has, by ratifying the Climate Change Convention (in December 1993),

---

9. It is widely acknowledged that global warming began to increase with the impact of the anthropogenic emissions consequent on the industrial revolution and that industrialised countries, as the authors of both historical pollution and the bulk of current emissions, have a special responsibility in dealing with global warming.
10. A two-tier approach is adopted by Art. 4, with more definite policy commitments being required of industrialised countries to adopt policies to mitigate global warming.
11. i.e. those natural resources which process carbon, for example forests.
12. Earthscan 1993; see chap. 11, 'The UK and the global environment'.

accepted both the seriousness of the global warming issue and, as an industrialised country, a leading role in acting to curb the problem. As a result, following detailed negotiation with domestic industry, environmental and other interest groups and the general public, the *Climate Change: the UK Programme*[13] was published in 1994.

Wide consultation was considered appropriate and necessary, since the decisions which affect the production of greenhouse gases, particularly carbon dioxide, are the province not just of government or even industry but also of individual citizens (through the emissions generated by domestic fuels and private transport). While the programme covers several greenhouse gases,[14] including methane and nitrous oxide, carbon dioxide makes by far the most significant contribution to global warming, amounting in 1990 to 67 per cent of all the UK's greenhouse gas emissions. The main sources of carbon dioxide emissions are energy and transport, accounting in 1990 for 35 MtC[15] and 84 MtC, respectively. The programme aims to decrease carbon emissions by 10 MtC on their 1990 level (106 MtC) by 2000; this is broken down into the following target areas and levels:[16]

| Sector | Reduction target (MtC) | Means of achieving reduction |
|---|---|---|
| Domestic energy consumption | 4 | Include tax on domestic fuel,[17] grants, and advice on energy-efficiency |
| Business energy consumption | 2.5 | Advice and information |
| Public sector energy consumption | 1 | Efficiency drive |
| Transport | 2.5 | Increased tax on fuel |

The Climate Change Convention has, therefore, already had a significant effect on the UK's energy policy, at least in respect of emission controls, but it will also have considerable resource implications. These general policy commitments have

---

13. (Cm 2427), published under the requirements of Art. 12 of the Climate Change Convention.
14. Some of the other gases which also have an impact on global warming are already covered by the Montreal Protocol on Substances which Deplete the Ozone Layer, 1987.
15. Million tonnes of carbon. The weight of carbon dioxide can be calculated by multiplying figures by 44 and dividing by 12.
16. The table summarises policy commitments expressed in 'Climate Change: the UK Programme', supra.
17. The controversial imposition of value-added tax on domestic fuel was originally planned in two phases, with an initial tax level of 8 per cent being imposed in the budget of 1994. The second phase, designed to raise VAT to the standard level of 17.5 per cent in 1995, was, however, defeated in Parliament. As a result, alternative charges (notably on fuel for transport) were made in the hope of curbing emissions.

been further fleshed out in the First,[18] Second,[19] Third[20] and Fourth[21] Annual Reports on the Government's environmental policy document, *This Common Inheritance*.[22]

Emission targets in the energy sector will be pursued through a two-strand approach. Firstly, as will be apparent from the table above, an important element in the Government's thinking involves the conservation and more efficient use of energy. As well as using energy more efficiently once it is produced, the state is also examining cleaner sources of energy; these include switching to fossil fuels which emit a lower proportion of carbon, such as natural gas. A second priority is the development of renewable energy sources, which are either responsible for comparatively low carbon emissions or even free from them altogether.

## EC action

General EC action on air pollution (covered in chapter 4) has of course had an impact on energy law in the UK. The Large Combustion Plants Directive,[23] which aims to reduce emissions of sulphur dioxide and the oxides of nitrogen, has had the greatest specific impact on the energy sector. EC legislation also deals with energy-efficiency issues through consumer protection law (see below). In the energy sector, though, EC legal action tends to follow the lead of wider international law, in much the same way as domestic policy within the UK has done.

## Energy policy in Northern Ireland

It seems that the UK has started to develop the roots of a national energy policy in recent years, motivated primarily by its international legal obligations. This policy has reached its most sophisticated form to date under the auspices of the Climate Change Convention.

Energy policy in Northern Ireland is, unlike some other areas of environmental activity, reliant for its motivation and primary content on the work of the Departments of the Environment and Trade and Industry in Great Britain. The reason for this will be readily apparent; the implications of energy use are not merely local or even regional but global and are necessarily the province of national government.

This is not to say, however, that Northern Ireland does not have its own distinctive energy strategy within that adopted by the UK. Northern Ireland presents a unique range of issues and problems in the energy sector, which require a specifically tailored policy approach. The task of developing an energy strategy for Northern Ireland has fallen to the Department of Economic Development; as a result, *Energy for the 90s and Beyond: An Energy Strategy for Northern Ireland*

---

18. *This Common Inheritance: First Year Report* (Cm 1655), 1991.
19. *This Common Inheritance: Second Year Report* (Cm 2068), 1992.
20. *This Common Inheritance: Third Year Report* (Cm 2549), 1994.
21. The 1995 report (Cm 2822) includes the first update on the Government's sustainable development strategy (adopted in 1994), which includes policies on energy and climate change.
22. *This Common Inheritance: Britain's Environment Strategy* (Cm 1200), 1990.
23. See chap. 4.

was published in 1992, setting out the Government's priorities for action in the Province for the rest of the century.

The energy strategy represents a considerable advance on the DED's previous approach to the energy questions facing Northern Ireland as expressed in the 1983 DED discussion paper, *Northern Ireland Energy Issues*. This paper, while designed to shape discussion on providing for Northern Ireland's energy needs in the medium to long term, was heavily influenced by the adverse impact of the oil crisis of 1973 and high price rises of 1979 on Northern Ireland's economy.[24] The focus of the discussion paper was on efficiency in the production and distribution of energy in order to facilitate a positive economic performance, with a 'true economic value' being placed on the fuels in question. As one would expect of a document of this period involving one of the public utilities, emphasis is clearly laid on maximising the role of market forces in controlling the demand for and use of energy.

The discussion paper examined the availability and economic practicability of the various power options available to Northern Ireland. These included assessing the viability of augmenting domestically produced power by gas and electricity links with Great Britain and Ireland and of exploiting energy from alternative and renewable sources.

The conservation of energy from traditional sources was a priority; not only were Government departments in Northern Ireland to take a lead in 'good housekeeping' where energy was concerned, but the energy conservation grant scheme was introduced to give practical encouragement to industry and commerce in the efficient use of energy. The scheme provided grant aid for projects including the insulation of premises and equipment, the promotion of projects using energy from renewable sources, and the provision of funding for more efficient equipment (for example combined heat and power generating systems).

Environmental considerations, however, played at best a peripheral role in the discussion paper, making a discreet appearance only on the penultimate page of the 159-page document—though they were at least highlighted as issues worthy of discussion. The discussion paper merely referred to the 'complexity of the issues' and gave a cursory mention to the effect on emissions of changing fuel sources. It was in many ways a typical product of its time—although it is arguable that it was somewhat outdated even by the standards of the early nineteen-eighties. The environment was, even in the early eighties, an emerging factor in the complex questions surrounding energy production and its consequences, although its rise to the top of the energy agenda was yet to begin.

If the discussion paper was a product of its time, the same is true of the *Energy Strategy* document produced almost a decade later. In the words of Peter Brooke, the Secretary of State, the 'energy scene' in Northern Ireland is set to be transformed as energy-efficiency measures take hold and interconnection with the national electricity grid and the supply of natural gas by pipeline from Scotland are imminent. Energy-efficiency is once again the by-word of the strategy document, but this time not only as an end in itself but also to 'help protect the

---

24. Northern Ireland, lacking indigenous fuel sources, has historically been dependent on imports of oil and coal to supply its energy needs.

environment.' Indeed Mr Brooke went as far as to say that '[t]he central premise is that energy use has consequences which could affect our environmental heritage.' Environmental considerations have therefore moved from the periphery to the very centre of energy policy in Northern Ireland.

The Government has laid out the following strategic objectives for energy in Northern Ireland:

- energy-efficiency and the clean production and use of energy;
- lower costs and the protection of consumer interests;
- diversification of supply; and
- security of supply.

Northern Ireland at present remains almost totally dependent on imported coal and oil to supply its energy needs; in electricity generation, oil accounts for 70 per cent and coal for 30 per cent of power generated. This situation is distinctly different from that in the rest of the UK, where the proportions of power generation are 8 per cent from oil, 70 per cent from coal, and 2 per cent from hydro-electric sources.[25]

The results of the heavy reliance on oil for power generation in Northern Ireland are two-fold. Firstly, electricity prices are on average 15 per cent higher than in the rest of the UK; secondly, since oil has a 3 per cent sulphur content, whereas that of coal is only 1 per cent, reaching EC emission targets under the Large Combustion Plants Directive is significantly more expensive in Northern Ireland than in the rest of the UK.[26]

## PART II ENERGY GENERATION AND THE ENVIRONMENT

### Electricity: solid fuel generation

The Government is committed to greater energy-efficiency as the central strand of its energy policy, subscribing to the widely held belief that it represents the quickest and most cost-effective means by which to combat global warming. Efficiency considerations were therefore brought to the fore in the legislation introduced to privatise Northern Ireland Electricity (NIE). Among the significant provisions contained in the Electricity (Northern Ireland) Order 1992 was the introduction of a 'revenue cap', limiting the incentive to increase sales and instead focusing on securing efficiency.

In addition, the DED itself and the Director-General of Electricity Supply for Northern Ireland are placed under a range of statutory duties with environmental implications. The DED is under a general duty imposed by article 4:

> to take into account [in exercising its functions] the effect on the physical environment of activities connected with the generation, transmission or supply of electricity

---

25. Figures taken from chap. 1 of *Energy for the 90s and Beyond,* supra p. 479.
26. See evidence given by the chief executive of Northern Ireland Electricity (appendix 36) to the House of Commons Environment Committee in its report *Environmental Issues in Northern Ireland* HC 39 (1990).

and a specific duty, by virtue of article 4(4)(*b*):

> to promote efficiency and economy on the part of persons authorised . . .
> to supply or transmit electricity and the efficient use of electricity supplied
> to consumers.

The Director-General is placed under identical duties by article 6.

Generators are also commercially obliged to supply NIE with electricity generated as efficiently as possible.

In addition to securing economic efficiency, the DED also favours what could be termed 'environmental efficiency' in its strategy for the generation of power. One of the key elements of the DED's approach is to work towards improved emission control in the electricity sector, and to this end it supports a four-strand approach, combining straightforward technological fixes with diversification of energy supply. Strategies adopted include:

- the Non-Fossil Fuel Obligation (see below), which requires NIE to purchase a small proportion of its power from generators using renewable technologies;
- the installation of nitrogen oxide abatement equipment at the Kilroot power station;
- the installation of flue gas desulphurisation equipment at Kilroot;
- the conversion of Ballylumford power station to gas (to be supplied by pipeline from Scotland).

Each of these strategies will bring about advantages concerning the environmental impact and security of power supply—but they will do so at a cost; flue gas desulphurisation alone could cost £100 million initially and have annual running costs of between £5 and 10 million,[27] and reducing nitrogen oxide is likely to add 1 per cent to generation bills over two years.[28] NIE is very unwilling to take on such costs and is hoping that the government will allow it to 'borrow' spare emission capacity from other parts of the UK which are well within their emission targets. While this would certainly solve NIE's economic difficulties with abatement measures, it would hardly secure optimum protection for Northern Ireland's environment, nor could it be described as securing equity between NIE and other UK energy producers, which is one of the Government's objectives in extending integrated pollution control to Northern Ireland in the proposal for a Draft Industrial Pollution Control Order 1996.[29]

### Electricity: gas generation

The Government has been eager to promote the reintroduction of gas as a source of energy in Northern Ireland. The expensive and import-dependent town gas system was phased out during the nineteen-eighties. The Government, however, in the light of its wish to diversify Northern Ireland's energy base and with an eye to the environmental advantages of generating power from gas (markedly less air

---

27. Walter McClay, electricity supply director, NIE, quoted in 'The cost of cleaning up power' by Martina Purdy, *Business Telegraph,* 3 Oct. 1995.
28. Ibid.
29. See chap. 4.

pollution is produced as a by-product of the generating process) has been eager to find a means of reintroducing gas as a viable power source.

The restructuring of the electricity supply system which accompanied the privatisation of the electricity industry has allowed the Government to give practical effect to the policy commitment to promoting gas expressed in *Energy for the 1990s and Beyond*. To this end, Ballylumford power station, having been purchased by British Gas, is being converted for gas-fired generation. Gas piped from Scotland by the official gas undertakers for the Province, Premier Energy Suppliers Ltd and Premier Transco Ltd.,[30] will power the converted station. The use of natural gas piped in from Great Britain is geared to promote maximum efficiency in the use of the gas resource. The project has also achieved EC backing to the tune of £56 million from the European Regional Development Fund[31] (the total cost is £259.2 million; the balance is to come from the private sector).

The main piece of legislation on energy generated by gas remains, however, the woefully outdated (particularly from an environmental point of view) Gas (Northern Ireland) Order 1977. The Order was perhaps even outdated at the time it was made, since it is almost totally devoid of environmental considerations.

The DoE(NI) is given a minimal role in regulating the activities of gas undertakers; its role is to superintend the digging up of roads, bridges, sewers, drains or tunnels for the laying of pipes and to approve the reinstatement of any of these that were disturbed by excavations (paragraph (1), Schedule I—also known as the Gas Supply Code). Paragraph (25) of the Gas Supply Code also provided some incidental environmental protection, by making it an offence to fail to prevent gas escapes.

The pipeline connecting Northern Ireland to Scotland (which is due to come on stream in late 1996) has had some interesting and unforeseen environmental consequences, in the form of disturbing the arms dumps established at Beaufort's Dyke in the Irish Sea following the Second World War. The activity on the seabed necessitated by the construction of the pipeline, which passes near the dyke, has been linked to approximately a thousand incidents of armaments being washed up along the Scottish and Northern Ireland coasts. The full scale of this problem has yet to emerge, it having been revealed that no complete records remain of the material dumped in the area. The proposed electricity interconnector with Scotland may run into similar problems.

## Diversification of energy generation

Energy-efficiency is not only geared to securing sound environmental practices, it also aims to provide a reasonably priced and good-quality service to consumers. The diversification of energy sources which is being introduced in Northern Ireland should go some way towards promoting this—although there are doubts about the role of the market in what is essentially a privatised monopoly.

---

30. These firms were declared gas undertakers by the DED under its powers contained in the Gas (NI) Order 1977 (SI 1977/596) and SI 1982/84 in the Gas Undertaker (Premier Energy Suppliers Limited) Order (NI) 1994 (SR No. 293) and the Gas Undertaker (Premier Transco Limited) Order (NI) 1994 (SR No. 41)

31. As reported by Desmond McCartan, 'Gas project wins Euro cash', *Belfast Telegraph,* 5 Jan. 1995.

Electricity prices in Northern Ireland have been the subject of comment and investigation by the House of Commons and its committees on more than one occasion in the relatively short period since privatisation.

A variety of means are favoured by the Government for achieving greater efficiency and decreased emissions in energy generation. These include the use of combined heat and power generation technology, the use of emission abatement, and the use of natural gas, referred to above. Unfortunately these can prove to be expensive; for example, it is estimated that energy supplied from natural gas will, when it comes on stream, add 2 to 3 per cent to power generation costs—which already account for 60 per cent of domestic and 80 per cent of industrial and commercial fuel bills. Diversification of energy sources, however, by whatever means, will also serve to secure Northern Ireland's energy production from the vagaries of the oil market (the fourth of the DED's strategic goals) as well as helping to conserve fossil fuel resources and to reduce polluting emissions.

It is in this particular part of the energy sector that the state has had to abandon a purely market-based approach to the supply of energy and provide specific statutory and financial intervention to promote its policy. The basic reason for this is fairly simple and was clearly expressed by Adam Butler (Minister of State) in the DED's 1983 discussion paper; energy developments tend to be costly, and profits tend to take a long time to absorb costs.

Diversification of the energy sector in Northern Ireland involves action on two distinct levels. The first is decreasing reliance on oil for the generation of electricity; interconnection with the national electricity grid and the supply of natural gas from Scotland will go some way towards achieving this end. While such moves will have some positive environmental side effects in the reduction of emissions, they are based primarily on securing efficiency objectives, and emissions will still occur in respect of generating activities.

The second aspect of diversification of energy supply, while also concerned with the preservation of scarce fuel resources, is more self-consciously environmental in its orientation; the development of energy from renewable sources.

### Energy from renewable sources

Policy in respect of renewable technologies in Northern Ireland has matured considerably over the last decade. One positive development has been the publication (in July 1993) of a report, *Prospects for Renewable Energy in Northern Ireland,* commissioned by the Department of Trade and Industry in collaboration with the DED and Northern Ireland Electricity PLC. The report set out to 'examine the technical and economic factors affecting the development of renewable energy resources in Northern Ireland' and the prospects 'of reducing Northern Ireland's dependence upon oil and coal . . . [which] will contribute to a cleaner environment.' The report opened official discussion on the introduction of a Non-Fossil Fuel Order for Northern Ireland (NFFO),[32] which had become a

---

32. The Non-Fossil Fuel Order was originally introduced in England and Wales in the Electricity Act 1989, (which privatised the industry) in order to ensure continued research, development and deployment of renewable energy technologies. The first Order was made in Sep. 1990.

possibility since the entry into force of the Electricity (Northern Ireland) Order 1992. Article 35 of the 1992 Order provides that the DED may, following consultation with the Director-General of Electricity Services, make an Order requiring those licensed under article 19(1)(*b*) and (*c*) (to transmit and supply electricity, respectively) to take up a specified amount of generating capacity from non-fossil fuel sources (article 35(2)). Failure to comply with such an order is an offence, punishable on conviction on indictment by an unlimited fine.

The Order then provides a guaranteed market for energy produced from renewable and alternative sources, even though they do not represent the cheapest means of producing energy. The NFFO was introduced to Northern Ireland in 1994 and is administered by NIE. It is a sophisticated instrument, attempting to take into account the fact that the various forms of renewable energy are at different stages of technical and market development by grouping them together in bands for the purposes of pricing and allocation.

The DED and the Director-General of Electricity Supply for Northern Ireland are placed under a duty by article 4(4)(*c*) of the 1992 Order

> to promote research into, and the development and use of, new tech-
> niques by or on behalf of persons authorised by a licence to generate,
> transmit or supply electricity,

which underpins continuing activity in this area.

The Secretary of State is also placed under a duty, by article 60 of the 1992 Order, to exercise the powers conferred on him by section 5 of the Science and Technology Act 1965. The Secretary of State is authorised to fund research and development in science and technology by the 1965 Act. The Order requires him to promote such research and development into new techniques for the generation, transmission or supply of electricity as appear to him to be necessary in the national interest; this of course can and will include research into renewable energy sources.

*Prospects for Renewable Energy* looks at the range of renewable sources available and at their potential viability in Northern Ireland. Renewable energy sources are defined as those which can be renewed or replaced within a relatively short time. The report predicts that in the short term—i.e. by the year 2000— viable contributions are possible from wind, bio-fuel, waste and hydro sources. The report estimates the maximum contribution of energy (allowing for public acceptability, market conditions, and penetration into the energy market) from non-fossil fuel sources by 2000 at 540 GWh/y;[33] total system demand is 6,500 GWh/y. The potential contribution therefore amounts to some 8 per cent of projected energy demand. This will represent a considerable change from the current pattern of power generation; in the UK as a whole in 1994 energy from renewable sources accounted for only 2 per cent of power generated (though in Scotland the figure was 15 per cent). The Government aims to produce 1,500 MW[34] of the UK's energy needs from renewable sources by 2000, which will result in an estimated 0.5 MtC saving in emissions.

---

33. Gigawatt [1,000,000,000 watts] hours per year.
34. 1 megawatt = 1,000,000 watts.

Tidal, wave and geothermal sources are rejected in the report as proving inappropriate to local conditions. In the long term—i.e. by 2025—short-rotation willow coppicing is likely to be a significant source of energy. The DANI has played a prominent role in developing the plantations and technologies necessary for willow coppicing and bio-fuels (i.e. agricultural wastes).

### Renewable energy sources in practice: the Non-Fossil Fuels Order

The Electricity (Non-Fossil Fuel Sources) Order (Northern Ireland) 1994[35] gives practical effect to policy priorities concerning the development of energy from renewable sources. The Order was made on 31 March 1994 and came into operation on the same day.

The approach adopted is a progressive one, beginning with the status quo and focusing on providing energy from those sources of alternative energy which are currently best developed and best suited to the prevailing conditions in Northern Ireland. Article 2 of the Order requires NIE to make arrangements, covering the successive periods outlined in Schedule 1 to the Order, to secure 'the aggregate amount of generating capacity available to it from non-fossil fuel generating stations of the description specified in that Schedule . . .' The types of generation, quantities of electricity (in megawatts) and periods specified in Schedule 1 are as follows:

| Power Source | Period 1 31/4/94– 30/9/94 | Period 2 30/9/94– 31/3/95 | Period 3 31/3/95– 30/9/95 | Period 4 30/9/95– 31/3/96 | Period 5 31/3/96– 31/3/97 | Period 6–17[36] until 2009 |
|---|---|---|---|---|---|---|
| Wind | — | 6.426 | 12.664 | 12.664 | 12.664 | 12.664 |
| Sewage gas | — | 0.001 | 0.560 | 0.560 | 0.560 | 0.560 |
| Water | 0.030 | 0.030 | 1.890 | 2.374 | 2.374 | 2.374 |

Thus by 2009 NIE will be required to obtain 15.598 MW per year of power from these three renewable sources.

### Conditions to be met by non-fossil-fuel generating activities

Article 3 and Schedule 2 to the Order require that certain conditions precedent be met before the required non-fossil-fuel energy may be purchased. Some of these conditions precedent have environmental implications, including the requirement that the necessary planning permission for the construction of the generating stations (paragraph (1)) has been obtained. In addition the NFFO requires that generating activities be duly licensed under the 1992 Order (paragraph (4)). The means of generating in question must also have been proved to be commercially, physically and technically viable (paragraph (5)). Indeed the Order goes so far as to require that the commercial standing of the generating company that undertakes to supply power from non-fossil sources is secure. Schedule 3 allows agreements with

---

35.   SI 1994/132.
36.   Periods run from 31 Mar. of one year to the same date the next year.

the generators of non-fossil fuels to be terminated by NIE in the event of default in supply (paragraph (2)) or the winding up of the company (paragraph (3)).

The provisions of the Non-Fossil Fuels Order do not appear to be onerous, although they do require that NIE pay a price greater than that which would be charged for the same amount of energy obtained from fossil fuel sources. The amount of energy involved remains a fairly small proportion of the annual total referred to above. Despite this, NIE cites the high cost of energy from renewable sources as a reason for the high energy prices which continue to be borne by consumers. It is worth setting against this claim the half-yearly profits of £46 million announced by NIE for the first part of 1995.

It is apparent that NIE views itself as an organisation committed to maximising its efficiency and therefore the dividends payable to its shareholders. This understandable market-based attitude does not, however, sit easily with the longer-term view of energy production espoused by the non-fossil fuels requirement. Indeed it is the intention of NIE's chief executive to request that the second tranche of the Non-Fossil Fuels Order, covering the period after 31 March 1997, be delayed and that the preferential prices it is obliged to pay to producers of energy from renewable sources be reduced.[37]

While the Non-Fossil Fuels Order shows that the law can actually support and develop energy practice and can indeed (to at least some extent) force technology to develop, this is not a typical situation, and the law can sometimes have problems keeping pace with technological developments in the energy sector. There are, for example, no regulations at present which control the production of bio-gas by anaerobic digestion, although general health and safety law covers gas control and use.

Using renewable sources can have broader positive impacts on diverse sectors of the environment. The use of bio-gas from agricultural and sewage sludges allows the controlled use of methane; coppicing allows the use of otherwise rather unproductive land for a valuable and useful crop; incineration of waste cuts pressure on landfill (at present 90 per cent of the UK's domestic and commercial waste is landfilled) and merely recycles (rather than adds to) the production of carbon dioxide.

### Renewable energy sources: some environmental drawbacks

Energy from renewable sources, although often representing a significant improvement as far as emissions (particularly of greenhouse and acid gases) are concerned, can have adverse environmental consequences of its own. Wind farms, for example, produce visual pollution and therefore adversely affect amenity, a defect shared by several other alternative technologies. Windfarms also generate noise and can interfere with communications networks. The potential for wind-based energy is limited by several factors, notably physical constraints such as populated areas, transport routes, and the natural environment; technical constraints also arise (see below). Finally, institutional constraints, for example protective designations such as AONB and ASSI,[38] can arise.

---

37. Letter to the chair of the Ulster Unionist Party Consumer Affairs Committee 17 Dec. 1995.
38. See chaps 7 and 8.

Integrating energy from renewable sources into the electricity grid can present technical difficulties, since it is often produced intermittently. The electricity system in Northern Ireland is small and characterised by low demand; peak demand is approximately 1,500 MW and minimum demand 300 MW; as a result it can be difficult to integrate energy from intermittent sources into the system. For example, wind power representing more than 10 per cent of minimum demand (30 MW) would in the opinion of NIE be likely to cause grid management problems. Technological progress in smoothing out some of the problems posed by renewables is rapid; at least some of the difficulties then would appear to be limited to the short term.

## Incidental protection for the environment from energy law

The energy sector can afford very specific protection to the environment, especially with regard to the imposition of emission standards and through the promotion of energy from renewable sources; but it can also provide benefits to the environment by less direct means. For example, the Electricity (Northern Ireland) Order 1992 provides protection to the physical environment as a by-product of its prime function of controlling electricity generation and supply.

The first incidence of protection afforded by the Order lies in the requirement in article 8 that the generation, transmission and supply of electricity be carried out only under licence (or a valid exemption). This of course has economic implications but it also has the valuable environmental function of preventing the adverse physical and pollution impacts that would result from an unrestricted proliferation of electricity-oriented activities.

Licences to generate, transmit or supply electricity are subject to a number of conditions, and these can have an impact on the environment. Conditions may, by virtue of article 11(1)(*a*), include those which in the view of the grantor (i.e. the DED in consultation with the Director-General of Electricity Supply) 'appear . . . to be expedient having regard to the duties imposed by Articles 4 and 6,' which, as detailed above, include a duty to take account of the effect of activities which they control on the physical environment.

Further environmental considerations come into play in the 1992 Order through the requirement that the DED give its consent for the construction of power stations with a capacity greater than 2 MW (article 39(2)) and other electricity infrastructure, including power lines with a voltage greater than 20 kilovolts (article 40(2)). Articles 39 and 40 and Schedule 8 to the Order provide for a (comparatively rudimentary) control mechanism to limit the environmental impact of power line developments. The DED's consent can be subject to such conditions as it deems appropriate (articles 39(5) and 40(3)); these can include conditions geared towards the protection of the environment.

Schedule 8 lays down the procedure for applications, which are to be in writing and accompanied by an illustrative map (paragraph (1)). The provisions of the consent procedure as laid down in Schedule 8 pay particular attention to the rights and interests of those whose land may be affected by electricity power line developments. More specific protection is offered by article 41 and Schedule 9 to the Order, which relate specifically to the preservation of amenity and fisheries.

The law dealing with gas has yet to be updated in Northern Ireland to include new environmental imperatives—though the provisions dealing with electricity could lead the way in developing a more environmentally sensitive approach to the wider energy sector.

## Smoke control programmes

In addition to protection offered to the environment from energy law in the true sense of this term, measures to prevent or minimise air pollution connected with energy are also worthy of consideration. One example is found in local authority promotion of the use of less-polluting domestic fuels since the middle of the nineteen-sixties. In Belfast alone 80,000 homes are covered by twenty-four designated smoke control areas. Northern Ireland is aiming to comply with Directive 80/779/EEC by the end of 1993.[39] The issue of local air pollution and the measures taken to deal with it are examined in detail in chapter 4 (Part I, section 5).

## *PART III* ENERGY CONSERVATION

### Voluntary action

Voluntary action promoting energy-efficiency by the business and commercial communities is encouraged by the work of the Northern Ireland Energy Efficiency Action Group, which has been established recently by the Government. This is a body made up of representatives of all sectors of the economy whose task is to encourage industry and commerce to set targets for energy-efficiency and to assess progress, advising on difficulties and effective strategies.

### The state and energy conservation

Article 44 of the Electricity (Northern Ireland) Order 1992 allows the Director-General of Electricity Supply, after consultation with public electricity suppliers (and other persons or bodies which appear to him to be representative of those likely to be affected), to determine the standards for efficient use of electricity by consumers to be attained by suppliers and to publish these standards. Once again this type of legislative approach applying to suppliers of energy, particularly when coupled with information and grant schemes to encourage the public as consumers of energy to use it more efficiently, could be used as a starting point for action covering the wider energy sector.

The energy advice shop, which has used an intensive media campaign to publicise general energy-efficiency issues and particularly the Domestic Energy Efficiency Grants Regulations (Northern Ireland) 1994,[40] has done much to raise the profile of energy-efficiency in the public consciousness.

The Energy Efficiency Grants Regulations were issued by the Department of Economic Development (with the consent of the Department of Finance and Personnel) using powers contained in the Social Security (Northern Ireland) Order 1990.[41] The Regulations provide grants for improving energy-efficiency in the

---

39. i.e. the end of the agreed UK derogation from the Directive.
40. SR No. 308.
41. SI 1990/1511.

home for pensioners[42] and those receiving certain social security benefits.[43] The Regulations provide an administrative regime for dealing with such grants, including making provision for a list of approved contractors to deal with approved works. (Applicants may also carry out the work themselves, though the grant levels[44] in this case are slightly lower than in relation to work carried out by recognised 'network installers', as defined by regulation 16.)

Those works approved for grant aid in the Regulations are outlined in regulation 3 as being those which are to improve the thermal insulation of dwellings and which otherwise reduce or prevent energy wastage in respect of space and water heating. Grants may also be made to cover the provision of advice on these classes of work.

Further detail of the types of work covered is provided by regulation 6(1). These include roof space insulation (paragraph (*a*)) and the draughtproofing of internal and external doors and windows (paragraph (*b*)).

## Appliance labelling and energy-efficiency

While the grant scheme outlined above has the potential to make a considerable impact on domestic energy use, particularly given the comparatively high level of reliance on state benefits in Northern Ireland, of wider application and in many ways more typical is the provision of information on the energy-efficiency of specific types of appliance. The EC particularly favours the provision of information to the public on the energy-efficiency of household goods[45] as a strategy for promoting sound choices by consumers which will in turn promote better use of energy.

A typical example of domestic implementation of the EC labelling scheme can be found in the Boiler (Efficiency) Regulations 1993,[46] as amended by the Boiler (Efficiency) (Amendment) Regulations 1994.[47] Under the Regulations, energy-efficient appliances are identified by the 'CE' mark (regulation 7), an example of which is provided in Schedule 1. The 'CE'[48] mark is awarded to appliances by a 'notified body' (which is appointed by the state and defined in regulation 8)

---

42. Reg. 4(1)(*b*) covers applications in respect of their dwellings by householders (reg. 4(1)(*a*)) who are pensioners (they may qualify either in their own right or through their spouse). Householders may be freeholders, lessees, or tenants (reg. 4(2)).

43. Reg. 4(1)(*b*) provides that householders in receipt (either in their own right or through the entitlement of their spouse) of the following benefits are eligible to make a claim under the regulations: disability living allowance; income support; family credit; disability working allowance; or housing benefit.

44. The grant levels applicable to each category of work are detailed in reg. 10.

45. See, for example, Directive 92/75/EEC OJ L297, 13 Oct. 1992, on the Energy Labelling of Household Electric Refrigerators, Freezers and their Combinations as implemented by Directive 94/2/EC OJ L45/1, 17 Feb. 1994, and Directive 92/42/EEC Concerning Efficiency Requirements for New Hot Water Boilers Fired With Liquid or Gaseous Fuels OJ L167, 22 June 1982 (as amended).

46. SI 1993/3083.

47. A broadly similar approach is taken by the Energy Efficiency (Refrigerators and Freezers) Regulations 1994 (SI 1994/3076).

48. The mark must be legible and affixed to the appliance in an easily visible and indelible manner (reg. 10(1)).

meeting objective criteria laid down in regulation 5. The notified body in the UK is the UK Eco-Labelling Board. In Northern Ireland enforcing the Regulations is the responsibility of the Department of Economic Development (regulation 12(*d*)).

The UK Eco-Labelling Board, as the body competent to award the 'CE' mark, has its role delineated by the contents of Schedule 4, which outlines the requirements of the 'EC type examination' to which appliances are to be subjected. The board will be required to look at a typical sample appliance (paragraph (1))[49] supplied by the manufacturer (paragraph 2(3)) on the application of the latter (paragraph 2(1)). The application must be supported by documentary evidence supplied by the manufacturer, including information to identify the manufacturer and his premises, and specified technical information (paragraph 2(2)).[50] The Board is required to examine the documents supplied and to verify that the sample supplied has been manufactured in compliance with them; it must then identify the features designed to fit EC requirements and test the equipment to verify its compliance with the relevant standards (paragraph (4)).

Where EC standards are met, the board must issue an 'EC type examination certificate' containing details of the manufacturer, the approved type of appliance, and the results of its examination (paragraph (5)(1)). Notified bodies throughout the EC are obliged to communicate relevant information in respect of the status of 'EC type examination certificates' to their counterparts elsewhere in the EC in order to promote a standardised approach to regulation (paragraph (7)).

It is forbidden to supply or put in service new appliances which do not bear the 'CE' mark and which are not accompanied by a 'certificate of conformity' stating (truthfully) that the energy-efficiency requirements laid down by the EC for the class of appliance in question have been complied with (regulation 6 and Schedule 2). False or misleading marking of appliances is an offence under regulation 7.

Failure to comply with the Regulations will be communicated by notice[51] to the manufacturers of the appliance in question by the notified body (regulation 9(2)), which will be required to ensure that the appliance is altered appropriately (regulation 9(3)(*a*)) and to ensure that no similar appliance is put into service unless it complies with the Regulations (regulation 9(3)(b)). If the manufacturer fails to take the requisite action within the period specified in the notice, EC approval for the appliance will be suspended (regulation 9(4)). In addition at this time it will be forbidden to supply appliances of the type referred to in the notice until compliance with its terms is secured (regulation 9(6)).

Manufacturers are obliged to keep records, of both technical and administrative data, for a period of ten years (following the last date on which the appliance received official approval), which are to be at the state's disposal (regulation 11). Conviction for the offence of failing to keep adequate records will result in a fine of up to £400. Other offences under the 'substantive' requirements of the

---

49. Para. 2(3) of Sch. 4 allows additional appliances to be requested by the notified body for the purpose of completing its test programme.
50. Para. 3 requires that the technical information supplied be sufficient to enable the product's conformity with the regulations to be assessed, and goes on in sub-para. (*a*)–(*f*) to specify the documents to be included.
51. The notice will give details of the failure (or failures) in question and will give reasons for the decision reached (reg. 9(5)).

Regulations will result in a fine of up to £2,000. Various defences to the range of offences established in the Regulations are available under regulation 14; these include dealing with second-hand equipment (regulation 14(1)(*a*)) and exercising 'due diligence' (regulation 14(2)); this defence is, however, subject to qualification.

# PART THREE

# CHAPTER ELEVEN

# Environmental Impact Assessment

This chapter is divided into four parts. Part I examines the history and evolution of the concept of environmental assessment. Part II looks in detail at the provisions of Directive 85/337/EEC on the Assessment of the Effects of Certain Private and Public Projects on the Environment.[1] Part III details provisions covering environmental assessment in Northern Ireland; the Planning (Assessment of Environmental Effects) Regulations (NI) 1989,[2] the Roads (Assessment of Environmental Effects) Regulations (NI) 1988,[3] the Environmental Assessment (Afforestation) Regulations (NI) 1989,[4] the Harbour Works (Assessment of Environmental Effects) Regulations (NI) 1990,[5] and the Drainage (Environmental Assessment) Regulations (NI) 1991.[6] Part IV outlines special assessment requirements in respect of wildlife sites of European significance under Directive 92/43/EEC[7] EC on the Conservation of Natural Habitats of Wild Flora and Fauna, as implemented by the Conservation (Natural Habitats etc.) Regulations (NI) 1995.[8]

## PART I THE ORIGIN OF ENVIRONMENTAL IMPACT ASSESSMENT

### The United States

Environmental impact assessment, although recently the source of some controversy in the UK, is by no means a novel weapon in the armoury of environmental protection. The concept of adding a special procedural element to decision-making processes affecting the environment and attempting to measure the impact of major development first came into use in the United States in the provisions of the groundbreaking National Environmental Policy Act 1969. While new in its thinking, the NEPA was heavily qualified in its impact, extending only to the agencies of the Federal government. It did, however, apply to the whole gamut of Federal activity, section 102 providing that all proposals for:

> legislation and other major Federal actions significantly affecting the quality of the human environment [should include] a detailed statement by the responsible officials on the environmental impact of the proposed action.

1. OJ L 175, 5 July 1985.
2. SR No. 20.
3. SR No. 344.
4. SR No. 226.
5. SR No. 181.
6. SR No. 376.
7. OJ L 206, 22 July 1992.
8. SR No. 380.

The range of activities covered is comprehensive, including legislative proposals, construction projects (both civil and military) carried out by Federal agencies or funded by them, and projects requiring a federal licence.

The potential impact of the innovation was curtailed, however, for while federal activities were and are significant in both number and scale, they constitute only a small fraction of activity affecting the environment. Government guidelines[9] issued by the Council on Environmental Quality[10] (CEQ) followed to add flesh to the bones of statutory provision. The guidelines aimed to provide a coherent approach to the difficult task of adding environmental value (which by their nature are often intangible and thus difficult to quantify) to the traditional economic and technical evaluation of federal proposals.

Environmental impact statements (produced by the sponsoring agency) are required by the guidelines mentioned above to cover the following elements:

- a comprehensive technical description of the proposed action and a cost-benefit analysis of its probable impact on the overall environment,[11] including ecosystems, land use and development, and the human community;
- a description of unavoidable adverse environmental impact and proposals to ameliorate this;
- description and analysis of the alternative courses of action considered and their environmental effects; and
- resource allocation issues.

Each of these potential impacts must be assessed in terms of their direct and indirect effects. The list of factors to be addressed, though by no means representing the full extent of what may be covered, illustrates how demanding (at least in theory) the environmental assessment package provided for by the NEPA is capable of being. Its effectiveness, however, has been considerably undermined by the willingness of Congress to waive the Act's requirements, particularly in relation to the vexed questions of power and energy. In addition, proposals must pass the 'threshold requirement' of 'significantly affecting the quality of the environment' before the environmental statement process will be brought into play. The CEQ has delegated the responsibility of determining whether the threshold has been reached to the Federal agencies and Departments (and even local government in community-based programmes) concerned, which have in turn published detailed guidelines to ensure uniformity of approach. The authorities concerned are required to give an undertaking that the assessment of environmental impacts of projects will be completed before funds are released to put them into effect. This requirement, as well as providing protection for the environment, ensures a degree of local democracy in the execution of federal projects, since the evaluation process provides the opportunity for informing the public and for community participation.

The importance on a theoretical and philosophical level of the introduction of environmental impact statements under the NEPA cannot be overstated, since, for

---

9.  Interim guidelines were introduced in 1970 and revised in 1973.
10. Established by s. 202 of the NEPA.
11. S. 101(*b*) lays down in broad terms environmental factors which may be considered in measuring environmental impact. Detailed provision as to coverage can be found in Appendix II of the CEQ Guidelines; included are physical impacts on all environmental media and species and qualitative aspects of the human environment, including recreation and the historical environment.

the first time, an overt attempt was being made to place value on the environment. This in turn adds a significant and entirely novel aspect to traditional cost-benefit calculations on the value of human activity, which the government is daily called to make in the public interest. The context of section 102 adds greatly to its value, for it is set against a legislative background seeking to introduce a new co-ordinated and comprehensive approach to the role of Federal government in the management of the environment. For example, section 101 of the NEPA requires that the planning and development plans adopted by Federal agencies minimise the long-term environmental effects of Federal actions. Strategies to be addressed include recycling, rational resource use, and the ultimate goal of securing the right of society to a safe, healthy and aesthetically sound environment.

The provisions of the NEPA have been upheld by the courts as providing a viable basis on which to challenge agency action on numerous occasions. The NEPA has also prompted state governments to adopt their own versions of environmental impact assessment, some of which are even more far-reaching than the Federal legislation (while this is encouraging in some respects, it does bring with it the dangers of conflict and overlapping of laws). The NEPA approach has also had a significant impact beyond the borders of the United States, as it provided the spur for governmental action on the impact of the state (and indeed that of private legal persons) on the environment on a global scale.

## The international dimension

There can be few innovations in environmental law which have spread with quite the rapidity and on quite the same scale as environmental impact assessment. By the time the Organisation for Economic Co-operation and Development turned its attention to the issue in 1979,[12] several of its member states had already adopted their own separate environmental assessment schemes or added elements of environmental impact assessment to their existing land use planning regimes. In addition, as scientific understanding of the environment began to grow in extent and sophistication, attention was increasingly focused on transnational environmental impact issues and information exchange in order to improve the quality of the procedures available to deal with them.

The OECD report, though limited in its application to development projects, provided a means of both focusing attention on environmental impact assessment and assuring it of a place on the international political agenda. The report provided a survey[13] which demonstrated a high level of acceptance for environmental impact assessment in most of the group of industrialised countries which constitute the OECD.[14]

While legal approaches to securing environmental assessment varied considerably (from the specific legal provision adopted in the United States to the inclusion of environmental considerations in the development and pollution

---

12. See *Environmental Impact Assessment,* OECD 1979.
13. By the report's own admission (p. 5), the information on the progress attained by member states was limited, relying on each state's own documentary evidence rather than independent research.
14. At the time the states involved were Australia, Austria, Belgium, Canada, Denmark, Finland, France, Federal Republic of Germany, Greece, Ireland, Italy, Japan, Luxembourg, Netherlands, New Zealand, Norway, Portugal, Spain, Sweden, Switzerland, Turkey, UK, and United States.

control regimes claimed by the UK), the idea that environmental impact assessment was valuable had, within ten years of the establishment of the NEPA, gained fairly wide acceptance. The OECD report was envisaged as only the beginning of more detailed investigation of the subject. The report readily recognised that the best means of securing effective environmental assessment procedures was essentially a matter for each member state but noted at the same time that states also had much to learn from each other in the development of this still novel branch of law. The report attempted to isolate key problem areas and to postulate some solutions.

### Key issues in environmental assessment as identified by the OECD

The first issue dealt with was the need for impartiality of the assessment; obvious difficulties could arise where the state agency promoting the project in question was also responsible for evaluating its environmental impact. The OECD suggested that this problem could be avoided, firstly, by ensuring that national standards were created, stipulating the appropriate form and content for environmental assessment, and thus in some measure ensuring at least a minimum standard of credibility. Secondly, effectiveness could be secured by rendering the decision-making process as transparent as possible, by providing for an objective supervisory body, and requiring wide consultation both of experts and the public.

The report was careful to acknowledge that while environmental impact assessment is a useful tool for gathering information about the possible consequences of a proposed project for the environment, it is not of itself sufficient to protect the environment. Its utility depends entirely on the role it is allowed to play in the decision-making process, which will determine whether or not development should take place.[15] An environmental assessment, it was concluded, must therefore be an authoritative documen (prepared by experts and scientifically and intellectually convincing) in order to play a significant role in influencing decisions that will have an impact on the environment.

In addition, it was agreed that assessment of the options available in each case needed to take place sufficiently early in the decision-making process to ensure that real options are being considered in order to choose that with the least adverse impact on the environment. This point is of central importance if environmental assessment is to avoid becoming a sterile administrative exercise offering a rationalisation after the event of the decision to back a particular proposal.

### A methodology for environmental assessment suggested by the OECD

Once the rationale and status of environmental assessment had been discussed, the report went on to identify a methodology which would secure a viable regime in practice. The elements of this methodology will each be addressed in turn.

### Identification of projects requiring assessment

The logical starting point was to identify those projects deemed to be in need of

---

15. Equally, an environmental assessment may be useful in determining the content of conditional approval for a particular project.

assessment. A list based on project type alone could not adequately determine this important issue; other issues, particularly the scale, location and complexity of the proposed development, were also deemed to be crucial considerations.

*Content of an environmental assessment*

The content of the environmental impact assessment itself is of course a key issue and goes right to the heart of the problem of evaluating the environmental costs of a particular course of action. The OECD provided a check-list of essential elements:[16]

- a description of the project being assessed, in particular its characteristics with regard to emissions to the environment etc.;
- a description of the environment into which the project is to be placed;
- a description and preferably quantified estimation of each separate impact of the project on the environment;
- a consideration of alternatives, if available, including comparison of 'with project' and 'without project' future situations; and
- an analysis of environmental impacts leading to an overall assessment and recommendations.

This list of factors to be considered is daunting in itself, and its practical application is even more demanding, requiring that all impacts of the project (from the transient and reversible to the permanent and irreversible, primary and secondary, direct and indirect) on all environmental media and on the natural and human environments and their inhabitants be identified and quantified. The process of carrying out an environmental assessment, if it is to be done well and so correctly serve the purpose for which it is designed, is then certain to be onerous and time-consuming.

# PART II THE EUROPEAN DIMENSION

The OECD was not alone in the international arena in focusing its attention on the new means of securing environmental protection which environmental assessment provided. The EC also concentrated its efforts in the area of environmental assessment as part of its wider environmental policy.

## The role of environmental assessment in EC environmental policy

Environmental impact assessment fitted extraordinarily well with three of the EC's key concerns in dealing with the environment, as well as having been the subject of an early and explicit policy commitment in its own right in the Second Environmental Action Programme.[17]

First, it is essentially a means of securing a proactive or preventive approach to the question of environmental damage, a general EC policy commitment enshrined in the First[18] and Second Environmental Action Programmes. Second,

---

16. See p. 20 of the OECD Report, supra, note 12.
17. Second Community Environmental Action Programme OJ No. C 139.
18. First Environmental Action Programme OJ No. C 112.

environmental assessment could be used to give effect to the 'polluter pays' principle, a key concern in EC environment policy, by placing the burden of evaluating environmental effects on those promoting development. Thirdly, the environmental assessment process is, at least in part, geared to securing informed, open and transparent decision-making in environmental issues. An active role is ensured for the citizen as well as the state, a policy commitment later expressed in the Fourth Environmental Action Programme.[19]

Securing EC action on environmental impact assessment was a long-drawn-out process. If the OECD has found difficulty in dealing with the complex issues involved at a theoretical level, it is understandable that the EC, in seeking to formulate environmental impact assessment in a workable legal form, should find drafting appropriate legislation less than straightforward.

Eight years of negotiation[20] finally culminated in Directive 85/337/EEC[21] on the Assessment of the Effects of Certain Private and Public Projects on the Environment. It will be immediately apparent from the title of the Directive that its provisions were at the same time narrower and wider than those of the pioneering NEPA; narrower in that environmental assessment was to be applied only to projects and not to plans, policies, and programmes, and wider in that all types of project (not just those which featured state involvement) would be included in its remit.

### Legal basis of Directive 85/337/EEC

The Directive's legal justification rested on Articles 100 and 235 of the EC Treaty. Action was justified on the basis of Article 100, on the grounds that disparities in the law of member states in this regard could 'create unfavourable competitive conditions and thereby directly affect the functioning of the common market.'[22] Differentiated environmental standards, allowing states with more relaxed environmental standards to act as 'pollution havens', thus attracting investment away from states exhibiting a more responsible approach to their environment, represented a threat to competition.

Article 235 was called into play justifying action where the original Treaty had given no specific powers, in order to promote the EC's objectives in securing environmental protection and promoting the quality of life of its citizens.

The EC's choice to legislate by Directive in respect of environmental impact assessment is significant in several respects. Since Directives are binding on member states only in terms of the objective to be achieved, such an instrument would be particularly appropriate for use in this context (in the light of the differences between member states' development control systems, of which environmental impact assessment was to form a part).

---

19. Fourth Environmental Action Programme OJ No. C 328/1.
20. Negotiations began in 1977, and the Directive was finally proposed on 11 June 1980, COM (80) 313 after the publication of no less than twenty internal drafts.
21. (OJ L175, 5 July 1985).
22. Introduction to Directive 85/337/EEC.

## The aims and objectives of Directive 85/337/EEC

As already mentioned, the concept of environmental impact assessment fits into the wider EC policy of, wherever possible, taking action to prevent damage to the environment in preference to allowing damage to occur and then taking remedial action. The development control process lends itself particularly well to this pre-emptive approach, since an informed planning decision can actually go a long way towards preventing serious environmental problems arising, whereas an ill-informed decision can actually aggravate the adverse environmental consequences of a particular development.[23]

Environmental assessment, as embodied by the Directive, attempts to provide an element in decision-making (for at least some projects) which will amplify the importance of environmental factors in the development control process (Article 2). The concept of environmental assessment aims to contextualise the costs and benefits of the development in question in terms of their impact on all aspects of the surrounding environment (Article 3). The decision-making process in development control is thus extended to cover environmental as well as more traditionally accepted social and economic costs.

The Directive also seeks to open up the development control process from the traditional, basically bipartite model of a developer petitioning a state authority (used in its widest sense to encompass both central and local authorities) to one which is inclusive of other informed opinion in the form of expert government agencies (Article 6.1) which are not directly concerned with the process of permitting development, and non-governmental organisations, and the wider public (Article 6.2). Provision is also made for consulting other member states where projects may have cross-border impacts (Article 7). Environmental impact assessment could perhaps be described as an exercise in environmental democracy on both a domestic and a transnational scale.

Environmental impact assessment, as currently practised in the EC, is essentially concerned with securing informed development and thus concerns itself primarily with information-gathering by those who wish to pursue a project and by decision-makers. This basic information-gathering is enhanced by the contributions of other state expert bodies whose opinion is volunteered or sought by either of the former parties and those who wish to object to a project on the basis of allegedly adverse environmental consequences.

## Requirements of Directive 85/337/EEC

### The environmental statement

The Directive places the onus of supplying the necessary information to enable the authorities to make an environmentally informed decision on a proposed project squarely upon the developer, through his responsibility for producing an environmental statement. (This term is not used in the Directive itself but has come to be commonly used as a form of shorthand describing the information provided by the developer in support of his project.) It is this statement that will

---

23. This point was highlighted by the Royal Commission on Environmental Pollution in its fifth report, *Air Pollution: an Integrated Approach* (Cmnd 6371), London: HMSO 1976

provide the state decision-making machinery with much of the raw material for the environmental assessment process. This could, if viewed in the most favourable light, be seen as an application of the 'polluter pays' principle, since the collection of full information, if properly carried out, would require considerable expenditure of both energy and financial resources.[24] Another, less indulgent view of the import of environmental assessment is possible, however. Cynics would argue that the Directive places the ball firmly in the developer's court but lacks detailed mandatory standards to ensure even a minimum quality for the information submitted.

Article 5.2 lays down minimum requirements for an environmental statement. These are:

- a description of the project, comprising information on the site, design and size of the project;
- a description of the measures envisaged in order to avoid, reduce and if possible remedy significant adverse effects;
- the data required to identify and assess the main effects the project is likely to have on the environment;[25] and
- a non-technical summary of the other information submitted; (this requirement is more than a mere cosmetic addition to the serious scientific business of the environmental statement, for it provides the means of making the information gleaned accessible to the public and thus has a crucial role to play).

Article 5.2 is further fleshed out by Annex III, which details some examples of what may be covered under the headings provided in the main body of the Directive. The specified information may, under Annex III, be accompanied by further information designed to amplify or explain it. This further information includes:

(i) the physical characteristics of the proposed development and the land use requirements;
(ii) the main characteristics of the production processes proposed;
(iii) the estimated type and quantity of expected emissions resulting from the operation of the proposed development;
(iv) the main alternatives studied by the applicant; and
(v) the likely significant direct and indirect effects on the environment resulting from: (*a*) the use of natural resources and (*b*) the emission of pollutants, the creation of nuisances, and the elimination of waste.

Article 5.3 places an obligation on state authorities holding information relevant to the environmental statement to disseminate this to developers on request.

*Qualifications on the minimum content of environmental statements*

Article 5.1 places certain qualifications on even the minimum amount of information required under Article 5.2 of the Directive, stating that member states

---

24. Because of the highly technical nature of many of the elements of environmental assessment, a whole sector of specialist environmental consultancy has developed.
25. Under Annex III, this must cover the direct and 'indirect, secondary, cumulative, short, medium and long term, permanent and temporary, positive and negative effects' of the project in question.

may determine how much information is relevant in a given case. Relevant factors include:

- the particular stage of the development control process in question;
- the characteristics of the proposed project and those environmental features likely to be affected by it; and
- what is reasonable given the current state of knowledge.

Much of the certainty of Article 5.2, therefore, is lost and replaced by state discretion.

In addition to the mandatory information outlined above, a developer may be asked 'where appropriate' to outline the main alternatives which he considered and his reasons for arriving at the choice of project which he has submitted for approval. Many environmentalists would argue that this evaluative exercise is central to the utility of environmental assessment and should be mandatory; for example, the Council for the Protection of Rural England complained that the Department of Transport's failure to consider alternatives to the roads programme and to particular routes under the Roads (Assessment of Environmental Effects) Regulations 1988[26] rendered the environmental assessment process farcical.

The Directive requires that information collected under the environmental assessment procedure be made public, although the means of securing the public input, which the Directive also requires, is left to the discretion of the member state. Likewise, while state authorities with environmental expertise must also be consulted, the means of securing this are also left to the member state.

## Scope of the Directive

The focus of the Directive is on securing procedural conformity throughout the EC; this is realistic both in terms of the nature of the content of the Directive itself and in terms of respecting the importance of leaving substantive decision-making to established state authorities, which are best fitted to secure the optimum outcome for the local environment in each case.

The Directive by no means serves to ensure that every proposed development will be subject to environmental assessment. Given the complex and often time-consuming nature of the assessment process, the Directive concerns itself only with major projects. Major projects are not classified for the purposes of the Directive by virtue of their size alone; the crucial factor is the potential for them to generate a 'significant impact' on the environment, a requirement which could equally well be satisfied by a small development of a dangerous or complex nature or a project proposed for a particularly sensitive location.

There is no requirement in the Directive that the conclusions reached as the result of the environmental assessment are to be decisive in determining whether or not permission is given for the project to go ahead. The focus of the Directive instead is on ensuring that the impact of a qualifying project on the environment is given measured consideration.

The definition of 'environmental factors' adopted by Article 3 of the Directive is broad, covering:

- human beings, fauna. and flora;

---

26. SI 1988/1241.

- soil, air, water, climate, and landscape;
- the interaction between all of these factors; and
- material assets and cultural heritage.

Projects are divided into those for which an environmental assessment is mandatory, contained in Annex I, and those for which environmental assessment is an option, contained in Annex II.

### Mandatory environmental assessment: Annex I

Annex I projects are grouped for our purposes as follows:
  (i) the energy sector: oil refineries; large thermal power stations, nuclear power stations and reactors; installations concerned with the storage or disposal of radioactive waste;
 (ii) the industrial sector: iron and steel works; installations concerned with extracting and processing asbestos; integrated chemical plants;
(iii) infrastructure projects: road, rail or air transport; projects concerning ports and inland waterways;
 (iv) waste treatment and disposal: projects dealing with the treatment, incineration or landfill of hazardous waste.

Annex I projects, while differing considerably in their nature, share a capacity to have a profound impact on both the human and natural environment, because of their inherently polluting nature and the inevitable by-products of their operation. The projects covered will generally be on a large scale and of considerable, even national, importance. They will very often be promoted or at least closely supported by the state or its agencies. Annex I could therefore be viewed as ensuring that states set a good example of probity in their dealings with and in considering their impact on the environment. This Annex has proved relatively non-controversial; the environmental implications of each of the classes contained within it are sufficiently apparent to support a consensus favouring a full assessment of potential impacts before a project is given the go-ahead.

### Non-mandatory environmental assessment: Annex II

Annex II to the Directive requires that an environmental assessment be carried out on listed projects only if member states are of the opinion that the characteristics of the project require it. It is left to member states to determine what these 'characteristics' may be. As a result, Annex II has proved to be much more problematic in practice than Annex I, simply because, by giving member states a degree of freedom of action, a concurrent element of uncertainty has been introduced into the equation. Annex II covers a range of classes of project:
  (i) the agricultural sector;
 (ii) the industrial sector, including extractive industry, metal processing, glass manufacture, the chemical industry, the food industry, the textile, leather, wood and paper industries, and the rubber industry;
(iii) the energy sector;*
 (iv) infrastructure projects;*
  (v) miscellaneous projects; and
 (vi) modifications to projects covered by Annex I.
*Projects not already covered by Annex I.

## *Implementation of Directive 85/337/EEC in the UK*

Implementation of the Directive was to prove controversial in many of the EC member states, not least the UK. The Government initially resisted the notion that the Directive required any specific legislative action, arguing that environmental quality had always been a 'material consideration' in the planning system, which was required to be evaluated in reaching a decision on whether or not to give a proposed project the permission required for it to proceed.[27]

Implementation when it did occur was tardy and piecemeal, in both Great Britain and more particularly Northern Ireland. Member states were required to have their environmental assessment mechanisms in place by 3 July 1988 (a three-year 'grace period' replacing the normal two-year limit), but the main legislation was not activated in England and Wales until 15 July 1988 under the Town and Country Planning (Assessment of Environmental Effects) Regulations 1988,[28] as amended. In Scotland the main legislation was the Environmental Assessment (Scotland) Regulations 1988.[29] In Northern Ireland equivalent legislation was delayed until the implementation of the Planning (Assessment of Environmental Effects) Regulations (NI) 1989[30] on 1 March 1989. Each of these sets of regulations was made under section 2(2) of the European Communities Act 1972.

The main regulations (which were issued to cover the planning system), while covering by far the most numerically significant part of environmental assessment (see below), did not by any means represent full implementation of the Directive. Other subject-specific legislation was required to cover those classes of activity, notably agriculture, forestry, roads and fisheries, which do not fall under the control of the planning regime in its usual form. Numerous[31] supplementary regulations have therefore been required to ensure that environmental impact assessment is applicable to all types of project which could 'significantly affect' the environment.

The problem of coverage would not have arisen had the Government chosen to fulfil its EC obligations by means of primary legislation applicable to all projects.

It is clear that the Government was initially of the opinion that environmental assessment would prove itself to be redundant, but the official view has changed in the years since the implementation of the Directive. Recent research has revealed that some 2,300 environmental impact assessments have been carried out in the period between October 1988 and September 1995; 75 per cent of these have been conducted within the Town and Country Planning system; 80 per cent of the total have been in England and Wales.[32]

The evident utility of environmental assessment in practice appears to have led

---

27. For an overview of the planning system in Northern Ireland see A. Dowling, *Northern Ireland Planning Law* Dublin: Gill & MacMillan, 1995.
28. SI 1988/1199.
29. SI 1988/1221.
30. SR No. 20.
31. These currently total nineteen in the United Kingdom, and gaps still remain, for example in respect of Crown immunity.
32. Figures quoted by John Zetter of the DoE in his paper 'Environmental Impact Assessment: Does It Have an Impact?' delivered at University College, London, on 3 Nov. 1995 as part of a conference organised by the Centre for the Law of the European Union. Source Research Project carried out by Oxford Brookes University on behalf of the DoE, publication pending.

to a substantial change in the Government's attitude towards the concept. In recent legislation the Government has actively promoted environmental assessment, for example through section 15 of the Planning and Compensation Act 1991 (inserting section 71A into the Town and Country Planning Act 1990). This provision allowed the Secretary of State for the Environment to make regulations under planning law to extend the scope of assessment beyond the categories listed in the Directive. Thus environmental assessment has (at least in England and Wales) finally gained a place in primary legislation, and its remit now has the capacity to expand to meet changing circumstances.[33]

# PART III THE LAW IN NORTHERN IRELAND

## SECTION 1. THE MAIN REGULATIONS

### The Planning (Assessment of Environmental Effects) Regulations (NI) 1989,[34] as amended: the main Regulations

#### Implementation

The Directive was primarily implemented in Northern Ireland by the Planning (Assessment of Environmental Effects) Regulations (NI) 1989, as amended by the Planning (Assessment of Environmental Effects) (Amendment) Regulations (NI) 1994.[35] The Regulations fit into the general planning control system. They extend the time for determining a planning application from the usual period of two months allowed by the General Development Order 1993[36] to sixteen weeks (regulation 14(1)(*a*)), calculated from the date of receipt of the developer's environmental statement (regulation 14(1)(*b*)). The Regulations require that a minimum period of four weeks elapse before the determination of a planning application where an environmental statement is required (regulation 14(2)).

#### Decision-makers

Environmental assessment, as embodied by the main Regulations, is in effect a supplement to the decision-making process already available under the planning system of development control. An environmental assessment is carried out by a state authority on the basis of the environmental information generated by the assessment process (this is made up of the promoter's environmental statement together with the additional environmental information contributed by other expert state agencies, non-governmental organisations, and the general public).

The DoE(NI) was designated as the competent body in measures relating to environmental impact assessment under the Directive in respect of town and

---

33. The Town and Country Planning (Environmental Assessment and Permitted Development) Regulations 1995 (SI 1995/417) and the Town and Country Planning (General Permitted Development) Order 1995 (SI 1995/418) have also served to extend the scope of environmental assessment in Great Britain.
34. SR No. 20.
35. SR No. 395.
36. SR No. 278.

country planning. The main Regulations are now tied to the Planning (NI) Order 1991[37] by virtue of the 1994 amendments.

## *Appeals*

Appeals from the decisions of the Department in planning matters lie, in respect of environmental assessment, as in all other cases, to the Planning Appeals Commission (regulation 6). The Commission will hear the applicant's case and make a report on it, which will then be considered by the Department, which may then amend, confirm or withdraw its original determination (regulation 6(2)).

The Department has the power under regulation 17 to direct that a specific development does not require the consideration of environmental information as a necessary prelude to a development control decision. This widely worded set-aside provision would of course create difficulties if applied to a Schedule 1 project where environmental assessment is supposed to be mandatory.

## *Application*

Regulation 3 states that:

planning permission shall not be granted pursuant to—

(*a*) a Schedule 1 application; or

(*b*) a Schedule 2 application where the proposed development is likely to have significant effects on the environment by virtue of factors such as it nature, size or location;

unless the Department or the Commission, as the case may require, shall first have taken into consideration environmental information.

This provision is parallel to Article 2 of the Directive. In Northern Ireland the 1994 Regulations insert a new paragraph, 1A, into the 1989 Regulations, requiring that where the Department grants planning permission to a project it will state, in communicating its approval to the applicant, that it has 'taken environmental information into consideration.' 'Environmental information' is defined in regulation 2(2) as:

• the applicant's (or in relevant cases the appellant's) environmental statement,

• representations by bodies that must be consulted under the regulations, and

• representations duly made by any other person

concerning the likely environmental effects of the proposed development.

Schedules 1 and 2 to the Regulations are in principle parallel to Annex I and II of the Directive, and, like the Directive, their content has been the source of some debate and controversy, particularly on the part of environmental pressure groups. One vexed question is that of the difficulties created by adopting a finite list of project types for coverage and the inevitable gaps which result. This problem is inherent in the drafting of the Directive and, the EC being what it is, amendment is slow. This has not, however, resulted in the Directive becoming moribund in England and Wales, as demonstrated by the extension of the domestic regulations to cover private toll roads[38] and wind-powered electricity generators, motorway

37.  SI 1991/1220.
38.  Added to Sch. 1.

service areas and coastal protection works[39] by the Assessment of Environmental Effects Regulations 1994.

There has recently been some similar, if less radical, progress in Northern Ireland with the passing on 16 October 1995 of the Planning Environmental Assessment and Permitted Development Regulations (NI) 1995,[40] implementing environmental assessment procedures (which follow the model adopted in the main legislation) in the previously exempted area of permitted development. Permitted development allows certain projects to proceed without the need to secure planning permission. The scope of permitted development is laid out in Schedule 1 to the Planning (General Development) Order (NI) 1993. Permitted development rights have also been removed by the Planning (General Development) (Amendment) Order (NI) 1995 in respect of those projects where an environmental assessment would be required if normal planning rules governed the project in question.

Schedule 2 to the main Regulations continues, however, to pose one important problem; it remains open to question whether a particular project that falls within the ambit of the Schedule will actually be deemed to require an environmental assessment. The Regulations do not in themselves shed much light on this question. Regulation 3(2) states that:

> a proposed development shall be taken to be likely to have a significant effect on the environment by virtue of factors such as its nature, size or location where—
>
> (a) the applicant and the Department agree that an environmental statement is required and the Department has notified its agreement in writing; or
>
> (b) the Department has determined that an environmental statement is required under regulation 4, 5, or 6.

### The preliminary stages

An environmental assessment may be instituted in one of three ways: on application by the developer to the DoE(NI) in order to find out whether the project in question falls under the Regulations; through the imposition of an environmental assessment by the Department; or by voluntary action by the developer.

### Applications by developers

Under regulation 4(1) a developer may, before applying for planning permission, ask the Department to determine whether his proposed development would fall within Schedule 1 or Schedule 2 and under which particular description it would be classified. If the proposed Development is deemed to lie within Schedule 2, the developer may ask whether the Department is of the opinion that it is likely to have a significant effect on the environment. When seeking such a determination, regulation 4(2) requires that the developer supply:

(i)   a plan that identifies the land concerned in the proposed development; and

(ii)  a brief description of the nature and purpose of the proposed project.

---

39. Added to Sch. 2.
40. SR No. 357.

The developer is also permitted to volunteer additional information in support of his application.

The Department is entitled under regulation 4(3) to consult the relevant district council (i.e. the council in whose area the proposed project is to be sited) and other relevant statutory authorities which appear to the Department to have an interest in the application (according to regulation 8(2)). These requirements aim to ensure that, even at this preliminary stage, the Department will arrive at an informed decision.

If the Department is not satisfied that it has been supplied with sufficient information to reach a determination, it is required by regulation 4(5)(*a*) to let the applicant know (in writing) what additional information he must supply. Under regulation 4(4) the Department is normally allowed four weeks[41] to arrive at a decision, although a longer period may elapse if the applicant agrees to this in writing.

If the Department decides that an environmental assessment is required, the applicant must be given notice in writing, with full reasons, that he is required to supply an environmental statement (regulation 4(6)). If the applicant is not minded to accept the Department's determination, he may avail himself of the opportunity to have his case heard by the Planning Appeals Commission. He is required[42] to inform the Department in writing (within four weeks of the original decision[43]) if he decides to take this course of action.

In England and Wales some clarification on threshold requirements indicating the applicability of environmental assessment is offered to applicants in DoE Circular 15/88 and in the booklet *Environmental Assessment: a Guide to Procedures*.[44] Similar publications are not at present available to applicants in Northern Ireland, although the DoE(NI) has recently introduced DoE(NI) Advice Note Number 10 (based on the current Scottish model) which will perform the same function. Advice to developers is currently available on a less formal level through discussion with Divisional Planning Offices, which in turn are made au fait with the more complex issues involved in environmental assessment through discussion with the Planning Service's central Special Studies Environment Unit. The latter body has, since the introduction of environmental assessment in 1989, gained particular expertise in the area.

## The role of informal consultation with decision-makers

Informal pre-application discussions on whether or not an environmental assessment is a live issue in respect of a projected development and, if it is, what information will be required of the developer, often proves invaluable. Timely informal consultation can save both the developer and the decision-making authority time and money in the long run.

---

41. Under SI 1988/1199, the parallel provision applicable in England and Wales (reg. 5 (4)), the period allowed is normally three weeks.
42. By reg. 4(7).
43. Under reg. 4(8).
44. DoE, 1989.

### Screening and scoping

Obviously, with the wide range of factors which could potentially fit into the scheme designed by the Directive and implemented in the Regulations, it is necessary to allocate a weighting and priority to the factors which are most important and appropriate for consideration in a particular application. This initial process is known as screening and is used to identify the most significant potential impacts so that their magnitude can be addressed. The second element in preparing an environmental statement will also involve discussion and negotiation with the Department. This process is known as 'scoping'. The task here is to identify the breadth and depth of examination to be allocated to specific effects in order to produce a valuable conclusion which will satisfy the Department's need for cogent environmental information. Scoping can also be affected by the outcome of consultation with the general public, which, although not mandatory at this early stage, can prove valuable, since the concerns generated (by what are often by their very nature 'bad neighbour' developments) will eventually need to be addressed as part of the overall assessment process; and here, once again, thorough groundwork can save time and money later on.

Further useful information, as in England and Wales, is to be found in the statistical and factual records kept by the DoE(NI) on environmental assessment determinations and the results of appeals on the environmental assessment process.

### Imposed environmental assessment

In the alternative, regulation 5 makes it clear that the Department may in any event decide that an environmental statement will be required. This will occur where an applicant has submitted a request for planning permission without an environmental statement and it appears to the Department that the proposed project has (or may have) Schedule 1 or 2 status. The decision-making process pursued by the Department in this instance is broadly similar to that used under regulation 4. The applicant here too has a right of appeal to the Planning Appeals Commission. If he fails to exercise this right (as outlined in the description of regulation 4(7)) his planning application will be deemed to have been withdrawn. If the applicant's appeal is successful and the Department withdraws from its original decision, the normal process and time limits for determining planning applications come into play from the date of that withdrawal (regulation 5(7)).

If a statement is required (and also if an appeal is lodged and the initial decision is confirmed) the applicant is given six months (or such longer period as may be agreed) from the date of the determination to submit the necessary information to the Department. If he fails to do so, once again his planning application will be deemed to have been withdrawn (regulation 5(5)). The applicant may take advantage of discussion with the Department to screen and scope his environmental statement here in the same way as under regulation 4.

If the planning application in question is deemed withdrawn under any of the provisions of regulation 5, it is to be returned to the erstwhile applicant along with any fee charged (regulation 5(6)).

The Department is obliged by regulation 7 to place a copy of any determination it makes under regulations 4 and 5 and which the Planning Appeals Commission makes under regulation 6 on a public register.

## *Voluntary environmental assessment*

The third and final way in which an environmental statement can be initiated is as a voluntary step undertaken by the developer and accepted by the Department (regulation 8(1)).

## **Compiling an environmental statement: the formal process**

Once the Department has decided that an environmental assessment will take place in a given case and has informed the developer that an environmental statement will be required of him (or has accepted the voluntary intention to provide one), official machinery designed to help the developer to provide an adequate contribution to the environmental information comes into play. Regulation 8(2) requires the Department to take the following steps:

(i) to notify the district council in whose area the proposed development is to be situated;

(ii) to notify other statutory bodies that appear to the Department to have an interest in the proposal;

(iii) to notify the bodies informed under paragraphs (i) and (ii) that they have a duty[45] to make available to the developer any information in their possession that they consider relevant to the preparation of the environmental statement; this information can be issued either in response to a request from the developer or as a result of contact initiated by the body concerned to ascertain whether it holds any relevant material (regulation 9(2)); these bodies are allowed to make a 'reasonable charge' covering the cost of making its information available to the developer (regulation 13(2));

(iv) to supply any of the bodies informed under paragraphs (i) and (ii) with any information the Department holds about the proposed development that such a body may reasonably request; and

(v) to inform the developer, in writing, of the names and addresses of any body so informed.

The Regulations make a considerable effort to aid the developer in compiling an informed and adequate environmental statement. These provisions constitute an official embodiment of the consultation process, though, as already pointed out, the unofficial components of screening, scoping and pre-compilation consultation with the public and others will by this stage already have played a very significant role in shaping the environmental statement.

Once the statement has been received by the Department, the process of compiling the rest of the environmental information begins.

---

45. Information held in confidence under reg. 9 (2) may, however, be withheld.

### Other environmental information

#### The public

Regulation 10(1) requires the Department to place a copy of the developer's environmental statement on a public register; this step is designed to facilitate the official consultation and collection of information from non-governmental organisations and the general public. In addition, regulation 11 requires that the developer must, as well as submitting the environmental statement to the Department, make it available to the public. The Department will, under regulation 11, publish a notice stating that a planning application has been made and that it is accompanied by an environmental statement. The notice will contain the address in the affected locality where the developer has made available copies of the environmental statement. The developer must supply a reasonable number of copies of the statement for public consumption (regulation 12). The developer may make a reasonable charge for copies of the statement, reflecting the costs of printing and distribution (regulation 13), and the Department will include the amount charged in the notice issued under regulation 11.

#### Other bodies

The Department must, on receipt of an environmental statement, consult the relevant district council and other relevant statutory bodies about the environmental statement and inform them that they have the right to make representations for the Department to consider. The bodies concerned must be given a minimum of four weeks notice that environmental information will play a part in determining a particular planning application. The Department may not consider such information until this period has elapsed (regulation 10(3)).

### The decision

The Regulations, like the Directive, do not require that an application for development be automatically turned down on the basis of an adverse environmental assessment. The information and environmental impacts must be considered, and they are given a certain amount of additional status among other material planning considerations as a result of the assessment procedure; they still, however, remain only one factor in a multi-faceted decision-making process. Environmental assessment may have a positive impact in encouraging the use of conditional planning consents with environmental safeguards built in—but the overlap between planning controls and other specific statutory environmental regimes, particularly in respect of pollution control, makes this issue problematic.

## SECTION 2. SUBJECT-SPECIFIC ENVIRONMENTAL ASSESSMENT
### REGULATIONS

The main Regulations are limited in their application to the remit of the Town and Country Planning system, which covers most but not all development which can affect the environment. As a result it was necessary to create supplementary regulations to deal with discrete classes of development that are not subject to planning controls. In Northern Ireland the specific provisions are as follows.

**The Roads (Assessment of Environmental Effects) Regulations (NI) 1988,[46] as amended by the Roads (Assessment of Environmental Effects) Regulations (NI) 1994[47]**

*Implementation and application*

The Roads Environmental Assessement Regulations added a new Part IVA to the then main legislation governing road building projects in Northern Ireland, the Roads (NI) Order 1980,[48] and are currently incorporated in article 67 of the Roads (NI) Order 1993.[49] The Regulations apply to new road projects (unless they fall under article 39(*b*)(9), where details of the project were published before the Regulations came into operation on 14 November 1988) and the improvement of the existing road network.

*Decision-makers*

Since the DoE(NI) is, through its Roads Service, the body with responsibility for promoting new road schemes but is also required, by article 39B of the amended Order, to:

> determine before the publication of details of the project whether or not it falls within Annex I or Annex II to Council Directive No. 85/337 . . .

the same apparent problem arises as when under the main Regulations the DoE(NI) is required to consider whether a planning project which it is itself promoting itself will require an environmental assessment, namely, that it could be perceived to be acting as a judge in its own cause.

*The environmental statement*

The Department controls the content of the environmental statement, which it must prepare under article 39B(2) of the 1993 Order if an environmental assessment is deemed necessary, supplying the information detailed in Annex III of the Directive:

> to the extent that the Department considers—
>
> (*a*)  that such information is relevant to the specific characteristics of the project and of the environmental features likely to be affected by it; and
>
> (*b*)  that having regard to current knowledge and methods of assessment the information may reasonably be gathered. . . .

This power to determine the content of the environmental statement is of course subject to the minimum information requirements stipulated by Annex III and outlined briefly above.

The 1994 Regulations amplify the previously somewhat cursory definition of an environmental statement offered by article 67(2), inserting the following provision describing a statement as:

---

46.  SR No. 344.
47.  SR No. 316.
48.  SI 1980/1085.
49.  SI 1993/3160.

identifying, describing and assessing in an appropriate manner, in light of each individual case and in accordance with Articles 4 to 11 of the Directive, the direct and indirect effects of the project on the factors mentioned in Article 3 of the Directive.....

### Other environmental information

#### The public

The Department is required by article 39B(3) to publish, by the date of publication of the details of the project, for two successive weeks in at least one newspaper circulating in the area where the project is initiated, a notice detailing the following:
 (i)   the general effect of the project;
(ii)  stating that an environmental statement has been prepared;
(iii) specifying the place in the area affected where the statement is available for inspection by any person, free of charge (for a period of at least thirty days following the last publication of the notice); and
(iv) stating that within those thirty days a person may express a written opinion of the statement.

This provision opens the way for input into the assessment process by the general public

#### Other Bodies

Article 39(B)(4) ensures that by the date of publication of the notice referred to above, the district council whose area will be affected and other statutory bodies whose interests appear to the Department to be affected will have been consulted. Indeed article 39(B)(5) allows the Department to require such councils and bodies to furnish it with any relevant information in their possession.

### The decision

The Department is required by article 39(B)(6) to consider opinions expressed in relation to the proposed project as a result of the preceding provisions and to hold a local inquiry if it appears necessary to the Department to do so. The inquiry is open to any person, and the Department must consider the report produced (article 39(B)(7)(*b*)).

In any event, the public is to be informed of the outcome of the decision-making process. The Department is required to publish a notice in one or more newspapers circulating in the affected area containing the following information (article 39(B)(8)):
 (i)  whether or not the project is to proceed and
(ii) specifying the place in the area where the reasons for the Department's decision may be examined by any person (once again free of charge and for thirty days following the publication of the notice).

## The Environmental Assessment (Afforestation) Regulations (NI) 1989[50]

### *Implementation and application*

The Regulations which implement the Environmental Assessment Directive in respect of afforestation projects funded by the state came into operation on 1 September 1989. The Afforestation Regulations, although not located within the sphere of planning, are much more akin to the main Regulations than to the Roads Regulations. Here once again what is involved is an application by an individual to a central state authority, though not for permission to plant trees but rather for grant aid 'for the initial planting of trees for forestry purposes.' The Department of Agriculture (DANI) is prohibited from making grants for afforestation projects:

> where it appears . . . that the project will be likely to have significant effects on the environment, and may lead to adverse ecological changes, by reason inter alia of its nature, size or location unless it has first taken into consideration environmental information in respect of that project [regulation 3(1)].

The classification of afforestation under Annex II of the Directive is clearly indicated by regulation 3.

### *Decision-makers*

The regulatory authority for forestry issues in Northern Ireland is the DANI, since such matters are not subject to conventional planning controls. The Regulations make the DANI responsible for environmental assessment as a part of its wider regulatory role in the forestry sector.

### *Preliminary stages*

#### *Applications*

As with applications under the main Regulations, the applicant may seek the Department's opinion on whether or not his project is likely to require an environmental assessment (regulation 4). As with the main Regulations, the applicant must support such a request with adequate information. Regulation 4(2) requires that the application be accompanied by:

(i)  a map or plan sufficient to identify the proposed site and showing the extent of the proposed planting, and

(ii)  a brief description of the nature of the proposed planting and its possible effects on the environment.

The applicant may volunteer further information if he sees fit. The Department, if it considers the information supplied inadequate to form an opinion, is required to notify the applicant in writing of the areas in which it requires further material (regulation 4(3)). Once again the usual time limit for this preliminary determination is four weeks, unless a longer period is agreed in writing between the parties (regulation 4(4)).

If the Department deems it necessary to consider environmental information in determining the applicant's grant application, it must inform him of the reasons in

---

50.  SR No. 226.

writing (regulation 4(4)). If the Department fails to supply the applicant with an opinion within the four week time limit it will be presumed that the consideration of environmental information will not be required in respect of the project.

### Imposition of environmental assessment

In addition to the applicant being able to request a determination on whether an environmental assessment will be required, the Department also has the power, by virtue of regulation 5, to insist that an environmental statement be produced to support an application. If the initial application is not supported by an environmental statement, the Department must notify the applicant within four weeks of receipt of the original application of its view that one is required and give reasons for its opinion. The applicant may then, within four weeks of the date of notification, inform the Department in writing either that:

(i)   he accepts the DANI's view and proposes to provide an environmental statement or

(ii)  he is requesting that the Department reconsider its original determination.

If the applicant fails to act within the four-week period, his application will be deemed to be refused (regulation 5(3)).

### Appeals

If the applicant is unhappy with the DANI's decision on the preliminary issue he can apply in writing for the Department to reconsider its opinion. Requests to the Department to reconsider its original determination under regulations 4 or 5 are governed by regulation 6. The applicant is allowed to accompany his request with any representations which he sees fit (regulation 6(1)). The Department may request that the applicant supply supplementary information in writing when it deems this necessary to its decision (regulation 6(2)). It must reach a decision within four weeks of receipt of the applicant's request or within such longer period as may be reasonably required (regulation 6(3)). The Department must then notify the applicant of its decision, stating its reasons where it is still of the opinion that environmental information is required.

The Department is left with no option but to refuse an application if the environmental statement, which forms an integral part of the environmental information it deems necessary, is not supplied.

### The environmental statement

The applicant is required to submit a minimum of five copies of his environmental statement to the DANI (regulation 7(5)). As under the main Regulations, provision is made under regulation 8 for the developer to obtain access to information held by state authorities that could help in the preparation of the environmental statement. Again, as under the main Regulations, a reasonable charge may be made for this service (regulation 10(2)).

If the DANI deems the information contained in the environmental statement to be inadequate, further information may be requested from the applicant (regulation 9). In addition, regulation 9(2) explicitly empowers the Department to require the applicant to produce 'such evidence as it may reasonably call for to verify any information in his environmental statement.'

## Other environmental information

### The public

Once the DANI has decided that an environmental assessment is appropriate and has received the environmental statement, this must also be duly publicised pursuant to regulation 7 if it is to form a valid basis for the appraisal process (regulation 5(4)).

Regulation 7(1)(*a*) requires that the applicant (in at least two local papers nominated by the DANI) give notice of the project and inform the public that they have at least twenty-eight days in which to make representations in writing to the Department. The developer must also, by virtue of regulation 7(1)(*b*), make a reasonable number of copies of details of the project and the environmental statement available at the Department's offices (or another agreed convenient place) for public consultation for at least twenty-one days after the publication of the advertisement under paragraph (*a*). The advertisement must also state the address from which copies of the environmental statement can be obtained and any charge to be made. The charge, as in the main Regulations, must be reasonable (regulation 10(1)).

### Other bodies

The DANI is required by regulation 7(2) to send a copy of the environmental statement to:
 (i) the appropriate District Conservation Committee,
 (ii) the appropriate district council, and
 (iii) any other public authority and any statutory body that appears to it to have an interest in the afforestation project,
and to consult each of these bodies about the statement.

Once again the bodies concerned are given a minimum of four weeks notice that the environmental statement is to be considered, and the DANI is not permitted to examine the statement before this period has elapsed (regulation 7(3)).

## The decision

The Department can only reach a decision after considering both the environmental statement and any representations or comments made on it (regulation 7(4)). The Department's decision whether or not to grant funding to the project must then be notified in writing to everyone who has made a representation on the project and must be further published in the newspapers used to advertise the application in the first place.

### The Harbour Works (Assessment of Environmental Effects) Regulations (NI) 1990[51]

*Implementation and application*

The Regulations extending environmental assessment to harbour works were made on 21 May 1990 and came into operation on 25 June 1990. By virtue of regulation 3 these Regulations apply to works below the low water mark of medium tides (which are not subject to normal planning controls).

*Decision-makers*

The competent authorities under the Harbour Works Regulations are, under regulation 2(2)(*a*) and 2(2)(*b*), the DoE(NI) (for works not relating to fishery harbours[52]) and the DANI (for works relating to such harbours).

*Preliminary procedures*

The applicants under these Regulations are harbour authorities. They are prohibited from beginning work without the appropriate Department having considered whether or not an environmental assessment will be required. If the appropriate Department decides that, either because the project falls outside Annexes I and II of the Directive or falls within Annex II but because of its characteristics does not require an environmental assessment, an environmental statement will not be necessary (regulation 4(4)). If this is the case the Department is required to inform the promoting harbour authority and may take no further action on the matter.

In addition, work may proceed after an environmental assessment has taken place and the appropriate Department has reached a decision on the merits of the application (regulation 8).

*Appeals*

The Regulations do not provide for any appeal against any of the appropriate Department's determinations.

*The environmental statement*

If the appropriate Department is of the opinion that an environmental assessment is required in respect of a particular proposal, it is required by regulation 5(1) to inform the applicant harbour authority of its decision. The Department must also direct the authority to supply it with that information detailed in Annex III of the Directive which in its opinion is necessary (given the characteristics of the project) and reasonable (given current knowledge) to the assessment process. The Department must also give the authority directions on the form in which the information is to be presented. Regulation 5(2) specifies the minimum information that can be required in line with Article 5.2 of the Directive.

---

51.  SR No. 181.
52.  'Fishery Harbour' is defined by art. 1(2) of the Ministries (Transfer of Functions) Order (NI) 1973 SR&O (NI) No. 129.

The environmental statement supplied under regulation 5 must in this case be accompanied by a copy of the notice of proposals and related information supplied to the public (see below) and a certificate confirming that the publicity requirements under regulation 6 have been complied with.

Once the environmental statement has been compiled, once again the stage is set for the collection of the rest of the environmental information.

## Other environmental information

### The public

Regulation 6 places an obligation on the promoting harbour authority to publicise its proposed works. This must be done not less than fourteen days before it supplies its environmental statement to the appropriate Department. The authority must publish the following particulars in a newspaper circulating in the affected area:

   (i) its name and the location and nature of the proposed harbour works;
  (ii) that it has applied for consent to carry out the proposed works;
 (iii) that it has been directed to supply the information referred to in regulation 5;
  (iv) that a copy of any information supplied may be inspected by members of the public at all reasonable hours;
   (v) an address, within the locality of the harbour where the works are proposed, where the documents that are open to inspection can be consulted; details of the last day on which they will be available are also required (this date being not less than forty-two days after publication of the notice);
  (vi) an address (fulfilling the same conditions as (v)) from which copies of the environmental statement may be obtained, together with details of any charge imposed; and
 (vii) that persons wishing to make representations on the proposed works should do so in writing, within seven days of the date specified in (v), to the appropriate Department.

In addition to this newspaper publicity, regulation 6(2) requires that on the same date the harbour authority post a notice at or outside its offices containing the same information. The notice must be left in place for at least forty-two days, be carefully and accessibly displayed, and be replaced if it is removed, damaged, or defaced (regulation 6(3)).

### Other bodies

The appropriate Department may, under regulation 7(1), direct the applicant authority to supply its environmental statement to bodies that appear to the Department to have environmental responsibilities. If the Department takes this step it is obliged by regulation 7(2) to consult any bodies in receipt of the information.

If the Department sees fit it can cause an inquiry to be held into the proposed works. The harbour authority, any individuals who have made representations and any bodies informed under regulation 7(1) may appear (regulation 7(2)).

## The decision

The Department, once the environmental information has been collected, may proceed to consider that information, i.e. the environmental statement, representations by the public, representations from state bodies, and the report of the public inquiry (if one has been held), and then reach a decision on the merits of the proposal (regulation 8(1) and (2)).

The Department may then either grant permission to proceed (either conditionally or unconditionally) or refuse its consent to the works in question (regulation 8(3)). The Department is required to notify its decision and its reasons to the harbour authority and to all those who made representations or were consulted as part of the assessment process and to publish (in at least one newspaper circulating in the affected area) the import of its decision and the place where copies of its full determination can be consulted (regulation 8(4)).

## *Enforcement*

One of the unique aspects of the Harbour Works Regulations is that they contain a specific enforcement mechanism which may come into play if the environmental assessment procedure is in any way contravened. The Regulations in this area therefore give environmental assessment, at least in theory, significantly enhanced importance.

If a harbour authority has proceeded, without obtaining the appropriate Department's consent, to carry out works for which in the Department's opinion an environmental assessment should have been carried out, the Department can, by giving notice in writing, order work in progress to be stopped (regulation 9) pending the supply of the requisite environmental information. If the authority fails to supply an environmental statement the Department is authorised to carry out the other aspects of an environmental assessment and to reach a determination on the merits of the project without it.

If work is carried out despite the appropriate Department's refusal of permission or in contravention of any conditions imposed, the appropriate Department is empowered by regulation 10 to serve notice in writing to the offending harbour authority requiring it to remove the works or make alterations to them and reinstate the site in a specified period of not less than thirty days. If the case appears to the Department to be one of urgency it is authorised to carry out the appropriate action itself. Equally, if the authority fails to act within the required time, the Department may act to remove or alter the works and to reinstate the site (regulation 10(2)). In either case the Department is entitled to recover the expense—as certified by itself—of remedial action (regulation 10(3)).

## The Drainage (Environmental Assessment) Regulations (NI) 1991[53]

### *Implementation and application*

The Drainage Regulations were made on 15 August 1991 and came into operation on 23 September 1991. The regulations are tied to the Drainage (NI) Order 1973.[54] The Regulations apply to all 'drainage works', exhaustively defined in regulation 2(1) as:

> any works for the purpose of draining land or of mitigating flooding or

---

53. SR No. 376.
54. SI 1973/69.

erosion to which land is subject, and includes the construction, cleansing, scouring, deepening, widening, straightening or diverting of any watercourse or outfall for water, the construction, installation or alteration of any pump, pump machinery or pump-house, the removal of any obstruction, natural or artificial, in any watercourse, and the construction, repair, raising, lowering, widening, straightening, altering or removal of any embankment, dam, barrier, sluice, weir, wall culvert or groyne or of any structure or erection for the purposes of defence against water.

The sweeping effect of this definition is countered by the provisions of regulation 3, excluding from these Regulations the following categories of drainage operation:

(i) operations begun before the Regulations came into operation;

(ii) operations carried out under a drainage scheme authorised by article 30(1) of the 1973 Order before the Regulations came into effect;

(iii) operations carried out under an agreement with persons outside Northern Ireland entered into under article 30(2) of the 1973 Order before the Regulations came into effect; or

(iv) operations carried out under a drainage scheme, whether prepared before or after the coming into operation of the Regulations, confirmed under article 13 of the 1973 Order or treated as if they had been so carried out.

### Decision-makers

The DANI is designated as the appropriate authority to deal with this aspect of environmental assessment. The DANI is also the body which proposes or supports the carrying out of drainage works under the 1973 Order and thus could be seen as acting as a judge in its own cause in respect of environmental assessment.

### Preliminary stages

The Regulations are split into two distinct sections. The first deals with general drainage operations—generally speaking 'one-off' projects; the second specifically with drainage schemes—larger-scale strategic operations.

### General drainage works

The DANI is prohibited from initiating drainage operations or co-operating with persons outside Northern Ireland in such works unless the environmental assessment procedure contained in the Regulations is first addressed (regulation 4(1)). Firstly, the DANI must consider whether the proposed works fall within that category of projects in Annex II of the Directive which require an environmental assessment. Regulation 5(1) requires the Department in each case so considered, to issue a notice in the *Belfast Gazette* and at least two local newspapers containing the following information:

(i) an announcement that it is proposed that the works in question be carried out;

(ii) a brief description of their size, nature, and location;

(iii) a statement as to whether or not the DANI intends to subject the works to environmental assessment; and

(iv) where no environmental assessment is proposed, notice that any person who wishes to make representations concerning the likely environmental effects of the proposed works may do so in writing to an address specified in the notice within twenty-eight days of its appearance in the *Belfast Gazette*.

Where the DANI deems environmental assessment applicable, it is obliged to prepare an environmental statement (regulation 5(2)). In addition, if the Department reconsiders its initial decision on the need for an environmental statement in the light of representations made as a result of publication of the preliminary notice, it must inform those who made the relevant submissions and proceed to draw up an environmental statement (regulation 5(3)). This provision is unique to this particular set of Regulations and potentially provides considerable enhancement to the role of public contributions in the assessment process.

The Department does, however, remain free to reject representations made to it and to proceed without carrying out an environmental assessment (regulation 5(4)).

Where the Department does provide an environmental statement, the foundation of the environmental assessment has been laid and the way is clear to collect the rest of the environmental information.

### Other environmental information

#### The public

Where an environmental statement is compiled, the DANI is required by regulation 6 to publicise it in the following manner. Firstly, a notice must be issued in the *Belfast Gazette* and at least two local newspapers announcing that the statement has been prepared and that individuals wishing to make representations about the environmental effects of the works may do so in writing within a specified period of at least twenty-eight days of the appearance of the notice in the *Belfast Gazette*. The Department must also make copies of the statement available for inspection, at a convenient time and place, for a period of at least twenty-eight days following the publication of the notice. Copies of the statement must also be made available to the public, and the venue and any charge to be made will be detailed in the notice.

#### Other bodies

Regulation 6(*d*) requires the Department to supply copies of its environmental statement to the Drainage Council (which operates under the 1973 Order), the appropriate district council, and any other public authority, statutory or other body or organisation that appears to it to have an interest in the matter. Regulation 7 places the DANI under an obligation to consult any body to which it supplies an environmental statement under regulation 6(*d*). Such bodies must be given at least twenty-eight days notice that an environmental assessment is to be carried out, and the DANI is prohibited from considering the environmental information before this period expires.

If the DANI enters voluntarily into consultation with another public body while preparing its environmental statement, regulation 9 requires that the respondent body make available to the Department any information (that is not confidential) which it possesses and that the Department considers relevant.

## The decision

The DANI is required to consider all the environmental information generated by following the procedures laid down in the Regulations before it may proceed with the works in question (regulation 10).

## Drainage schemes

The Regulations in respect of drainage schemes are broadly similar to those concerning general drainage works. There are, however, some important differences.

Firstly, the preliminary publicity requirement has an additional element; as well as publication giving notice of the scheme in the *Belfast Gazette* and two local newspapers, a copy of the scheme (and an estimate of its cost) must be sent to the district council covering the area or areas in question (regulation 13(1)(c)). The district council is placed under a duty to provide access to the details of the scheme (regulation 13(4)(a)) and to consider the scheme itself (regulation 13(4)(b)) with a view to making representations concerning it. The DANI must also serve official notice that it intends to make a drainage scheme on every other authority which appears to it to be likely to be affected by the execution of the scheme (regulation 13(5)).

Secondly, the scope for making representations in respect of the scheme is not confined (as with general drainage works) to dealing with environmental impacts. Under regulation 13(3)(b) an individual may make a representation if he considers that his interests will be prejudicially affected by the scheme.

The requirements of publicity for an environmental statement itself are similarly extended in respect of drainage schemes. Drainage schemes can only be confirmed where an environmental assessment has been initiated following consideration of all the environmental information (regulation 13).

## Concluding thoughts on the implementation of the Environmental Assessment Directive in Northern Ireland

While each of the sets of regulations outlined above purports to implement the Environmental Assessment Directive, it will be immediately apparent that there are considerable differences between them. The stages of the assessment process are broadly similar, each exhibiting a preliminary step where the need for assessment is considered, the compilation of the environmental statement, consultation to provide the rest of the environmental information, and the assessment process itself. Once the environmental information is collected and evaluated as part of a consideration of the merits of the project, the decision-making authority is free to act as it sees fit. Only in the Harbour Works Regulations will the absence of an environmental assessment prove crucial; this arguably goes further even than the Directive itself.

The preliminary stage, and the publicity and appeals mechanisms differ significantly in each of the regulations, and while each satisfies the very general requirements of the Directive, they also represent a confusing range of options for compliance. Environmental assessment is hardly a user-friendly, standardised procedure.

The implementation of the Environmental Assessment Directive is by no means watertight in Northern Ireland; some of the gaps, for example in respect of

Crown immunity and the assessment of offshore oil and gas installations,[55] are shared with the rest of the UK; others, such as the failure to extend environmental assessment to wind farms, remain an issue in Northern Ireland but not in Great Britain.

One problem—at least on a theoretical level, as its practical significance has diminished with time—is the idea expressed in each of the sets of regulations examined that the Environmental Assessment Directive did not apply to projects which were already 'in the pipeline' when the Directive was implemented. This very issue was litigated in Scotland in *Kincardine and Deeside District Council v. Forestry Commissioners.*[56] The facts, briefly stated, are thus. The Environmental Assessment (Afforestation) Regulations 1988 came into force in Great Britain on 15 July 1988; Directive 85/337/EEC, however, came into force on 3 July 1988. An application for an afforestation grant was received by the Commissioners on 13 July 1988 and approved on 9 November 1990. The issue of environmental assessment was not considered by the Commissioners, who relied on regulation 1(2), which stated that the Regulations would apply only to applications received on or after 15 July. The decision was challenged on ecological grounds by Kincardine and Deeside District Council, which claimed that the lack of environmental assessment invalidated the decision to allow the project to proceed. Lord Coulsfield, however, upheld the Commissioners' contention that the Regulations were not applicable at the date of the application concerned, and he also denied that, as far as Annex II applications were concerned, the Directive was capable of direct effect on the basis of the discretion accorded to the member state by the Directive. The approach taken by the court was not calculated to promote the EC's intentions with respect to the Directive.

The European Court of Justice has, however, since been called on to deal with a broadly similar situation and has given short shrift to attempts to avoid the application of the Directive in Case 396/92 *Bund Naturschutz in Bayern et al.*[57] The Bundestag adopted a law transposing Directive 85/337/EEC on 12 February 1990. This law contained, in paragraph 22, provision for transitional rules excluding environmental assessment procedures for projects already initiated and brought to public notice before the Directive was transposed. The complainants (a number of private individuals, the Government of the Netherlands, and the Commission) argued that the Directive required that all projects yet to be approved by the deadline for implementation be subject to environmental assessment. In this case the complainants were challenging road schemes approved without an environmental assessment that were initiated and publicly notified, though not finally approved, before the implementation of the Directive. In fact the projects were initiated after the date on which Germany should have transposed the Directive into their domestic law.

Advocate-General Gulmann was sympathetic to the complainants' arguments to a degree, pointing out that excluding projects initiated before the implementation date would remove a significant number of projects from control. The Court in its judgment did not, however, really deal explicitly with the 'pipeline projects'

---

55. The government admits that it is in breach of the Directive as regards offshore oil and gas installations and has promised to formulate regulations within the next year.

56. [1991] SCLR 729.

57. ECRI–3717.

issue, instead invalidating the decision to allow the projects to proceed on the grounds that the Directive ought already to have been transposed by that point and denying the member state in any event the capacity to waive the application of an active Directive by means of adopting transitional provisions. The Court was of the opinion that to allow member states to adopt transitional provisions at will 'would result in an extension of the deadline . . . and would be contrary to the obligations under the Directive.'

If another case, therefore, like *Kincardine and Deeside District Council v. Forestry Commissioners* should arise in the UK it is unlikely that the provisions of the Directive could be thwarted with such impunity.

### Challenging environmental assessment decisions

The appeal mechanisms adopted by the Regulations implementing Directive 85/337/EEC are of variable nature and quality, ranging from the non-existent in the Harbour Works Regulations through a simple requirement that a Department reconsider its initial decision in the Afforestation Regulations (an administrative exercise) to the quasi-judicial access to the Planning Appeals Commission under the main Regulations. In any event only the applicant may challenge a decision by appeal, if the Regulations in question provide one.

It could be argued that, since environmental assessment is designed to open up the decision-making process to the public (to at least some extent), the appeal process could be wider. The Directive itself, however, does not take such an ambitious step; indeed the Drainage Regulations in their current form could arguably go beyond the Directive on this point.

Another method of challenge, judicial review, is, however, available to the concerned and aggrieved third party—though it may be of doubtful value given the outcome of cases to date. Thus far several battles have been fought by environmental interest groups and their members seeking the judicial review of decisions concerned with environmental impact assessment—usually with little success. A case in point is *R. v. Swale Borough Council, ex parte Royal Society for the Protection of Birds.*[58] The RSPB wished to challenge the council's decision (made without conducting an environmental assessment, which it deemed inapplicable to the application in hand) to allow land reclamation on the Medway mudflats. The area in question was a breeding ground of international significance for wild birds and one already protected, at least in part (and this protection was due to be enhanced and extended) by EC law. The RSPB managed to surmount the hurdle of *locus standi* by establishing that it had a sufficient interest in the matter to which the application related to gain a hearing before the courts. It was, however, refused relief, on the grounds that it had failed to bring its action 'promptly', despite acting within the three-month time limit set out in order 53 of the Rules of the Supreme Court. It would appear that the Court's reasoning on the timing of the application was strongly influenced by the facts subsisting at the time of the hearing.

Development had already started; to halt it would have affected third-party rights, and the relief sought would have proved extremely expensive in terms of compensation to the developers and lost jobs in an area greatly in need of

---

58. [1991] JPL. 40.

employment. On a more general level, Simon Brown J placed an important limitation on the utility of judicial review in challenging a competent authority's decision on whether or not a project required environmental assessment, saying:

> The decision whether any particular development was or was not within the scheduled descriptions was exclusively for the planning authority in question, subject only to *Wednesbury*[59] challenge. Questions of classification were essentially questions of fact and degree, not of law.

Even more worrying was the approach taken to environmental assessment by Schiemann J in *R. v. Poole Borough Council, ex parte Beebee et al.*[60] The local authority in this case gave permission for its own housing development on Cranford Heath. An area of special scientific interest for nature conservation was included in the affected site. The applicants argued that there had been a breach of the Town and Country Planning (Assessment of Environmental Effects) Regulations 1988, on the grounds that the project fell within Schedule II and the council had not even considered whether or not an environmental assessment should be carried out. Schiemann J was of the opinion that the failure to consider the environmental assessment issue was not fatal to the grant of permission, since:

> the substance of all the environmental information which was likely to emerge from going through the formal process envisaged by the regulations had already emerged (through the submissions of environmental pressure groups) and was apparently present in the Council's mind.

This view essentially allows environmental assessment as a discrete process to be ignored and surely frustrates the aims of Directive 85/337/EEC. It would appear, then, that while environmental assessment offers greater public input to environmental decision-making to at least some degree, it represents, at least in its present form, fairly limited progress, particularly when assessment issues come before the courts.

**Environmental impact assessment: the way forward**

It is difficult to quantify the effect that environmental assessment has had on the shape of our environment to date—indeed research in this area is only really beginning to get off the ground,[61] and conclusions tend to be impressionistic rather than scientific. This area of legal and environmental endeavour is still in its infancy, and changes need to be made in order to improve the quality of the process. Many suggestions have been made as to how this could be achieved. One idea of particular value (and currently used in the Netherlands) is placing the control of environmental assessment in the hands of a single centralised body, thus allowing for objectivity, the development of expertise, and in turn greater quality control over environmental information. It can be argued, however, that while such a development would optimise the impact of the existing environmental assessment regime in Europe it would not deal with the central conceptual flaw at the base of the system. Put simply, this is that the environmental assessment of

---

59. Associated Provincial Picture Houses Ltd. v. Wednesbury Corporation [1948] 1 KB 223.
60. [1991] JPL 643.
61. See for example K. Fuller and M. Binks, 'The effectiveness of environmental assessment' *Environmental Assessment* (1995), vol. 3, issue 3, 88.

projects occurs too late in the development process to offer more than token protection to the environment. It is argued that truly valuable environmental assessment can only exist if it permeates the system of government from top to bottom; from plans, policies and programmes down to the projects that eventually give them substance. To this end the European Commission is working on a draft Directive to promote Strategic Environmental Assessment; however, given the record of extremely slow progress experienced by the much simpler and less controversial Directive 85/337/EEC, it is unlikely that such a radical instrument will emerge this century, if indeed at all.

## PART IV  SPECIAL PROVISION FOR THE ASSESSMENT OF EUROPEAN HABITAT SITES

While not involving environmental assessment proper under Directive 85/337/EEC, a related strategy has been adopted as part of the matrix of techniques[62] available to offer protection to habitats under the Conservation (Natural Habitats etc.) Regulations (NI) 1995.[63]

### Obligations placed on environmental authorities

Part IV of the Regulations adapts planning[64] and other environmental controls[65] in order to secure enhanced protection for wildlife habitats of European significance, as defined by Directive 92/43/ EEC on the Conservation of Natural Habitats and of Wild Flora and Fauna (which promotes the Natura 2000 scheme). Environmental authorities are required by regulation 43, before deciding to undertake, or permit or authorise, plans or projects which are likely to have a significant effect on a European site,[66] to 'make an appropriate assessment of the implications' for the site in view of its conservation objectives.

### *Applications in respect of European sites*

Applications which touch on European sites must be supported by such information as the decision-making authority concerned deems appropriate (regulation 43(2)) in order to carry out the necessary assessment.

---

62. For details of other control strategies see chaps 7 and 8.
63. SR No. 380.
64. Specific provisions dealing with both individual planning decisions and strategic planning policies are made by regs. 49–61; these follow the ethos of the general provisions discussed infra.
65. For example, reg. 62 ensures that special protection is applicable to European habitat sites in both the granting of waste disposal licences under Part II of the Pollution Control and Local Government Order 1978 and the passing of strategic waste disposal resolutions by district councils under art. 13 of that Order (see chap. 6). Adverse effects on European habitat sites should be avoided by the use of relevant conditions in new licences and resolutions under the 1978 Order and by variations in existing licences and resolutions.
66. The activity in question must not be directly connected with or necessary to the management of the site in question if reg. 43 is to apply (reg. 43(1)(*b*)).

### Assessment of applications in respect of European sites

The assessment should take account of the manner in which the plan or project is to be carried out and any conditions or restrictions that are proposed in relation to the consent or permission (regulation 43(6)).

Having carried out the assessment, the decision-making authority may grant the application which has been made to it only if it is of the opinion that to do so would not adversely affect the site (regulation 43(5)). The only exception to the requirement imposed by regulation 43(5) occurs if the situation falls under regulation 44, where considerations of overriding public interest arise. If there are no alternatives available and there are 'imperative reasons of overriding public interest,' which may be social or economic,[67] a plan or project may go ahead even in the face of a negative assessment. If a decision is reached to allow a plan or project to go ahead (or affirming an existing decision, consent, or other authorisation) under regulation 44, then the DoE(NI) is required by regulation 48 to take compensatory measures to ensure that the overall coherence of the Natura 2000 scheme is protected.

### Consultation

#### The DoE(NI)

Decision-makers are required to consult the DoE(NI) and consider any representations the Department makes in carrying out the assessment (regulation 43(3)).

#### The public

The competent authority is empowered by regulation 43(4), if it considers such measures appropriate, to make arrangements to consult the public.

### Reviewing existing consents

In addition to dealing with new applications in respect of European habitat sites, provision is also made for the review of existing consents and decisions etc. which are applicable to sites which have been newly designated (regulation 45). An assessment process under the same terms and conditions and with the same consequences (regulation 46) as is applicable to initial applications must be carried out. The decision in question may be affirmed by the decision-making authority which is reviewing it (regulation 46(3)) if it is ensured that the integrity of the site is not being adversely affected. Decisions may also, if the integrity of the site is threatened, be revoked or modified (regulation 46(5)).

---

67. Unless the application concerns a priority habitat site or a priority species, in which case only considerations relating to public health, public safety or beneficial consequences 'of primary importance to the environment' or other reasons which the Commission regards as sufficient will allow a project to go ahead in the face of an adverse assessment (reg. 44(2)).

# CHAPTER TWELVE

# Public Access to Environmental Information

## Introduction

The question of public access to environmental information is one of the most important and controversial issues currently raging in the field of environmental protection. Environmental laws throughout the UK have traditionally been enforced primarily by statutory enforcement agencies, with only very limited rights being granted to the public in this regard. In recent years public rights to enforce environmental standards have increased considerably; however, without adequate access to environmental information these rights are rendered virtually ineffective. Pollution control authorities have extensive powers to procure often very specific environmental information, and although such information is essential in determining whether environmental standards have been violated in a given situation, it has traditionally been withheld from the public in response to pressure from industrial interests. Industry has continued to insist that the public disclosure of information concerning discharges etc. would involve the release of confidential commercial information and would also encourage litigation from fanatics or so-called 'green nutters'.[1] Despite industry's continued resistance, increasing pressure for reform in this context, exerted at both national and EC levels, has resulted in the gradual emergence of a vitally important system of public access to environmental information.

The Royal Commission on Environmental Pollution has championed the case for free public access to environmental information within the UK since the early nineteen-seventies and altogether has addressed this issue in five separate reports,[2] beginning with its Second Report in 1972. The Tenth Report, published in 1984, which provided the fullest discussion of the issues raised in this context, essentially stated that the public had a 'beneficial interest' in the environment and therefore had a right to know the extent to which it was being polluted. The Royal Commission recommended that the public should be:

> . . . entitled to the fullest possible amount of information on all forms of environmental pollution, with the onus placed on the polluter to substantiate a claim for exceptional treatment. Accordingly, we recommend that a guiding principle behind all legislative and

1. For a more detailed discussion of the history of secrecy in relation to environmental information see Ball and Bell, *Environmental Law,* 3rd ed., London: Blackstone Press, 1995, pp 140–8.
2. Second Report, *Three Issues in Industrial Pollution* (Cmnd 4894), 1972; Third Report, *Pollution in Some British Estuaries and Coastal Waters* (Cmnd 5054), 1972; Fifth Report, *Air Pollution Control: an Integrated Approach* (Cmnd 6371), 1976; Seventh Report, *Agriculture and Pollution* (Cmnd 7644), 1979; Tenth Report, *Tackling Pollution: Experience and Prospects* (Cmnd 9149), 1984.

administrative controls relating to environmental pollution should be a presumption in favour of unrestricted access for the public to information which the pollution control authorities obtain or receive by virtue of their statutory powers, with protection for secrecy only in those circumstances where a genuine case can be substantiated.[3]

Despite Royal Commission recommendations that a uniform system of public access to environmental information be established, the Government remained reluctant to depart from its traditional opposition to the concept of public access to such information.[4] Although the Government has more recently accepted, subject to certain conditions, that the public should have free access to environmental information obtained by pollution control authorities,[5] the dominant stimulus for the introduction of a comprehensive regime of free public access to environmental information has undoubtedly come from the European Community, particularly since the adoption of its Fourth Environmental Action Programme (1987–92) in which the need for EC legislation in this regard was highlighted as a matter of priority. Whereas the UK has primarily implemented its policy of free public access to environmental information by means of a system of public registers, the Community has supported a system of general access which provides a potentially greater level of access to environmental information than the public register approach which provides access to specifically defined categories of environmental information. Directive 90/313/EEC on freedom of access to information on the environment is undoubtedly the most important EC measure introduced in this context thus far, guaranteeing, subject to certain exceptions, a right of access to 'any' environmental information held by public authorities responsible for the environment. In addition, the EC has introduced a number of other important measures which provide public access to various other categories of environmental information; these include access to environmental information held by Community institutions, information submitted to the Commission concerning national implementation of EC environment Directives, information submitted to the European Environment Agency concerning the state of the environment throughout the territories of each of the member states, information concerning the environmental impact of various products, and information

---

3. Royal Commission on Environmental Pollution, Tenth Report, *Tackling Pollution: Experiences and Prospects* (Cmnd 9149), 1984.
4. In this regard see the views expressed by the Interdepartmental Working Party established to respond to the Royal Commission's Tenth Report in DoE Pollution Paper 23, *Public Access to Environmental Information*, London: HMSO 1986. For a more detailed treatment of the historical development of public access to environmental information in the UK, see Ball and Bell, *Environmental Law*, 3rd ed., London: Blackstone Press, 1995, p. 141 and pp 147–50.
5. For more detailed discussion of the UK's position concerning access to environmental information see Rosalind Malcolm, *A Guidebook to Environmental Law*, London: Sweet and Maxwell, 1994, 92; Birkenshaw, *Government and Information*, London: Butterworths, 1990; DoE, *Green Rights and Responsibilities: a Citizen's Guide to the Environment*; and the White Paper on Open Government (Cm 2290), 1993; DoE, Pollution Paper 22, *Controlling Pollution: Principles and Prospects*, London: DoE 1984; DoE Pollution Paper 23, *Public Access to Environmental Information*, London: HMSO, 1986; House of Lords Select Committee on the European Communities, *Freedom of Access to Information on the Environment*, First Report, session 1989/90, London: HMSO.

concerning the environmental performance of those industrial concerns that participate in environmental management and audit schemes.

The purpose of this chapter is to identify and explain the principal rights to and sources of environmental information currently available in Northern Ireland. This chapter is divided into the following parts:

- Part I: Public access to environmental information held by public authorities responsible for the environment under Directive 90/313/EEC
- Part II: Public registers of environmental information operating in Northern Ireland
- Part III: Public access to local authority meetings
- Part IV: EC and UK eco-management and audit schemes
- Part V: Eco-labelling
- Part VI: Other sources of environmental information in Northern Ireland.

## PART I FREEDOM OF ACCESS TO ENVIRONMENTAL INFORMATION HELD BY PUBLIC AUTHORITIES RESPONSIBLE FOR THE ENVIRONMENT

In 1990 the EC adopted Directive 90/313/EEC[6] on the freedom of access to information on the environment, which represents the EC's most important initiative thus far in the context of public access to environmental information. The objective of the Directive is to 'ensure freedom of access to, and dissemination of, information on the environment held by public authorities and to set out the basic terms and conditions on which such information should be made available' (Article 1). In essence, the Directive requires that public authorities which hold information relating to the environment are obliged to make such information available to the public on request, thereby creating a right of access to environmental information. Although the obligation to provide access to environmental information is wide-ranging, it is not absolute. Public authorities governed by the Directive are permitted, and in some cases are required, to refuse access to environmental information in specified circumstances. It is important to note that while the Directive itself does not grant public access to environmental information held by Community institutions, public access to documents held by the Council and Commission was granted in late 1993.[7]

Member states were required to implement the Directive by 31 December 1992. Directive 90/313/EEC is implemented in Northern Ireland partly by means of a system of public registers (Part II of this chapter) and partly by the Environmental Information Regulations (NI) 1993[8] which came into operation on 31 March 1993. A detailed guidance note on the application of these Regulations in Northern Ireland has been published by the DoE(NI). Although the Environmental Information Regulations (NI) 1993 are likely to provide a fruitful source of litigation in the coming years, there are as yet no Northern Ireland

---

6. OJ L 158, 23 June 1990.
7. OJ L 340/43 1993 and OJ L 46/58 1994.
8. SR No. 45.

decisions concerning the ambit of their provisions. Only a handful of decisions has been delivered by courts in Great Britian concerning the scope of the equivalent provisions. As a result, the most detailed guide available thus far as to the obligations imposed by the Directive is contained in the DoE(NI)'s guidance note on the implementation of the Information Regulations. It should be noted, however, that decisions of the European Court of Justice and national courts will prevail in relation to the proper interpretation of the Directive and the Information Regulations. The Directive requires member states to report to the Commission on their experience gained in relation to the operation of the Directive. National reports must be submitted by the end of 1996.

## What information is covered by the Information Regulations?

Regulation 3 provides that the Information Regulations will apply to any information that:

(*a*)  relates to the environment;

(*b*)  is held by a relevant person in an accessible form and otherwise than for the purposes of any judicial or legislative function; and

(*c*)  is not (apart from these regulations) either—

(i)  information which is required, in accordance with any statutory provision, to be provided on request to every person who makes a request; or

(ii)  information contained in records which are required, in accordance with any statutory provision, to be made available for inspection by every person who wishes to inspect them.

In effect, the Information Regulations apply to 'information relating to the environment' which is held by 'a relevant person'. The Information Regulations do not apply to environmental information which must be made available to the public under other statutory provisions; in effect, such information is available already. However, environmental information which is available pursuant to other statutory provisions is not entirely beyond the control of the Information Regulations (see page 544).

The concept of 'information relating to the environment' is quite complex. Article 2 of the Directive provides that information relating to the environment will include 'any available information in written, visual, aural or data-base form.' Regulation 2(2) of the Information Regulations defines the 'information' as including 'anything contained in any records'; the term 'records' includes 'registers, reports and returns, as well as computer records and other records kept otherwise than in a document.' Although 'information' is defined widely for these purposes, regulation 2(3) (which implements Article 2 of the Directive) provides that information will only be deemed to be 'information relating to the environment' if it relates to any the following:

(*a*)  the state of any water or air, the state of any flora or fauna, the state of any soil or the state of any natural site or other land;

(*b*)  any activities or measures (including activities giving rise to noise or any other nuisance) which adversely affect anything mentioned in sub-paragraph (a) or are likely adversely to affect anything so mentioned;

(c) any activities or administrative or other measure (including any environmental management programmes) which are designed to protect anything so mentioned.

The DoE(NI)'s guidance note on the application of the Information Regulations highlights the following points concerning the concept of information that relates to the environment:

1. Environmental information will be governed by these Regulations 'whether or not it was obtained as a result of [the] body's environmental responsibilities' (paragraph 15).

2. Information collected before the Information Regulations were enacted will also be governed by these Regulations. This also includes information passed to the Public Record Office for safekeeping (paragraph 15).

3. The Regulations will apply to environmental information held 'within the body's building or elsewhere' (paragraph 15).

4. Environmental information does 'not include new information that could be created by manipulating existing information' (paragraph 15).

5. The guidance note states that environmental information does not include 'information destroyed in accordance with established office procedures'; however, it goes on to provide that 'bodies must ensure that important data sets no longer in operational use will continue to be available beyond their normal destruction date' (paragraph 15).

6. No geographical limitation is placed on the information in question, in that the information may relate to matters outside Northern Ireland or indeed to any part of the world. However, the disclosure of information concerning territories outside the UK may be exempted from the application of these Regulations (paragraph 18). (Exceptions to these provisions are outlined at page 539).

7. Although the Information Regulations do not specifically refer to information relating to human health, the guidance note states that as the environment undoubtedly has an impact on human health, either directly or indirectly, 'information affecting the state of human health' should be regarded as coming within the ambit of these Regulations' (paragraph 19).

8. Bodies which might be called upon to provide information relating to the environment are advised to issue a disclaimer where appropriate in order to protect themselves against any inaccurate information that might be released to the public (paragraph 21).

9. As outlined above, regulation 2(3) of the Information Regulations (which implements Article 2 of the Directive) provides that information will only be regarded as relating to the environment if it concerns any of the subjects listed in regulation 2(3). Paragraph 17 of the guidance note provides assistance with the meaning of the criteria listed in regulation 2(3)(*a*), namely 'the state of any water or air, the state of any flora or fauna, the state of any soil or the state of any natural site or other land.' The term 'state' is regarded as including 'physical, chemical and biological conditions at any moment in time (i.e. past, present or future).' The term 'water' is regarded as including 'underground and surface waters (both natural and in man-made structures).' Surface waters

are regarded as including 'inland waters (i.e. rivers, canals, lakes), estuaries and seas.' The term 'air' is regarded as extending to 'the limits of the atmosphere and should be taken to include the air within buildings and other natural and man-made structures above or below ground.' The terms 'flora and fauna' refer to all species, live and dead. The term 'land' is regarded as including 'all land surfaces, buildings, land covered by water, and underground strata.' 'Soil' should be interpreted as including 'the *in situ* upper layer of the mantle rock in which plants grow', and the term 'natural site' should be interpreted as including 'areas identified by reason of their flora, fauna, geological or physiographical features' (for example, the 'area of special scientific interest' and 'European sites' designations, discussed in chapter 7) or 'general environmental quality' (for example, the 'area of outstanding natural beauty' designation, discussed in chapter 8).

10. References to 'activities' and 'measures' in regulation 2(3)(*b*) and (*c*) are interpreted to include 'administrative measures and environmental management programmes', for example, 'planning and transport development' (paragraph 20).

In 1995 the Queen's Bench Division of the High Court considered the meaning of the term 'environmental information' as used in the Environmental Information Regulations 1992[9] (the British equivalent to the Northern Ireland Information Regulations) during the course of its decision in R. *v. British Coal Corporation, ex parte Ibstock Building Products Limited*[10] The case concerned two applications for planning permission in relation to waste disposal in quarries owned by Ibstock. During the consultation process for the second application, British Coal stated that it had received reports from a member of the public that munitions had been dumped down mine-shafts which ran under and alongside the quarry. Ibstock requested that British Coal release the name of the person who had made these reports, but it refused to do so. The Ministry of Defence informed Ibstock that it had no record of any munitions dumped in the quarry. The planning application could proceed no further until the munitions question was resolved. Ibstock obtained leave to bring proceedings for judicial review, at which point British Coal released the information. British Coal, however, refused to pay costs to Ibstock, on the grounds that as the information did not relate to the state of the land it did not constitute 'environmental information' within the meaning of the Environmental Information Regulations 1992 and therefore it was under no obligation to make the information available. The High Court rejected this argument and ruled that the concept of environmental information must be interpreted broadly. In the court's opinion, information about the person's name did constitute information about the state of the land, because it was impossible to assess the weight to attach to the reports of munitions dumping without information about the source of the reports.

---

9.  SI 1992/3240

10. [1995] Env LR Digest D22. See also the case commentary on this ruling in Environmental Law Monthly, June 1995: Monitor Press, Suffolk.

## Which bodies are required to provide access to environmental information?

The Information Regulations apply only to environmental information that is held by 'a relevant person' (regulation 3(*b*)). Regulation 2(4) identifies two categories of 'relevant person' in this context:

(*a*) all government Departments, district councils and other persons carrying out functions of public administration as, for the purposes of or in connection with their functions, have responsibilities in relation to the environment; and

(*b*) any body with public responsibilities for the environment which does not fall within sub-paragraph (a) and is under the control of a person falling within that sub-paragraph.

The first point to note concerning the definition of a 'relevant person' in this context is that the Information Regulations, like the British equivalent,[11] do not contain a definitive list of bodies affected by the Directive. The Northern Ireland guidance note states that because circumstances continue to change, it would be impossible to provide a 'definitive list' of organisations in Northern Ireland that are subject to the provisions of the Information Regulations.[12] In effect, it is up to individual organisations to decide for themselves whether they fall within either of the categories of relevant persons, and in the event of a dispute the onus is on the body in question to prove that it does not fall within the provisions of the Regulations.

In relation to the first category of relevant persons identified by regulation 2(4), the DoE(NI) guidance note points out that 'Government Departments and their respective offices' would clearly fall within this group, but goes on to state that 'any constituent advisory and *ad hoc* groups or committees not having a separate legal identity and other organisations that carry out functions of public administration and have responsibilities relating to the environment' will also be included in this category (paragraph 9).

Paragraph 10 of the guidance note points out that the second category of relevant persons identified by regulation 2(4) would include bodies that have public responsibilities for the environment but which do not fall into the first category and which are under the control of a person in the first category. In this regard, the guidance note states that 'control is taken to mean a relationship constituted by statute, rights, contracts or other means which either separately or jointly confer the possibility of directly or indirectly exercising a decisive influence on a body'. In the DoE(NI)'s opinion such a relationship would exist in the case of 'most public sector bodies (e.g. Non Departmental Public Bodies and

---

11. Environmental Information Regulations 1992 (SI 1992/3240). The DoE issued a guidance note concerning the application of these Regulations in 1992: *Freedom of Access to Information on the Environment: Guidance on the Implementation of the Environmental Information Regulations 1992 in Great Britain.*

12. When introducing the draft British Environmental Information Regulations 1992 to the House of Commons, the Minister for the Environment stated that the Government 'had carefully considered' whether a list of bodies affected by the Regulations should be included. He explained that it decided not to include such a list, because it would soon become outdated and thereby expose the UK to the possibility of enforcement proceedings for failure to implement the Directive (Official Record 1992, House of Commons, 16 Dec. 1992).

Government owned companies) but could also be the case for private sector bodies placed under some statutory duty' (paragraph 10).

It is important to note, however, that in order to be bound by the provisions of the Information Regulations and the Directive, a body must have a public responsibility for the environment. Paragraph 11 of the guidance note highlights a possible source of confusion concerning the nature of public responsibility for the environment required by the Directive. Articles 3–5 of the Directive contain the essential obligations to provide access to environmental information. Article 2 defines those public authorities to which the Directive applies as having 'responsibilities relating to the environment.' However, Article 6 of the Directive requires member states to ensure that the obligations laid down in Articles 3–5 also apply to environmental information held by public authorities with 'public responsibilities for the environment.' The guidance note states that Article 2(*b*) suggests an 'indirect responsibility' for the environment, which in the DoE(NI)'s opinion would include every Government department and public body, because, for example, under article 4 of the Nature Conservation and Amenity Lands (NI) Order 1985,[13] all are deemed to have responsibilities relating to nature conservation. On the other hand, the guidance note states that Article 6 of the Directive suggests the need for a 'direct responsibility' for the environment such as 'development, management, regulation or inspection of aspects of the environment on behalf of the public; such a responsibility might be established through statute.' At the time of writing, this ambiguity has not been authoritatively resolved by judicial means.

## Who may rely on the Information Regulations?

Article 3 of the Directive states that member states must ensure that public authorities are required to make environmental information available 'to any natural or legal person at his request and without his having to prove an interest.' This provision is implemented by regulation 4(1) of the Information Regulations, which provides that the relevant bodies (defined above) must make environmental information available 'to every person who requests it.' In effect, the applicant may be a private individual or any form of organisation (including a company), and it is irrelevant whether they possess UK citizenship or not. The applicant does not have to explain the purposes for which he wants the information, and similarly, paragraph 39 of the guidance note states that, in determining whether the request is reasonable, the body providing the information is not entitled to attach any importance to any interest which might be stated in the request or to a failure to state an interest.

## What is the scope of the obligation to provide environmental information?

The scope of the obligation to provide access to environmental information is wide-ranging, but, as already stated, it is not absolute. Article 3.1 of the Directive requires member states 'to define the practical arrangements' under which environmental information will be made available. Rather than imposing one

---

13. SI 1985/170.

uniform arrangement for the provision of environmental information, paragraph 22 of the DoE(NI)'s Guidance Note points out that the Information Regulations place this obligation on each individual body, thus enabling each one to introduce arrangements which are suited to their individual 'functions, responsibilities, and procedures'. This being stated, regulation 4(2) of the Information Regulations imposes certain controls on the nature of these arrangements. In effect, the relevant bodies are under a statutory duty to 'make such arrangements' for providing access to the environmental information in their possession as to ensure:

(i) that 'every request' for such environmental information is responded to 'as soon as possible';

(ii) that every such request is responded to 'within two months of the request being made'; and

(iii) that 'where the response to such a request contains a refusal to make information available, the refusal is in writing and specifies the reasons for the refusal.'

Regulation 4 goes on to make the following provisions concerning the obligation to make practical arrangements for the provision of environmental information:

1. The arrangements for the provision of environmental information may entitle the body to refuse a request for environmental information where the request 'is manifestly unreasonable or is formulated in too general a manner' (regulation 4(3)). The guidance note states that examples of an unreasonable request might be when an 'excessive' amount of information is requested or where 'significant processing of information is necessary before . . . [the information] can be released' (paragraph 42). Where a request for information is refused on the grounds that the question is formulated in too general a manner, the guidance note states that the body holding the information requested should make this clear to the applicant so that the question can be reformulated in such a manner that the information can be isolated and released (paragraph 43).

2. These arrangements may make provision for the imposition of a reasonable charge and may make the supply of the information in question conditional on payment of the charge (regulation 4(4)(*a*) and (*b*)). Although the guidance note acknowledges that it is impossible to prescribe a 'standard charge' for all bodies governed by the Information Regulations, it emphasises that bodies holding environmental information 'will need to avoid the accusation that they are setting unreasonable barriers to access. It is open to an applicant to appeal against any charges levied' (paragraph 30). Paragraphs 30–5 of the guidance note give more detailed advice about the nature of the charges that may be levied for the supply of environmental information.

3. The obligation to provide access to environmental information only obliges the relevant body to provide access in 'such form, and at such times and places, as may be reasonable' (regulation 4(5)). In this regard, the guidance note states that although practical arrangements for the provision of environmental information are for each individual body to decide, '[t]hey should be administratively practicable, efficient and should not represent an unjustified bureaucratic or financial burden.' In addition, such arrangements 'should not be

based upon an unrealistic expectation of the demand for access to environmental information' (paragraph 22).

4. The duty to provide access to environmental information is owed to the person who has requested the information (regulation 4(6)).

5. Any 'statutory provision or rule of law' which restricts or prohibits the disclosure of information will not apply to the disclosure of information which is governed by the Information Regulations, i.e. environmental information held by a relevant person (regulation 4(7)). This provision is, however, subject to the exceptions laid down in regulation 5 of the Information Regulations (discussed at page 539).

6. The guidance note also stresses that each body governed by the Information Regulations should ensure that the public is aware of the 'range and extent' of the environmental information held by the body so that requests for information can be formulated in the most effective manner. To this end, the guidance note advises that 'special mention should be made of any statutory public registers maintained by the body, giving the subject matter covered and the location of each register' (paragraph 23). The guidance note suggests that a statement of this nature could be contained in the body's 'annual report or a similar document'. It is also suggested that it would be helpful if bodies holding environmental information 'publicised the name and address of a contact point or information co-ordinator' for enquiries and assistance. Paragraph 24 of the guidance note also addresses the implication of the obligation laid down in Article 7 of the Directive, namely, that member states are obliged to 'provide general information to the public on the state of the environment by such means as the periodic publication of descriptive reports.' In this regard the guidance note states that Article 7 does 'not require the comprehensive publication of environmental information.' In effect, each body has a discretion to publish any environmental information it holds and to levy an 'appropriate charge' for these reports. As examples of reports published in pursuance of Article 7, the guidance note lists the annual *Digest of Environmental Protection and Water Statistics* produced by the DoE, the annual *Statistical Bulletin,* and *The UK Environment,* all of which contain information concerning the state of the environment in Northern Ireland. Finally, paragraph 25 provides guidance on the issue of copyright in reports on environmental information that are commissioned by public bodies from outside organisations.

7. Where a request for environmental information does not require the collation or editing of information—in other words, where the information requested is 'readily available'—paragraph 27 of the guidance note suggests that 'it should be possible to give a quick verbal or written response or allow inspection to personal callers on an *ad hoc* basis; no special arrangements need be made.' However, in the event that a request for environmental information does require 'significant staff time' to answer, the guidance note suggests that such requests are 'probably best handled through correspondence.' Finally, it is suggested that a special reception facility be established where requests are 'plentiful or repetitive;' however, the guidance note points out that arrangements of this nature would be 'unwise' until there is evidence of 'a high level of demand and adequate cost-recovery procedures.'

8. Article 8 of the Directive requires member states to report to the Commission

on 'the experience gained' in relation to the operation of the Directive; this report must be submitted by the end of December 1996. The DoE(NI) will be required to prepare the Northern Ireland report and in doing so will seek assistance from bodies holding environmental information concerning the practical implementation of the Directive. Paragraphs 36–8 of the Guidance Note point out that the Commission will use the national reports to prepare any proposals which might be necessary to improve the system of access established by the Directive; bodies are advised to note any shortcomings in the operation of the Directive which may then be included in the Northern Ireland report. The guidance note emphasises that this monitoring function need not be onerous and in particular should assess 'the total number of requests for environmental information received; and the total number of these requests that are refused.' It is also suggested that requests for environmental information under other statutory powers (i.e. environmental information contained in statutory registers) should be included in these figures, on the grounds that the information could have been requested under the Information Regulations.

### Exceptions to the right to information

Although there is a general presumption that environmental information should be released unless there are 'compelling and substantive reasons to withhold it' (paragraph 40, guidance note), the Information Regulations set out a number of exceptions to the right to environmental information. However, before addressing these exceptions, it is important to note, as a general matter, that the recent High Court decision in *R. v. British Coal Corporation, ex parte Ibstock Building Products Limited*[14] suggests that national courts will favour the disclosure of environmental information and will interpret exemptions to the obligation to disclose such information narrowly. It should also be noted at this juncture that Article 3.2 of the Directive provides that 'information held by public authorities shall be supplied in part where it is possible to separate out information on items concerning the interests referred to [in the exceptions listed below].' Regulation 5 (4) implements this provision by providing that the Information Regulations cannot authorise a refusal to provide access to environmental information which is 'contained in the same record as, or otherwise held with, other information which is withheld by virtue of this regulation unless it is incapable of being separated from the other information for the purpose of making it available.'

The exceptions to the obligation to provide environmental information are as follows:
  (i) The Information Regulations do not extend to information relating to the environment that is held by a public authority for the purposes of 'any judicial or legislative functions' (regulation 3(*b*)).
 (ii) As already explained, a body holding environmental information may refuse a request for such information where the request is 'manifestly unreasonable or is formulated in too general a manner' (regulation 4(3)).
(iii) Regulation 5 provides that the Information Regulations cannot require the release of 'confidential' information. However, a distinction is made between

---

14. [1995] Env LR Digest D22. See also the case commentary, supra note 10.

those circumstances where information is 'capable' of being treated as confidential and those where information 'must' be treated as confidential. In circumstances where information is capable of being treated as confidential, bodies have a discretion in deciding whether or not to release the information in question. However, in circumstances where the information requested must be treated as confidential, refusal is mandatory. Regulation 5(2)(a)–(e) provides an exhaustive list of the circumstances in which environmental information *may* be treated as confidential; regulation 5(3)(a)–(d) lists those circumstances in which environmental information *must* be treated as confidential. Each will now be addressed in turn.

Regulation 5(2) provides that environmental information is to be capable of being treated as being confidential 'if, and only if,' it is information:

(a) relating to matters affecting international relations, national defence or public security;

(b) relating to, or to anything which is or has been the subject-matter of, any legal or other proceedings (whether actual or prospective);

(c) relating to the confidential deliberations of any relevant person or to the contents of any internal communications of a body corporate or other undertaking or organisation;

(d) contained in a document or other record which is still in the course of completion; or

(e) relating to matters to which any commercial or industrial confidentiality attaches or affecting any intellectual property.

The meaning of each of these circumstances will now be addressed in turn.

*Re (a):* In this regard, paragraphs 46–8 of the guidance note give assistance on the role of the Official Secrets Act 1989, which governs the power of Crown servants to release information which might endanger the interests of the UK or its citizens abroad, the power of the Secretary of State to refuse the inclusion of information on statutory registers in the interests of national security, other non-statutory agreements which might lead bodies to refuse access to information on the grounds that it might be harmful to national security, the withholding of properly classified documents, and the extent to which public order may be invoked as a ground for refusing access to environmental information. It should also be noted that the High Court in *R. v. British Coal Corporation, ex parte Ibstock Building Products Limited*[15] (outlined above) rejected the argument that the disclosure of any named source was exempt on the grounds that it was a matter affecting national defence or public security. In coming to this conclusion, the court pointed out that the Ministry of Defence had not attempted to raise this issue when asked for any information in its possession concerning possible munitions dumping at the quarry in question. In addition, the court stated that the existence of munitions dumping at the Ibstock quarry was not necessarily a matter that currently affected national defence or public security.

*Re (b):* Regulation 5(5) provides that the phrase 'legal or other proceedings' includes 'any disciplinary proceedings, the proceedings at any local or other public inquiry and the proceedings at any hearing conducted by a person

---

15. Ibid.

appointed under any enactment for the purpose of affording an opportunity to persons to make representations or objections in respect of any matter.' Paragraph 49 of the guidance note suggests that examples of proceedings falling within regulation 5(5) might include 'information collected and to be used for the purpose of investigative proceedings (e.g. police proceedings); the subject matter of appeals to the (DoE(NI)); information which could reasonably be expected to interfere with enforcement proceedings; information which would deprive a person of a right to a fair trial or an impartial adjudication.' However, paragraph 49 continues to note that 'every effort should be made to release information once legal proceedings have been concluded unless there are statutory restrictions to the contrary.' The High Court in the *British Coal* case also ruled that as no appeal had been lodged concerning the planning application, there were no 'prospective' legal proceedings, and therefore the information could not be exempted from release, regardless of the fact that the information sought related to a planning application.

*Re (c):* In this regard paragraph 50 of the guidance note points out that 'bodies must be allowed to think in private,' but advises that while 'background deliberations, papers and reports leading up to policy statements or decisions . . . [and] other classified documents' would not normally be released, this exemption should not cover purely 'administrative or routine' transactions. In addition, paragraph 51 of the guidance note suggests that while the Local Government Act (NI) 1972 confers a right of access to any environmental information held by a district council via the public right of access to council, committee and sub-committee meetings and to the papers and background papers relating to those meetings, the Information Regulations may confer 'wider rights of access' to such information. The guidance note does not elaborate any further in this regard. Finally, paragraph 52 suggests that 'information relating to the contents of any internal communications of a body corporate or other undertaking or organisation may be withheld.' In the DoE(NI)'s opinion these would include 'Ministerial and Member correspondence, letters to and from members of the public, information passed between officials in the course of their duties, internal minutes and submissions to Ministers and Members.'

*Re (d):* In this context paragraph 53 of the guidance note points out that while it is reasonable that access to information being used by a body in the carrying out of its own 'studies including, inspection, testing, evaluating, monitoring and research' should be denied during the course of any of these processes so that 'analysis or interpretation' can proceed without obstruction, there may be difficulties in defining the point at which data can be considered as complete and therefore ready for public release if requested. In this regard, paragraph 54 attempts to provide assistance in relation to when various types of studies might be considered complete for the purposes of the Information Regulations (e.g. studies based on scientifically selected samples and longitudinal surveys). As a general point it is stressed that information which forms part of 'regular routine monitoring should not be regarded as part of an unfinished [data] set but should normally be released as soon as practicable after it is collected, or according to a planned and published timetable.'

*Re (e):* Where the information requested relates to any matter to which commercial or industrial confidentiality attaches, or the information relates to matters affecting any intellectual property, the body has a discretion to refuse access to the information. However, the position is different if the release of such information is the subject of existing statutory restriction (see below). Paragraphs 55–62 provide detailed advice on how bodies holding environmental information of this nature should determine whether or not to provide public access to such information. Overall, bodies are advised to be 'careful not to restrict the release of information unreasonably.' In particular, the guidance note suggests two courses of action which might be adopted by bodies receiving environmental information of this nature from third parties under contract or statute, namely, to classify the information either when it is received or to do so when a request for access to the information is first received. More detailed advice concerning each option is provided. A general point made in relation to both options is that handling commercially confidential information in the manner suggested in the context of both options could be time-consuming, and therefore it is likely that the two-month limitation period within which a response must be made under regulation 4(2) will be breached. Paragraph 62 suggests that where this is likely, the body in question should give the applicant written warning of the delay before the response deadline expires.

Regulation 5(3) provides that environmental information *must* be treated as confidential 'if, and only if':

(*a*)  it is capable of being so treated and its disclosure in response to that request would (apart from regulation 4(7)) contravene any statutory provision or rule of law or would involve a breach of any agreement;

(*b*)  the information is personal information contained in records held in relation to an individual who has not given his consent to its disclosure;

(*c*)  the information is held by the relevant person in consequence of having been supplied by a person who—

   (i)  was not under, and could not have been put under, any legal obligation to supply it to the relevant person; and

   (ii)  did not supply it in circumstances such that the relevant person is entitled apart from these regulations to disclose it; and

   (iii)  has not consented to its disclosure; or

(*d*)  the disclosure of the information in response to that request would, in the circumstances, make it more likely that the environment to which such information related would be damaged.

The meaning of each of these circumstances will now be addressed in turn.

*Re (a):* In essence, sub-paragraph (*a*) provides that where the disclosure of the information requested is prohibited by an existing statutory provision or a rule of law, the body holding the information must not release it to the public if the information in question is capable of being treated as confidential within the meaning of regulation 5(2) of the Information Regulations (outlined above). Paragraph 64 of the guidance note describes this provision as a 'catch-all case designed to exempt from disclosure information required or permitted to be kept secret by other statutes etc.' However, it is important to note that information of this nature must only be withheld on the grounds of confidentiality if 'it is capable of being so treated,' meaning that the information must fall into one of the categories listed in regulation 5(2) (discussed above). If the information requested does not fall into one of these categories, it must be released.

*Re (b):* This provision is relatively self-explanatory. However, paragraphs 65–7 of the guidance note make the following general points in this regard. First, paragraph 66 states that 'personal information should not be withheld where there are provisions to the contrary'. The guidance note cites the Dogs (NI) Order 1983 as an example in this regard. The Order imposes a statutory duty on district councils to maintain a register of prescribed particulars of dog-licensing and breeding establishments. This personal information would be supplied under the Dogs (Licensing and Identification) Regulations (NI) 1983 and the Dogs (Breeding Establishments and Guard Dogs Kennels) Regulations (NI) 1983. In addition, the guidance note emphasises that 'care should be exercised when handling information containing the addresses of individual properties. When that information relates to an individual occupant, it should be treated as personal information and not released without the occupant's consent.' However, the guidance note also suggests that 'it should be possible to release summary information or remove reference to the actual address and release the remaining information.' The High Court in the *British Coal* case also rejected the argument that the information requested (i.e. the name of the informant) could be exempt on the grounds that it was personal information and that the informant had not consented to the information being released. In the court's opinion, the name of an informant held by British Coal could not be considered as personal information for the purposes of the Environmental Information Regulations 1992 (which mirror the Northern Ireland Information Regulations); such information was deemed to be simply part of a broader category of information which was held in British Coal's records.

*Re (c):* In essence, sub-paragraph (c) provides that where a body holds information which was supplied voluntarily (i.e. by a person who 'was not under, and could not have been put under, any legal obligation to supply it' to the body), the body is obliged to refuse access to such information unless the person who has supplied the information consents to its disclosure or there are overriding powers of release. The protection of environmental information which has been volunteered is designed to prevent the inhibition of 'open and constructive discussion between environmental control authorities and industry and the gathering of information on which environmental statutes are based' (paragraph 68). It is important to note, however, that paragraph 69 identifies two exceptions to the protection afforded to volunteered information. First, information which is volunteered is not exempted from disclosure if it falls within a category of information which the body could be obliged by statute to release, unless the information in question is exempted from release by some other statutory provision. Second, where a statutory obligation to provide information is introduced, 'any information previously supplied on a voluntary basis for the same purpose should be released as long as it is not covered by other exemptions (e.g. on grounds of commercial confidentiality).' Finally, although the guidance note emphasises the importance of protecting volunteered information, it also states that 'it would not be in the spirit of the Directive to refuse to release all volunteered information as a matter of principle' (paragraph 70). To this end, the guidance note urges bodies to encourage suppliers of voluntary information to consent to the release of the information. In the event that access is permitted, bodies are advised to mark the information accordingly for future reference.

*Re (d):* Although the grounds of confidentiality set out in sub-paragraph (*d*) are self-explanatory, paragraph 71 of the guidance note provides instructive examples of instances where the release of environmental information would increase the likelihood of damage to the environment. In particular, paragraph 71 cites the release of information concerning the 'location of nesting sites, rare habitats or endangered/protected species' as information which should be withheld on these grounds. In addition, paragraph 71 notes that information concerning possible areas of special scientific interest under the Nature Conservation and Amenity Lands (NI) Order 1985 (discussed in chapter 7) should not be released to the public until formal notice of the DoE(NI)'s intention to designate is served, the rationale being that premature release of such information could create the risk that the site would be damaged before it was protected under the 1985 Order. However, it should also be noted that paragraph 71 advises bodies to 'exercise careful judgment when restricting information in this way.'

### Control of access to environmental information under statutory provisions other than the Information Regulations

Regulation 3(*c*) provides that the Information Regulations do not apply to information which must be provided on request to every person who makes a request, nor do they apply to information contained in records which must be made available for inspection by every person who wishes to inspect them. In both instances the obligation to release the information must be contained in an existing statutory provision other than the Information Regulations themselves. However, it is important to note that information which must be released under other statutory provision does not escape the control of the Information Regulations entirely. Regulation 6 provides that the practical arrangements made for the provision of information which must be released subject to other statutory provision must be such as to secure conditions identical to those required under regulation 4 for the provision of environmental information governed by the Information Regulations. In effect, every request for information relating to the environment whose release is governed by other statutory provisions must be responded to as soon as possible; a response must be made within two months of the request being made; where the response contains a refusal to release information, the refusal must be in writing and must specify the reason for the refusal; and finally, only a reasonable charge may be levied for the provision of such information.

In effect, regulation 6 operates to control the provision of information relating to the environment contained, for example, in public registers which various public bodies with responsibility for the environment are required by statute to maintain (see Part II of this chapter). To ensure compliance with the Information Regulations (as far as they govern the provision of such information), paragraph 26 of the guidance note advises bodies, which are under a statutory obligation to maintain registers of environmental information, to 'keep registers up to date and strive towards greater standardisation and consistency of contents' so as to 'maintain and improve their user friendliness.'

## Appealing against a refusal to release environmental information

As already outlined, the obligation to release environmental information is not absolute. A body may refuse to release information for a number of reasons, for example, because the request concerns information which falls into one of the exceptions, or the body concerned does not consider itself to be governed by the Information Regulations, or the information is not held by the body in question, or the information does not relate to the environment and is therefore not information governed by the Information Regulations, or the release of the information has to be delayed. Article 4 of the Directive provides that 'a person who considers that his request for information has been unreasonably refused or ignored, or has been inadequately answered by a public authority, may seek a judicial or administrative review of the decision in accordance with the relevant national legal system.' The Information Regulations do not make formal provision for taking an appeal against a refusal to release environmental information; however, paragraphs 72–4 of the guidance note address the requirements laid down in Article 4 of the Directive and provide advice on the means by which a person who 'is dissatisfied with a refusal' to make information available or who considers that a request has been 'inadequately answered or delayed' may seek a remedy. Paragraphs 72–4 provide as follows:

1. The applicant may request that the body concerned review its stated reasons for delaying or refusing access.
2. The guidance note states that where some other statutory measure confers a right of appeal, the refusal letter should not only contain the reasons for the refusal but should also inform the applicant of their right to appeal. Where there is no statutory right of appeal, the applicant might appeal to the head of the body concerned.
3. Where a district council refuses access to environmental information, the applicant may apply to the Ombudsman for a remedy, on the grounds of 'maladministration giving rise to injustice.'
4. The guidance note suggests that aggrieved applicants should also invoke 'the usual democratic channels', for example ask their local MP to pursue the matter.
5. Finally, the guidance note suggests that 'if all else fails,' the applicant may take an action before a national court to enforce the statutory duty owed to the applicant under regulation 4(6) of the Information Regulations (outlined above); the body in question would then have to defend its reasons for refusing access. A national court hearing such an action may refer questions concerning the proper interpretation of the Directive to the European Court of Justice under Article 177 of the EC Treaty (Preliminary References Procedure).
6. Although it is not referred to in the guidance note, it should be noted that an aggrieved applicant may also inform the European Commission of any failure to implement the Directive correctly in Northern Ireland and urge the Commission to take enforcement proceedings under Article 169 of the EC Treaty against the UK. Although the Commission retains complete discretion to

decide whether or not to take such an action, there are no formal procedures or time limits governing such contact with the Commission; a letter explaining the nature of the alleged failure will suffice to alert the Commission. The Information Regulations follow the wording of the Directive closely; however, one possible area of weakness in the implementation of the Directive arises in the context of the practical arrangements which member states are required to make for the release of environmental information. Article 3.1 of the Directive provides that member states 'shall define the practical arrangements under which such information is effectively made available.' Nigel Haigh points out in relation to the British implementation of the Directive[16] (which mirrors the Northern Ireland Information Regulations), that 'it is debatable how far the Regulations implement [this] obligation.'[17] Although the British and Northern Ireland Regulations both require bodies governed by the Directive to make environmental information available and require that they make practical arrangements for the provision of the information, the Northern Ireland Regulations, like the British Regulations, do not require such bodies to define the arrangements in detail. The Government, for its part, considered that it would be impractical to define these practical arrangements in detail, and so the question remains whether the Directive has been implemented fully, and therefore correctly, in the UK.

## PART II  PUBLIC REGISTERS OF ENVIRONMENTAL INFORMATION

As explained at the beginning of this chapter, statutory registers are one of the principal sources of environmental information throughout the UK. The following is a list of the statutory registers which must be maintained in Northern Ireland under the legislation discussed in this book. It should be noted, however, that much of Northern Ireland's primary legislation governing pollution of land, air and water is currently under review, and all the proposed provisions contain requirements for the establishment of public registers. It should also be noted that this section does not list many of the other statutory requirements concerning public access to information and public consultation, for example requirements to publish reports concerning the implementation of particular Directives in Northern Ireland, or requirements to advertise applications for consents to discharge polluting substances into water; such provisions are discussed in the specific context of individual chapters. Two types of registers are referred to in this list, namely, the 'Statutory Charges Register' maintained under the Land Registration Act (NI) 1970[18] and registers created and maintained by the DoE(NI)'s Environment Service.[19] These registers must be available for public consultation at all reasonable times. (See also the requirements laid down by the Environmental

---

16. Environmental Information Regulations 1992 (SI 1992/3240).
17. N. Haigh, *Manual of Environmental Policy: The EC and Britain,* London: Longman, 1992, chap. 11.5, p. 3.
18. c. 18.
19. The Environment Service can be contacted at Calvert House, 23 Castle Place, Belfast BT1 1FY, for further information as to the times at which these registers can be consulted.

Information Regulations (NI) 1993 concerning the release of environmental information under statutory provisions other than the Information Regulations, pages 544–5.)

1. Article 33 of the Nature Conservation and Amenity Lands (NI) Order 1985 requires that declarations, made and confirmed under article 24, that an area of land is an area of special scientific interest be registered in the Statutory Charges Register. The declaration must include a statement of the scientific interest of the area and the notifiable operations for that area. In the event that an ASSI is also designated as a 'European site', the DoE(NI) has the power under the Conservation (Natural Habitats etc.) Regulations (NI) 1995 to alter the ASSI declaration in terms of its statement of the scientific interest of the site and/or the notifiable operations concerning that site for the purposes of ensuring compliance with the Habitats Directive. The amendment to the ASSI declaration must be registered in the Statutory Charges Register.

2. Article 33 of the Nature Conservation and Amenity Lands (NI) Order 1985 requires that any management agreement entered into under article 24 for the management of an ASSI must be registered in the Statutory Charges Register.

3. Article 33 of the Nature Conservation and Amenity Lands (NI) Order 1985 requires that any agreement or covenant entered into under article 8 and any management agreement entered into under article 17 for the management of a nature reserve must be registered in the Statutory Charges Register. Similarly, any waiver of the conditions thereof must also be entered in the register.

4. Regulation 10 of the Conservation (Natural Habitats etc.) Regulations (NI) 1995 requires the DoE(NI) to compile and maintain a register of 'European sites' in Northern Ireland; i.e. special areas of conservation (SACs), special protection areas (SPAs), sites of Community importance, and sites subject to the consultation procedure laid down in Article 5 of the Habitats Directive. Entries concerning European sites in the DoE(NI)'s register must also be made in the Statutory Charges Register.

5. Regulations 13 and 14 of the Conservation (Natural Habitats etc.) Regulations (NI) 1995 require that any management agreement entered into in respect of a European site must be registered in the Statutory Charges Register.

6. Article 9 of the Nature Conservation and Amenity Lands (NI) Order 1985 requires that any management agreement entered into by the DoE(NI) for the management of an area of outstanding natural beauty (designated under article 14 of the Order) must be entered in the Statutory Charges Register. It should be noted that while the DoE(NI) is not required to maintain a public register of designated AONBs, it is obliged to ensure that copies of individual designations are kept at the offices of relevant district councils and that these are available for public consultation at all reasonable times. Any agreement or restrictive covenant entered in by the DoE(NI) under article 8 of the Nature Conservation and Amenity Lands (NI) Order 1985 concerning the manner in which land designated as an AONB can be developed or used must be registered in the Statutory Charges Register, and any waiver in the conditions thereof must also be registered.

7. Article 56 and Schedule 3 to the Access to the Countryside (NI) Order 1983 provide that all public path creation orders, public path extinguishment orders

and public path diversion orders made by district councils under the Order must be registered in the Statutory Charges Register.

8. Article 56 and Schedule 3 to the Access to the Countryside (NI) Order 1983 require that all access agreements made under the Order must be registered in the Statutory Charges Register; similarly, any order which varies or revokes an access agreement must be registered.

9. Article 56 and Schedule 3 to the Access to the Countryside (NI) Order 1983 provide that any access order made under the Order must be registered in the Statutory Charges Register; similarly, any instrument or order which varies or revokes that order must be registered.

10. Article 40 of the Access to the Countryside (NI) Order 1983 requires district councils to maintain maps, available for public consultation, which show: (i) areas of land within the council's district which is subject to an access agreement or access order, (ii) any land therein which is exempted from public access and the provisions under which such restrictions have effect, and (iii) any land acquired by the council for the purposes of providing public access.

11. Section 9(9) of the Water Act (NI) 1972 requires the DoE(NI) to create and maintain a public register of the discharge consents (and attached conditions) which are currently in force; these consents permit discharges of trade and sewage effluent and other polluting matter into Northern Ireland's inland, coastal and groundwaters.

12. Section 25 of the Water Act (NI) 1972 requires the DoE(NI) to create and maintain a public register which contains all the particulars of sampling points fixed by the Department under section 25.

13. Section 20 of the Water Act (NI) 1972 requires the DoE(NI) to provide facilities for the public inspection of records of data or information collected by or on behalf of the DoE(NI) concerning the exercise of its functions under the Act (i.e. the prevention and control of water pollution in Northern Ireland's inland, coastal and ground waters).

14. Regulation 26 of the Water Quality Regulations (NI) 1994 requires the DoE(NI) to maintain records of the quality of water intended for human consumption. Such records must be made available for public consultation.

15. The DoE(NI) is required to create and maintain a public register which contains a full set of water quality results (for all of the prescribed parameters) in respect of all bathing waters designated in Northern Ireland under the Bathing Water Directive.

16. The DoE(NI) is obliged under regulation 12 of the Urban Waste Water Treatment Regulations (NI) 1995 to keep maps of all waters identified as estuaries and areas of water identified as sensitive areas and as areas of high natural dispersion (less sensitive); such maps must be available for public consultation at all reasonable times.

17. The Alkali &c. Works (Registration) Order (NI) 1981 requires the DoE(NI) to maintain a register of those works in Northern Ireland which are permitted to carry on an 'alkali work' or a 'scheduled work' under the Alkali &c. Works Regulation Act 1906. Although the 1981 Order does not specifically require this register to be available for public consultation, it is likely that this

information will fall within the Environmental Information Regulations (NI) 1993 considered in Part I of this chapter.

18. Article 8(4) of the Pollution Control and Local Government (NI) Order 1978 requires district councils to keep a register containing all prescribed details of all the current waste disposal licences it has issued; these registers must also contain details of resolutions passed by the council in question under article 13 in respect of its own waste disposal sites.

19. Regulation 14 of the Pollution Control (Special Waste) Regulations (NI) 1981 imposes a series of obligations on producers, carriers and disposers of 'special waste' to maintain registers of all consignment notes of special waste produced, transferred and disposed and the locations of disposal sites. Regulation 14 also prescribes the length of time for which these registers must be kept and the format of the register (specific details of which are provided in chapter 6).

## PART III PUBLIC ACCESS TO LOCAL AUTHORITY MEETINGS

Article 23 of the Local Government Act (NI) 1972[20] gives the public a right of access to district council, committee and sub-committee meetings and to the papers and background papers relating to those meetings. This includes a right of access to environmental information held by councils, which is supplemented by the Environmental Information Regulations (NI) 1993, outlined in Part I of this chapter.

## PART IV ECO-MANAGEMENT AND AUDIT SCHEMES

In recent years voluntary environmental management and auditing schemes have been introduced at national, EC and international levels for the purpose of promoting continuous improvement in the environmental performance of those commercial and industrial concerns which participate in these schemes and also to make information on the environmental performance of participating concerns available to the public.

Environmental management and auditing schemes, which were first developed in the United States, are essentially designed to implement the concept of 'sustainable development', which requires, among other things, that the responsibility for environmental protection be shared by all sections of the community. In 1993 the EC adopted Regulation EEC/1836/93,[21] which established a voluntary eco-management and audit scheme (EMAS), whereby companies involved in industrial activities can submit one or more sites, rather than the company as a whole, for registration.[22] Once a company wishes to register a site under the scheme, it is obliged to establish environmental policies, programmes and management systems for the site and to submit them for

---

20. c. 9.
21. OJ L168, 10 July 1993.
22. For further information concerning the EC eco-management and audit scheme see Haigh, supra, chap. 11, s. 8; Freshfields Environmental Group, *Tolley's Environmental Handbook: a Management Guide*, London: Tolley 1994, chaps. 8 and 14. An updated edition of the Tolley's publication is due in late 1996.

systematic, objective and periodic evaluation, the results of which must be made public in the form of an environmental statement. It is important to note that although Regulation EEC/1836/93 was adopted in July 1993, it did not come into operation until 2 April 1995. The UK has also developed its own voluntary standard for environmental management systems (EMS), contained in BS 7750.[23] BS 7750 can be applied to organisations of any size or type and is designed to help organisations 'establish an effective management system for sound environmental performance, and to form a basis for environmental auditing.'[24] As with the EC scheme of environmental management, participation in EMS is voluntary. BS 7750 complements the EC scheme and is an extension of the quality accreditation scheme laid down in BS 5750. BS 7750 was reviewed in February 1994 to bring its requirements into line with Regulation EEC/1836/93. The International Organisation for Standardisation (ISO) is also in the process of developing a similar environmental management scheme (ISO 14001); at the time of writing, however, it remains in draft form.

To avoid competition between the Community, national and international systems, the EC Regulation provides that companies which comply with a 'recognised environmental management standard', either national, EC, or international, will be accepted for registration under EMAS. It should be noted, however, that there is considerable controversy about whether the considerably weaker ISO 14001 draft should be approved as a means of obtaining EMAS registration.[25] Although the ISO, UK and EC standards differ in many respects, there are two main areas of concern. First, Annex IC of the EMAS Regulation lists specific issues which must be addressed by companies' environmental policies and programmes and environmental audits; the ISO standard lacks detail in this area. Second, Annex II of the EMAS Regulation prescribes in detail the means by which environmental audits should be carried out; the ISO standard provides only minimal guidance in this regard. The European standards body CEN is now under considerable pressure to adopt ISO 14001 to avoid creating a trade barrier which would open up avenues for litigation.

### Regulation EEC/1836/93 (EMAS)

The EMAS scheme set up under Regulation EEC/1836/93 is open to companies operating a site or sites at which an industrial activity is performed. Article 2(i) of the Regulation defines the term industrial activity as meaning 'any activity listed under sections C and D of the classification of economic activities in the EC (NACE rev. 1) as established by Regulation EEC/3037/90[26] with the addition of electricity, gas steam and hot water production and the recycling, treatment, destruction or disposal of solid or liquid waste. Article 3 of the Regulation sets out the conditions which must be satisfied by any such company in order to have a site registered in the EMAS scheme. They are as follows:

---

23. Copies of BS 7750 may be obtained by post from BSI Sales, Linford Wood, Milton Keynes MK14 6LE; tel. (01908) 221166.
24. Croner's *Environmental Management*, July 1994, 1.
25. Environmental Data Services (ENDS Report 240, p. 25 Jan. 1995) provides a detailed discussion of the nature of conflicts between the UK, EC and ISO standards in this context under the headline 'Weak ISO draft threatens Europe's environmental management standards'.
26. OJ L 292 24 October 1990.

1. The company must adopt an environmental policy in accordance with the relevant requirements set out in Annex I to the Regulation. The company's environmental policy must not only ensure that the site in question is in compliance with all relevant environmental standards, it must also include commitments aimed at the reasonable continuous improvement of the site's environmental performance, with a view to reducing the site's environmental impact to levels not exceeding those corresponding to the economically viable application of the best available technology.
2. Article 3 then provides that the company must conduct an environmental review of the site in question which addresses those issues specified in Annex I, part C to the Regulation, namely:
    (i)     assessment, control and reduction of the impact of the activity concerned on the various sectors of the environment;
    (ii)    energy management, savings and choice;
    (iii)   raw materials management, savings, choice and transportation and water management and savings;
    (iv)   waste avoidance, recycling, reuse, transportation and disposal;
    (v)    evaluation, control and reduction of noise both within and outside the site;
    (vi)   selection of new production processes and changes to production processes;
    (vii)  product planning (design, packaging, transportation, use and disposal);
    (viii) environmental performance and practices of contractors, sub-contractors and suppliers;
    (ix)   prevention and limitation of environmental accidents;
    (x)    contingency procedures in cases of environmental accidents;
    (xi)   staff information and training on environmental issues;
    (xii)  external information on environmental issues.
Once the review is complete, the company must then introduce an environmental programme for the site and an environmental management system applicable to all activities at the site. Both the programme and the management system must be drawn up in light of the review. The programme must be aimed at achieving the commitments contained in the company's environmental policy concerning the continuous improvement of environmental performance; the management system must comply with the requirements set down in Annex I, part B to the Regulation.
3. Next the company must have the environmental performance of the site audited either externally or internally. The audit must satisfy the requirements laid down in Article 4 of the Regulation. Article 4 governs the persons authorised to conduct the audit, the issues which must be addressed during the audit and the frequency of the audit. The audits must be carried out at maximum intervals of three years; however, the specific frequency for individual sites will depend on the nature and scale of the emissions etc. being carried out on the site.
4. Once the audit has been conducted, the company must set objectives at the 'highest appropriate management level' which are aimed at the continuous improvement of the environmental performance of the site. These objectives will be drawn up in light of the findings of the audit and, where necessary, the site's environmental programme must be altered to enable these objectives to be achieved.

5. The company must then prepare an environmental statement for each audited site. The statement must comply with the requirements laid down in Article 5 of and Annex V to the Regulation. In essence, the environmental statement must be prepared in light of the initial environmental review of the site and each subsequent audit or audit cycle for the site. The statement must be designed for public consumption and to this end must be written in a concise and comprehensible form; technical material may be appended. In particular, the statement must draw attention to any significant changes since the previous statement and should include an assessment of the figures on pollutant emissions, waste generation, consumption of raw material, energy and water, noise and other significant environmental aspects of the site in question. Article 5.5 provides that a simplified environmental statement must be prepared annually in the years between each environmental audit. Such statements should be based on the criteria listed above.

6. The company must then have the environmental policy, programme, management system, review or audit procedure and environmental statement or statements examined by an independent accredited environmental verifier (who must also be independent of the site's environmental auditor).[27] The verifier must assess the specific issues laid down in Article 4 and Annex III. Once validated, the company must forward the site's environment statement to the competent national body which must register the site and make the statement available to the public. It should be noted, however, that the site will be registered only when the competent body receives the validated environmental statement and the registration fee (Article 8). Once registered, the site is entitled to use one of four 'statements of participation' (contained in Annex IV) and the relevant graphic or symbol. The statement of participation and graphic will indicate the level of participation in the scheme. It should be noted that the graphic cannot be used without the statement of participation and the statement cannot be used to advertise products, or on products themselves or on their packaging. They may be used, for example, on the company's stationery. Any site which violates any of the requirements laid down by Regulation EEC/1836/93 will be refused registration or will be suspended from the register until such time as the violation is remedied.

Member states were required to establish a system of accreditation for environmental verifiers by 2 April 1995. In the UK the verifier must be accredited by the UK Accreditation Services (UKAS)[28] (formerly known as the National Accreditation Council for Certification Bodies) and must prove to the UKAS that they have the requisite qualifications, training, and experience. An EC-wide list of all accredited environmental verifiers will be published in the *Official Journal*. In addition, member states were required to have designated a 'competent body' by July 1994 to register participating sites in a register which is to be updated annually and communicated to the Commission. The Northern Ireland 'competent body' is the UK competent body for the Eco-Management and Audit Scheme

---

27. The simplified environmental statement will require validation only at the end of the audit or audit cycle.
28. The UKAS can be contacted at tel. (0171) 2337111.

(DoE) London.[29] This body holds the register of companies which have attained the EMAS standard in the UK, and its register is open to public consultation; thus far, no Northern Ireland companies have been registered on their list. A list of all sites registered under the scheme throughout the EC will be published annually by the Commission. Finally, it should be noted that the Commission will endeavour to promote collaboration between the various national accreditation systems so that the procedures and criteria for accreditation employed throughout the EC will be consistent, and also that the EC scheme will be reviewed in July 1998.

## BS 7750 (EMS)

The first point to note about BS 7750 is that it does not set out specific environmental performance requirements. Instead it states that sector application guides will be issued; these guides will be of BS code of practice status. Although it is not a prerequisite of BS 7750, it is expected that organisations which comply with quality accreditation schemes contained in BS 5750 will be able to extend their system to comply with the environmental accreditation scheme contained in BS 7750.

The steps for implementation and maintenance of BS 7750 are very similar to those laid down under Regulation EEC/1836/93 for the EC EMAS. In effect, an organisation seeking to comply with BS 7750 must carry out an initial or preparatory review where there is no existing environmental management scheme in operation. The initial review will address the statutory and regulatory requirements governing the organisation and will examine the organisation's previous environmental management practices. Next the organisation must produce an environmental policy statement concerning its activities and products which is comprehensible to those involved. The structure of the organisation and location of responsibility must be clearly defined; the requirements contained in environmental legislation relevant to the company's activities must be listed; the significant environmental effects of the company itself and the environmental performance of its suppliers must be considered; environmental objectives and targets must be established; and finally, those activities and processes carried on by the company which are likely to affect the environment must be identified, and operational controls must be set in place for such activities and processes.

Next the company must establish an environmental management programme which is monitored by a senior manager. The management programme must be able to address the company's past activities and also the effects of new products at all stages of their life-cycle. The company must produce a sufficiently detailed environmental manual to enable the environmental auditor to assess whether the environmental management system exists and whether it is appropriate in relation to the environmental impact of the company. In addition, the company must establish a system of recording maintenance work which is carried out, inspections which have been conducted, any failures to comply with the company's environmental policy, and any corrective action which has been taken. As is the case under the EC EMAS scheme, participating companies should normally be

---

29. This body can be contacted at the DoE, room C11/21, Marsham Street, London SW1P 3EB; tel. (0171) 2763377; fax (0171) 2763731.

subjected to an environmental audit at least every three years, or annually where there is particular danger of environmental damage; BS 7750 details the issues which should be addressed by an environmental audit plan. Under the EC EMAS scheme, participating companies are registered site by site rather than as a company as a whole; however, under the BS 7750 scheme, all parts of the participating company will be reviewed in the audit. Compliance with BS 7750 may require that the environmental audit be subject to external, independent verification.

The UK Accreditation Service (UKAS) (formerly known as the National Accreditation Council for Certification Bodies) acts as the UK accreditor for those who issue verification certificates under BS 7750. Where an environmental consultant deemed competent by the UKAS issues a certificate verifying the environmental audit, that certificate will also be valid under the EC EMAS scheme. As already stated, the UKAS also acts as the accreditor for verifiers under the EMAS scheme. The Government also intends that organisations which comply with BS 7750 will be able to obtain certification from an independent organisation, as is the case for those which comply with the quality standard under BS 5750. However, any company or individual which wishes to carry out certification under BS 7750 must first be accredited by the UKAS.[30] Finally, it should be noted that the UKAS also maintains public records of the companies certified to BS 7750.

**Further information and assistance concerning participation in EMAS or EMS**

Organisations in Northern Ireland wishing to participate in either the EC or national scheme should contact the Environmental Audit Support Scheme and the Environment Management Support Scheme, both of which are operated by the Northern Ireland Department of Economic Development, Industrial Research and Technology Unit.[31]

---

30. Croner's *Environmental Management* (July 1994), p. 4; Department of Trade and Industry, *Consultation Paper on the Implementation of the EC Eco-Management and Audit Regulation and Accreditation Arrangements for Certification to BS 7750,* London: HMSO 1993.
31. The DED can be contacted at the Industrial Science Centre, 17 Antrim Road, Lisburn BT28 3AL, Co. Antrim; tel. (01846) 623000; fax (01846) 676054. Both the Environmental Audit Support Scheme and the Environmental Management Support Scheme offer companies grants towards the cost of commissioning an environmental audit or towards the cost of employing an independent consultant to assist in the development of an appropriate environmental management system. All companies and organisations operating commercially in Northern Ireland are eligible to apply. Advice is also available from the following organisations concerning the types of consultants that are available: Environmental Auditors Registration Association, the Old School, Fen Road, East Kirkby, Lincolnshire PE23 4DB, tel. (01790) 763613; the Confederation of British Industry, Fanum House, 108 Great Victoria Street, Belfast BT2 7DP, tel. (01232) 326658; the information officer, Local Enterprise Development Unit, Upper Galwally, Belfast BT8 4FY, tel. (01232) 491031. Finally, it should be noted that in Jan. 1996 the Commission released guidelines for companies wishing to reflect environmental considerations in their annual accounts ('Environmental Issues in Financial Reporting'). The guidelines were drawn up by the Accounting Advisory Forum and include recommendations on the definition and disclosure of environmental expenditure and on the recognition, measurement and disclosure of environmental risks and liabilities. The guidelines are not legally binding. Copies can be obtained from the Commission's Financial Information Unit, tel. +32 2 2953470; fax +32 2 2994745.

## PART V ECO-LABELLING

Whereas environmental management and auditing schemes are designed to encourage commercial and industrial concerns to improve their environmental performance as a company, or the environmental performance of individual sites, the concept of eco-labelling focuses on the environmental impact of products produced by the commercial and industrial concerns.

The concept of eco-labelling, as applied throughout the EC, has two main objectives. Firstly, it is designed to encourage the production of products which cause the least possible damage to the environment from the point where raw materials for the product are extracted right through to the point of disposal. Secondly, it is designed to provide reliable information to consumers about the 'green credentials' or environmental impact of those products registered under the scheme. As public concern about the state of the environment has increased, so too has the market for products that are 'environment-friendly'. However, because many of these claims can be misleading, several countries have introduced official eco-labelling schemes in addition to national legislation concerning false and misleading trade descriptions and advertising codes of practice. The first official eco-labelling scheme was established in Germany in 1978, which employed the 'blue angel' symbol; today official eco-labelling schemes are in operation in several countries around the world, including the UK.

The German scheme provided the stimulus for an EC eco-labelling scheme, which was finally established, after extensive discussion, in 1992 by Regulation EEC/880/92.[32] Article 1 of the Regulation states that the objective of the EC eco-labelling award scheme is to 'promote the design, production, marketing and use of products which have a reduced environmental impact during their entire life cycle, and provide consumers with better information on the environmental impact of products.'[33] Although it was originally proposed that an EC 'jury' would assess eligible products and award the eco-label, it was decided that competent bodies, designated at national level, would assess the environmental performance of products and award the eco-label. However, the Regulation provides that in order to obtain the EC eco-label, products must be tested according to specific ecological criteria established by the Commission (assisted by an advisory committee of experts) for each product group.[34]

Article 5.4 of Regulation EEC/880/92 provides that the specific ecological criteria established for each product group must be devised using a 'cradle-to-grave' approach based on the objectives set out in Article 1 and with reference to the indicative assessment matrix contained in Annex I to the Regulation. The concept of 'cradle-to-grave' assessment means that the entire life-cycle of a product will be assessed in terms of its environmental impact, including the choice of raw materials, the distribution, consumption, use and ultimate disposal of the product after use. In addition, Article 5.4 provides that the ecological criteria

---

32. OJ L99/1, 11 Apr. 1992.
33. It should be noted that the Regulation seeks to ensure that product and workers' safety are not compromised nor does it significantly affect the properties that make the product fit for use.
34. Art. 6 of the Regulation requires that the Commission consult widely when establishing the ecological criteria for any given product group. In particular it is required to consult 'the principal interest groups'.

established for each product group must be 'precise, clear and objective so as to ensure uniformity of application' by the national bodies designated for the task of assessing individual products under the scheme. The criteria must also 'ensure a high level of environmental protection, be based as far as possible on the use of clean technology and, where appropriate, reflect the desirability of maximising product life.' Products which satisfy these criteria and EC health, safety and environmental requirements will be awarded the EC eco-label. Article 2 provides that Regulation EEC/880/92 will not apply to food, drink or pharmaceuticals. Article 4 provides that an eco-label cannot be awarded to either: (i) products which are substances or preparations classified as dangerous in accordance with Directives 67/548/EEC[35] and 88/379/EEC[36] or (ii) products manufactured by processes which are likely to cause significant harm to human life and/or the environment. The eco-label logo is contained in Annex II to the Regulation.

In November 1992 the UK Eco-labelling Board Regulations 1992[37] came into force and established the UK Eco-labelling Board as the competent body for the purposes of assessing products for the award of eco-labels under the EC eco-labelling scheme. The UK board must assess eligible products according to the eco-labelling criteria adopted by the Commission under Regulation EEC/880/92.[38] Article 9.2 requires that member states must ensure that the composition of the competent body is such 'as to guarantee their independence and neutrality.' The competent body is obliged to apply the ecological criteria for each product group in a consistent manner. In effect, Regulation EEC/880/92 establishes a system of mutual recognition of the decisions of national competent bodies. Where a national competent body decides that a product should be awarded an EC eco-label, it is obliged to notify the Commission of its decision and must enclose the full results and a summary of the results of its assessment of the product in question. The Commission must then notify other member states of this decision. Member states are entitled under the Regulation to raise objections to the award of an EC eco-label; however, a reasoned objection must be submitted to the Commission within thirty days of receiving notification of the decision to award, otherwise the award will proceed. In the event that objections to the award of an eco-label cannot be resolved by informal consultation, the Commission, acting through its advisory board, will take the final decision.[39] Where a national competent body decides to award an eco-label to a product which has already been rejected by the competent body of another member state, the national body must highlight this fact when notifying the Commission of its decision to award; in such a situation the Commission, acting through its advisory board, must in all cases

---

35. OJ L196/1, 27 June 1967.
36. OJ L187/14, 7 June 1988.
37. SI 1992/2383.
38. The Governmental debates concerning the establishment of a UK eco-labelling scheme are contained in the following reports: Department of the Environment and Department of Trade and Industry, *Environmental Labelling: a Discussion Paper,* London: HMSO 1989; House of Commons Select Environment Committee, Eighth Report HC (1990–91), 474–1, London: HMSO; DoE, *The Government's Response to the Eighth Report from the House of Commons Select Committee on the Environment* (Cm 1720), London: HMSO 1991; National Advisory Group on Ecolabelling, *Giving Guidance to the Green Consumer: Progress on an Ecolabelling Scheme for the UK,* London: HMSO 1991.
39. The procedure governing this decision-making process is contained in Art. 7 of the Regulation.

take a decision on the award of the label.[40] Where a national competent body decides to refuse an application for an EC eco-label the Commission must be notified immediately, and the applicant must be informed of the reasons for the refusal. Member states are required to make provision for appeals against refusals of awards.

Companies which apply for an eco-label will have to pay an application fee, and if the label is awarded they will be required to pay an annual licence fee for use of the label and also sign a contract governing the use of the eco-label. The label logo may be used to advertise the product which has been awarded the eco-label but may not be used until the label has actually been awarded. Any false or misleading advertising or use of a label or logo which leads to confusion with the EC eco-label or logo is prohibited.

The Commission has now adopted 'indicative guidelines' as to costs and fees in this context; these are laid down in Decision 93/326/EC,[41] and competent bodies may set their actual fees for testing etc. within 20 per cent (plus or minus) of these rates. It should also be noted that the Commission is required to maintain separate records of all applications received, all applications approved, and all applications rejected. Article 10.9 of Regulation EEC/880/92 specifically states that the registers of applicants received and rejected may only be accessible to the competent bodies of the member states. When an application is made for an eco-label, the UK Eco-labelling Board will be required to check the application against the central register of all applications, approvals and rejections for the EC as a whole. Member states are required to ensure that consumers and undertakings are informed of the objectives of the eco-label award scheme, the product groups which have been selected, the ecological criteria for each product group, the procedures to be followed when applying for an eco-label, and the competent body or bodies in the member state for assessing products for award of the eco-label (Article 15).

When Regulation EEC/880/92 was first adopted in 1992, the Council of Ministers agreed that ecological criteria for an initial group of fifteen products should be established, namely washing machines, dishwashers, paper products, laundry detergent, dishwasher detergent, household cleaning products, batteries, paints and varnishes, insulating materials, light bulbs, soil improvers or growing media, and hair sprays. Thus far EC criteria have been adopted for washing machines and dishwashers; these criteria are contained in Decisions 93/430/EC[42] and 93/431/EC,[43] respectively. Work is in progress for EC criteria concerning the other products; however, certain member states, including the UK, have already adopted national criteria in relation to some of these products.[44]

## PART VI OTHER SOURCES OF ENVIRONMENTAL INFORMATION

In addition to the more formal sources of environmental information or statutory obligations to provide such information discussed throughout this chapter, there

---

40. Ibid.
41. OJ L129, 27 May 1993.
42. OJ L 198/35 ,28 June 1993.
43. OJ L198, 7 Aug. 1993.
44. See Haigh, supra, chap. 11.7, p. 6.

are also numerous other sources of information concerning the state of the environment in Northern Ireland. It is impossible within the context of this chapter to be absolutely comprehensive; however, the following is a list of significant further avenues for obtaining environmental information.

## DoE(NI) Environment Service

The House of Commons Environment Committee report *Environmental Issues in Northern Ireland*, published in 1990,[45] stated that 'our general impression was that environmental data for Northern Ireland is less comprehensive than for England and Wales.' The report concluded that this position was unsatisfactory but acknowledged that it was probably the result of under-resourcing of the environmental protection aspects of the DoE(NI)'s work. The report expressed the view that 'broadly the same information ought to be produced for the United Kingdom as a whole' and recommended that 'the Government publish annual environmental statistics for the whole of the United Kingdom. We also recommend that, as soon as the necessary resources are made available, the DoE(NI) produce an annual report on the environment.' Since the publication of the House of Commons report the DoE(NI)'s Environment Service has produced the following reports: *Environment Service Report, 1991–1993*; *Environment Service Report, 1993–95*; *The Environment in Northern Ireland, 1993–94*; *Environment Service Corporate Plan, 1994–1997*, the *Environment and Heritage Service Corporate Plan, 1996–1999* and the *Environment and Heritage Service Information Pack, 1996* (containing Framework Documents etc.). Each of these reports explains the nature and extent of the Environment Service's work (or Environment and Heritage Service) on environmental protection and sets out its targets for the coming years in this regard. These reports also provide useful statistics covering the main sectors of the Environment Service's work. All are available free of charge. In addition, the Environment Service has produced a wide variety of more specialised publications concerning its work in relation to specific issues, for example, the designation of areas of special scientific interest and areas of outstanding natural beauty and river and estuary quality in Northern Ireland. Reference is made to more specialised publications throughout this book. The *Environment Service Corporate Plan, 1994–97* states that the Environment Service has commissioned the Northern Ireland Environment Link to carry out a feasibility study into the establishment of an environmental information centre for Northern Ireland; at the time of writing, the results of this study are not yet available. It should also be noted that many of Northern Ireland's statutory registers of environmental information (listed above) are held and maintained by the Environment Service. The head office of the Environment Service is at Calvert House, 23 Castle Place, Belfast BT1 1FY; telephone (01232) 254754; fax (01232) 254700.

## Council for Nature Conservation and the Countryside

The CNCC was established as the DoE(NI)'s statutory advisory body in 1989 on matters concerning nature conservation and countryside conservation and

45. *House of Commons Environment Committee First Report, Environmental Issues in Northern Ireland* HC 39(1990).

management. Thus far, the CNCC has produced three reports (all published by HMSO) on its activities since its establishment and has also published a considerable number of more specialised reports putting forward the council's views and recommendations in relation to specific issues within its remit. The most recent report covers the period 1992–93 and contains a list of specialised CNCC reports published to date; an updated CNCC report is forthcoming. At the time of writing the CNCC secretariat is located with the Environment Service's Countryside and Wildlife Branch at Commonwealth House, 35 Castle Street, Belfast BT1 1GH, however, this may change in the near future with the establishment of 'Next Step' agencies throughout the DoE(NI) in April 1996.

## Department of Economic Development

The Industrial Research and Technology Unit (IRTU) within the DED publishes a free periodical bulletin, *Point: Environmental News and Opportunities for Business,* which contains environmental information relevant to companies and organisations involved in commercial activity in Northern Ireland. To receive copies of *Point* contact IRTU, Industrial Science Centre, 17 Antrim Road, Lisburn, Co. Antrim BT28 3AL, or the IRTU's Environment Line at (01846) 623000; fax (01846) 676054. In addition, the IRTU undertakes a wide variety of other environmental initiatives and provides environmental information services. For further information in this regard contact the Environmental Enquiry Point 0800 262227.

## Northern Ireland Environment Link

NIEL acts as a forum for voluntary organisations concerned with conservation of the countryside, wildlife, and the environment. It essentially operates as a link between members and the government and provides information to the public on environmental matters. The NIEL published a summary of *An Environmental Strategy for Northern Ireland* in 1995 designed for public consultation; the final strategy document was launched in May 1996. All Northern Ireland's principal environmental interest groups are member of the NIEL. The NIEL is located at 47A Botanic Ave., Belfast BT7 1JL. Tel: 01232 314944; Fax: 01232 311558.

## Environmental Agencies

The functions of the Environment Agencies for England, Wales and Scotland and the EC Environment Agency are addressed in Chapters 1 and 3 respectively. These agencies are valuable sources of environmental information.

## Other sources of environmental information

'Business in the Environment NI' and Cleaver Fulton and Rankin, solicitors, published *The Green Triangle* in 1994, which provides a brief summary of environmental legislation for business in Northern Ireland and contains a wide variety of useful addresses etc. of bodies involved in environmental protection. A second edition will be published in October 1996 in conjunction with Arena Network NI. *Who's Who in the Environment: Northern Ireland,* published by the

Environment Council, London,[46] provides a more comprehensive directory of organisations involved in environmental protection and other sources of information in this context.

## Environmental information concerning the Republic of Ireland

For environmental information concerning the Republic contact the Environmental Information Service (ENFO), 17 St Andrew Street, Dublin 2; telephone 01-679 3144; fax 01-679 5204. ENFO provides very useful fact sheets (free of charge) concerning environmental law and the state of the physical environment in the Republic. An excellent monthly Environment Bulletin is produced by the Department of the Environment (Dublin). For inclusion in the mailing list contact Air/Environmental Awareness Section, Department of the Environment, Custom House, Dublin 1. Tel: 01-679 3377 ext. 2601; Fax: 01-874 2710.

---

46.  The Environment Council can be contacted at 21 Elizabeth Street, London SW1 9RP.

# CHAPTER THIRTEEN

# Strategies Governing Environmental Liability

This chapter is divided into two Parts. Part I discusses regulation based on command and control mechanisms and identifies some problems posed by this control strategy in the environmental sector. Part II looks at some of the alternative mechanisms available to control human conduct relating to the environment; these are strict liability, environmental insurance policies, market-based controls, environmental information, and environmental education.

## Introduction

It is now recognised that a variety of strategies are available to tackle the varied practical and regulatory problems that can arise in the context of the environment. While the traditional command and control approach favoured by the UK since the days of the Alkali Act 1863[1] seems set to continue to play the dominant role in regulatory theory and practice for the foreseeable future,[2] it is no longer operating in isolation. Administrative controls are, however, envisaged as continuing to provide the basis for 'delivering environmental policy goals,' defining property rights, and monitoring and enforcement activity.[3] As the twenty-first century approaches, regulatory innovation will ensure that alternative control mechanisms, such as market-based strategies and self-regulation, will increasingly be used and developed to supplement more established and traditional legal controls.[4]

## PART I  TRADITIONAL COMMAND AND CONTROL STRATEGIES

Command and control strategies have been the subject of much academic debate, both in the context of general regulatory theory[5] and specifically in the environmental sector.[6] While it is not possible within the confines of this book to deal in detail with the many issues that have arisen, it is nonetheless instructive to

---

1. Centralised state regulation in Britain and Ireland was already well established by the nineteenth century. A brief history of the factors governing its emergence can be found in A. I. Ogus, 'Regulatory law: some lessons from the past', Legal Studies, vol. 12, 1992, 1.
2. This point is clearly made in chap. 1 of *This Common Inheritance: Britain's Environmental Strategy,* (Cm 1200) 1990, para. 1.26–1.27.
3. Ibid., para. 7.
4. Ibid., para 1.28–1-32. See also Appendix A for a brief examination of some alternative regulatory strategies.
5. See, for example, A. I. Ogus, *Regulation: Legal Form and Economic Theory,* Oxford: Clarendon Press, 1994, for an examination of both command and control mechanisms and their alternatives.
6. See for example K. Hawkins, *Environment and Enforcement: Regulation and the Social Definition of Pollution,* Oxford: Clarendon Press, 1984, for a detailed critique of command and control strategies in regulating the aquatic environment.

examine the main aspects of this fundamental branch of regulatory technique in order to attempt to assess its efficacy and shortcomings.

## Reasons for diversification of regulatory techniques

In 1990 the Government estimated that pollution control cost between 1 and 1.5 per cent of Britain's gross national product (about £7 billion).[7] This sum was primarily accounted for by the cost of regulatory authorities policing compliance with the terms of statutory licensing regimes and initiating the prosecution of environmental offences under the relevant legislation. Securing economic efficiency in regulation is therefore one of the Government's priorities in developing its future regulatory strategy.[8] Where traditional rule-based control systems or alternatives are used, the state aims to ensure that polluters pay the cost of regulatory control.[9]

## Securing compliance with environmental laws

In the mainstream policing of unlawful activity, compulsion and coercion and the vigorous use of available legal sanctions are actively pursued; indeed a successful prosecution is the hallmark of the effectiveness of the policing system. In the regulatory sector, however, for example in 'policing' the environment, a compliance and compromise strategy is more likely to be pursued, and recourse to the legal sanctions provided for in statute tends to be viewed by regulators as a last resort, a sign of the failure of the regulatory strategy. Internal views of the success of environmental regulation tend to differ markedly from the public's perception of the issue; society tends to view the success of a regulatory regime in terms of the number of successful prosecutions pursued—rather like 'ordinary' policing— and a low prosecution rate is thus equated with failure. Public expectations tend to be aroused by the passing of high-profile environmental statutes, but they are often doomed to be disappointed by the emergence in practice of what is known as the 'implementation gap' between what the statute promises on paper and what regulatory agencies can deliver in practice. A low prosecution rate is often taken as an indication of the phenomenon known as 'agency capture', where the necessarily close relationship between the regulator and the regulated is deemed to have paralysed the regulatory regime.

While the public perception of the efficacy of regulatory regimes and agencies is perhaps understandable, it is also somewhat unfair, since the comparison made between regulatory activity and mainstream policing is not necessarily an appropriate one.[10] There are several important distinctions that must be drawn between administrative regulation and policing. The first is the relationship

---

7.   *This Common Inheritance,* supra note 2.
8.   Development of the tax-based strategies, however, will be subject to other social and economic imperatives, as expressed for example in the Advisory Council on Science and Technology paper *Innovation and the Tax System,* London: HMSO 1994, which emphasises the need to ensure that tax strategies promote rather than stifle innovation.
9.   *This Common Inheritance* at para. 1.25.
10.  Nonetheless the Government itself drew attention to low prosecution rates in respect of the aquatic environment in its White Paper *Crime, Justice and Protecting the Public* (Cm 965) 1990.

between the regulator and those regulated. In a traditional policing situation, even allowing for the effects of recidivism, there is no continuing relationship between the parties; instead there is 'one-off' or at worst relatively infrequent repeated contact. In the regulatory context, however, there is a continuing relationship between the parties; they are inevitably associated with one another on a periodic basis over many years, and prosecution is hardly an attractive option when a future relationship between the parties cannot be avoided. Indeed the quality of the continuing relationship between the parties is also important, because of the financial and staffing constraints that weigh heavily on regulatory authorities and because of the geographically dispersed nature of the industry that is the subject of regulation. The co-operation of those regulated is essential to the smooth running of the system.

In addition, prosecution is an expensive strategy for agencies to pursue; yet the level of the penalties imposed by the law[11] is (comparatively speaking) low.[12] Fines also disappear into the coffers of the state rather than going back directly into the regulatory system; arguably there is little incentive for agencies to run the risk of going to court. Agencies are accountable to the state for the funds they spend and are under an obligation to make the most efficient use of them; prosecution may simply not represent an efficient option.

Moral problems have also arisen in the context of environmental regulation in the past, since, despite the criminal nature of environmental offences, pollution of the environment has long been regarded as morally neutral, unlike many of the more obvious aspects of criminal behaviour. Environmental offences have tended in the past to be regarded as less than 'real' crimes.[13] Indeed environmental pollution and even pollution-based offences are the by-product of otherwise beneficial and legally sanctioned industrial activity.

Conciliation and education, for these and other reasons, tend therefore to be the preferred tools of regulatory agencies, representing a solution to the problem of ensuring a 'good' continuing relationship with their regulatory constituency and a relatively cost-effective approach to ensuring compliance with both general statutory and licence-specific standards.

## Extension of the criminal law in dealing with the environment

By the late nineteen-eighties, however, the environment had risen to such prominence on the political agenda and in popular consciousness that it was also high on the legislative agenda. The new legislation, most notably the Water Act 1989 and the Environmental Protection Act 1990, in addition to dealing with technical pollution control issues also reflected changed public attitudes—

---

11. The 'new wave' of statutory provision for the environment in Great Britain, including the Environmental Protection Act 1990 and the Water Resources Act 1991, has significantly increased the level of fines available on summary conviction to up to £20,000 and an unlimited fine or up to two years' imprisonment on indictment—although the average penalties imposed by the courts tend to be only a small fraction of this.

12. The Government itself drew attention to the derisory level of fines in respect of aquatic pollution in *Crime, Justice and Protecting the Public,* supra.

13. See G. Heine, 'Environment protection and criminal law' in O. Lomas ed., *Frontiers of Environmental Law,* London: Chancery, 1991.

including a changed view on the morality of environmental offences.[14] Within a fairly short time pollution ceased to be regarded as a morally neutral and natural consequence of industrial activity. Both the aforementioned pieces of legislation abound in offences involving breaches of the substantive licensing regimes created and requirements to provide the information which underpins the operation of each regulatory system.

An additional dimension to criminal liability in environmental law has also been created by not only making firms liable as legal persons for the regulatory offences they commit but also imposing criminal liability on senior company officers.[15] As Waite comments:

> nothing is more likely to concentrate the minds of senior company officers whose companies, however much they may benefit the economy, are the cause of serious environmental degradation.[16]

Company officers may be liable as primary wrong-doers, as accomplices, for conspiracy, and under specific statutory provisions.

Command and control regulation then seems likely to benefit in the longer term from more vigorous social attitudes towards environmental offences and from enhanced legislative powers and regulatory machinery.[17]


## PART II  ALTERNATIVES TO COMMAND AND CONTROL

In addition to changes that will have a direct impact on command and control regulation, the wider system of environmental governance stands to be greatly enhanced by the development of new strategies (and the adaptation of existing ones not before employed in this area) to tackle the unique challenges of environmental regulation.

### Strict Liability

Common law civil liability, like criminal liability, can act to influence the behaviour of polluters; the practical and financial effects of civil liability are not dissimilar to those of market-based strategies (in that they ensure that the 'polluter pays') and for this reason are dealt with along with other alternative control strategies in Annex A of *This Common Inheritance*. Strict civil liability for pollution offences is already a feature of several Continental legal systems[18] and

---

14. The new moral view of environmental offences is not confined to the UK: see, for example, S. Raucher, 'Raising the stakes for environmental polluters: the *Exxon Valdez* criminal prosecution', Ecology Law Quarterly, 1992, 147.

15. For a discussion of the liability of individuals for corporate offences see A. Waite 'Criminal liability of company directors', Land Management and Environmental Law Report, June–July 1991, 74, and F. Addison and E. Mack, 'Creating an environmental ethic in corporate America: the big stick of jail time', Southwestern Law Journal ,1991, vol. 44, 1427.

16. Waite, op cit. at p. 74.

17. See chap. 1 and 2, supra.

18. For example, strict liability is used by public authorities to deal with soil pollution problems in both the Netherlands and Denmark.

international agreements. It is also the subject of draft legislation[19] in EC law, which will be discussed in some detail below.

Essentially, under a strict liability regime it is unnecessary to prove that the defendant has been negligent or otherwise at fault in order to establish liability for damage. Strict liability is at present a feature of criminal liability in the UK, though in a civil action proof of negligence is the norm. One exception is the rather limited application of strict liability under the rule in *Rylands v. Fletcher*.[20] This case imposed strict liability on landowners for damage caused by the escape of things which were likely to do mischief if they escaped and which had been accumulated by them on their land. In order for liability to be imposed the use to which the land was put had to be characterised as 'non-natural'.[21]

The limitations of the rule in *Rylands v. Fletcher* as a modern dynamic source of liability were clearly revealed in the case of *Cambridge Water Co. Ltd v. Eastern Counties Leather PLC*.[22] The case involved historical contamination—by spillages of the solvent perchloroethene (PCE) onto the ground at Eastern Counties Leather's tannery—of one of the neighbouring Cambridge Water Company's boreholes from which it obtained groundwater for domestic consumption by its customers. The claim based on the rule in *Rylands v. Fletcher,* together with claims based in nuisance and negligence, failed at first instance[23]— much to the disgust of environmentalists, who railed at the law's evident unwillingness or, worse, inability to deal with the question of historical pollution. The Cambridge Water Company was, however, successful in the Court of Appeal on another closely related head of strict liability, the court being of the opinion that Eastern Counties Leather was liable under the authority of *Ballard v. Tomlinson*.[24] for the contamination of water percolating under Cambridge Water Company's land.

*Ballard v. Tomlinson,* imposing strict liability for the contamination of groundwater, dates, like *Rylands v. Fletcher* itself, from the time before the tenets of fault-based negligence liability came to dominate the law of torts in the UK and is therefore equally out of step with modern thinking on liability. The Court of Appeal's ruling in *Cambridge Water* caused a brief crisis of confidence in the environmental insurance sector, with visions of unlimited liability for contamination caused by historical pollution peppering the general and professional press. The crisis was, however, short-lived, since Eastern Counties Leather's appeal to the House of Lords on the question of strict liability proved successful. Lord Goff in his speech was of the opinion that the decision in *Ballard v. Tomlinson* did not raise any legal principles distinct from those contained in *Rylands v. Fletcher.* He pointed out that liability under *Rylands v. Fletcher,* while

---

19. See L. Sheehan, 'The EEC's Proposed Directive on Civil Liability for Damage Caused by Waste: taking over where prevention fails', 1991, vol. 18, Ecology Law Quarterly, 405, for discussion of factors that have caused the EC to pursue strict liability strategies.

20. (1868) LR 3 HL 530.

21. The 'non-natural use' proviso was added to Blackburn J's original formulation of the rule in *Rylands v. Fletcher* by Cairns LC on appeal.

22. [1994] 2 WLR 53.

23. The claim under *Rylands v. Fletcher* failed because Kennedy J was of the opinion that the operation of the tannery constituted a natural use of land and therefore did not fall under the strict rules introduced in that case to cover dangerous activities.

24. (1885) 29 Ch D 115.

strict, was not absolute, alluding to the 'non-natural user' proviso attached to liability to illustrate his point. He was unwilling to agree with Kennedy J's opinion that Eastern Counties Leather's activities constituted a natural use of land, though the company escaped liability in any event on the grounds that at the time when the spillages of PCE which caused the damage occurred, Eastern Counties Leather was not in a position to foresee that contamination of Cambridge Water Company's aquifer would result.

The prime problem which the courts appear to have with the rule in *Rylands v. Fletcher* seems to be the fact that strict liability is fundamentally opposed to the general tenor of civil liability in modern UK law, which is based, more or less exclusively, on the fault-based tenets of negligence. The unwillingness of the courts to interfere with current orthodoxy in this area is clearly illustrated in the words of Lord Goff in *Cambridge Water*:

> It is more appropriate for strict liability in respect of operations of high risk to be imposed by Parliament than by the courts. If such liability is imposed by statute, the relevant activities can be identified and those concerned can know where they stand. Furthermore, statute can, where appropriate, lay down precise criteria establishing the incidence and scope of such liability.

The Government has so far failed to rise to this challenge; on the other hand, it has not ruled out strict civil liability as a potentially useful means of further developing environmental regulation. The suggested benefits of such a regime include providing industry with a further incentive to conduct its activities with care; one drawback is that strict liability will inevitably serve to create extreme difficulties for industry in obtaining insurance coverage in respect of environmental risks. Self-insurance by industry or policies underwritten by the state as suggested by the EC Commission in its communication to the Council and the European Parliament on environmental liability could provide a solution to this difficulty.

### EC Draft Directive on Civil Liability for Environmental Damage

The EC's proposals for a Directive introducing strict civil liability for environmental damage may eventually lead (although progress in reaching agreement is likely to be slow) to the concept playing a major role in environmental control. The impetus for legislation was, as is so often the case, to be found in environmental disaster, specifically the Seveso incident[25] in 1983 and the contamination of the Rhine in a spillage of toxic chemicals near Basel in 1986. These incidents raised a series of issues, both general and specific, and called into question the whole focus of EC-based environmental regulation.

The EC has in the past tended to concentrate its regulatory efforts on the prevention of future environmental damage. Attention was now also directed to examining the need to ensure that remedial action would be undertaken to restore the environment in the wake of environmental damage caused by waste.

---

25. The discovery that forty-one barrels of highly toxic dioxin-based waste had been transported undetected from Seveso, Italy, to a barn in Saint-Quentin, France.

Civil liability is identified as the appropriate legal instrument for ensuring that the polluter pays for environmental damage. The EC favours a strict liability approach (as a supplement to other forms of regulation) for several reasons; prime among these is the removal of the current difficulties posed by proving fault in cases involving environmental damage. In environmental law (liability being based on fault) it is at present sufficient for polluters to argue that they have acted within the confines of the appropriate regulatory regime in order to absolve themselves from any finding of fault and thus liability—even though environmental damage may still occur under statutory dispensation.

Strict liability for environmental damage involves an incentive effect for industry to adopt effective environmental protection strategies, otherwise industry's deep pocket will be called on to pay for any damage that is caused by its activities.

Strict liability regimes do, however, raise several important problems, not least being the need to define the scope of liability and to determine who may be held liable in a given situation. One suggested strategy is to link the defendant's liability to activities carried out by him which constitute a risk to the environment. An alternative approach would be to designate certain particularly dangerous activities (though defining what exactly constitutes a 'dangerous' activity is in itself controversial) as appropriate subjects for strict civil liability; the latter is the strategy favoured by the EC.

Strict liability may offer a useful addition to the range of options available to ensure environmental protection, though it must not be viewed as some sort of universally applicable panacea; it cannot, for example, deal with chronic pollution problems, nor can it be used to deal with untraceable pollution incidents.

Supplementary regimes, such as industry or state-based compensation programmes, may offer useful back-up to a strict liability regime.

### Insurance for environmental liability

As is all too clearly revealed by the Court of Appeal decision in *Middleton v. Wiggins*,[26] coverage for environmental liability under current public liability policies is severely limited. The case concerned an explosion caused by methane gas close to a site formerly used by Hargreaves Clear Waste Ltd to landfill waste. The site had closed and been sold to Mr and Mrs Wiggins. Gas from the site migrated (though this was unexpected) to the ground under the plaintiffs' house, and an explosion eventually occurred destroying the house and injuring the plaintiffs.

The court was called on to decide whether the plaintiffs' loss could be covered by Hargreaves' public liability insurance policy. The wording of the policy carried an endorsement that made liability conditional on damage being caused 'from an accident in the method of disposal.' At first instance liability was imposed. On appeal, Hargreaves argued that the policy provided coverage only for accidents occurring as 'part and parcel' of the actual process of waste disposal and not for accidents consequential on the method of disposal; the majority of the Court of

---

26. 1995 Environmental Law Monthly, vol. 4, issue 10, 1.

Appeal agreed.[27] The decision itself was strongly opposed by McCowan LJ in his dissenting judgment on the limited interpretation given to the concept of 'disposal' but such an approach could, however, be justified on the bare wording of the policy. The extent of liability under insurance policies will doubtless continue to be a vexed question and the subject of further litigation.

The insurance industry itself recognises that the status quo cannot possibly continue, and potential legal intervention, together with new industry strategies to deal with pollution issues, have been the subject of heated debate.[28] In a survey[29] of the top fifty insurance firms in the UK carried out in 1992, it was found that fifteen carried no pollution cover policies. Of the remaining thirty-five, 94 per cent offered coverage for 'sudden and accidental' pollution. Only three firms offered wider environmental impairment liability (EIL) insurance (though a further ten stated that they planned to provide such coverage). This type of policy covers gradual environmental pollution, such as leachate from landfill sites contaminating soil or groundwater. EIL policies are, however, subject to extremely rigorous conditions; they represent a bad risk for insurers, since with many environmental problems it is not a question of 'if' but rather 'when' environmental damage will occur.

In the light of the obvious difficulties faced by the insurance industry in dealing with environmental liability, it would seem likely that self-insurance schemes (such as those common in the high-risk petrochemical industry) or state-financed insurance schemes[30] will play an increasingly prominent role in this area of law.

**Market-based controls**

As mentioned above, the Government expressed a strong commitment to developing market-based regulatory strategies in *This Common Inheritance*. While it may seem at first that this move is the direct result of the particular ideological preference for 'pushing back the frontiers of the state' espoused by the Conservative Government over the last few years, this would be unduly simplistic, since the diversification into market-based initiatives is actually a global phenomenon. Privatisation,[31] the hallmark of modern conservative ideology has, however, played an important role in raising the profile of regulatory issues[32] in the UK and has aroused considerable debate, particularly concerning the

---

27. This outcome is in sharp contrast to that reached in the American courts, where liability has been imposed under general insurance policies, although this has had the disastrous consequence of causing insurers to withdraw all coverage for environmental damage.
28. The insurance industry's main weekly publication, Post Magazine, has given a huge amount of coverage to environmental liability: see, for example, J. Monteith, 'How green is your valley?' 23 Apr. 1992; P. Falush, 'Few like it hot', 7 Jan. 1993; and C. Sheppard, 'Back to the polluter', 20 May 1993.
29. Monteith, ibid.
30. Such as those in Italy, France, and the Netherlands: Monteith, op. cit.
31. For a critique of privatisation see C. Graham and T. Prosser, 'Privatising nationalised industries: constitutional issues and new legal techniques', vol. 50 MLR 1987, 16.
32. See, for example, B. Sas, 'Regulation and the privatised electricity supply industry', vol. 53 M.L.R 1990, 485, and R. Macrory, 'The privatisation and regulation of the water industry', vol. 53 M.L.R. 1990, 78.

difficulties in reconciling the interests of shareholders with other needs, notably those of consumers and general environmental standards.

The strategies suggested in *This Common Inheritance* and examined in detail in Annex A of the Report include using traditional regulatory controls to improve the operation of the market by ensuring that consumers are sufficiently well informed to make environmentally sound use of their purchasing power. The Government gives eco-labelling schemes as an example of this approach in action (this also forms a part of the wider strategy of environmental control by information).

More generally, market-based instruments are designed to correct the distortions in the market that have evolved over the years whereby environmental pollution has long been regarded as having no economic cost. For many years the environment has been regarded as a 'free' economic good, though this is beginning to change with increased consciousness of the true impacts of pollution. One example of this type of approach is exhibited in the area of waste disposal, with increased charges being made for landfill disposal in order to make the financial cost at least begin to reflect some of the environmental costs involved and to encourage waste minimisation and the use of alternative disposal options, such as incineration (see chapter 6).

The Government favours charging polluters to cover the costs of running regulatory systems; both HMIP[33] and the NRA[34] in Great Britain are authorised to make charges for the authorisation and monitoring procedures for which they are responsible. Paying for the regulation of pollution represents a small element of the 'polluter pays' ideal; it does not, however, reflect the wider social costs of pollution in the same way as clean-up costs (which also feature in modern UK environmental legislation) do. Charges vary with the complexity of the polluting activity and in the case of water pollution with the complexity of the pollutant and the volume discharged.

Another group of market-based strategies, used with some success on the Continent, involves industry levies, product levies, and deposit and refund schemes. Industry levies involve the identification of a homogeneous group of polluters, levying a charge on these firms on the basis of output and using the proceeds for environmental ends.

Product levies (imposed by the state) and deposit and refund schemes (undertaken voluntarily by industry) can be used to tackle the waste disposal problems associated with particular products; this is another example of the 'polluter pays' principle in action.

Taxes can be levied directly for environmental damage; local pollution charges, such as the differential landing fees imposed by some airports based on noise levels, represent this type of charge, if on a small scale. Taxes can also be imposed on particularly environmentally damaging raw materials or products. Differential taxing, such as that applied to leaded and unleaded fuel, can be used to encourage environmentally sensitive consumption.

The United States has seen some particularly advanced development in the use of market mechanisms for environmental regulation, and the Government in *This*

---

33. Under the Environmental Protection Act 1990.
34. Under the Water Resources Act 1991.

*Common Inheritance* expressed a particular interest in the concept of tradeable emissions permits. Tradeable emissions permits emerged on a large scale in the United States in the context of securing reductions in emissions from power plants under the Clean Air Amendment Act 1990. The principle is simple; the state sets a ceiling for emissions of a given pollutant. Permits are then produced dividing pollution capacity among the participants in the industrial sector to be regulated. Individual plants may only emit that quantity of the controlled pollutant for which permits are held; emissions in excess of this level will incur punitive fines. A cheaper alternative to paying fines will be to purchase excess permit capacity from other plants. Progressive lowering of the emissions ceiling and thus of the available capacity of pollution permits ensures that tradable emissions schemes are 'technology-forcing'—though, in contrast to command and control systems, the onus for pushing technology forward lies with industry itself; innovation, emission reductions and consequent spare permit capacity are in the best interests of individual firms. In addition, firms are free to use their own special knowledge of their own operations to decide how best to operate within their permit capacity and thus will arguably meet targets more efficiently than under strategies imposed from without.

Tradable permits also serve to decrease the regulatory burden of the state, running the permitting system and monitoring being the chief roles for state authorities, with the labour-intensive role of prescribing abatement techniques and technologies being removed.

Finally, Annex A of *This Common Inheritance* discusses the viability of subsidy and public compensation schemes as a means of securing pollution control. The view expressed of these devices is overwhelmingly negative, a major reason being that they discourage firms from taking responsibility for their polluting activities.

The panoply of potential regulatory techniques available in the form of market mechanisms provides the opportunity for a more tailored approach to environmental regulation, since it is obvious that, in respect of particular environmental problems, alternatives to traditional command and control-based liability regimes may be more appropriate and therefore more successful.

### Control by information strategies

Environmental information provisions are examined in some detail in chapter 12, but their significance as a means of environmental regulation will, for the sake of completeness, be examined briefly here.

### *Registers*

The command and control version of environmental regulation has in the UK, particularly since the passing of the Control of Pollution Act 1974, frequently included provision for registers of environmental information. These registers generally contain details of relevant consents and monitoring information. They are designed primarily to open up the generally rather closed arena of environmental regulation to the public, in whose interest the system is supposed to be run. The contents of registers, by providing for at least some transparency in the regulatory system, allow checks to be made on the conduct both of industry and of the regulatory agencies concerned.

Environmental information issues also arise in the wider administrative context; for example, environmental services were added to the Government's Citizen's Charter initiative in 1992.[35]

Domestic initiatives in improving access to environmental information—an essential back-up to consumer-oriented market-based regulatory strategies—were brought more sharply into focus by international initiatives, most notably the EC's Directive on Freedom of Access to Environmental Information 90/313/EEC[36] and Local Agenda 21 (a product of the Rio Earth Summit). Attempts have been made to use registers of environmental information in a more proactive manner, as a guide to conduct, rather than just as a conduit for the facts and figures generated by the regulatory system. This was the case in the so-called registers of contaminated land[37] proposed by section 143 of the Environmental Protection Act 1990, which were abandoned in the face of implacable opposition from the building and related industries.[38]

### *Eco-labels*

The EC has, under the auspices of Regulation EEC/880/92, establishing the EC Eco-Label Award Scheme,[39] provided for a recognised mark[40] indicating that goods carrying it satisfy EC agreed standards of environmental quality.[41] The quality standards promoted are ambitious—design, production, marketing and use, i.e. the entire life-cycle of products covered are subject to scrutiny. Subject specific Regulations will eventually apply to most classes of goods available to consumers,[42] though such wide coverage will be attained only gradually.

Goods are first divided (by Article 3.1(*c*)) into more manageable 'product groups' applicable to products serving similar purposes and having equivalence of use. Products are (under Article 3.1(*d*)) assessed on the basis of their environmental impacts 'from cradle to grave'.[43] Goods must conform to both general and specific health, safety and ecological requirements (Articles 4 and 5). No goods that pose a threat to the environment through the production of

---

35. *Green Rights and Responsibilities: a Citizen's Guide,* DoE London 1992.
36. See chap. 12, infra for a detailed discussion of the Directive.
37. What was actually to be recorded was 'land which may have been subject to contaminative uses,' on the basis of a relatively cheap 'document based' desktop survey, rather than land that had actually been contaminated, since securing the latter information would necessitate hugely expensive and extensive scientific site survey. For an outline of the new provisions that will deal with this issue see chap. 6.
38. For an examination of the problems raised by the registers proposed under s. 143 of the 1990 Act see R. Lewis, 'The abandonment of registers of contaminative uses', Environmental Law and Management 1993, 26. The issue was finally readdressed by Parliament in the Environment Act 1995.
39. 1992 OJ L 99, 1.
40. A daisy emblem, the petals of which are made up of stars representing each of the member states of the EC; see Annex II to the Regulations.
41. See ch. 12 for a detailed discussion of the Regulation.
42. Food, drinks and pharmaceuticals are specifically excluded from the remit of the Regulations (Art. 2).
43. This phrase, as defined by Art. 3, covers the choice of raw materials, distribution, consumption, and waste disposal.

dangerous substances, or the use of dangerous production methods, may qualify for an eco-label.

Member states are obliged (by Article 9) to appoint a 'competent body' responsible (subject to certain powers of supervision and intervention exercised by the Commission) for the domestic running of the eco-label scheme. In the UK this role is performed by the Eco-Labelling Board. The label is awarded for a fixed period (Article 8.5); the process is initiated by voluntary application by manufacturers.

One of the major aims of the scheme is to satisfy the public's interest in access to relevant environmental information that can facilitate the making of sound environmental choices by consumers.

### *Eco-auditing*

Eco-auditing and other industry initiatives instituting voluntary checks on environmental practices and standards within individual firms and industrial sectors have shown themselves to be influential in shaping new approaches to environmental regulation.

One example of an industry-led initiative has emerged in the expansion of the internal examination of environmental management systems within firms to become the subject of external recognition and verification through satisfying the good practice requirements under the British Standards Institution in BS 7750. Likewise, internal industry initiatives on the eco-auditing[44] of practices, procedures and production processes carried out by businesses for their own ends; including improving efficiency and securing better compliance with regulatory requirements, have been influential in the adoption of the EC's Regulation on Eco-Management and Auditing.[45]

Building upon established internal industry practice, the EC's EMAS scheme allows industry another route whereby to establish its 'green credentials'. The EC has provided a Community wide network to give external validation and recognition to eco-management and audit practices. Responsibility for the registration of qualifying firms and sites lies in the hands of member states[46] which are also required to transmit this information to the EC Commission and to the public.

New developments of this nature, while still in their infancy, represent another strand in the increasing coverage and sophistication that appear to be the hallmark of environmental regulation in the nineteen-nineties.

### *Environmental education*

The Government has expressed a commitment to ensuring that environmental issues are the subject of public education, for those of school age and well beyond. Public education, such as that outlined above, through the 'green' Citizen's Charter, together with media-based information programmes, has become common.

---

44. See the International Chamber of Commerce pamphlet *Environmental Audit,* 1992.
45. EEC/1836/93 (EMAS). See chap. 12 for details of the EMAS scheme.
46. This function is carried out for the United Kingdom by the DoE(London).

The environment has also found a place within the school system, notably through coverage in the National Curriculum. Environmental skills can also form the basis of national vocational qualifications (NVQs).

## Conclusions

It will be apparent from even the brief summary of developments above that the regulation of environmental concerns is at present the subject of both debate and innovation. The need to supplement traditional command and control regulatory strategies has long been apparent, and it would appear that industry, the UK Government, the EC and the wider international community have all been active in promoting new approaches to the problems that have emerged in environmental control.

The prospects of success for these new strategies are very difficult to assess, though with such a diverse range of instruments available it would appear that the law is better equipped to deal with the vast problem of environmental regulation than ever before.

# Appendix A

## The Environment and Heritage Service

### *Status, structure and remit*

On 1 April 1996 the Environment Service was renamed the Environment and Heritage Service (EHS) and internally reorganised as an executive agency under the 'Next Steps' initiative. The EHS is headed by a Chief Executive and is organised into four directorates, each headed by a director — Natural Heritage, Built Environment, Environmental Protection and Corporate Affairs. Responsibility for the day-to-day running of the EHS lies with its chief executive. The Agency's functions are, briefly,[1] 'to regulate air, water and land pollution, conserve the countryside and protect and record historic monuments and buildings'[2] and are divided as follows:

- The Directorate of Natural Heritage encapsulates five divisions, each headed by an assistant director—conservation science; conservation designations and protection; countryside and coastal management; regional operations; and information and education.
- The Directorate of the Built Heritage encompasses three sub-directorates—protection of historic monuments; protection of historic buildings; and recording the built heritage.
- The Directorate of Environmental Protection is made up of—the alkali and radiochemical inspectorate; the local environmental quality unit; the water quality unit; the drinking water inspectorate; and the waste management inspectorate.
- The Directorate of Corporate Affairs is divided into units for finance operations; finance accounting; administration, central management and legislative matters; personnel and human resources; and directorate and secretarial services.

The EHS's functions are more or less identical to those which it carried out under its previous title, the only substantive change being an enhanced role in waste regulation which will come into its own on the making of the proposal for a draft Waste and Contaminated Land (Northern Ireland) Order 1996.

The EHS has produced a Corporate Plan[3] for the first three years of its existence, stating a commitment to follow up on national and international environmental policies and legal commitments as they apply to Northern Ireland. Key domestic developments will include the overhaul of waste controls (to be in place on the ground by 1997/98), the implementation of air and industrial pollution controls (to be in place by 1997/98) and updating water law.[4] Efficiency

---

1. For a more detailed view of the EHS's remit see the agency's Framework Document, DoE(NI), March 1996.
2. A Corporate Framework for the Department of the Environment for Northern Ireland, DoE(NI), March 1996, p. 12.
3. DoE(NI) March 1996.
4. Detailed plans for 1996/97 can be found in Section 2 of the EHS Corporate Plan (supra).

in its operations and effective customer service are the watchwords of the EHS
*Corporate Plan.*

With its work under its previous title to build on, the EHS seems to be in a good
position to achieve its environmental and human aims. Much of the sorely needed
legislative innovation required to equip a modern system of environmental
governance is now in place (or set to come on stream in the near future). Perhaps
the time is right for a new start and a fresh identity for environmental institutions
in Northern Ireland.

# Index